Medicine at Harvard

FRONTISPIECE. *Holden Chapel. The basement, formerly used for storage, became the site of the Medical School. In 1805 the anatomy course was moved to hired rooms over an apothecary shop in Boston, and in 1815 the whole Medical School was moved there. At that time the School was variously called Medical School or Medical Institution of Harvard College or Harvard Medical School. Hand-colored engraving in the Harvard Medical Archives.*

The University Press

of New England

Sponsoring Institutions

Brandeis University

Clark University

Dartmouth College

University of New Hampshire

University of Rhode Island

University of Vermont

Medicine at Harvard
The First Three Hundred Years

Henry K. Beecher, M.D., and
Mark D. Altschule, M.D.

The University Press of New England

Hanover, New Hampshire, 1977

The quotation on the following page is from
Archibald MacLeish, *The Next Harvard, as Seen by
Archibald MacLeish* (Cambridge, 1941), quoted
with permission of the author and the
Harvard University Press.

FRONT END PAPER. *The Great White Quadrangle on Longwood Avenue, Boston,
dedicated September 25 and 26 and occupied on September 27, 1906. There were
no adjacent hospital buildings at that time. The School was surrounded by
dwellings.*

BACK END PAPER. *An aerial view by Laurence Lowry of the Harvard Medical
School in 1973, showing the School overshadowed by nearby hospitals, the new
buildings of the Harvard School of Public Health, and those of several other
educational institutions.*

From the beginning of its history the next Harvard has been in process of evolution, and the next Harvard is in process of evolution now. Harvard, like other universities, is committed to one time and one time only—the future toward which the American Republic moves.

—Archibald MacLeish

MASSACHUSETTS MEDICAL COLLEGE.

Massachusetts Medical College, the medical division of Harvard University, 1815–46. It was on Mason Street near the Massachusetts General Hospital. Print from the collection of Mark D. Altschule, M.D.

Preface

An oarsman who steers by his wake knows where he has been and can define his direction. But if he wants to know where he is heading, he must turn around. A history must not only contain the data that describe past events but organize these data so as to reveal trends that, from their direction in the past, can be usefully projected into the future. This has been our endeavor.

What follows is an account and an assessment not so much of the Harvard Medical School per se as its contribution to medical education and to the practice of medicine. The reader will find no chronologies of names, dates, and discoveries; for these one should go to Harrington or Garrison. Our purpose has been to describe the Harvard past so as to reveal the trends leading to the most significant developments, and to define the ideas that made them possible. To further that end, we subscribe to Hegel's phrase that ideas have hands and feet. The emphasis is upon both the men themselves—in the classroom, in the laboratory, in the hospital—and the medicine they made.

Recent events cannot yet be evaluated with sufficient perspective to warrant inclusion of many important matters. Systematic treatment of the Harvard past has therefore terminated with the end of Dean George Packer Berry's tenure in June of 1965. Certain trends that began before or during his tenure have been dealt with, however, if they continued under the deanship of his successor, Robert Higgins Ebert.

The period covered by this book is long and rich, but space is limited. Certain omissions should some day be given monographic treatment: the degree to which foundation money influenced Harvard's growth; the reasons behind the change from the sensible good-doing of Harvard's earlier faculties to the irrational social activism of some of today's faculty; the criteria for tenure appointments over the years; the qualities and qualifications of a good dean. Also the extent to which Harvard graduates or men trained at Harvard hospitals influenced outstanding students to choose Harvard; the manner and degree to which interactions between Harvard and the other Boston medical schools and the proprietary clinics (Lahey, Overholt, Joslin) affected the history of Harvard medicine; and how students have been chosen for admission.

Since the present work is intended to present the developments that occurred at the Harvard Medical School in the framework of medical education, the undoubtedly outstanding research accomplishments of the increasingly swollen departments will not be discussed unless they specifically bear on the training of physicians as physicians. Moreover, they are all sufficiently well known to other basic research men.

Similarly, there will be no discussion of the current superstitious belief that a subject can be taught only by a man who has spent his entire scientific life studying one narrow aspect of it, although this belief has contributed to the swelling of the faculties.

It is impossible to formulate criteria to define the quality of a medical school, but certain things seem important: innovation and leadership, academic standings of the candidates for admission, and the records of its graduates. By all these criteria Harvard has been an excellent school. It has, since 1782, been associated with most of the world's developments in medicine, often either as creator or as challenger. It brought European medicine—whose leader was then French medicine—to this country.[1] It was, of course, peculiarly Bostonian in personnel and in philosophy for most of its history.

The life story of Harvard medicine is made up of periods each of which has a specific character of its own. Within each period it is easy to see the connections between separate developments and trends. Although in occasional instances bridges connecting areas of seemingly detached happenings have had to be constructed, there is an organic unity evident from the origins of medicine in Boston until after World War II, at which time social and scientific changes began to make themselves felt and the School's character likewise began to change. It will remain for future historians to describe these events.

Two individuals more than others have given wide-ranging help during its writing: Professor Donald Fleming of Harvard University, and Mr. Richard J. Wolfe, Rare Books Librarian in the Countway Library of Medicine. Professor Fleming read the entire manuscript and made many helpful suggestions. Mr. Wolfe read much of the manuscript and with his intimate knowledge of the Countway Library was always a source of help. We could not have written the book, at least not in its present state, without the guidance and scholarship of these two gentlemen. At the same time, we must acknowledge that we did not always take their advice. Neither is in any way, of course, responsible for the final outcome.

It is necessary to give special acknowledgement to Marjorie Vara, who has worked not only as a most skillful secretary but also as a research assistant throughout most of the writing.

Our research was conducted in ten libraries and archives (nine in the United States, one in London).[2] We are especially indebted to the following individuals for the help and many courtesies that have been extended: Ruth Linderholm, Rare Books Department, Catherine Binder-up, Reference Librarian, and Janet Regier, Rare Books Department, Francis A. Countway Library of Medicine; Harley P. Holden, Curator of the Archives, Archives of Harvard University (Widener); Erika Chadbourn, Treasure Room of the Harvard Law Library; Carolyn E. Jakeman, Assistant Librarian for Reference, Houghton Library of Harvard University; Leo Flaherty, Curator of the Archives, Commonwealth of Massachusetts Archives (State House); and J. William Hess, Archivist, Rockefeller Foundation. Jean Alonzo Curran was always helpful when it came to questions that overlapped from the Medical School to the School of Public Health. Professor Saul Benison was a never-failing source of stimulation and encouragement. We have already acknowledged in the appropriate places those who very kindly furnished us with technical data arising from their own work. Henry C. Meadow and Priscilla M. Hubbard were great sources of help with the financial history of the School.

Financial support was received from the Massachusetts General Hospital, the Commonwealth Fund, and the National Endowment for the Humanities. Dr. George Farrar also made a contribution from Wyeth Laboratories. The book could not have been written without this help, for which we are grateful.

Boston, Massachusetts   H.K.B.
June, 1976   M.D.A.

Contents

Preface   IX

Illustrations

Part I
The Earliest Stages

Chapter One

Awareness of Need

ON September 19, 1782, the Corporation of Harvard College, adopting a plan set forth by President Joseph Willard and Professor Edward Wigglesworth, founded the Harvard Medical School, the third in the country.[1] What led to this decision? The question can be answered only by considering the state of medicine before and during this period.

The recorded medical history of the colonists is imprecise, conflicting, and filled with uncertainties. It could scarcely be otherwise, for records were few and diagnoses often inaccurate or confused. Many disease patterns were not clearly identified. Many outbreaks, especially those away from the cities, were not even recorded. True, the dramatic onslaughts of smallpox or yellow fever were viewed with horror, for the consequences were devastating, but the influence of these calamities on the history of the period has often been considerably overrated. On the other hand, the colonists newly arrived from Europe were especially susceptible to dysentery and malaria, which probably exacted a heavier death toll of "fresh Europeans" than all other epidemics combined. Duffy places respiratory ailments—colds, influenza, pleurisy, and pneumonia—as the third most important killer.[2]

Malnutrition and famine prepared the way for infectious disease, and war aggravated the situation. The "white man's diseases" were highly effective in reducing the Indian menace: the natives had no immunity to the diseases newly introduced from Europe; they had no concept of isolation of the patient, and their methods of treatment were no more effective than those of the colonists. Although Negro slaves generally had more immunity to smallpox, malaria, and yellow fever than did the colonists, they were highly susceptible to respiratory ills. The loss of life and the cost of disease, economically and in terms of suffering, cannot be estimated with accuracy; clearly, both were enormous and greatly hindered the development of Colonial America.[3] Notwithstanding the adverse effects of disease, however, the colonists steadily increased in numbers and in wealth.

The inadequacy of available medical care was widely recognized. Articulate comment by John Eliot and President Henry Dunster could be heard within a decade of the founding of Harvard College. In 1647 John Eliot wrote to Thomas Shepard and various clergymen and educators that he was desperately aware of the shortcomings of the available medical resources and the inadequacy of medical care. He prayed that "our young Students in Physick may be trained up better than yet they bee, who have onely theoreticall knowledge, and are forced to fall to practice before ever they saw an Anatomy [Autopsy] made . . ."⁴ These views accorded with those of President Dunster, who was aware of the shortcomings of the Harvard Library and the need for medical instruction at the College (1647). In writing about Harvard College in 1651, Edward Johnson also commented on the need for the study of Physick. It was probably Eliot's letter that led the General Court of the Bay Colony to acknowledge in 1647 the necessity of medical study.

What medical care was available at that time was almost always administered by laymen. That busy man Cotton Mather, for example, found time to write medical treatise. His *Angel of Bethesda* was the first important effort to produce a medical treatise in America.⁵ The remedies he recommended were those of the period. Most of them were remarkable: he advocated the use of dung and wine as excellent for many ills, and it was his opinion that human excreta was "A remedy for Humune Bodies that is hardly to be paralleled." The drugs most often used were calomel, mercury, opium, ipecac, rattlesnake root, and "Jesuit's bark." One can imagine the Protestant colonists' reluctance to use a remedy with such a name as that last, but its effectiveness in treating malaria under the more satisfactory label of cinchona bark or Peruvian bark led to its popularity.

Purging was essential to medical treatment. A bill sent as late as 1747 to a patient by a Dr. Pasteur of Williamsburg itemized thirty-two drugs used during his illness, and of these, eighteen were purgatives. The compounding of prescriptions was haphazard: "use as much as can lie on a pen-knife's point," "the bigth of a walnut," "a pretty draught." Such niggling details as exact quantities were beneath the attention of these worthies. Bleeding of twenty to forty ounces or until the patient became unconscious was an indispensable remedy, or so the colonial physician thought. Some patients did not survive the loss of blood, and it is a testament to man's tenacity of spirit that some *did* survive. Malnutrition, chronic disease, deficiency diseases—such was the lot of the poorer people, who were "much afflicted with Scurvy, and many Die, especially at Boston . . ."⁷ Meddlesome and destructive therapy prepared the way for the ravages of epidemics.

Since there were no medical schools in the colonies, and the English situation was hardly better, it was necessary to go as far as Leyden or

Padua to obtain adequate medical training, which few were able to do. In 1721, of the ten "physicians" practicing in Boston only one held a doctor's degree. It has been estimated that as late as the time of the Revolution only 400 of the 3500 practitioners had a medical degree.[8] Obviously, the English tradition of physicians as university men and surgeons as craftsmen could not be maintained. The colonists had to depend on the apprentice system but had few physicians to serve as preceptors.

The medical scene was confused not only by those earnestly striving to do their best for ailing humanity, but also by an abundance of quacks. In 1706 William Byrd said: "There be some men indeed that are call'd Doctors: but they are generally discarded Surgeons of Ships, that know nothing above very common Remedys." John Oldmixon, who considered it a blessing that Virginians had but few doctors among them, fancied that "the Number of their Diseases would increase with that of their Physicians."[9] "He that sinneth before his Maker Let him fall into the hand of the physician" (Ecclesiasticus 38:15).

Not surprisingly, there were two points of view, the clergyman's and the patient's, as to the value of the missionaries of the Society for the Propagation of the Gospel. The Reverend Henry Lucas wrote in 1716: "My little Knowledge in Physick has given me a great Optunity of conversing with Men by which I have done that which by preaching I could not have done and by it I have saved our People more Money than ere they proposed to allow and have not taken any thing for all I have done."[10] But the minister-physician was not always appreciated. The wardens of the church at Perth Amboy, New Jersey, wrote in 1769 to the Society that they did not want a pastor who practiced Physick, for a preceding one had been "bred to Physick" and it had interefered with his pastoral duties.[11]

It is ironic but not at all surprising that the confused state of medicine in the colonies prevented, for a considerable time, the acceptance of treatments proven to be effective for two of the most highly fatal diseases that the colonists experienced: scurvy and smallpox. The Canadian Indians had a cure for scurvy—apparently the bark of a species of spruce —and informed the French of it in the sixteenth century. Spanish seafarers also had an effective (dietary) treatment for the disease. Scurvy, however, remained a dreaded enigma to the English-speaking world until the British Naval surgeon James Lind showed in 1757 that it could be prevented by including citrus fruit juice in the diet. Smallpox was more complicated, and we will use it as a case history to show some of the problems and methods in the practice of medicine at the time.

Unlike some of the afflictions that could not be diagnosed, smallpox was easily identified. It was distinguished early from the great pox (syphilis), which at first had been thought to be a form of smallpox. The appearance of smallpox in North America occurred simultaneously with white settlements there. In the mid-eighteenth century its mortality rate was variously estimated at 15 to 40 percent. A belief existed, probably erroneous, that American colonists were more susceptible to smallpox than were the English at home. This superstition grew out of the conflict between those who believed Africa and North and South America to be paradises inhabited by noble savages—François de Chateaubriand was a leading exponent of this idea—and those who held the opposite view, notably Comte Georges de Buffon. Buffon's position as the world's greatest naturalist of his time permitted him to persuade most people that not only were the savages not noble but that any human or animal that settled in these lands degenerated. The opposite may have been true, at least in respect to smallpox, for in the colonies the death rate from this disease was often lower than in England. Indians were extraordinarily susceptible, however: half a tribe would sometimes die in short order. For reasons not clear, there were often long intervals between smallpox epidemics, but when the disease did strike again, many succumbed. That smallpox could be prevented had been known in Africa and the Middle East for hundreds of years, at least since the time of Rhazes. The method used was to induce a mild attack of the disease by pricking into the skin a small amount of matter from a pustule. The method was called variolation, and although occasionally fatal, it could otherwise be relied on to produce a lasting immunity. The technique reached the English-speaking world when letters to the Royal Society from Turkey and Greece described the successful use of variolation there.[12] Lady Mary Wortley Montagu, wife of the English Ambassador to Turkey, successfully experimented on her son. Mary was a close friend of Princess Caroline and through her influenced the royal family. But it was not long before variolation ran into stormy weather; in both England and America, judgment as to the worth of the practice was divided.

Cotton Mather learned about this method of inoculation for smallpox from several direct sources. His black servant Onesimus told him of practices in Africa. In addition, Dr. Emanuel Timonius, graduate of Oxford and Padua, wrote a letter that was published in the *Philosophical Transactions* of the Royal Society concerning his experience with inoculation during his practice in Constantinople, as well as the experience of others there. Mather read this letter, and it unquestionably influenced him. He came out for inoculation and urged it on the physician William Douglass.[13] Douglass, a conservative, refused to have anything to do with it for thirty years (at least as far as a public recantation is concerned), and this attitude was shared by nearly all Boston physicians.[14]

Dr. Zabdiel Boylston held otherwise. He learned of variolation from hearing the many arguments for and against it. Experiences with some Boston slaves reinforced his determination to study the matter. He tried it out when the great epidemic of 1721 provided the necessary opportunity for trial. He inoculated not only his own children but Mather's as well. Many of the good folk of Boston held that this was a heathen practice, one, they said, to be abhorred by Christians. Mather confided to his diary his view of the "monstrous and crying Wickedness of this Town, (a Town at this time strangely possessed with the Devil,) and the vile Abuse which I do myself particularly suffer from it, for nothing but my instructing our base Physicians, how to save many precious Lives . . ."[15] A bomb was thrown through Mather's window. Luckily, it did not go off. The intemperate bombardier appended a note: "COTTON METH-ER, YOU DOG, DAM YOU. I'll inoculate you with this, a Pox to you." Although Mather was filled "with unutterable Joy at the prospect of . . . approaching martyrdom," he was denied this final ecstasy. Many clergymen like Boylston and Mather supported the practice and it became widespread, though still with underlying clerical opposition. A Mr. Masley, for example, objected to this "unjustifiable act, an infliction of an evil, and a distrust of God's overruling care."[16] A colleague affirmed that inoculation tended to promote "Vice and Immorality," for those freed from disease were likely to lead intemperate lives. Another, in London, asked, "Is it not unlawful to make oneself sick?"[17]

One can only speculate on why Mather's and Boylston's attitudes led to such violent opposition. Donald Fleming suggests jealousy: Douglass' jealousy of Mather and other physicians' jealousy of Boylston.[18] It is doubtful, however, that jealousy alone could have aroused such virulent attacks without support from the community at large. For one thing, there was skepticism concerning the efficacy of the procedure. The dogmatic insistence, on the basis of meager experience, that it could not fail was an unhappy claim, coming especially from the abrasive Cotton Mather. Failures when they occurred were attributed to infection *before* inoculation.

Boylston's data should have cleared the air: some 280 individuals were inoculated during the 1721 epidemic in Boston; six, or 2 percent, died ("some of these may have also been infected in the natural Way before being inoculated"). Of those infected by natural means in Boston in the epidemic of 1721–22, 5759 contracted the disease, and of these, 844 or 14.6 percent, died—a sevenfold increase. Boylston adds, "None of our inoculated Patients afterward took the Small-Pox, tho' they were continually expos'd."[19]

After the furore surrounding the 1721 epidemic had quieted down, not much was heard from the variolation battlefront until the next major epidemic, nearly a decade later, which struck Boston, New York, and Philadelphia. In Boston some 400 persons had accepted variolation, of whom twelve died, a death rate of about 3 percent. Of the 4000 who contracted the disease naturally, 12.5 percent died.[20] Variolation received the robust support of Benjamin Franklin, and in 1759 he prevailed upon Dr. William Heberden to write an account of the success of inoculation. Franklin wrote the introduction to this pamphlet, wherein he urged parents to "no longer refuse to accept and thankfully use a discovery God in his mercy has been pleased to bless mankind with."[21]

Notwithstanding the remarkable success of variolation, outcries against it continued. Insofar as one can get at the reasons for this remarkable behavior, they were in part owing to the fact that those who were inoculated had light cases and mingled with their friends. "Ordinarily the Patient sits up every Day and entertains his Friends, yea ventures upon a *Glass of Wine* with them,"[22] all the while distributing his infection. The opponents of variolation finally got the upper hand in New England—for reasons far from clear but perhaps because uncontrolled inoculation was responsible for spreading the disease—and by 1790 variolation was forbidden in all of the New England states. When epidemics occurred, however, the restrictions on variolation were inconsistently relaxed. William Cheever observed in his diary on November 24 that during the epidemic of 1776 "Permission was given for Inoculation of the Small-Pox." This was also true in the outbreaks of 1778 and 1792.[23] Dr. John Morgan, chief physician of the American armies, recommended, and Washington ordered, general inoculation of the Army.[24] When the British army in Boston was forced to leave, it was because of smallpox raging in Boston, not because of American military strength. When the British departed, Washington ordered one thousand of his men who had had the smallpox or who had been inoculated previously to enter the town, forbidding all others to do so. On the other hand, smallpox among Benedict Arnold's forces prevented any effective action in the invasion of Canada.

The half-century from 1721 to 1776 showed a remarkable change. James Warren wrote from Boston, July 17, 1776, to John Adams: "this town is now become a great Hospital for Inoculation . . . so it is that the rage for Inoculation prevailing here has whirled me into its vortex & brought me . . . into a Crowd of Patients with which this Town is now filled . . ."[25] John Adams replied a week later, July 24, 1776: "This, I suppose, will find you at Boston, growing well of the Small Pox. This Distemper is the King of Terrors to America this year. . . . I could wish, that the whole people was inoculated,—it gives me great Pleasure to learn that . . . Inoculation is permitted in every town."[26] Unquestionably, variolation was an important medical advance of the eighteenth century and was so recognized by the end of the colonial period. Its early failure of acceptance in New England was symptomatic of the lack of medical standards.

Although the history of smallpox in New England is alone highly dramatic, one should not forget that other serious diseases occurred. Diphtheria and scarlet fever were commonly lumped together as "throat distemper." Its cause, like that of yellow fever, a deadly and terrifying scourge that repeatedly struck coastal cities, was unknown.

Not much attention was paid to measles in the eighteenth century. Deadly though it could be to Indians, its mortality rate was low when compared with smallpox among the colonists. Mumps and whooping cough were recognized but did not often appear in early times. Diseases of the respiratory system flourished among the inevitable hardships of the colonial period. Deficient food, crowded housing, poor sanitation, ignorance, inadequate nursing, and poor medical care were factors in all of these epidemics—and were especially important in the spread of respiratory disease.

Fevers and poxes seemed to arrive simultaneously with the early settlers. Judging from their diaries, the colonists were always talking about fevers, and reports loomed large on dysentery, typhoid, typhus, yellow fever, malaria, respiratory ailments, etc. The cause of neither the fevers and lung diseases nor the dysenteries could be diagnosed. It is probable that typhoid fever was present. Its differentiation from typhus was not easy or certain. Typhus was widespread and often fatal in Europe, but it was not a great problem in New England.

Venereal disease was not unknown to the seventeenth-century colonists. The Puritans were evidently a more earthy people than tradition has implied. No seventeenth- or eighteenth-century Kinsey was on hand to provide us with quantitative data. In 1646 there was an outbreak of syphilis in Boston.[27] "Lues venerea" was brought to the city by a sailor who infected his wife. She was a wet nurse, and many persons drew milk from her ulcerated breast. At least sixteen persons were infected by this new and odious disease. The energetic Cotton Mather would not have kept out of this scene:

> I am informed of several Houses in this Town, where there are
> young Women of a very debauched Character, and extremely Im-
> pudent; unto whom there is a very great Resort of young men,
> [which] are extremely poisoned by such conversation as these enter-
> tain them withal. I must address our Society, that by suitable Admo-
> nitions . . . this Mischief may be extinguished.[28]

It is evident that the medical scene in Boston was characterized by ignorance, confusion, and superstition. In Europe precise diagnosis was developing rapidly, owing to the writings of Thomas Sydenham and Thomas Willis in England and Herman Boerhaave and his disciples, trained in Leyden but later established in Edinburgh, Vienna, and other cities. In view of the absence of effective specific agents for the treatment of disease, however, diagnosis was not much of a gain. In New England, not only was effective treatment unavailable, but the morale of the sick was impaired by the medical practitioners' evident ineptitude with respect to diagnosis. Despite the fact that the high birth rate made up for the losses brought about by diseases (the population doubled about every twenty-three years) [29] and the wealth of the land led to material development, the state of medical care was not satisfactory. This backwardness of medicine not only prevented effective clinical practice, but also hampered the development of institutions for the care of the helpless sick.

INSTITUTIONAL CARE OF THE SICK

Pestilence, famine, and death dogged the footsteps of the colonists, rich and poor alike. The welfare level depended on the community's extent of need, available resources, and degree of social consciousness. The immigrants brought with them the practices of poor relief in their homelands (England and Holland), together with the principle of local responsibility derived from the English Poor Law of 1601. Local responsibility was the keystone, whether in religious matters or civil affairs. The sick poor were therefore a local responsibility. Strangers without local rights could be ousted. "Warning out" notices were everywhere. The seriously ill presented grave problems both of conscience and of practice. Even so, some, especially pregnant women, homeless and friendless, were expelled without mercy.[30]

> February 15, 1715/16. Sarah Hinks Single woman belonging to Salem who sayes She came last from thence into this Town abt Sixteen dayes Since, and is at the House of Widdow Warren at the South of Boston and is reported to be with Child and nigh ready to lye in, being this day by Mr. John Mayon at the direction of the Sel. men, warned to depart out of this Town to Salem where she belongs.[31]

Care of the sick had to be determined in part by the number of available physicians, but these were scarce until late in the eighteenth century. Colonizing companies sent some contract physicians and barber surgeons, but to escape death in the colonies, many returned home. The clergy carried on as well as they could with saving both body and soul.

It is interesting that unlike the situation which prevailed until recent decades, there did not seem to be any prejudice against women practicing medicine. Their activities were comparable to the work of male physicians and were not confined to midwifery.[32]

There is a petition dated June 18, 1688, to Governor Andros from one William Hutchins of New Hampshire, stating that he had been afflicted with the scrofula, or king's evil, for six years and had exhausted all of his resources with "the Most Learned & Scilfulest phisitians" but without cure. He begged to be sent to England, where the King's touch would doubtless give relief.[33]

The town of Boston erected two "guest houses" in 1658, where those newly arrived from England could be sheltered until they could find or build their own permanent housing.[34] There is no indication that these were used to house the sick.

With the growth of the population, it became impractical for the larger towns to take up each case of need. From this situation evolved the town physician. Dr. Stone in 1671 became Boston's first town physician, with salary paid by the town. The Selectmen's minutes for November 29, 1671, state:

> Upon the motion of Doctr Daniell Stone for pay for Chirurgery & phisicke administered to severall poore of this town the select men see cause to abate him his rate this yeare for what is done for the time past . . .[35]

This contract was renewed annually for several years following, and other towns adopted the practice. The fixed salaries were very low, and extra funds were not usually provided for medicines or appliances. Certainly, there was no great incentive to efforts beyond the minimal. Only a dedicated doctor could have been expected to fulfill his contract. At times, a physician was not able to discharge all of his responsibilities.

One can summarize the lines of development as the colonists endeavored to accept their responsibilities: care for the body, either at home or "boarded out"; provision of nursing and medical care paid out of the town treasury if the patient was unable to pay; farming out medical care to a salaried physician; caring for the sick poor in almshouses or work houses, sometimes with medical care; jailing of the insane; and, finally, provision of general or special hospitals for the sick poor. One principle stands out; it was derived directly from the Elizabethan Poor Law of 1601: society is responsible for providing for the sick poor. There was, nevertheless, toward the end of the colonial period a definite shift from governmental responsibility to private enterprise, and private philanthropy in large part took over the care of the indigent.[36]

Few of the eighteenth-century colonists had ever seen a general hospital, although people who lived in seaports were familiar with quarantine hospitals, whose function was to prevent the entry of infectious disease, especially yellow and other fevers, smallpox, measles, diphtheria. The General Court of Massachusetts at the March session, 1647/48, established a strict quarantine over all vessels coming from the West India Islands, where an epidemic was raging, perhaps "the plague or like In[fectious] disease."[37] (It may have been yellow fever.) But a year later, at the session beginning in May 1649, it was recorded: "The Courte doth thinke meete, that the order, concerning the stopping of West India ships at the Castle should hereby be repealed seeing it hath pleased God to stay the sickness there."[38]

In 1716 the Newport (Boston Harbor) Town Meeting authorized the construction of a quarantine hospital on Coaster's Island in Boston Harbor. It was excellently equipped. The Massachusetts General Court in 1717 built a hospital on Spectacle Island, also in Boston Harbor. Later it was moved to Rainsford Island, where it functioned for over a century, until 1849.

It is not clear if the quarantine hospitals in the early days were used exclusively for quarantine of incoming disease or whether, as seems likely, they were also used for diseases arising in the colonies. At any rate, Dr. James Lloyd (1728–1810) wrote in his ledger that the barracks at Castle William became, on February 24, 1764, a "Hospital for Inoculating," where he worked with Joseph Warren.[39]

Almshouses had existed from antiquity and were a characteristic feature in the principal New England towns. The sick were cared for in them, but they did not exist for such care alone. Helpless paupers of all varieties were accepted. In Boston the almshouse was under the supervision of the Overseers of the Poor, who were elected each year by the local citizens. It was customary for distinguished men to serve on this board; they included Thomas H. Perkins, Joseph Coolidge, Jr., and Edward Tuckerman (all of whom eventually became Trustees of the Massachusetts General Hospital). The Overseers took turns inspecting the almshouse and thus became familiar with the misery of the poor and acutely aware of the need for a genuine hospital. The Boston almshouse can hardly have been more than a symbolic medical gesture: it provided only eight beds for the care of the sick and insane of the entire town.

The shortcomings of the almshouse were set forth in the first promotional pamphlet published by the Trustees of the Massachusetts General Hospital:

An Alms-house is, in its nature, merely an *asylum for poverty.* Here the poor, without respect of age or sex, have a right to find shelter.

If it provide medicine and professional attendance, it is because these are inevitably *incidental* to such an establishment, and not because they are the objects of it. *The care of the* sick is, almost necessarily, a secondary consideration in an Almshouse . . .[40]

The roots of the hospital as we know it today can be found in the latter part of the eighteenth century, as a place where bed care of the sick could be provided, where teaching could be carried out, and where, in a modest way, disease could be studied and treatment improved. But how was such an establishment to be staffed?

Chapter Two

Education of Physicians

BEFORE the establishment of medical schools in the colonies, the young man who wished to learn "physic" could follow one of two routes: If he had the necessary financial resources—and only a few were so lucky—he could go to Leyden, Padua, or, later, Edinburgh or London, for the best available instruction of the times. Great emphasis was placed on a classical education, and a fluent use of Latin was usually required. Theses were written in this language, as were many textbooks. Or, the course followed by the majority, the student could apprentice himself to a well-known practitioner for a period of years.

APPRENTICESHIP

Until nearly the beginning of the nineteenth century, the majority of physicians in the United States were men without formal medical education. "They had heard no lectures, performed no experiments, and, more than likely, seen no dissections. They called themselves 'Doctor' not because they were graduates of a university, with a diploma to show, but because they were in fact practicing what doctors of a university usually did."[1] They were apprentices to a practicing physician for a variable period, often from one to five years, after which, with their master's certificate, they moved on, more or less prepared to care for the injured, the sick, the dying.[2]

The apprenticeship system has received its share of criticism, but it is only fair to take a look at the high quality of many of the distinguished practicing physicians of the time who accepted apprentices and who had themselves been products of the system. Apprenticeship was, whatever might be said against it, an effective method and, in principle, not very different from some of today's clinical training of interns and residents.

Philadelphia had the best-developed system of medical education in the colonies. The students who began to frequent the Pennsylvania Hospital for instruction as soon as it was open were primarily apprentices of the staff members, although some were simply "pupils of the Hospital." After completing their prescribed activities, Thomas Bond (a distinguished physician of Philadelphia) gave them a certificate.

Notwithstanding John Morgan's later harsh words in his *Discourse* (below, p. 20) about the apprentice system, the training could be exacting. Some hint of its severity can be obtained from Benjamin Rush (1745), who was apprenticed to the busiest Philadelphia doctor, John Redman, 1761–66. Redman took only two apprentices at a time and kept them busy. Rush recounts that in his five years of training he was absent only eleven days, and was out of Redman's house on his own time only three nights. He had many duties: compounding medicines, taking sick call, making home visits, sometimes acting as a nurse. He was in charge of Redman's records and accounts. He read all the medical books he could get his hands on. He mentioned especially Sydenham, Van Swieten, and Boerhaave. Most important, he had daily association with his master, who, in turn, had been educated by the severe John Kearsley. Redman's pupils had distinguished careers. Rush became a well-known American physician of his time, and Morgan and Rush were among the first professors in the Medical School of the University of Pennsylvania.

Among the distinguished individuals who had started as apprentices in the Boston area, one in particular stands out: Dr. James Lloyd (1728–1810). He undoubtedly had great influence, indirectly, on the Harvard Medical School, for he was a mentor of the founder of the School, John Warren (1753–1815). After completing his apprenticeship in Boston and following a year as a dresser at St. Thomas' in London, Lloyd quickly made a name for himself, especially in surgery and midwifery. He introduced Cheselden's method of amputation, and he may have been the first practitioner in Boston to perform the hazardous operation of lithotomy. While assisting Dr. John Clark, he became an ardent follower of Zabdiel Boylston in advocating inoculation for smallpox. With Dr. Clark he was able to show remarkable results: one death from smallpox in three hundred inoculated individuals, whereas five deaths had occurred in one hundred individuals who had not been inoculated, a fifteen-fold difference in favor of inoculation.[3]

By all accounts Lloyd was the busiest physician Boston had ever seen; yet despite his heavy responsibilities, he found time to accept apprentices—for example, one Oliver Smith, "at 14 or 15 years old." Lloyd speaks of having "engaged [his] Apothecary to take him for the first three or four years, when he will be under my Eye, the two or three last years will take him with me, was he my Son I should take the same steps."[4] In many cases, his trainees became distinguished—Major General Joseph Warren and John Jeffries, for example. When, later, Benjamin Waterhouse learned of Edward Jenner's discovery of vaccination and received from Jenner material for carrying it out, he immediately submitted the material to Dr. Lloyd, with whom he had long been acquainted and on whose experience, frankness, and good judgment he had long relied. Lloyd was fully persuaded of the importance of the discovery and played an important part in introducing the practice of vaccination into the United States. One of the first diplomas of Doctor of Medicine by the University at Cambridge, Massachusetts, was granted to him. He was an excellent product of and participant in the apprentice system. At the same time it must be noted that there were few laws governing who could or could not practice medicine, and the loose reins of the apprenticeship system—or lack of system—invited charlatans and quacks as well as the grossly incompetent.

Although in the early days of the country, the system was, for the majority, the only type of training available, it was not immediately supplanted by the medical schools; rather, the two systems reinforced each other. Thus, fifteen years after the founding of the Harvard Medical School, James Jackson, later a cofounder of the Massachusetts General Hospital, was, in 1797–98, an apprentice of Professor Edward A. Holyoke. Even today the internships and residency programs in hospitals are descendants or at least variants of the apprenticeship system. Even more direct is today's common practice among young physicians, following the completion of a residency, of associating themselves for a period of years with a distinguished, or at least experienced, physician.

TRAVEL ABROAD

In the first half of the nineteenth century, there was no place in America where a graduate physician could improve his knowledge of any branch of medicine as well as he might in several of the European centers. Bonner suggests that the real problem confronting American medicine at that time was not graduate education but an urgent need to improve undergraduate instruction.[5] For various reasons foreign travel had a considerable influence on American medicine. From the colonial days onward, a steady stream of medical students left America for European schools. A distinguished roster of American physicians, including Benjamin Rush, John Morgan, and Philip Syng Physick from Philadelphia, and Benjamin Waterhouse from New England, studied abroad for varying periods, principally at Edinburgh and London. By this time Padua had lost its preeminence, as interest in anatomy began to take second place to that in clinical medicine and chemistry. Edinburgh at this time was becoming the center of a Scottish Enlightenment. Medicine participated in this development and benefited especially from Edinburgh's traditional ties with Leyden. That city was the leader of European clinical medicine, a position that it maintained for some time despite the loss of much of its faculty to Vienna, at the invitation of Maria Theresa. Many of the leading physicians of Edinburgh spent part of their professional lives at Leyden, even to the point of serving as professor, alternating at each (as Pitcairn did).

That Edinburgh had entered its gayest and most cultured period beginning about 1750 was evident in the sudden burst of intellectual activity which thrust the city to the top position among the medical schools of Europe, as the reputation of Leyden declined. Vienna had not yet established itself, and the controversy in France between the orthodoxy of Paris and the more daring theoreticians of Montpellier was yet to be settled by the liberalization of Parisian medical thought. Later Edinburgh also declined, partly because of its loss of outstanding physicians to England.

Between 1749 and 1800, 117 Americans received their degrees from the University of Edinburgh. These potential leaders usually obtained a medical degree first at Pennsylvania, Harvard, Yale, or the College of Physicians and Surgeons, and then went to Europe for postgraduate study in one or more medical specialties. After 1830, when German medicine began to have a powerful attraction for New Yorkers, Harvard men flocked to Dr. Pierre Louis in Paris. Soon Louis supplanted John Hunter in Edinburgh and later London as the most sought-after teacher. Henry I. Bowditch walked the wards of La Pitié with Louis, and as a special mark of consideration Louis allowed him to enter the wards out of the usual hours.[6] Oliver Wendell Holmes and J. Mason Warren were associates in Paris at that time.

In one letter, written from Paris on May 12, 1833, Bowditch expressed his great enthusiasm for Louis. Bowditch had a considerable altercation on this subject with Holmes, who confided to a friend the next day that according to Bowditch, Louis "was the greatest man that ever lived in medicine, or I was crazy."[7] Bowditch called him the "first man for knowledge of disease."[8] Indeed, Louis taught the Americans the meaning of bedside observation, how to conduct clinical examinations, the true importanace of pathological anatomy, and the maintenance of statistical records. Bowditch translated Louis' important work on phthisis, as well as his studies on typhoid fever, and had this to say about him in a letter to his mother written in January 1833:

> I shall always love him, and look upon him as the one who is to be
> a renovator of the science of medicine. He marks out a path for him-
> self and his disciples, but if it be followed closely it can't fail of mak-

ing medicine a little more certain than it is now and them more powerful in distinguishing diseases. He has raised in me a higher feeling than I had in regard to my profession. I always looked upon it as one of the noblest in the world; but now I have driven off some of the lower feelings which influenced me while in America, and am prepared to study it as one requiring for a proper acquaintance of it the highest and most laborious exertions of which man is capable.

When James Jackson, Jr., had completed his stay with Louis, Louis wrote to his father, pleading that the son be allowed to study scientific matters for four or five years before beginning practice. The father would have none of it. Such a move would separate his son from other physicians in an undesirable way: "We are a business doing people. We are new. We have, as it were, but just landed on these uncultivated shores; there is a vast deal to be done; and he who will not be doing must be set down as a drone."[9] Bonner points out that despite the large number of Americans who studied pathology with Louis, no pathological research patterned after the French school ever took root in America. There was a widespread belief that attention to pathology was less important than the cure of the patient. This view was to prevail in Boston until Eliot, President of Harvard University after the Civil War, forced a reform.

In the meantime, although many leaders of American medicine in the pre-Civil War period valued their training in the great clinics of Europe, the problem of providing a rapidly growing America with adequate numbers of physicians remained unsolved. It is sad to recall that when attempts were made to cope with this problem, only a few schools in the European model were established, and over a hundred whose only aim was financial gain for their owners were opened instead. In the western states the extreme shortage of qualified physicians led to the abandonment of qualifications entirely. The commercial aspect of many of these ventures was plainly to be seen in their competition for students. Western schools especially attempted to outrival one another in shortening curricula, cutting fees, and establishing easy requirements for degrees. Bowditch was right: there was a great contrast between his American background and Louis' in Paris, and this contrast became more marked with time.

THE FIRST MEDICAL SCHOOL: PENNSYLVANIA

The Medical School of the University of Pennsylvania, first in the country, was established in 1765 in the College of Philadelphia, later the University of the State of Pennsylvania. It antedated by three years the second school, established in 1768 in King's College, New York City, now the College of Physicians and Surgeons of Columbia University, and, by some seventeen years, the third school, Harvard's, in 1782. Where the first two led, Harvard, to some extent, followed.

Philadelphia was a fitting place for such a venture: In 1765 it was the largest town in the North American Colonies, with some 25,000 inhabitants. Strategically situated as a seaport and merchant area, it was growing rapidly. Since the Pennsylvania Hospital had been chartered in 1751 and had begun receiving patients the next year, the prior existence of this institution must have been a strong element in the determination to create a school of medicine in Philadelphia.

Two classmates, William Shippen, Jr., and John Morgan, went to Edinburgh to attend the lectures of Alexander Monro (the first) and William Cullen. In 1761 Shippen took the degree of M.D. there; Morgan took his also in Edinburgh, in 1763. One of the great friends of the Colonists was the celebrated London physician, Dr. John Fothergill, of Whitehall Court, London. During 1750–60 every American physician or medical student was certain to be warmly welcomed by him. The young Shippen, whose father was a governor of the Pennsylvania Hospital, may have delighted his host with detailed accounts of medical practice in Philadelphia. Familiar with the principal practitioners in Philadelphia, Shippen recognized the shortcomings of the apprentice system and discussed them with Fothergill, who had never traveled to America but was extraordinarily well informed of conditions there.

The first recorded mention of a medical school at Philadelphia is in a letter from Dr. Fothergill to James Pemberton (one of the managers of the Pennsylvania Hospital).

> I have recommended it to Dr. Shippen to give a Course of Anatomical Lectures to such as may attend, he is very well qualified for the subject and will soon be followed by an able Assistant Dr. Morgan both of whom I apprehend will not only be useful to the Province in their Employments but if suitably countenanced by the Legislature will be able to erect a School for Physick amongst you that may draw many students from . . . parts of America and the West Indies . . .[10]

An agreement was apparently reached that Shippen would become professor of anatomy (this included surgery and midwifery) and that Morgan would have the chair of physic.[11]

Shippen returned to Philadelphia late in 1762 and opened a private school of anatomy in a building adjacent to his father's house. This kind of teaching he could carry on alone while he awaited the return of Morgan to join him in the creation of the school. John Morgan returned to

Philadelphia in April 1765, and medical affairs began to hum. He had distinguished himself at Edinburgh. Aggressive and ambitious, he had a well-thought-out scheme for affiliating a faculty of medicine with the College of Philadelphia. Clearly, Morgan was determined to go down in history as the founder of the first medical school in America, and in this he pretty well succeeded. Animosities between Shippen and Morgan created at this time persisted for the rest of their lives. The reputations of both were injured, and their institution's development hampered. Notwithstanding the Quakers' peaceful intentions, the leading physicians of Philadelphia were committed to war on one another.[12] Ambition had prevailed over candor and generosity, as it often does in academe.

Present at a special meeting of the Trustees of the College, held on May 3, 1765, were Drs. John Redman, Thomas Cadwalader, Thomas and Phineas Bond, but, notably, *not* Shippen Senior. Morgan's proposals were studied, and The Minutes of the Meeting record that "The . . . proposals being duly weighed, and the Trustees entertaining a high sense of Dr. Morgan's abilities, and the honors paid to him by different learned bodies and societies in Europe, they unanimously appointed him Professor of the Theory and Practice of Physic in this College."[13] In an atmosphere of academic treachery thus began academic medical education in America. The new professor was invited to address the Commencement to be held four weeks later on May 30. At the morning session on that day, Morgan, in the academic robe of a professor, began to read his now celebrated *Discourse upon the Institution of Medical Schools in America*, which he had worked on for more than a year, but the day being hot and the discourse long, the meeting was adjourned until the next morning.[14] Since the paper disparaged the apprenticeship system, one can hardly avoid the suspicion that it may have been owing to the heat of his audience, distinguished practitioners who had achieved their eminence through what Morgan described as the unworthy apprentice route.

Morgan set out to define the boundaries of medicine in America, "to show its present [1765] condition . . . the difficulties which accompany its study, and the impracticability of making any great progress therein, till it is put on a better footing." He found it important to separate the practice of physic from surgery, and in accordance with European ideas he divided the "science of medicine [into] Anatomy, Materia Medica, Botany, Chymistry, the Theory of Medicine, and the practice." There followed an examination and description of each of these, which, he said, should be studied in that order.

Morgan proposed that the medical school be established in the College of Philadelphia. Close ties with the Pennsylvania Hospital were to be sought. He then took a thrust at Shippen Junior, claiming that he, Morgan, had learned "with the highest satisfaction" of Shippen's intention to deliver some medical lectures, but Morgan did not "learn that [Shippen] recommended at all a collegiate undertaking of this kind." He seems never to have missed an opportunity to put down his old friend. Despite his objectionable personality, however, Morgan's underlying good sense, his wide experience, and his wider view of the needs of the present and the future shine forth. His small book, a classic, marks a milestone in the development of cultural life in America. It also served as a guide in the development of later medical schools, including Harvard.

Morgan, as if surprised by the immediate hostility his *Discourse* evoked, promptly wrote, to be inserted in the published book, a twenty-five-page "Preface containing, amongst other things, the Author's apology for attempting to introduce the regular mode of practicing Physic in Philadelphia." He was charged with reflecting adversely upon other practitioners, evidently those educated only by apprenticeships. This he denied. Others felt he had exaggerated the difficulties of the physician's training. This, too, he discounted. He emphasized, possibly with Shippen in mind, the inadequacy of a knowledge of anatomy as a background for the complete physician. He was envisioning a superior class of physicians as a goal toward which he would strive. Yet he offended many local physicians who combined medical and surgical practice and acted, as was the custom, as apothecaries, compounding drugs. Morgan seemed to claim for himself a higher station than that of the general practitioners. He condemned Shippen Senior, Thomas Bond, and John Redman, who were proud of the apprentices they had trained even though the system was inadequate. Morgan, labeling surgery an unintellectual art, seemed willing to leave it to apprentice training and did not propose a chair. Nor was midwifery mentioned. He knew well that the professor-designate of anatomy, Shippen Junior, practiced and taught both. (Shippen kept quiet for several months, but finally, on September 17, 1765, asserted his own priority in planning a medical school and said he would graciously accept a professorship. The appointment was made at once by the trustees, and Shippen gave his first lecture November 14, 1765.) Morgan's curious preface, prepared in a few weeks, unlike the main body of the *Discourse*, which took a year, diminished but did not destroy its message, which was how a medical school should be organized.

The rivalry between Morgan and Shippen continued and actually spread. Benjamin Rush, chosen for the Chair of Chemistry by Morgan, also disliked Shippen. The day after Shippen died, Rush wrote in his diary, "He was my enemy from the time of my settlement in Philadelphia in 1769 to the last year of his life."[15] The Morgan and Shippen antagonism did a "great hurt," as William Smith put it.

In summary, Morgan's plan comprised nearly all of the elements of medical teaching since found to be essential: affiliation with a university, qualified professors, thorough premedical preparation, a carefully planned curriculum with well-defined studies before clinical work was undertaken, close affiliation with a teaching hospital, a library, laboratory-type demonstrations in anatomy, botany, and chemistry, and high standards for graduating. He even suggested that a medical school might become a center for research. As Corner points out, if Morgan's plans had been truly followed, American medicine might have advanced much more rapidly than it did.[16] Morgan's plan failed only to grasp that lectures were not enough, that each student should dissect for himself and carry out chemical tests and physiological experiments. These ideas, today considered essential, were to go unrecognized for many years, both in Europe and in America.

KING'S COLLEGE

The second medical school in America was founded in New York. As a student at Edinburgh, Samuel Bard (1742–1821) learned what Shippen and Morgan were planning. Other physicians, too, watched the Pennsylvanians with considerable envy, but except for Bard they seemed powerless to do anything about it. Bard expressed his thoughts to his father:

Edinburgh, Dec. 29th, 1762.

Honoured Sir,
     You no doubt have heard that Dr. Shippen has opened an anatomical class in Philadelphia; his character here as an anatomist is very good, and no doubt he appears equally so in America. You perhaps are not acquainted with the whole of that scheme; it is not to stop with anatomy, but to found, under the patronage of Dr. Fothergill, a medical college in that place: Mr. Morgan, who is to graduate next spring, and will be over in the fall, intends to lecture upon the theory and practice of physic, and is equal to the undertaking . . . I am afraid that the Philadelphians, who will have the start of us by several years, will be a great obstacle; and another almost insurmountable one is, the religious and party feeling which exists in New-York; for if such a thing was to be undertaken, it ought to be in conjunction

with the college. This perhaps you may think a wild scheme; but it is at least an innocent one, and can do no hurt to have such a thing in view . . .

Your affectionate son,

S.B.

His father replied: "I much approve of . . . the establishing of a proper medical institution in this city; but I think it should be commenced by a public hospital."[17]

This exchange gives substantial basis for crediting John Bard with the original concept of the "hospital of New-York; a design which his son subsequently effected; an institution . . . creditable to its author." Samuel Bard was greatly influential in establishing the New York school in 1768. Unlike the one in Philadelphia, it was less influenced by "physic" and more by surgery. The College did not prosper, however, and before long the Revolution had destroyed it, scattering its students and faculty. When finally the British evacuated New York, several attempts were made to revive the school. They were not successful, in large part owing to the jealousies of rival contending groups, a state of affairs that seems to plague academic institutions in a manner that appears to have become traditional.[18] It was not until 1810, when the College of Physicians and Surgeons was formed, that the school was resurrected, later to become a part of Columbia University.

Whereas the Philadelphia experience, involving as it did the Morgan *Discourse* and the efforts of a considerable number of distinguished physicians, clearly influenced the events that led to the creation of the Harvard Medical School, it is unlikely that the ephemeral organization in New York City played any such role.

COLONIAL MEDICAL SOCIETIES

The medical societies were also an important element in the medical environment. The first in the country was launched in Boston in 1735–6. Despite the illustrious names of its members, all that is known of it for certain is contained in a letter from Dr. William Douglass of Boston to Dr. Cadwalader Colden of New York, February 17, 1735–6:

> . . . we have lately in Boston formed a medical society of which this Gentleman [Dr. Clark, the bearer of this letter] a Member thereof can give you a particular account. We Design from time to time to publish some short pieces: there is now ready for the Press No. 1 with this Title page.[1]

It is not clear whether a letter signed "Philanthropos" and published in the *Boston Weekly News-Letter* of January 5, 1737, referred to the Douglass-Colden Society just mentioned:

To the Judicious and Learned President and Members of the Medical Society in Boston.

At present we are infected with an Empiricomany or, An Infatuation in favour of *Empiricism* or *Quackery*. To put a stop to the growing Evil . . . [even though our laws do not cover this situation. It would be absurd that] there should be no Remedy against Quack, who, attempting to remove some slight Ailment, thro' downright Ignorance poisons me . . . [In England, they did it better, for] in the Tenth year of King Henry VIII [the College of Physicians was incorporated in London, and confirmed by Parliament in the Fourteenth year of the same King] that no Body shall exercise the Faculty of Physick in *London*, or within seven Miles around it, unless he be admitted there by the President and Community of said College . . . [Parliament added the need for] Letters Testimonial [and examination, except when the candidate was a graduate of Oxford or Cambridge. So much for England.] Methinks it would be a Matter of no great Difficulty to concert some proper Measures for regulating the Practice of Physick thro' out this Province . . . so that no Person shall be allowed to Practice Physick within the Limits of this Province, unless he be first examined by regular, approved and learned Physicians and Surgeons as the Honourable Court shall see meet to appoint.

Philanthropos

There is little record of the activities of this society. It was heard from as late as November 13, 1741, for in that issue of the *Boston Weekly News-Letter* is this statement:

A Medical Society in Boston, New England, with no quackish view as is the manner of some; but for the Comfort and Benefit of the unhappy and miserable Sufferers by the excruciating Pain, occasioned by a Stone in the Bladder, do Publish the following Case . . .

The next mention of an American medical society of record is in a manuscript in the Library of the New York Academy of Medicine: "A Society of Gentlemen in New York, founded about 1749, for the weekly discussion of Medical Subjects." The title of the manuscript is "An Essay on the Nature and Cause of ye MALIGNANT PLEURISY, that proved so remarkably Fatal to the Inhabitants of Huntington, and some other places on Long-Island; in the Winter of the Year 1749; Drawn up at the request of a Weekly Society of Gentlemen in New York, and Addressed to them at one of their Meetings . . . by Dr. Jno. Bard, New York, 1749." Nothing more is known of this organization.

John Morgan understood the importance of medical societies in medical education. When he returned to Philadelphia from Europe in 1765, he immediately organized the Philadelphia Medical Society. Very little is known about it beyond the fact that it is referred to in the correspondence of Benjamin Rush in 1768. In that year it became part of the American Society for the Promotion of Useful Knowledge. Benjamin Franklin had founded the American Philosophical Society in 1743, "for the promotion of useful knowledge among the British plantations of America." The American Society was also headquartered in Philadelphia, and since its purpose was the same, the two were united on January 2, 1769.[20]

To return to Boston: In 1765 Cotton Tufts of Weymouth attempted to organize a state medical society in Massachusetts but was not then successful, although his persistent efforts finally bore fruit. The Massachusetts Medical Society was established in 1781, just a year before the founding of the Harvard Medical School. It is the oldest medical society in the United States with a continuous record of meetings. (The Medical Society of New Jersey was established fifteen years before the Massachusetts Society, but it held no meetings from 1775 to 1781 and again suspended meetings for a twelve-year period, 1795–1807; its continuous activity, therefore, dates from 1807, not 1766.) The Bostonians learned two lessons from the experiences of the New Jersey society: first, that a state medical society should have nothing to do with fee tables, and second, that the state society should oversee the laws concerning the practice of medicine. The formation of the Massachusetts society was part of a wave of intellectual activity that swept over Boston soon after the restraints of the Revolutionary War were released. Emerging from the ferment were, in addition to the Massachusetts Medical Society (1781), the American Academy of Arts and Sciences (1780), the Harvard Medical School (1782), and the Massachusetts Historical Society (1791). Their origins were similar and their purposes related.[21] However, the formation of the Massachusetts Medical Society was preceded by the formation of a Boston society a year and a half earlier.

The famous 1765 "Graph. Iatroon Letter" (letter of a writing physician—author unknown) is important.[22] It gives cogent reasons for the establishment of medical societies.

Sir: There has been some time on foot a proposal forming medical Societies or Associations of Doctors analogous to those of the Clergy for the more speedy Improvement of our Young Physicians.* To get the Profession upon a more respectable footing in the Country by suppressing this Herd of Empiricks who have bro't such intolerable

contempt on the Epithet *Country Practitioner*. And to increase Charity
& good will amongst the lawful Members of the Profession that
they may avoid condemning & calumniating each other before the
Plebians as it is too common for the last that's call'd in a difficult
Case to do by those that preeceded him which we apprehend to be
highly detrimental to the Profession and the chief Root from whence
these very Empiricks spring.

We don't know what Objections there may, there have been such
Societies in Boston and where medical Academies are established &
Empiricks are punished by Law there is not so much need of them.
We should esteem it a favor to be convinced of the impracticability
of such a Scheme if it is so, & if not why it may not immediately
take place ——

If you, like our Design as all do to whom we have proposed it, we
humbly conceive that the only way to effect it is for you to join heartily in the Cause & agree upon some certain time & Place to meet in
which all the Physicians *digni honore* must be notified and to bring
with each of them a written Plan of Regulations if they please, at
the Meeting to chuse a Moderator and after hearing each Plan that
to be adopted which shall obtain a Majority of votes &c. &c. &c.:

Presuming upon your Concurrence we desire you to promote the
Design by circulating this Paper thro' the Hands of all the under mentioned Physicians, or others beyond their Limits, but we must be careful that it falls not into the Hands of any but orthodox Physicians,
and to prevent it you should deliver it yourself or send it by a trusty
Person carefully seald & superscribed lest a telltale wife or Child di-
vulge that which must be as secret as Masonry till some Societies are
established.

The Gentlemen within compass of our knowledge whom we think
it necessary to invite are as follows . . . [names omitted]

You are desired to repair to Gardners Tavern on Boston Neck at
the hour of two P.M. precisely on the third Monday in March 1765.

It is hoped that the elder and established Physicians will promote
this Affair by their Influence that cannot by their Presence.
            Yrs.
(signed) Graph. Iatroon [writing physician]
Utopia 2d. of 2d. Moon [1765. Year of Christian Era. 2nd of
February 1765]

---

* as by communicating to each other any Discoveries in any of the
Branches of Physick, especially Botany, for which this Country is an
ample Field.

For reasons not now clear, these plans were carried out without any publicity.

This second Boston Medical Society was founded May 14, 1780—a year and a half before the Massachusetts Medical Society and ten days after the American Academy of Arts and Sciences. Burrage believed that the state society had its inception in the Boston Medical Society.[23] At any rate, all the founders of the state Society save one had been members of the Boston Society.

The latter organization had several functions: it set a fee table which, with appropriate changes over the years, lasted until modern times. It involved itself in medical affairs of concern to the public. And it actively participated in the founding of the Harvard Medical School. In the Warren Papers there is a note on the meeting of November 30, 1781. "Voted, that Dr. John Warren be desired to demonstrate a course of anatomical lectures the ensuing winter." Warren had given the previous winter a similar course at the military hospital near the present site of the Massachusetts General Hospital.[24]

There was, according to Ephraim Eliot, some jealousy of the young Warren in the Boston Medical Society.[25] His lectures were nevertheless successful, and a foundation stone of the Harvard Medical School was thus laid, through the good offices of the Boston Medical Society. It would be unreasonable to assert that the vote launched the School, but it was the first of a series of actions that led directly to the establishment of that institution fewer than ten months later.

Doubtless the ground had been prepared, in part, by the so-called "Anatomical Society" shortly before the Revolution, when a group of Harvard students of the classes of 1770–72, including John Warren and Samuel Adams, Jr., had formed this organization, which met secretly for the dissection of cats and dogs and perhaps cadavers. When the war came, these and many other Harvard graduates who were apprenticed to physicians for training, or were practicing physicians, became military surgeons. Their common experiences made them aware of the shortcomings of New England medicine. (A similar experience was encountered by the military physicians of World War II, who in wartime had better anesthesia, for example, and better supportive therapy for their patients than they were accustomed to get in their civilian practice.) They resolved to do better after the War, and to this end the Boston Medical Society was formed in 1780 and the Massachusetts Medical Society on November 1, 1781.

Although Cotton Tufts's efforts to form a society in 1765 did not immediately flower, the "Regulations" he laid down were incorporated in 1781 in the Massachusetts society. In one sense the Society's origins, then, go back to 1765. Several individuals associated with the former period were incorporators. In 1782 Dr. Tufts, along with Dr. James Lloyd and Dr. Samuel Holten, was charged with drawing up the bylaws. The archives of the Massachusetts Medical Society contain a draft of these first bylaws in Dr. Tufts's handwriting. The official history of the state society contains the curious and, in the light of the above, manifestly unfair statement that "the documentary evidence points to him as the guiding spirit *after* [emphasis added] the society had been started." It is unmistakably clear that Cotton Tufts had labored with single-minded purpose for sixteen years (1765–81) to establish the state society and was its true founder, if any one man is allowed to have that honor.

The establishment of the Massachusetts Medical Society was a group affair, with fourteen "Founders" and/or thirty-one "Incorporators." (Confusingly, Burrage at times refers to the thirty-one as Founders.)[26] The Charter of the Society was approved by the Legislature on November 1, 1781, and the first meeting was held in the County Court House on November 28, 1781.

LETTER TO THE PUBLIC UPON THE INSTITUTION OF THE
MEDICAL SOCIETY

The design of the above institution is, "to promote medical and surgical knowledge, inquiries into the Animal Economy & the Promotion & Effects of Medicine," by encouraging a free Intercourse with the Gentlemen of the Faculty throughout the United States of America, and a friendly Correspondence with the eminent in those Professions throughout the World: as well as to make a just Discrimination between such as are duly educated and properly qualified for the Duties thereof, and those who may ignorantly and wickedly administer Medicine, whereby the Health and Lives of many valuable Individuals may be endangered and perhaps lost to the Community . . .[27]

Through all the waxing and waning of the several societies, a common purpose persisted: to better medical education and medical practice in America.

Chapter Three

Beginnings of the Harvard Medical School

O F transcendent importance in the development of medicine at Harvard was the adoption, on September 19, 1782, by the President and Fellows of Harvard College of a plan submitted by the new President, Joseph Willard, and former Acting President Edward Wigglesworth.

The proposal for a school was first made at the meeting of the Boston Medical Society of November 30, 1781. It surfaced when Dr. John Warren was asked (with some guidance from himself) to repeat a course of anatomical lectures similar to those he had given the year before at the military hospital. In accord with his request, this was officially approved, and the lectures were a success despite some unwarranted (presumably jealous) sniping. Warren had also suggested that since there seemed to be a sufficient number of students desiring lectures, a medical school be established. At about the same time (1780–81), the Corporation of Harvard University began itself to think seriously of setting up a medical institution. An alumnus of Harvard (A.B. 1728), Dr. Ezekiel Hersey, a practicing physician of Hingham, Massachusetts, had bequeathed in 1770 £1,000 toward the support of a "Professor of Anatomy and Physic," when such post should be established. (Twenty years later his widow bequeathed a like sum, and in 1793 Hersey's brother, Dr. Abner Hersey, left £500.) Dr. Hersey's legacy was considered to be an excellent foundation, but on the suggestion of those who were favorably inclined, an enlarged plan, including professors of anatomy, surgery, and chemistry, was adopted. As already noted, the Massachusetts Medical Society came into being November 1, 1781, evidently out of the Boston Medical Society. Dr. John Warren, who had won the approval of the Boston Society, explained the purpose of the new society.[1] Some months later the Corporation appointed a committee to consider the matter. These developments indicate that John Warren deserves credit for the actual founding of the Harvard Medical School, even though the idea was already in the air.

The committee appointed by the Corporation on May 16, 1782, described the establishment of professorships of physic at the University.

Professors were to be elected by the Corporation and confirmed by the Overseers. The professors were, at all times, to be "under the inspection of the President and Fellows and of the Overseers . . ." Further details were set down as to the proper procedure in the case of death or removal of the professors. Detailed instructions for the activities of each were given.

Each professor was to have the use of the Library and to be treated as all other professors in the University were. A rather unusual proviso for those times stipulated that students in physic residing in the halls of the University or in the Town of Cambridge who had put themselves under the instruction of the professors were also to have access to the Library. Many similar details were spelled out concerning the conduct and privileges of faculty and students.

The business-like report was promptly followed by action: Warren, 29 years old, was appointed on November 22, 1782, as the first Professor of Anatomy and Surgery (after 1791, he was Hersey Professor).[2] It was clear to Warren that the greatest needs were for systematic instruction and clinical experience. Shortly afterward, December 24, 1782, Dr. Benjamin Waterhouse of Newport, Rhode Island, also 29, was appointed Professor of the Theory and Practice of Physic. The original faculty of three professors was completed May 22, 1783, when Aaron Dexter, at the age of 33, was named Professor of Chemistry and Materia Medica. He had graduated from the College in the Class of 1776.

Harvard had been recognized as a university by the state constitution, October 25, 1780, a year before President Willard took office. In 1782 Harvard became a university in fact by its provision of instruction in medicine. This had been anticipated as early as 1647, in the time of President Henry Dunster, when John Eliot wrote to Thomas Shepard and clearly stated the need for such an institution (see above, p. 4).

Curiously, the University had considerable difficulty in choosing a name for the fledgling faculty. The first name was the Medical Institution of Harvard College. Later, it was spoken of as the Medical School of Harvard College or Harvard University. Sometimes journalists referred to it as the Boston Medical School. After the School moved from Cambridge, it was at times called the Massachusetts Medical College, the name given to the building erected for the use of the School in Mason Street.[3] It was only in the 1850's that its present name came into general use.

The Medical Institution of Harvard University was declared open on October 7, 1783. On that day two of the professors, Warren and Waterhouse, were publicly inducted into office. The President and other officers of the University and the Medical Society and the Consul and Vice Consul of France were invited to attend the ceremony. On October 16 Dr. Aaron Dexter was inducted before the Overseers and the Corporation.

At its meeting of September 18, 1783, the Corporation had indicated that each professor was to be expected on his induction to subscribe to the following pledge:

> I .... elected Professor of
> .... in the University of Cambridge
> declare myself to be of the Christian religion as maintained in the
> churches of the Protestant communion. * * * I promise to discharge
> the trust now reposed in me, with diligence and fidelity, and to the
> advantage of the students in my particular department. * * *
>
> I promise to promote the interests of virtue and piety by my own
> example and encouragement. * * * I declare and promise that I will
> not only [support] the advancement of medical knowledge in the
> University, but consult its prosperity in every other respect. * * *

No other oath was ever taken by any member of the faculty (probably because there was none whose principles could be questioned) until 1935, when faculty members were required by law to take an oath to support the Constitution.[4] This disgraceful requirement was withdrawn by vote of the Corporation on March 6, 1967, the law having been declared invalid by the Supreme Judicial Court of Massachusetts.

Warren evidently started his lectures on anatomy as soon as possible after his appointment. That would have been easy enough, for he had given similar lectures before. Morison assumes that Waterhouse and Dexter did not begin their lectures until 1785, inasmuch as the first two medical graduates did not receive their degrees until 1788, following a three-year course.[5] If we can believe President Willard, however, the three professors were already lecturing when he applied to the General Court on February 5, 1784, for the creation of an infirmary.[6]

ANATOMY AND SURGERY

Dr. John Warren, in his youth, had been much interested in dissection of animals (and perhaps cadavers). During and following the War of Independence, he had opportunities for human dissection. In 1780 he had given a course in anatomical demonstrations at the military hospital in Boston. He was vigorous in his determination to promote and provide excellent training in medicine and its sound practice. His activities involved not only clinical duties and teaching but policy-making as well:

John Warren. A chief motive force in the founding of the School and the Massachusetts General Hospital. First Professor of Anatomy and Surgery. From a painting by Rembrandt Peale, lithographed by John Pendleton.

He was a petitioner for the incorporation of the Massachusetts Medical Society in 1781 and the founder of the Harvard Medical School in 1782. His youth and his ardent pursuit of his goals inevitably led to hostility on the part of his less-favored peers. He was buffeted by many adverse winds: His health was not very good, and as a young man he thought he was a subject for pulmonary disease. During the Revolutionary War he had a violent fever, and still another in 1783 just after the founding of the Medical School. There was widespread fear that he would not survive this ailment. An optimistic exception was Dr. Joseph Gardiner, who said, "that young man is so determined to recover, that he will succeed in spite of his disease."[7] He was the victim of "sick headache," presumably migraine.

His determination to succeed did pull him through, and he gave his first course of lectures in the autumn of 1783. They covered six weeks. He was described as a fine lecturer, who attracted especially by his excellent voice and great earnestness. Oliver Wendell Holmes commented, "The driest bone of the human body became in his hands a subject of animated and agreeable description." After Warren's death, his lifetime colleague, Dr. James Jackson, wrote that the special attractions of his teaching "were derived from the animation of delivery, from the interest he displayed in the subject of his discourse, and from his solicitude that every auditor should be satisfied both by his demonstrations and by his explanations." He rarely used notes.[8]

On assuming the Professorship, his charges from the Corporation were to "demonstrate the anatomy of a human body with physiological observations and explain and perform a complete system of surgical operations." It is clear from Dr. Warren's lectures in 1790, for example, that his focus was primarily anatomical rather than surgical.

At that time the period of instruction was lengthened to eight weeks and the next year was extended once again. The anatomical course was then split into two: In one part, for medical students, the relationship of anatomy to surgery was given prominence, and the second part, a course of twenty-six lectures on anatomy, was given in the spring for students of the undergraduate department.

The plan for surgery adopted in the earliest days followed that of the University of Edinburgh, where instruction in anatomy was controlled by the three Monros, Primus, Secundus, and Tertius, who together held the Chair in uninterrupted succession for a period of 126 years (1720–1846). The three were original characters, authors of many unusual works, and were said to be morbid in their controversies but entirely worthy of the confidence reposed in them by their fellow townsmen. In the years 1720–90 some 12,800 students were taught by Monro Primus and Secundus alone.[9] These teachers were principally responsible for the acclaim achieved by Edinburgh in those years. It was customary for anatomists to be also surgeons. The Edinburgh School, as has been noted, had great influence on the development of surgery in the Harvard Medical School, but by 1835 Harvard had felt the need for separate attention to the field of surgery, beyond anatomy.

The Harvard Corporation had recognized early that lectures were not enough: there had to be involvement in clinical situations as well. As early as 1784 a vigorous attempt had been made to obtain clinical material for teaching. Application to the Town of Boston was made for use of the infirmary at the Almshouse for both the Professor of Surgery and the Professor of the Theory and Practice. Dr. Waterhouse also pleaded for a marine hospital, where he would have control of clinical material for teaching. This was presented in arguments as cogent today as they were then. There was indeed need for the School to have control of hospital wards, but the effort came to nothing, and in the end the Almshouse was utilized for teaching purposes. The instructions laid down by the College authorities were that "the professors demonstrate the anatomy of the human body on recent subjects if they can be procured; if not, on preparations duly adapted to the purpose. That they elucidate this by physiological observations on the parts and explain and perform a complete system of surgical operations."

This utilization of the Almshouse was opposed by the Town in a typical Town and Gown hassle, and success was not achieved until 1810. In the long interval (1782–1810), surgery was taught by lectures, textbooks, and the example of an occasional surgical operation. As a field for study, surgery was not adequately recognized until 1835.

The lectures were given in the basement of Harvard Hall and moved to Holden Chapel as soon as three separate rooms could be arranged for the three departments, Anatomy and Surgery, Theory and Practice, Chemistry and Materia Medica. The difficulties encountered by the School were far greater than could reasonably have been anticipated. Part of the difficulty was owing to the problem posed by the Charles River. The surgeons could cross to Cambridge by ferry or could take the nine-mile ride through Roxbury.

John Warren must bear the primary responsibility for the shift of the Medical School to Boston. Although access to Cambridge in those days was difficult, it is regrettable that the School, with its later associated hospitals, was not established in proximity to the rest of the University.

When the School was moved to Boston in 1810, the lives of the surgeons, including John Warren's, were simplified. Now they could avoid the sometimes difficult and always tedious journey through the Charles River marshes to Cambridge. These pioneers in surgery were, for the most part, self-taught men. (John Warren's reputation was enhanced by devising a procedure for operating successfully on a dermoid cyst of the ovary.) Their knowledge of illustrious surgeons who had gone before was gleaned from those who had had the advantages of study in Europe. Books were scarce and expensive and newspapers and periodicals almost unknown. Teaching was by word of mouth and by example, a system like the present-day self-teaching of surgical residents, with one resident passing down his views to his successor. The trouble is that once an error is introduced into the closed system, it, too, is perpetuated. In the view of many, there is far too little checking of the residents by more experienced physicians, even today. In the early years, teaching of sections was common and the apprenticeship system persisted. These approaches had the advantage of bringing the preceptor into close relationship with his pupil.

In Warren's early period, after the creation of the School, he was more than once at the point of succumbing to the great effort required to fulfill his obligations. Twice he offered to resign his professorship; twice he was prevailed upon to retain it. While operating, he was cool and composed, with sound judgment, and his preeminence, according to James Thacher, was unrivaled.[10] He introduced the primary healing of wounds long before this important concept was adopted by his European colleagues. Healing time was thus greatly shortened, and pain relieved. Once, while demonstrating a brain, one arm suddenly became paralyzed; he never fully recovered. He was long a sufferer from chest pain, probably because of arteriosclerosis—a view that autopsy supported. But Warren was still actively engaged in his profession when he died on April 4, 1815, in his sixty-second year. His leadership in teaching and in practice was an important factor in the development of Harvard medicine for years afterward.

The appointment in 1809 of John Collins Warren as Adjunct Professor of Anatomy and Surgery relieved his father, John Warren, of some of his heavy obligations. At the beginning of the nineteenth century, John Collins returned from Europe, where he had studied under Sir Astley Cooper, Antoine Dubois, and others. He immediately resumed his teaching career and at the same time opened a private dissecting room in Boston. His clinic at the Almshouse was a most valuable aid in the slow development of surgery in the Medical School.

When the School was moved to Boston, John Collins Warren began to assist his father in surgery and midwifery. When his father died, John Collins was elected Professor of Anatomy and Surgery (May 10, 1815), and Walter Channing was elected to the new lectureship on midwifery.

John Collins Warren not only had six years as a professor but also the advantages of foreign study and familiarity with the teaching of

John Collins Warren. He succeeded his father, John Warren, as Professor of Anatomy and Surgery. His collection of specimens became the Warren Museum. He was the surgeon who performed the first operation under ether anesthesia in Boston. Photograph from the collection of Henry K. Beecher, M.D.

anatomy in Europe. He was an experienced, skillful, and enthusiastic dissector, but there is some doubt whether his abilities as a teacher were equal to those of his father. Writers of the time indicate that as he was strict with himself, so also he was exacting toward others. Unlike his father, he was primarily a surgeon, with a secondary interest in anatomy. He held the Hersey Professorship for thirty-two years. Since he had begun dissections as early as 1802 (not including his student days), he actively participated in anatomical instruction for forty-five years.

Knowing that he lacked his father's facility as a lecturer, Warren prepared himself with exquisite care. Since he was engaged in heavy surgical practice, he doubtless depended upon young prosectors for dissected materials used during his lectures. Throughout his busy surgical life, he collected many interesting and unusual specimens. As early as 1799 (when he was a medical student at Guy's Hospital, London), the value of such collections was recognized in Europe, and he had realized the importance of such material. In 1809 he and a colleague formed the Anatomical Theatre and Dissecting Room at 49 Marlborough Street; and as various collections of human specimens came on the market in Europe or America, they were purchased. By 1834 the need for space was so great that Warren applied for more to the Corporation. They agreed that if he would contribute $1,000, the Corporation would erect new space for the anatomical collection. Warren did not comply.

Warren's interests broadened to include wax representations of smallpox and other skin diseases made in Paris. Skeletons of fish fascinated him, and he collected them, too. President Quincy expressed the wish that the Museum be made available to medical students "and others"; even the public was later allowed to visit it; but the Corporation remained, for a time, loath to spend further money on better accommodations. Warren used his fees from lectures for its support. When he resigned his professorship in 1847, most of his collection was presented to Harvard College and with it the sum of $6,000 (or $5,000—the accounts vary) for preservation and development of the collection. His intention was that all diseases should be represented at various stages. In recognition of this, the Corporation of the University gratefully accepted the collection and voted that the Museum be named after its founder, John Collins Warren.

Following Dr. Warren's initial gift, the collection continued to grow from year to year, and it moved whenever the School did. Dr. Oliver Wendell Holmes contributed many valuable preparations, especially chosen to illustrate healthy anatomy, including many microscopical specimens. Professor Henry Jacob Bigelow was an ardent collector. So also, in the early days, were Professors George Hayward, John Ware, and R. M. Hodges.

An interesting item in the Museum is the so-called crowbar skull. An improperly controlled explosion had sent an iron bar, several feet long, through the central part of a man's head. He recovered but, not surprisingly, was said to have had a change of personality thereafter, from a gentle good nature to irritable profanity. This may have been the first frontal lobotomy.

The Massachusetts General Hospital, founded in 1811, first began to receive patients in 1821. The intervening ten years were devoted to financing and housing. John Collins Warren had been chosen Surgeon to the Hospital, and students at the Medical School were admitted to operations on payment of a fee. Not many operations were carried out in this period. Anesthesia was still a quarter of a century in the future. The Faculty issued a circular in 1823 calling attention to the fact that in twenty months, from September 21, 1821, to June 11, 1823, forty-six operations had been carried out in the Hospital. It is likely that the types of operations the students were permitted to see provided adequate material for the times. Most of the surgical procedures were minor, and most of the instructor's attention was given to this kind of material.

In 1835 a professorship of the Principles of Surgery was established, with the proviso that "It shall be the duty of the professors to give elementary lectures on the principles of surgery and clinical lectures on the surgical cases in the Massachusetts General Hospital." It required "the same attendance on the lectures . . . of the candidate for the degree of Doctor of Medicine in the University as is required on the lectures in other departments of the Medical Faculty." This new post was filled by Dr. George Hayward, with the proviso that Warren should teach operative surgery and Hayward clinical surgery. The distinction between the two fields is not clear. The term for surgical instruction was extended to four months.

When the Medical School moved in 1847 into the North Grove Street building adjoining the Massachusetts General Hospital, a large room was made available for the Museum material. The specimens were especially valuable in the mid-nineteenth century, when bodies for dissection could be obtained only with difficulty. Dr. Warren wished to present himself as an example to medical students and to the public: He bequeathed his body to the School. The skeleton is present in the Museum but can be seen only by members of the Warren family.

One of the problems that troubled all teachers of anatomy was the shortage of cadavers. Body snatching was by no means rare. There are no helpful data to describe exactly how bodies for dissection were procured, but some undoubtedly were brought into the state from outside. Corpses were even spirited away from funerals by sham mourners. In

1825 the Faculty of Medicine appropriated $300 annually to be used at the disposition of the Professor in order to encourage the study of anatomy. No accounting of this expenditure was required, and what the money was to be used for seems evident. All of this was most unsatisfactory. Popular indignation was rising to the extent that the Medical College was threatened, and Warren, who had been appointed Adjunct Professor in 1809, had reason at times to expect attacks on his dwelling house.

"An Act to Protect the Sepulchres of the Dead" was passed by the General Court and was approved by the Governor on March 2, 1815.[11] Grave-robbing or kindred activities were to be severely penalized. In 1825 the problem was faced when Harvard appointed Dr. Warren and Dr. Jacob Bigelow a committee whose purpose was to draw up an Act of Dissection. What became of this is not known, but it seems probable that it directly supported the efforts of Dr. John Collins Warren to get on the statute books the first anatomical law in the United States, which preceded by a year Lord Warburton's English Anatomy Act of 1832. It provided that all unclaimed bodies might go to the medical schools for dissection.

On February 4, 1829, the Council of the Boston Medical Society appointed a large committee to prepare a petition to the Legislature to modify the existing laws covering anatomical dissection. The petition stressed that anatomical knowledge could be acquired only by dissection, and on February 28, 1831, the General Court of Massachusetts approved "An Act more effectually to protect the Sepulchre of the Dead, and to legalize the Study of Anatomy in certain cases."[12] It provided that if any person were to dig up or convey away, or assisted in the digging up or conveying away, any human body or the remains thereof, such person would be adjudged guilty of a felony, to be punished by solitary imprisonment for a term not exceeding ten days, and by confinement afterward to hard labor for a term not exceeding one year, or punished by a fine not exceeding $2,000. After the passing of this act, it was declared lawful for the Board of Health to surrender the unclaimed bodies to a duly licensed regular physician to use for the advancement of anatomical science. After such bodies had been used, they were to be decently inhumed.

Helpful as the 1831 legislation was, it was far from satisfactory, primarily because it was left to the civil authorities to determine whether they would surrender the body in question to the schools. Warren's prestige was very great, and it may be that this accounted for the early good effects of the law, at least for a time. But difficulties arose, and the number of available cadavers fell off. In March 1845 the law was radically emended: The word "shall" was inserted.[13] Release of bodies, that is, was no longer permissive but mandatory, provided the deceased had not stipulated that he was to be buried without being dissected.

Notwithstanding opposition of some senior members of the Medical School, the Legislature in 1859 voted a revision of the statute.[14] The key word "shall" release bodies once again became "may," making it necessary to depend upon the decision of a superintendent of a board of health whether unclaimed bodies would be delivered to the School. It was easier for a superintendent to refuse bodies than to take action that might place him in an awkward situation. There was also the ugly possibility that dead bodies might be a source of profit to those who controlled their destiny. It is known that Harvard received bodies from out of state during this trying period, although the offended Harvard Corporation refused to provide funds for them. In consequence, the Legislature in 1895 reversed itself once more, the word "may" being displaced by "shall."[15]

Bodies could not now be applied for by individual practitioners, but arrangements were made for a fair division among the schools. Moreover, a body could not be used for fourteen days after death; it was required that it be kept available for inspection.

THE THEORY AND PRACTICE OF PHYSIC [16]

The charge to the Professor was to

> teach the students by directing and superintending, as much as may be, their private studies; lecturing of the diseases of the human body, and taking such of them as are qualified to visit their patients; making proper observations on the nature of the diseases and the peculiar circumstances attending them, and their method of cure; and, whenever the professors be desired by any other gentlemen of the Faculty to visit their patients in difficult and uncommon cases, they shall use their endeavors to introduce with them their pupils who are properly qualified.[17]

The intention was that a "theory" of medicine was to be developed in the lectures, and the principles involved applied to patients in the presence of the students.

The first professor, Benjamin Waterhouse, was born in Newport, Rhode Island, in 1754 (and died in 1846). His great uncle was the celebrated London physician John Fothergill, a staunch friend of Colonial-American physicians. This distinguished connection may have

Benjamin Waterhouse, first Professor of the Theory and Practice of Physic. An outstanding botanist and mineralogist, and a pioneer in Boston in inoculation for smallpox prevention. Engraving by R. Reeve.

cost Waterhouse more in emotional terms than it was worth. In addition to this advantage, he was probably the best trained physician of his time in America. How much these credentials had to do with his abrasive behavior one can only surmise, but abrasive he was said to be. He told his son that he loved energy, even in quarreling. Why anyone of that period in Boston should be criticized for being abrasive or, indeed, how abrasiveness could be recognized in a resident of that era must remain mysteries. Other reasons for disliking him must be considered. For one thing, he was a foreigner, having been born in another state—one founded by outcasts from Massachusetts. For another, because he was one of the few men in Boston with an earned medical degree, he was accused of feeling superior. In any case, he was always in trouble with his associates, and his exceptional abilities were clouded by constant quarrels.

Waterhouse had begun his medical studies at sixteen under Halliburton at Newport. Six years later, on his way to Edinburgh, he was among the passengers on the last ship to escape from Boston Harbor (1775). Directed by Fothergill, he passed his first nine months in Edinburgh under William Cullen, Joseph Black, and Monro Secundus. He returned to London and became part of his great uncle's household. Fothergill continued to guide his study of medicine thereafter.

Waterhouse's interests were broad: experimental philosophy, mineralogy, and botany were a part of his education. These were especially important in his later life. After three years in London, he had four years at Leyden, whence he graduated in 1780. He entirely avoided the war, but so far as one can tell, this did not injure his career. He returned to Newport in June 1782, expecting to take the place of his old preceptor, who was out of favor with current attitudes in Newport. Almost at once, however, he was elected Professor of the Theory and Practice of Physic at Harvard. He was twenty-nine years old.

The scholarly Dr. Waterhouse, in his inaugural address, dealt with the various branches to be brought together under the umbrella of his professorship—not only anatomy and chemistry, insofar as he could disengage this material from his professorial colleagues, but also botany, materia medica, and natural philosophy. Toward the end of the address he made a remarkable appeal for the scientific study of insanity. This amazing man had at least as much or more to offer than any of his colleagues, not least of which was his understanding of the need for a scientific approach to clinical research. Some historians have claimed that Waterhouse had an exalted idea of the task before him, but his understanding of his responsibilities was not beyond his capacity to carry them out; furthermore, it was traditional throughout much of the nineteenth century for the Professor of the Theory and Practice to sum up the activities of many diverse departments and to give to them a practical interpretation. This extraordinary man, aided by his friend, Dr. John C. Lettsom of England, also founded the Botanical Garden at Cambridge, Massachusetts, and formed a collection of minerals.

In 1786 and 1787, at Providence, Rhode Island, Waterhouse gave a course of lectures on natural history, botany, and mineralogy, and in 1788 the course was transferred to Cambridge. He gave the series for twenty years without fees and is said to have derived more acclaim from them than from his lectures on the Theory and Practice of Physic.

The most important advance in clinical medicine in America up to the end of the eighteenth century was the basis laid for the ultimate conquest of smallpox, first through "inoculation" and then "vaccination." The latter, of course, was derived from Edward Jenner's work published in 1798 as an *Inquiry into the Causes and Effects of the Variolae Vaccinae or Cow Pox.* Dr. Waterhouse received a copy of Jenner's book from his friend, Dr. Lettsom. This was probably the first copy to reach America. Waterhouse was immediately impressed by it. He used words felicitously.

> This publication shared the fate of most others on new discoveries.
> A few received it as a very important discovery, highly interesting to
> humanity; some doubted it; others observed that wise and prudent
> conduct which allows them to condemn or applaud, as the event might
> prove; while a greater number absolutely ridiculed it as one of those
> medical whims which arise today and tomorrow are no more.[18]

Later in the year, Dr. Waterhouse received a considerate hearing when he presented a report at a meeting of the American Academy of Arts and Sciences presided over by President John Adams (President at the time not only of the Academy but of the United States), and before an audience of many eminent men.

There was doubt in Boston as to the efficacy of vaccination. In order to settle the matter, Dr. Waterhouse made a brilliant proposal to the Board of Health of Boston that a public experiment be made, in which a number of children were to serve as subjects. They were to be vaccinated and later inoculated with smallpox virus. (A similar proposal made by Dr. James Jackson on his return from Europe had been previously refused.)

Waterhouse's experiment was carried out under the observation of a committee of seven of the most reputable physicians in the town. Nineteen children were vaccinated in August 1802. The following November, the children were inoculated, on two different occasions, with a variolous matter and exposed for twenty days to the contagion of smallpox. This was done at the smallpox hospital, Noddle's Island in East Boston. The experiment was a great success and showed that the cow pox gave complete security against the smallpox: not one of the nineteen children came down with the disease. Whatever modern-day ethicists might say about the impropriety of using children for such a study, this must stand as a fine example of soundly controlled experimentation, not inferior in scientific insight to Lind's conquest of scurvy.[19]

In 1804 Dr. Waterhouse closed the medical course with a lecture in Holden Chapel on "Cautions to Young Persons concerning Health, containing the general doctrine of Chronic Disease, showing the evil tendency of the using of tobacco upon young persons, more especially the ruinous effects of smoking cigars, with observations on the use of ardent and vinous spirits in general." In this lecture Dr. Waterhouse pictured the rapid deterioration of the Harvard student of that day. "Six times as much ardent spirits were expended here (in Cambridge) annually as in the days of our fathers. Unruly wine and ardent spirits supplanted sober cider."

Indeed, there was evidence that the general health of the College had deteriorated: in the twenty-seven years from 1769 to 1796, there were nine deaths among the students. In the subsequent eight years there were sixteen deaths, mostly from tuberculosis. Never in his twenty-three years of experience had Dr. Waterhouse seen "so many hectical habits and consumptive affections as of late years." All of these he ascribed, of course, to the evil effects of smoking and drinking. During the next decade and a half, six editions of his lecture were printed. It was translated into several foreign languages. For some obscure reason the fame of this lecture always annoyed him.

Benjamin Waterhouse was probably the intellectual superior of his two colleagues, John Warren, the Founder, and Aaron Dexter, the Professor of Chemistry. The origin of his difficulties related perhaps to his belief that his superb training of over seven years in Europe and his close association with the great Fothergill entitled him to special consideration. For whatever reasons, he attracted ridicule and created enemies. From the very beginning, his relations with John Warren were difficult, each accusing the other of lying, deceit, double-dealing, and slander.[20] Wherever the fault, the University suffered from the lack of cooperation between the two top professors.

Waterhouse was something of a radical also. He believed in the primary role of environment in the formation of personality traits. Unfortunately, he applied this dogma to an evaluation of Samuel Thomson, the sensational quack from rural New Hampshire, who was his contemporary. He stated, "Had John Hunter, whom I well knew, been born and bred where Samuel Thomson was, he would have been just such another man; and had Samuel Thomson been thrown into the same society and associations as John Hunter, he would, in my opinion, have been his equal, with probably a wider range of thought, but both are men of talent and originality of thought."[21]

By the autumn of 1811 the other medical professors had become so exasperated by Dr. Waterhouse that on November 11, 1811, they presented to the Corporation a memorial detailing his sins.[22] At this late date it is manifestly impossible to sift the charges, but his participation in the petition for the new College of Physicians was the last straw in a series of angry confrontations. The Corporation seems to have examined these matters with care, but finally concluded on May 8, 1812, that harmony and confidence had been destroyed and that the "interest and reputation of the University require that he [Dr. Waterhouse] be removed from the office of Hersey Professor of the Theory and Practice of Physic." Among his other distinctions then, Dr. Waterhouse holds one of great rarity: being discharged from a professorship solely because his fellow professors disliked him.

In 1812 James Jackson of Boston, a former apprentice of Edward Holyoke and the first physician to the Massachusetts General Hospital, was promoted to succeed Waterhouse. Dr. Jackson belonged to the small category of truly outstanding men. His influence on the medical and social life of the Commonwealth was exceedingly broad. He had a fine and judicial grasp of the needs of medicine and medical education of his time. He was evidently not an original man in terms of research and writing, but he was a "good, safe teacher." On his return from study in Europe, he had hoped to be the one to introduce vaccination into the Boston community. In this he was forestalled by Dr. Waterhouse.

During their long professional lives, Drs. Jackson and Warren worked so closely together that it is difficult if not impossible to determine which, in a given instance, was the originator of new developments for the good of the community. Dr. Jackson understood perfectly well that "a hospital is an institution absolutely essential to a medical school, and one which would afford relief and comfort to thousands of sick and miserable." This plea he sent to the benevolent citizens of Boston, and it led directly to the founding of the Massachusetts General Hospital. It is possible that the new building for the Medical School on Mason Street was also erected chiefly through his efforts. His talented son, James Jackson, Jr., came to a tragic end very shortly after returning to Boston from Paris, where Professor Louis had considered him an outstanding man. James Jr. writes of his father to Dr. J. B. S. Jackson: "You will not deem it an affectation in me, I am sure, to say that I listen to him with infinite delight and satisfaction. The object of attending lectures is to be taught—and my word for it, he does understand the art of teaching better than any man with whom it has been my good fortune to

James Jackson, second Professor of the Theory and Practice of Physic. He was one of the organizers and the first physician of the Massachusetts General Hospital. Photograph in the Locke Collection, Boston Medical Library.

meet." Dr. Jackson Sr. was a friendly and sympathetic man, both with students and with patients. A careful observer, he was methodical in his study of the patient's symptoms. Much later, in 1822, he wrote that in addition to his formal lectures it was always his practice to give one or two afternoons each week to subjects that otherwise would have been crowded out. Oliver Wendell Holmes commented on his conduct at the bedside: "I have seen many noted British, French and American practitioners, but I never saw a man so altogether admirable at the bedside of the sick as Dr. James Jackson."

Dr. Jackson clearly was a man of affairs and a learned physician. He had a zeal for scientific truth, and he inspired others with it. Although it would have been too much to expect this man to have been a leader in investigation, he did come near to discovering appendicitis, recognizing that a serious disorder sometimes occurred in the right lower quadrant. It remained for Reginald Heber Fitz, Sr., to clinch the discovery in 1886.

James Jackson continued in office until 1836, when he resigned his professorship and, the next year, his chiefship at the Massachusetts General Hospital.

CHEMISTRY AND MATERIA MEDICA

As long ago as 1783 Dr. Waterhouse, in his inaugural address, had called attention to the various sciences that were adjuncts of his professorship. One can see how instruction is needed to guide the students in their use of laboratories. The students' limited understanding of the usefulness of the laboratory pointed up the need for clinical lectures and clinical instruction that would help to train the neophytes in the ways of accurate observation.

Dr. Aaron Dexter, the first professor, was born at Chelsea in 1750, graduated from Harvard in 1776, and studied medicine under Dr. Samuel Danforth. He was called "the most scientific chemist then on the stage." Toward the end of the Revolutionary War he married Rebecca Amory and began to practice in Boston. His name does not appear, however, in the list of medical men of the Revolution. (He may have been confused with William Dexter, a surgeon's mate from Massachusetts.) On May 22, 1783, Dr. Dexter was elected Professor of Chemistry. The Corporation voted in 1784 the sum of £80 for the purchase of medical books and clinical apparatus for his use.[23] Aaron Dexter was an incorporator of the Massachusetts Medical Society and its first treasurer. He is said to have been a member of many learned societies, but unfortunately, none is named save the American Academy of Arts and Sciences, to which he was elected in 1784.

Professor Dexter seems to have had limited financial means until 1791, when he was the recipient of £1,000 designated in the will of Major William Erving (Harvard College, 1753). This large sum was explicitly "for the sole use and purpose of enlarging the salary of the Professor of Chemistry." The professorship became the Erving Professorship of Chemistry and Materia Medica. In 1816 he became Emeritus Professor.

There is, unfortunately, very little more known about Professor Dexter. He was notable for his urbanity and kindness and his lifetime quiet and unassuming service to the medical school he had helped found. He died of old age at his home in Cambridge, February 28, 1829. He was reliable, steady, and well-connected.

Dr. John Gorham, in 1809, had been appointed Adjunct Professor, and upon Dexter's resignation in 1816 was chosen Professor of Chemistry. Gorham was born in Boston in 1783. He received the A.M. at Harvard in 1801 and studied medicine with his future father-in-law, John Warren. Following his graduation with the degree of Bachelor in Medicine in 1804, he spent two years studying in Europe. As a teacher he was popular and successful; Dr. James Jackson said of him, "During twenty years and more, I know not that he has made an enemy." He was the author of two books on chemistry.

The wandering Medical Department, which had begun in the basement of Harvard Hall and had then moved to nearby Holden Chapel in Cambridge, once more moved, this time to 49 Marlborough Street in Boston (now 400 Washington Street), where it remained for half a dozen years and then moved again to its own building in Mason Street.

Not only was Dr. Gorham obliged to give a course to the seniors at Cambridge, but it was announced that he would "give a private course to the gentlemen at Boston after the conclusion of the medical lectures." The Corporation authorized in 1812 expenditure of the hardly reckless sum of $170 to set up a laboratory suitable for the needs of the Professor of Chemistry. Dr. Gorham asked that materia medica be separated from his department and taken over by a younger man. The lectureship in materia medica and botany was established in 1815 and given to the distinguished Dr. Jacob Bigelow. At the same time, Dr. Gorham was required to give a full course in Chemistry and Mineralogy to the students at Cambridge. He had charge of the laboratories and apparatus there.

Possibly, the Corporation felt that it was losing control of the medical professors. Whatever the reason, in 1824 it required that the Erving

Professor should live in Cambridge. Dr. Gorham refused to accept this condition. A Professor of Mineralogy and Geology was then appointed who was to give instruction in Chemistry in Cambridge, while Dr. Gorham's activities were to be related to the Medical School in Boston. Dr. Gorham resigned in 1827, and the Corporation voted that the Erving Professor of Chemistry should again reside in Cambridge and give lectures to the undergraduates and also at the Medical School in Boston. Dr. Gorham died in 1829, to be succeeded by the notorious John White Webster.

THE PHARMACOPOEIA OF THE MASSACHUSETTS MEDICAL SOCIETY

Dr. Gorham's tenure witnessed an interesting development. Although various pharmacopoeias had been published in foreign countries, the Massachusetts volume was the first in the United States (1808). It was a production of the Massachusetts Medical Society, but those principally involved were also professors in Harvard University and founders of the Massachusetts General Hospital—namely James Jackson and John Collins Warren.

There was considerable interest in following the plan of the British or the Edinburgh books. The latter had been recently revised and seemed best; however, there was a major difficulty: it was in Latin and therefore not suitable for use by American apothecaries. The Society nevertheless resolved to accept the Edinburgh plan, with such changes as might be indicated for local American practices.

The Council of the Massachusetts Medical Society voted October 3, 1805, that "a committee be raised to draw up and lay before the Councillors at their next meeting a pharmacopoeia, or formulae for the preparation of compound medicines with names affixed to the same to be called the *Massachusetts Pharmacopoeia*."[24] Drs. Aaron Dexter, Edward Holyoke, James Jackson, J. C. Warren, and Benjamin Oliver were chosen for this committee.

At the next meeting of the Counsellors "at the room of the American Academy of Arts and Sciences in Boston, holden June 5, 1806," Dr. Dexter said that he had asked Dr. Jackson and Dr. J. C. Warren to see to the preparation of the manuscript and to follow it through the press. At the meeting of June 4, 1807, Warren and Jackson presented their manuscript. It was accepted and forthwith voted that the *Massachusetts Pharmacopoeia* be printed for the Society. Warren and Jackson were directed to publish the work on the best terms obtainable.

At the meeting of October 7, 1807, it was voted that the pharmacopoeia "shall be adopted in practice by the Fellows of the Society" as of June 1808, the year of publication. It was a modest volume of 272 pages. A letter of thanks for the Society's *Pharmacopoeia* was received from the President of Harvard University. A contemporary historian said of it:

> It effected a complete change in the language of a branch of medical science; it produced an exactness in the names of medicinal substances, and a protection in their preparation, which have greatly relieved practitioners of medicine, and contributed to the safety of the community.
>
> The *Pharmacopoeia* of the Society has been adopted by the apothecaries in Boston and throughout the state, so far as we are informed; and with most cordiality by the most eminent of them. There is therefore good reason to expect we shall avoid the embarrassments and dangers, which have been produced by a multitude of names and by the variations in strength of the same preparations of medicine made by different apothecaries.[25]

Dr. Lyman Spalding (Harvard, 1797), a student of Nathan Smith and later his assistant in the Dartmouth Medical School, in a paper read before the New York County Medical Society on January 6, 1817, presented the need for a National Pharmacopoeia. Spalding, also a Fellow of the Massachusetts Medical Society, was informed by J. C. Warren that a Committee had been appointed to revise the 1808 *Massachusetts Pharmacopoeia*. This committee had received a request from the New York State Medical Society to cooperate in making a National Pharmacopoeia.[26] The Massachusetts Medical Society voted to cooperate, and a delegation to the proposed National Pharmacopoeial Convention was approved. The first edition of the Pharmacopoeia of the United States of America was published in Boston, December 15, 1820. The preface was long thought to be the product of others, and Dr. Glenn Sonnedecker of the *United States Pharmacopoeia* has recently, through checking with Mr. Richard Wolfe's material in the Countway Library of Medicine, discovered that the preface was in fact written by Jacob Bigelow. The two first paragraphs are as applicable to the modern scene as they were 150 years ago:

> It is the object of a Pharmacopoeia to select from among substances which possess medicinal power, those, the utility of which is most fully established and best understood; and to form from them preparations and compositions, in which their powers may be exerted to the greatest advantage. It should likewise distinguish those articles by

convenient and definite names, such as may prevent trouble or uncertainty in the intercourse of physicians and apothecaries.

The value of a *Pharmacopoeia* depends upon the fidelity with which it conforms to the best state of medical knowledge of the day. Its usefulness depends upon the sanction it receives from the medical community and the public; and the extent to which it governs the language and practice of those for whose use it is intended.[27]

NEW ENGLAND JOURNAL OF MEDICINE

The New England Journal of Medicine and Surgery and the Collateral Branches of Science, 1812, is the oldest medical periodical in continuous publication in the United States, perhaps in the world.[28] Its auspicious start in life was a direct consequence of the imagination and vigor of that remarkable pair of Harvard professors, John Collins Warren and James Jackson. Jackson was in 1812 Hersey Professor of the Theory and Practice of Physick. Warren was, after 1815, Professor of Anatomy and Surgery. He proposed the establishment of a medical journal in Boston about 1811.

The founders of the new journal included, in addition to Warren and Jackson, six other Harvard professors: John Gorham, Jacob Bigelow, Walter Channing, and, later, George Hayward, John Ware, and John W. Webster. They were accustomed to meet together each month "to sup and read the papers submitted."

The first issue of 434 pages, published in January 1812, had as its lead article "Remarks on Angina Pectoris" by John Warren, father of the editor. This remarkable volume is a veritable *Who's Who* of doctors of the period. James Jackson was represented by "Some Remarks on morbid effects of dentitian" and a second article "On Croup." John C. Warren described "Cases of apoplexy with dissections." Jacob Bigelow's was "Observations and experiments on the treatment of injuries occasioned by fire." Walter Channing presented "Remarks on Diseases resembling Syphilis." John H. Dorsey sent a letter from Philadelphia describing the "Case and dissection of a blue female child"; at the postmortem examination of this child, it was found that the aorta, of unusual size, communicated with both ventricles. Various practitioners dealt with "Remarks on the petechial, or spotted fever." There was an account of operations for lithotomy and aneurysm. Further reports dealt with gunshot wounds. There were remarks on cold bathing. B. C. Brodie, F.R.S., was represented by "Physiological researches, respecting the influence of the brain on the heart." In another communication from the Royal Society, the Davy brothers, Humphry and John, disagreed with M. M. Gay Lussac concerning action between an oxide of carbon and chlorine. Dr. Benjamin Rush's "Sixteen Introductory Lectures," published in Philadelphia, were reviewed. Other subjects varied from hydrocele to comments on ancient manuscripts recently discovered in Herculanaeum, and scores of other fascinating subjects. A chronological list covering the first hundred years of editors, proprietors, publishers, and arresting events has been recorded by Joseph Garland.[29]

Of the papers published in *The New England Journal of Medicine* since 1812, "hardly a score qualify as contributions of sufficient importance . . . to illustrate the progress of medicine." This was the harsh judgment of Henry Viets in 1962.[30] One could expect that there would be few important original contributions during the first 100 years. During most of that period it was not customary to document one's unusual experiences, and most of the papers were personal reports from private practice or, after 1820, practice on hospital wards. But the most important event ever celebrated then or now in the pages of the *Journal* was reported by Bigelow (November 18, 1846), whose account curiously beat that of J. C. Warren (December 9, 1846): it was on insensibility to pain, produced by breathing ethereal vapors.

The New England Journal of Medicine and Surgery, founded in 1812, was edited by the original group of eight until 1825, at which time the editorial duties were assumed by two other Harvard professors, Drs. Walter Channing and John Ware. They held office until 1828, when the *Journal* was renamed the *Boston Medical and Surgical Journal,* a title borne for a hundred years. Almost without exception, the editors were Harvard graduates or Harvard Faculty members or both.

One of the most productive innovations of the *New England Journal of Medicine* was the establishment of a weekly clinicopathological conference which had its origin in teaching at Harvard. While an undergraduate of Harvard College, Walter B. Cannon had as roommate a law student.[31] Through him, Cannon became familiar with and much impressed by the case method of teaching law, a method derived from Professor Christopher C. Langdell in the 1870's—the inductive method.[32] Cannon applied the system to medicine. Facts were obtained from recorded examples, and generalizations or principles induced from skilfully recorded cases. Success depended upon (1) accurate observation, (2) exact recording, (3) the exactly limited inference. President Eliot has told of his early teaching experience (ca. 1865) in the Harvard Medical School, where uninterrupted lectures for six hours were the rule. Inasmuch as some of the students could hardly write, that method of teaching was not successful: how much better the case method, where the student participates in a lively discussion.

Dr. Richard C. Cabot, quick to see the advantages of the method (as did others), introduced it into the clinical conference in the Department of Pathology at the Massachusetts General Hospital, where it has flourished for more than fifty years. In 1915 Cabot had the cases recorded by a stenographer. He then sent the material to a list of physicians who had indicated an interest in receiving it. Since 1923 the material has been published weekly in the *Boston Medical and Surgical Journal* and, since 1928, in its successor, *The New England Journal of Medicine*. To Cabot the case method was a device for drawing together clinicians and pathologists and for teaching students and staff. Cabot was followed by Dr. Tracy B. Mallory and he by Dr. Benjamin Castleman, who, with distinction, kept the traditional practice alive. At the present time (1976) a new problem has arisen which considerably threatens the publication of the clinicopathological conference: In a major hospital like the Massachusetts General hardly anyone dies undiagnosed. Although that statement is sweeping, the fact remains that it is increasingly difficult to find suitable material for presentation.

TENTATIVE ARRANGEMENTS IN OBSTETRICS

The feeling of satisfaction that the founding and successful functioning of the Medical School engendered did not lead to the desire to keep things as they were. Change, when it seemed desirable, was welcomed.

An interesting development—one not readily understandable in terms of today's thinking—occurred in 1815. In this year Walter Channing was appointed Professor of Obstetrics and Medical Jurisprudence. Today this seems an odd combination, but at the time it was eminently reasonable. Harvard did not make the first appointment in the field, as commonly stated but was a very early pioneer, having made the second appointment when Channing was given the post. According to Professor William J. Curran, there has never been a good historian of legal medicine at Harvard, and so one can only surmise the circumstances.[33] It will be recalled that this period was one in which psychiatry was almost solely a French development. Philippe Pinel, his pupil Jean-Étienne-Dominique Esquirol, and the numerous pupils of both of them shaped modern psychiatry. The clinical descriptions of mania, depression, and what today are called schizophrenia and catatonia were fully outlined. Pinel and those who came after him noted that one patient in ten in their female wards had just had a baby. In addition, abortion and infanticide were also discussed as evidences of mental disease. A brilliant offshoot from early nineteenth-century French psychiatry was medical jurisprudence, which spread to include other elements of criminal behavior whose etiology might be medical. Nevertheless, the role of pregnancy was most spectacular, in that previously normal women might become psychotic or sociopathic. These relationships were noted even earlier. Many concepts in the medicolegal field go back to the influence of Paulo Zacchia (1584–1659), a leader. The problems in the field were then generally associated with childbirth, abortion, and mystical beliefs about demons and sex. Demonology was frankly sexual in character.

At about the time, then, that modern medical jurisprudence was being recognized as a specialty, obstetrics also came to the fore, as male "midwives" began to be accepted.

It is perhaps for all these reasons that the two subjects, obstetrics and medical jurisprudence, became the responsibility of one man, Walter Channing. Dr. Channing (1786–1876) had entered Harvard College in 1804; while there, he took part in the undergraduate Rebellion of 1807 and as a consequence failed to receive his bachelor's degree in the regular course. (Fifty-nine years later it was granted to him as a member of the Class of 1808.) The University of Pennsylvania had granted his M.D. in 1809, and Harvard an M.D. in 1812. He returned to Harvard at that time, following study in Edinburgh and London. In 1812 he began to practice obstetrics. In 1828 he shared with Dr. John Ware the editorship of the *Boston Medical and Surgical Journal*. He participated in the founding of the Boston Lying-in Hospital in 1832.[34] Although Walter Channing was appointed Lecturer in Obstetrics in 1815 (his lecture notes are in the Countway Library), there is little or nothing in the Harvard catalogues which describes the early methods of instruction.

The first definite statement about the obstetrics course was contained in the catalogue of 1830:

> The Midwifery Department contains models from Florence to illustrate the practice and to teach the nantomy of this branch of the profession. Besides these, it is well supplied with plates and preparations to aid its study.[35]

By 1841 some fifty lectures on midwifery were offered, and still others on "operative midwifery."

> The class is formed into divisions, and these meet the professor in the afternoon and as often as may be necessary, and are examined on

what has been taught, and with the professor perform the operations with instruments on a suitable machine. The lectures are illustrated by models made in Florence and by every truly valuable work with plates as it appears.[36]

No practical instruction was offered in the early days except as this might accidentally occur, presumably owing to the presence of an especially interesting case. Commonly, the professors in this field provided living space in their houses for medical students who were expected to absorb learning by proximity. It is probable that these students had the opportunity to take charge of the labor of poor patients, or at least to be present during their labor. Such was the policy until modern times, with the difference that the labors of the poor were in the early days probably supervised by old women, and presumably some practical instruction was given to the students before they were allowed to take on cases themselves. By the 1830's for some reason not clear, the close association with older physicians had pretty much died out. It is difficult to understand why this situation developed. According to Dr. Malcolm Storer, for some time, beginning about 1835, it was seemingly a rare thing for a man to observe a woman in labor until, as a practitioner, he suddenly had to face the problem of how to help a recalcitrant baby out.[37]

It is said that Dr. Channing's lectures were interesting and amusing, but doubtless they were not very scientific. Evidently no textbook was in use. The "models made in Florence" may have been more a happy thought as far as their practical use went than anything else. Storer could not find any of Channing's pupils who remembered ever having seen them. Channing held his double title until 1854. The two dissimilar parts continued together until 1877.

The Harvard Medical School in its early days, as has been noted, reflected the character of the New England community, particularly Boston. In that city the cultural, financial, and political leaders were largely related by blood, marriage, or both. A genealogical study of the Harvard Faculty, both at the College and at the Medical School, would show much inbreeding, or, if one wanted a more optimistic term, preservation of good blood-lines. Hard work, a sense of duty to God and man, respect for the accumulatioon of knowledge, good works, and hard cash characterized the Medical School Faculty. Except for Waterhouse, the outsider, none showed outstanding interest in or talent for other branches of learning. In politics, again except for Waterhouse, they were all patriots. The faculty functioned as a high-principled, conscientious, and optimistic club. This atmosphere was to prevail a long time.

Nevertheless, the earnest, practical idealism that motivated these men could not remain confined within this group. Its dissemination took two forms, illustrious alumni, and the organization of medical teaching and medical-care delivery.

NATHAN SMITH AT DARTMOUTH AND ELSEWHERE

Today the alumni of the Harvard Medical School are found largely among the leaders of medical practice, teaching, and research. The expert, illustrious alumni appeared only a few years after the School was founded. The story of Nathan Smith (1762–1829), founder of Dartmouth Medical School and influential in the establishment of three more of the earliest schools in the country, exemplifies this.

The Dartmouth Medical School at Hanover, New Hampshire, founded in 1798, was the fourth such institution in the United States, preceded only by the Medical College of Philadelphia, King's College, and Harvard. The first of a long line of country medical schools—founded as it was in a village of fewer than a thousand—it was established by Dr. Smith, a worthy colleague of the redoubtable Eleazar Wheelock (1711–1779), founder of Dartmouth College. A curious provision in the College's charter allowed the President to appoint his successor. He did: his son, John, aged twenty-five. The son's administration lasted thirty-six years, and it was during his tenure that the Medical Department was established. Its own building was erected in 1811. (A closely associated hospital, the Mary Hitchcock, was not built until 1890–97.)

Nathan Smith was born of poor parents in Rehoboth, Massachusetts, September 30, 1762.[38] Very soon the family moved to Chester, Vermont, where he received such education as the country schools afforded. A turning point in his life came when he heard that Josiah Goodhue, a famous surgeon, was coming to Chester to amputate. Goodhue was then President and Trustee of the Berkshire Medical College. A group of spectators had assembled at the patient's house, including Smith—"a strange and rather ungainly backwoodsman looking youth [who] stepped up boldly and offered his aid"—when the surgeon asked for someone to hold the leg to be amputated.

The youth's steadiness and concentration impressed the surgeon. After the operation was finished and the crowd gone, Smith approached the surgeon. "To him the surgeon was a ministering angel of comfort, the workings of the human body more marvelous than he had dreamed: To understand the latter, and to merit the honor of the former, was henceforth to be the hope of the man." He asked to be an apprentice of Goodhue. Goodhue told the young man that he must first get more education.

This he did during a year's tutelage by the Rev. W. Whiting, after which he was for three years an apprentice to Goodhue. He entered practice in Cornish, New Hampshire, in 1787 but soon realized the inadequacies of his preparation and at great sacrifice entered the Medical School of Harvard College, where he was graduated three years later with the degree of Bachelor of Medicine, the fifth man to receive that degree from Harvard. Returning to Cornish, he practiced there six years. Once again, dissatisfied with his opportunities and labors, he set out to provide medical education for other local youths. To this end he applied to the Trustees of Dartmouth College (1796), "asking their encouragement and approbation of a plan he had devised to establish a Professorship of the Theory and Practice of Medicine in connection with Dartmouth College."

This plan was approved by the President and Trustees, but such a bold innovation was not to be hurried; final action was to be postponed for a year. In the meantime, Smith was to travel in Europe, gathering modern ideas and materials—all evidently at his own expense. Since his resources were meager, he went to Scotland, where the fare from the United States was $75, whereas travel to London cost a surprising $170. The journey was a profitable one.

While in Edinburgh he sent to Dartmouth books costing £30, which he hoped the Trustees would pay for. He returned to Boston early in September 1797 on his way to Hanover, where he was to begin teaching even before an appointment had been approved. In August 1798 the Trustees came through and appointed him Professor "whose duty it shall be to deliver public lectures upon Anatomy, Surgery, Chemistry, and the Theory and Practice of Physic." Smith was awarded a Master's Degree in 1798; the College added the M.D. in 1801.

Smith's first assistant was Lyman Spalding, another Harvard graduate, M.B. 1797, who lectured on Chemistry and Materia Medica. In 1812 Spalding was to attain distinction as President and Professor in the Medical School of the Western District of the State of New York. He shared honors with Jacob Bigelow for preparing the *American Pharmacopoeia* (above, page ooo).

The early years of the new school at Dartmouth were fraught with difficulties. One can only admire Smith's steadfast courage and persistence. Harvard had not received the support expected from the surrounding medical profession; neither did Dartmouth. Smith was doubtless buoyed up by the knowledge that he was doing something not previously done: carrying formal medical education into the wilderness. Except for the two years when Spalding assisted him (1798–99), Smith bore the entire burden until Dr. Cyrus Perkins came to carry part of the load in 1810. Students were plentiful. Finally, he petitioned the New

Hampshire legislature for help. In 1804 he was voted an annual salary of $200. He was granted (1809) $600 for apparatus and $3450 for a building, provided "he would give the site for it, and assign to the State his Anatomical Museum and Chemical Apparatus." He did so in June 1811, after eight years had intervened, but he was discouraged. A year before, on May 14, 1810, he had written to George Cheyne Shattuck in Boston and declared his intention to leave Hanover:

> The political parties are so very jealous of each other in this state
> and so near a balance that I have nothing to expect from either as some
> ignorant persons might be offended at any grant or assistance voted
> by the Legislature to promote what they term the "Cutting up of
> dead bodies."

He had not finally determined where he would settle, but Boston seemed increasingly attractive, and he went there, to teach at Harvard. He apparently had some difficulty over a misunderstanding concerning fees. Abuse was heaped upon him. At the same time he was being pressed to go to the new Medical School at Yale, and he did in fact accept an appointment as Professor of the Theory and Practice of Medicine and Surgery in the Medical Department at Yale College in 1812. He began his teaching there in 1813 and continued until his death in 1829. In 1814 he obtained $20,000 from the Connecticut legislature, with which he purchased a stone building, started a library, and founded an anatomical museum.

Dartmouth and Yale were progressing. The State of Maine also saw the need for a medical school, and once again Nathan Smith was summoned. In 1820 an annual appropriation of $1000 was made on condition that Dr. Smith would found the new school. This appealed to him as an opportunity to develop a school in new territory, "where neither habit nor party have laid their ruthless hands on the public institutions and where the minds of men are free from the poisonous influence." The Medical School of Maine, in conjunction with Bowdoin College, was opened in 1821. Nathan Smith had established two flourishing schools, proof enough that his principles were sound. In the years 1822–25 he gave four courses of lectures at the University of Vermont.

According to Harrington, his career as a teacher of medicine covered thirty-one years, 1797–1828. In that time he was involved in forty-two general courses and gave instruction in 138 special courses. He wrote on typhus and recognized that the disease has a specific course and is self-limited. His "Observations on the Pathology and Treatment of Necrosis" were valuable. He carried out an ovariotomy July 5, 1821, without knowledge of McDowell's achievement twelve years earlier. In the words of William Henry Welch:

Dr. Nathan Smith, when he came to New Haven from Dartmouth, was already a star of the first magnitude in the medical firmament . . . Nathan Smith shed undying glory upon the Yale Medical School. Famous in his day and generation, he is still more famous today, for he was far ahead of his times, and his reputation, unlike that of so many medical worthies of the past, has steadily increased, as the medical profession has slowly caught up with him. We now see that he did more for the general advancement of medical and surgical practice than any of his predecessors or contemporaries in this country. He was a man of high intellectual and moral qualities, of great originality and untiring energy, an accurate and keen observer, unfettered by traditions and theories; fearless, and above all, blessed with an uncommon fund of plain common sense.[39]

MASSACHUSETTS GENERAL HOSPITAL

The other way in which the Harvard Medical School faculty spread its principles outside its walls was through its relationships with certain hospitals. Reference has already been made to the efforts exerted by the earliest faculty, especially Waterhouse, to secure access to clinical material for teaching. These early efforts failed, and the faculty had to be satisfied with the Almshouse until, confident of their influence and believing in the validity of their alms, they undertook the formation of a general hospital.

The founders of the Massachusetts General Hospital were men of great vision. The Reverend John Bartlett, in 1810, wrote to "fifteen or twenty-five [sic] of the wealthiest and most respectable citizens of Boston." In his letter he urged the building of a hospital. The individuals written to were, for those times, men of economic power and political influence. Many belonged to established well-to-do families. Others represented the rising merchant and industrial class. Leadership in civic improvement was close to their hearts. Even at that early date they recognized that prosperity was accompanied by a distinct social obligation.

The Reverend Mr. Bartlett was joined in his aspirations by Dr. John C. Warren and Dr. James Jackson. In 1811 they had very few precedents to guide them, although the Pennsylvania Hospital in Philadelphia and the New York Hospital in New York were already in existence. Upon receiving a charter from the General Court in 1811, they at once formed a corporation and wrote the bylaws which, with very few changes, guide the Hospital today.

In 1811 the population of Boston was just a little more than 33,000.

The Trustees set about planning the building and obtained the services of the distinguished Charles Bulfinch. Their decision was that there should be no restrictions as to race, color, creed, or ability to pay. This was more remarkable in 1811 than it would be today. All those in need of hospital care were welcomed.[40]

The staff was comprised of leading practitioners in the City of Boston. Most of its founding members were already connected with the Harvard Medical School and interested in teaching. Those who had had the privilege of training in France were much interested in research.

Some years were to elapse before its building was ready. In the meantime, the Trustees purchased the Barrel estate in Somerville and there established the McLean Hospital, which later became a psychiatric division of the Massachusetts General Hospital. A few years later Bulfinch and Alexander Parris completed their building across the Charles River, in Boston. From then on, the development of the Harvard Medical School was closely tied in with the development of the Massachusetts General Hospital. Although the two maintained their independence, each was involved symbiotically in the affairs of the other.

Chapter Four

The Second Phase

B Y the time the Harvard Medical School had established itself as a well-organized, well-functioning entity, New England had shown marked changes. The Industrial Revolution had brought to the region, with its resources of waterpower, native inventiveness, and (compared with New York and Philadelphia) nearness to Europe, great wealth. Although a considerable portion of this wealth went for fine houses, fine furnishings, and foreign travel, little went for high living. The habit of hard work together with unfailing awareness of the value of a dollar provided the resources for what Van Wyck Brooks aptly named *The Flowering of New England.*

The intellectual preeminence of New England was bound to have an effect on its schools, including the Harvard Medical School. Dissent and social experimentation was in the air. The social experimentation petered out, as such experiments often do, but the spirit of doing good in a dissenting way, if anything, grew stronger. The Abolitionist movement is perhaps best known, but that Vermont's state legislature passed two strongly worded resolutions condemning the Mexican War is even more indicative of the strength of social conscience. Intellectual curiosity led physicians and medical students to Europe instead of to Edinburgh, formerly the medical Mecca of Americans. France was then in a golden age of physics, chemistry, and, most important for this history, clinical observation.

Jean-Nicolas Corvisart, René Laennec, Jean-Baptiste Bouillaud, Pierre Louis, and others of lesser note were at that time dominating clinical thoughts and methods of measurement. Pierre Louis was the man who seemed to have had the greatest influence on Boston physicians. It is regrettable but understandable that some of the ideas held by François Broussais were not accepted. Head of the equivalent of our Veterans' Administration (L'Hotel des Invalides) and professor at Paris, he became notorious for his dogmatic belief that the cure for almost all disease was to bleed, and bleed again. His method of treatment was reported to have killed more people than had all of Napoleon's campaigns. His destructive therapeutic notions obscured his positive contributions. His sensible comments on the *ego* in psychiatry, and his scornful disparagement of then current ideas about the unconscious and the use of free association to study it, would, if accepted, have saved Boston medicine some bad times a century later.

In any case, it is clear that the character of the Harvard Medical School during the second phase of its growth was strongly influenced by French medicine, and remained so affected at a time when other American medical schools came under the influence of German medicine. It also remained flagrantly proprietary, and its faculty was a closed group. Despite this, it accepted and indeed accelerated the diversification of medicine and the beginning of its division into specialties.

ANATOMY

When Dr. John Collins Warren resigned in 1847, the Professorship of Surgery was separated and made a distinct chair. The Hersey Professorship of Anatomy moved then to Cambridge, and Dr. Oliver Wendell Holmes became Parkman Professor of Anatomy and Physiology, the chair having been named after George Parkman, the victim in the Webster-Parkman murder case. Holmes, like many of his contemporaries, had studied in France after graduating from the Medical School. The Countway Library has his notes taken in French during lectures by Gabriel Andral. Before coming to Harvard, he had two years of teaching at Dartmouth Medical School, and while there was co-author, with Jacob Bigelow, of a revision of the Englishman Marshall Hall's textbook of medicine. This work is today notable for the history-taking form it contained. Evidently, the medical history taken by students in the mid-nineteenth century was much the same as the one used in the mid-twentieth. Holmes's interest in broader aspects of clinical medicine was shown in another direction when on February 13, 1843, he read to the Boston Society for Medical Improvement his paper "On the Contagiousness of Puerperal Fever."[1] He held that women at childbirth should never be attended by physicians who had been caring for women with puerperal fever, erysipelas, or peritonitis, or conducting autopsies, for those diseases could be transmitted from one to the other by bodily contact. He held that changing one's clothes and thorough washing would likely prevent the transmission of the disease. Holmes gives a "long catalogue of melancholy histories" of cases of puerperal fever. He re-

Oliver Wendell Holmes, Parkman Professor of Anatomy and Physiology. He introduced the microscope into medical-school teaching. Wrote on "child-bed fever." A leading literary figure during the flowering of New England and the most photographed man in America at mid-century. Photograph in the collection of the Boston Medical Library.

counts the similar experience of many others, going back to Dr. Gordon of Aberdeen, who, in 1795, had recognized the contagiousness of the disease. Notwithstanding the experience of many and the widely held belief that puerperal fever *was* contagious, current medical teaching did not recognize the fact until after Holmes. Even then, there was great hostility to Holmes's views.

It is curious that in the 1906 *History of the Harvard Medical School*, Ignaz Semmelweis, not Holmes, is credited with one of the truly great medical advances of all time, great not only because of its effect on care of patients, but also for what it foreshadowed: that childbed fever could be attributed to a contagion and was spread by lack of cleanliness. Holmes's remarkable Harvard demonstration of 1843 antedates Semmelweis' by more than four years. Holmes's report might also be acknowledged as recognizing the importance of asepsis long before Joseph Lister (1867 *et seq.*).

When Dr. Holmes came to Harvard to teach after his two years at Dartmouth, he was thirty-eight years old and had already acquired a considerable reputation as a writer and lecturer. Not only was he well grounded in anatomy, but he was equally at home in physiology. In those days, however, physiology was not concerned with living organs, studied, as we do today, with highly specialized instruments. Rather, it was a system of physiological interpretation based on what was observable through a microscope. When Matthias Schleiden and Theodor Schwann provided the substrate for the cell theory in the 1830's, this approach was quickly taken into medicine as a course in microscopy. Today it is called microscopic anatomy or histology, but it was considered physiology almost until the end of the nineteenth century. Holmes brought back from France a microscope, which he subsequently modified, and his instrument was widely used in America for decades.

He was an enthusiastic microscopist. It is said that he gave more attention to the construction of the microscope and the resolving powers of lenses than he did to the subject matter of science. Actually, he first gave a course on microscopy in the summer of 1858, and this was continued for many years. Physiology was finally made a separate department in 1871.

In earlier times Dr. Holmes lectured five times a week in the winter term at 1:00 P.M. to a class nearing exhaustion. Perhaps only Dr. Holmes could have been tolerated at such a time. Dr. Cheever said "As a lecturer he was accurate, punctual, precise, unvarying in patience over detail, and though not an original anatomist in the sense of a discoverer, yet a most exact descriptive lecturer; while the wealth of illustration, comparison, and simile he used was unequalled." Cheever records that

Holmes likened the mesentery to the shirt ruffles of a former generation, a sweat-gland to a fairy's intestine, and the brain and its membranes to an English walnut in its shell. He was also a careful lecturer on osteology.[2]

Holmes was interested in still other medical matters. He was phrenologically oriented, as were other physicians who could not accept the dogma but were unwilling to reject the possibility that it might contain some truth. (Today, Boston physicians who learn about another Viennese dogma, the Freudian, and who harbor similar ambiguities, refer to themselves as analytically oriented.) Holmes's comments on the mind in his Phi Beta Kappa address are of greater interest. He made sensible observations about the ego, and firmly believed in the reality of unconscious thought. Among other things he said that the conversation of women proved the existence of the unconscious.

By 1882 Dr. Oliver Wendell Holmes's literary reputation was so secure that his publishers induced him to resign his professorship. He intended to resign without ceremony, but faculty and students insisted on a final lecture, which was given on November 28. Great enthusiasm and emotion were aroused by this closing chapter of his medical career. His term of service, thirty-five years, was almost exactly coterminous with the building on North Grove Street (1883) where he taught. The two Warrens and Holmes together had occupied the Chair of Anatomy for almost one hundred years.

During Dr. Holmes's time, there was a gradual rise in the importance of the demonstrators. They were young men chosen for their skill in dissection, who prepared the material of a given day for presentation to the students by the lecturer. Under Dr. Holmes, demonstrators were F. S. Ainsworth, 1849–1851; Samuel Kneeland, 1851–1853; R. M. Hodges, 1853–1861; David W. Cheever, 1861–1866; C. B. Porter, 1868–1879 (assistant 1867–1868); H. H. A. Beach, 1879–1882 (assistant 1869–1879); and M. H. Richardson, 1882–1887. The position of demonstrator came to be regarded as a likely stepping-stone to a hospital appointment. Having demonstrators and other assistants teach in the course made Anatomy much less a matter of lectures than it had been at first. In 1862 Dr. David W. Cheever instituted anatomical conferences in the dissecting room. These conferences were continued under C. B. Porter and H. H. A. Beach. Dr. Cheever was appointed Assistant Professor of Anatomy in 1866; after two years he was transferred to the Surgical Department, where he established a popular course in regional anatomy. He is famous for having established a medical dynasty, successors who were usually members of a given family and noted for their outstanding work and their own influence on ensuing generations.

PHYSIOLOGY

From 1847 to 1882 the Parkman Professorship was held by Oliver Wendell Holmes, but only until 1865 was he responsible for instruction in Physiology. Dr. Josiah Stickney Lombard was appointed Lecturer in Physiology (1865), and the next year he was elevated to an assistant professorship. Dr. William Thompson Lusk, as Lecturer, instructed in Physiology in the year 1870–71. It is not possible now to be precise about the amount and type of instruction given during this period: the School's announcements are stated only in general terms. Writing some forty years later, Dr. Porter noted significant variation in statements of the earlier day students.[3] Some thought only three or four lectures were developed by Dr. Holmes; others said twenty. This uncertainty may have been owing to the less than complete separation between Anatomy and Physiology. Dr. Holmes actually gave few demonstrations.

Although conclusions drawn from gross and microscopic anatomic findings provided the inferences that comprised much physiological thinking at that time, one can discern the beginnings of actual studies of function. For example, in 1865 Josiah Lombard reported his finding that the temperature of the forehead rises during thinking and concluded that thought caused increased blood flow to the head. In this he was a pioneer not only in physiology but in experimental psychology. Insofar as one can judge from the catalogues of the period, Dr. Lombard's instruction seems to have been limited to the summer term, and no attempt was made to include the whole of Physiology. Rather, such selected subjects as glycogenesis, circulation of the blood, and respiration were given a good deal of attention in lectures assisted by demonstrations. Original research was becoming fairly common during this period. There was, however, no laboratory to which students had access. Dr. Lusk's instruction (1870–71) was limited to three lectures a week during the winter term.

In 1864 the distinguished Dr. Charles Edouard Brown-Séquard, a native of Mauritius and primarily identified with French medicine, was named Professor of Physiology and Pathology of the Nervous System. This celebrated physiologist held office in the School for three years. According to the catalogue of 1866–67, he lectured twice a week during the winter term of four months. He has been described as a most enthusiastic lecturer, and he was highly successful in imparting his enthusiasm for experimental science. Brown-Séquard was a pioneer well in advance of his colleagues elsewhere. W. T. Porter comments:

> Thus, eighteen years before the publication of the wellknown work of Goldscheider on the specific energy of the temperature-perceiving

nerve terminations in the skin, we find Brown-Séquard teaching that the sensibility of the skin to cold and to heat was probably dependent upon two separate sets of nerve terminations.[4]

The need for additional knowledge about physiology and how to study and teach it had inspired the importation of a Frenchman to satisfy the demand. This clearly was not going to be enough, however, and the next step was taken—sending a Bostonian to Europe specifically to get this kind of training. Henry Pickering Bowditch was the man. He was graduated from the School in 1868, after which time he spent three years in Paris, Bonn, Leipzig, and Munich, preparing himself for a career in Physiology. After serving five years as Assistant Professor, Dr. Bowditch was named Professor of Physiology during the Eliot era, and discussion of his subsequent career properly falls into those chapters (below, pages 97–100).

CHEMISTRY

The confused history of chemistry in the early days of the Harvard Medical School exemplifies the difficulty that has always existed in trying to decide whether a basic science course belongs in the undergraduate college or in the Medical School. When Dr. Gorham resigned in 1827 (above, page oo), the Corporation voted that the Erving Professor of Chemistry should again reside in Cambridge but should give lectures both to the undergraduates and at the Medical School in Boston. Dr. Gorham was succeeded by the later notorious John White Webster. Born in Boston in 1793, Dr. Webster graduated with the Harvard Class of 1811 and the Medical School Class of 1815. He practiced medicine in Cambridge and in Boston, was a member of the American Academy of Arts and Sciences, and held associate membership in several foreign scientific societies. His lectures in the Medical School were given at the Mason Street Building until 1847, when the School moved to its new location on North Grove Street. It was there he murdered Professor Parkman, a crime for which he was hanged. Dr. E. H. Horsford was named Lecturer in Chemistry at the Medical School for the academic year 1849–50—as the record shows, "in the absence of the Erving Professor."

In 1850 Josiah Parsons Cooke (Harvard College, A.B., 1848) was elected Erving Professor of Chemistry and Mineralogy. He, too, was required to live in Cambridge as a member of the College Faculty but to lecture in Boston as well. About 1853 a laboratory was fitted up in the basement of the North Grove Street building; six desks were provided, and for the first time students studied analytical chemistry under the eyes of an instructor. Only a small group took the course, using *Galloway's Analysis* as their laboratory manual. Professor Cooke was able to obtain from abroad Lehmann's *Physiologische Chemie.* No textbooks in English were available. Cooke had been the first medical student to carry the study of chemistry farther than simple organic analysis, and he had taken an advanced degree at Cambridge, England.

Professor Cooke gave in his regular course a few lectures on the urine and on toxicology. At his own request, in 1856, he was relieved from his duties of lecturing at the Medical School. Dr. John Bacon and Mr. Charles W. Eliot (later President) were appointed Lecturers in Chemistry in the Medical School for that year. During his tenure Cooke did much to extend the character of chemical instruction, especially when he introduced laboratory teaching into the curriculum.

After Professor Cooke's resignation in 1856, the Corporation reexamined the arrangements it had previously insisted upon. In 1857 Dr. John Bacon, who had received an A.B. degree at Harvard in 1837 and the M.D. degree in 1840, was elected University Professor in Chemistry for the Medical School, and the time-honored, preexisting connections were severed between the teaching of chemistry in the undergraduate and the Medical departments. The request was made in 1858 that the income from the Erving Fund originally provided for Dr. Dexter be transferred to the Medical School, but the Corporation decided, one fears somewhat typically, that at least the existing arrangements should not be disturbed. Dr. Bacon had given instruction in chemistry at the Boylston Street Medical School, and he restored and enlarged the students' laboratory in the basement of the Medical College. This expansion embraced sixteen desks. In 1858 summer school was established, and thereafter recitations in chemistry took place throughout the year. Dr. James C. White (Harvard, A.B., 1853; M.D., 1856) was appointed in 1866 Adjunct Professor of Chemistry. When Dr. Bacon resigned in May of 1871, University law required the automatic termination of the Adjunct Professorship held by Dr. White. In the five years preceding, however, much more attention had been given to physiological, toxicological, and clinical chemistry. Demonstrations in clinical chemistry were also introduced for the students at the Massachusetts General Hospital.

MATERIA MEDICA

The ambiguous position of Materia Medica in medical thinking of the period is shown in that, originally an offshoot of the Department of

Chemistry, it became more or less independent under Jacob Bigelow. The School's second period up to the Eliot era was dominated by him, and he continued to lecture on Materia Medica while serving as Rumford Professor in the University. He was promoted to Professor of Materia Medica in 1824, and in 1836 had the further title of Lecturer in Clinical Medicine conferred on him. A year after Dr. Bigelow resigned in 1855, Dr. Edward Hammond Clark succeeded him as Professor of Materia Medica. He was assisted by Dr. Fitch E. Oliver from 1861 to 1869. Dr. Oliver had the title of Assistant in Materia Medica, changed in 1870 to Instructor. Until the third period there was no evidence of any effort to teach pharmacology as an experimental field, although experiments began to be used for didactic purposes.

SURGERY

Although John Collins Warren was the teacher of surgery at the Medical School when he succeeded his father in the early days, a separate Professorship of the Principles of Surgery was established in 1835, with the proviso that "It shall be the duty of the professors to give elementary lectures on the principles of surgery and clinical lectures on the surgical cases in the Massachusetts General Hospital." It required that "The same attendance on the lectures in this Department shall be required of the candidate for the degree of Doctor of Medicine in the University as is required on the lectures in other departments of the Medical Faculty."

This new post was filled by Dr. George Hayward, with Dr. Warren teaching operative surgery and Hayward clinical surgery. The distinction between the two fields is not clear. The term for surgical instruction was extended to four months. However, Hayward resigned his professorship after holding it two years. What stress prompted this action is not known. A month after his resignation, Henry Jacob Bigelow (1818–1890) was elected Professor of Surgery. Dr. Bigelow was, notwithstanding the distaste of the Warrens and his own aggressive personality, one of the most distinguished surgeons of his time. He graduated from Harvard in 1837 and began his medical studies under his father and at Dartmouth with Oliver Wendell Holmes. In 1838–39 he was house pupil at the Massachusetts General Hospital. A bout with pulmonary tuberculosis forced him to go to Cuba for his health; afterward he studied in Paris and then returned to Harvard to get his medical degree in 1841. He then took another trip abroad for study in London and Paris. On returning to Boston in 1844 he began practice and, ever the innovator, opened with Dr. Henry Bryant a "Charitable Surgical Insti-

Henry J. Bigelow, Professor of Surgery. He was a skilled clinician, noted particularly for his orthopedic innovations and for his outstanding lectures. His strong personality created conflicts with his colleagues and many others. Photograph of portrait in oil by F. P. Vinton (1889) in the portrait collection, Francis A. Countway Library of Medicine.

tution for Outdoor Patients." The two advertised this by means of circulars and thus precipitated petty criticism from some of their colleagues. Nevertheless, shortly after Bigelow's return from Europe the second time, his great skill as an operator and lecturer became acknowledged. The amphitheater and lecture room were always crowded when Bigelow was performing (essentially the right word for it).[5] Also in 1844, he won the Boylston Prize Essay with the treatise "Manual of Orthopedic Surgery." He became an Instructor in Surgery at the School and in 1846 was appointed Visiting Surgeon to the Massachusetts General Hospital. A few months afterward he is said to have participated in the first public demonstration of anesthesia, but his participation seems to have been limited to observation and a shrewd understanding of the meaning of the phenomenon he had witnessed.

Bigelow's most distinguished work probably was his "Mechanism of Dislocations and Fractures of the Hip with the Reduction of Dislocations by the Flexion Method." His discovery of the Y-ligament was crucial to an understanding of the pathology of dislocation of the hip. This versatile man was also interested in surgery of the bladder, and in 1878 he published a "Lithotrity by a Single Operation." In this he described his lithotrite, an instrument by which he crushed the bladder calculus and removed the detritus at the same time. When present at the first public demonstration of anesthesia, Bigelow was a young man with an open mind. Two decades later he had lost much of that flexibility and is said to have opposed the introduction of Listerism into his clinic. Finally, so the story goes, his colleagues pressed him, after ten years of Listerism in other places, to try it out in one of his fracture cases. He did so, and the fracture mended well. When this was pointed out to him, he said, "But, *our* fractures do well," and it is said he ignored Listerism for a further decade.

Bigelow resigned his professorship in 1882 and was made Emeritus Professor of Surgery. But younger teachers came along, notably Drs. R. M. Hodges and David W. Cheever. Under their auspices clinical teaching was advanced. Dr. Cheever's strictly clinical exercises were given at the Boston City Hospital. Small classes were the rule, and it was possible for him to demonstrate with care the procedures he wished to teach. On January 27, 1866, Hodges was elected Adjunct Professor of Surgery, and Cheever on January 5 attained the rank of Adjunct Professor of Clinical Surgery. Bedside teaching was at last coming into its own. As the amount of material increased, the course had to be lengthened, and in 1867 it was continued through the spring months. Even so, the surgery of that day was for experts to carry out and rarely attempted by the ordinary practitioner. Students had few opportunities to participate as clinical clerks and dressers. Even the opportunities for minor surgery in the Out-Patient Department were few. Ward visits were not thorough in the German sense, and students had reason for dissatisfaction.

The John Collins Warren–Henry Jacob Bigelow era at the Harvard Medical School and the Massachusetts General Hospital was a time of great advance in surgical theory and practice. Just as the intellectual life of Boston flowered, so did the development of surgery. At this time, the influence of the French School was dominant. As the early nineteenth-century masters of surgery progressed, operating techniques improved. However, emphasis had to be given to speed and dexterity, and one can well understand the vested interest in haste on the part of strapped-down patients. Prior to the development of surgical anesthesia, operative surgery was principally limited to the surface. It was rapid and spectacular, a great field for the showman. (Surgeons of today are more subdued, by force of public opinion, but it is doubtful if there has been a basic change in their nature. The change in their behavior came in the late nineteenth century with the influence of William Halsted of Johns Hopkins.) In any case it was for the future surgeon to enter the major cavities of the body. "The pose of the operator as the only actor on the scene emphasized the fact that surgery was amphitheatre surgery," John Collins Warren emphasized. Two advances greatly altered the activities of the surgeon: anesthesia (1846) and antisepsis (1867). Both greatly extended the range and character of surgical operations and increased their number.

The history of the introduction of anesthesia is particularly Bostonian, although the idea of inducing insensibility to pain by inhaling a chemical to produce anesthesia had interested many, in different parts of the world. The contentions and controversies that marked the first ninety years of the anesthesia era are dutifully recorded in the Bowditch (1851) and Washburn (1939) histories of the Massachusetts General. Bowditch's opening sentence of more than a hundred years ago is apt: "The patience of the public has been long since thoroughly wearied out by the ether controversy." Even the claim of Georgians that Crawford Long was first is today open to doubt, for one Clarke of Rochester, New York, seems to have preceded him, and Humphry Davy had used nitrous oxide before both of them. The inscription on the wall of the Hospital's Ether Dome concludes with the moving phrase that with anesthesia, "a new era for surgery began," and that is the important consideration at present, not the senseless pursuit of claims for priority— assuming that one can define that word so as to please everyone.

The first public demonstration of clinical anesthesia occurred while the School was being transferred from the building in Mason Street to the building just finished on North Grove street. The dentist William

T. G. Morton applied to the head of the Department of Surgery at the Massachusetts General Hospital for permission to try his new method of relieving pain in surgery. It is essential that one realize how courageous not only Morton was, but also the aged John Collins Warren. Both of them risked their careers to carry out the public demonstration of anesthesia. If disaster had occurred, the introduction of clinical anesthesia would doubtless have been delayed for decades. Dr. William Thomas Green Morton came to this demonstration with the enthusiasm of a young man with a brilliant discovery. Warren approached the test full of honors and a position of great prestige. The courage of both men was adequate to the test. How much was told the patient, Gilbert Abbott, is not at all clear. Perhaps modern-day ethicists would have stopped the whole business. At any rate the demonstration succeeded, and the news of it was published. So great was the enthusiasm aroused that ether anesthesia spread throughout the western world. Within a year after the publication, Nikolai Pirogoff, Surgeon-General of the Russian army, made use of ether anesthesia standard in all forces under his command.

The introduction of Listerism and the development of the concepts of antisepsis and, later, asepsis in operations was slower.

Both changed surgery.

MEDICINE

James Jackson was a pioneer at the Medical School and a founder of the Massachusetts General Hospital. Dr. Jackson continued in office until 1836, when he resigned his professorship, and the next year, when he relinquished his chiefship at the Massachusetts General Hospital.

Five years earlier, in 1832, Jackson had asked for an assistant, and Dr. John Ware was named Adjunct Professor with the understanding that this should not increase the expense to medical students. Dr. Ware succeeded Dr. Jackson. Ware was a very pleasant man, modest and hard-working as a physician. He was popular and a good fellow, able to sing a song and tell a good after-dinner story. As a physician his judgment was considered sound, and in dealing with human life it was his firm conviction that conservatism must be the order of the day. John Ware fully appreciated the importance of the medical profession and of a dignified approach to it. He understood clearly, however, that he was not likely to achieve any great fame. He compared Harvey and Newton, whom he considered to be men of the same type of mind, capable of producing great discoveries. "But," Ware asked, "who knows of Harvey as compared with the popular fame of Newton?" "A physician's permanent reputation must be given to him by the profession." He held that a little learning was not a dangerous thing if part of general study. He felt that there was a danger of practitioners becoming simply students of the natural history of disease. Thus he warned against specialization, which was to him a threat to the well-developed man: "The student comes to the Medical School for the first time to study and acquire for himself . . . Previous defects of education can be overcome by the man who now cultivates his powers of observation . . . The studies of the humanities and of language are not to be despised, rather much to be desired . . . Before, we have been taught by others, now we are to learn for ourselves." He warned against scientific studies for their own sake and advised his students not to get so interested in them that there might be neglect of the physician's calling. These views would not find universal approval today.

In the School circular of 1841–42 it was announced that fifty plaster casts had been imported from Paris. It was supposed that these would be useful in the Department of Theory and Practice, for they illustrated many elementary forms of disease. As a matter of fact, they were rarely used in teaching, because they were heavy and it was difficult to move them to the lecture rooms.

In 1850 Theory and Practice included lectures on the general principles of pathology and therapeutics, as well as the history and treatment of particular diseases. Clinical lectures were given at the Massachusetts General Hospital. In the years 1852–53 Dr. J. B. S. Jackson, besides holding a professorship in his own department of Morbid Anatomy, was associated with Dr. Ware in Theory and Practice. The next year, 1853–54, Dr. Morrill Wyman became Adjunct Professor of Theory and Practice; he held this office until 1857. That year saw the first attempt to present a graded course at the Medical School. A two-year course included anatomy, pathological anatomy, practical anatomy, surgery, chemistry, and physiology—all studied during the first year. The second year included botany, zoology, theory and practice, midwifery, diseases of women and children, medical jurisprudence, materia medica, practical anatomy, and clinical observation. For the first time, chemical analysis and the use of the microscope were spoken of. The subjects that formerly were in the charge of the Hersey Professor were now divided among three professors. The lectures and examination were held at the Medical College by Dr. John Ware and Dr. George Cheyne Shattuck. The books principally used in the department at that time were Watson's *Theory and Practice* as the principal textbook and, for collateral reading, books by Wood, Stokes and Bell, Graves, and Williams.

After a time Dr. John Ware resigned, and in a circular published in 1859 Dr. George C. Shattuck was spoken of as the Adjunct Professor. In the fall of that same year he was listed as Hersey Professor.

George Cheyne Shattuck held the Hersey Professorship of the Theory and Practice of Physic until 1873. At that time the didactic lecture was the principal agent of instruction, and although Dr. Shattuck went along with this approach, he had advanced ideas as to what the student must have if he were to become a practical physician. As Dean of the Faculty, 1864–69, he was a true progressive; he encouraged the development of the School and was active in introducing young men into the ranks of instructors. Dr. Shattuck was an outstanding man noted for his genial manners and kindliness, his invariable gentleness and courtesy. He made great efforts to help those who were striving for a medical education. He very early gave up active practice and confined his work to the hospital service. Great changes in the method of teaching occurred at the close of his period of service. They will be discussed later.

The history of clinical medicine at Harvard does not reside wholly in the Hersey Professorship, the first chair in Medicine established at the School. Another chair, the Professorship of Clinical Medicine, was established later under circumstances indicative of the controversies and ill will that characterized the early years of the School. One of the problems was to find a niche for the growing number of men of talent and position who were appearing on the scene.

Dr. Richard Cabot has provided various details concerning the Department of Clinical Medicine.[6] In the Quinquennial Catalogue it is said that the Professorship of Clinical Medicine was established in 1854 and four years later named the Jackson Professorship, a tribute to Dr. James Jackson. Although Medical School catalogues refer to the Professor of Clinical Medicine at a much earlier date, James Jackson seems to have been the first to receive the title. This grew out of the fact that when the Medical School was moved from Cambridge to Boston in 1810, Dr. Waterhouse, who held the title of Hersey Professor of the Theory and Practice of Physic, was adamant in his refusal to be moved from Cambridge. It was therefore essential to create a new professorship to replace him in Boston. The Professorship of Clinical Medicine was thus created for Dr. James Jackson, who seems to have been dealt with rather harshly in that his only compensation was from such fees as he could collect, and the only clinical facilities available to him were those of the Boston Almshouse. Jackson held the office for two years before Dr. Waterhouse resigned or, more accurately, was forced out, in 1812—at which time, James Jackson succeeded to the title "Professor of the Theory and Practice of Physic." He continued, however, "to perform the duties of Professor of Clinical Medicine until another should be chosen." Then, as now, these things do not ever seem to be hurried, and James Jackson continued to teach unaided for twenty years.

Little effort seems to have been made to provide the students with clinical instruction at this time. If they got any, it was mainly from private instructors not connected with the School. In effect the situation was very like that of the apprenticeship, where private patients of these instructors were seen in their homes or offices by the students. It was, of course, of great advantage to the students of those days to be drawn into such intimate observation of the private practice of medicine. In some cases the instructors provided no clinical experience; under very limited supervision the students educated themselves as well as they could by reading.

The entire description of Clinical Medicine in the Catalogue of 1833 consisted in the statement "The lectures for medical students are delivered at the Massachusetts Medical College in Boston. They continue four months. During the lectures the students may find in the city *various opportunities* (italics inserted) for practical instruction." It is strange that the first mention of the Hospital is in 1835, when it is stated in the Catalogue that students who attended the lectures in Theory and Practice might also attend the medical visits at the Massachusetts General Hospital. In the then current catalogue, there was no separate Department of Clinical Medicine, and the phrase "Clinical Medicine" does not occur in any catalogue between 1835 and 1844. But in the Catalogue of 1844–45 there is a statement that in the Department of the Theory and Practice of Clinical Medicine, Professors Ware and Jacob Bigelow gave, for $15.00, a course of clinical lectures, two hours each.

Cases at the Massachusetts General Hospital were presented twice a week. The Catalogue of 1844–45 states:

> Abundant opportunities are thus furnished for most important practical observation and study. Students have an opportunity of visiting *all the cases*, of observing and learning the symptoms and treatment of each case, and particularly of the exploration of the body for the PHYSICAL SIGNS of disease by *palpation, auscultation, and percussion.*

During this period and up to the appointment of Dr. George C. Shattuck, in 1855, no separate examination in Clinical Medicine was held.

Dr. Jacob Bigelow united the Professorships of Materia Medica and Clinical Medicine during 1847–55. Like many other physicians of the period, he was a man of many talents and great ingenuity. Since there was no book of American plants useful in medical treatment, he set about creating one. (Unknown to him, William Barton was doing the same thing in Philadelphia.) Initially, the illustrations, printed in black and white, were hand-colored by a corps of young ladies in Boston. This method proved slow and unreliable. Accordingly, in order to produce the book in adequate numbers and with uniform quality, Bigelow engaged a Boston printer to develop a method of color printing. His book was sold widely along the eastern seaboard.

Later, when Dr. Shattuck took over, "the subjects formerly in charge of the Hersey Professor of Theory and Practice were divided among the professors, Professors Ware (theory and practice), Shattuck (clinical medicine), and J. B. S. Jackson (pathological anatomy)."[7]

Teaching seems to have improved a good deal, for "lectures, recitations and examinations" were held by Dr. Shattuck at the Medical School and medical visits were made at the Massachusetts General Hospital.

> These medical visits apparently constituted what we should call the clinical part of the teaching. They occurred "twice a week during the winter months, and four times a week during the summer term. Students have an opportunity of practising physical exploration and of *learning the uses of chemical analysis and of the microscope in the study and treatment of disease . . .*"[8]

According to Richard Cabot, the number of students was too great and the time too limited to allow many of the students to get firsthand acquaintance with cases until near the end of the term, when the number of students attending the visits was greatly reduced. The faithful student, if he stuck it out, could learn a great deal.

Examinations were oral and were placed at the end of the three-year course of study under the direction of a "regular practitioner of medicine." Eight months of lectures with each professor was required, but there is no evidence that very much attention was paid to the students as far as grading or estimating their progress is concerned.

For reasons not now clear, Henry I. Bowditch became Jackson Professor of Clinical Medicine, replacing Dr. George C. Shattuck, who was transferred to the Hersey Professorship of the Theory and Practice. At this time (1859) there is the first mention of the clinical lectures given at the Hospital. In the course of a lecture a patient would be brought from the wards to the Jacob Bigelow Lecture Room, situated in the northeast corner of the Massachusetts General Hospital. The case was demonstrated and explained to the students, and some of them, at the close of the lecture, were able to examine the patient. Dr. Bowditch continued instruction in the wards during the winter term, and in the summer Dr. J. B. S. Jackson, Dr. Gould, and others carried on. One wonders how this situation can be overlooked when the claim is made, as it so often is, that William Osler, more than others, originated bedside teaching at the Johns Hopkins, 1899–1904. In the Catalogue of

1859–60 there is also the first mention of clinical teaching by physicians who did not hold an official position in the School. Harvard has never had a University hospital, and all hospitals maintained their independence except the Collis P. Huntington Hospital, not now functioning as such.

The policy of grouping studies first began, according to the Catalogue, in 1857–58. This took place in the first and second years. The grouping, however, concerned nothing but lists of studies until 1860. At that time clinical observation by groups was to be found in the Massachusetts General Hospital and the Dispensary. The system of apprenticeship continued until 1871, but more and more, as time went on, this approach was given up and men spent three years under the Harvard Medical School as the only instructor.

Of the men of this time, Dr. Henry I. Bowditch and Dr. Calvin Ellis were outstanding. These two held in common certain similarities as well as contrasts. They were conscientious and faithful; they fulfilled their function as teachers with painstaking thoroughness rather than by brilliance or eloquence. Their presentations were not noted for their literary polish. In these things the two were alike. One of Dr. Bowditch's outstanding characteristics was his contagious enthusiasm. On the other hand, Dr. Ellis was quiet and not easily aroused to any kind of outburst. Dr. Bowditch occasionally introduced kindly humor into his lectures, while the earnest Dr. Ellis was never humorous. Dr. Bowditch had many interests; he was as much concerned with antislavery legislation as with medicine. It was natural for him to associate himself with such public works as the Sanitary Commission and the Massachusetts Board of Health. Dr. Ellis' whole energy was devoted to his one interest, teaching. Dr. Bowditch, for all of his activities, was later able to fill the Chair of Clinical Medicine in a satisfactory way. After Dr. Bowditch retired as Jackson Professor, he joined the staff of the Boston City Hospital, where he continued to serve and teach from 1867 on, without title.

The first mention of the clinical conference is in the 1862–68 Catalogue. It took place during Dr. Bowditch's term as Professor of Clinical Medicine, although a somewhat similar course had been given by Dr. George C. Shattuck. These earlier exercises were not part of Medical School instruction and are not referred to in the Catalogue. Inasmuch as the School was still a proprietary institution, there was no sharp distinction between stated and private instruction.

The School began to give more attention to clinical instruction in 1865. Before that time the Faculty, composed of only eight teachers, had conducted all activities in the Medical School. In 1865 ten professors and nine assistants were on hand. In these years the Faculty was expanding rapidly, and in 1866–67 the number of teachers was increased to more than twenty. Fourteen were professors, two were assistants, and the others were instructors.

Judging from the Catalogue, instruction was limited to about nine hours a week from November to March. There were two clinical lectures, one clinical conference, and six medical visits, two of which took place at the Massachusetts General Hospital, two at the Boston Dispensary, one at the Marine Hospital, and one at the Boston City Hospital. Special instruction was now given in hygiene, ophthalmology, dermatology, syphilis, and "psychological medicine," whatever that was. For the first time, stethoscopes, ophthalmoscopes, and laryngoloscopes were mentioned in the Catalogue of 1868–69. The stethoscopes had been in use, however, since about 1839–40. The first mention of the microscope is in 1870.

PATHOLOGICAL ANATOMY [9]

The development of pathology as a specialty in France naturally led to its expansion in Boston medical teaching. In France at that time pathological anatomy was more than a branch of medical knowledge—it was an integral part of clinical medicine and absolutely essential in teaching.

This department was established with the appointment in 1847 of Dr. J. B. S. Jackson, who was given the title of Professor of Pathological Anatomy. He was also named Curator of the Warren Anatomical Museum. Until this specialist came on the scene it was customary for the clinicians to teach such pathological anatomy as the students learned. Not much official attention was paid to the field until 1856, nor was it required for a degree until that time. It is of some historical interest that Harvard was the first Medical School in the country to present Pathology as a special course. George Cheyne Shattuck endowed the Professorship in 1854, and the Chair was then named the Shattuck Professorship of Morbid Anatomy. In 1879 the title was changed once again to the Shattuck Professorship of Pathological Anatomy.

J. B. S. Jackson had studied in Paris under several distinguished men, Dupuytren, Roux, Lisfranc, and others. In London his masters were Bright, Addison, Hodgkins, and others. Like all the other professors, Jackson was a practitioner of medicine throughout his life, although his chief interest always lay in Pathological Anatomy. As Curator of the Boston Society for Medical Improvement he developed a "cabinet" or museum, and in 1871 the collection was given to Harvard College under the name of the Jackson Cabinet. It was then placed in the Warren

Anatomical Museum, of which he had long been Curator, having built the museum to a high degree of usefulness. Professor Mallory estimated that Dr. Jackson's fame "will rest chiefly and securely on his work as Curator, a position in which he showed unusual powers of intelligent observation and great zeal in the collecting of useful and instructive pathological specimens." In 1847 a *Descriptive Catalogue of the Museum of the Society for Medical Improvement* was published, and in 1870 a *Descriptive Catalogue of the Warren Anatomical Museum.*

Throughout Dr. Jackson's tenure, the Professor of Pathological Anatomy—or of Morbid Anatomy, as he was sometimes called—shared the duty of teaching medicine with the Hersey Professor of the Theory and Practice of Physic and the Professor of Clinical Medicine. This is interesting in light of the fact that several of Harvard's leading professors of medicine of the late nineteenth and early twentieth centuries were first professors of pathology.

OBSTETRICS

In the years from 1835 to 1860, according to Dr. Malcolm Storer, it was seemingly a rare thing for a man to observe a woman in labor until as a practitioner he was brought face to face with the awful problem of how that twelve-pound baby was to emerge through such a small opening. The babies were always twelve-pounders before scales were introduced into the clinic. The neophyte, to his happy surprise, found at length that nothing he could do would prevent the arrival of the new citizen. A great relief.

In the 1850's the inadequacy of didactic lectures alone became apparent. It was clear that supplementary clinical teaching was necessary; Channing, who was then in charge of Obstetrics, had been impressed by the effects of ether. Very soon after the first public demonstration of anesthesia at the Massachusetts General Hospital in 1846, he began to use ether in childbirth, cautiously at first. After two cases, he published a note: "The ether did just what was looked for from its use. It did it at once, and with no circumstances of embarrassment or difficulty. When its influence was no longer needed, its effects passed quickly away, and left a repose . . ."[10] By the next year, he had accumulated 581 similar cases and published a book about them, dedicated to James Jackson, then Emeritus Professor of the Theory and Practice of Physic.[11]

Dr. D. H. Storer, who had been teaching Obstetrics at the "Tremont Street Medical School," took over the chair in 1855. The headquarters were in a room at 39 Tremont Street. This institution was started in

1838 by Bigelow, Reynolds, Storer, and Holmes. Its purpose, according to a statement in its catalogue, was to give "a full course of instruction to private pupils, principally during that part of the year not occupied by the public lectures of the University." It was supplemental to, not in opposition to, University instruction. In effect, the Tremont Street School was a summer school, lectures being given only during vacation periods of the University. As time passed, the material of the summer school was used to augment Harvard instruction and thus became more and more closely tied to the School, until finally it frankly became, in 1858, the Harvard summer school.

It is said that a motivating factor in the creation of the Tremont Street Medical School was a reaction against the conservative methods advocated at the University. Young men of this period felt strongly the importance of work in the clinic. Very little of such activity was offered in any Harvard department.

In an early catalogue of the Tremont School (1847), it is said that the mannikin was used; and during the last year of study arrangements were made for the student to become familiar with the practical management of labor. It was only many years later that Harvard provided any such opportunity. Storer took the chair at Harvard coming directly with his advanced ideas of instruction obtained in the Tremont Street School, convinced of the importance of practical instruction. He very soon gave some students cases to manage. The Boston Dispensary was a principal source of supply. The catalogue of 1855 stated that

Lectures in the Department of Midwifery comprise the anatomy of the pelvis and organs of generation, the functions and diseases of the external and internal organs, the physiology of generation, the symptoms and diseases of pregnancy. The different classes of labor are minutely dwelt upon, and the use of instruments employed demonstrated upon the manikin. Particular attention is paid to diseases of the puerperal state. The lectures will be illustrated by specimens and plates. A distinct course is given on medical jurisprudence, those subjects receiving special attention which have a bearing on obstetrics; namely, impotence, superfoetation, retarded gestation, abortion, pretended pregnancy, rape, infanticide, etc.

The 1858 catalogue of Harvard announced that "arrangements were made by which the student is enabled to become acquainted practically with the management of labor." Cases were still too few, and it was a lucky man indeed who got one. Separate instruction was given in 1858, but few took advantage of it. The horrible possibility that puerperal fever would take over was always present. By that time, textbooks were used, particularly those by Churchill and Ramsbotham.[12] The principle operating here was that nature should not be interfered with. Ramsbotham explained that the only equipment needed in labor was a lancet and a catheter. It was not customary for an assistant to be present at a delivery.

NEW HOSPITAL FACILITIES

The important role of the Massachusetts General Hospital in the teaching of Harvard Medical School students has been noted. During the pre-Eliot years under consideration, however, several other institutions came to be used in a similar way. This was at least partly owing to the fact that not all of the Harvard instructors were on the staff of the General Hospital. There may have been other reasons as well, such as the availability of additional types of clinical material at other institutions.

Boston City Hospital

In 1849 a great epidemic of cholera struck the City of Boston. In order to care for the victims, a Cholera Hospital was established on Fort Hill, and it had a great deal to do with the later establishment of the Boston City Hospital. The Cholera Hospital was well run and made it evident that the sick poor needed such an institution for their proper medical care. It is true that the Massachusetts General was already established, but it was also already overcrowded. In the mid-nineteenth century Boston's strong feeling of civic pride, in its medical aspects, was based upon a long history of accomplishment in caring for the ill and poor, not only in the Fort Hill institution but by the practitioners of the City of Boston. The first patient was received in the Fort Hill hospital on June 29, 1849. The last was discharged on November 15, at the end of the epidemic. Of the 262 patients treated in the hospital during the epidemic, 166 died. The total number of deaths in the City was over 600.

Because of the great success of the Cholera Hospital in saving lives during the epidemic, there was a considerable feeling that the institution should be preserved, but the general opinion of Boston physicians was against maintaining it. At that time there was doubt that cholera was an infectious disease, a view allegedly borne out by the fact that the staff caring for the epidemic victims rarely became infected themselves. The reasoning involved was erroneous, because cholera *is* infectious. Nevertheless, the example set by the Cholera Hospital was a very powerful element in the determination of some of the leading physicians in Boston that a full-fledged hospital should be established as soon as possible to care for the sick poor; yet from 1850 to 1857 nothing significant happened. Early enthusiasm, for reasons not clear, had waned. In 1856, however, leading physicians of Boston enlisted the support of progressive citizens, and the municipal hospital was revived, with Alexander Hamilton Rice in charge.

The staff was chosen from the most distinguished physicians and surgeons in Boston. The names are familiar: D. W. Cheever, A. Coolidge, D. Thaxter, C. Homans, C. Buckingham, C. Stedman. Each of these men had been graduated from the Harvard Medical School between 1828 and 1858. It was helpful that they belonged to the families that had been or had become social and financial leaders since the Revolution. Six physicians and surgeons formed the Board of Consultation: A. A. Gould, S. D. Townsend, W. Lewis, E. Reynolds, J. Jeffries, and S. Durkee. They had great influence on the choice of younger staff men.

The Boston City Hospital, with 200 beds for medical, surgical, and ophthalmological patients, was ready to be opened on June 1, 1864. A resident staff of five young men had been chosen as house officers. None had as yet received his M.D. degree from the Harvard Medical School, by which they were appointed.

With its auspicious beginning, it is a pity that in subsequent decades the institution became a political football; that unfortunate fact ultimately checked its academic development. However, it served for more than a century as one of Harvard's leading teaching hospitals.

Boston Dispensary

Some teaching was carried on at this institution beginning in the 1850's. It seems not to have played a great role in the development of Harvard medicine, although in the nineteenth and twentieth centuries its staff included distinguished physicians. In the twentieth century, in combination with the Boston Floating Hospital (founded to care during the summer for sick children from the hot slums) and several other institutions, it became, as the New England Medical Center, the main teaching hospital of Tufts Medical School.

DEVELOPMENTS IN THE PRE-ELIOT YEARS

Harvard medicine, from its beginnings to the post-Civil War period, can be characterized as going through a period more of expansion and consolidation than of innovative development. Its physician-teachers were outstanding—some brilliantly so—but most of the ideas came from France. The exception to this statement lies in the remarkable development of surgery, but that was due to two adventitious factors, anesthesia and Listerism. The first was, of course, a Boston phenomenon, although it, too, had been brought in from the outside. On the whole, however, the School continued the policies and in large measure the practices of the founders and their immediate successors. Administrative changes accommodated the increased number of students, the move from Cambridge to Boston, and the acquisition of clinical facilities. The School was still a proprietary institution, however, run by men who were mostly related by blood and marriage. There were quarrels even within this seemingly homogeneous group, and outsiders did not fare at all well. One such, Benjamin Waterhouse, was cast out, although his daughter married a Ware and their descendants became important persons in the Boston establishment. Another outsider—a Dartmouth man, Henry Jacob Bigelow—became involved in an earthshaking quarrel with the Warrens, but in the end his brilliance was recognized, and his descendants, too, became leaders in the Boston medical establishment. The murderer Webster became such when pressed by his fellow physician Parkman to pay a debt of money, but this act fortunately did not become the established way of settling disputes within the Harvard Faculty.

The first eighty years of the Harvard Medical School witnessed steady professional development but were deficient in one respect. When the School was founded, students had been changed from servants (as apprentices) to observers, but they did not to any great degree become participants. That change would have to wait for another kind of reform. The students, as in any proprietary school, paid their money and took their courses with little or no checking on them. Until the School ceased to be a proprietary vehicle that supported—in some cases enriched—an oligarchic faculty (however distinguished and public-spirited), and until it instituted a system that guided and closely supervised students, it could not become great. Those changes were soon to come.

Part II
The Eliot Years, 1869–1909

Chapter Five

A New Broom

WHEN the Medical School of Harvard College, founded in Cambridge in 1782, moved to Boston in 1810, arrangements for clinical teaching remained exceedingly vague.[1] The Harvard move was planned merely to provide convenient access to the clinical material in the hospitals of Boston.

State regulatory laws did not yet exist, and the School diploma constituted a license to practice. Examinations were brief, oral, and secret, and as long as a candidate could gain the approval of a majority of nine professors, he was assured of his degree—if he could pay his tuition bill. No applicant for instruction who could pay his fees or sign his note was turned down, though all candidates for admission were obliged (with a few exceptions) to pass a nominal examination in English, Latin, Physics, Chemistry, and an elective subject, which could be any one of the following: French, German, algebra through quadratic equations, plane geometry, or botany. Written examinations were required. Candidates were especially welcome who presented a degree in Letters, Science, or Medicine from a recognized college or scientific school. The size of classes was nevertheless restricted. Henry J. Bigelow, Professor of Surgery at Harvard in 1871, in a statement revealing a limited outlook, said, "it is safe to say that no successful school has thought proper to risk large existing classes and large receipts in attempting a more thorough education."[2]

Until Charles William Eliot became President of Harvard University, the Medical School remained a proprietary institution run by a few families, its leaders supporting the interests of themselves and their relatives and friends. It was, to speak plainly, a money-making institution not much better than a diploma mill. In Eliot's words, the School was "a sort of trading corporation as well as a body of teachers."[3]

When he began his tenure as President, Eliot found the Medical School in the worst condition of any part of the University. Once installed, he turned his attention to it, with far-reaching results. From a reading of the record, one cannot believe that Eliot, in his earliest years, had time for many other activities, nor were any of his activities then or later of more consequence than his achievements in the field of medical education. A generally sympathetic Corporation was to make it possible for him to impose his ideas for change despite the resistance of most of the Faculty, only a small segment of which favored the changes he suggested. Mr. Eliot's later views were the result of conversations with Edward Hickling Bradford, who gave him strong support in his stand. Eliot's first move "startled the bewildered Faculty of its Medical School into the first of a series of reforms that began [1870] with the grading of the existing course and ended in 1901 with the requirement of an academic degree for admission" (later modified).[4]

Eliot increased the study period from four months to nine, instituted progressive and graded advancement in courses that were increasingly complex, and substituted written for oral examinations at the end of each year. At that time a wave of commercial exploitation was sweeping over the field of medical education. University departments were, in effect, separated from their University affiliation for all practical purposes. Harvard, Yale, and Pennsylvania became, as they grew, essentially independent of the institutions with which they were legally united.[5] A first step toward correcting the virtual autonomy at Harvard occurred when the University set out to collect the fees and to administer finances of the departments through an annual budget. This took place at Harvard in 1871, and later at Yale and Pennsylvania.

Eliot's first formal confrontation with the Faculty was dramatic, not to say traumatic. Professor Henry Jacob Bigelow said that he didn't see why so many changes were being proposed by the new President when everything in the School was prosperous and quiet. For a moment there was dead silence, then President Eliot, speaking softly, replied: "I can tell Dr. Bigelow the reason; we have a new President." The President was in attendance at subsequent medical faculty meetings also—an unprecedented and shocking circumstance, even though it was the outcome of a unanimous vote on October 28, 1869, on the motion of Dr. White, to invite the President to attend meetings.[6] Dr. White was one of the few progressives.

Oliver Wendell Holmes commented to a friend: "Our new President, Eliot, has turned the whole University over like a flapjack. There never was such a bouleversement as that in our Medical Faculty." Holmes, antagonistic at first, was, in the end, completely won over by Eliot—no small achievement. One has the impression that Holmes enjoyed hugely the continuing struggles between Eliot and Bigelow.

Bigelow exploded when he learned that Eliot had carried to the Corporation the move for revision of the entrance requirements. "Does the Corporation hold opinions on medical education? Who are the Corporation? Does Mr. Lowell know anything about medical education? or

Charles William Eliot, President of Harvard. Great educational reformer in general and a powerful influence on educational policy at the Medical School. From an engraving printed by J. A. Lowell and Co.

Reverend Putnam? Or Judge Bigelow? Why, Mr. Crowninshield carries a horse-chestnut in his pocket to keep off rheumatism! Is the new medical education to be best directed by a man who carries horse-chestnuts in his pocket to cure rheumatism?"

The marvel is that Eliot, then little known and little experienced, had the strength of character to take on this sometimes overbearing giant which threatened his career.[7] He was beginning his tenure against a background of imminent revolt by the entire Medical Faculty.

Their first differences were over the higher admission standards Eliot proposed; these required that candidates chosen for admission must have shown evidence of academic achievement. Bigelow countered that this criterion was arbitrary, and might exclude a genius who had not fitted into an approved academic pattern. Moreover, said Bigelow, academic performance was irrelevant, since physicians and surgeons are born and not made; and besides, great medical discoveries were not born in the academic environment of university laboratories. Something of a key to the famous Dr. Bigelow could have been seen nearly a quarter of a century earlier, when he brashly capitalized on the first public demonstration of anesthesia, October 16, 1846. A mere bystander on that famous occasion, he rushed into print with the first published account. Bigelow, with his eye on the main chance, recognized better than most, or perhaps sooner than any, the meaning of that event. No wonder the Warrens disliked him.[8]

In the battle between Eliot and Bigelow, a very great deal was at stake, and both men knew it. Eliot understood the increasing importance of science in medical education and practice. Bigelow did not. This interest is probably what prompted Eliot to attempt in 1870 to combine Harvard with "Boston Tech"—as the Massachusetts Institute of Technology was then called.[9]

Until Eliot arrived on the administrative scene in 1869, the Harvard Medical School was a poor thing, unworthy to be associated with Harvard College. Yet great names are associated with the mid-nineteenth-century faculty. James Clarke White described them[10] on entering the Tremont Medical School in late September 1853: At Harvard there were seven professors lecturing: Oliver Wendell Holmes on Anatomy and Physiology; Materia Medica and Clinical Medicine by Jacob Bigelow; Theory and Practice of Physic by John Ware; Obstetrics and Medical Jurisprudence by Walter Channing; Morbid Anatomy by J. B. S. Jackson; Surgery by Henry Jacob Bigelow; and Chemistry by J. P. Cooke. These men were not only distinguished, they were powerful. They controlled the curriculum—content as well as breadth—by controlling the charges made to students, arranged through a business agent. Each candidate for a degree was obliged to buy tickets to each of the courses for at least one year. Twice a week there was a "clinical medical visit" at the Massachusetts General Hospital for one hour, and on Saturday morning an operative session. (Of the 127 students attending, 31 held a college degree.) There was no gradation of studies, no laboratories, no private courses, no individual instruction. There were two courses of lectures of four months each. The remainder of the students' work was, theoretically at least, supervised by the outside instructors to whom the students were apprenticed, more or less, for three years. How much this apprenticeship amounted to depended upon the habits and inclinations of the instructor involved. It might be great or it might be essentially useless. Some students were able to see many cases of disease, and some none at all. In the crucial year of 1871 the three-year graded course was adopted and the apprenticeship terminated.

The Medical School Faculty were quickly polarized on Eliot's arrival in 1869.[11] There were two camps: (1) the progressives, led by James Clarke White (A.B., 1853), who opposed (2) the conservatives, who had Henry Jacob Bigelow (A.B., 1837) as spokesman. White paved the way for Eliot by publishing three bold editorials in the *Boston Medical and Surgical Journal*.[12] In the first he commented favorably on the Legislature's action whereby Harvard University was allowed to sever its connection with the Commonwealth of Massachusetts. Harvard's first independent act was the Alumni's selection of the Overseers to fill the places previously held by the old State Board. "Thus in four years the entire government of the University will be in the hands of those who are chosen by a body supposed to be her best friends and the best judges of her interests." He warned against filling the governing posts as an expression of thanks for gifts of money. He warned, too, against rule by a clique! "Such a body may entirely defeat the unsuspecting efforts of the great mass of the Alumni who would see a more liberal spirit manifested in the management of this seat of learning." He warned against an omnipotent Corporation with the power to thwart the wishes of the large majority of the Faculty. He urged the Medical Alumni to get their fair share of Overseers' posts, so that the Faculty could be protected. White deplored the low estate of some of the examining committees, which "are in many instances a disgrace to her. Men have been placed upon some of them who know nothing whatever of the subjects thus associated with their names, and whose appointment is an insult to the men of learning and science who properly occupy this important position."

The second editorial, "Medical Education"[13] called attention to the rapidly changing medical scene: only a few years earlier, the entire public medical instruction was limited to three annual four-months' courses of lectures, plus a three-year probationary period and the passing of a "ridiculously easy" examination. In 1867 only five out of nine really essential courses had to be passed and a thesis[14] presented, then the M.D. would be conferred.

> Probably none were more sensible of, or more regretted the defects in our system of medical education, than those who have been professionally engaged in it here in New England, and efforts were made by them under the only general authority recognized, our national Association, to raise its character by a mutual agreement on the part of all the schools in the country to insist upon a full three-years' course of study and a more thorough examination before conferring degrees; but such a change threatened the financial prosperity of some of them by interfering with the chief source of their popularity, and nothing was effected. It was evident that without a central governing power all action in this direction must be individual. Harvard University had already taken the first important step by extending its course of instruction so as to cover the whole year in the medical, as required in all its other great departments of study, and this system has been quite generally imitated within a few years by other large schools.

The second editorial closed with a plea for diversified specialists teaching the several branches of medicine:

> Our own University has been among the first to recognize the necessity of such division of labor, and has accordingly created the system of adjunct professors, assistant professors, and assistants, so that more than twenty instructors are now engaged in teaching in this department, in which seven were considered sufficient less than ten years ago.

The third editorial was concerned with "Censorial Duties—Medical Education."[15]

> Not until the profession throughout the country shall awake to the deplorable deficiencies of our present system and shall insist upon the establishment of some uniform standard, either through the general government or our National Association, can medicine in America raise itself to a level with that of foreign countries, or even with other branches of learning at home.

White was realist enough to recognize that very little could be accomplished by a single school. One school alone could hardly extend the medical course to four years; but what could be done was to elevate the quality of teaching in the accepted three years.

Another safeguard was at hand: Suppose, White said, Yale College purports to change a boy into a physician in two years, the Massachusetts Medical Society can refuse to recognize him as such, just as this Society prevented Harvard University from shortening the curriculum to four months. White believed it would be best if a State board of impartial examiners could be set up.

Here indeed was a voice crying for excellence forty-four years before Flexner came along with his sweeping report. Many members of the Faculty, practitioners and friends, considered White's heresies dangerous to the profession and dangerous to his career. Even the brave Dr. Ellis warned White, although he was sympathetic to White's views, that he was liable to be decapitated. White replied, "Well, it will still remain a talking head if they do."

It is not difficult to imagine Eliot's appreciation of such a stalwart colleague. Eliot summed up his broad view of the situation:

> It would be difficult to overstate the importance of the effort which this single School is making, with no support except the approval of the profession, to improve the system of medical instruction in the United States. The ignorance and general incompetency of the average graduate of American Medical Schools, at the time when he receives the degree which turns him loose upon the community, is something horrible to contemplate, considering the nature of a physician's functions and responsibilities. The early mistakes of a young lawyer or a young minister are no great matter; not much is staked upon his skill and wisdom, and the community does not suffer irremediable losses and multiplied miseries, if novices in these professions are left by the Schools in such a condition that they have to learn some pretty elementary lessons by practice. In the medical profession it is far otherwise. The mistakes of an ignorant or stupid young physician or surgeon mean poisoning, maiming and killing, or, at the best, they mean failure to save life and health which might have been saved, and to prevent suffering which might have been prevented . . . The Harvard Medical School has successfully begun a revolution in this system.[16]

Eliot had two definite avenues in mind for the rehabilitation of the Harvard Medical School. Both had to do with quality: of students and of the teaching. The first was to be achieved by exclusion of the weak by difficult entrance examinations. His expectation was that a bachelor's degree would eventually be required for entrance. In the second category he intended to eliminate the apprenticeship. Although these goals seemed laudable then, with the passage of time the second has been found to be not entirely sound. It is a curious thing that the apprentice system was (and sometimes still is) spoken of in terms of disdain, yet it still cares for at least 50 percent of medical education through the four to six years of intern and resident programs. The difference is that in the eighteenth and nineteenth centuries, the student was guided usually by a single preceptor, whereas in the late nineteenth and twentieth centuries there were and are multiple preceptors for each student. The principle is the same, and the difference is not important. If Eliot were alive today, he could argue that what he was talking about was within the Medical School proper. Today we see that the residency, a modern-day apprenticeship—albeit an impersonal one—is as important as medical school training. And with prolongation of the residency it has seemed necessary to reduce the entrance requirements. Many today do not consider the bachelor's degree necessary.[17]

Eliot understood that medicine cannot be taught without patients suffering from disease or injury. Such teaching requires a hospital staff approved by the hospital trustees, chosen by the Faculty, and approved in the higher levels by the Corporation.

Notwithstanding Henry Jacob Bigelow's contemptuous reference to laboratories, in Eliot's early years as well as later, the scientific revolution was burgeoning and had to be reckoned with. Faculty appointments and departmental rearrangements were to recognize this. One result of the attempt to improve teaching was the appointing of the first full-time professor in the Medical School, Henry Pickering Bowditch, whose leadership in the development of physiology will be described later.

Eliot had achieved great advances in the scholarship of the Medical School's staff, and his aim for the students had been, in considerable part, achieved. He could report that

> An American physician or surgeon may be, and often is, a coarse and uncultivated person, devoid of intellectual interests outside of his calling, and quite unable to either speak or write his mother tongue with accuracy . . . In this University, until the reformation of the School in 1870–71, the medical students were noticeably inferior in bearing, manners, and discipline to the students of other departments; they are now indistinguishable from other students.[18]

Advancement far beyond the single course of lectures repeated each year had been achieved. They were now, as early as 1871, graded courses through which the student progressed step by step, his proficiency challenged by examinations. By 1872 the Faculty had voted to offer postgraduate instruction to those who were already practicing but who wanted to remedy deficiencies. In 1874 it was recommended that the M.D. curriculum be lengthened to four years, and it was, temporarily.

As Eliot planned, new teachers were added without raising the tuition fee. This led to deficit spending over a period of some years, after which, the news having got around that Harvard's teaching had improved, more students were attracted. In 1872, 170 students were in attendance; by 1879 the number had risen to 251, and the students from outside of New England had doubled. The financial situation was greatly improved.[19] There was a touch of Harvard arrogance in Dean Calvin Ellis' 1878 report: "Some time since, an invitation was received to join the Association of American Medical Colleges, established to secure a greater uniformity in medical education; but, as the standard proposed was lower than that already adopted by the School, the invitation was declined."[20]

Although the revolution in medical education was initiated by White, Eliot also had important support from Dean Ellis, about whom Eliot wrote in 1883, a year before Ellis' death: "He actively furthered all the many improvements made by the Faculty during his long term of service, and the changes made in 1870–71 could not have been effected without his support."[21]

Improved standards of Faculty and student body led, as mentioned, to increased numbers of students, and that in turn, to increased revenue. There was still a need for more clinical material, supplied after 1864 by the Boston City Hospital. All of this brought with it a need for an expansion, and a new school was located on Boylston Street at the corner of Exeter, halfway between the Massachusetts General Hospital and the Boston City.

It was expected that the new building would provide the necessary space far into the future. In fact, space ran out in twenty-three years. The formidable task of raising money for the 1883 building weighed heavily upon the Administration. The Corporation denied that it had funds "appropriate" for such building. The public had not yet been initiated into their responsibility for support of medical developments. In his annual report for 1876–77, Dean Ellis reported only that "two valuable donations have been received—one of a microscope . . . the other of a skull . . ."[22] President Eliot had, as usual, a clear view of the problem: "So long as medical schools are conducted as private ventures for the benefit of a few physicians and surgeons who have united to form a corporation or faculty, the community ought not to endow them."[23]

The Harvard Medical School was no longer a private "corporation" but, from that time onward, a part of the University. Valiant attempts had been made by a distinguished group of citizens in 1874 to raise $200,000. The drive failed, at least in part, because of a hangover from the financial panic of 1873. Seven years later a similar drive succeeded, this time with the wholehearted support of Henry Jacob Bigelow (who knew a winner when he saw one), President Eliot, Holmes, and others.

In the meantime the expansion and diversification of teaching went on. The departments already in existence when Eliot took office gradually changed in response to new developments in content, the coming of outstanding teachers, and the increase in the size of the student body.

ANATOMY

Dr. Thomas Dwight began to teach histology in 1874 and was made an Instructor in Topographical Anatomy in 1880. His superb dissections are still of interest and use. While the famous Dwight Room no longer exists as such, a portion of the Dwight dissections are in the Warren Museum and the rest in the Department of Anatomy.

The 1906 *History of the Harvard Medical School* contains an unconsciously ironic statement: Every effort, the *History* says, was made by the Faculty to find a worthy successor to Dr. Holmes; "these efforts failing, it became necessary in June, 1883, to appoint Dr. Thomas Dwight to the professorship." Just what Professor Dwight's feeling in the matter was is not recorded. Inasmuch as Dwight was the great-grandson and grandson of the first two professors, no very substantial departure from high standards was expected by the authorities.

The demonstrators after 1883 were M. H. Richardson, 1883–1887; S. J. Mixter (Assistant), 1884–1887; S. J. Mixter, 1887–1893; William M. Conant (Assistant), 1890–1893; Franklin Dexter, 1893–1895; W. A. Brooks, 1895–1901; John Warren, 1901. The old family names are much in evidence. Some of them reached higher ranks. At this period, gross anatomy was in its heyday. Many instructors and assistants were appointed. There was an ever-increasing prestige in the office of demonstrator.

Under Dr. Dwight, for the first time, original work was carried out in the Department. It consisted mainly of statistical observations, with a great deal of attention being given to anatomical variations. Of especial interest were variations of the human spine and the hand and foot. Great enthusiasm was engendered by the finding of an "absolutely new occasional bone (the intercuneiform) . . ."[24] Series of frozen sections were prepared and placed in the Warren Museum in order to further the study of anatomical relations in the body.

The development of anatomical teaching was steady and continuously progressive. In 1888 histology was greatly developed under Assistant Professor Minot. The high point of anatomical instruction was achieved in 1897–98, at which time Professor Dwight gave three lectures weekly to the first class throughout the term, and the dissecting room was carefully supervised. In the second year there were two lectures weekly. In the fourth year Professor Dexter gave an elective course, and there was a volunteer dissecting course by the Demonstrators. The time allotted to anatomical studies began to be curtailed sharply in 1903 as interest in the subject began to flag and other subjects simultaneously began to demand more time. As might be expected, Professor Dwight protested bitterly this reduction, but the trend was clearly evident and continued in later years.

PHYSIOLOGY [25]

In accordance with Eliot's new arrangement, Physiology was classified as a first-year study. Its importance was recognized, and a large laboratory was added on top of the North Grove Street building. It is important to recognize that the nature of physiology required that it be separated from anatomy, with which it had previously been united.[26] Studies in this department were then, as now, largely limited to experimentation in animals, whereas previously the course had consisted of lectures and a few demonstrations.

Sir Henry Dale in writing an obituary minute on Walter B. Cannon for the Royal Society asks who are physiologists and what is physiology. He answers his question:

> Its followers have been concerned with the systematic description and provisional interpretation of the functions of living beings as seen, for the most part, in vertebrate animals. Their ultimate aim has been to create a physiology of man, as one of the foundations of medical science, though their immediate objective has more often been the analysis of animal functions more accessible to experiment. Their methods have had a background of human and vertebrate anatomy, and they have called in aid only the more readily available teachings and methods of physics and chemistry, with such instrumental aids as their own ingenuity could devise from these. This tradition goes back to William Harvey, but its proximate origin, or revival, in the mid-nineteenth century can be traced to the laboratories of Claude Bernard in Paris and Carl Ludwig in Leipzig; and the large contribution which has been made by the English-speaking countries to this stage in the development of physiology has been due, in the main, to men who had studied under one or other of these leaders, or received the tradition as handed down by those who were thus directly their pupils.[27]

These *post hoc* comments may be valid, but they do not explain the rise of physiology at Harvard at the time it occurred. The rise was, in fact, associated with the appearance on the scene of a most unusual man, Henry Pickering Bowditch, brilliant member of a brilliant family, and

Henry P. Bowditch, first full-time Professor of Physiology in America.
He was expected to earn an adequate income from his Beacon Street
medical practice. Photograph in the Harvard Medical Archives.

related peripherally to other outstanding persons. Dr. Bowditch had been graduated from Harvard College in 1861 and had enrolled in the Lawrence Scientific School. His academic career had been interrupted by the Civil War while he served as a cavalry officer in the Union Army until June 1865. When the War was over, he resumed his studies, receiving a Master's degree in 1866 and an M.D. degree in 1868. Following this, he went to Paris and later to Leipzig, where he worked under the distinguished physiologist Carl Ludwig. In December of 1869 President Eliot asked him to return to Harvard to lecture in physiology. He refused this invitation because he was uncertain that he could afford the life of a true scientist.[28] He was also aware that it was Harvard's happy custom to permit the incumbent of a new chair of science to furnish his own apparatus. Luckily in this case, Bowditch was assured by his father that he would have adequate support for a scientific career, and when Eliot extended a second invitation, it was accepted. In the spring of 1871 he came home to serve as Assistant Professor of Physiology and to organize the Department. When he was asked to whom he was assistant, he replied, "Myself." He rose rapidly from assistant professor to become the first Professor of Physiology. He was the first Harvard Medical School Faculty member to restrict himself to research and teaching and was the first full-time medical school teacher in America. Physiology emerged from its subordinate position relative to anatomy with the appointment of Henry Pickering Bowditch.[29] There was, however, no physiological laboratory—a problem that was partly solved by reconstruction of two attic rooms in the old Medical School Building. Thus the first physiological laboratory for the use of students was created. These two small rooms were, in fact, the first laboratory for experimental medicine in the country.

Henry Bowditch was not content to become America's premier physiologist. Notably, he had a desire to know more about growth in children. His remarkable pioneering study of Boston school children was begun in 1875, published in 1877, and revised in accordance with John Galton's new statistical methods in 1890. This superb study, although praised by a few physicians, was treated by most with total neglect.[30]

Professor Bowditch worked alone except for such assistance as he could obtain from his students, who either volunteered for the work or whose fees were forgiven. An Assistant in Physiology was appointed for the first time in 1877, Dr. George Minot Garland, who was succeeded by Dr. Joseph Weatherhead Warren. Following him, more than twenty assistants and instructors held office in the Physiology Department up to 1906, although no officer of high rank was added to the teaching force until 1892. At that time Professor William Henry Howell, who occupied the Chair of Physiology at the University of

Michigan, was invited to assume the position of Associate Professor of Physiology at Harvard. The famous Professor Howell worked only a year at Harvard, when he was called to take charge of the Department of Physiology in the Johns Hopkins University. His successor was Professor William Townsend Porter, who came from the St. Louis Medical College and who, after five years as Assistant Professor, was made Associate Professor of Physiology in 1898. In 1902, one of the greatest professors of all time at the Harvard Medical School was appointed Assistant Professor of Physiology, Dr. Walter Bradford Cannon, after two years' service as an Instructor. In 1906 his title was changed to the George Higginson Professor of Physiology. The children of George Higginson had established this professorship in 1903.

With the establishment, in 1871, of a Physiological Laboratory, there was available, for the first time at Harvard, the possibility for systematic study of physiological problems. Evidence that the staff availed themselves of the opportunity is demonstrated by the fact that in 1879 it was possible to issue a volume of some eighteen collected papers on work carried out in the Physiological Laboratory. In 1886 a volume of twenty-two papers was issued. The students themselves were allowed (1892–96) to carry out physiological experiments. Except in the year 1892–93, these experiments were entirely chemical, and in 1896 they were transferred to Professor Hills of the Department of Chemistry. Their place was taken by work in other fields, such as study of the circulation and the nervous system under Professor Porter's direction. By 1896 each student was spending two afternoons in such experimentation. This having proved successful, in 1897–98 the requirement was increased until each student was working two to three hours on twelve afternoons. The class was divided into sections. One difficulty was that, according to the system then in vogue, it was not possible to coordinate the physiological teaching with the teaching of anatomy. Many years passed before Harvard recognized that such coordination was not only feasible but essential.

Professor Porter maintained the superiority of teaching characterized by concentration and sequence. In 1899 he took over the responsibility for first-year instruction when Professor Bowditch decided to withdraw from such activity. Professor Porter was largely responsible for a "new" method of teaching physiology: the provision of apparatus that made laboratory teaching possible. This new method ensured that didactic instruction would be closely preceded by relevant experiments carried out by the student himself. The classical experiments in physiology were arranged in the new method in the most helpful sequence, performed by the student, and, after this, discussed by the lecturer, whose responsibility was then to coordinate the students' experiments with those of like observers. The old method stressed didactic teaching; the new method stressed observation. By 1900 a remarkable increase in activity in the Physiology Laboratory was present during four months when 220 students carried out work in the Physiological Laboratory every day except Saturday. Clearly, experimentation on this scale requires thousands of pieces of apparatus. Recognizing the fact of this great need, plus the fact that even simple apparatus is costly, the Harvard Medical School made its own apparatus, and in such quantity as to leave a surplus available for sale to other universities. By 1906 Harvard physiological apparatus had been sent to more than 160 laboratories in the United States and to more than fifty in foreign countries, including Syria, Russia, Japan, and Australia.

Because experiments in physiology are sometimes tedious and time-consuming, the students were divided into groups of eight, a plan that has persisted down to the present. In studies of metabolism, for example, an experiment would be assigned to the entire group, two members of which were the subjects of the experiment while others of the group divided up the labor of the analyses.

A broad approach was taken to the field of Physiology and because of the complexity and variety of subjects belonging to this field, all methods of instruction were employed: the didactic lecture, the text-book, the recitation, the laboratory experiment, the demonstration, and the conference. Physiological conferences were patterned after the clinical conference method employed by the famous French clinical teacher Louis.

Beginning in 1870, lectures were given twice a week by Dr. Robert Amory on the physiological action of drugs on man and lower animals. He illustrated the lectures by animal experiments, in the course of which he showed the physiological action of ether, chloroform, chloral, nitrous oxide, the bromides, cyanides, belladonna, aconite, veratrum viride, potassium iodide, caffein, and thein. This was the beginning of interest in pharmacology.

The lucky students of the period also had available Professor Jeffries Wyman's lectures on Comparative Anatomy and Physiology, delivered in Cambridge, but available to medical students. Wyman was one of the most distinguished biologists of his time.

CHEMISTRY

At the Harvard Medical School the relevance of the chemistry course to medical studies in general seemed to fluctuate. Under Eliot in 1871 the Chemistry Laboratory was greatly enlarged. It could then accommodate nearly one hundred students. Professor John Bacon in 1871 generously presented all of the chemical apparatus, cases, and furniture in the laboratory to the Corporation for use in the Medical School. It was voted in 1873 that a satisfactory examination in general chemistry and qualitative analysis should be accepted as equivalent to an examination in those areas in the Medical School. Professor James C. White decried this as "the first step towards the elimination of general chemistry from the curriculum."

After the resignation of Dr. Bacon, who died in 1881, Dr. Edward S. Wood (Harvard A.B., 1867, M.D., 1871) was appointed Assistant Professor of Chemistry. At the same time Dr. James C. White was made Instructor, responsible for the course while Dr. Wood took a year of study in Europe. Dr. Wood became full professor in 1876.

The School moved to its new building in Boylston Street in 1883. Two large laboratories had been constructed for the Chemistry Department. Dr. William B. Hills (Harvard, A.B., 1871, M.D., 1874) was chosen in 1884 Assistant Professor of Chemistry, and in 1889 he was elevated to the position of Associate Professor.

The Faculty voted in 1890 that students who had passed a satisfactory examination in general chemistry in the undergraduate department might pursue the study of medical chemistry, a new subject, in their first year. From this time onward, the character of the instruction in chemistry became almost entirely medical. A course on pharmaceutical and physiological chemistry was established in 1898 under Dr. Franz Pfaff. A course in elementary organic chemistry was required in 1903 for admission after September 1903. After Professor Hills resigned in 1904 and Professor Wood died in 1905, the teaching was carried on by Drs. Carl L. Alsberg and L. J. Henderson, each with the title Instructor in Biological Chemistry.

The full development of biological chemistry at Harvard took place after the Eliot years, in the early and mid-twentieth centuries. Harvard was not ready for it before then, and only the tentative beginnings took place.

THE CLINICAL CURRICULUM

We have seen how the beginning of President Eliot's tenure produced drastic, even revolutionary, changes in the administrative practices that regulated teaching and, more strikingly, in the standards of admission and academic appraisal of Medical School students. He also began to modify the curriculum, creating a separate department of physiology, with a full-time physician at its head. On the other hand, he was remarkably uncertain about the role of his own subject, chemistry, in medical teaching. Perhaps this foretold the confusion of nonphysician teachers of basic sciences in medical teaching in the mid-twentieth century, a confusion that led to imperfections in their own teaching and seriously distorted medical teaching in general.

Let us now consider the changes that occurred in the clinical curriculum after Eliot took over. In general, they were few and unsensational, and in fact might have occurred as part of a natural evolution rather than as a result of presidential intervention. We shall never know to what extent he introduced specific changes in this curriculum, although it is probable that his own progressive attitudes and his support of the views of the progressive members of the faculty created an intellectual environment that favored improvement.

SURGERY

In the reorganization of the School "surgery" and "clinical surgery" (one wonders exactly how they were differentiated) were assigned to the second and third years. Later, the curriculum underwent extensive revision and with it, changes in the Faculty.

J. Collins Warren was designated Instructor in Surgery in 1872. The following year Charles Burnham Porter received a similar appointment. These were Faculty appointments, and as such entitled the recipient to a seat in the Faculty, among the first of their kind in surgery.

The full Professorship of Clinical Surgery was established in 1875, with Dr. Cheever elected to fill that post. David Williams Cheever characterized himself: "I never thought I excelled as an operator, but rather as a painstaker." As a matter of fact, however, Dr. Cheever was equally skilled in surgical practice and in lecturing. Although his father was a respected physician, David was not encouraged to study medicine. In his early years he had thought of a literary career. He was educated in the classics at home and took pleasure in writing essays on medical subjects for the prestigious journals of the time: the *Atlantic Monthly* and the *North American Review*. He was graduated from Harvard Medical School in 1858.

Oliver Wendell Holmes offered Cheever the position of demonstrator in anatomy in 1860—the beginning of a thirty-three-year teaching career in the Medical School. Cheever introduced competitive student dissections and quizzes. In his day this was a revolutionary idea in the dissecting room. He was appointed visiting surgeon at the Boston City Hospital in 1864, the year it was founded, and in 1875 he became Professor of Clinical Surgery, directly succeeding Henry Jacob Bigelow on the latter's retirement in 1882.

David Cheever originated or revised unusual operations. When he began his medical career, there was no antisepsis or asepsis. Gangrene and suppuration were common. The hospital thermometer was not in use. The X ray did not exist. Among his surgical achievements, he displaced the upper jaw for nasopharyngeal tumors, removed tumors of the tonsil by external incision; pharyngotomy or esophagotomy was carried out for foreign bodies in the esophagus. He devised a radical cure for hernia. He performed the first two consecutive successful ovariotomies in Boston and was one of the first to carry out Caesarean section.

Cheever wrote and published widely. He edited the first five volumes of the Hospital reports at the Boston City Hospital and himself wrote much of the surgical text. For a time he served as editor of the *Boston Medical and Surgical Journal*.

In Cheever's view the hospital surgeon had two major responsibilities: to succor the patient and to share his advantages with students and fellow physicians. He was by nature a reformer. He instituted the class conference and a weekly clinical essay by a student, presented for criticism by his colleagues and instructors. During his long life he was noted for his vigorous mind and body. His simple dignity moved all who became acquainted with him. He died in 1915 just after his 84th birthday, in full possession of his faculties. Of his six children, David Cheever, M.D., became Associate Professor of Surgery at the Harvard Medical School and a noted surgeon at the Peter Bent Brigham Hospital. Many honors accrued to him in his lifetime.

An examination in clinical surgery for students was established in 1875. Dr. Porter later assumed David W. Cheever's post. Dr. Cheever moved over to become Professor of Surgery in 1882. Drs. Charles Porter and John Collins Warren became Assistant Professors of Surgery at that time, the latter being promoted to Associate Professor in 1887. Dr. Cheever became Emeritus Professor of Surgery in 1893, and John Collins Warren became Professor of Surgery. Subsequently, in 1899, this title was changed to Moseley Professor of Surgery, a title that persists to this day.

The professorship of clinical surgery remained in Dr. Porter's hands until 1902. Maurice Howe Richardson, of later fame in the field of operative surgery, was added to the teaching corps as Assistant in Surgery in 1883. Richardson continued his advance and was elected Assistant Professor of Clinical Surgery in 1892. One sees the continuation of established medical family dynasties or the beginnings of new ones. There is, strangely, little said about Henry Jacob Bigelow in this era.

In the early 1870's the surgery course consisted of recitation in the first term and second term, with an additional course on minor surgery and practical instruction in surgical anatomy. The weekly exercises in clinical surgery were two in the first term and three in the second. Later, it became possible to develop teaching in an advantageous way by increased cooperation between the two departments of Surgery and Clinical Surgery. Heretofore, these two courses had been relatively independent. With the passage of time they were gradually combined. The lectures on surgery were expanded in order to cover more ground in surgical pathology. The available cases increased from 44,000 examples in 1870 to 100,000 in 1892, at which time the four-year course was established.

Under Professor Porter's skillful management, the scheme of teaching small sections at the Massachusetts General Hospital and Boston City Hospital was adopted, to his great satisfaction. This became a predominant feature of the surgical courses in many medical schools. The clinical conference case report gradually developed into the requirement of an elaborate paper on the subject dealt with. Coordination was planned and attempted in the field of surgical demonstrations. Cases were now selected with a view to illustrating different topics rather than limiting such demonstrations to the peculiar interests of the teacher. Ward visits burgeoned in importance, and the students began to get much sounder instruction at the bedside than heretofore had been the case. This was made essential by the great increase in medical knowledge.

Around 1872 instruction in surgical histology was offered for the first time. At the other intellectual extreme, a course in bandaging was now available. Dr. J. Collins Warren gave both of these courses and also heard recitations in surgery and surgical pathology in the second-year class.

There were other changes in the curriculum, a reflection of the increase of knowledge in surgery, its techniques, and the basic sciences related to both. In 1885 a course in operative surgery was instituted. It comprised systematically demonstrated surgical operations, under the auspices of Professor Porter. Following this, there was laboratory work in carrying out operations by students under the guidance of an assistant for each group of six. An elective course in operative surgery described in the early twentieth century was based on carrying out surgical procedures on cadavers.

In 1881 specialization within the general field of surgery, such as orthopedic surgery, was taught separately from general surgery and was placed under the charge of Edward H. Bradford, who had the title Assistant in Clinical Surgery. Following the retirement of Professor Henry Jacob Bigelow, separate instruction was given for the first time in Genito-Urinary Surgery, under the charge of Dr. A. T. Cabot. When Dr. Cabot was made a member of the Corporation of Harvard University, Dr. Watson gave the lectures in the genito-urinary field. He was joined by Dr. Paul Thorndike. Lectures were given to third-year students, who also received practical instruction in the clinic.

In 1897 Dr. E. H. Nichols was appointed Demonstrator of Surgical Pathology and gave an elementary voluntary course to second-year men. Included here were exercises on inflammation and repair, as well as the pathology of various regions of surgical interest and importance. In 1901 a Laboratory of Surgical Pathology was established in the charge of Dr. E. H. Nichols, who had become Instructor in Surgical Pathology. In 1904 he became Assistant Professor of Surgical Pathology. Opportunity was provided in the Laboratory of Surgical Pathology for surgical research.

By 1906 the two surgical divisions became, with Orthopedic Surgery, Genito-Urinary Surgery, and the Department of Surgical Pathology, a unified Division of Surgery. At this time instruction imparted by the Division of Surgery began with the second year. A series of clinical lectures followed, in which the conditions studied in the primary course were illustrated three days a week during January at the Boston City Hospital. In the second half of the second year and the first half of the third year, systematic lectures on surgery were given at the Medical School. Not only were specimens studied at the two hospitals, but from time to time instruction was given in the Warren Museum, based on the preserved material there. Instruction was offered in the use of enemas, hypodermic injections, heat and cold, and poultices—certainly a low level of intellectual activity. The student as surgical dresser put these techniques to work in the Outpatient Department. In his third year, the student was brought into personal contact with the patient at his bedside and had practical experience in diagnosis, prognosis, and treatment. At this time considerable pride was taken in the fact that there was "blending of instruction" in systematic surgery, clinical surgery, genito-urinary surgery, and orthopedic surgery. The fourth-year courses were entirely elective in the fields just mentioned.

The purpose was to acquaint the students in the Division of Surgery with the underlying conditions of disease, physiological changes as well as pathological, and to emphasize the importance of consulting reliable authors. There was evidently also an intention to give the student an opportunity to increase his technical skills in surgery. Today this is no longer the case.

MEDICINE

As Richard C. Cabot has noted, President Eliot made little change in the teaching of clinical medicine.[31] It may be assumed that no appointments to the faculty were made except by him, both technically and in fact, but these appointments continued or served to establish the medical dynasties of the old Boston families.

After Dr. George C. Shattuck's retirement, Dr. Francis Minot became Hersey Professor. He had been an Instructor in the same Department (1869–70), and in 1872–73, Adjunct Professor. He was the first lecturer in the School on diseases of women and children. The field of diseases of women and children was not a popular one. The conservative members of the profession didn't like it, nor did the older ones care much for specialties other than their own. But the activities of men outside the School forced the Faculty to recognize the need for instruction in the field of diseases of women and children. Dr. Minot's instruction was based on lectures derived from his own experience. He also gave ward instruction to large groups of students.

In 1868, on Dr. Bowditch's retirement, Dr. Calvin Ellis was named Jackson Professor of Clinical Medicine, but illness forced him to retire only twelve years later. The duties during this hiatus, while a new Jackson Professor was awaited, were divided between Dr. Francis Minot, Professor of the Theory and Practice of Physic, and Dr. R. T. Edes, who had become Professor of Therapeutics. In 1884 Dr. Edes became Jackson Professor. Among the younger men in the department were George B. Shattuck and George C. Sears. The latter became a powerful figure at the Boston City Hospital and was the donor of the Sears Laboratory there.

An outstanding figure during the Eliot years was Dr. Frederick Cheever Shattuck. Dr. Shattuck had a long-range view of the probable course of the development of medicine. Six years after his graduation from the Harvard Medical School in 1873, he was appointed Clinical Instructor in Ausculation and Percussion, and as Instructor in those subjects and later in Theory and Practice, he continued in these roles for nine years until 1888. In that year he became Jackson Professor of Clinical Medicine, a title he honored through nearly a quarter of a century of distinguished service. In the amphitheater his lectures and demonstrations were notably characterized by the wisdom of their selection and by emphasis on the most significant features present. Noted for his wit, Dr. Shattuck was also a shrewd and kindly man, an excellent judge of human nature, a wise physician. In the decade 1898–1909 he was a member of the Faculty Committee on the Course of Study. His interest in excellent

Frederick Cheever Shattuck, brilliant clinician and teacher before the era of full-time physicians. From the crayon portrait by John Singer Sargent owned by the Shattuck family, who donated this photograph to the Boston Medical Library.

instruction led him to recognize not only the difficulties of the rotating service in the Hospial, where his service visited only four months in the year, but also the possibilities of duplication and omission. He was convinced that continuity of policy, both in the Hospital and in the Medical School, was required for medical progress and for adequate medical instruction.

Frederick Cheever Shattuck cooperated heartily in a plan that gradually evolved into continuous service of a single directing head at the Hospital and into one Department of Medicine in the Medical School. His foresight basically made possible the present satisfactory arrangements between the Medical School and the several affiliated hospitals in Boston where Harvard students are taught.

Out of a high regard for Dean Edsall, Dr. Shattuck founded, in his name, a satisfactorily large revolving loan fund. In 1910, Dr. Shattuck established the Henry Pickering Walcott Fellowship in Clinical Medicine, and in 1913 the Arthur Tracy Cabot Fellowship in Surgery. He retired, more or less, in 1912.

In fact, his retirement at the end of the Eliot era did not mark the end of his work in medicine. When, in his 65th year, Dr. Shattuck resigned the Jackson Professorship, he had served for a third of a century. He might reasonably have looked forward to years of comfortable retirement, but that was not in his nature. Although Professor Emeritus, he was destined to continue his service for sixteen years more. In some ways his most distinctive contributions were made in this later period of medical activities.

The proposition was presented to the faculty in 1913 that a Department of Tropical Medicine be established for an experimental period of five years, during which the question of its permanent establishment would be determined. With characteristic energy, Dr. Shattuck immediately undertook the necessary fund-raising. His judgment and his wisdom were so well known in the community and his advice had been so often followed successfully that his efforts were soon successful. In addition to such general success, he, himself, generously endowed the Chair of Tropical Medicine and thereby ensured its permanence. His interest in the development of this field of medical undertaking was constantly supported and encouraged to the end of his life.

An amplification of the above can be seen in Dr. Shattuck's interest in medical research to the industries of New England. He collected a fund (1916) to be used during five years to demonstrate the usefulness of medicine in promoting the health of the working people. A Committee on Industrial Hygiene was created to administer the fund, with Dr. Shattuck acting as Chairman. He had a vigorous interest in this enterprise and was especially interested in devising ways to render the skill and insight of medical investigators available for solving the problems of industrial hazards. This early work had a large influence on the establishment of the Harvard School of Public Health.

In all, Dr. Shattuck served the Harvard Medical School for nearly fifty years. Courtesy, simplicity, and directness of thought and speech, a penetrating humor, complete frankness, and sincerity stood forth in what might have been considered his declining years. ". . . he showed the freshness and enthusiasm of youth . . ."[32] When he passed away on January 11, 1929, he left a rich heritage of example and good deeds and a memory of human character and of unselfish devotion to professional ideals which will be long cherished in the Harvard Medical School. He was more than a person—he was the personification of the best of Boston medicine of his era.

The growth of the student body and the consequent move to the large new building in 1883 led to the expansion of the course of formal lectures in clinical medicine. Dr. F. C. Shattuck, although not yet Professor of Clinical Medicine, presided over discussions of Flint's *Theory and Practice of Medicine.* He apparently did this by rote, questioning the students on the pages covered since the last lesson. One book at least was read thoroughly. At this time, assistantships at the Hospital were not eagerly sought after, and the cutting of lectures in clinics for the sake of seeing patients in the outpatient department was considered to be a very doubtful proceeding by the students. By 1900 the Department consisted of the Jackson Professor (Dr. F. C. Shattuck), five instructors, and six assistants, including Dr. Richard Cabot. In these years not only were there quantitative increases, but so also the quality of teaching was improved.

In 1890 Dr. Minot resigned, and Reginald H. Fitz, in 1892, transferred to the Professorship of Theory and Practice. Dr. Fitz promptly gave up the "hospital visit" as a means of teaching and in its place organized a clinical exercise in which the student was put in front of the patient and required to obtain a history, make an examination, and call for or make examinations of blood, urine, or sputum. (All of this was being done years before the practice was initiated at the Johns Hopkins.) At the end of such an exercise, Professor Fitz would sum up the principal points of the case, treating the subject from the broadest possible viewpoint. The clinical conference was arranged so that each student made a detailed examination of one case in the course of a year. There was clearly need for an increase in such opportunity, and in 1895 this approach was required for the degree of Doctor of Medicine.

In their second year the students were taken fresh from laboratory courses and taught the value of symptoms and how to take histories. Emphasis was given to the special common symptoms. Diseases were considered in the order of their relative frequency and importance. General symptoms, such as cough, jaundice, dropsy, constipation, and diarrhea, were taken up and considered, following which the limitations as well as the strengths of laboratory methods were considered. Later in the year students were given cases to study and were encouraged to apply laboratory methods. This teaching was continued through the first half of the third year, with more complicated cases and with even sharper criticism of the work carried out by the individual student.

The clinical lecture had not changed much in the preceding fifty years, but after 1901 Dr. Shattuck allowed groups of students to examine patients, under the supervision of Dr. W. H. Smith, while the lecture was going on.

Ward visits formed part of the instruction from 1835 until 1902, when, astonishingly, they were discontinued. The ward visit had grown in favor until about 1880, when visits were being made to the three hospitals by eighteen physicians, supervising sections of students. After this high point "medical visits" gradually fell off, having been abandoned at the Massachusetts General Hospital in 1897. They were continued at the Boston City Hospital until 1902, when they were terminated, although in 1906 they were reinstituted at the Boston City Hospital. The instruction in ausculation and percussion was continued from 1872. In the years 1895–1902 there was also a requirement that four Dispensary cases be taken by each student, who followed the patients at their homes. This was supervised by Dr. Henry Jackson. The students were required to write brief reports on all four cases. The upshot was that each student had opportunity to get some feeling for the realities of private practice.

Although the system was good for the students, administrative duties were heavy, so in 1902 the system was replaced by required outpatient work, one month for each student in a clinic of one of the School's teachers. This was not necessarily under the Department of Clinical Medicine, but by this new system students got to see more outpatient material than was the case when they were previously limited to home visits. On the other hand, family problems could not be understood as well in the Outpatient Department as when the student went into the patient's own home.

In both cases the goal was to get the student into firsthand contact with the sick, so that he might learn to recognize relevant signs and symptoms and understand their development from day to day. To this end, there were clinical lectures, ward visits, personal instruction in the techniques of eliciting signs and symptoms, and the clinical conference. The twenty-minute oral examination used for evaluating the students had

The Harvard Medical School, 1846–83. The small structure on the left was built over the Charles River mudflats. The dismembered body of the murdered Parkman was disposed of by Professor Webster through this structure. The Massachusetts General Hospital was built at the river's edge a few hundred feet downstream. Although all the senior faculty were also staff members at the Hospital, there was no administrative connection between the two institutions. This was as close as Harvard came to having a University hospital. Engraving by Russell Richardson.

Harvard Medical School, 1883–1906. This building at Exeter and Boylston Streets represented a move away from geographical association with the Massachusetts General Hospital. The building was an architectural gem; it had a central open stairwell, with supporting cast-iron pillars in classic Greek style, leading to corridors, each of which housed a department, but all remaining with easy access to one another. In 1906 the building became the College of Liberal Arts of Boston University. It was demolished in the 1960's to become the site of an addition to the Boston Public Library. Drawing by F. Myrick, engraving by Moses King.

been dropped in 1872, and the new system consisted of a series of twenty written questions, somewhat like those given in Theory and Practice. This was continued until 1876 and was supplemented by bedside examinations. In 1876, however, these bedside examinations were discontinued, and the written questions were replaced by a series of detailed histories of actual cases. From these the student was obliged to work out diagnosis, prognosis, and treatment.

After about 1900 four new assistants were appointed—Dr. Mark W. Richardson, Dr. Elliott P. Joslin, Dr. Franklin W. White, and Dr. George S. C. Badger. The names are familiar, either as the family names of medical dynasties or else because the individuals were later to become famous. In 1903 Dr. Joseph H. Pratt (for whom the Pratt Diagnostic Hospital was later named) was added to this group.

In 1904–06 Cabot could say that instruction for graduates by the Department "has never been taken very seriously." The head of the Department had nothing to do with it, the instruction was provided by subordinates and suffered grievously from lack of a system. The announcement of graduate instruction was presented in 1872 when Dr. F. I. Knight offered his course in auscultation, percussion, and laryngoscopy, continued until 1879. This was the only so-called graduate instruction before 1906. When Dr. F. C. Shattuck became Jackson Professor in 1889, an announcement concerning courses for graduates was once more presented, the first since Dr. Knight had dropped his graduate teaching in 1879. Two more courses in physical diagnosis were added, and in 1891–92 eight courses were announced, consisting of some eight to twenty-four exercises. They were conducted at the Massachusetts General Hospital, the Boston City Hospital, and the Boston Dispensary. Over the next half dozen years there was a decline in interest in such courses, but by 1906 new interest had been aroused and eight courses were again offered. Interest in this aspect of teaching has fluctuated ever since.

One can look back at the Eliot years and realize that then the foundation was laid for subsequent developments. Clinical methods and firsthand contact of student with patient was their ideal, one that holds even today. Insofar as one can judge at this late date, the personality of the teacher seemed to account for a great deal, perhaps more then than now.

In 1906, Cabot had this to say:

The modern teacher of medicine reverences the facts so much that he is afraid of interposing his personality between them and his pupils, and so draws himself more and more into the background. This is as it should be, provided the teacher does not forget that facts [alone] mean nothing, and that it is his business to see to it that the student knows what to do with his facts when he has gathered the crude mass. In the interpretation and application of data personality is as important as ever; hence the great teacher of medicine, in the future as in the past, will be first of all a great man.[33]

PATHOLOGY

In 1879 R. H. Fitz became head of the Pathology Department, a position he held until 1892, when he was named Professor of the Theory and Practice of Physic. Trained by Virchow and Orth, as a teacher of pathology and a pathological anatomist he had strong leaning toward clinical medicine. Dr. Fitz's fame rests secure on his identification of appendicitis and pancreatitis with fat necrosis.

He was succeeded by W. T. Councilman. Following a study of medicine at the University of Maryland, Dr. Councilman received his M.D. degree in 1878. He was considerably influenced by the distinguished Henry Newell Martin, Professor of Biology at the Johns Hopkins University. It was Martin who stimulated his interest in research. From 1880 to 1882 he worked under Hans Chiari in Vienna, Julius Cohnheim and Carl Weigert in Leipzig, and Friedrich von Recklinghausen in Strasbourg. In 1886 he joined Welch at Johns Hopkins as Associate in Pathology. Following another year abroad, he became, in 1888, Assistant Professor of Pathology and Resident Pathologist at the Johns Hopkins Hospital. In 1892 he was called to Harvard as the third Shattuck Professor of Pathological Anatomy and was that year appointed Visiting Pathologist at the Boston City Hospital, where he organized the Department.

Dr. Councilman induced the Massachusetts General Hospital to acquire a building for pathology and, in 1896, to engage a full-time pathologist, recommending (the later very distinguished) James Homer Wright for the position. He was insistent that the development of pathology required a special department. Dr. Councilman is described as kind, tolerant and observant; his appraisal of men was rapid and accurate. He enjoyed the amenities of life "unadorned by formalities or artificialities."[34]

Dr. Councilman was an able pathologist, as were many others at the Hopkins in his time. He lived a pleasant, informal life, devoted to his family, and was not a major scientific force, although he had some important achievements to his credit: the discovery of the so-called Councilman Bodies in the liver in the presence of hepatitis. Another achievement was his research on inflammation of the cornea, then a controversial subject. He upheld Cohnheim's view that the pus cells are "emigrated" white corpuscles from the blood. Dr. Councilman saw a great deal of malaria and was among the first in America to confirm Alphonse Laveran's finding of the malarial parasite; but he was more interested in developing his young colleagues than in independent research. His major publications were more often than not published with his colleagues.[35]

To his everlasting credit, Dr. Councilman attracted the excellent Frank B. Mallory to the field of pathology. And in due time this led directly to his two sons, Tracy and Kenneth, becoming important clinical pathologists. Dr. Mallory was graduated from the Harvard Medical School in 1890. He worked his way through medical school, in large part, by doing technical work in the Department of Histology. Doubtless this experience was what led to his lifetime of activity in the development of special tissue stains. He served some kind of internship at the McLean Hospital in Waverley, where, insofar as one can learn, he spent most of his time feeding uncooperative patients by stomach tube. He then opened an office for the practice of medicine. After the passage of several months without a patient, a young woman paid him an office visit to request an abortion.

In 1891, he embarked on his true career. At the same time that Dr. Councilman was appointed Pathologist at the Boston City Hospital, Dr. Mallory was made his assistant, both in the Medical School and at the Hospital. The activities of these two were made difficult by the fact that the morgue and autopsy room of the Boston City Hospital were located in the boiler room of the Hospital, on the other side of Albany Street, and dead patients had to be carried from the Hospital on stretchers across the busy thoroughfare. When the objectionable practice could no longer be tolerated, the morgue and autopsy room were moved to the Hospital grounds, oddly to the second floor of the laundry building. No streets had to be crossed, but bodies had to be carried up a long, winding, narrow stairway. Through the persistent efforts of Drs. Councilman and Mallory, the Boston City government finally agreed to the construction of a separate laboratory and mortuary building. When completed, however, the structure was one of the best in that part of the country. In 1893 Mallory worked a year with Hans Chiari in Prague and Ernst Zeigler in Freiburg. Upon returning, in 1894, he was made an Instructor in Pathology at Harvard.

In 1896 a series of far-reaching events was initiated. Dr. Mallory was promoted to Assistant Professor of Pathology at the Harvard Medical School, and the new laboratory building at the Hospital was formally opened. The previous year, J. Homer Wright had come from Baltimore and was appointed second assistant to Dr. Councilman and Assistant at the Medical School. Dr. Mallory's friendship with Dr. Wright continued throughout the remainder of their lives. They collaborated in many scientific and literary adventures.

It was early in his career that Dr. Mallory developed a keen interest in staining methods, and the first of a long series of papers on this subject appeared in 1895. He always stressed the importance of precision in histological procedures and established high standards for his laboratory.

Dr. Wright was Director of the Clinico-Pathological Laboratory at the Massachusetts General Hospital from 1896 to 1925. He received much less attention during his lifetime than he deserved. His first assignment at Harvard was in Dr. Councilman's laboratory at the Sears Laboratory of the Boston City Hospital. Two important papers, dealing with the pathology of diphtheria, emerged from his work there. A principal goal of this work was to answer the question whether the organisms that remained in the throats of those who had convalesced were less dangerous than those that had killed the host. Wright found no decrease in virulence between the organism that killed the host and those that did not but were obtained from people who had convalesced from the disease.

Wright had other bacterial interests, especially those associated with an epidemic of spinal meningitis, with malaria, and with the culturing of gonococci. In 1903 he described the organism *Leishmania tropica* in the skin lesion of a 9-year-old Armenian girl. He did this six months after visceral *Leishmaniasis* was described by Donovan.

His great forte was staining, his work in 1902 with the polychrome stain of Romanowsky, the stain now referred to as "Wright's stain," shows his skill. The stain could mark malarial parasites as well as blood cells. The technique has stood the test of time, as he predicted in one of his papers: "It is confidently believed that by following out with reasonable accuracy the procedures detailed below this simple method will not fail to give constantly the results from it even in the hands of beginners in hematology."

So apparently simple a matter as tissue stain opened the way for Wright's major contribution, the discovery of the origin of blood platelets. This enabled him to stain tissue sections of the spleen and bone marrow and to observe the similarity of the megakaryocyte cytoplasm with the platelets that were present in the peripheral blood, and to conclude that the platelets were derived from megakaryocytes. The basis for his theory of platelet histogenesis is as follows:

1. The cytoplasm of the megakaryocytes has an identical appearance to the cytoplasm of the platelets.

2. Megakaryocytes have pseudopods projecting from their cell surface of similar size to platelets.

3. Megakaryocytes lose cytoplasm as they grow older.

4. The number of megakaryocytes with pseudopod formation could account for the number of platelets in the peripheral blood.

5. Blood platelets and megakaryocytes share similar amoeboid motion.

6. Blood platelets and megakaryocytes exist only in mammals, whereas lower forms of animals have a nucleated cell that functions in the circulation.

7. When blood platelets appear in the developing stage of the mammal, megakaryocytes are also present at the same time.

8. Certain diseases with decreased or increased platelets, that is, pernicious anemia with decreased platelets and bleeding and chronic myelogeneous leukemia with increased platelets, have a similar decrease or increase in the number of megakaryocytes in the bone marrow.

Wright's work on the histogenesis of platelets brought him an honorary Doctor of Science degree from Harvard University at the very young age of 35. He received the Boylston Prize in 1908. Most of all, he was highly acclaimed by William Henry Welch and William Osler.

In 1900 Wright, in dealing with the histogenesis of cells, reported a case of multiple myeloma and reviewed eight other cases, proving for the first time that the cell origin of this tumor was the plasma cell that was normally present in bone marrow. Another outstanding work of histogenesis dealt with the origin of the malignant tumor, which he named neuroblastoma. In doing this, Wright depended on his knowledge of the neuroblast from the histology of the embryo and pointed out the similarity of this group of tumors, previously referred to as sarcomas, with the cells of the developing sympathetic nervous system.

In 1909, Wright reported the finding of treponema spirochetes by using *Leviditi* stain in five cases of syphilitic aortitis, which made it possible for him to point out that the primary involvement of the aorta was one of the necrosis of the media and that the subsequent repair of connective tissue led to aneurysmal formation.

Frank B. Mallory and James Homer Wright collaborated on the *Textbook of Pathologic Technique*, which went through seven editions during Wright's lifetime. For many years the book remained the standard reference for pathologists, and it stands today as a thorough and well described book for the practice of hospital pathology.

In the beginning, Pathology was not deemed worthy of much space in the Harvard Medical School for a laboratory and workshop. The chief activities consisted of the collection and preservation of gross anatomical specimens, which were stored in the Warren Anatomical Museum. After microscopes were introduced, however, a large room was fitted up in 1871 in the attic of the North Grove Street building for the use of students. When the School moved to the Boylston Street Building, the Pathology Laboratory consisted of only a desk room for students, and was used in common with the Department of Embryology. In 1890 Dr. Henry F. Sears's gift made possible the large Sears Laboratory, which was given over to the Departments of Pathology and Bacteriology.

By this time it was clear that Pathology was no longer to be circumscribed by the "narrow anatomical point of view which dominated it so long." Of course, the anatomical view was important as long as the chief work in pathology consisted of the classification of diseases and description of the series of anatomical changes which were associated with defined clinical conditions.

A great conceptual advance was made in the last years of the nineteenth century and the first few years of the twentieth century, for at this time pathology began to concern itself with the causes of disease and the manner in which these causes act in the production of their characteristic lesions. Workers in the field of pathology then began to concern themselves with the relation between the anatomical changes and clinical phenomena. The Department of Pathology was greatly enhanced by having within it men highly competent to work in special fields, for example neuropathology and surgical pathology.

As long ago as the beginning of the twentieth century, Professor Mallory recognized that the "sure foundation for [successful work in Pathology] lies in the experiment. Its relations with the other branches of medicine become closer each day." He well recognized that there must always be the closest relationship between the clinic and the Pathology Laboratory. At the same time, it was essential that Anatomy and Embryology be equally close to pathology. How was one to understand abnormal development unless normal development was clear? Tumors were then (as now) almost entirely an unknown field.

In addition to work with the microscope, lectures were presented on a wide variety of relevant matters, stimulated by the receipt of organs obtained from autopsies at the different hospitals in addition to the information obtained from preserved specimens. Students in small groups were allowed to attend the post-mortem examinations, and in some cases, they were allowed to take an active part in them. The students received some instruction in histological technique. For fourth-year students who elected Pathology, the emphasis was on correlating the clinical symptoms of the patient's disease with the lesions found post-mortem.

The Department of Pathology was similar to the clinical departments in that its usefulness depended on the hospitals from which specimens of pathological material were obtained. It was evident that the closest possible relationships between the several hospitals and the Department of Pathology was essential. The Department initiated the practice of charging modest fees for autopsies and the examination of pathological specimens for private physicians. The funds so obtained were used for laboratory expenses connected with the work.

At this time the Department of Pathology, in addition to its own laboratory, had control of the Pathology Laboratories of the Massachusetts General Hospital, the Boston City Hospital, Long Island, the Children's Hospital, and Carney Hospital. Teaching in the Department of Pathology made it possible for the students to study and see for themselves the basic changes produced in the several tissues and organs by a wide variety of injurious agents. Full understanding of these changes enabled the student to understand more intelligently the findings of autopsies, and such a background made it possible for students to identify the cause of the signs and symptoms present in disease.

The policy of the Department of Pathology after about 1890 was to give young men interested in the field an opportunity to obtain a deeper knowledge of the subject than could be expected in the routine courses of the Medical School. The object was to develop men who might become leaders of distinction, and the success of the policy is indicated by the individuals who emerged from that experience. It was Professor Mallory's observation that the best men require little, if any, direction; their need is unhampered opportunity for self-development.[36]

Owing to the generosity of Dr. Henry F. Sears, the Pathology Laboratory possessed a large library, which was available to all men working in the hospital laboratories and to graduate students. It was customary for members of the various laboratories in Boston to meet once a week in the evening in order to review the literature, to discuss interesting cases, and to present findings of special investigations. The esprit generated by these arrangements was of a very high order. It was always the policy in this Department to encourage research work as the best way to develop teachers and to keep them in a position to understand and to value the work going on in this field. In line with this, every instructor was expected to produce a certain amount of original work each year. At the present time, many leaders would object to this universal research requirement.

The required work of the period from about 1893 to 1906 can be summarized. It is most impressive.

> ... three monographs on the subjects, epidemic cerebrospinal meningitis, diphtheria, and smallpox; a text-book on pathological technic; and many papers on the causal agents of certain diseases such as ac-

tinomycosis, Madura foot, Aleppo boil, gonorrhea, glanders, and scarlet fever; on the histological changes in various pathological processes
such as acute and subacute nephritis, typhoid fever, and necroses of
the liver; on bacteriological and microscopical technic; and on tumors
in general and gliomata in particular.[37]

LEGAL MEDICINE

As Professor F. W. Draper has noted, by 1877 a needed reform was
under way.[38] The Legislature of Massachusetts provided means for investigation of deaths suspected of being the result of violence. To improve this work the Office of the Coroner instituted the position of Medical Examiner. Medical men noted for their "discretion, ability and
learning in the science of medicine" combined with authority to investigate cases of deaths possibly by violence. It was their responsibility to
determine the manner of death. Legal Medicine was then separated from
Obstetrics.

The senior Medical Examiner for Suffolk County, the southern section of the City of Boston, was appointed Lecturer in Medical Jurisprudence in Harvard University and was given charge of Forensic Medicine,
which was then established as an independent department. Thus he had
opportunity to examine all varieties of death by violence. One of the advantages of this course in Legal Medicine was the opportunity to demonstrate through autopsies the cause for violent deaths. Such autopsies were
performed in the pathological amphitheater of the Boston City Hospital.
Thus, with the passage of time, the Department of Forensic Medicine, as
it was then called, came into the possession of extensive material exem-
plifying the problems in the Boston area, with special attention to abor-
tions, various kinds of mechanical trauma, suicides, homicides, sudden
mysterious deaths from natural causes, and infanticide. Examples were
provided by the fatal effects of electricity, heat, cold, starvation, poisonous gases, burns, and scalds as well as accidents of various kinds.

In 1877 Dr. F. W. Draper was appointed Lecturer in Forensic Medicine. Seven years later, he was promoted to Assistant Professor, and in
1889 to Professor of Legal Medicine. In 1903, owing to failing health,
he resigned his professorship, and the vacancy was not filled. During his
tenure he and his assistants conducted a most impressive course. The
lectures were arranged according to the following syllabus:[39]

   1. Definitions and limitations of the subject. Special training re-
      quired of medical jurists. The calls to practice forensic medicine

come without warning. Self-reliance, a result of medico-legal training. Proceedings of a criminal prosecution at law.

2. Medical evidence and the medical witness. Dying declarations an exceptional form of ordinary testimony. The value and use of notes. Expert testimony. Rights and demeanor of the medical witness.

3. Age as an element of identity. Dentition.

4. Sex and doubtful sex. Hermaphrodites.

5. Personal identity. Scars. Tattoo marks. Identification of multilated remains.

6. Impotence and sterility.

7. Rape. Age of consent. Violation of little girls.

8. Rape of young women. Proofs of virginity. The hymen. Defloration. Seminal stains.

9. Rape of matrons. Anesthesia in rape.

10. Criminal abortion. Proofs of recent childbirth. The corpus luteum. Drugs used as abortifaciants. Abortion induced by traumatism. Objective evidence of abortion. The usual causes of death.

11. The signs of death. Scientific tests. Loss of animal heat. Postmortem lividities.

12. Rigor mortis; time of manifestation, cause. Cadaveric spasm. Putrefaction.

13. Sudden death due to natural causes. Heart disease. Brain disease. The pancreas.

14. Death by drowning.

15. Death by hanging and strangulation.

16. Death by suffocation. Punctate suppurative ecchymoses.

17. Wounds in their medico-legal relations. Incised wounds. Contused wounds.

18. Punctured wounds. Pistol shot wounds.

19. Wounds of regions. Wound inflicted some time before death. The manner and purpose of the wounding.

20. Infanticide. Was the child born alive or was it dead at birth? The hydrostatic test. The cause and manner of the death.

21. Human blood in its medico-legal relations. Identification of suspected stains. The haemin test. The microscope as an aid. The serum test.

22. Death by electricity. Lightning.

23. Death by heat, cold, and starvation.

24. Murder by poisoning.

25. Death by illuminating gas.

26. The physician's legal relations to his patients. Malpractice.

27. The technic of a medicol-legal autopsy.

OBSTETRICS

In the year 1867, Dr. S. L. Abbot came on the scene, and Dr. C. E. Buckingham was appointed Adjunct Professor to assist D. H. Storer, who resigned in 1869, at which time, Buckingham became the full professor. Also at this time J. P. Reynolds took the place of Dr. Abbot. Dr. Reynolds wrote that he "gave brief teaching, pursuing an individual course with the approval of the professor, and superintending the assignment of cases obtained from the Dispensary and encouraging students to call upon him for counsel and assistance." W. L. Richardson, later distinguished, became an Instructor in 1871.[40]

Although the catalogue stated that students woud be allowed to take charge of cases in their third year, there were still too few cases available. Remarkably enough, students were allowed to buy cases in the public market, "paying the regular fee of two dollars." This augmented the School's supply of teaching material. At about this time the announcement was made that instruction in obstetrics could be provided for graduates. Schroeder's book was added to those approved.[41]

Dr. Richardson returned from a leave in 1874 and was given the title of Clinical Instructor. An advance was made in the establishment of a course in Operative Midwifery, and a cadaver was used for practical illustration. "Modern" obstetrics dated from the early 1870's. The importance of antisepsis, then asepsis, after many years, had finally begun to be recognized, some thirty years after first Holmes (not mentioned) in 1843, then Semmelweis (1847–49), had called attention to infection as a cause of puerperal sepsis. Stubborn resistance to the germ theory was as common when applied to obstetrics as to surgery.

Dr. Buckingham died in 1877, and Dr. Reynolds succeeded him. Playfair's text was approved, as were the books of Winckel, Parker, and Barnes.[42] A voluntary fourth year was established in 1880. In this course the students received one lecture weekly by the Professor and two clinical and operative exercises were given each week by the Instructor throughout a four-month period. Charles M. Green's "summer course" in Obstetrics was made available. While Dr. Green did not officially become connected with the School until 1883, it is fair to consider this as part of the Harvard teaching from its beginning. This course was described as invaluable for the lucky few who could take it. Not only did these young men profit from Dr. Green's lectures, but as a favored few they had much greater opportunities for clinical work than the School alone could possibly provide. An aggressive young man could manage to get some fifty cases during the period of the course, and this summer course became in reality the Outpatient Department of the Boston Lying-in Hospital. Under the auspices of that institution, students delivered some 1800 women in 1900.

Dr. Richardson was appointed Assistant Professor in 1882, and Lusk was added to the approved texts.[43]

In 1883 every third-year student was required, for the first time, to attend and conduct not fewer than two cases of labor before his degree would be granted. It was at this time that Dr. Green was appointed Clinical Assistant in order to provide the necessary instruction.

When Dr. J. P. Reynolds resigned in 1886, Dr. Richardson became Professor in his place. At this time the requirement for a degree had been advanced to three cases. Dr. Edward Reynolds was added to the staff, and another assistant, Dr. C. W. Townsend, was added in 1887. The books of Schauta and Kucher were recommended as collateral reading. The case requirement was advanced to four in 1888, and in 1890 raised to six. At this time also a clinical conference in obstetrics was arranged. Thus three courses were offered to graduates. In 1892 written reports were required on the six cases.

Dr. George Haven's name was added to the roster of assistants, and Dr. Green became Assistant Professor. The rule was laid down that each student had to receive instruction in at least one case. Before this time, if a student's cases were all normal deliveries, it is unlikely that he got any bedside instruction.

Dr. F. A. Higgins and the later celebrated F. S. Newell, "Uncle Chub," became assistants. Dr. Higgins became an Instructor in 1901, while Drs. Howard Townsend Swain and L. V. Friedman were appointed assistants. Swain and Newell were for many years rivals. Each succeeded in his own area. Newell went farther than Swain in the academic world, but Swain triumphed with a large practice in the Back Bay social milieu.

In 1904 the teaching force consisted of one Professor, Dr. W. L. Richardson, one Associate Professor, Dr. Charles M. Green, one Instructor, Dr. Newell, and three assistants, Drs. Swain, Friedman, and Torbert. An elective course in Operative Obstetrics was provided under Professor Green in 1899. In this, twelve practical exercises were available, and each student received three two-hour exercises.

In the third year attendance at sixty-four lectures on the Theory and Practice of Obstetrics was required. Thirty-two recitations on these lectures were also required. While the Instructor was allowed to refer principally to the textbooks, it thus became possible for the Professor to give most of his attention to special subjects. Each student received four hours of instruction in Clinical Obstetrics at the Boston Lying-in Hospital from the members of the teaching staff. Each student served ten days on externe duty for the Hospital, at which time he conducted some six to twelve cases of labor and cared for these patients during their convalescence. The student was required to present written reports on each of his patients, and personal instruction in one case was essential. He could ask for it in the five other cases required for a degree. Students had the new privilege of observing the care of normal deliveries at the Hospital before being required to take care of cases themselves, a practice that afforded great relief to the student. In 1905 a somewhat capricious new rule made the entire fourth-year course an elective.

Chapter Six

Appearance and Growth of New Specialties

MEDICAL knowledge continued to accumulate and was given order and, to some extent, meaning by the data of basic sciences. It was a natural evolutionary process that men would become interested in one part of medicine to the exclusion of others. Growth and diversification were given stability by the administrative strengthening that President Eliot instituted.

DERMATOLOGY

As early interest in this subject continued to grow, the Professorship of Dermatology was created in 1871, the first in the country. Graduate courses in dermatology and in syphilis were offered for the first time in 1872. James Clark White's graduate course at the Massachusetts General Hospital consisted of two weekly exercises, with the opportunity for examining cases presented in the Outpatient Department.

Dr. White graduated from Harvard College in 1853 and was a contemporary of Charles William Eliot. They studied chemistry together, and Dr. White, while on the medical staff of the Massachusetts General Hospital, became its Chemist. He then went to Vienna to study dermatology under Ferdinand von Hebra, Josef Skoda, and Carl Rokitansky. Upon returning to America, he became the first professor of dermatology in the United States (1871). His career in this field was outstanding, and he became the first president of the American Dermatological Society in 1876 and then a second time in 1897. He had a long drawn-out feud with Henry Jacob Bigelow in his attempt to establish beds for the treatment of skin diseases in the Massachusetts General Hospital. White also achieved a major role in upgrading teaching at the Harvard Medical School, and was a valiant supporter of President Eliot—all of which is beautifully described in his autobiography.[1]

Dr. White's systematic lectures and demonstrations were repeated each year for many years. There were two exercises a week, and one exercise might be spread over two days. There was an afternoon lecture throughout the year, illustrated by photographs, wax models, and specimens covering the entire field of dermatology. The lecture was given at the Medical School, and the following morning at 10:00 the lecture of the preceding day was illustrated, insofar as was possible, by patients in the hospital. This course was given for the entire thirty-one years of Dr. White's professorship, beginning in 1871.

Further specialization was evident here, for in 1871 Drs. Edward Wigglesworth and Francis B. Greenough were named Lecturers on Syphilis, and in 1875 both were made Clinical Instructors in Syphilis. Dr. Wigglesworth retired in 1881, and Dr. Greenough carried on the post alone until the next year, 1882, at which time Dr. Abner Post received an appointment as Clinical Instructor in Syphilis. He and Dr. Greenough shared the teaching responsibilities. An optional fourth-year course was established by Dr. White in 1880. Courses here consisted of three exercises a week at the Massachusetts General Hospital; also Drs. Greenough and Wigglesworth offered exercises in Syphilis once a week in the Marine Hospital and the Boston Dispensary. The fourth-year course in Syphilis became obligatory in 1892, but dermatology was elective. In 1900 to 1901, Syphilis was merged with Dermatology. The Department then became that of Dermatology and Syphilis under the jurisdiction of the Professor of Dermatology.

Dr. James C. White resigned the Professorship of Dermatology in 1902, at which time Dr. White's outstanding services to the Medical School received a vote of recognition by the Corporation. Dr. Bowen said of Dr. White, "A pioneer in Dermatology, he has contributed more to the upbuilding of the specialty and to the advancement of dermatological education than any individual in the country."[2] Dr. White's services thus extended far beyond his professorial activities. He occupies a prominent place in the modern development of the medical curriculum.

In 1893–94 instruction in cutaneous diseases was given for the first time at the Massachusetts General Hospital by Dr. John T. Bowen in July and August. These summer courses were quite informal, strictly clinical, and attracted a considerable number of students. Dr. Bowen was appointed head of the Department of Dermatology and Syphilis with the title of Assistant Professor of Dermatology. When the new Outpatient Department of the Massachusetts General Hospital was opened, and with it a ward for the care of skin diseases, teaching and study in Dermatology was greatly advanced. This ward was established by a gift from Dr. Charles G. Weld, and it contained sixteen beds for skin diseases in separate single or double rooms. These facilities meant that teaching could be carried out in a much improved fashion. In 1904, in accord with general moves in the School, the number of didactic lectures was reduced from thirty-two to eight. It was found advantageous to break up the large classes into small sections.

OPHTHALMOLOGY[3]

No attempt had been made to give special instruction in ophthalmology in the Harvard Medical School until 1869, when the Faculty named Dr. Henry W. Williams and Dr. Gustavus Hay as University Lecturers in this field. A few lectures were given by each of these men. The situation was about the same in 1871 when Dr. Hasket Derby was added to the teaching staff. Dr. Williams was made Professor of Ophthalmology in October of 1871. At this time, the Catalogue described a complete course on diseases of the eye. Lectures were given once a week during the School year at the Boston City Hospital, and clinical instruction was given once a week for six months. Evidently, this Department had not yet felt the impact of the new President (Eliot), for no examination was held, and the students' attendance was occasional. This condition persisted until the school year of 1880–81, when an advisory fourth year was established and Ophthalmology was made an elective for the fourth-year students. At this time however, few students remained in the School for the fourth year, and even fewer elected Ophthalmology. Dr. O. F. Wadsworth was appointed Clinical Instructor in Ophthalmology in 1881, and the next year a voluntary course in Ophthalmology was established. A half dozen students attended. In 1888–89 Ophthalmology was made an elective for students of the third class, and a small number chose it.

Dr. Williams resigned in 1891, and Dr. Wadsworth was appointed Professor. Several were added to the staff, and lectures were given at the Medical School with clinical instruction at the Boston City Hospital, Massachusetts General Hospital, and the Massachusetts Charitable Eye and Ear Infirmary. The teaching limped along until the fall of 1895. Previous to this, Ophthalmology had been an elective study, but on the establishment of the fourth year, Ophthalmology was placed on a required basis. The lecture course offered comprised a brief review of the anatomy and physiology of the eye. The basic facts of refraction were made available, and the "simpler" diseases of the eye and its appendages were presented in the lecture course. In 1900 the examination, which had been entirely written, was made partly clinical. The number of Assistants was increased to five so that clinical instruction could be given to small groups. In October of 1904 studies in this field were rearranged. The required Ophthalmology was placed in the third year, with an elective course continuing in the fourth.

It is evident that Ophthalmology was not yet ready to participate in the developments that occurred in other specialties in the late nineteenth century.

HYGIENE

The first mention of this in the Harvard University Catalogues occurs in 1869–70, as noted by Professor C. F. Harrington.[4] Dr. George Derby's name appeared as Lecturer on Hygiene in 1870. The only information given was that lectures in this field were placed in the same category as those on Ophthalmology, Laryngoscopy, Otology, and "the Physiological Action of Drugs on Man and the Lower Animals," a strange bag of unrelated disciplines. In 1871–72 Dr. Derby was described as Professor of Hygiene. The Catalogue states tersely "Hygiene—a course of lectures on Hygiene will be given." For a fee of $5.00 graduates could attend lectures on this subject until Dr. Derby's death in 1874. What "hygiene" then consisted of cannot be judged from the Catalogues. The subject was dropped for a year until Dr. Frank W. Draper was appointed Lecturer. Dr. Harrington asserts that lectures were given to third-year students on Thursdays "after April 15th." He points out that such a brief course could scarcely have placed a severe tax on the instructor. Eight lectures were given on Hygiene. About 1875 there were two Lecturers, Dr. Frank Draper and Dr. Charles F. Folsom. A year later Dr. Folsom's title was changed to "Lecturer on Hygiene and Mental Diseases." The next year Dr. Folsom's title was changed once more. This time, he became "Lecturer on Mental Diseases." Some eight lectures on Hygiene were given by an unnamed instructor.

Not much was done about Hygiene until Dr. Samuel H. Durgin was announced as Lecturer in Hygiene in 1882–83. He offered a voluntary course of sixteen lectures and demonstrations for first-year students. Dr. Durgin gave instruction to fourth-year men by means of sixteen lectures on the application of Hygiene to practical municipal sanitation, presumably a forerunner of modern courses on Preventive Medicine. This, apparently, was the substance of the course.

In 1897–98 Hygiene was listed as a required study. Especially qualified students were permitted to elect a laboratory course offered to fourth-year students. Just what this consisted of is not clear. In March 1906 Dr. Harrington was named Professor of Hygiene.

HISTOLOGY AND EMBRYOLOGY

Dr. C. S. Minot has described the first Department of Histology and Embryology (1887).[5] Its beginnings, reasonably enough, were in the Department of Anatomy, and it owed much to the stimulation of Dr. Oliver Wendell Holmes. Even though Holmes had retired from the School five years earlier, his influence persisted. He was accustomed "to give more or less attention to histology and embryology in his lectures and demonstrations." Holmes, with his considerable interest in microscopy, had arranged a wooden frame to hold a microscope and a kerosene lamp to provide illumination. This somewhat unusual apparatus could then be passed around the class during the lecture so that the students had at least some idea of what microscopic structures looked like. Holmes had the foresight to understand the importance of histology, and he occasionally inserted questions on that subject into his examinations.

For some reason, the value of the microscope as a scientific tool was not recognized in America nearly as early as in Europe. The students who went aboard after the Civil War learned to appreciate the instrument, and under the influence of Dr. Calvin Ellis the use of the microscope was stimulated in the Harvard Medical School. Its value was especially appreciated in pathological examinations, and Dr. R. H. Fitz was the leading spirit in emphasizing its usefulness. He was in charge of the laboratory until 1874, when he gave instruction in normal as well as pathological histology. The alterations in the old North Grove Street Building allowed for the inclusion of a microscope room. In 1873 Dr. Fitz became Assistant Professor of Pathological Anatomy, and Dr. Thomas Dwight received an appointment as Instructor in Histology. Thus the teaching of Histology was carried out by the appropriate instructor. This was the first move toward the establishment of a new department. For nine years Dr. Dwight continued as Instructor in Histology. Also, during part of this time, he gave a short course on Embryology.

In 1880 Dr. Charles Sedgwick Minot was appointed Lecturer in Embryology. A distinct course in Histology and Embryology was offered as voluntary work shortly after moving into the new building on Boylston Street about 1883–84. Unfortunately, in the new School building no separate place for normal Histology and Embryology had been provided. As one can understand, Dr. Holmes did not allow *this* oversight to pass unnoticed in his remarks at the dedication of the new building.

The School limped along for ten years with inadequate space until the Sears Building provided space for the Departments of Pathology and Bacteriology, when the old laboratory was then available for Histology and Embryology. For the first time the Department of Histology and Embryology was definitely recognized, and Dr. Minot became Assistant

Professor in 1887 and Professor in 1892. At long last, the Department had become entirely independent. All was not yet smooth sailing, however. When the new building was opened, the entire equipment of the Department of Histology consisted of eighteen Hartnack microscopes, no instructors, and no assistants. The Department was allowed an annual appropriation of $50.00. From these modest beginnings, by 1906 the Department had grown in a sound way and at that time had a considerable library, two hundred and fifty microscopes, a variety of microtomes, and other apparatus. Even more important, it had an extensive collection of embryological preparations. In 1906 this collection was thought to be the finest in the world.

The stated purposes of the Department were to train the students in exact observation and reasoning, to give them expertise in the use of the microscope, and for information to rely on preparations rather than a textbook.

In helping to meet the practical requirements of medical education, the students learned the microscopical structure of the body as well as the laws of development. Scientific research was now given a high place. A close alliance was maintained between the work in Gross Anatomy and that on Minute Anatomy; it was especially fostered by Dr. Thomas Dwight.

While every effort was made to pursue a scientific course, the Department chose, insofar as this was possible, human material, and the aim was "to pay especial attention to such parts of the subject as shall be of greater value to the men in their subsequent practice." One month of the course was devoted to Embryology.

LARYNGOLOGY

Laryngology, according to Professor Algernon Coolidge, Jr., was first taught as a special subject in 1866, although occasional mention of it had been made earlier in courses in Medicine.[6] The establishment of Laryngology as a special subject can be dated from the appointment (1866) of Dr. H. K. Oliver as University Lecturer in this field. Lectures and demonstrations of apparatus were carried out in the Medical School building on North Grove Street. Dr. Oliver was Lecturer in Laryngoscopy until 1873, except for the year 1870–71, during which time Dr. F. I. Knight was in charge. Instruction was not limited to lectures but included, somewhat surprisingly, supplementary instruction in ausculation, percussion, and laryngoscopy. The attempt was to present "thoroughly practical knowledge of these methods of exploration."

While Dr. Knight was in Europe in 1872, he was made Instructor in this field, and with the support of Dr. Calvin Ellis preparations were made to establish a special clinic dealing with diseases of the nose and throat at the Massachusetts General Hospital. These arrangements were to be completed by the time Dr. Knight returned from Europe.

This clinic was the first in New England to include laryngology. It was opened by Dr. Knight in 1872 in a small room in the Hospital's amphitheatre building. In association with this clinic a course in laryngology was started in 1873 for the second class. Instruction consisted principally in methods of examination with the laryngoscope, rhinoscope, and nasal speculum. Conditions of disease were dealt with only incidentally as far as the teaching went. No examination was required. A graduate course was offered. Percussion and ausculation were separated from laryngology in 1879. Dr. Knight's title then became Instructor in Laryngology. In 1880 a fourth-year course was given in the field, three exercises a week for two months. In this situation instruction was "both clinical and systematic." It was followed by a written examination. When the new Outpatient Building was opened, much more material became available for study and treatment.

Dr. Knight became Clinical Professor in 1888 and served until 1892. His successor, Dr. F. H. Hooper, after four years of service, died. He had done a considerable amount of original work in connection with the physiology of the larynx. It was he who introduced into this community the operation for the removal of adenoids under general anesthesia. His death was a considerable loss to the School.

Following Dr. Hooper's death, the Department of Clinical Medicine again took charge of instruction in laryngology. Dr. Coolidge and several others were appointed Clinical Instructors in Laryngology, and the work was divided among the City Hospital, the Boston Dispensary, and the Massachusetts General Hospital. In 1905 the later distinguished Dr. H. P. Mosher was appointed.

GYNECOLOGY

According to Professor C. M. Green, before the reorganization of the Medical School in 1871 by Eliot, diseases of women were not given any prominence in the Medical School.[7] The Professor of Obstetrics had, of course, made occasional passing reference to pelvic disease as related to his field. Then, too, the general surgeon was accustomed to carry out a few gynecological operations. This is still the system at the Massachusetts General Hospital. Professors of medicine dealt with symptoms that were believed to proceed from the diseases of women. However, the pathology of the female pelvic organs had not yet been written, and gynecology as a science did not exist. There were few pioneers in this new field of research either in this country or in Europe. The literature was meager.

It should be noted, however, that in 1871, Dr. Francis Minot, on being appointed Assistant Professor of the Theory and Practice of Physic, was also Clinical Lecturer on the Diseases of Women and Children, as announced in the Catalogue of 1872. No textbook was recommended, probably because none of a satisfactory quality existed. Dr. Minot's appointment lasted only three years and was chiefly related to the diseases of children.

The first appointment limited to diseases of women was that of Dr. James Read Chadwick, who was appointed Lecturer on Diseases of Women. Except for the wards of the Boston hospitals, no facilities existed for clinical teaching of diseases of women, but in 1873 Dr. Chadwick established on Staniford Street the first dispensary in Boston for such cases. He taught here officially and unofficially for many years. Dr. Chadwick was appointed in 1874 to the newly established Outpatient Department for Diseases of Women at the Boston City Hospital.

Dr. William Henry Baker, in 1877, was appointed Instructor in Gynecology without limit of time, thus being made a member of the Faculty. For the four ensuing years, Dr. Baker was the only teacher in the Department. Dr. Baker was able to obtain some outpatient material in the Boston Dispensary and at the Free Hospital for Women, which he had established in 1875. Students were thus afforded their first opportunity in Boston for instruction in operative gynecology. A voluntary fourth year had been established in the Medical School. The year 1881–82 showed considerable gains in the development of this area. For the first time a textbook and other books for collateral reading were recommended in the Catalogue and a general plan of instruction announced. According to this, one lecture a week was given to the third and fourth classes. Clinical instruction was given to the third class in small sections at the Boston Dispensary or at the Free Hospital for Women. Dr. James Read Chadwick gave twelve lectures to the fourth-year class and clinical instruction to small sections at the Staniford Street Dispensary and the Free Hospital for Women. Dr. Baker held a clinical conference once a week. Clinical facilities appropriate for teaching were greatly increased in 1881 when, at the Boston Dispensary, a Department of Diseases of Women was established. This accomplishment must be attributed largely to Dr. Baker, who in 1882 was promoted to the rank of Assistant Professor.

No significant change in the teaching in gynecology occurred until

1886, when the amount of clinical teaching provided for fourth-year students was greatly increased. At about this time Dr. Baker, with an associate, offered a course in operative gynecology. When a full professorship was conferred on him in 1888, Gynecology was definitely established as a Department.

Dr. Francis Henry Davenport had published in 1889 a textbook on diseases of women. In 1892 Gynecology was required study in the third year with a one-hour examination; the subject remained elective in the fourth year. In 1895, Professor Baker resigned after twenty years of service. At that time the Faculty of the Department of Gynecology was placed under the Professor of Obstetrics. Clinical teaching in the fourth year was assigned to Dr. Charles Montraville Green in 1895, who was Assistant Professor of Obstetrics. The fourth-year instruction dealt with clinical and operative exercises in the gynecological wards of the City Hospital. In 1899 Dr. Malcolm Storer was appointed, and the School was able to sustain a daily clinic for six months at the Boston Dispensary in addition to the triweekly clinics in the Outpatient Department of the Boston City Hospital throughout the year. Reconsruction was underaken and completed at the City Hospital for the benefit of the Gynecological Department, which then had a service of sixty beds with up-to-date operating rooms and equipment. Thus the simpler operations all the way up through major procedures could be carried out and demonstrated to students.

Dr. Franklin S. Newell, who had served as Assistant in Obstetrics since 1897, was, in 1901 appointed Assistant in Gynecology. In 1895 Green was named Assistant Professor. He had taught Obstetrics and Diseases of Women officially and unofficially for nearly twenty-five years. He was made, in 1904, Associate Professor of Obstetrics and Clinical Gynecology. Professor Mallory and his associates cooperated with the Gynecological staff by their supervision of the pathological work. In 1906 the Department of Gynecology remained under the direction of the Professor of Obstetrics, Dr. William Lambert Richardson.

OTOLOGY

Up to and through most of the Eliot years, the Harvard Medical School remained largely French in outlook and training. However, German influences began to become evident. This has already been alluded to with respect to physiology; it became even more striking in otology.

When this field began to be recognized as a valid area for research and teaching, it was because of the German example. European aural clinics had already been formed and by the late 1860's were beginning to attract American students. Of special importance to the Harvard Medical School was the influence exerted by the German universities, Adam Politzer and Josef Hyrtl in Vienna and Nikolaus Rüdinger in Munich. Actually, a special lectureship was created in 1869 to cover disease of the ear.[8] This came about because of one of the most interesting of Harvard's pioneers, Clarence John Blake. He was born in Roxbury, Massachusetts, the son of an industrial chemist. After attending the Lawrence Scientific School at Harvard, and then the Medical School, he received the M.D. degree in 1865. He was from the first interested in ear diseases and finding no place in this country in which to be trained in otology, he went to study under Politzer in his clinic in the Vienna Krankenhaus. He distinguished himself sufficiently to be made Dr. Politzer's assistant, not only in the clinic but in his laboratory. Back in Boston in 1869, he joined the recently founded American Otological Society, made up largely of European-trained otologists. He also became Lecturer in Otology at Harvard and Aural Surgeon at the Massachusetts Charitable Eye and Ear Infirmary, where he established the aural clinic. Its only equipment was an old dinner bell, used to test hearing. (At that time, otology was considered far inferior to ophthalmology.)

The Clinic consisted of Blake and only one other physician, but the two saw over 1,600 patients in the first year. Dr. Blake invented a new speculum and a snare for removing aural polyps. He also began to work with Alexander Graham Bell in his research on hearing. Dr. Bell needed a device for recording tracings of the voice, and, since none was available here, Clarence Blake built one for him in accordance with principles he had learned in Vienna. Alexander Bell went on to develop the telephone, but it was Dr. Blake's notes on their studies together that enabled Dr. Bell, who kept few records, to obtain his patent.

Dr. Blake later became Professor of Otology at Harvard and Chief of the Aural Service at the Infirmary. He trained scores of physicians in otology and when he died in 1919, he was recognized by all as the father of Boston otology and a pioneer in the science of hearing.[9]

When the new department was founded in 1888, it represented a direct transplantation of German methods of instruction in the clinic. There was little anatomical or pathological material available here, and little time was allotted to the new study; hence, the practical instruction of the students was limited chiefly to lecures with a little clinical training in diagnosis and treatment of diseases of the ear. Nevertheless, the students were eager to learn about this new field. When one really sought for it, it was evident that considerable clinical material could be found in the Outpatient Department. The difficulty was that only a short time was allotted to each student, and it was therefore impossible for the students to follow major cases. At this time one lecturer held the position of Aural Surgeon to Outpatients at the Boston City Hospital, and the other instructor worked in the Aural Surgery Department in the Massachusetts Eye and Ear Infirmary.

Twelve or so lectures were given at the Medical School. Both instructors participated in these, and once again, for clinical teaching, the class was broken into sections with eight to twelve students in each group. Little graduate instruction was available. Beginning around 1888, the work of the Department in clinical teaching was advanced by the admission of aural patients to the wards. The Aural Surgeons to Outpatients continued to supervise the care of the bedpatients. This in-house material made it possible for the students to witness major aural operations, but it was not until the new building for the Eye and Ear Infirmary was opened that adequate provision was made for this type of patient. In the end, thirty beds, with others available for emergency cases, were placed under the service of the aural outpatient surgeons.

The importance of this teaching was officially recognized when the Board of Managers of the Eye and Ear Infirmary expressed their willingness to permit the use of the clinics and wards for instruction in the Harvard Medical School. The City Hospital clinic was then given up. The increase in available pathological material required the appointment of further assistants. In 1906 the Department consisted of a Professor of Otology and four Assistants in the field. The Department, although popular, seemed to lack organization and direction at this time. Later, through combination with related departments, it came to function more positively.

PEDIATRICS

Although the development of the Department of Pediatrics extended over a period of many years, perhaps thirty-five, it was not really recognized as a separate entity until 1888, when an assistant professorship was granted to the Department with representation on the Faculty, as Professor T. M. Rotch has pointed out.[10] The teaching of diseases of children was first officially announced in 1871 shortly after the Eliot upheaval. In that year Dr. Francis Minot, who had the title Assistant Professor of the Theory and Practice of Physic, was given also that of Clinical Lecturer on the Diseases of Women and Children. Professor Rotch commented that the centuries-old idea persisted that children's diseases should be taught with obstetrics and gynecology.

On assuming the added role, Dr. Minot was requested to say some-

thing about medical problems of children. He selected measles and scarlet fever, omitting the ubiquitous problems of feeding, saving the lives
of premature infants, and lowering the tremendous mortality of diseases
of the gastrointestinal tract in the infant. On the other hand, much could
be said in favor of his choices, for the exanthemata were prominent
enough in the infant and young child, in contrast with their frequency in
adults, hence had a special place in pediatric teaching.

The two most prominent figures in this early period of the development of the Department were the then Professor of Physic, Dr. Minot,
and the Professor of Clinical Medicine, Dr. Calvin Ellis. They maintained that physicians who made a special study of the diseases of children and controlled hospitals whose patients were limited to the early
years could better answer vital questions associated with infants and children than could those whose teaching and clinical experience was limited to adults. The concept was growing that the student should receive
practical training in what he would need in this area when he was in
practice.

Professor Rotch commented:

> Those who were interested in obtaining for the students a means to
> acquire a more exact knowledge of the clinical medicine of early life
> have always taken the position that it was not diseases *of* children
> which was in most cases to be taught, but the manifestations of disease
> as it occurred *in* children and how the symptoms of the disease varied
> at different ages according to the stage of development.[11]

Once the importance of special teaching in children's diseases had
been assimilated, the problem was to insert it into the curriculum in a
way that would not conflict with but would supplement teaching in the
other branches of medicine.

When in 1873 Dr. Charles Pickering Putnam was appointed Lecturer
on Diseases of Children, a course limited to the problems of children was
given for the first time. Dr. Putnam lectured on clinical matters once a
week during the second term at the Dispensary for Women and Children
on Staniford Street. Dr. Minot discontinued his lectures on children in
1874, for reasons not clear. However, in addition to Dr. Putnam's lectures
once a week in the second year, beginning in 1875 Dr. Joseph Pearson
Oliver, who had been appointed Instructor, began to lecture to the third-
year students. Dr. Oliver assigned cases to the Dispensary Districts in
what today would be called triage. Reports on these cases were made to
the entire class. In 1874–75, for the first time, questions appeared in the
examination paper on children's diseases. In 1876 some questions concerning children appeared in Professor's Minot's examination on Theory
and Practice. No questions on children's diseases appeared on any exami-

nation papers for a time. Presumably, this presents one more example of the never-ending scramble for allotted time in the medical curriculum.

Following the retirement of Dr. Putnam from the school in 1878, Dr. Joseph Pearson Oliver and Dr. Thomas Morgan Rotch, later celebrated for his pioneering studies on infant feeding, were appointed clinical instructors the next year. Dr. Rotch's clinical lectures utilized the large and varied material available in the Dispensary Clinic. Thus it was becoming possible to outline the beginnings of the system which, in later years, was developed in the Department, an important feature of which was always that special attention in the teaching should be given to the normal condition of infants and children in the several stages of their development. This was fundamental to an understanding of the disease conditions found at each stage.

Again, in 1879, questions concerning infants and children appeared on the examination papers. In 1880–81 instruction in the third year was carried out as before, with the addition of a voluntary course for students of the fourth year. At that time Dr. Rotch introduced teaching in children's diseases at the Boston City Hospital and gave the fourth-year men three exercises a week followed by a special examination oriented to pediatrics. This marked the first completely separate examination given in children's diseases in the School. In 1882 Dr. Rotch began to utilize the teaching material available in the new Children's Hospital. Probably, as an early recognition of his coming distinction, he was allowed to increase the time devoted to the Pediatrics course by giving an additional lecture during the second term. One cannot call this overwhelming generosity, but at least it represented progress.

A further milestone can be seen when Dr. Rotch was, in 1885, given entire charge of the teaching, with the title Instructor in Diseases of Children. A considerable battle obviously had been won. Close oversight was kept of the extensive material in the Dispensary Districts. Students were, at that time, allowed to visit the homes where these diseases could be found.

Great efforts were made to permit the student, as part of his course on children, to see as many cases as possible of infectious diseases. This had long been considered vital to a full understanding of diseases in early life. The material for the lectures was drawn not only from the Boston City Hospital but also from the Children's Hospital, the Children's Room at the Boston Dispensary, and the Infant's Hospital. At this time too students began to receive instruction in nursery hygiene. Practical points were made in regard to bathing, clothing, ventilation, rest, and sleep. The feeding of infants was dealt with in detail, especially at Infants' Hospital, which among its other advantages contained a well-equipped clinical laboratory. It was possible in this institution to make serious studies of diseases of the gastrointestinal tract and to study various aspects of nervous phenomena. There was in Europe and Great Britain widespread interest in the possibility that most diseases were, or were manifested as, disorders of the sympathetic nerves. Children who were believed to have nervous systems that were particularly delicate, unstable, and vulnerable, were studied with this in mind, especially in regard to nursery practice. Attention was given to problems of the skin in health and disease. Three clinical exercises a week were given to the fourth-year students.

The Pediatrics endeavor had become almost too successful, and it became difficult for the instructors to keep up with their obligations. Junior members were added to the staff until, in 1888, the title of Assistant Professor of Diseases of Children, including a Faculty seat, was given to Dr. Rotch. The course was now offered to graduates, and graduate teaching in the Department was carried on continuously after 1888.

It is interesting to observe that many decades before women were welcomed in the Harvard Medical School, the various instructors in the Pediatrics Department had been willing to receive in their courses women physicians who were graduates. Thus the practice in the Pediatrics Department with regard to women long preceded the eventual situation at the Harvard Medical School.

It was clear that the type of instruction presented in the years around 1888 was worthy of a Department. Nonetheless, its smooth development was greatly interfered with by the system of electives, which allowed the student to take his degree without any regular or systematic program of courses. The only continuity of instruction in this field, one lecture and one clinical conference a week, began at the end of the second year. A course of study was arranged so that the student took the elective course starting in March and April of the second year and continued into the third year.

In 1889 contagious wards were opened at the Boston City Hospital, and instruction in diphtheria, measles, and scarlet fever was immediately started by the Children's Department. Dr. Buckingham and Dr. Rotch by virtue of their staff positions at the Hospital had some control over the wards. It must be noted that this was the first systematic teaching of contagious diseases in a hospital given at the Harvard Medical School, and it superseded the earlier system of seeing cases at irregular intervals in the Dispensary Districts.

Dr. Rotch was made full Professor of Diseases of Children in 1893, and sectional teaching in the wards was again started under the direction of the department. By that time considerable information had been obtained in the Infants' Hospital as to the best methods of care of premature infants, and emphasis was given in the Department to this branch of

Pediatrics. This led to still further advances in knowledge of feeding problems, and interest increased in the establishment of a system of milk laboratories, to ensure that pure milk would be availbale. The same thing happened in Canada and England. It was recognized that careful supervision and easily maintained equipment was essential in the dairies, especially those connected with the laboratories. Members of the staff of the Children's Department gave particular attention to these matters in the summer months. At long last, significant advances were being made in the understanding and control of diseases of the gastrointestinal tract during the early years.

A problem given particular attention at this time was whether an infants' hospital should be separated from a children's hospital. The conclusion was that there were sufficient reasons for such separation. One reason was that the expense of caring for young infants in the best possible way was so much greater than that for older children. In a children's hospital, more care, comparatively, was spent on the younger individual at the cost of the older. A book was published in 1895 based on the clinical data, which presented actual cases. It served as a textbook for discussion.[12]

In 1900, Dr. John Lovett Morse and Dr. Maynard Ladd were added to the teaching staff, and both brought great distinction to the Hospital in the years to come. Dr. Ladd became the premier surgeon in the field of Pediatrics.

All teaching in the field of contagious diseases in the fourth year, previously under the direction of the Department of Clinical Medicine, was, in 1903, transferred to the Department of Pediatrics. It had become evident that far and away the majority of patients in the South Department of the Boston City Hospital were children and that the diseases were so closely related in the early years that they, too, should be especially taught in the Pediatrics Department. Didactic lectures were made introductory to the problems encountered in the Pediatrics world, problems that the students later on had to deal with at the bedside. The lectures principally dealt with the anatomical, physiological, and developmental characteristics of the different stages of growth in infancy and childhood. Not many recitations from the textbook were required, although some memorizing was considered to be essential. A little later, case teaching became a prominent feature of the instruction. Three principal areas were dealt with: the exanthemata, feeding, and gastrointestinal diseases. Whenever possible, actual cases were demonstrated to the students.

It was fairly well recognized that teaching in Pediatrics at Harvard before 1900 covered more ground and gave greater opportunities to the individual student than was true in any other school in the country.

In 1905–06, the course was greatly expanded and remodeled so as to present more teaching. These courses were offered in the Outpatient Department of the Children's Hospital, the Thomas Morgan Rotch, Jr., Memorial Hospital for Infants, and in the contagious wards of the Boston City Hospital. Pediatrics was now considered such a rich field that a student might take all eight courses then offered and grant a full year to Pediatrics.

BACTERIOLOGY

Instruction in Bacteriology was first offered in the autumn of 1885 when six lectures were delivered to the second-year class by Dr. Harold C. Ernst, later (1895) Harvard's first Professor of Bacteriology.[13] He was born in Cincinnati, Ohio, July 31, 1856. His grandfather fled to this country from Germany in 1804 with his eldest son, Andrew Henry Ernst, the father of Dr. Ernst, because his principles forebade him to comply with the harsh Napoleonic restrictions. Dr. Ernst's mother, Sarah H. Otis, was a direct descendant of General Otis of the Revolution. She was a great worker during the Civil War, an abolitionist, and a pioneer advocate of suffrage for women.

Harold Ernst was graduated from Harvard College in 1876 and from Harvard Medical School in 1880. He received a Masters degree, also from Harvard, in 1884.[14] Following graduation from the Medical School and hospital service, he began to practice medicine in Jamaica Plain. From the very beginning he was interested in bacteriology. His first papers, published in 1883 and 1884, were on the tubercle bacillus. In 1884, he was made an Assistant in Bacteriology in the Harvard Medical School, and in 1885 he went abroad to study the bacteriology of tuberculosis with Robert Koch. His lectures were the first in this country on bacteriology as a part of the regular instruction for medical schools.

Dr. Ernst steadily maintained the importance of the new science of bacteriology in the service of medicine and surgery. This he did notwithstanding considerable opposition on the part of some of his older colleagues, who wished to deny him laboratory space and the privilege of teaching. Dr. Ernst won out, however, and in 1888 laboratory work became a part of the bacteriological instruction to medical students. In 1889 he was promoted to Instructor, in 1891 to Assistant Professor, and in 1895 he was made Professor of Bacteriology.

Dr. Ernst's scientific activities are demonstrated by publications on tuberculosis, suppurative bacteria, rabies, diphtheria, photomicrography with ultraviolet light, and the infant field of immunology. He carried out, in 1895, important research on the "infectiousness of Milk from

Tuberculous Cows with no Lesions of the Udder," a report that was published in book form by the Masaschusetts Society for Promoting Agriculture. His important conclusion was that milk from tuberculous cows with no appreciable lesions of the udder may and not infrequently did contain the bacillus of the disease.

Dr. Wolbach agreed that Dr. Ernst possessed the true spirit of investigation and had the abilities of a great investigator, but his temperament, perhaps derived from the Ernst-Otis inheritance, led him to work of immediate usefulness.[15] Dr. Ernst was a true pioneer in placing laboratory resources at the command of practicing physicians. He very often acted as consultant on bacteriological programs. It was he who introduced sterilization of milk for infant feeding. It was he who prepared dry-sterilized (that is, baked) surgical dressings, which Dr. J. C. Warren used at the Massachusetts General Hospital. In an informal way his laboratory for a time served as the city bacteriological laboratory for Boston, as well as some other cities. He first manufactured tuberculin and diphtheria antitoxins for the City of Boston.

In 1890 Ernst returned to Koch's laboratory in order to learn about tuberculin. Then he served as physician to outpatients at the Massachusetts General Hospital for about ten years, until 1900. His therapeutic use of tuberculin was given a cautious and careful trial. When this country became involved in World War I, he immediately volunteered his services and was placed in charge of laboratory work of the Northeastern Division with the rank of major.

Beginning in 1914 and until his death in 1922, he was visiting Bacteriologist to the Children's Hospital. He derived great satisfaction from it and especially liked the sense of being directly useful to patients. For many years, he was in charge of opposition to legislation in Massachusetts which attempted to outlaw animal experimentation.[16] Over the years he accumulated an important library concerned with bacteriology, which has now been incorporated into the library of the Medical School.

> His high ideals, direct speech, promptness to action and punctiliousness in personal relationships and everything pertaining to the amenities of life, made him an outstanding personality in each of the groups he served. Throughout his professional life he gave freely of his time to his colleagues and his assistance and encouragement are gratefully remembered by many practitioners of medicine as well as by laboratory workers.[17]

Theobald Smith, Professor of Comparative Pathology, was also involved in bacteriologic teaching and research. Whether the two professors recognized their responsibilities and found some way to divide them is not known. There was also some coordination with the Department of

Theobald Smith, world-famous pioneer in microbiology. He was Professor of Comparative Pathology, a post established in order to bring Smith's genius to Harvard. Photograph from the Harvard Medical Archives.

Pathological Anatomy, then in the charge of Professor R. H. Fitz. The establishment of the Department of Bacteriology was another first for Harvard in that these were the first lectures on bacteriology given in this country as part of a medical course presented by a special teacher. The first laboratory teaching was not extensive and was carried out in a previously unoccupied room of the Boylston Street Building of the Harvard Medical School. It was not possible to give practical teaching to any except special students, interestingly enough, but the number of these increased as rapidly as space could be found for them. In 1889 Dr. Ernst was promoted to Instructor, in 1891, to Assistant Professor; he achieved professorial rank in 1895 in the field of Bacteriology.

Since there was no prototype anywhere else, the plan of instruction had to be worked out *de novo*. The first lectures were offered to the second-year class. In 1888 required laboratory work was added in the second term of the first year. Later, with increase in activities in this area, the entire required bacteriological instruction was placed in the first term of the second year where it remained in 1906.

The intention here was to give every student some familiarity with the principles controlling the action of bacteriological microorganisms, together with some knoweldge of the necessary techniques. This was done in the hope that such principles and methods might be of practical clinical value.

Later, electives were offered to fourth-year students. These were tailored to the students' desires and could be brief or might extend for as long as a year. In additon, graduate courses were offered to those who had the M.D. degree, as well as to special students whether beginners or experienced persons. The system followed in the Medical School was like that which had been accepted in the Division of Biology in the Faculty of Arts and Sciences.

Research by qualified persons was encouraged, and all the resources of the Department were made available as needed. Summer courses were given. The research work carried on between 1891 and 1906 dealt with tuberculosis, rabies, glanders, smallpox, diphtheria, typhoid fever, as well as inflammation associated with suppuration and septicemia. The finances of the School were not adequate to support these many activities, and consequently money had to be obtained from the outside.

Some practical matters which originated out of the research in this department: The application of "baked" dressings (Dr. J. C. Warren at the Massachusetts General Hospital), for which an oven especially constructed for the purpose was necessary; the sterilization of milk for babies; the value of a bacteriological examination of material from the throat in suspected cases of diphtheria (J. H. McCollom). The laboratory became involved in the practical work of making such diagnoses for a number of cities and towns. The Department was also engaged in the study of methods of ultraviolet photomicrography employed in the rapid diagnosis of rabies, and became involved in the preparation of the new curative agent, diphtheria antitoxin. Very soon, routine activities of this kind became so burdensome that serious injury to the Department was threatened, especially in the field of research.

Professor Ernst took an active part in the formation of the American Association of Pathologists and Bacteriologists and participated in the editorial control of the *Journal of Medical Research*. In 1906, the Department consisted of one professor, one instructor, five assistants and one Austin Teaching Fellow.

NEUROLOGY

American neurology grew out of the medical experiences of the Civil War. The common occurrence of disability produced by wounds of the brain or nerves and the specific localizing manifestations of these lesions became an essential part of miltary medicine. Men such as Weir Mitchell led the way. Another factor at this time was the enormous development of neuroanatomy, stimulated originally by the Viennese Franz Joseph Gall, who later became the founder of phrenology (which took Boston by storm; Boston seems to have a fondness for Viennese music and medical superstitions). A third factor in the growth of interest in neurology was the development of electrical medicine, begun in the mid-eighteenth century when Desbois de Rochefort described how the application of electricity to the head might cure depression. In the 1850's the publication of Guillaume-Benjamin Duchenne's great book on electrical medicine in France produced a spark that started things moving in Boston. As Dr. E. W. Taylor pointed out, the teaching of diseases of the nervous system was first recognized in 1872 when Dr. James Jackson Putnam received the remarkable but understandable title of Lecturer on the Application of Electricity in Nervous Diseases.[18] Two years later he was named Lecturer on Diseases of the Nervous System. Presumably this shortening of the title broadened his field and therefore represented a step up. Until 1895 such lectures and demonstrations as Putnam prepared were presented under the auspices of the Department of Clinical Medicine, from which Neurology in the Harvard Medical School, as well as elsewhere, was derived. In 1875, the year William James apparently founded at Harvard College the first psychological laboratory in America, Drs. Putnam and S. G. Webber of Harvard were appointed Clinical Instructors at the Medical School. At that time, and for many years, a small room in the Outpatient Department of the Massachusetts General Hospital served the purposes of the Neurological Service. The Harvard University Catalogue offered each year "Lectures and Demonstrations at the Massachusetts General Hospital." At the end of some ten years the clinic had so outgrown the quarters mentioned that two rooms were made available in another part of the building. These also soon became inadequate to meet the growing requirements of patients and physicians.

In 1885 the later distinguished Dr. Putnam was advanced to the position of Instructor. In that year, teaching was continued at the Massachusetts General Hospital under the general direction of Dr. Putnam, assisted by Dr. George L. Walton. Dr. P. C. Knapp was appointed Clinical Instructor in 1888, and through his association with the Boston City Hospital, the Neurological Clinic of that institution was available for teaching.

Gradually, recognition of the special importance of neurological work became widespread, culminating in the establishment of the Chair of Diseases of the Nervous System in 1893; and Dr. Putnam, having outstandingly fulfilled his obligations in minor positions over a period of twenty-one years, was made the first professor. From 1895 to 1898 Dr. Morton Prince served as Clinical Instructor, but resigned at the end of the three-year period.

Dr. Putnam gave his principal attention to the instruction of students in the third year. Neurology, however, was not a required study until 1895. About 1901 the teaching force in the Department had been increased by the appointment of several assistants. The year 1896 saw a considerable expansion in the teaching of Neurology when an instructorship in Neurological Pathology was created under the Department of Pathology.

With the cooperation of Dr. W. T. Councilman, a course evolved which was concerned with the pathological anatomy of neurological disease. This was planned for the second-year students. It extended over sixteen exercises of three hours each. The purpose of this course was to make clear to the students knowledge of the alterations responsible for the important neurological disease processes, as well as to serve to introduce the students to the clinical work of the third year in this field. The good feeling and cooperation between the Departments of Pathology and Neurology illustrated very well the advantages of a close relationship between "scientific" and clinical departments. The upshot was a considerable broadening of practical neurology and a new interest in pathological anatomy.

The opening of the new Outpatient Building at the Massachusetts General Hospital in 1903 had great significance for the teaching of Neu-

rology, as well as for many other subjects. Adequate room for patients
and physicians and the possibility of privacy in teaching and examination
clearly conferred great benefit on the Neurological Department of the
Medical School. It also led to postgraduate work.

The clinical material appearing in the Massachusetts General Hospital
and the Boston City Hospital provided excellent opportunities for the
study of neuroses, as well as all types of structural diseases in their early
manifestations. The Weld Ward in the Massachusetts General Hospital
was designed chiefly for patients with skin diseases, but two beds were
reserved for neurological patients. The Long Island Hospital, an institution for paupers from about 1896 onward, was a possible resource for
the study of chronic and late stages of nervous disease, but difficulties of
transportation (it was on an island in Boston Harbor) prevented courses
of instruction from being held there. Nevertheless, enterprising students
often availed themselves of the opportunity to see the patients, and that
Hospital became an increasingly important institution for neurological
teaching.

Neurology having begun as a small offshoot of general medicine, had
become, by 1893, virtually independent. Instruction was extended, and
made, in part, compulsory until by 1906 it was involved in three years
of the medical course, although considerable puzzlement was expressed
over just what and how much neurological knowledge the medical student should have at his graduation. At any rate, no longer could Neurology be neglected. A command of the subject was made difficult by the
complicated anatomical and pathological knowledge required, especially
since the time allotted was sharply limited. Teaching included the lecture system with presentation of patients, a method that was not wholly
satisfactory, inasmuch as the numerous students could not easily be
brought into close contact with the patients. That situation led to the division of the classes into small sections for clinical instruction. The So-
cratic method of teaching had been fairly satisfactory, but the students
were not wholeheartedly in favor of this approach, preferring direct
methods with clinical demonstrations. The case system as introduced by
Dr. W. B. Cannon (above, page 000), was found to be a valuable adjunct in neurological teaching. Drs. J. J. Putnam and G. A. Waterman
published a book of cases in 1902, which served as a modified textbook
for the third-year course.

The future of Neurology as a separate discipline was a matter of considerable interest. Here, although the lecture was important and textbooks and the use of the case system was useful, the central object in
clinical instruction was recognized to be the study of disease as it appears
in the individual patient. It was clear that a study of the nervous system
by those who expected to specialize in it was inevitable. In the end, that

could only mean a growing independence of neurological departments. Professor Putnam's thesis was, however, that Neurology must remain an inseparable part of the general subject of internal medicine, notwithstanding the fact that its boundaries must be pushed beyond what is ordinarily encompassed in that term. The unfortunate separation existing in the student's mind beween structure and function should be overcome by systematic instruction in anatomy and pathology under the direct supervision of the Professor of Neurology. The anatomy of the nervous system should, in Dr. Putnam's view, be as much a part of general neurological instruction as the study of the cases. At the same time, the rights and privileges of other departments should not be encroached upon. An essential requirement of neurological teaching always is an adequate number of hospital beds for patients suffering from diseases of the nervous system. These beds, in Putnam's view, should be under the control of the head of the Department of Neurology. The advantages of such an arrangement had been amply demonstrated in foreign universities.

In the 1906 description of this Department, it is interesting to find the statement that the future of Neurology is "undoubtedly to see in this Community a development of the somewhat neglected field of psychiatry," a field which also requires special students, which "should be brought into closer relationship, not only with its nearest neighbor, neurology, but also with the more remote field of research represented by the general subject of Internal Medicine."

ORTHOPEDICS

Orthopedic surgery developed at the Harvard Medical School as an outgrowth of the Department of Surgery. Professor E. H. Bradford has pointed out that while the establishment of a full professorship of orthopedic surgery was relatively recent in 1906, the interest in this branch of surgery in Boston had been active for more than fifty years.[19] The first efforts here were contemporary with the work of William Little of London and Dr. Buckminster Brown of Boston. The latter, as early as 1850, was devoting himself entirely to the treatment of deformities and was the first in this country to open a public hospital ward for this purpose. He became the first American specialist in this field. He presented his valuable collection of specimens and casts, especially of deformities of the feet, to the Harvard Medical School. He also willed a considerable sum for the foundation of an endowed Professorship of Orthopedic Surgery. He was effective in opening the way for a generation of distinguished orthopedic surgeons to succeed him. The ground work was laid by him for what, in subsequent generations, was to become one of the most celebrated Departments in the Harvard Medical School.

In the early part of his career, Dr. Henry J. Bigelow, later Professor of Surgery at the Harvard Medical School, also devoted himself to problems of orthopedic surgery. Bigelow had a considerable capacity for inserting himself into areas that were rapidly expanding in terms of contemporary interest. It is said that his monograph on orthopedic surgery was the "best exposition of French orthopedic surgery of the day."

After Dr. Bigelow's occasional safaris into the field of orthopedics, the next distinguished figure was Edward Hickling Bradford. This direct descendant of William Bradford, the second governor of Plymouth Colony, was born in 1848 and died in 1926. He received the Doctor of Medicine degree from Harvard in 1873 after a year's internship at the Massachusetts General Hospital. Following this, he passed two years in serious study in Vienna, Berlin, and Strasbourg. Early in his career, he saw the possibilities of orthopedic surgery and studied under Charles F. Taylor (1827–1899) in New York. In Boston the leader at this time was Dr. Buckminster Brown, and the relationship of the two men was cordial. Both had worked at the House of the Good Samaritan, the first institution in Boston to make special provision for children afflicted with joint disease.

Bradford early recognized that specialism had to be based on the parent discipline of general surgery or medicine—in his case, surgery. In 1880 he was appointed Surgeon to the Outpatients at the City Hospital and later became Full Surgeon, and resigned only when the Children's Hospital teaching and private practice dominated his interest. As a surgeon at the Children's Hospital he kept in close touch with general surgery, finally becoming Surgeon-in-Chief there. In 1881 he was appointed Assistant in Surgery in the Harvard Medical School, and orthopedic teaching was entrusted to him. In 1899 he continued to be Instructor in Surgery but had the added title "and Orthopedics." In 1893 his title was changed to Assistanat Professor of Orthopedics, and in 1903 he became the first Professor of Orthopedic Surgery and filled the chair which later was designated as the John Ball and Buckminster Brown Professorship (1915). By that time Bradford had become Emeritus (although he carried on as Dean for six years, 1912–1918).

Bradford was a man of the highest principles, noted for his capacity and devotion to work. He was constant in friendship. When he was nearly 75, failing sight led him to learn to read braille, and he taught himself to use the typewriter by touch. He dominated blindness and led, even in his last years, a happy life with his wife and four children. To him belongs credit for establishing Orthopedics as a discipline separate from Surgery.

Edward H. Bradford, the next to the last part-time Dean. An outstanding orthopedic surgeon. He was Dean during the period when the newly constructed Peter Bent Brigham Hospital was incorporated into the Harvard curriculum, at a time when the first attempt was made to provide for the School a University hospital. He also guided the School during the trying times of World War I and the difficult period of the furor over the Flexner Report. Photograph from the Locke Collection, Boston Medical Library.

As with all other courses, teaching in the Harvard Medical School in orthopedic surgery began as a small voluntary course given by Instructors in Surgery to those who were interested in this special field. In the beginning, this specialty was overshadowed by the great expansion of general surgery, owing to the introduction of general anesthesia and the aseptic technique. Deformities remained, however, as a special incentive to the pursuit of orthopedic surgery until, as Professor Bradford says, with perhaps a not entirely unbiased point of view, "orthopedic surgery is regarded as one of the most important of the specialties in the Surgical Department . . ." In 1906, while the Department of Orthopedic Surgery was still organized as a branch of the Division of Surgery, it had its own full professor, Bradford, and a corps of four assistants. By 1906 those interested in this specialty functioned on the wards and outpatient departments of the Children's Hospital, the Carney Hospital, and the Massachusetts General Hospital.

COMPARATIVE PATHOLOGY

Not long before the move of the School to Longwood Avenue was undertaken, President Eliot became interested in insects and animals and their role in the causation of diseases in man. To further knowledge in this area, he established the George Fabyan Professorship of Comparative Pathology (1896), with Theobald Smith as the incumbent.[20] George Frazier Fabyan, a lover of horses, wished to endow a Chair that might be of benefit to animals and at the same time honor his father. Mr. Fabyan handsomely endowed the Chair with a first gift of $100,000. Two years later he added $25,000 to the permanent endowment. It was Mr. Fabyan's intention that the Professor should not engage in private practice unless this was recommended by the Medical Faculty and with the consent of the President and Fellows, a rather sophisticated policy for those early days.

Since no space was available at the time of the creation of this professorship, Comparative Pathology was housed in the Bussey Institution of Harvard College, near the Forest Hills rapid-transit station. Provisions were made for the study of both human and animal disease. Professor Smith took an active interest in developing and directing the Massachusetts State Board of Health Laboratory for the production and free distribution of antitoxins and vaccines. These activities are continued to the present time. When, in 1904, a new laboratory was built for the exclusive purpose of preparation of antitoxins and vaccines and the investigation of associated problems, this building was leased to the State Board of Health. The Professor of Comparative Pathology was able, owing to the broad range of his interests, to provide a stimulus for research into practical problems, "a stimulus likely to be wanting when contact with actual disease is not provided for." An active program of teaching and research has been carrried out there. Professor Smith's primary interests were in infectious and parasitic diseases, and two courses were given, one devoted to a broad discussion of the principles underlying infectious diseases, while the other was devoted to those protozoan and higher animal parasites which are important in human pathology. It was Professor Smith's policy to open his Institution to a few advance students, for special research.

There was a great need for assistants, somewhat ameliorated by the assignment, in 1900, of an Austin Teaching Fellow. One reason for the shortage was simply a lack of available good men. In the first ten years of existence of the laboratory, papers published dealt with general methods in bacteriology, special studies of diphtheria bacilli and toxins, and the standardization of diphtheria and tetanus antitoxins and bovine as well as human tubercle bacilli. Several papers were published on the epidemiology of malaria in relation to mosquitos in Massachusetts, and several studies were concerned with sporozoan parasites, which infest lower animals.

Rather remarkably for this early date, papers were published on the role of heredity in the resistance of animals to diphtheria toxin and on the resistance of red corpuscles. In the first decade of the existence of the laboratory, a great deal of unpublished work (before 1906) had been carried out on animal diseases, but it was held back for further checking.

Why a Department of Comparative Pathology? First, the need for bacteriology or microbiology had to be accommodated, and, second, the comparative method of studying disease processes was gaining in importance. At that time the enormous importance of parasitism was just beginning to be appreciated, and the study of animal and vegetable parasites was mandatory. It had become clear by 1906 that all phenomena in animal life concerned with infectious disease could throw important light on human ailments. Studies in this area have also promoted the development of biology and biochemistry.

It was generally accepted, at that time (1906), that disease processes were essentially the same in animals and in man. Field work under Professor Smith's direction was especially concerned with pathology in the higher animals. It was his belief that in such work new leads might be found which would be of importance in human medicine. He summarized the approach:

This method was of the greatest influence in ridding the medicine of the last century of its rigid conceptions of health and disease and replacing them with the more flexible biological conceptions of to-day. To learn that any given microbe which produces a well-defined disease in man is harmless to animals, that a disease germ, dangerous to one species, has no effect upon a closely-related species, and that a human being may carry dangerous microbes which are held in check by unknown forces within him are lessons which in themselves have had a great influence in making medicine begin to appreciate the flexibility as well as the enormous complexity of the processes which protect us from disease or which lead to recovery.

Departments in medicine as in other institutions of learning may be considered as having a past, a present, and future value. Unless made over or remodeled some may have only a past value, others are at their best in the present, and still others have only the future to point to. The study of animal diseases, the use of their resources and the resources of animal life in general in the elucidation of human maladies and their amelioration, is largely a future task.[21]

It is a remarkable fact, notwithstanding the almost overwhelming domination of Pasteur and Koch on medical thinking in the late nineteenth century, that Theobald Smith interpreted the then available evidence to argue against overinsistence on the doctrine that maintained the specificity of cause in disease. The proponents of the view tried to make it applicable to a wider area of diseases than was supported by the facts.[22]

Professor Smith's policy was to begin with general biological phenomena and to trace them in an ascending scale from lower forms of life on into pathological processes of the highest forms, though working from the top down could, on occasion, be useful. As far as the Department of Comparative Pathology in the Medical School is concerned, only the second of the above approaches could get much attention.

Professor Smith closes his account on a plaintive note

In estimating the relative output of useful knowledge by any department, it is necessary to bear in mind that it is almost wholly at the mercy of equipment and material in the choice of problems. This is especially true of such as have a future value and whose work for a time must be chiefly research. It should also be added that in the study of the diseases of animals, as well of human beings, the time cannot be chosen, but the student must be ready when the disease presents itself.[23]

Theobald Smith was one of the greatest scientists America has ever produced. It is clear that persuading him to come to Harvard was a great coup. It is also clear from his own comments that he was given a free hand in developing his own department and in formulating the concepts that underlie his subject.

MATERIA MEDICA AND PHARMACOLOGY

Dr. Robert T. Edes was appointed Assistant Professor of Materia Medica in 1871 to succeed Dr. Clark and was made full Professor of Materia Medica in 1875. In 1884, he became, in addition, the Jackson Professor of Clinical Medicine. In addition to the duties associated with that professorship, he continued to teach Therapeutics for a year under his new title. Dr. Edes described his course as follows:

> Materia Medica is taught by recitations, as this mode of instruction is best adapted for imparting that practical knowledge of drugs and their properties which can only be obtained from the examinations of specimens and pharmaceutical preparations, of which there is an extensive collection. Therapeutics or the physiological action of drugs and their application to disease is taught in the third year by lectures.[24]

Dr. Edes gave all of the instruction in the Department until 1874, with the exception of 1871, when an Instructor took over the teaching in Materia Medica while Dr. Edes limited his teaching to Therapeutics. Three lectures a week were given in the third year from 1874 to 1884.

Dr. F. H. Williams was, in 1885, placed in charge of this department with the title of Instructor in Materia Medica. There seemed to be no hesitation in giving minor titles to departmental heads. He was made Assistant Professor in 1886 and kept this title for five years, when he resigned. In 1885 Williams' instruction in Materia Medica consisted of two lectures a week during the second half of the first year and two recitations or demonstrations a week throughout the second year. In the third year one lecture a week on Therapeutics was given. This included demonstrations in which there was little or no student participation.

Dr. Charles Harrington was placed in complete charge of the Department of Materia Medica and Therapeutics in 1891. He gave two lectures a week in this field in the second-year term, and then continued until 1898. In 1894, Mr. James O. Jordan was appointed Assistant in Materia Medica for the purpose of giving a course in Pharmacy and to illustrate for the students the compounding of prescriptions, obviously filling an urgent need. Dr. Franz Pfaff was appointed Instructor in Pharmacology in 1895 and gave one demonstration a week. He succeeded Dr. Harrington in 1898 with the rank of Instructor in Pharmacology, Dr. Harrington becoming Assistant Professor of Hygiene. In 1905 Dr. Pfaff was named full Professor of Pharmacology. His course consisted in a series of lectures on drugs—their physical and chemical properties, their action, and, finally, their use in the practice of medicine. Whenever he could do so, he demonstrated the action of drugs by appropriate experiments. Dr. Pfaff was much interested in research and in having his assistants also carry out research in the Pharmacology Laboratory of the School and the Chemical Laboratory of the Massachusetts General Hospital, then under the direction of Dr. Pfaff. Dr. A. W. Balch was appointed First Assistant in Pharmacology under Dr. Pfaff. He conducted the course in Pharmacy with Mr. Jordan and was in general charge of the laboratory under Dr. Pfaff. Dr. M. Vejux Tyrode succeeded Dr. Balch in 1901. He worked as a volunteer assistant to Dr. Pfaff for some five years, until in 1900 he was appointed Dalton Fellow at the Massachusetts General Hospital, where he was Dr. Pfaff's assistant.

In 1902 Materia Medica was separated from Pharmacology. Dr. Tyrode had charge of Pharmacology while Dr. Pfaff gave lectures in Pharmacology and Therapeutics during the second half of the second year. The course was changed again in 1904, with Dr. Pfaff giving one lecture a week in the first half of the third year on General Therapeutics and two lectures a week in the second half of the second year on Pharmacology. Emphasis was given under Dr. Tyrode to practical prescription writing.

An examination took place on the completion of the course in June. This was unsatisfactory from the point of view of both students and instructors who believed that not enough time was allotted to assimilation of such a rich field. In order to overcome this, a separate course in Therapeutics was introduced in the third year, and by 1906 this approach was considered to be sound and successful.

The many changes of the course here, as in the other departments, are understandable because, important as Therapeutics was in treatment, it developed slowly:

> Pharmacology is one of the youngest of the medical sciences; it is, indeed, a growth chiefly of the twentieth century, and in consequence has very little history. Only three discoveries of major importance to pharmacology were made in the nineteenth century—namely, anaesthetics, antiseptics and endocrine therapy . . .[25]

THE HARVARD SOCIAL SERVICE
AT THE MASSACHUSETTS GENERAL HOSPITAL

At its founding, the Massachusetts General Hospital showed a great interest in patients' problems, an interest that has led to a humane attempt to lighten their burdens. To this end, when the Hospital was small the Trustees themselves regularly visited the patients, and, in many instances, they provided comfort beyond the medical care. The doctors and patients of the Hospital were a small family and the troubles of the patients and their diseases were an interest of all.[26] This care extended beyond the period of discharge. The Ladies' Visiting Committee on making friendly rounds not infrequently found a need of assistance and quietly gave it.

The Resident Physician (in this case, Dr. F. A. Washburn) or his associate went to great pains to see that discharged patients were properly escorted to their homes, and that patients who had no home to go to were suitably placed. Administrative problems were handled as well as the Hospital's means and facilities permitted. The problems were not so difficult in the early days, when the population of New England was lower and homogeneous. The standard of living was high, but with unrestricted immigration in the latter part of the nineteenth and the early part of the twentieth centuries, difficulties emerged. Medicine itself changed, owing to the increase in knowledge of the causes and treatment of disease. Treatment with drugs alone was no longer sufficient. What was sometimes required was reeducation in the manner of living, opportunities for a rest and for relief from worries, proper food, and sometimes special diets. It was clear that an organized approach toward the handling of these problems was absolutely necessary.

Dr. Richard C. Cabot, a member of a Boston family widely known for its independent thinking and acting, indicated a weak point in Hospital work, and so it was, in 1905, that he, with the backing of public-spirited men and women, employed two full-time social workers, who, with the help of volunteers, established themselves in the Outpatient Department. The main divisions of work were outlined:

1. Tuberculosis. The proper disposition of cases in hospitals, classes, etc.

2. Hygiene teaching for some of the multitude of cases who need it.

3. Infant feeding and the care of delicate children. Demonstrations and directions to mothers.

4. Vacations and country outings for those who need them as part of their treatment.

5. The care of unmarried girls, pregnant, morally exposed, or feeble-minded.

6. Help for patients needing work or a change of work.

7. Provision for patients "dumped" at the hospital.

8. Assistance to patients needing treatment after discharge from the hospital wards.[27]

This ambitious and sophisticated plan was more than a paper scheme. The history of the service—another first for the Harvard Medical community—will show how fruitful the course of action was to become.

This development was by no means an isolated phenomenon. It was of a piece with the establishment of other evidences of concern for the needs of the unfortunate poor, such as the Home for Little Wanderers, the charitable hospitals, etc. The development of interest in the social aspects of medicine—not as a broad concept but as an approach to the specific problems of individual patients—occurred in the period under discussion here. However, its participation in the teaching of medical students came later, hence will be discussed in detail in the appropriate place.

PSYCHIATRY

The early history of neurology and psychiatry at Harvard is the history of two men, James Jackson Putnam and Morton Prince. Both were of old Boston families, but their preoccupation with mental phenomena did not entitle them to the label "proper Bostonian." Interest in mental phenomena long antedated these two, however, and in fact is to be found in the writings of the most Bostonian of them all, Oliver Wendell Holmes, M.D. Holmes, although not a phrenologist, was phrenologically oriented, as were many others in the Harvard community of his time. Johann Spurzheim, one of the early leaders in phrenology, visited the Harvard commencement in 1832 by special invitation of President Quincy, and when Spurzheim was unfortunate enough to die a few days later (the Commencement collation was blamed by some, probably unjustly), he was given a public funeral at which the Handel and Haydn Society sang an anthem specially composed by one of Boston's leading clergymen. Spurzheim's skull is in the Warren Anatomical Museum at the Medical School. His body is said to rest six miles away in the Mt. Auburn Cemetery in Cambridge, the resting place of Boston's elite. Phrenology was popular in Massachusetts, and the second woman to graduate in medicine in this country, Lydia Folger, a member of the Nantucket family, married L. N. Fowler, America's leading phrenologist.

Concerning Holmes himself, he was very much into discussion of the unconscious mind. In his novel *The Guardian Angel* he wrote: "The best thought, like the most perfect digestion, is done unconsciously." In his Phi Beta Kappa lecture of 1870, he remarked that the unconscious continuous flow of thought was "well illustrated in a certain form of dialogue which seems to be in a measure peculiar to the female sex." His 1871 essay *Mechanism in Thought and Morals* also emphasized unconscious thinking: "We know very little of the contents of our minds until some sudden jar brings them to light." He said that in dreams, "we do battle with ourselves unconscious that we are our own antagonists." He used terms like "latent consciousness," "unconscious cerebration," and "the reflex action of the brain," terms that various of his predecessors invented, as synonymous. Less than a century later Boston's psychoanalysts claimed him as their own. When they admitted him to their pantheon, they thereby avoided a heresy that resembled the one that led to the condemnation of Paul of Samosata, who held that there was a time when Christ was not.

Neuropsychiatry began officially with James Jackson Putnam, who was born in Boston, Massachusetts, in 1846. He came from old New England stock and was a descendant of John Putnam, who emigrated to Salem, Massachusetts prior to 1641. He was graduated by Harvard College in 1866 and the Harvard Medical School in 1870. He held an internship at the Massachusetts General Hospital, following which, he studied neurology in Leipzig, Vienna, and London, but, surprisingly, not in France. After these studies, he returned to Boston and promptly identified himself with the field of nervous diseases. He was Lecturer at the Harvard Medical School in 1874. Putnam served as Professor of Diseases of the Nervous System, 1893–1912, and founded, in 1872, one of the first neurological clinics in the United States at the Massachusetts General Hospital. He developed a neuropathological laboratory in his own house. Putnam was closely attached to Henry P. Bowditch, Professor of Physiology at the Harvard Medical School.

Putnam had a great capacity for work, and his interests were wide. Perhaps one can identify as his most important contribution a study of paresthesia which he published in 1880. This has been described as the first adequate description of a condition which subsequently has become generally recognized. In 1895 he published his first paper on the psychoneuroses. He had a special interest in this branch of neurology throughout the remainder of his life.

James Jackson Putnam published at least two very important public addresses. The first was the Shattuck Lecture for the Massachusetts Medical Society, *Not the Disease Only, but also the Man*, 1899[28]—the physician is a healer of the mind as well as the body. His other famous address dealt with the broader aspects of neurology and was delivered at St. Louis: *The Value of the Physiological Principle in the Study of Neurology* (1904). In his Shattuck Lecture Dr. Putnam chose as the text for his address:

Remember, when you go to see your patients, that it is after all the man, not the disease, that you are called upon to treat.

It is much more common nowadays to voice this sentiment; it was less common in the nineteenth century. In his concluding remarks he emphasized that every physician is an educator whether he intends to be or not and should strive to be a good one. He works with a present objective in view: to cure his patient, to leave him better able to cure himself another time, and to establish systems of treatment that reflect sound and liberal views.

By his very nature, Putnam was an analytical and philosophical man. Undoubtedly, he was greatly influenced by his friends, William James and Josiah Royce. The German school of philosophy appealed to him. He first noticed the work of Sigmund Freud in 1909. Freud's point of view appealed to him. In the last decade of his life, he set about reconciling the views of Freud and the moral purpose of the world.

Putnam was one of the founders, in 1875, of the American Neurological Association and served as its president in 1888. He is principally remembered for his pioneer work in neurology.[29] He contributed important papers to the fields of both structural and functional neurology, frequently in advance of his time. President Lowell of Harvard characterized him at the time of his death as "a man of science, eminent in his field, a philosopher and a saint."

The other important early figure was Morton Prince, who became late in life Associate Professor of Abnormal and Dynamic Psychology at Harvard College. Dr. Prince, as a proper Bostonian, exhibited typical independence of thought and action, which, in the end, at times supported, and at other times nullified, what he was trying to do. In his youth he was an avid sportsman and the originator of various secret societies. Nowadays, he would undoubtedly be called a "swinger."

After graduating from college in 1875, Prince entered the Harvard Medical School. Before long, he had distinguished himself by winning the Boylston Prize with his essay on "The Nature of Mind and Human Automation." This foreshadowed his interests in the years to come. For a while, he worked at the Boston City Hospital and, after receiving his medical degree, departed in 1879 for the traditional grand tour of Europe. On this tour he hoped to receive clinical instrutcion at Vienna and at Strasbourg, but as he said, "I managed not to overdo it." [30]

It is probable that his mother, who suffered from a mysterious neurotic ailment, influenced the later interests of his career. He took his mother to the renowned Master of La Salpetrière, and remained throughout his subsequent life in profound admiration of Jean-Martin Charcot.

His wife, to whom he was married in 1885, also suffered from psychogenic symptoms. Thus Prince, whose early interests were in the prosaic field of otolaryngology, began to specialize in nervous and mental disorders and to embark on a series of startling observations and experiments. In the course of these activities he went far beyond the limits of Charcot's concepts[31] to a preoccupation with unconscious psychic processes.

The course of his career was bolstered further by the influence of William James's paper on automatic writing. In Europe there were the papers of Charcot's great pupil, Pierre Janet, who had published in 1887 his classic studies of hysteria and thus opened that path to the unexplored territory of mental operations. These findings and reflections were significant leads which culminated in Prince's publication, in 1905, of *The Dissociation of a Personality*. This study is based on a single case of a young woman whom Dr. Prince had treated over seven years. The patient, during the course of treatment by means of hypnosis, suggestion, and sedation, displayed eventually two, three, and finally four different personalities. As Otto Marx points out, notwithstanding the great detail presented concerning the patient's action, letters, and stories, the actual treatment embarked on can often only be guessed at.[32] The patient's overall problem is defined in Janet's terms of dissociation, and the goal of therapy was evidently sought in the reintegration of these personalities into one. It is evident that Prince thought this best accomplished through education in traditional terms.

One of Dr. Prince's goals was certainly to arouse public interest in psychopathology. The widespread acceptance by the popular press of the book mentioned is evidence of his success.[33] He was fortunate in attracting the interest of many distinguished individuals who wrote with enthusiasm about his book, not the least of whom was William James. A second edition came out in 1908, and it has been reprinted seven times, the last time in 1957.

Through all of the discussion of *The Dissociation of a Personality*, it became clear to Prince that psychopathology would necessarily have to join with psychology. To this end, Prince worked for the establishment of a clinic in the Department of Psychology at Harvard. In the meantime, he had been serving as Professor of the Diseases of the Nervous System at Tufts University. The clinic and laboratory Prince envisioned found a place in the Department of Abnormal and Dynamic Psychology in Cambridge. He considered this to be the most meaningful accomplishment of his life and the only monument he wanted.

As Henry Murray points out:

Prince's favorite concepts—innate and acquired dispositions, automatisms, complexes and their integrations, conflict and repression, meanings, symbols, root experiences and memories, and finally suggestion (as a therapeutic measure for the reorganization of personality)—were largely derived from other theorists. But he excelled in operationally defining and supporting them through a series of what must have been the most ingenious psychological researches of a fundamental nature ever performed.[34]

In 1914 Prince summed up his investigations to that date and published them in *The Unconscious*. This treatise went far to establish his reputation as the leading experimental psychiatrist in America, possibly in the world.

In examining the scientific contributions of Morton Prince, it is important not to lose sight that although the medical profession as a whole was giving its complete attention to the physical origins of disease, he was almost alone in upholding the theory of psychogenesis, and he was constantly occupied in putting this theory into practice. The validity of the approach was shown by the success of his treatment for many of the ill who came to him.

Many of Dr. Prince's medical colleagues resented and resisisted his concepts as heresy, but gradually as other workers confirmed his views, a fairly wide acceptance occurred, and as Murray points out, he was just about to be accorded a grand place in the sun when his domain of thought was overwhelmed by the libido theory.[35] Freudian psychology taxed him and his views. Prince was unique in his ability to see the good in psychoanalysis and yet to be not wholly overcome by that approach. His psychoanalyst colleagues could scarcely understand a man who, on one hand, supported their efforts but, on the other, continued to criticize their theories and never joined their ranks.[36]

In Prince's most active period he received numerous appointments—for example, Physician for Diseases of the Nervous System, Boston Dispensary; United States Examining Surgeon for Pensions; City Physician of Boston; Physician for Nervous Diseases at the Boston City Hospital; and, in 1902, Professor of Diseases of the Nervous System at Tufts Medical School. In 1914 he became Consulting Physician to the Boston City Hospital. In 1906 he established the *Journal of Abnormal Psychology* and founded the American Psychopathological Association. In 1925 a *Festschrift* was published by his students and colleagues.

Diffuse in his enthusiasms, one can liken him and his professional career to that of Alexander Forbes, who had a similar breadth of interest, with great emphasis on sports. He was not basically a contemplative man. As Murray says: "In his experience there were no dark shadows, no all-pervading skepticisms, no tragic depths, and hence with age he did not ripen to a mellow wisdom, but remained youthful and zealous and experimental and optimistic."[37]

Morton Prince's driving ambition was to make Harvard a great center of psychopathology. His goal was to establish a group who would engage in fundamental research and who would train men to carry it on at other centers. In his seventy-second year he was appointed Associate Professor of Abnormal and Dynamic Psychology at Harvard College.

RADIOLOGY

Radiology in America came into medicine late in the Eliot era, but its development occurred in hospitals rather than in medical schools. Wilhelm Konrad Roentgen (1845–1922) communicated his discovery of a new type of ray to the Würzburg Society December 28, 1895. Roentgen modestly called the new rays X rays, but upon motion of Albrecht von Kölliker they were named Roentgen rays in honor of their discoverer. Kölliker predicted their great usefulness in medicine and surgery.

The application of Roentgen rays to surgery and medicine followed very swiftly on the announcement of their discovery. Not only were they used to diagnose fractures, dislocations and foreign bodies, they were also utilized by the physiologist. Professor H. P. Bowditch of Harvard suggested, in the autumn of 1896, less than a year after their discovery, that the use of Roentgen rays should be helpful in studying gastric motor activities under normal circumstances. Walter B. Cannon, at the beginning of one of the greatest careers in American science, took up Bowditch's suggestion, with the result that he could present classic studies of the movements of the stomach.[38] Cannon's work was presented in May 1897.

In spite of the brilliant introduction of Roentgen rays into clinical medicine and the use of them in a major scientific undertaking, the subsequent scientific use of the rays lagged far behind their clinical application.

At the Boston City Hospital, Dr. Francis H. Williams was given permission to set up an X-ray apparatus in 1896, and he did so despite the difficulties he had in getting the proper apparatus. By 1898 a photographer, Mr. E. E. Fewkes, had been hired to do the technical work. He soon was given an assistant, and the medical staff likewise increased, reaching a total of three physicians by 1905. In this year it was established as an official department. It had begun to use primitive shielding devices before that. By the end of 1905 Dr. Williams had published forty-four papers on various topics, and there were others, chiefly on bone lesions, by F. J. Cotton, F. B. Lund, and others. Some papers on treatment were also published by Dr. Williams.

At the Massachusetts General Hospital it was Walter J. Dodd, the Hospital's pharmacist and photographer, who, after Roentgen's announcement, began to experiment and to gather together equipment for the production of X rays. In the beginning he met with constant failure, but in March 1896, with the help of the Hospital's assistant pharmacist, Joseph Godsoe, he succeeded. Power was generated by the hand-cranked Holtz static machine, a machine that, remarkably enough, had been used to give electrical shocks for nerve disorders.

Before long, Dodd was able to obtain an induction coil for the production of X rays from the General Electric Company. This apparatus was demonstrated during the 50th anniversary of the celebration of Ether Day. It was a resounding success, so much so that the Trustees donated enough money to purchase a coil. The apparatus was moved from the brick corridor near the pharmacy to the space beneath the Bulfinch steps. Dodd continued to carry out experiments with various tubes. His usual method of testing was a deadly one: fluoroscopy of one's hand until a satisfactory image was obtained.

As early as 1897 Dodd had already developed dermatitis, produced by the X-rays, that was severe enough to require hospitalization. This was followed by a series of hospital admissions and operations for the next nineteen years. By 1902 it was necessary to amputate a part of a finger to remove a carcinoma. The fingers were removed bit by bit during some fifty operations. By 1900 it was apparent that lead shielding was necessary to protect the operator from radiation. In 1901 Dodd finally constructed a machine which, for the first time, gave satisfactory results. By 1904 systematic fluoroscopy was under way.

Some critics described radiology as merely a new photogrpahy. It was easy to see how such a denigration occurred: radiographs were usually made by physicians who had a hobby of photography. Dodd very early appreciated that he never would be considered on a par with his medical colleagues as long as he remained the Hospital's photographer, so in 1900 he entered the Harvard Medical School (though he left it after one year). He was constantly being asked to help with problems at the Hospital. He finally received the degree of Doctor of Medicine in 1908 from the University of Vermont and then received the title of Roentgenologist at the Massachusetts General Hospital, the Department of Roentgenology being finally established in the same year. Dodd went to France in 1915 with the first Harvard Medical Unit, where he was sought out as a specialist in handling X-ray machines. He died December 18, 1916, from metastatic carcinoma. Over his grave in the Mount Auburn Cemetery is the phrase, "Pioneer Roentgenologist and Martyr to Humanity."

Presumably, the students at the two hospitals saw some of the pictures in conjunction with their case studies, but there was no attempt to formalize instruction in roentgenology for many years.

Chapter Seven

The Era Ends—Brilliantly

W HEN John Warren, Benjamin Waterhouse, and Aaron Dexter were installed as
the Medical Faculty of Harvard, they had
few books, no collections, no hospital. They
began to lecture in some small rooms in the basement of Harvard Hall
and soon moved to Holden Chapel.

When the North Grove Street building was erected in 1847, it contained one small laboratory (for anatomy). At the one hundredth anniversary, a third of a century later, student laboratories were available for
each of the fundamental subjects—anatomy, physiology, chemistry, histology, and pathology. The Faculty had grown to 47: 10 professors, 6
assistant professors, 9 instructors, 13 clinical instructors, and 9 assistants,
working in the fine new building on Boylston Street, with laboratories,
dispensaries, and hospitals. These were the early friuts of the Eliot era.

Eliot recounts that there was

a grave question whether the profession, the community, and the
young men who, year by year, aspire to become physicians and surgeons, would support the Faculty in making these improvements. The
answer can now be recorded. The School has received by gift and
bequest three hundred and twenty thousand dollars in ten years; it
has secured itself in the centre of the city for many years to come, by
the timely purchase of a large piece of land; it has paid about two
hundred and twenty thousand dollars for a spacious, durable, and
well-arranged building; it has increased its annual expenditure for
salaries of teachers from twenty thousand dollars, in 1871–72, to
thirty-six thousand dollars, in 1882–83; its receipts have exceeded its
expenses in every year since 1871–72, and its invested funds now ex-
ceed those of 1871 by more than one hundred thousand dollars. At
the same time, the School has become a centre of chemical, histological,
and sanitary research, as well as a place for thorough instruction; its
students bring to the School a better education than ever before; they
work longer and harder while in the School, and leave it prepared, so
far as sound training can prepare them, to enter, not the overcrowded

lower ranks of the profession, but the higher, where there is always room.[1]

The chief act of celebration of the one hundredth anniversary was a long lecture by Oliver Wendell Holmes, erstwhile Professor of Anatomy, in which he reviewed the preceding one hundred years. Perhaps the task was imposed on him. Although the address contains useful lists of texts studied, discerning comments on the Faculty, and description of advances in medical care over the century just closed, it is devoid of any sparkle so characteristic of Holmes's usual writing—altogether a pedestrian account. President Eliot came off better in his brief remarks on this occasion.

The Boylston Street building was occupied in 1883 with suitable exercises to mark the 100th Anniversary of the founding of the Harvard Medical School. Along with these brave activities, the Corporation appointed Henry Pickering Bowditch as Dean. Thus a great milestone— not everywhere recognized at the time as such—was passed on the road to excellence. Heretofore, the Deans had been drawn from the clinic, but now a scholar was chosen to guide the developing institution, a man whose interests and abilities were scientific. The Faculty had been educated to the realities and needs of scientific medicine, where mechanisms, where studies of cause, where deviations from normal were of primary interest, rather than treatment of disease. A half century or so was to pass before the concidence, at times, of the two areas was to be evident.[2]

Notwithstanding the poor general state of the Medical School, some great men had been present. This was a time for homage to the great names of the past, honor through named professorships: Henry Willard Williams Clinical Professor of Ophthalmology, W. H. Baker Professor of Gynecology, James Jackson Putnam Professor of Neurology, Thomas Morgan Rotch Professor of Pediatrics, and the J. B. and Buckminster Brown Professor of Orthopedics. Then there was, as already mentioned, the Parkman Professorship of Anatomy and the Hersey Professorship of Anatomy and Surgery (1782, with title and endowment coming in 1791). The first two Warrens held the latter chair until 1847. On that date the word "Surgery" was omitted and the chair moved to Cambridge, to the Department of Comparative Anatomy, with Jeffries Wyman the occupant. In 1866 the Medical Faculty regretted that they had allowed the Hersey endowment to slip through their fingers. They insisted that the fund had always been intended for the Medical School. The Corporation, not always noted for its Solomon-like decisions, in this case came through and directed that Professor Wyman be added to the *Medical* Faculty. At the next appointment the chair reverted to the College. (Only one familiar with academic politics can surmise what machinations went into these changes.) The Hersey Professorship of the Theory and Practice of Physic remained in the Medical School. The Jackson Professorship of Clinical Medicine was created, as was the Shattuck Professorship of Pathological Anatomy and the John Homans Professorship of Surgery. The Fabyan Professorship of Comparative Pathology was also established at the Medical School, although its locus of action was elsewhere.

The James Stillman Chair of Comparative Anatomy (1902) was founded for Charles S. Minot. The Chair of Comparative Physiology was founded for W. T. Porter, and the Professorship of Biological Chemistry for Otto Folin. The latter was soon endowed to honor Hamilton Kuhn.

In furtherance of President Eliot's interest, the Medical Faculty proposed the creation of a School of Veterinary Medicine. This was done in 1882, but its life span was brief. Notwithstanding the valiant efforts of its Dean, Charles P. Lyman, the School languished, apparently for lack of sustaining interest. It expired in 1901. The Dental School was hardier; founded in 1867 as a separate department of the University, it had an arrangement with the Medical School whereby some instruction of the dental students was provided by the Medical School.

When it became evident that the overcrowded Boylston Street building would no longer suffice, plans were made for a move to Longwood Avenue. As in past moves, the problem was how to meet the cost. When, in 1898, the University recognized the Medical School's need, unrestricted University funds were for the first time assigned to the Medical School.[3] The new move was, from a financial point of view, frightening. A large tract of land had to be bought, some 23 acres. This was done in the hope that the several hospitals would also build there and create a great medical center, where the School would control the higher positions.

As usual in the growth of the School, a Warren was a motivating force, in this case, J. Collins Warren, great-grandson of the Founder. Associated with him was Henry Pickering Bowditch. The bold plan was theirs. Bowditch had given up the Deanship in 1893 but still retained the Professorship of Physiology. Warren was the Moseley Professor of Surgery. Eliot's guiding hand was there from the beginning, which took place at an informal meeting held in J. Collins Warren's house on Beacon Hill. In addition to the President and Warren, several members of the Corporation and Professors of the Medical School were present. There is something awe-inspiring in the un-Bostonian devil-may-care determination of Warren and Bowditch to proceed with this multimillion-dollar project despite the lack of funds. It is no wonder that the usually intrepid Eliot had doubts.

It is evident from a study of the history of this period that the expectation was that a University Hospital would be erected there. (The fact that it was not did not in the least deter the celebrated Harvey Cushing and his successor, Elliott C. Cutler, from promoting the view that the Peter Bent Brigham Hospital was indeed the envisoned University hospital. To this day, the Harvard Medical School has no hospital—unless one counts the Huntington, a hospital that exists on paper and is encompassed by the Massachusetts General Hospital complex. Rather, the Harvard Medical School is served by affiliated hospitals, as will be discussed later.)

The Brigham brothers, Robert Breck and Peter Bent, saved the day: They had left funds that were to accumulate for twenty-five years and then were to be used to establish two hospitals, one for general purposes and the other for chronic diseases, specifically for "the suffering poor of Suffolk County," an instruction not precisely followed in the ensuing years. The Warren-Bowditch combination saw in the Brighams a means of getting their proposed University Hospital for free—as far as they were concerned.

It was Bowditch who was instrumental in obtaining the land for the School and the neighboring hospitals. It was he who initiated the construction of the white marble quadrangle with his friend, John Collins Warren. As Cannon has put it, this was "a monument to the vision and faith and devoted efforts of these lifelong companions."[4]

A member of the Corporation, Henry Lee Higginson, ever the public servant, formed a syndicate to buy the land for the Medical School. Unfortunately, in the view of many, the Francis estate in Roxbury was considered the most desirable, even though this meant a permanent and quite unnecessary cleavage of the Medical School from the University. Other earlier acts in that direction could have been rectified, but not so after this decision. The die was cast: the Medical School was to be forever separated.

That irresistible pair, Warren and Bowditch, went right ahead with their plans just as though the money to execute them was on hand. A five-unit building was sketched and shown to J. Pierpont Morgan. On Commencement Day, 1900, President Eliot read Morgan's cablegram from London. He had agreed to build the three central units in memory of his father, Junius Spencer Morgan, "a native of Massachusetts." At about this same time, John D. Rockefeller, Jr., was approached. With customary thoroughness, he sent an agent to Boston to examine the plans. A thirty-page report said, in essence, "I am satisfied that Harvard is an institution well qualified to manage a large Medical School and to do the best grade of work." The famous Dr. W. H. Welch of the Johns Hopkins Medical School assured Mr. Rockefeller that major support for

Harvard would in no way interfere with the activities of the newly established Rockefeller Institute and might abet them. A further large gift sufficient to take care of the cost of the remaining building was made by Mrs. Collis P. Huntington, to match an equal Rockefeller gift. Thus the completion of the new Medical School was assured.

It was dedicated in September 1906 by President Eliot.

> I devote these buildings, and their successors in coming time, to the teaching of the medical and surgical arts which combat disease and death, alleviate injuries, and defend and assure private and public health, and to the pursuit of the biological and medical sciences on which depends all progress in the medical and surgical arts and in preventive medicine.
>
> I solemnly dedicate them to the service of individual man and of human society, and invoke upon them the favor of men and the blessing of God.[5]

At the time of the move into the Longwood Avenue buildings, Dr. William L. Richardson had been Dean. He resigned and was succeeded as Dean of the Medical Faculty by Dr. Henry A. Christian. By this act another tradition was broken. The election of Christian as Dean and simultaneously as Hersey Professor of the Theory and Practice of Physic was the first time an outsider, that is, one whose early training was not at Harvard, had been given the Deanship. It was done in a deliberate effort to broaden Harvard's vision, an effort to overcome the provincialism of the early years.

These years were marked by difficulties. The 1901 decision to require a bachelor's degree prior to admission to the Harvard Medical School exacted a considerable financial hardship: it resulted in fewer students and decreased income from fees. Transportation was a problem, too. The Peter Bent Brigham Hospital was not yet built, and much of the clinical instruction took place at the distant Massachusetts General Hospital or Boston City Hospital. In those essentially pre-automobile days, much time was wasted in transportation. Some help was obtained by the development of an Outpatient Department in a School building, which functioned until the Peter Bent Brigham was opened.

Once more the wisdom of President Eliot and his successor (in 1909), A. Lawrence Lowell, successfully carried the institution safely over what might have been a hazardous question of principle. Mr. Lowell faced up to it in his first annual report.

> The relations between the Medical School and the Peter Bent Brigham Hospital have at last been placed upon a basis wholly satisfacfory to both institutions. The University has no desire to manage the Hos-

pital, nor have the Trustees of the latter an ambition to manage the School. But it is essential to the efficiency of a Medical School that its clinical instructors should have positions in hospitals, and hence an eminent surgeon or physician cannot be called from a distance to a chair in the School unless he can be offered at the same time a clinic in a hospital. This is impossible unless the appointments in both institutions are made jointly. On the other hand, the Trutees of the Hospital believe that the welfare of their patients will be promoted by having at their disposal the scientific resources of a great school, and by the ability to call to their service the best man from any part of the country by a joint offer of a chair and a clinic. The two institutions are convinced, therefore, that the interests under their charge coincide, and can be attained only by an unbroken mutual understanding in the matter of appointments.[6]

In 1908 the Massachusetts General Hospital had worked out a joint relationship with the University: F. C. Shattuck, who held the Jackson Professorship of Clinical Medicine, was placed in continuous charge of the Hospital's general medical wards. Other professorships followed this pattern. The Children's Hospital soon followed suit. The pattern was well set by the time the Brigham was completed in 1912. The practice has been widely followed throughout the country, and what had loomed as a difficult teaching problem was resolved to Eliot's satisfaction.

In 1905 or '06 the Surgical Division was provided with a laboratory in the newly constructed David Sears Building in the Quadrangle. Seven rooms, set aside for this purpose, consisted of one large laboratory and a small operating room, with a library and secretary's room across the hall. The large laboratory was well equipped for pathological studies, and the operating room provided the essentials to make possible aseptic surgery. A department library was provided to serve as a meeting place for members of the Surgical Division. Records of this department were kept in the secretary's room, which could also be used by an artist. The management of the Surgical Laboratory, while under the Professor of Surgery, was in the hands of a Committee on Surgical Research. It is clear that by the beginning of the twentieth century, widespread recognition was given to the importance of surgical research. Qualified undergraduates or graduate students were allowed to investigate surgical problems whether in pathology or operative surgery.

The Laboratory of Surgical Pathology, under the charge of the Assistant Professor of Surgical Pathology, was also admirably equipped. It was in the Collis P. Huntington Building, now torn down. In this laboratory there were special rooms for the Director and his assistant and rooms for special investigation, which included an excellently equipped operating room as well as space for an artist and secretary.

The accommodations for operative surgery were in the Anatomical Building. Here there was one large operating room, large enough for six tables, and another with four tables. An Instrument Room was provided with a room for the prosector and another for the instructors. Two large rooms in the Administrative Building were devoted to the course in Surgical Technique; the necessary appliances were present with thirty models for bandaging; benches with the necessary tools for the construction of metal and wooden splints were provided, as were conveniences for the application of plaster of Paris dressings and a storeroom for materials used in the course.

The previous crushing space shortage suffered by the Department of Physiology was widely recognized, and in 1906 it was planned that one half of the Collis P. Huntington Laboratories would be assigned to this department, a great change from the small corner of the Physiology Laboratory on Boylston Street, where work was unofficially undertaken by the permission of Professor H. P. Bowditch.

Concerning histology and embryology, no serious attention could be given to training in the technique of section-cutting, owing to the crowded condition of the laboratory in the old building. This situation was considerably ameliorated by the move into the white marble Quadrangle. Students were then expected to be able to make preparations for themselves, with the thought that they would be capable of using them in independent work.

The increase in space also benefited the Pathology Department, which moved into the Huntington Building. The fittings were elaborate. Professor Mallory related that the "only criticism that can be made in regard to the arrangements in the new buildings is that it is unfortunate that it has seemed advisable to place the pathology collection in the Warren Anatomical Museum, which is so far distant from the Pathology Building."

The new space also made it desirable to extend teaching in new directions—for example, roentgenology. An X-ray laboratory was placed in four rooms in the basement of the Administration Building. The equipment consisted of a static machine, simple induction apparatus, and a high-frequency apparatus. A dark room for the development of photographic prints was provided.

In the X-ray laboratory two kinds of teaching were carried on. First, routine instruction was given to every student. The aim was that each student who graduated from the Medical School should at least understand the general theory of the production of X-rays, the method of taking an X-ray picture, and the practical uses, dangers, and fallacies of

X-ray work in medicine and surgery. It is regrettable that there was far too little appreciation of the dangers present. Professor Walter B. Cannon suffered throughout the latter years of his career from early X-ray injuries, especially of his hands. The plan was also to provide all graduates who were competent the possibility of carrying out original investigations. This was done in the hope that able men would thus take up the X-ray field as a specialty. All this only a few years after the discovery of X rays.

Thus the closing of the Eliot era was marked by the creation of a locus that not only housed the greatly expanded activities of the Harvard Medical School but also provided for maintaining a forward-looking stance with respect to new developments. When Eliot retired as President of Harvard, he could look upon his role in the phenomenal development of Harvard medicine with satisfaction, if not pride.

He died in 1926. It is ironic that the time of his death almost coincided with that of Rudolph Valentino, a motion-picture actor. They were given equal space and position on the front page of the *Boston Evening Transcript* for the 23rd of August—thus a commentary on prevailing values.

Throughout his presidency, Eliot had maintained a keen interest in social and political as well as educational affairs, but it was in his retirement that the true stature of this great man could be seen. He became, as William Allan Neilson said, to a remarkable degree the giver of counsel to the nation at large. He has been linked with Emerson and Lincoln as a benefactor of his time and nation.[7] We remember him best as the man who guided the Harvard Medical School through its difficult adolescence into its confident adulthood.

What of the future? Everything seemed to foretell a period of brilliant performance and growth in the new century. Other changes would also occur. The appointments to high position of Drs. Theobald Smith and Henry Christian, men with no roots in the great Boston medical families, was the trickle that was later to wash away the dam of family influence in the destinies of the School. Another seemingly small phenomenon was the growing tendency of the Faculty to go to Germany, Austria, and England for advanced training, thereby lessening the French influence on the School. In time this was to have great consequences also.

Part III

The Great White Quadrangle: From 1906

Chapter Eight

Changing Harvard, The Flexner Report,

and the Emergence of New Leadership

THE move to the Great White (Longwood Avenue) Quadrangle was celebrated in speech and writing, all of it inspired and hopeful and most of it glaringly inaccurate in its failure to appreciate in any detail the substance of the great years to come. These great years were basically the expression of Harvard's unusual resources, both spiritual and intellectual. The form that the greatness was to take was determined largely by the leadership of one man, David Linn Edsall, Dean of the Harvard Medical School for eighteen crucial years.

The years were crucial for several reasons. Harvard was ceasing to be the creature of a small number of (interrelated) Boston medical families, which, however highly motivated, were inevitably dedicated to preserving their own world—because it clearly was the best of all worlds. The introduction of new ideas and approaches was becoming more important. It was essential, however, that the change come about without destroying the qualities that made Harvard great, if unwilling to perform on a national stage.

There was a growing awareness in Boston of the increase in the importance of German medicine, and these Germanic elements would have to be engrafted on the then predominantly French influence. Most of today's readers are unaware of the situation in European medicine up to the middle of the nineteenth century. French medicine dominated medical thinking and teaching. However great that French pathology and other basic subjects were, they were nevertheless considered as no more than handmaidens to clinical medicine.[1] This school of thought was established in Dublin, where Robert Graves, Caleb Parry, William Stokes, Robert Adams, John Cheyne, and Sir Dominic Corrigan became the leaders; in London, with Thomas Hodgkin and Richard Bright; and even in Edinburgh, although it had maintained its ties with the declining Leyden. The Parisian influence extended to Vienna, where the "New Viennese School" developed, to supersede the old school established by Maria

Theresa when she bought most of Leyden's faculty after the death of the great Hermann Boerhaave.

At around mid-century, however, another approach began to develop, this time in Germany. It held that the only rational approach to medicine was through the basic experimental sciences, especially physiology. The movement was given status by the authority of Johannes Müller, a magnificent physiologist and teacher. Three newly established journals indicated the situation by their names: *Archives for Physiologic Healing, Journal for Rational Medicine,* and *Archives for Pathological Anatomy and Pathological Physiology and for Clinical Medicine.* German views of the nature of medicine and the development later of the German Ph.D. programs, with their emphasis on huge amounts of data on some narrow subject, began to change the thinking about medicine in America.

Hence in Boston two basic changes were imminent, and the success with which they came about would necessarily depend on the leadership available. Fortunately for Harvard and the medical world in general, superior leadership was standing ready in the wings. Nevertheless, the shift from the old to the new was beset with difficulties. There was, naturally, resistance to change. The new ideas were not only revolutionary, but also highly expensive. And in a curiously American way the issues were to become clouded by the less-than-responsible clamor in the lay press in support of a *Noble Experiment.* It was outlined in the now historic Flexner Report, a document praised by many but scrutinized by few. Harvard could not ignore the Report, although it could not accept whatever of its major recommendations it had not already put into force decades previously. David Edsall's unshaken conviction of the inadequacies of the Report permitted him to lead Harvard to continued and expanded greatness along lines determined more by its traditional values than by the uproar of a sensation-seeking lay press. Accordingly, the first part of this section will show why the Report did not and could not have any primary effect on Harvard's development.

There seems today to be a view widely held that the reform in medical education initiated by the Flexner Report was the first serious effort of the kind.[2] As a matter of fact, it was the third. Charles William Eliot, President of Harvard University, labored with great success for forty-one years before the appearance of the Flexner Report to correct the inadequacies of medical education at Harvard and, by example, in all American medical schools. But his efforts had only local authority, and their effects were not widely recognized in the early years.

Secondly, the American Medical Association had realized that medical education in America needed study and improvement. To this end the American Medical Association, in 1902, appointed a committee to study the problems of medical education in this country and to make recommendations concerning them. In 1904 the Council on Medical Education of the American Medical Association was created.[3] Dr. Arthur Dean Bevan was its first chairman.

A report of the Council made in 1905 showed that only five of the 155 medical schools then existing in the United States and Canada required two or more years of college training prior to beginning medical studies: Johns Hopkins Medical School, from its establishment in 1893, required a college degree before medical training could start. Harvard was moving in that direction. In 1909, the year Flexner made his inspections, sixty out of sixty-two members of the Harvard class entered that year with college degrees. The Harvard students were well prepared by any standards.

The Council collected information and separated the schools into four groups according to the success of their students in passing state board examinations. This was apparently the first attempt made in America to rank graduate activities on a qualitative basis, although it seems to have been more quantitative than qualitative. Dr. Bevan and colleagues went in for increasingly elaborate schemes of data collection. At the meeting held in Chicago, on April 29, 1907, a progress report was given and the need for further study was discussed.

It was Dr. Bevan's hope that Henry S. Pritchett, President of the Carnegie Foundation, might be interested in supporting such an inquiry. Pritchett insisted that the subject was not basically a medical problem but a broadly educational one. In 1908 he recommended to the Executive Committee of the Carnegie Foundation that it undertake studies of medical, legal, engineering, and theological education. Pritchett singled out Abraham Flexner as his choice for the planned study of medical education.[4] The result was the famous Flexner Report, published in 1910. Pritchett wrote in 1913, "Credit for the progress achieved in the field of medical education in the United States belongs in the first instance to the American Medical Association and its Council on Medical Education."[5] With the abandon of the dogmatist, he passed over the forty-one years of successful labor to improve medical education carried out under President Eliot by the Harvard Faculty.

Flexner spent the year of 1910 studying European medical schools. About this time Frederick T. Gates, principal adviser in business and philanthropy of John D. Rockefeller and later one of the original trustees of the Rockefeller Foundation, named in the act of incorporation, invited him to lunch, and during it said abruptly, "What would you do if you had a million dollars with which to make a start in reorganizing medical education in the United States?"[6] Flexner's retort was to the general effect that any funds could be most wisely spent in developing the Johns Hopkins Medical School. This was, to say the least, tactful, since

Gates was a close friend and admirer of Dr. William H. Welch, Dean of that institution. In the fall of 1913 a sum was voted by the Rockefeller Foundation which would provide a yearly income of $65,000 to the Johns Hopkins Medical School for "full-time" clinical teaching departments.

Flexner visited every one of the 155 medical schools then active in the United States and Canada. In order to overcome any possible handicap by his layman's status, he studied with care the reports of the Council on Medical Education of the American Medical Association and had many conferences with Dr. Bevan and his associate, Dr. N. P. Colwell, who had been visiting medical schools year after year with the hope of stimulating improvement in their own ways. Flexner then spent a considerable amount of time at the Johns Hopkins Medical School and the Rockefeller Institute for Medical Research. He very early chose the Hopkins School as a model. One guess as to why might be that he found the firmly established German tradition there sympathetic. If that is so, it is easy to understand why he was blind to the advances made during Harvard's experience with the French influence. Another likely reason might be the influence of Flexner's famous brother, Simon, a well-known medical scientist who had much the same approach to medical affairs.

From time to time in his excursions around the country, Flexner returned to New York to report to President Pritchett. What Flexner calls *Bulletin No. 4,* "which Dr. Pritchett characterized in a letter to me shortly before his death as the most important educational report of the period judged by what it accomplished . . . was a candid and absolutely accurate summation of the conditions in every medical college in the United states and Canada."[7] The words "by an opinionated layman enamored of the German Ph.D. tradition" should perhaps be added. Flexner summarized the results of his observations in the first part of the *Bulletin* (published in June 1910), and "created a tremendous furor." In the second part of the *Bulletin*, he "dissected the institutions state by state, school by school, giving names and places."[8] Pritchett wrote an "urbane" introduction. "The press of the country did the rest. It accepted the report and Pritchett's recommendations as true and in news columns and editorials denounced the prevailing system. The schools tried vainly to excuse or explain the situation. No one listened to them. In a short time, resentment subsided."

The 155 schools in 1901 were by 1943 reduced to about 60, largely because of the findings of the AMA Council. Subsequently, hundreds of millions of dollars were obtained for the reorganization of the surviving schools, and here the propagandistic writings of Flexner carried great weight.

If America now [1943] holds the first place in the world of medical education [Flexner generously concludes], the credit is due to four great leaders: President Eliot, who from his inauguration in 1869 was interested in the medical school and who had already provided at Harvard splendid laboratories for work in the underlying medical sciences; President Gilman of Johns Hopkins, who from the day he was called to Baltimore in 1873 conceived of the medical school, laboratories and clinics alike, as scientific faculties made up, like the faculty of arts and sciences, of the best talent to be found anywhere in the world; Dr. Welch, who shared Gilman's ideals and knew who and where the men were who should constitute the original faculty of the Johns Hopkins Medical School; and finally Dr. Pritchett, the layman, who comprehended the idea when it was presented to him and who had the courage to pursue a straight course, who enlightened both laymen and the profession, and who in all this won friends for himself and the cause.[9]

It is evident from the context that Flexner had in mind a fifth great leader—himself—but modesty, for once, had the upper hand. It is worthy of note that he credits Eliot only with providing laboratories, Gilman and Welch with making medicine scientific (apparently meant in a technical and not a procedural sense), and Pritchett with favoring this approach.

Pritchett recognized very well, and so did Flexner, that an important shortcoming of their study was that they had no adequate measuring stick with which they could decide the kind of institutions that should have a share of Mr. Carnegie's benefactions. Although the standards of the New York State Board of Regents were adopted, it was plain that this test was in effect quantitative and not qualitative. Gradually, the course was steered in the direction of qualitative test values.

From vague personal reports it is evident, and not surprising, that the Flexner Report evoked considerable annoyance at Harvard, but no documentary evidence for this reaction can be found. A diligent search in many places—the Minutes of the Meetings of the Faculty of Medicine, the Minutes of the Administrative Board, the Countway Library Archives, the Widener Archives at Harvard College, the Minutes of the Harvard Corporation, in correspondence of President A. Lawrence Lowell—has not turned up a single word about the Flexner Report. In fact, this was appropriate, for the Report had little relevance to Harvard. Some years later, when David Edsall was Dean at Harvard, he commented on the furor caused by the Report everywhere but at Harvard (below p. 194).

The docket for the Faculty of Medicine in its meeting of February 4, 1911, contained a report of the Committee to consider means of lessening the rigidity of the medical curriculum. It is possible that it was stimulated by the Flexner Report, but this seems unlikely, as evidenced by the fact that Hopkins, whose Flexnerian ideas about what medicine should be exceeded Harvard in rigidity, continued its same course for years to come.

Here and there, other changes were introduced which may or may not have been evoked by the Flexner Report but which continued policies that had long been recognized at Harvard. For example, in the February 26, 1913, Report of the Overseers Committee to Visit the Medical and Dental Schools, the statement is made that

> ... great development of the laboratory departments of the medical schools in this country has been a marked feature of the last two decades of progress. Clinical teaching, although greatly elaborated and varied in character and better adapted to the students' needs, has remained upon what might be termed an amateur basis. It is only quite recently that medical teaching bodies have come to the full realization of the fact that clinical instruction must be placed, like laboratory instruction, on an academic basis.[10]

The Committee pointed out the need for a large sum of money to place the clinical departments of the Medical School on an equal footing with the laboratory departments. An additional endowment of $1,500,000 would be needed, it was estimated, first, to pay University salaries to clinical professors who had given a large part of their time to University work, and second, to provide for assistants who would devote all of their time to teaching, clinical work, and investigation in the laboratories and hospitals for a period of five years. It is doubtful, though possible, that this recommendation of the Overseers' Committee was activated by the Flexner Report. More likely, it reflected the natural growth and development of the Harvard Medical School.

Flexner's Report, *Medical Education in the United States and Canada*, is justly famed but is clearly biased in favor of the Johns Hopkins Medical School, which he calls "the first medical school in America of genuine university type."[11] That sweeping and erroneous claim has often been asserted, before and since the Report, but the notion is conclusively refuted by the evidence Flexner himself published on the two schools. It is evident that Johns Hopkins and Harvard were the two best schools, although each arrived at that position by a different route. Flexner praised one route enthusiastically and ignored the other, which did not coincide with his fervent and narrow views about medical education. The present work is not intended as a history of the Hopkins, however, and we comment only to emphasize the uniqueness of Harvard's approach.

University control of the Medical School had been a goal of President Eliot from the beginning of his tenure in 1869, but "he was anticipated," according to Flexner, by the establishment in 1893 of the Johns Hopkins Medical School, which required a bachelor's degree. Flexner goes in for some fine hair splitting here: In Harvard's first-year class at the time of Flexner's visit (October 1909), sixty of sixty-two of those who entered possessed a bachelor's degree. (It is ironic that today efforts are made to do away with the requirement.)

Harvard was not and is not troubled by the lack of a university hospital: there was and is no lack of clinical material. From very early years the Harvard system of affiliated hospitals has been a great boon. Flexner seems to have misunderstood the situation. He says, "But the conditions to which [those without university hospitals] submit in order to gain access to it at all, though varying somewhat from place to place, are alike fatal to freedom and continuity of pedagogic policy."[12]

He extolls the clinical success of the Germans "in proving that freedom is the very life-breath of scientific progress—freedom on the part of the university to choose its own teachers, finding them where it may; freedom on the part of the teachers to strike out along whatever path they please."[13] These lyrical and inspiring thoughts are more indicative of Flexner's state of mind than of the character of the institutions he was writing about. However accurately the words represent the situation at the Germanic universities, they totally misrepresent what prevailed at the Germanic university medical schools. Here whatever freedom there was resided only in the heads of departments. Their subordinates were never the senior authors of their own papers and often were not permitted to add their names to that of the professor at the head. Subordinates were not permitted to have ideas—they could only dutifully express those of the head man. If there was any striking out along a new path, the path quickly led to the outside of the school.

There was some correspondence—a half-dozen letters—between President Lowell and Dr. Flexner, in which they argued the merits of a classical versus a scientific preparation for the study of medicine. Flexner held to the importance of a scientific training as a basis for medical study. From a letter of Flexner to Lowell, October 18, 1911:

> The medical student has at the very least to be trained in the following branches: physics, chemistry, biology, anatomy, physiology, pharmacology, bacteriology, pathology, internal medicine, surgery, gynecology, obstetrics, dermatology, pediatrics, ophthalmology, psychiatry,

hygiene, legal medicine, etc. He has fours years in which to get the absolutely essential rudiments and interrelations of these topics. If the two years of college, probably all that can be generally counted on, are to be given mainly to Latin and Greek, then all the subjects named must go into the medical curriculum. This involves an utter impossibility. Part of the burden has got to be anticipated. That appears to me to settle the question as to whether the student is to do the classics or the sciences in college.

Flexner seems to have won this round, yet today many medical educators believe that a nonscientific interest at the college level, with a minimum of scientific courses, is to be preferred, and in a remarkable paper given in 1936 and received with almost total neglect, one of the greatest medical scientists this country or any other has ever produced, L. J. Henderson, warned about regarding medicine as a branch or a kind of science. He preferred to regard it as a branch of sociology.

Lawrence S. Kubie was well acquainted with Abraham Flexner. On the basis of published material and personal discussions with Dr. Kubie, it seems clear that Flexner had three major goals in mind: (1) an increase in preclinical research in the field of human biology, (2) greater sophistication in clinical research, and (3) better teaching and training in clinical medicine. He believed that the route to these goals was through the full-time system in medical education.[14] It was believed that under that system the full-time clinicians, like full-time basic scientists, would not have to do their teaching and research with left-over time and energy. Kubie believes that it is precisely here that the full-time system has failed, as Henderson predicted it would.[15] Although it led to some reduction in the pressures of private practice, other demands took over, such as committee work, so that the full-time professor was in actuality still a part-time clinician. Kubie quotes a sardonic comment that "the difference between the full-time professor of medicine and the part-time clinical professor is that the full-time professor is away full-time, whereas the part-time professor is away only part-time." Thus the "full-time absences of the full-time faculty have shortchanged students . . ."

The full-time clinical system is responsible for another major shortcoming: to an increasing extent, full-time clinical research and clinical teaching have passed into the control of inexperienced beginners—a disastrous situation. One can see common evidence that preclinical scientists very often dominate school policy, the dominant role having passed from the clinician to the "preclinical medical scientists." Kubie believes that "This unbalanced domination of medical school policies by the preclinical faculty has been complicated still further by the failure of the preclinical scientist to understand the complex nature of clinical maturity . . ."[16]

Kubie also believes that the force of the full-time system has failed in three ways: (1) the original intention was that establishment of the full-time system would create opportunities not for the novice but for mature and experienced clinicians, freed from the burdens of private practice; (2) the goal was that the mature clinician and his behavior toward patients would represent an ideal relationship between the two; and (3) withdrawal from private practice, it was hoped, would make it possible for the full-time clinician to have time to exercise his mature clinical judgment in the choice of significant clinical problems for study. This did not happen. The result has been that under the full-time system clinical chairs are often filled by clinically inexperienced young men. Although they may have shown promise in various fields of preclinical research, they have had, too often, no adequate clinical experience to prepare them for their clinical chairmanships.

> In short, by plucking pre-clinical scientists out of their pre-clinical laboratories and placing them in charge of clinical departments, the full-time system has stunted many promising careers in the pre-clinical sciences, while at the same time re-enforcing in our medical culture that very clinical traditionalism from which it was supposed to free us.[17]

W. H. Welch engrafted a rigid full-time system on the Hopkins over the bitter opposition, in his active years, of Sir William Osler, among others. Osler, one of the greatest clinicians of this era, left Johns Hopkins to become Regius Professor at Oxford. (However, he later came to agree with Welch's ideas.)

Many kinds of tests can be leveled at medical schools. One such is recognition by the Nobel Committee: Six faculty members of the Harvard Medical School, half of them clinicians, have shared in three Nobel Prizes; at the Johns Hopkins, none while there. This hardly supports the idea of scholarly blessings envisioned under the full-time system.

In the end, it matters very little who achieved leadership in the reform of medical education in this country—Eliot, the American Medical Association, or Flexner. The fact is that essential reform did come, and with far-ranging benefit to the medical establishment in this country and in other countries. There is honor enough for many. What is important is that the Eliot reform strengthened medicine and the Flexner reform deformed it. Today's criticism of the shortsightedness of government agencies that spend billions to support research at medical schools and zero to support clinical teaching is not warranted. The blame lies not with these agencies but with the Flexnerian educators who told them what to do. Today's medicine, which many find irrelevant to patients' needs, is the fruit of Flexner's report. This was not the first time, nor will it be the last, that medical educational policy has come under the influence of a well-informed but short-sighted reformer supported by an enthusiastic but deluded lay press.

Fortunately, Harvard was able to profit from the efforts of a great education leader, a man who skillfully combined the old with the new in accordance with the special needs and circumstances of this School. David Edsall led the School into its next great phase, and he did this largely by avoiding the disadvantages that would have accrued by instituting Flexnerian recommendations foreign to Harvard's traditions.

Chapter Nine

David Linn Edsall, Dean of Deans, 1918–1935

D AVID LINN EDSALL was born in 1869 and died in 1945.[1] The bare facts concerning him can be stated very simply. He was graduated from Princeton University in 1890 and received the Doctor of Medicine degree from the University of Pennsylvania in 1893, and an honorary Doctor of Science degree from Princeton in 1913. He received another honorary Doctor of Science degree from Harvard Univeristy, in 1928. It was conferred by President Lowell with the following words: "Dean of our Medical School in the progress of medical education in America, the leader."

Dr. Edsall had been Professor of Therapeutics and Pharmacology at the University of Pennsylvania from 1907 to 1910 and Professor of Medicine there from 1910 to 1911. He was Professor of Preventive Medicine at Washington University in St. Louis, 1911 to 1912. In the latter year he came to Harvard University as the Jackson Professor of Clinical Medicine (1912–1918). The plottings, duplicities, foundation pressures, and frustrations involved in his movings make depressing reading. He was Dean of the Harvard Medical School from 1918 until he retired in 1935. He became Dean of the School of Public Health in 1922 and of the Faculty of Dentistry in 1924 at which time all the health faculties were united. Among other things, he was a fellow of the American Academy of Arts and Sciences, a member of the Association of American Physicians, and a member of the American Philosophical Society. He was the author of some 111 published papers.

Edsall's Philadelphia years were distinguished mainly by his contributions to clinical investigation. Before 1908 he had published more than 50 papers dealing in large part with the relation of metabolism to disease. At the University of Pennsylvania he was looked upon as something of a curiosity, for he was not only interested in chemistry and working in a laboratory, but was admittedly a good clinician—a combination as rare then as now. In December of 1908 he wrote a paper entitled "A Disorder Due to Exposure to Intense Heat." This was his first public expression of interest in industial hygiene in America. Soon there-

David L. Edsall, the first full-time dean at Harvard and one of the greatest medical educators of the twentieth century. His uncanny ability to detect budding geniuses brought many men to Harvard, where they developed into outstanding teachers, practitioners, and researchers. From his biography by Joseph C. Aub and Ruth K. Hapgood, published in 1970 by the Harvard Medical Alumni Association.

after he published another one: "Some of the Relations of Occupations to Medicine." Many papers followed, several of which showed increasing interest in industrial medicine and pointed to the extraordinary opportunities for research which this area presented. Nonetheless, the general field of industrial medicine was considered in 1908 to be hardly worth serious study. Unfortunately, many of the men then entering it had been rather unsuccessful in the pratice of medicine and were glad to accept a salaried post. While Edsall's special interest remained centered on the problems of metabolism and nutrition, his interest in public health problems was maintained. He was in this way far ahead of his time during the Philadelphia period.

Dr. Edsall encountered great obstacles in Philadelphia, owing to a major conflict there over general policy in the organization of the medical school.[2] He wanted more emphasis on scientific training and research, and more people devoted to full-time or nearly full-time work in hospital activities and teaching. This clashed directly with the views of the more conventional Philadelphia doctors. The Harvard Medical School later wanted Edsall precisely because he stood for the very things that had led to sharp opposition in Philadelphia. Personal incompatibilities may also have had some share in the local problems. His St. Louis period, where he served as Professor of Preventive Medicine, lasted, as noted, only a single year and was a time of extreme frustration for him. At this juncture he found an opportunity to work for a while at the Carnegie Nutrition Laboratory in Boston, and as a result became interested in the application of Benedict's "universal respiration apparatus" as a tool to use in studying clinical problems in respiration and respiratory metabolism. He described his experience in this field in the Shattuck Lecture of 1912.[3]

In the early years of the twentieth century, medicine underwent a renaissance of activity. To understand Dr. Edsall's contribution to medicine at Harvard, one must understand the components of that period. Several factors played a part in initiating what was, for Harvard, an era of medical prosperity: (1) in 1897 "an intelligent layman" (F. T. Gates) read word for word Osler's *Textbook of Medicine*. As a result, the Rockefeller Institute and Foundation were created.[4] (2) In 1904 the Council on Medical Education of the American Medical Association was created and by 1907 had inspected and classified in four groups (based upon their success in passing state board examinations) all of the then-existing schools, pointing out the urgent need for reform.[5] (3) In 1905 the Interurban Clinical Club was established by Dr. William Osler, who had a great deal to do with choosing the charter members. Its first meeting was held at the Johns Hopkins Medical Clinic. Among those present were Richard Cabot, Edwin Locke, Joseph Pratt, and David Edsall. (4)

As part of the ferment of the times, a group of Young Turks, somewhat bored by the dull nonphysiologic discussions of the American Association of Physicians, formed in 1908 an organization of their own to cultivate clinical research. Thus the remarkable American Society for Clinical Investigation was born, and among its founders were several local notables: Henry Christian, Edwin Locke, Joseph Pratt, and, again, David Edsall. (5) The Trustees of the Carnegie Foundation, realizing the inadequacies of much of American medical education, appropriated, in the autumn of 1908, funds for further study of medical schools. The ticklish job of inspection was given to Abraham Flexner (see above, Chapter 8). The long-standing Boston complacency was disturbed by all these events.

The main criticism of Flexner was of Harvard's method of appointing the heads of the clinical services at hospitals. At this time, although the University was free to secure laboratory men whenever it chose, it nevertheless was bound to make clinical appointments very much according to seniority. If this system were ignored, the newly appointed professor was likely to be without a hospital post. Flexner was correct in calling attention to this evil (which was, of course, not limited to Harvard). The common practice by which the man appointed to the hospital service was also appointed to the University clinical chair led to a "noticeable lack of sympathy" between the laboratory and the clinical men.[6] Their ideals were different.

Henry Christian, Richard Cabot, Edwin Locke, and Joseph Pratt were familiar with active teaching clinics through their membership in the Interurban Clinical Club. They attended these meetings and returned to Boston full of the new gospel that there were excellent facilities at hand for the investigation of disease if only sufficient sense and vision were present to make use of the opportunities. The preclinical faculty were to be encouraged to make the discoveries and devise the approaches that clinical investigators could use in making disease understandable.

As a result of these new trends, Walter Cannon became Professor of Physiology in 1906; in 1908 Henry Christian became Professor of the Theory and Practice of Physic, and the next year Dean of the School. Otto Folin became Professor of Biological Chemistry (1909) and Milton Rosenau, Professor of Medicine and Hygiene (1909). Francis Weld Peabody went to the Rockefeller Hospital in January 1911 and returned to demonstrate to skeptical New Englanders that serious clinical research was here to stay. Harvey Cushing became Professor of Surgery at Harvard in 1912. In 1912 another important position became available: Dr. Shattuck retired from the Massachusetts General Hospital and from the Jackson Professorship of Clinical Medicine. The School and Hospital staffs had, for the preceding two or three years, been observing David Edsall.

Dr. Frederick Cheever Shattuck had been, in considerable part, responsible for attracting Edsall to the Massachusetts General Hospital in 1912. There was clearly a desire for new blood there. Upon his retirement as Professor, there was a lively discussion about who his successor should be. Some believed that Richard C. Cabot should have the post. He was a brilliant clinician in the Oslerian tradition, an excellent laboratory man interested in the use of the laboratory not for itself but as an aid to understanding clinical problems, and a forward-looking medical philosopher, as shown by his introduction of organized social service into clinical hospital practice. Cabot was a distinguished member of an old New England family, as were Bowditch, Minot, Peabody, and a dozen other professors. But outsiders were breaching the walls—Theobald Smith, Henry A. Christian, Otto Folin—all professors recently appointed. There was a feeling that new blood was needed at the Massachusetts General Hospital, that perhaps a more physiological approach in medical thinking might advance medicine more than did the study of the infinite variations and subtleties inherent in clinical observation. Many rejoiced when Edsall accepted the post vacated by Shattuck. Richard Cabot showed no sign of disappointment and loyally supported the new chief.

When Edsall assumed the Harvard professorship at the Massachusetts General Hospital in 1912, he recognized that he had an opportunity to work in a constructive way in the industrial field. One of his first moves was to require that outpatient histories at the Massachusetts General Hospital give a better account of the industrial life of the patient than had been the case. Edsall went even further and established an industrial clinic at the Hospital. This lasted for several years under the leadership first of Dr. Harry Linenthal and then Dr. Wade Wright. Although cessful, the clinic was closed during World War I, and when the was over the material formerly utilized was spread to the Division dustrial Hygiene. Because the School of Public Health was fund and the *Journal of Industrial Hygiene* was available, the need clinic's pioneering efforts had passed.

Edsall reorganized on a sound basis the Department of M the Massachusetts General Hospital. A few years later he did Surgery, and still later the same for Psychiatry. Edsall was s not stubborn, and through his membership on the Gene Committee of the Massachusetts General Hospital had a c erful influence on the Hospital's policies. His aim was prove the methods involved and the physical equipment ticularly, to develop a strong staff, especially young showed promise of productive scholarship in medicine. He later pursued this aim for the School as a whole after he became Dean.

Edsall's concept was that medicine could best advance through the physiological approach; study of the mechanisms of disease was in order.

> [We] have recognized that these disorders of functions must be clearly appreciated individually before we can comprehend any disease as a whole. It is through this change of conceptions that general physiology, physiological chemistry, the study of the normal reactions of immunity and similar questions have become so lively a part of clinical investigation. Not many years ago the physiologist was, so to speak, the mere acquaintance of the medical and surgical clinician ... Now in his daily work the physiologist is quite as important to him as the pathologist ...[7]

Although Dr. Edsall's Deanship spanned the years 1918–1935, Reginald Fitz[8] would like to believe that preparation for Edsall's labors at the Harvard Medical School, in truth, began on the evening of May 1, 1909, for on that auspicious occasion, the Faculty assembled at the Medical School to attend its last meeting under the leadership of President Eliot. (Certainly, Edsall was not present at that meeting. Perhaps Fitz meant that the atmosphere generated then was sympathetic to Edsall's ideals and prepared the way for their later adoption.) It was a solemn and dignified occasion, during which President Eliot spoke movingly of his concern for the welfare of the Medical School. This was not unnatural for one who, when 22 years of age, had given his first course in chemistry lectures in the Medical School as a substitute for Professor Cooke. Eliot described three principal reasons for his interest in the School. First, its work lay in the field of natural science, with which he had some familiarity. Second, the purpose and object of its instruction had to do with improvements in the conditions of human life—individual, family, industrial, and social. Third, its "methods of instruction were capable of ... improvement."[9] But the comment of President Eliot which applied particularly to Edsall's own ideas was that, to Eliot's way of thinking, medicine had been a long time the most altruistic of the professions, and in recent times had developed a second method of serving the people: through medical research. Edsall, like Eliot, held that individuals who are engaged in the actual treatment of the sick and injured, as well as those who are studying the sources of disease and the modes in which diseases are transmitted and spread, are all actuated by the desire to make the world "wiser and happier"[10] because they lived in it. Eliot believed that the coming years would hold more possibilities of progress in medical education than had ever been true in the past.

"Money is going to be poured out for the promotion of medicine, and especially of preventive medicine."[11] These predictions seemed to herald the coming of Edsall. To an uncanny degree, Edsall seems to have been, consciously or unconsciously, an intellectual descendant of Eliot, although the problems Edsall faced were clearly different from those of Eliot's day. (One reason was that Eliot had solved, or started to solve them.)

Dr. Edsall became Dean at a time when he was most needed, when by training and temperament he was exceptionally well prepared for some of the tests that confronted him. He was one of the younger group of scholars who, under the leadership of Christian Herter and Graham Lusk, were introducing precise studies of metabolism into American physiology. Edsall was thus a trained laboratory worker who, when he entered clinical study, became one of the pioneers among academic clinicians. He was, however, well informed and sympathetic to the points of view of both the investigator and the clinician. At the same time, although in full sympathy with the new enthusiasm for the "scientific method in clinical study," he did not disregard the art of medicine, like some of the young enthusiasts whose efforts led a number of excellent laboratory investigators to become mediocre professors of medicine.[12] This appreciation for the role of the clinician was to stave off at Harvard the trend that led some institutions to regard medicine as a branch of basic science. When carried to its extreme, this attitude seemed to create hospials with the slogan "Diseases welcome. Patients stay out!"

With the particular support of President Abbott Lawrence Lowell and Dr. Henry Christian, Edsall became Dean of the Harvard Medical School in 1918, and the first full-time Dean in 1923. It was a time of considerable uncertainty but was, all the same, a period characterized by reorganization.[13] Many problems confronted Edsall. For example, there was need for reorganization of Medical School–Hospital relations, the question of full-time clinical activities, the adjustment of preclinical departments to the expanded clinical laboratories (a subject of controversy to the present day), and the function of medical schools in relation to public health.

Clinical expansion was occurring at the School also. The year 1912 marked the opening of the Peter Bent Brigham Hospital, soon followed by the Children's Hospital and the Infants' Hospital. The School had thus become the center of a group of hospitals all with policies in full accord with it. In 1912 Dr. Christian resigned the deanship in order to devote more time to the Medical Service of the Peter Bent Brigham Hospital and his professorship. This action was clear evidence that one man could not serve effectively in two such important capacities as Professor of Medicine and Dean of the Medical School. Dr. Edward H. Bradford succeeded Christian as Dean and held this office from 1912 to 1918. The latter part of his term coincided with the war years, when about half the teaching staff had gone into public service of one kind or another.

When Edsall arrived on the scene as Dean in 1918, he set himself a policy of observation without comment for a year. During this period he accumulated data which went into a "Statement of the Dean to the Faculty of Medicine," April 7, 1919. Edsall had been in office long enough to develop certain convictions about the School and its peculiarities. He went into action. The April 7th speech described the School as he saw it, and made clear his hopes for its future development and suggested how these hopes might be attained.

This report (originally labeled "Confidential" but now declassified) constitutes one of the great milestones in the history of medical education and marked the beginning of a profoundly new approach to medical education. The masterly document has been too little appreciated. More than fifty years ago, for example, Edsall foresaw the "strong possibility of socialization" of medicine and pointed out that this possibility would have great effect on the public organization of the profession of medicine.[14] He noted the influence of the war recently ended; the prevalent social disturbance, which tended to involve medicine sooner than other professions; the rapid rise in public recognition of the importance of health and its preservation. All of these things together made it probable that great reorganization would take place in medicine. These reasons were among the factors that made a review of the Medical School in the postwar world extremely urgent.

Edsall emphasized that although the Dean had only one vote when it came to determining policy, he was nonetheless charged with the duty of proposing and executing policy. He took the occasion of his report to describe for the senior faculty the direction in which he proposed to go. His practice would be to share with the senior faculty his plans; he had already seen the bad results of secret academic diplomacy when important changes were undertaken. He proposed a policy of frankness.

Some things stood out in Edsall's mind regarding Harvard as contrasted with the two other schools he had been associated with—the University of Pennsylvania and Washington University at St. Louis. He spoke first of certain things which appeared to him to be open to criticism, or at least in need of improvement. He believed that the potential opportunities, taking into account the available facilities, should make Harvard a leading school, a status not yet fully achieved. He admired some of the procedures used at the Johns Hopkins and commented on that School's influence in the recent past. Hopkins had a small and remarkable faculty, with more attention paid to the development of junior men than was the case at Harvard. Harvard had not had such rigorous standards in the choice of young men or comparable facilities for their work. At Hopkins positions of importance were rarely filled until repeated, unhurried, and frank discussion by the senior faculty had taken place. This, Edsall found, was not often true of Harvard, where discussion was far too limited. Edsall commented that he had rarely heard frank discussion of candidates for posts. As he said, "We have had a kindly but dangerous shyness of what seems like criticism of candidates."[15] Decisions at Harvard were very often reached by an almost automatic acceptance of a committee report. There was too much feeling that it is discourteous to question a professor's recommendation of a man as associate or assistant professor in his own department. "The most important of all policies is the manner in which the personnel is chosen."[16] Edsall believed that there should be a report in writing describing the training positions held by the candidate, work done, and papers published, and a report on the candidate's personality. (This was doubtless the forerunner of the present thorough *ad hoc* committee procedure.) In general, no names should be acted upon at the meeting in which their consideration was first proposed.

Although Edsall found that the relations with the hospitals had been progressing satisfactorily in recent years, that the hospitals were managed by boards having little or no organic connection with the School made cohesive and systematized effort difficult—and the problem urgently needed a solution.

It was Edsall's view that there had been less real contemplation and study of general policy by the Faculty of Full Professors at Harvard than was true of any other school he had been associated with. There were several reasons: a considerable number of men in these bodies had scattered spheres of action and consequent lack of frequent academic association. The limited form of organization Edsall found at Harvard was such as to force the Dean to be an autocrat or to compel him to depend upon the Administrative Board as an oligarchy. He believed that the Faculty and the entire Committee of Full Professors should give frequent and serious consideration to general matters affecting the School. This, however, had not been the custom.

Dean Edsall listed the policies which, at that time, seemed to confront the government of the School. They had to be looked at from four chief standpoints:

(1) what product should be furnished to the public; (2) what shall we be essentially forced to do owing to pressure caused by public demand or by activities of what I may speak of as competitive schools; (3) what are the peculiar opportunities of this School to modify or expand its activities in such a way as to contribute conspicuously to public service and thereby to its own present and future prestige; (4) what currents and countercurrents in medicine in general and in this

School in particular seem to be sufficiently apparent to make it necessary for us to consider at least what influence they may have within a few years? In other words, what activities should we be in a position to assume without very difficult expansion or reorganization . . .[17]

Edsall found soon after his arrival that such great growth of special departments had recently occurred, owing in part to Harvard's hospital connections in the clinical field and the burgeoning of research, that even a large budget had been stretched so that it could cover only thinly the current needs. He pointed out that Hopkins, with a smaller budget expended upon fewer objects, went further in general than did Harvard.

Of all of the problems that confronted the new Dean, the most urgent and severe was the financial one. In 1908 Harvard Medical School's budget was $251,389. When Dean Bradford resigned ten years later, the budget had increased only to $270,000, despite the fact that the cost of living had greatly increased and despite the fact that there had been considerable growth of special departments with important new hospital connections. It was urgent that the School obtain more funds. In some ways, however, Harvard seemed calm. Edsall continued:

> . . . I cannot quite see what is the matter with Medicine in general at this moment throughout the country . . . Part of it is due to the influence of Mr. Flexner I am sure, but there is also more than that and I think it is in part the neurotic effects of the war . . . I have never seen anything that even approached the present state of excitement and unrest and unsteadiness in most places. I heard a very distinguished man say the other day that Harvard seemed to be the only medical school of importance in the country that was not having a brain storm . . .

Things were calm at Harvard only by comparison. Ten years later Edsall would look back on this period and see what a razor's edge he had traversed. "Many of the senior staff, and most of the junior staff, were in a state of dangerous dissatisfaction and depression," he wrote in his 1927–28 Dean's Report, and the school was "in so precarious a condition that it was quite uncertain whether it would not go downhill rather than forward. The funds provided for the very able personnel to do their work were, in a number of instances, not more than one-half of what other schools were providing, sometimes less than that. There was . . . strong effort made on the part of a large number of other schools to take away the major number of the distinguished personnel in the School . . . The School had been in such financial condition that it had even been obliged to allow its plant to run down to an extent that has necessitated expending within the past five years . . . about $200,000 to rehabilitate it . . . The condition at that time was really rather alarming."[18]

Edsall's presence went far to correct the financial problems. It was, in fact, directly responsible for a golden shower of financial support during his early years as Dean. The DeLamar Fund alone (1919) brought in more than $5,000,000. (Evidently the Fund had been earmarked for the Medical School before Edsall's advent to the Deanship, but Edsall's presence went far to ensure that the large gift would be available.)

With all of the many problems Edsall accepted on becoming Dean, close to his heart was the ever-recurrent one of Public Health and how best to provide for its development. He found on looking over his resources that a "school for health officers" (the Harvard-Tech School of Public Health) was in existence at Harvard, having been established through the energy and foresight of Dr. Milton Rosenau and Professors George Whipple and W. T. Sedgwick, in 1913. This was a joint activity of Harvard University and the Massachusetts Institute of Technology. Dr. Edsall had no direct part in this school, but from the very beginning of his association with the Medical School he was intensely interested in Dr. Rosenau's course in Preventive Medicine and Hygiene for medical students. His ambition was to see that medical students gained an understanding of the importance of preventive medicine and public health. Dr. Edsall had been an active governmental consultant in industrial hygiene. He was, therefore, continuously and deeply involved in all that the new field of industrial hygiene undertook.

During World War I, Dr. Frederick C. Shattuck had become interested in this area and quite typically had set himself the task of obtaining funds so that teaching and research could be offered in the field. He was successful, obtaining $125,000, which was administered by a small committee in the Medical School, with Edsall as a member. In 1918, therefore, when Edsall became Dean, there were two well-established activities in hygiene, the Harvard-Tech School and the enterprise in industrial hygiene, associated with Physiology and with Professor Rosenau's teaching in Preventive Medicine in the Medical School. These endeavors attracted attention to activities in teaching and in research in this field.

The first study of an industrial hazard carried out under the new auspices by Edsall and Cecil K. Drinker (1919) involved consideration of cases of manganese poisoning, investigated at the request of the New Jersey Zinc Company.[19] This disease was newly recognized in the United States and not well understood in Europe. Studies in animals in collaboration with the Medical School's Department of Neurology finally established that manganese affects certain of the basal ganglia. Harvard's recommendations were accepted by the Company and resulted in the elimination of the manganese hazard in all of its operations.

About this time, the spring of 1919, an ancient tradition was overcome by the appointment to the Faculty of Dr. Alice Hamilton as Assistant Professor. A great deal of coming and going by President Lowell, Dean Edsall, and his adviser, Henry P. Walcott was involved. In a letter to President Lowell (December 20, 1918), Edsall assured the President that Dr. Hamilton's studies were unquestionably more extensive and of finer quality than those of anyone else at work on public health hazards.[20] Harvard had not really thrown its cap over the windmill in recommending the appointment of Dr. Hamilton. President Lowell went out of his way to indicate that this dangerous recommendation was not to be construed as a precedent for admitting women as candidates for Harvard degrees. Lest too many shibboleths be broken, the President stipulated that Dr. Hamilton must accept three limitations: she was not to enter the Harvard Club; she was not to participate in the Commencement academic procession; and she was not to expect professorial privilege in obtaining football tickets.[21] The conservatives were finally reassured. She was never advanced in rank.

Dr. Edsall became the first editor of the *Journal of Industrial Hygiene* (1919), which was published by the new division of the Medical School in order to provide a medium for publication in this field. This journal was important in establishing the standards of research which Dr. Edsall knew were required. All of these activities had an important secondary effect: they brought Dr. Edsall into contact with the International Health Board of the Rockefeller Foundaton, from which in 1921 resulted a proposal from the Foundation that a School of Public Health be established in Harvard University. C. K. Drinker and Richard Strong were important figures in this development.

The rich opportunities available in the new Harvard School of Public Health can be indicated by the fact that serious students could work under Alice Hamilton (the first woman to receive a Faculty appointment in the Harvard Medical School) or under Philip Drinker. The student could write a thesis on vital statistics under E. B. Wilson, on circulation and fatigue under Cecil K. Drinker, on physical chemistry of the blood under L. J. Henderson, on respiration under Alfred C. Redfield, on metabolism and nutrition under J. C. Aub, on endocrine glands under Walter B. Cannon, on physical chemistry and physiological processes under Edwin J. Cohn, on demonstrations of mammalian physiology under W. T. Porter, and on fundamental principles underlying the activity of the nervous system under Alexander Forbes. These matters involved joint activities of the Harvard Medical School and the School of Public Health and are well described by Jean Alonzo Curran in his delightful book, *Founders of the Harvard School of Public Health* (New York, 1970).

Although the School of Public Health, administratively, has had a separate faculty, it has never been, from the very beginning, really cut off from the Medical School in terms of staff, research, and administrative activities. Involved in these activities have been study of the hygiene of infants, the Fatigue Laboratory, the study of the effects of temperature and pressure, the Dental School, and the study of nutrition. Sanitary engineering has come to have a prominent place.

Dr. Drinker records that owing to his close relationship with these early activities leading to the establishment of the School of Public Health, he could say, with certainty, that an important part of the background was the confidence of those concerned that Dr. Edsall would indeed be a leader who would provide sound guidance throughout the problems of organization and establishment and would see that the School operated with scholarly standards and not as a simple trade school.[22] From the beginning, Dr. Edsall required that the new school be closely associated with the Medical School and the other Departments of the University. It was his strong belief that public health would advance first by virtue of research in the area, and, secondly, by determining that the departments of the Medical School, the Engineering School, and even the Business School would be steadily confronted with the possibilities of *preventive* work. A Rockefeller Foundation gift provided for a building fund. Dr. Edsall suggested that the Infants' Hospital be purchased. This was done with advantage not only to the School of Public Health but to the Infants' Hospital. The economy effected by the purchase of a building already standing was appreciated by the Foundation, and it was agreed that the money saved should be used gradually for the construction of laboratories and equipment.

The relationships between the Medical School and the School of Public Health were far wider than those established between the School of Public Health and the School of Engineering, for example. Thus a new period within the Medical School was at hand during Edsall's regime. For some years a Committee had existed at Harvard on Industrial Physiology. Dr. Edsall was the Chairman. The Dean of the Business School and the former Dean of the Bussey Institution were members.

Dr. Edsall's studies of industrial medicine had been important also to sociology, and the School of Public Health went much further in the same direction. Its problems are, in the broadest sense, sociological.

In the original budgets for the School of Public Health, Dr. Edsall allotted funds to certain Medical School departments, among them Bacteriology, Preventive Medicine, Hygiene, Tropical Medicine, and Comparative Zoology.

Dr. Edsall's activities in the field of public health were so impressive that he was invited to become a member of the International Health Board of the Rockefeller Foundation. After the Board was disbanded in 1927, he became a trustee of the Foundation and shortly thereafter a member of its Executive Committee. These posts he still held at his retirement in 1935. His interest in the area was increased by the request of the Foundation that he make various trips to England, China, and Mexico, and to the southern states. These journeys added immensely to his competence in developing educational standards in the field.

Cecil Drinker records that the early days of the School of Public Health were discouraging: there were few students and their preparation was, he said, woefully bad. There was considerable interest on the part of some to establish short courses of instruction, with a lowering of standards, so that those with at least some training in public health could be hired by departments of health. Dr. Edsall was opposed to such proposals. The new school was a University activity, and he had every intention of seeing to it that the standards of instruction were of University caliber. He was confident that students would come eventually. He saw clearly that the country could have a real profession of public health not hampered by political interference, and that the principal positions would go to men who were especially trained.

Community responsibilities did in fact grow with the increased availability of trained practitioners. Public recognition of the value of health and the recognition of the social and economic relations of medicine increased rapidly. In 1919 there was, for example, a growing demand for graduates trained as experts in fields of public health work.

Edsall discussed with his colleagues an attack on public health problems with personnel already on hand. A good start in the establishment of public health teaching had already been made through the Departments of Preventive Medicine, Pathology, Bacteriology, Physiology, Biological Chemistry, and Pharmacology, aided also by special facilities in Comparative Pathology, Tropical Medicine, and Industrial Medicine, and with cooperation by the Department of Sanitary Engineering and other Cambridge departments. In addition, there were the State and Municipal health departments, all of which were the equivalent of what hospitals are to clinical teaching. There were, in addition, remarkable facilities covering contagious diseases and mental hygiene. No better opportunities existed in any other medical school.

The department, already established, dealing with preventive medicine was going in the right direction. Edsall likened the current status of teaching in preventive medicine in 1918 to a "department of pharmacology and no further discussion of treatment."[23] He saw here a great opportunity for the School to take a leading role, with the inevitable result of enhancing its own prestige. It was his observation that most medical graduates in 1918 thought less about their responsibilities in the field of preventive medicine than they did of the application of pathology, anatomy, and chemistry to their clinical work.

Edsall observed that there was a strong tendency in the United States and an even stronger tendency in other countries toward organization of the medical profession under some form of public control. He predicted that in a few years there would be interesting and "probably radical" results. It was likely, he believed, that a number of physicians would go at once into desirable salaried positions of a great variety of kinds in which they would deal with groups of people or even with whole communities. Even in 1919 the doctor's community relations were far more important than they had been a few years earlier. It was evident that the preventive side of medicine would thus become more important—perhaps even the dominant side of medicine. Notwithstanding these changes in the public arena, medical teaching had changed very little over many years, Edsall found that in 1918 the teaching of medicine was still almost entirely concerned with the care of the individual sick man.

Edsall said that as the socialization of medicine progresses, a great deal will be demanded of the medical profession. The movement was surely one to be watched. As time passed, Edsall witnessed the development of social legislation of advantage not only to the University but to the entire country. Whatever direction one's sympathies took with regard to the socialization of medicine and the increase in public health work, one could only agree that the whole movement would be more safely conducted through men who have had specific training in schools equipped for graduate instruction in public health of university caliber. The fact that the University was prepared for this situation is chiefly owing to the vision of Dr. Edsall.

Edsall turned his attention to a discussion of countercurrents and reactions that the then present tendencies might lead to: Advances in medical knowledge had occurred more through developments in fundamental medical science than through the clinical areas, he thought. Scientists are dependent on the University's provision for their care, whereas clinicians have other sources of income as well as other useful and interesting activities. If neither the scientist nor the clinician is adequately provided for, the scientist would suffer more and have greater cause for dissatisfaction than the clinician. The clinician has a higher market value than the laboratory man, simply because he can make more money through some private practice. Practice also provides a refuge if academic advancement does not come.

The failure to provide the laboratory man with increased financial support as the cost of living rose had the result of attracting fewer able men into the fields of basic science than was previously the case. Edsall commented that about 1910 there was a rather wide choice of desirable men as candidates for professorships in the basic sciences. Ten years later he found the choice much narrower. The opposite held true in clinical medicine. This situation threatened the future development of medicine to a serious degree, he believed: "Inability to secure or to hold the personnel desired is the worst misfortune that could befall us." [24] Combatting this situation should have a high priority.

Edsall held the view that of any funds available to the School, a considerable amount should be kept constantly mobile and used for temporary purposes, not mortgaged to any given department. It is true that inefficiency and suffering should be relieved when this is possible, but limited resources should be expended for limited purposes. His principle was that it is essential to build up one thing at a time and to make the given development truly first class, and that new ventures not absolutely necessary were not to be added until the requirements had been satisfactorily provided for.

It was essential that the governing body at Harvard have a clear view of what it wished to accomplish. At the Johns Hopkins, for example, the belief was rigidly held that major clinical departments and a large proportion of junior men would devote nearly all of their time and thought to their University duties. The radical and inflexible rules imposed at Hopkins had been questionably successful and were very likely to be lessened in rigidity, Edsall supposed. (This was not the case, and Hopkins suffered for its failure to lessen its rigidity.)

As happened so often in times of conflict, there was danger of going too far or of going headlong in directions suggested more by the condemnation of old difficulties than by wise consideration of the total needs for future reconstruction. Edsall avoided the trap. In a report to the Carnegie Foundation he summarized his views: The development of a rigid and inflexible full-time system in the clinical departments did not seem to be the wisest plan. He believed that several types of opportunities should be presented. First, men highly trained in teaching and in organizing the teaching and hospital staffs upon which teaching depends should be available, and should be trained also in developing and guiding research. The major part of the time of these individuals should be given to academic pursuits. These men should have opportunity to add to their incomes by association with private patients. Separation from practice among the well-to-do classes, Edsall believed from personal experience, would cause these men to get a distorted view of clinical teaching.[25] The rigid full-time plan made no provision for junior men who decide not to commit themselves to a full-time academic career but choose a consulting practice along with part-time teaching of practical medicine. Edsall's view was responsible for the establishment of the "Harvard Full-Time System," wherein a man could increase (double) his academic salary in private practice.

This decision was in some ways costly, as the history of Harvard's negotiations with the General Education Board of the Rockefeller Foundation was to show. Harvard requested $2,500 a year for salaries for each of fifteen full-time assistants over a period of five years, in order to strengthen the clinical departments. The particular targets of this support were to be the medical, surgical, and pediatric services, followed by obstetrics, gynecology, neurology, and psychiatry. Simultaneously, William H. Welch applied for funds for the Johns Hopkins, which would provide an annual income of $65,000 to make it possible for the professors at Hopkins in Medicine, Surgery, Pediatrics, and subsequently other branches, to give *full time* to teaching, research, and patient care. Immediately, difficulties arose over the questions of (a) whether a single university hospital, like Hopkins, was better than one with multiple hospitals, like Harvard, and (b) full-time staff as opposed to part-time. The Hopkins "team" consisted principally of W. H. Welch, A. Flexner, and F. P. Mall. The Harvard antagonists were D. L. Edsall, H. Cushing, H. Christian, A. L. Lowell, and the then retired C. W. Eliot.

It is clear that neither William H. Welch nor Abraham Flexner understood the great value of having a number of affiliated hospitals with their clinical riches against the single university hospital, as at Hopkins. The charge was made that Harvard did not adequately control the academic programs of the hospitals affiliated with it. President Lowell and the leaders in the Medical School continued to press the fact of Harvard's wealth of clinical material. Harvard had clearly underestimated the vigor of the opposition to its ideas, however, and it lost.

As early as 1904 the Harvard Faculty had accepted the principle of full-time salaried heads of Medicine and Surgery, just like professors in scientific fields. Bearing in mind that direct contact with hospital patients is undoubtedly beneficial in the clinical areas, such consultation practice could be accepted, the faculty believed, if it would not interfere with the efficacy of the individual's teaching and research.[26] Harvard proposed that its new concept would include an office in the hospital and a basic salary for the physician, who also could collect fees under certain limitations. But full-time teaching under these conditions was vigorously opposed by Henry Christian, Hersey Professor of Physic, and Harvey Cushing, Moseley Professor of Surgery. One can get a pretty good idea of just how severe this opposition was from reading four letters, Dean Edsall to Abraham Flexner, January 22 and 28, 1914 and Flexner to Edsall, January 26 and 31, 1914.[27] The Medical School did not meet the guidelines for full-time status of professors in clinical departments that the General Education Board of the Rockefeller Foundation used in deciding who would receive funds. The Rockefeller Foundation was evidently strongly influenced by the views of Flexner and his Johns Hopkins supporters.

Flexner was invited to dine at the Maryland Club in Baltimore with Drs. Welch, Halsted, and Franklin P. Mall, the distinguished anatomist. Mall expressed his opinion frankly:

> If the school could get a sum of approximately $1,000,000, in my judgment there is only one thing that we ought to do with it—use every penny of its income for the purpose of placing upon a salary basis the heads and assistants in the leading clinical departments. . . . That is the great reform which needs now to be carried through.[28]

At a meeting of the Trustees in January 1914, a resolution was set down which described the Board's attitudes for a period of some years: "the Board does not consider it expedient at present to aid medical education except insofar as it concerns the installation of full time clinical teaching."[29]

Retired Harvard President Eliot was a leader who carried great influence with the General Education Board of the Rockefeller Foundation but not quite enough to achieve his desires. Harvard had applied to the Board in 1913 for an endowment of 1.5 million dollars for the purpose of placing "all its clinical departments . . . on a satisfactory university basis."[30] Under its plan, the professors would be expected to devote the major part of their time and attention to school and hospital work, but they were not to be denied the privilege of receiving fees from private patients. Eliot wrote:

> The authorities of the Harvard Medical School regard the full-time policy as a great improvement in clinical teaching . . . but they believe that in its most intelligent application it will permit the continued employment as teachers of men who accept private practice as well as hospital practice; and they observe that great improvements in medical treatment have in recent years proceeded from men who were in private practice . . .[31]

Harvard refused to sell its independence.

The policies advocated in the April 7, 1919, address of Dr. Edsall to the Faculty were, in large part, carried out. It was widely agreed that his recommendations would lead to success. In support of this view, the budget quadrupled from 1918 to 1935 during his administration, exactly as President Eliot had predicted. Money flowed into the worthy medical institutions. It was in truth a golden age.

In this period, the Harvard School of Public Health moved into the building which had been originally intended to house the Infants' Hospital. The Infants' Hospital became associated with the Children's Hospital. The Beth Israel Hospital and the Lying-in moved to the vicinity of the School, thus making available clinical facilities. Vanderbilt Hall was constructed, with great advantage to the medical students not only for the housing provided but for the physical-exercise facilities included. A reasonably good library available to the students and Faculty was established on the second floor of the Administration Building. Fitz wrote in 1935:

> Spiritually—and this is more important than any physical growth,—the personality of the School has changed. Gone are the days of uncertainty, apprehension and dissatisfaction on the part of many of the staff, and instead there has arisen a general feeling of stability, confidence, loyalty and reasonable contentment, which is reflected from department heads downwards. Such a spirit, so intangible, and so difficult to define, and yet one of the reasons why many people like to work in the Harvard Medical School, has been a not unimportant factor in attracting eminent new Faculty members to the School and in holding others who have been urged to go elsewhere.[32]

As the resources of the Harvard Medical School increased both physically and intellectually, it was evident that Dr. Edsall's hope was that superior departments in the fundamental medical sciences would be developed, and first, a "school" of Physiology and Biochemistry. They were already leading departments before Edsall became Dean. By 1935 they had become conspicuously more productive than any similar departments in the country.

Also, by 1935 some thirty professorships in physiology or similar subjects had been established over the country by men who had received most of their training at Harvard. By 1935 similar opportunities were being made available in pathology, bacteriology, immunology, and protozoology. The Department of Anatomy at that time had become a recognized center for neuroanatomical training.

Harvard had always had a strong clinical orientation. Not surprisingly, the clinical departments shared in the School's ascendancy. Many hospitals had developed and were brought into a satisfactory working relationship with the School. Their organization was now on a much more academic basis than formerly was the case. All Massachusetts General Hospital men worked with pride in the development of laboratories and the great increase in investigative work which made it necessary to take over the Bulfinch Building. All City Hospital graduates realized the importance of what had happened there through the opening of the Thorndike Memorial Laboratory (1921), the Neurological Unit (1925), and the Mallory Institute of Pathology (1933). The Children's Hospital, which purported to offer no more than a sound clinical training in Pediatrics, had developed so that its clinical activities, research, hygiene, and sociological relations were now considered to make it one of the leading pediatric clinics in America. The Huntington Hospital (now incorporated into the Massachusetts General Hospital), the Massachusetts Eye and Ear Infirmary, the Peter Bent Brigham Hospital, the Beth Israel Hospital, and the Lying-In all became distinguished parts of the School in the sense of the interchanging relationships to be found there.

In 1910 only about twenty professors and as many junior men could be said to be occupied in serious scientific medical research. In 1935 there were some 200 men constantly at work along these lines. The School's reputation was enhanced. These things are tangible evidence of the growth and expansion made possible by Dean Edsall's broad views. "Investigation at Harvard has flourished. The teaching of clinical medicine has improved." [33] In fact, striking improvement was evident in the teaching of medicine to undergraduates.

Important in medical education was the fact that the students were entirely free of specific obligations two afternoons a week, or three counting Saturday, and the tutorial plan was established for men of superior ability. The subtle change can be described by the fact that the majority of the men present worked as students of medicine and not, as they had formerly, as applicants for a license through examinations.[34] Their interests were wider; their reading and advanced work were far beyond the requirements. They were interested in acquiring knowledge, and there was little studying for grades. The breadth of their activities was indicated by the knowledge of elective or voluntary courses where close relationships with a stimulating teacher could be found. Their training as clinicians had greatly improved. Provision for the financially poor student had alleviated many of their problems through development of loan funds and increase in scholarships. In 1935 nearly half the students received some form of financial help during their medical careers. The superior student had come to be widely recognized as a most precious resource of the School; he received encouragement, help, and guidance as he needed it. In 1910 two thirds of the undergraduate group came from the neighborhood of Boston; in 1935 only about one third came from that area. The Harvard Medical School had finally become a national medical school.

Dr. Edsall was happy to see the stream of young Americans going abroad for further training during his dispensation, matched by an equal stream of Europeans coming to Harvard.[35] Doubtless a large factor in the foreigners' coming to this country was to be found in the facilities for research. Young men were no longer barred by low salaries from a career in investigation. In the case of very young men of promise, Edsall was remarkable in his ability to provide full-time salaries for them. He was constantly hunting for superior human material.

In a discussion (1929) with a journalist, Mason Ham, Edsall states that he believed that the eminence of the Harvard Medical School was built on the foundations laid by President Eliot and Professors Henry P. Bowditch, J. Collins Warren, and Frederick C. Shattuck in the early years of the twentieth century.[36] In this interview he also made the perceptive comment that more highly developed investigation and instruction in the cause and control of mental disease were needed, a most important illness in terms of cost to the community and the least yielding so far to attempts to alleviate it. Edsall likened past movements in this field to religious movements that depended largely on the generosity of the individual who leaves behind no residue of measurable accomplishment on which further accomplishment may be founded. He urged the adoption of the scientific method—which, in the end, should leave a body of definite information useful to future workers.

In addition, Edsall's efforts caused a change in the relations with the University. Before his tenure, the Medical School was an isolated activity far away from the College proper and having little relationship to it. In Dean Edsall's time the School became a definite part of the Harvard world. There was great progress in the biological sciences, in economics, sociology, and even law and business.

According to Means' obituary, Edsall was at his best at the bedside.[37] He demonstrated to the students that the best care of a patient is that which is planned with a clear understanding of the basic principles of the medical sciences involved. He showed that it was possible to integrate research, teaching, and the care of the patient. He was well aware of the social factors involved and the role of environment in determining the clinical picture.

The years have shown that Edsall lives not only through his works but through his many pupils. In his years at the Massachusetts General Hospital prior to his assumption of the Deanship, his influence was such that it could be said of him that he created a school—the mark of a great teacher. His disciples combined investigative insight with clinical skill. Numbered among them, to name only a few, are Francis Weld Peabody, George Minot, James Howard Means, Joseph C. Aub, Paul Dudley White, Fuller Albright, Walter W. Palmer, Herrman L. Blumgart, Chester W. Keefer, and William B. Castle.

At a meeting at the Tavern Club where the advance of the School was discussed (about 1934), President Lowell remarked that all constructive labor is in the nature of a work of art (reminiscent of Thomas Jefferson's observation that talk is an art form), and all of those engaged in work at Harvard are more aware of its difficulties than anyone else, but when a given task is completed, he has the right to say, "This is the best I could do under the circumstances." David Linn Edsall was, in these terms, a great artist. In his seventeen years as Dean of the Harvard

Medical School and the thirteen as Dean of the Harvard School of Public Health, he established in those institutions the principles he had earlier tested and proved valuable in clinical medicine. He had also participated, usually as a leader, in the formulation of educational policies that were to increase Harvard's greatness. His stewardship coincided with the period of some of Harvard's most notable medical accomplishments.

For convenience, Edsall's chief policy concepts (1919) can be summarized:

1. Secret academic diplomacy is undesirable; Edsall preferred a policy of frankness.

2. The most important of all policies is the manner in which the personnel are chosen.

3. It is essential to have a report in writing on the candidate for a faculty post (forerunner of the present *ad hoc* committee procedure).

4. The senior Faculty must participate in determining policy and have a clear view of what it wants to accomplish.

5. The physician and the School have community responsibilities.

6. There is a new (1919) public recognition of the value of health and the social and economic relations of medicine.

7. It is the obligation of the School to train men for public health work.

8. The medical profession will probably be placed under public (legal) control.

9. The doctor's community relations are far more important (1918) than they were only a few years earlier.

10. Prevention of disease is bound to expand greatly, perhaps even to become the dominant side of medicine.

11. "Inability to secure or hold the personnel desired is the worst misfortune that could befall us."

12. It is essential that some funds should be kept mobile for emergency use.

13. It is important to promote one development at a time.

14. Limited resources should be expended for limited purposes.

15. A rigid or inflexible full-time system in the clinical departments is not desirable. Some private practice is highly useful, both for

financial reasons and also for the teacher's balance (the Harvard "full-time" system).

16. It is important to provide for the gifted student. (Edsall did so in his creation of the tutorial system.)

A cursory examination of these concepts might suggest that they are innocuous. It would be a mistake to dismiss them lightly. For example, Dean Edsall's insistence on some private practice for all clinicians has made a great difference between Harvard and the Johns Hopkins, where, as indicated, a rigid full-time system prevailed, with only a few exceptions (Osler, Dandy, for example). Occasionally, attempts have been made to promote such a rigid system at Harvard. Luckily, so far, they have failed.

One measure of the validity of the concepts is that they have persisted to the present time (1975). They represent the major guiding principles on which the Harvard Medical School has functioned for more than fifty years.

It is true that through the wisdom and foresight of President Eliot and the eminence of a group of leaders—Drs. Frederick Shattuck, Walter Cannon, Otto Folin, Harvey Cushing—the Harvard Medical School, like the Johns Hopkins, had for some years been moving in the direction of new concepts. But these two institutions stood in need of far less reformation than most other American medical schools. It is well to remember that this preparedness of Harvard for the new era in American medical thought was owing as much to the unselfish spirit of men distinguished in the older clinical school, men such as Shattuck and Bradford, as it was to the foresight of the new leaders.

Edsall was characterized by his trust of those whose competence was in fields outside of his own experience. He often sought advice but gave it only when asked, and then helpfully and considerately. When asked for financial support for research, he did his best to further the success of any worthy effort. It was clear to him that investigation and teaching were inseparable. A successful administration required sympathy with the ambition of scholars to develop productive departments. In these matters, he was cooperative in the encouragement of the younger men of talent.

The capital funds of the School increased enormously under Edsall, from less than five million dollars in 1918 to about seventeen million dollars in 1935. He was a compelling money-raiser.

During Dean Edsall's career, he witnessed the establishment of the Wassermann Test; the control of diphtheria, hookworm, and malaria; and the use of the X ray in the diagnosis and of insulin in the treatment of diabetes—to mention a few of the advances that have altered the individual practice of medicine. The social significance of well trained medical men was recognized and accepted. During Dean Edsall's earlier years it was considered unethical for a doctor to take a contract appointment.[38] This contrasts sharply with the situation that obtained in 1935 at the end of his tenure. The growth of social obligation of physicians was apparent from many points of view. Dr. Edsall recognized time and again the importance of the physician's personality in terms of warmth and human sympathy. Without this, the technical advances of the clinician are sorely crippled.

Great progress was made in the control of disease through the coordinated efforts of the public health worker and the physician. The Harvard Medical School took a leading position under Dean Edsall and with the stimulation of M. Rosenau, C. K. Drinker, Richard Strong, and others, to meet the need for public health education. He made clear the value of sound public health policies in industry, commerce, government, and society.[39] He also made abundantly clear the attractiveness of a career in the public health service. It was his insistence that has provided a background for public health care in pure science, chemistry, physics, biology, and bacteriology, as well as the increments of knowledge turned up in the fields of economics, sociology, and psychology.[40] He even proposed that some public health workers might well be sociologists, chemists, and psychologists.

The Flexner Report, published in 1910, showed that Harvard possessed one of the most richly endowed medical schools of the day. During the years that followed, the School carried its share of the responsibility for leadership. The burgeoning impact of science on medicine placed a great new responsibility upon the University as a whole for the training of doctors who understood the concepts of science. The coordination of clinical and laboratory staffs was no easier at Harvard than elsewhere, but Harvard early saw the importance of such liaison, thanks to Edsall. It would be wrong to overlook the difficulty that clinical men found in their efforts to adjust themselves to the academic traditions of the University. Dean Edsall was acutely aware of this problem throughout his administration. He was notably successful in coordinating the clinical and laboratory phases of medical education:

> the clinical work has been illumined by the laboratory work in Harvard College as well as in the laboratories of the Medical School itself. The complexity of the administrative problems of a medical school is not fully realized: how to utilize leadership wherever it may be found; how to encourage brilliance in unexpected places; how to remain sufficiently unconventional to give free sway to new ideas.[41]

As mentioned, it was during Edsall's dispensation that the Medical

School became a national instead of local institution, in both its composition and its outlook. The scholarship among students and Faculty was elevated. The advances derived from research were greatly enlarged.

It was nearly everywhere recognized that with the death of David Edsall a truly great figure had departed from American medical education. In his obituary, published in the *New England Journal of Medicine* and written by his disciple and younger colleague, James Howard Means, he was described as large in body as well as mind, with a strong will and great breadth of vision.[42] His objectives were clear to himself, and they were pursued with untiring vigor. His great goal was to improve the teaching of medicine and the promotion of medical research. He achieved these goals to a quite remarkable degree.

Lawrence J. Henderson points out that the "practice, teaching and science of medicine have never been isolated from the other affairs of men but have modified them and been modified by them."[43] During the course of Henderson's tribute to Dean Edsall, his subject was the interaction of these activities as they existed at the end of Dr. Edsall's administration. Henderson identified three periods of the interaction from and toward medicine: First, a long period when the influence was directed chiefly from medicine outward; second, a period of transition, sharply marked by the influence of biology, of chemistry, and of physics upon medicine, and a third complex period when actions and reactions between medicine and other human affairs were so numerous, so ever present and intricate, that it was almost impossible to follow relations of cause and effect. Although Henderson was writing about the conditions as they obtained in 1935, when he believed that the third period had arrived, his comments are even more relevant at the current time (1975). In the seventeenth century, physicians contributed disproportionately more than their share to a movement of great importance in the growth of science: the founding of academies. The requirements of medicine have created new sciences. Medicine has throughout the ages stimulated new developments. It is true that in 1918, when Dr. Edsall became Dean, many new conditions, especially immaterial and intellectual conditions wherein the teaching and the science of medicine were evolving, were already present.[44] Great institutions change slowly. Evidence of this is the still (1975) not quite complete integration of the Medical School with the rest of the University, although great strides have been made in that direction, especially during the tenure of Edsall.

Opportunities were established under Edsall for a direct influence of the more abstract sciences on those of the Medical School. For example, from the first establishment of the School of Public Health, a *professional mathematician* and a *mathematical physicist* occupied the Chair of Vital Statistics (1935, E. B. Wilson). Moreover, an experimental physicist was, during Edsall's period, a regular officer of the Cancer Commission. Other factors have strengthened the influence of the abstract sciences on the Medical School. A Department of Physical Chemistry was established. There were close relationships between the Medical School and the Division of Biology: Professor Redfield, who taught for years in the Medical School, later became Director of the Biological Laboratories at Cambridge. During Edsall's period an economist was added to the Faculty of Medicine. Close relationships were developed between the laboratories of the Medical School and those of the great Boston hospitals, where formerly relationships were few indeed.

The Edsall era was clearly one of great change in medical education, but we must recognize that it is actually only a period of transition. It initiated but rarely completed the changes that made twentieth-century American medicine what it is.

THE THREE POST-EDSALLIAN DEANS

The Dean of the Harvard Medical School has great though restricted powers. Although most of his decisions have to be ratified by the Faculty or by the Committee of Professors, some do not. By his power to appoint some highly important committees, such as those on Admissions and on the Curriculum, he can shape the School to a significant degree. He also plays a large but by no means solitary role in determining the composition of *ad hoc* committees to recommend persons for tenure appointments. He usually has the deciding voice in negotiations with foundations and other donors.

The three Deans who followed Dr. Edsall were C. Sidney Burwell, George Packer Berry, and Robert Higgins Ebert. The first served as Dean of the Faculty of Medicine from 1935 to 1949, after which, he resigned to become the first Samuel A. Levine Professor of Medicine. His career encompassed forty years of teaching and research, chiefly on cardiovascular diseases. He was particularly interested in the circulatory adjustments which take place in women during pregnancy. His studies brought assurance to women with heart disease that in the great majority of cases, they can be carried successfully through pregnancy and have a baby of their own. With Dr. James Metcalfe of Harvard and the Boston Lying-in Hospital, he published, in 1958, *Heart Disease and Pregnancy*, a definitive book describing the specific problems presented by heart disease in pregnant women and outlining the modern method of management.

Dr. Burwell's medical research bridged the gap between basic physiology and the clinical problems of the respiratory and cardiovascular systems. He was concerned largely with the measurement of cardiac output in various diseases and with the natural, self-limiting mechanisms controlling disease. As early as 1940, with Drs. Eugene Eppinger and Robert Gross of Harvard, Dr. Burwell described methods for measuring the volume of blood passing through the patent ductus of the heart. These measurements antedated those made by cardiac catheterization. Later he worked on the physiologic and clinical problems of aging.

As Dean of the Faculty of Medicine at Harvard from 1935 to 1949, Dr. Burwell guided the Medical School through the hectic days of World War II, when Harvard's medical teaching program was stepped up by wartime demands at a time when its Faculty was depleted by military service. During this period he not only maintained the traditions of Harvard medicine but also, with President James B. Conant, laid plans for the future growth and development of the Medical School after the war.

This planning encompassed four major areas. One was the problem concerned with replacement of a group of distinguished members of the Faculty of Medicine who were reaching retirement age. A second challenging problem was the integration of the Medical School and the academically associated hospitals. With a "Committee of Eight" prominent members of the Faculty of Medicine, objectives were defined and the groundwork laid for the present closer affiliation of the teaching hospitals and the School. With President Conant, Dr. Burwell's third concern was the reorganization of the Harvard School of Dental Medicine. The basic decision involved a major change in orientation for the Dental School from one that was primarily clinical to one based on the laboratory sciences, with emphasis on research and preventive dentistry. The growing importance of the basic medical sciences and the need to strengthen instruction and research in these areas at the Medical School was the fourth item to occupy Dr. Burwell's attention during and following the war years.

He will be remembered forever for his statement to a graduating class on the occasion of their final formal convocation: "Half of what we have taught you is wrong. Unfortunately we do not know which half." After his retirement as Dean, assumed infallibility became more common in high places.

In 1935 Dr. Burwell had been appointed both Dean of the Faculty of Medicine and Research Professor of Clinical Medicine. By accepting these important posts he was forced to exchange must of his research and teaching for administrative duties. He maintained a research laboratory at the Peter Bent Brigham Hospital, however, where studies he had begun in Nashville were continued. After his resignation from the Deanship, he resumed full-time teaching and research in medicine at the Peter Bent Brigham Hospital.

Dr. Burwell was succeeded in 1949 by George Packer Berry, who served until 1965, holding the titles of Dean of the Faculty of Medicine of the Harvard Medical School, Professor of Bacteriology, and President of the Harvard Medical Center. Dr. Berry received the A.B. degree with highest honors in biology from Princeton University in 1921 and the M.D. degree from Johns Hopkins University School of Medicine in 1925. Following this, he had postdoctoral training in medicine at the Johns Hopkins Hospital, and from there in 1929 he went to the Rockefeller Institute.

In 1932 Dr. Berry left the Institute to become Professor of Bacteriology and head of the Department of Bacteriology and Associate Professor of Medicine at the University of Rochester School of Medicine and Dentistry.

As Dean of the Faculty of Medicine and Professor of Bacteriology in Harvard University, and, for a time, President of the Association of American Medical Colleges, Dr. Berry has accomplished a great deal in terms of shaping the quality of medical education in a difficult period. During his tenure, he more than doubled the School's endowment and has made several remarkable achievements, not the least of which is the building of the magnificent Countway Library of Medicine. His major report, "Medical Education in Transition," is considered to be one of the few definitive statements concerning modern American medicine.

Scientifically, Dr. Berry was for years interested in the mechanisms of virus infections, and he was particularly interested in the role of viruses in causing cancer. He was the first to demonstrate that the virus causing one disease can be changed into a virus causing a distinct but related disease.

The citation he received when he was made a Doctor of Science at Boston University characterizes the man very well:

George Packer Berry, physician, educator, scholar, whose leadership in medical education is unique in this generation. You have brought dynamic support to the basic sciences while insisting on the education of the whole person for significant service in medical practice. As foundation trustee, consultant to public and private agencies, uniting force in creating a great medical library, you have devoted your talents and energy to the improvement of higher eductaion in all of its aspects.

This statement, accurate as far as it goes, does not mention his most prominent characteristic, his phenomenal dynamism. Nevertheless, his attitudes and beliefs concerning medicine were greatly influenced by two factors: (1) he was a basic scientist and not a clinician, and (2) he was a product of the Flexner mentality to the extent that he seemed determined to carry out its recommendations, heretofore not accepted by Harvard.

Robert Higgins Ebert, on his appointment as Dean in 1965, was given the titles of Professor of Medicine at the Harvard Medical School, Dean of the Faculty of Medicine, and Member of the Faculty of Public Administration. Dr. Ebert received the B.S. degree from the University of Chicago in 1936. During the following three years, he was a Rhodes Scholar at Oxford University, working in the laboratory of Sir Howard Florey. In 1939, he received the D.Phil. from Oxford. He subsequently received the M.D. degree in 1942 from the University of Chicago Medical School and became Professor of Medicine there in 1955. In 1956 he was appointed the Hanna-Payne Professor of Medicine at the Western Reserve University and then became the John H. Hord Professor of Medicine at the same University.

Dr. Ebert was brought to Boston through his appointment as Jackson Professor of Clinical Medicine and head of Harvard's Department of Medicine at the Massachusetts General Hospital. His clinical interests had been in the field of respiratory disease, primarily tuberculosis. His basic research in the past, reflecting his clinical concerns, was directed toward better understanding of tuberculous infection, including the effects of antimicrobial agents on the metabolism of the tubercle bacillus. More recently, he had been concerned with a study of inflammation. During his tenure, the erosion of bedside medicine at Harvard has continued, as laboratory medicine displaced it. Requirements for admission to the School were modified, so that sociologic deprivation became a qualification for admission. The view was held that since some men were unqualified through no fault of their own but solely as a result of societal inequities, their deficiencies could not be held against them. Hence, less than optimally qualified students were not only accepted—they were recruited. Perhaps as a result, for the first time in history Harvard students failed the National Board Examinations in significant numbers. The quality of the School was sacrificed in order to make it an instrument of societal reform. This change has not, however, demonstrably improved society. In this respect Harvard was no longer a leader but had become a weathervane, as it already had in its acceptance, finally, of the Flexnerian concept of medicine.

During Dean Ebert's tenure the Boston City Hospital was finally lost from the Harvard orbit. It had been founded by Harvard men a century earlier to serve exclusively the most impoverished and deprived groups in Boston, and while doing so had created a glorious tradition of outstanding medical care and clinical investigation.

Chapter Ten

Curriculum Changes

THE preceding pages have made it clear that as new aspects of medicine began to develop in Europe in the nineteenth century, they were adopted —some quickly, some after a lag—into the Harvard Medical School curriculum. The prevailing view, however, contin· ued to be the nineteenth-century French belief that medicine was a discipline in itself and that the incorporation of new material, both from the laboratory sciences and from other branches of human knowledge, must serve the ends of bedside medicine and hence must be selected to further those ends. Around the turn of the century there was a trend toward the Germanic university principle that medicine is applied physiologic science and must be taught as such.

This revolution, which has caused important changes in medical education, is usually ascribed to the activities of the reformers, both within and outside of medicine, who were given ammunition by the Flexner Report (above, p. 176). However, the possibility that medical education might be improved by tying it even more closely to a university than Eliot's reforms had accomplished was being discussed at Harvard before Flexner burst upon an astonished—and humiliated—America. As long ago as 1909 an unsigned article had appeared in the *Harvard Bulletin*.[1] The subject was education in medicine. The author clearly believed that the relationships of the Medical School and Harvard College needed re-examination. As medicine became "scientific" under the German influence, and as some medical schools began to be assimilated by universities, the problems of medical education, as seen in that far-off day, became increasingly complicated. Medical schools should not be permitted to be mere trade schools. The writer commented that the advent of science had, at that time, already "wrought powerful changes in the medical curriculum, while the demand for culture and general training in our medical graduates grows daily in strength."[2] He went on to say that whatever mixture of culture and specialism might ensue, there was an "irresistible demand" that a year or two more of hospital work be added to round off the practitioner. He was of the opinion that "qualitative improvement in medical education is far more desirable than those forms of quantitative alteration now going on, far more desirable than either cramming or lengthening the curriculum. That which counts in a medical course is not the number of hours but the number of ideas conveyed to the student; and again, not so much the number of ideas which are conveyed as their wisdom. Therefore let us refine and not cram, strengthen rather [than] lengthen, the medical curriculum."[3] It is interesting to observe that biochemistry and biophysics were casually referred to.

The writer makes the point again and again that much of the work of the Medical School appeared, in fact, to have become comparable to that of the Graduate School of Arts and Sciences. He points out that some of the subjects embraced in medicine—for example, physiology—are of great value in a general education and from any standard help to develop a cultured student. The writer indicates that courses having to do with diagnostic and therapeutic matters are truly medical and that the so-called fundamental courses are not merely medical but, in a broad sense, biological. He believes that there is room at the Harvard Medical School for different classes of subjects for students who have different goals in mind. He proposes that the following arrangements be made:

1. Count towards the A.B. suitable courses in medical sciences. 2. Admit unconditionally to the Medical School all holders of a respectable bachelor's degree. 3. Grant the M.D. (a) after not less than a fixed minimum of residence; (b) upon evidence of theoretical and practical attainment in the medical sciences (including the present admission requirements) and in the clinical branches. 4. Establish a simple administrative mechanism for the degree of M.D., modelled after the present mechanism for the Ph.D. 5. Execute the above arrangements in the broadest spirit, to establish and preserve academic freedom, as exemplified in the greatest variety of preparation, of medical course, and of finished product. 6. Relax the present rigid organization of the Medical School curriculum and lay stress upon the quality of our doctorate rather than the means of its attainment. 7. In all ways encourage the better students. Permit them to advance at their own rate and in their chosen paths.[4]

The unknown author's expressed concern for the differing needs of students was at that time unique.

It is apparent to medical educators that the success or failure of a medical school depends on four factors, listed in order of decreasing importance: (1) the *students*—their intelligence, their motivation, and the quality of their premedical training; (2) the *faculty*—their knowledge, their ability to inspire and communicate, and their curiosity concerning ambiguous or unexplored aspects of their subjects; (3) the *facilities*—clinical material, libraries, and laboratories; and (4) the *curriculum*—

primarily with respect to its permitting students to develop each according to his interests and potential, and, secondarily but clearly in relation to the primary role, with respect to its content.

One can say nothing about the optimal methods of securing the best *students*. This very difficult subject has been made even more difficult in recent years by the insistence of some governmental agencies—supported by some foundations—that students be chosen not only on the basis of intelligence, motivation, and premedical preparation, but also by sex, race, and previous condition of deprivation in social and educational opportunities.

The choice of *faculty* has also changed to minimize the importance of clinical interests and skills. Many men are given high clinical rank on the basis of outstanding work in the laboratory itself or in the application of laboratory methods to a narrow clinical problem. Some of these men, to their credit, voluntarily become adequate—occasionally outstanding—clinicians. Because of those who do not, medical education, not to mention patient care, must suffer. Some of these laboratory-oriented men do not become good teachers either, and a curriculum can be no better than its teachers.

Dr. James Howard Means, while Acting Dean in 1946, made the following suggestion to C. Sidney Burwell, the Dean, on his return from two months absence:

> it occurred to me that it would be an interesting thing to organize a
> course of instruction for our Faculty on the subject chiefly of how to
> teach. It occurs to me that some foundation might be interested in
> such a novel enterprise and put up some money to bring lecturers
> here. I would visualize something from authorities on interviewing,
> something on teachers who could instruct us in the proper use of seminars, colloquia, quizzes, and lectures and examinations, something on
> the choice of students and also the Faculty with respect to social medicine, the quality of evaluation of persons, their talents as well as their
> symptoms. Jacques Barzun might be an interesting fellow to talk to
> us, or Carl Binger on the doctor's job perhaps, and then some professional educators. Another thing that occurred to me while attending
> this ad hoc committee's meetings was: why not use the Student
> Health system to teach personal hygiene, both physical and mental,
> while taking care of these needs for each student?[5]

This problem has yet to be solved. Outstanding teachers are not made. They are born, but must have the opportunity to develop their God-given potentialities. A way of compensating for the marked lack of interest in human values evidenced by some clinical teachers was through the development of social services for patients. The organization of the Social

Service Department at the Massachusetts General Hospital and the association of this service with the teaching of Harvard Medical students occurred during the last days of the Eliot era.

The report for 1907 shows in a most impressive way the distribution of patients to the hospitals, convalescent homes, and relief societies, as indicated by their needs. The first official mention of these activities was contained in the report by Dr. Herbert B. Howard, then Resident Physician. It is clear that the initial purpose of the Department was to assure proper care after discharge of the patients from the Hospital.

In 1908 the Hospital employed a graduate nurse as Executive Assistant to work in the wards. Her responsibility was to arrange for the discharge of patients and their transfer to suitable institutions when this was necessary. In addition she had to find out which patients needed the attention of the Lady Visitors. This was an early indication of recognition of the need of nonmedical care of hospital patients.

The Social Service Supervisory Committee was organized in February 1909. The teaching of medical students had begun in 1913 in the presentation of medical social clinics; the first students in the Boston School of Social Work, four in number, were accepted in 1909, and in 1913 a definite affiliation with that School was arranged.

In the report for 1914 the Trustees say that they "have at length recognized the Hospital Social Service as a part of the Hospital System by the creation of the office of Chief of the Hospital Social Service. They have long realized the importance of this Service and its admirable and efficient management." [6]
In this same report, the Resident Physician says:

> The House Social Service work has been placed upon a basis of better relationship with the out-patient work during the year. Your Board has created the position of Chief of Hospital Social Service, and Miss Ida M. Cannon, the Head Worker in the Out-Patient Department, has been nominated for this position by me and appointed to it by your Board. It is believed that this will be a desirable arrangement and useful to the Ladies of the Visiting Committee. [7]

This rather primly expressed comment marked, in a New England manner, the typically New England concern with the less technical and more humanitarian aspects of medicine.

Miss Ida Cannon, sister of the distinguished physiologist Walter B. Cannon, was made Chief of the Social Service Department at the Massachusetts Charitable Eye and Ear Infirmary in 1915. In 1918 Miss Cannon became Associate Director in the Department of Civilian Relief in the New England Division of the Red Cross. The 1918 report states that social workers have been trained at the hospital.

1. To know what it is that the doctor wants to get across to the patient.

2. To phrase the doctor's ideas in simple plain words without technicalities.

3. To gain the patient's confidence so that he really believes that the source has been found and the way to relieve it and prevent its recurrence is in sight.

4. To make use of all the sanitoria, convalescent homes, vacation funds, employment agencies and charitable agencies that may at need help the patient or his family to pay for the medicine, apparatus or vacation that may assure recovery.

5. To teach good hygienic habits.[8]

The financial statement of the Department in 1918 shows that the annual expenses were some $25,000. At the same time, the Hospital was paying the salaries of the ward workers.

In 1919 the Trustees voted "That the Social Service Department be, from this time forward, considered as an integral part of the Hospital, both administratively and financially; and that the present Supervisory Committee be continued, and that due regard be given to its recommendations."[9] Miss Ida Cannon's report for 1930, the twenty-fifth anniversary of the founding of the Social Service Department, contains much valuable material:[10]

It is of some interest to observe that for the first twenty-five years the activities of the Department were confined to aiding the poor in the general hospital and the Outpatient Department. The Department engaged iself in a new approach when a hospital for people of moderate means was built (Baker Memorial). It was necessary to staff this new unit, and Miss Josephine C. Barbour was appointed to that post. Throughout this period, Harvard Medical students worked informally with the social workers and also participated in formal case conferences, co-chaired by a senior visiting physician and a chief social worker.

A program for theological students was established in 1930 and in 1933 was put on an improved educational basis. In 1934 seven theological students from four different seminaries spent some months in the Hospital. While acting as attendants on the wards, they studied how the resources of religion may be made availble for persons involved in life crises—for example, handicaps or bereavement.

It is clear that in 1905, organized medical social service was unknown, whereas in 1935 no hospital in the United States worthy of the name was without such a department. The example of the Massachusetts General

Hospital was followed throughout the western world. Providing this approach to medical problems today adds an invaluable new dimension in the education of medical students.

In 1925 another member of old Boston families, Francis Weld Peabody, generated a remarkable discussion of the essentials of medical care. It was evidently written not to displace but rather to put into proper perspective the new "scientific' medicine that was growing in popularity in the academic world. Francis Peabody, who had been chosen as the first director of the Thorndike Memorial Laboratory at the Boston City Hospital—a laboratory that was to become world-famous for its scientific work—emphasized the humanitarian needs of sick people. He concluded simply that the essence of patient care was caring for patients. This work was enthusiastically received and widely read before World War II. It is, alas, rarely mentioned today.

In 1935 a startling document appeared from the hand of Lawrence J. Henderson, a world-renowned physical chemist who had interpreted respiratory physiology in terms of physical-chemical systems.[11] This scientist here revealed his brilliance in another field, as a social philosopher. Instead of expounding the thesis held by some that medicine is, or at least should be, a branch of physical biochemistry, he chose rather to warn against the effects of this belief. With the same logic of thought and precision in language that had placed his physiological writings among the classics of modern medicine, he developed the idea that the doctor-patient duo formed a unique social system. In his analysis he used the more mathematical and less romantic approach to sociology espoused by Vilfredo Pareto. This made his paper an even greater humanitarian medical document than it might have been if it had been written in the floridly emotional language of many medical sociologists. After a brief flurry of interest—it could hardly be called excitement—his paper fell into total neglect. Nevertheless, his description of how even then the absorption (but not the digestion) of laboratory science into medicine had changed the latter, and how it was bound to change it even more drastically, should be read by all who today are bewildered by the dissatisfactions of patients receiving medical attention and the unhappiness of students who entered medicine in order to care for people.

The question of the physical *facilities* (the third factor in the success or failure of a medical school) needs little discussion. The preclinical years, spent mainly in the Longwood Avenue Quadrangle, are continually being expanded to meet the needs. The clinical teaching is maintained at the various affiliated hospitals. These are required to provide not only clinical case material but also conference rooms and clinical and research laboratories if they are to maintain their Harvard connections. It is possible that some of the hospitals are oversupplied with respect to laboratories, for the proper allocation of funds to patient-care, teaching, and research is a matter that has never been discussed, much less studied.

The fourth factor, the *curriculum*, really involves two subfactors, viz. presentation and content. Education everywhere has had to overcome one basic handicap, the convoy system, whereby as in a wartime convoy of ships, the speed of the whole group is determined by the slowest vessel accepted into the group. The problem of the superior student's place in medical education is perennial. One solution is the tutorial system. In 1928 David Edsall introduced into the School a modification of the Oxford preceptorial (tutorial) system. It is not difficult to identify the probable origin of his interest in this method of teaching. During a summer holiday while in his last year in the Medical School of the University of Pennsylvania (1894–95), he worked in the Surgical Outpatient Department, carrying out simple routine duties. He was working under "one of the ablest young men in Clinical Medicine" in the University at that time (whose name has been lost).[12] He described in a letter to Samuel Eliot Morison how important the experience was. The stimulating opportunity consisted essentially of a chance to talk with his older mentor. Edsall said in his manuscript Autobiographical Notes, "I look back upon it [this period] as a really quite exceptional opportunity which was beyond all question the most valuable thing to me in the whole undergraduate medical period, because of the point of view of independent thought, reading, etc., which it gave."[13]

Dr. Edsall's hope was to establish a system that allowed for the fullest development of the greatest number of able students. He was troubled by the apparent effort of American medical schools to train the best *average* doctors. He had no choice but to approve this, but at the same time, he recognized that in efforts to turn out merely sound doctors we do not give sufficient attention to some of the finest material in each class. He believed that our teaching methods should be flexible enough to promote the best development of the unusually intelligent man as well as the mediocre. He deplored the failure of a thoughtful approach to learning so common in the School but realized that the Faculty must bear considerable responsibility, since the Faculty spent so much time telling the students what they must do and what they must think. This surely discourages the inherent initiative of some and silences the bold.

Edsall was sent aboard by the Rockefeller Foundation to study medical education, particularly in Great Britain. He described this experience to the Association of American Medical Colleges:

> One thing which impressed me very much indeed was that in every medical school I visited, some students stood out a great deal in their general mental poise and their attack upon subjects and their whole

attitude toward the work, quite differently from the rest of the students. Whenever I inquired into them, I found they were always men who had been through some of the great universities, and in a great majority of the cases they were men who had gone to Oxford or Cambridge. It seemed that there was one thing which might readily explain this, and that was the influence of the kind of training that they had had with tutors in those two institutions . . .

In Great Britain this method is used in Oxford and Cambridge in connection with that course which men take there preparatory to taking medicine, that is the Honors School of Physiology, (which includes bio-chemistry, and they usually get their anatomy there also). The men there seemed to me to get in that time a degree of comprehension and poise in the subject that is quite unusual in students of that age in this country. It seemed to me also that since it is not used at any further stage in the medical course in Great Britain, that I could actually see these results falling away from many of these men during their clinical training in Great Britain. Now, if it is of any use at all, (and it seems to me likely to be of a great deal of use) the time in medicine to develop the best there is in most of them, is more in the clinical departments than in any other. I don't think it has ever been anywhere used thoughout the whole course and I am particularly anxious to see that it is done in the clinical branches.[14]

Edsall described the tutorial system to the Massachusetts Medical Society in 1924. In his view about 20 percent of the students would do well on this type of "individualized" work. The great problem was to find the right tutor. Edsall said, "We must do justice to the mediocre and the inferior, [but] we must not by doing justice to them do injustice to the most important material of all."[15] In a report accompanying a letter to Dr. E. A. Locke,[16] he commented that the record of the 15 percent of the top students who were allowed tutorial privileges showed that it had been of great advantage to them.

Every man is endowed with natural curiosity to learn, but at the time Dr. Edsall was the new Dean, this curiosity had been pretty well overwhelmed by the burden of course work. Edsall sought for some means to overcome this situation. Some superior students were easily enough detected, but at the same time it was quite certain that there were "sleepers" who, under the right circumstances, would show great promise. The Dean hoped that the introduction (1923) of the tutorial system into the Medical School would make it possible to awaken these individuals. Edsall understood very well that a radical departure of the kind he was proposing was a gamble and that no good would come of failure here.

In 1922 the top 15 percent were allowed certain privileges. The next year, 1923, Edsall presented to the Administrative Board his plan for a tutorial system like that in vogue at Oxford and Cambridge Universities. The purpose was to provide for the best development of the exceptional student. He submitted the proposal to the Rockefeller General Education Board. This Board agreed to pay the tutors' salaries and expenses for two years. Dr. Alfred C. Redfield was named Tutor in Physiology and Dr. Arlie V. Bock, Tutor in Medicine.

In the first experimental year, Dr. Redfield worked with twenty-five students, some from the fourth year and some from the first and second years. While most of the students were in the highest category, some were in the lowest. Eight men from the first-year class were provided with what was in reality a seminar in Physiology instead of the usual course. In the first year of the system Dr. Redfield devoted his entire time to tutorial work during the period when students were taking Physiology. For the second semester he chose a small group of students who, he thought, showed promise of exceptional capacity. These men were not required to carry out the routine physiological work. Men who had had precious suitable training were assigned to work under the direction of a member of the Physiology Department. Dr. Redfield carried, as a group, the promising men who had not had previous experience. These men worked as a team. One experiment was performed each week. It usually required a day's effort and was planned to illustrate some general type of physiological activity.

Several hours were devoted at the end of each week to a conference in which the experiment and the reading which pertained to the general subject of the experiment were both discussed informally. Plans for the next week's work were given out and discussed at this time, together with lists of recommended reading. More references were suggested than could possibly be covered in the available time. Thus the student was obliged to select original material for himself to study. The tutor was always ready to give guidance as to the choice of the material. Notwithstanding the fact that no special effort was made to prepare these men for their regular examinations in Physiology, they compared favorably with their classmates when tested. The men all agreed that their broad reading, the informal discussion periods, and the limited experimental activities were most valuable. (H.K.B. as a former tutee agrees.) The problems made medicine seem more real, and the result was that the students' imagination and initiative were awakened. The men who had participated in the arrangement as first-year students were encouraged to work under the tutorial system in the second and third years. They were aided by the fact that two free afternoons were available. The second- and third-year men were able to work in any one of the fundamental sciences directed by a sympathetic Faculty member. Although many students did not engage in valuable research, the system demonstrated that given a suitable problem to work on, creditable achievement could be made by the determined student in the time available in his second and third years. It was deemed inadvisable to present an organized series of lectures or conferences inasmuch as the regular curriculum already offered a great deal of clinically oriented intellectual activity. Experience showed that it was better to present a definite problem for experimental attack associated with wide reading than the reverse. In the case of those who had done continuous research work along a specific line in the fourth year, the Faculty permitted a limited number, whose cases were individually approved, a great deal of freedom in allocating their time. In some cases this amounted to as much as four or five months.

Dr. Bock started out with six men. With these he conducted two bedside clinics and one evening conference each week. In addition, they were assigned to laboratories at the Brigham or the City Hospital or the Massachusetts General. His first thought was to assign a considerable course of reading, but he decided against this in order to leave requirements as few as possible, "with the idea of permitting them to find their own way of working things out, with the aid only of suggestions from me."[17]

Following a trial of a year and a half for the new experiment, Edsall asked the General Education Board for help in putting the tutors on a permanent basis.[18] He explained to the Board that in addition to the two tutors in Physiology and Medicine then active, he hoped to add one in Surgery and one in Pathology. If the Rockefeller funds would cover half the expense, he planned to use funds from the DeLamar Bequest for the other half. Edsall considered that the "tutorial method . . . is the most important thing that has arisen," presumably during his deanship.

As an experimentalist, Edsall struck out forcefully, notwithstanding the disapproval of a good many Faculty members, and went ahead with his plans determined to permit exceptional students enough leeway to develop their intellectual powers by certain freedoms not accorded to the mass.

> The students chosen are those showing evidence of superior capacity who are desirous of and capable of doing extra and advanced work along some definite line in any one of the medical sciences or major divisions of medicine. As a pure experiment, a few mediocre men have been chosen from time to time. No one tutor attempts to direct the work of each man in his group but does place each student in intimate contact with the particular member of the faculty best fitted for his needs . . .[19]

Tutorial students were eventually placed in Anatomy, Bacteriology, Physiology, Biological and Physical Chemistry, Neurology, Medicine, and Surgery. Another good side of the new system was that more Faculty members were challenged by the plan to improve their teaching.

It is not the purpose of the tutorial service to wean men away from medicine into the medical sciences, but to aid in what must become more and more the general purpose of education: to develop scientifically trained minds. Dr. Bauer's study, in 1925, of the personnel involved indicated that the majority of the men in the tutorial planned to practice medicine.

Very often, the students who elected the system anticipated most of the prescribed regular work by two or three months of summer work. Many fourth-year students continued with advanced work in the medical sciences as preparation for their anticipated future clinical activity. Some became members of established research groups and thus achieved pleasant acquaintanceships with those of similar interests. It was made explicitly clear to the students "that the laboratory is not a sanctuary for the worship of authorities or heroes, but a free dwelling for students of medicine conscious of the faults and the virtues of those who surround them."[20] In the fourth year, informal weekly conferences with the subject matter chosen by the student were arranged.

Of the sixty-two men in the classes of 1925–29, inclusive, three have died and thirty-four of the remaining fifty-nine graduated with honors; fourteen are now (1976) in full-time work; and six have remained in the medical sciences. Those remaining are engaged in practice, and twelve are active in teaching hospitals. Of the twenty-five men who graduated with a grade of C, seven are in full-time work, and eighteen are in practice, of whom nine are in teaching hospitals.[21] Although this series is not large, the results suggest that

(1) Medical students can engage in special extracurricular work without danger to their regular work.

(2) As might be expected, men of superior capacity perform better than the mediocre, but the latter group also benefits from this type of teaching.

(3) A considerable percentage of the men exposed to this type of scientific training contribute to the advancement of medicine. The record seems to indicate that Dr. Edsall's original view that men of real capacity may go undiscovered unless specific efforts are made to flush them out was accurate.

Edsall commented[22] on the changes that had been made in the teaching program. These included not only the development of comprehensive examinations but also the use of tutors in the English style (as Edsall had worked with his tutor at the University of Pennsylvania), the requirement of a thesis, a new system of elective courses, and, of importance in the present context, opportunities for the top 15 percent of the senior class to do independent work, even in some cases at another school.

Eugene Landis, Professor of Physiology, devised an ingenious plan for permitting students to find their own pace. He arranged each exercise so that the slowest could finish the required portion. He added graded increments of work that superior students could, but did not have to, finish in proportion to the degree of their superiority. It is evident from the votes of the Faculty of Medicine that the need for advice and counsel for the average student was recognized.

While the tutorial system was operating for the superior student, the system of advisers was being worked out for the entire school. At the meeting of October 13, 1921, of the Harvard Medical Faculty Administrative Board, it was evident that considerable thought had been given to the *adviser* problem prior to the meeting of October 13, 1921. On that date, however, a Dr. Day "appeared before the Board to present his plan for an *adviser system*. He proposed that some Faculty member who was well acquainted with the whole staff of instructors and who was quick to grasp the boys' point of view, should interview every student within six months of his arrival. He would then, provided the student wished an adviser, decide to what instructor he might most successfully be assigned. If the instructor thus selected proved an unfortunate choice, the student might return to the original Faculty member for reassignment."[23]

Dr. Worth Hale, Assistant Dean, reported that the third-year class believed that a general adviser system would not be successful, "but urged that a man in danger of failure be assigned to an adviser, who could perhaps find out where the difficulties lay . . ." Dr. Hale also reported that the first-year class thought it would be well to give the plan a trial.

At a Meeting of the Faculty of Medicine on March 10, 1922, it was voted

> that an *adviser* be selected for every twenty-five men of the first class to confer with them regarding methods of work, use of free time, et cetera, and that each adviser continue associated with his group until the end of the second year when he shall be replaced by another adviser who shall serve similarly for the last two years of medical course.[24]

The system does not seem to have accomplished much.

Another aspect of the problem of the curriculum is to make the basic subjects pertain, or at least appear relevant to, the clinical interests and ambitions of students. The problem became increasingly troublesome as the preclinical curriculum became more specialized and more extensive, and as fewer of its teachers were physicians with clinical experience. This was a development of the twentieth century.

During Harvey Cushing's tenure as Professor of Surgery at Harvard and Chief of Surgery at the Peter Bent Brigham Hospital during the 1920's, the first-year students were given frequent clinical demonstrations in the operating room, the patient used having a condition related to that part of the course in gross anatomy then being taught at the School. In the 1930's and subsequently, Dr. Herrman L. Blumgart and his colleagues at the Beth Israel Hospital gave comparable clinical demonstrations in physiology. These were particularly interesting because at the insistence of Dr. Eugene Landis, Professor of Physiology, the clinical demonstrations were given before each group of physiology laboratory sessions. Later, clinical demonstrations were also given in the second-year courses in Bacteriology and Pharmacology. And, of course, the clinical-pathological conferences played a similar role in second-year Pathology (below, p. 270). In the third and fourth years a different approach obtained, in that the basic science material was used to help teach clinical medicine specifically.

Concerning the content of the curriculum, it is evident that struggle with it has been going on for a long, long time. See, for example, the Minutes of the Meeting of the Faculty of Medicine of fifty years ago (specifically February 3, 1922, and March 10, 1922). In the last decades, a great increase in the content of the laboratory bio-sciences, combined with the by then established notion that the way to learn clinical medicine is solely through laboratory science, has led to attempts to revise the curriculum so as to organize the basic data in a comprehensive manner. Such attempts suffer from a number of fundamental disadvantages, not the least of which is the erroneous belief that knowledge is absolute and not derived from the methods used to obtain it. At any rate, these attempts are currently under critical scrutiny and will not be discussed here.

For many years, graduate teaching in medicine has been carried on in Harvard University. In the beginning, it was informal. Students were simply encouraged to continue their studies beyond the regular curriculum prescribed for the degree of Doctor of Medicine. They were also offered opportunities to engage in research. As early as the 1870's there were university medical centers in the United States which were rapidly catching up with, and in some cases even surpassing, their European counterparts.

On November 29, 1872, the Faculty approved a comprehensive scheme for the establishment of "a special course for physicians." This course of study was publicized in the official Catalogue of the University: "For the purpose of affording to those already Graduates in Medicine, additional facilities for pursuing clinical, laboratory, and other studies, for which they had not previously found such subjects as may specially interest them; and as a substitute in part for the opportunities heretofore sought for in Europe." Courses were outlined in physiology, medical chemistry, pathology, surgery, and some of the specialties.

The action that led to the establishment of the Courses for Graduates in the Harvard Medical School occurred in a Faculty meeting held at the home of Dean Calvin Ellis, who also served as the Jackson Professor of Clinical Medicine. Also present was President Charles William Eliot and eleven other members of the Faculty of Medicine attended.

Although women were not admitted to the formal courses as degree candidates in the Medical School until 1945, a statement by the Faculty for the School of Medical Graduates noted in 1915 that women were not excluded from the courses, their admission being a matter "that rests with the Department." Three women were listed in that year.

On recommendation of the Faculty of Medicine in 1911, the Graduate School of Medicine of Harvard University was formally organized with a separate Dean, Dr. Horace David Arnold, and Administrative Board. In 1919 the Faculty of Medicine considered that a closer relationship between the undergraduate and graduate schools was desirable, and the Faculty voted to recommend to the Corporation that all instruction given under the Graduate School of Medicine should be grouped as "Courses for Graduates." The Corporation approved, and it became effective at the beginning of the fall term in 1919. In 1945 further reorganization of the Courses for Graduates took place, and the separate Faculty of the Courses was abolished. Then, all of the formal instruction to graduates in medicine became the responsibility of the Faculty of Medicine. There was a Standing Committee to supervise the Courses for Graduates, and all courses of instruction were placed under the direction of the heads of the Departments, as had been the case in the past.

In 1968 the Courses for Graduates carried out a considerable expansion of its activities by initiating programs of continuing education in community hospitals. In line with this change and the further broadening of its functions implicit in the changes just mentioned, the department was renamed "Department of Continuing Education."

Today, one can find a reversal of the trend of the preceding hundred years. Physicians from many foreign countries enroll in the Continuing Education courses. In 1971–72 the Department offered its first overseas course, "Diabetes Mellitus in Relation to General Medicine." It was given in Buenos Aires by a combination of Harvard and the University of Buenos Aires, and some 500 physicians from South America attended. The course was repeated in 1972–73 in Mexico City.

Chapter Eleven

The Preclinical Curriculum, I

B Y World War II Harvard medicine had reached a peak, characterized by the outstanding quality of a large number of senior students, particularly in terms of motivation and clinical maturity. The War put a stop to all this, accelerating in time and retarding in quality the students' curriculum and removing a large segment of teachers, who entered military service. After the War the return of these teachers and of students who believed they had been deprived of normal opportunities for education and training, created a short-lived renaissance of academic training.

George Packer Berry had been Dean after the war years, and his judicious and efficient analysis of how to keep academic medicine functioning, if not flourishing, during this difficult period of readjustment was helpful, but it could not prevent or even foresee the changes that were occurring. On the one hand, his planning—which was widely accepted—permitted students to remain free from military service until they had graduated and had finished from one to three years of internship and residency. This limitation on training was compensated for by a large number of fellowships, governmental and other, available to those who had fulfilled their military obligations. Approximately 25 percent of all fellowships in the medical sciences were held at Harvard and its hospitals. Since federal money was available to support these training programs—money that paid an institution and provided salaries for teachers—there was a strong stimulus to increase the teaching staffs of clinical services by adding men who belonged to a now fashionable group. They had written papers on basic-science applications to clinical problems, with more emphasis on the former than the latter. At the same time, the development of the National Institutes of Health, which poured many millions of dollars annually into the support of research with not one cent for purely clinical studies, began to change medical teaching. Huge government grants began to pay faculty salaries, some of which required that 80 percent of the time be spent in research. The Faculty at Harvard, as at all other medical schools, expanded by hiring men with little or no interest in clinical medicine.

The removal of the School in 1906 to the elegant Longwood Avenue Quadrangle permitted education within it to proceed free from the irritations caused by physical crowding but with an increase in tension caused by the need to change the curriculum almost daily. The change in content and method of each course had to be readjusted not only to the laboratory division's new quarters, but to the continuous growth of knowledge. Today it is impossible to imagine the spaciousness of the laboratories. It is also impossible for those who did not experience it to appreciate the vast amount of detail that the students were required to learn. As rapidly as the content was shown to be wrong or incomplete, it was replaced by other material, much of which soon was also shown to be wrong or incomplete. This process is going on at a more rapid pace today, a fact that should confound the creators of homogenized, so-called "integrated" (a greatly admired word today) curricula. In the first half of the twentieth century, each department had its hours, which it filled as dictated by its own judgment of what was not only important but likely to last for a reasonable time. Naturally, the content of each course as taught to medical students reflected the status of the corresponding science in general. But at that time there was no widespread conviction that the science was the thing, regardless of whether the way it was taught was demonstrably applicable to man. The latter view, of course, prevails today.

ANATOMY

There is no doubt that interest in gross anatomy was decreasing, and for three reasons: (1) the possibility of new discoveries was remote, hence the subject was not attractive to many young men; (2) even among surgeons or future surgeons, interest in surgery was narrowing, because the specialization that was rapidly developing was likely to limit interest to one area or system in the body. In the mid-1920's, because gross anatomy was taught entirely by clinicians, the subject had another reason for its loss of status as an area for research; (3) with the rise of histology and embryology new ways of looking at familiar structures came to the fore, and these new findings, though based on the old, often overshadowed them.

The science of mammalian embryology owed much of its development in this country to Charles Sedgwick Minot. He not only developed and taught the subject, but collected one of the greatest array of serial sections of human embryos—down to ten millimeters in size and smaller. This amazing collection, still largely intact, for decades served researchers into human embryology and the origin of congenital malformations.

Regardless of its diminished usefulness today, this collection remains a monument to human devotion to scholarship.

The course of histology and embryology—both highly important as the bases of human pathology—was maintained and advanced by the fortunate presence in the Anatomy Department of Professors John L. Bremer and Frederic T. Lewis. At that time the leading histology text was in German—Philipp Stöhr had been its author. Professor Lewis translated and revised it, and it became Lewis and Stöhr's *Histology.* Subsequent editions broke away from the old German material and became Lewis and Bremer's *Histology.*[1] The Department therefore had a large investment in both embryology and histology. The next professor was to be expert in both. In a highly imaginative way, he added the new techniques of histochemistry to the more traditional methods then in use.

Professor George Wislocki, Parkman Professor of Anatomy, has given an account of his stewardship of the Department of Anatomy from 1931 to 1943.[2] In a report covering these years, he prepared a statement of his ideas concerning future developments in the Department, especially in relation to his primary intention of attracting talented young investigators. His research policy was not to define a program with himself at the peak of a rigidly constructed pyramid in which his associates were obliged to participate. He sought, rather, to select men of ability and imagination, allowing them wide and independent scope of selection of problems for study. Professor Wislocki emphasized the need to evaluate constantly the channels in which productive research in anatomy might proceed. For example, developments in biochemistry and physical chemistry already provided opportunities for a new approach to the study of cells and tissues.

Likewise, recent advances in physical chemistry, he predicted, would offer far-reaching opportunities for their application to cells and tissues —for example, studying living and dead cellular systems by means of polarizing and fluorescent microscopes, microspectrography and X-ray diffraction, and the electron microscope. His predictions have come true to a remarkable degree, and today's anatomy is largely as he then envisioned it.

After World War II, Professor Don W. Fawcett became active in research. In the early 1950's the electron microscope was first being applied to mammalian tissues. The results were full of distortion and artifact, but Dr. Fawcett felt that he had to have firsthand experience with this new instrument in order to judge its potenial for biomedical research. He therefore obtained a leave of absence and went to the Rockefeller Institute to work as a Visiting Investigator in the laboratory of Dr. Keith Porter. Returning to Boston as an Assistant Professor of Anatomy, Fawcett successfully applied for funds for the first electron microscope at the Medical School. Later, in 1955, he accepted the Chair of Anatomy at Cornell Medical College in New York, where he continued electron microscopic studies of various tissues and organs. In a notable study of the Lucké tumor of frogs, he was able to find virus particles and reconstruct various stages in their assembly. This seems to have been the first electron-microscopic description of a herpes-type virus associated with a cancer. He then developed a strong interest in reproductive biology, being especially fascinated by studies of spermatogenesis and sperm structure. In 1959 he returned to Harvard as Hersey Professor of Anatomy and proceeded to modernize the teaching of microscopic anatomy.

A vigorous predoctoral and postdoctoral program was developed in cell biology and ultrastructure. Two books, *The Cell and Its Organelles and Inclusions. An Atlas of Fine Structure,*[3] and a *Textbook of Histology*[4] have been significant contributions to teaching in this field. (The latter has sold 90,000 copies in its last edition.) The Anatomy Department at Harvard is now one of the most productive in the country in research on biological structure. In more recent years it has become obvious that other than the quest for lasting peace, no problem facing mankind is more urgent than the control of his own numbers. Dr. Fawcett therefore joined with Dr. Claude A. Villee, Jr., Dr. Roy O. Greep, and others in creating a center for basic research relevant to the population problem. This has now come to fruition in the Laboratories of Human Reproduction and Reproductive Biology.

Today, Elizabeth D. Hay is Louise Foote Pfeiffer Professor of Embryology.[5] Her interest in cell and development biology was awakened at Smith College, where she did an honors thesis. In 1958 Professor Hay published the first ultrastructural study on the state of differentiation of blastema cells in the amphibian. In the same year Charles P. Leblond and others first reported the usefulness of tritiated thymidine for autoradiography, and Dr. Hay began at once to apply autoradiographic techniques to the study of the origin of the regeneration blastema.

Moving to Harvard in 1960 with Dr. Fawcett, she began a collaboration with a young biochemist who had joined the Department as a postdoctoral fellow, a collaboration that led to one of the first successful applications of autoradiography at the electron microscopic level. With this technique, Jean-Paul Revel and Hay subsequently studied the cellular sites of synthesis of DNA, collagen, and mucopolysaccharides. The fine structure and histochemistry of embryonic and regenerating tissues are under intensive study, and teaching based on this new information is now part of the first-year course.

When Professor Fawcett returned to Harvard as Chairman of the Department, he recognized the need to have more forceful representation in the field of neuroanatomy, and he therefore arranged for the appointment of Dr. Sanford Palay as Bullard Professor of Neuroanatomy. This subject has become important in anatomical research. Well over 50 percent of the papers presented at the annual meetings of the American Association of Anatomists are now devoted to neuroanatomy. Palay's own contributions have been based upon the application of electron microscopy to the study of the organization of the nervous system and the development of the field of neurocytology.

The increase in the size of the Department has turned it more and more in the direction of research and postgraduate training, but it still contributes importantly to the preclinical curriculum.

PHYSIOLOGY

Professor William T. Porter occupies a unique place in the history of Harvard physiology. The course had been established at Harvard by Bowditch, who had earned his reputation in Germany as an outstanding physiologist. Dr. Porter fitted perfectly into the company of scholars who functioned in the last part of the Eliot era. In his youth, the latter part of the nineteenth century, physiology was almost entirely talk and textbook,[6] and it was the general custom for students to put off their work on the subject until about six weeks before the final examination at the year's end. Stenographic notes of Dr. Bowditch's splendid lectures could be obtained for a price. Nearly all of the students passed.

It is easy enough to say that physiology should be taught by experiments carried out by the students themselves. In 1900, 220 students worked four months in the Physiology Laboratory and could have used more than 100 kymographs, typically a power-driven smoked drum on which various kinds of action can be recorded. They were made principally in Leipzig and cost $200 each delivered in America. It took five or six months to obtain the apparatus ordered. As rich as Harvard was, comparatively speaking, it could not undertake to equip 200 students at such prices. A solution was for the Department of Physiology to make its own essential apparatus.

A new Department of Comparative Physiology was established for Professor Porter in 1906, in order to train investigators. The department had, otherwise, no teaching obligations. In order to support the enterprise, it would be necessary to sell some of the apparatus, but there was a difficulty in that: profit-making could not be allowed on untaxed property. Therefore, President Eliot himself raised the original capital when the Harvard Apparatus Company was founded in 1901 by Professor Porter.

Various Boston philanthropists, as well as professors, came to the Company's aid, and in 1929 the Company was offered as a free gift to the American Physiological Society. The Council of the Society went on record as saying that in its judgment it would not be practicable for the Society to undertake or to supervise the management of the Company. The Council also stated, however, that no other agency during recent years had contributed more to the development of sound teaching in experimental physiology in this country than had the Company.

There was no desire that the Harvard Apparatus Company should interfere with commercial instrument-makers. In fact, the Harvard inventions were available to them at all times. They were not patented. The Harvard physiological apparatus has now been sent to more than 160 laboratories in the United States and to more than 50 laboratories in such foreign countries as Syria, Russia, Japan, and Australia.

Professor Porter retired in 1928 but continued as active head and guide of the Company until a few months before his death in 1934 at the age of 87. A few years afterward a charter was obtained from the Commonwealth of Massachusetts, which incorporated the Harvard Apparatus Company as an educational institution for the promotion of physiology and similar sciences. It was essential that "accidental" profits be used for fellowships controlled entirely by the American Physiological Society. The apparatus made was sold only to physiologists and to persons themselves engaged in physiological work. The Company was and is a financially sound organization. In twenty-eight years, 1921–49, it contributed a total of $38,453 to the American Physiological Society for the Porter Fellowship in Physiological Research. Dr. Porter twice offered the Company to the Society, which refused to accept it. The Harvard Apparatus Company still exists—in fact, flourishes.

In 1897 Dr. Porter had started the *American Journal of Physiology.* As the sole responsible editor and publisher, he carried the financial and intellectual burdens until 1914, by which time thirty-four volumes of the *Journal* had been published. In 1914 he presented the *Journal* to the American Physiological Society. The *Journal*, like the Apparatus Company, will always remain as a monument to Dr. Porter's devotion to the requirements of students and scholars everywhere.

Dr. Porter's accomplishments in teaching were overshadowed, however, by the brilliant performance of his younger colleague, Walter Bradford Cannon, who had succeeded Bowditch as George Higginson Professor of Physiology. Cannon was born October 19, 1871, of Scotch-Irish descent, in Prairie du Chien, Wisconsin. He was an only son. Of his three sisters, Ida became well known in the medical world as one of the founders, with Richard Cabot, of hospital social service—the first in America, or for that matter the world. He attended public schools in

Milwaukee and St. Paul and with more courage than support enrolled at Harvard. In 1896 he was graduated *summa cum laude*. In his undergraduate years he was greatly influenced by William James—so much so that he seriously considered a career of philosophy. James himself advised him not to do it. "You will be filling your belly with the east wind," was James's warning. Cannon then returned to his original plan of entering the Medical School. From the very beginning he carried on research; for example, in his first year, he conducted original experiments, observing the process of deglutition and peristalsis, as revealed by X rays, using opaque substances, starting with pearl buttons passing down the esophagus of a goose. His interest in the case method of teaching law and how he applied it, with the wholehearted support of President Eliot, to medicine has been discussed (above, p. 52). This became the basis for the Cabot Clinics at the Massachusetts General Hospital.[7]

He held low rank from 1900 to 1906, then was appointed the second George Higginson Professor of Physiology, succeeding Bowditch as head of the Department. Mrs. Cannon, according to her son Bradford, often mentioned a comment by Mrs. Irving Babbitt, who, when Dr. Cannon was made a full professor, said, "I hope he'll now discontinue those disgusting researches on the stomach and intestines."[8]

Dr. Cannon considered himself "one of Bowditch's sons, and a grandson of Ludwig on one side and Jeffries Wyman on the other, with perhaps a great uncle, Claude Bernard." The Mayo Clinic tried very hard to get him and Otto Folin to join their staff. Cannon wrote: "Where could I as a physiologist be of greatest service to medicine?" thereby indicating his decision to remain at Harvard.

In 1930 the Rockefeller Foundation made a gift of $175,000 to Harvard "for research in physiology under Dr. Cannon, and for physical chemistry." Previous to this, the Foundation had always supported projects, not persons.

Cannon's early work on gastrointestinal motility provided a practical as well as theoretical groundwork for an understanding of digestive activity. It was from these observations that the immensely practical barium meal as a diagnostic tool was devised. Perhaps more important, these observations gave Cannon a lifelong interest in the way the autonomic nervous system helps to sustain the constancy of the internal environment.

At the beginning of his studies on gastrointestinal motility Cannon was frustrated by the fact that sudden termination of all gastrointestinal movement would sometimes occur in the animal under study. It soon became evident that these cessations of activity could be correlated with emotional tension. Pain, fear, anger—all had the same result. He was able to show the initiation of digestive activity is effected largely through the splanchnic nerves, which constitute the sympathetic supply to a large part of the abdominal organs, including the adrenal glands. The parasympathetic nerves, especially the vagi, were shown to bring about an increase in motility, and, as Pavlov had described a little earlier, an increase in gastric secretion.[9] Cannon then elaborated the hypothesis that the sympathetic nervous system and the adrenal glands together form an elementary arrangement for adjusting the body to emergency situations. On the other hand, the parasympathetic pathways include control of a number of more discrete elements, each of which is primarily concerned with a specific part of the body's normal activity. As mentioned, this material was gathered together in a book, *Bodily Changes in Pain, Hunger, Fear and Rage* (1915). The concept that an endocrine gland, such as the adrenals, could be turned on or off according to circumstances encountered severe opposition, and a long controversy ensued. In the end, Cannon's view prevailed.

Cannon prepared the denervated heart for use as a sensitive indicator of the action of the adrenals in the otherwise undamaged animal. Three important lines of investigation grew out of this experimental preparation. First, Cannon demonstrated with it that the sympathetic nerves produce their effects through the mediation of an adrenalin-like substance, called sympathin at that time but now known as norepinephrine. Second, his students were able to show subsequently that many organs and even individual nerve cells become more susceptible to chemical influences after the normal nerve supply has degenerated. Later, the same series of experiments led to the preparation of animals without any sympathetic nervous system. These animals were capable of leading satisfactory lives as long as they were protected by the environment of the laboratory. They were, on the other hand, unable to adjust to abnormal or threatening circumstances, such as extremes of temperature, severe exercise, blood loss, and a number of other stresses. Cannon combined his observations with those of Claude Bernard, whose famous statement was that constancy of the internal environ is a condition of free life.

Cannon also carried out extensive work on the autonomic neuroeffector systems with Arturo Rosenblueth as collaborator. Years later the Nobel Prize in Physiology and Medicine was awarded to others for an elaboration on this work.[10] Cannon was several times considered to be of Nobel quality.

When World War I came, Cannon, although 46 years old, enlisted in April 1917 as a first lieutenant in the Harvard Hospital Unit, whose special interest was the study of wound shock. An unhappy aspect of his experience is described below (p. xxx).

For his work he received many honors, despite the seriously erroneous conclusion part of the work contained.

Walter Bradford Cannon, Higginson Professor of Physiology. A found-er of modern physiology and the first to use opaque material for gastro-intestinal X-ray studies. From a portrait by Marie Danforth Page in the Harvard Medical Portrait Collection.

Cannon coined the term "homeostasis"—the tendency of all complex organisms to maintain a steady internal state. Cannon's view greatly influenced clinical practice as well as theoretical aspects of physiology and psychology. His primary experiments were mainly concerned with the role of the autonomic nervous system in regulating the course of assimilation, circulation, respiration, and excretory reactions. As Morison has pointed out, Cannon's influence on the behavioral and social sciences persists in an important way. Thus what he was really creating was a background for psychosomatic medicine. He attempted to extend the theory of homeostasis into the social and economic sphere, described most fully in *The Wisdom of the Body* (1932), which today is considered to be principally a stimulating but limited analogy.

Evidence that creative activity is not limited to youth were his studies of wound shock carried out when he was 46–51 years of age, homeostasis when he was 51–59, chemical mediation of nerve impulses at 59–68, and the phenomenon of a pacemaker in the rhythmic pulsations of the cerebral cortex when he was over 70 years of age. Two other books by Cannon should be mentioned: *Digestion and Health* (Norton, 1936) and *Autonomic Neuro-Effector Systems* (Macmillan Co., 1937).

Cannon's influence on students in college was very great indeed. His philosophy of science was chiefly a matter of ordinary common sense. Rather than defining knowledge, his writings concentrate on its acquisition. Cannon was clearly a liberal in his attitude toward the Soviet Union. Although he was fully aware of the many restrictions on political liberty and the ordinary basic human rights found there, he concerned himself chiefly with efforts to improve the health, education, and general welfare of the Soviet peoples. His fast friendship with a fellow physiologist, Juan Negrín, caused him to take an active interest in the Spanish Loyalist cause, for which he suffered severe criticism.

He was, as Morison has pointed out,[11] basically an enlightened nineteenth-century liberal, and his attitude toward life as a whole was similar to his approach to laboratory investigation—simple, direct, devoted, and optimistic. In Philip Bard's introduction to a special edition of *The Way of an Investigator*, published for the 1968 International Congress of Physiological Sciences, he mentioned the man's "whimsical humor, his modesty, fairness, and helpfulness [which] drew the abiding affection and loyalty of his students and fellow workers, his great energy and zeal for the establishment of truth their wondering respect."

It was Cannon's belief in the international brotherhood of man, the universality of science, that took him to the Peking Union Medical College, and to his involvement in the American Bureau for Medical Aid to China and the United China Relief, to the formation of the Medical Bureau to Aid Spanish Democracy, and to the organization of the American-

Soviet Medical Society. In *The Way of an Investigator* he concluded the chapter entitled "Being a Citizen" with the following remarks:

All these considerations have a direct bearing on the role of the scientific investigator as a citizen. The unchecked pursuit of his most cherished desires depends immediately on the liberty which a democratic government most reliably provides. He does well, therefore, to watch over it and, if necessary, to go forth from his "serene attachment to the processes of inquiry and understanding" to battle for its security.

I am grateful that fortunate conditions gave me opportunities to test democratic methods by opposing the efforts of antivivisectionists at destroying freedom of medical investigation; to attempt aiding republican forces in Spain and in China as a struggle against oppressors; and to promote deeper sympathy and understanding between Americans and the Russians as they look forward to a better world.[12]

Dr. Cannon retired to Emeritus status in 1942, having been thirty-six years head of the Department. He died in 1945. It seems very clear now that the damage inflicted on Dr. Cannon by X rays played a dominant role in his eventual death. Not only was there widespread carcinoma of the skin, but a malignant lesion was found in his eye.

Another notable Harvard physiologist was Alexander Forbes, a grandson of Ralph Waldo Emerson. He was a pioneer in the early development of electrophysiology and continued to exert leadership in that field for more than fifty years. Dr. Forbes was a man of great versatility. While publishing more than a hundred papers on the nervous system, he was writing articles and books on the geography of Labrador, on oblique photogrammetry from the air, and on offshore navigation. He excelled in figure skating, skiing, sailing, and riding when he was more than eighty years of age. For thirty years he piloted his own airplanes. Much to his annoyance, the night flying provisions of his license were revoked when he reached the age of seventy.

Young Forbes was influenced by Professor G. H. Parker in deciding to make his career in neurophysiology. He was graduated from the Harvard Medical School in 1910, and then, at the suggestion of Walter Cannon, he went directly to work under Sir Charles Sherrington, then of Liverpool, on the physiology of the splinal reflexes. After a brief visit to Keith Lucas and E. D. Adrian at Cambridge, his interests broadened to include the peripheral nerves. This visit to Cambridge led him to the concept of applying precise biophysical studies to the peripheral nerves. These techniques, developed by the Cambridge workers, also led Forbes to attempt interpretation of the relatively complex spinal reflexes by the new biophysical approaches then being studied by the Sherrington school.

On Dr. Forbes' return from England, he brought with him a Sherrington guillotine and a Lucas pendulum, to which he soon added a string galvanometer, certainly one of the first in New England.[13] His earliest studies of the flexion reflex, using the new electrical techniques, were published with Alan Gregg in 1915.

With the onset of the first World War, Dr. Forbes joined the Navy, where he was assigned first to radio research and later to radio compass duty. Although these activities seemed to be an interruption of his career, in actuality they were important in his development: Forbes became expert in the new art and science of electronics. When the War was over, he applied this knowledge to study of the nerve.

The circuit of the first vacuum tube amplifier to be used for recording action potentials was published by Forbes and Thacher in 1920. With this tool they carried out a series of studies of the electrical characteristics of spinal reflexes. The work culminated in an extraordinarily fine article in *Physiological Reviews*, "The Interpretation of Spinal Reflexes in Terms of Present Knowledge of Nerve Conduction." In this paper Forbes presented reasonable explanations for many properties of the central nervous system, stated in terms of the fundamental properties of peripheral nerve. This review, published in 1922, brought widespread recognition that a new school of neurophysiology had developed at Harvard, and led to the unusual promotion of Dr. Forbes from Instructor to Associate Professor in one move. His laboratory, from then until the outbreak of World War II, was a center for research students and neurophysiologists from all over the world. Concerning the 1922 review, Hallowell Davis said, "This article can justly be described as one of the foundations of the new science of cybernetics." The opinion was based on the great influence which the article had on Norbert Wiener and others who were interested in theoretical problems of organization and control.[14]

Forbes's work ranged from biophysical studies on excitability and conduction in peripheral nerve to pioneer investigations of electroencephalography. It complemented work on the autonomic nervous system being carried out simultaneously by Professor Cannon. During this productive period Forbes published papers with more than sixty colleagues and students, many of whom went on to become distinguished professors in various fields at Harvard and elsewhere.

He also obtained (with McPherson) what were probably the first photographic records of spontaneous electrical activity of the exposed cerebral cortex of an animal, although, like his predecessors with more primitive instruments, he failed at the time to appreciate their full significance. Later, he turned to problems of spinal shock and muscle tonus and also to sensory systems, notably the proprioceptive and the auditory.

Improvements in recording technique were a continuing interest. Alex pioneered in the application of the electron-tube amplifier in the days when a condenser-coupled amplifier was a new idea, and he is credited with the first reported application of an electron-tube amplifier in nerve physiology (1920), using his string galvanometer as the recording instrument. Later he (with Renshaw) was one of the first to explore the brain with microelectrodes.[15]

Professor Forbes rightly considered his most important contribution to science to be the paper published with Hallowell Davis and others in 1926, on "Conduction without progressive decrement in nerve under alcohol narcosis." Before this paper had appeared, the standard teaching "inferred that under narcosis conduction occurs with progressive decrement, the impulse becoming gradually smaller in the narcotized region." ". . . it follows that the energy of the impulse comes not from the stimulus but from the fiber . . ."[16] (The all-or-none law was thus more firmly established than ever.) Quite independently, G. Kato of Japan had published a similar study.[17] Professor Forbes was wryly amused when Kato asked him to propose him (Kato) for the Nobel Prize.

With the approach of World War II, Dr. Forbes joined the Navy again, in 1940 before Pearl Harbor, when he was nearly sixty years of age. While he entered the Medical Corps, he was soon detached from that service to undertake the exceedingly important mission of laying out a northern air route to Europe.

Dr. Forbes became Professor Emeritus in 1948, but he continued his physiological investigation as a guest in the Biological Laboratories in Cambridge. In this work he produced a fine series of electroretinographic studies of color vision in the turtle. This work was published in the *Journal of Neurophysiology* fifty-six years after his first publication as a medical student. He left a great tradition in neurophysiology to Harvard as well as vivid memories of his warm personality, his everlasting vigor and enthusiasm, his versatility, and above all his firm adherence to the highest principles of science, ethics, and the art of living.[18]

Hallowell Davis was long a collaborator of Alexander Forbes. In 1926 the view was still widely held that postural muscle tonus was a special kind of contraction controlled by the sympathetic nervous system. This led, in turn, to the development of the surgical procedure of "ramisection" for the relief of spastic paralysis. They collaborated in a series of experiments, and in a critical review of experiments and theories of others they effectively put an end to ramisection for the relief of spasticity.[19]

The "ovulation potential" caused a flurry of excitement about 1936 when it was claimed that ovulation in the human caused a long-lasting difference in DC potential between the two hands. If true, it could be the basis of a great improvement in the rhythm method of birth control. Unfortunately, it was not true. The Group (Forbes, Davis, and their co-workers) did confirm the presence of a small short-lasting ovulation potential in the rabbit, but a clinical study on women, in collaboration with Dr. John Rock, showed that ovulation potentials could not be detected reliably by external electrodes because of the much larger potentials that originate in the skin.[20]

For several years Hallowell Davis' own major interest and objective was to map and study the nervous activity in the auditory tracts. He assessed the activity by listening through earphones and later by viewing on a cathode ray oscilloscope. During this period, three attempts were made to assess activity in human patients on the operating table. It was not until many years later that their laboratory studies of the auditory nerve led to diagnostic tests based on the recording of action potentials in human subjects.

A major contribution to medicine and specifically to neurology was undoubtedly the recognition of seizure patterns in epilepsy and the technical development of the inkwriting electroencephalograph. They were the first group west of the Atlantic to confirm Hans Berger's description of the alpha rhythm, as recorded from scalp electrodes. This came about almost by accident, as a result of the curiosity of a graduate student, A. J. Derbyshire, and a second-year medical student, Howard Simpson. Their electrical equipment, developed for study of action potentials of the auditory nerve and including a cathode ray oscilloscope, was sufficiently sensitive and had a wide enough frequency band to look for the alpha waves. Davis is still not sure who first came upon Berger's description, hidden in a German journal of psychiatry, but after several initial failures they satisfied themselves that Berger's claim was real. Davis decided to study the phenomenon further but realized that to do so effectively one needed an immediate on-line write-out which would also provide a permanent record. The visual image on the oscilloscope was too fleeting, and the delay imposed by photographic recording made experimentation too tedious. Lovett Garceau was the electrical engineer who provided a Western Union "undulator" with stronger magnets and stiffer springs to give an inkwriting electroencephalograph. (Tönnies in Germany made a better instrument earlier, but the Group was unaware of his work at the time.) With the available equipment, the Group demonstrated the Berger rhythm to a medical audience in the Building

C amphitheatre. Don Lindsley was the subject who provided the alpha waves. It was the first such demonstration west of the Atlantic.

Fred and Erna Gibbs joined the Group shortly thereafter with the explicit objective of applying the method to the study of epilepsy. Dr. William Lennox provided patients who had frequent petit mal seizures. On the very first try, one evening in the Building C laboratory, the Group identified a characteristic pattern that was clearly associated in time with the subject's seizures. The pattern was so large that the Group was afraid it was an artifact, and, indeed, Hans Berger, who had seen the pattern, did dismiss it as artifact, but the Group was able to establish its validity. It is pathognomic for petit mal epilepsy.[21]

The inkwriting EEG machine was soon greatly improved by Albert Grass, who succeeded Lovett Garceau and who has continued to manufacture them and other electromedical equipment ever since that time. The Group took its instruments to many hospitals in a search for the patterns in epilepsy (the Gibbses had studied 1,000 cases by 1943) and also (Hallowell & Pauline Davis) for other patterns that might relate to neurosis or psychosis. The latter effort was unsuccessful, but the inkwriting EEG has become a standard piece of neurological diagnostic equipment. One of the original "undulator" EEG inkwriters and some early records are now preserved in the Countway Library for their historic interest.

An incidental discovery made in 1938 has led, many years later, to another clinical application of the EEG, in electric response audiometry. The discovery was the evoked potential, which can sometimes be detected in the raw EEG trace in response to acoustic or other abrupt sensory stimulation.[22] It was not feasible to use this response clinically, however, until small average-response computers became available.

Quite another chapter was the study of acoustic trauma or temporary deafness following exposure to loud sounds that the Group undertook early during World War II under the auspices of the National Defense Research Committee. The work was heavily classified at the time and was published only a number of years later.[23] Both guinea pigs and human subjects were used. The study was part of the beginning of activity in several institutions which led to modern ear protectors and how to protect hearing against permanent impairment by noise exposure.

A final problem, in which Alex Forbes participated, was a study of the control of the depth of anesthesia, using the brain waves as indicators of the depth of anesthesia. Henry K. Beecher participated in these experiments.[24] Feedback control of anesthesia was shown to be possible, but as far as Davis and the writers know, the method has not been widely employed.

With Eugene M. Landis' acceptance of the George Higginson Professorship at Harvard (1943), he set about the establishment of a greatly broadened approach to the teaching of Physiology with emphasis on *human* physiology and correlation of laboratory experimentation with theoretical problems.[25] Eugene Landis was a young genius who by the age of twenty-seven was quoted in the medical literature around the world for his studies of capillaries. He had been a professor of medicine before coming to Harvard. Landis also excelled in teaching and was a great force in bringing teaching methods in the field of physiology up to date. For him both laboratory and lectures had a prime goal: the creation of physicians out of medical students. Essentially, the techniques employed in clinical investigation or diagnosis are used in the laboratory. As a matter of fact, it is very often easier to study human beings than it is laboratory animals. The broadening of the scope of the first-year course in Physiology required new apparatus and new laboratory space. The renovation of the building was completed in March 1944. The space was broken up into "units for human physiology."[26] They involved four rooms on the third floor of Building C, two of which were large enough to accommodate easily a group of half a dozen students. Each of these two rooms had its own temperature control, so that the effect of temperature on metabolism could be studied. To this end, simple thermocouples and a portable galvanometer were used for determining skin temperatures and for following cutaneous vasoconstriction and vasodilatation in response to body warming and body chilling. The other two rooms of the group of four did not require constant environmental temperature. They contained plethysmographs for measuring blood flow. The effect of graded exercise on blood flow through the muscles of the forearm could be studied. In another experiment the students measured blood flow through the skin of the hand in response to heat, cold, pain, deep breathing, reactive hyperemia, and smoking. An adjacent forearm ergograph was used for contrasts by subjective symptoms and objective records of physiological fatigue which occurs in muscles with normal blood flow from the pain of experimentally produced intermittent claudication. Another unit allows the students to determine for human erythrocytes the isotonic and the hemolytic concentrations of sodium chloride, glucose and sucrose and the effects of venous congestion on their own hematocrit readings. In still another unit a three-channel, ink-writing oscillograph records graphically under several experimental conditions and in sequence the human electrocardiogram, venous and arterial pulses, pulse wave velocities, reaction times, reflex times, muscle action currents, and electroencephalograms.

Gastrointestinal physiology is studied with a fluoroscope. A tilt table is utilized for study of the circulatory events that precede syncope. A treadmill used to the point of exhaustion gives information about physical work. The students are rotated in groups of five through these units. In these studies, the students become familiar with the errors of standard methods which they will encounter in years to come. The same apparatus may be used during certain periods by graduate students or house officers who wish to return for short periods of special work.

It was necessary to prepare a new laboratory manual, inasmuch as the old manual did not include the types of study just mentioned. In Landis' experience, something over half of the laboratory work can be devoted to detailed and quantitative observations of function in man. In his judgment half of the time granted to the study of man is about all that should be utilized at the present time, lest the omission of the animal tissue experiments weaken rather than strengthen the course. At the end of each day's experimentation, some discussion of elementary pathological physiology was carried out.

Landis raised an essential question: "Should medical students be introduced to physiology by a detailed study of one tissue, e.g., the frog's gastrocnemius muscle—or should they be introduced at once to the human being as a complex, integrated, functioning organism?"[27] He answered it by saying that to begin the first laboratory hours in the course in medical physiology with the brief general study of certain gross and easily observable responses of normal man is not only logical but also of advantage for medical students. The effect is that future physicians learn very quickly, with a minimum of unfamiliar apparatus and a maximum of observation, that carefully planned, controlled, and systematically recorded studies can be quantitative and revealing. Very often the answers themselves produce still more questions. Among other things, the student learns to look for "the normal state," "biological variation," "controlled observations," "control period," and "reaction to stress."[28]

Each day's work was terminated with an introduction to pathological physiology, e.g. in the turtle heart, heart block, and induced fibrillation; with the frog's capillaries, the local effects of mechanical trauma and the effect of severe hemorrhage for the anesthetized cat. Thus study of the effects of hemorrhage and the value of fluid replacement could be observed.

After a general point of view is developed, the laboratory work varies. One section studied the effects of rotation through the units for special human physiology, a second studied respiration and acid-base equilibrium in man, and a third and fourth undertook analyses of normal and abnormal function in muscle and nerve. Rotation continued until all sections had covered all of the topics.

In the lecture room itself, principles were stressed, along with points of view and recent work, rather than facts available in textbooks. Conferences were held on each laboratory day at 4:30 P.M. with the intention of bringing together and comparing the results of various groups in each section. If aberrant results were obtained by one group or another, they were carefully contrasted with the average results obtained by the majority of groups.

Physiology is indeed only one of the preclinical sciences, but it should assume special responsibility for the establishment of proper habits in observation and interpretation of interlocking functions. "In the physiology laboratories, for the first time in their long education, students can logically be faced with the whole human being."[29]

Landis had been one of August Krogh's students. It is impossible to think of the modern status of the Department of Physiology in the Harvard Medical School without some thought of Krogh, who trained many students who achieved prominence, even distinction, in the Faculty of the School. In 1899 Krogh was working as an assistant to Christian Bohr at the Physiological Institute in Copenhagen. He was above all an experimentalist, and his finest work was done in a simple, original laboratory only later supplanted by fine buildings built by the Rockefeller Foundation. He carried out his observations on the capillaries under primitive circumstances, yet his work led to the Nobel Prize in 1920.

After 1910, Krogh became independent in the Ny Vestergade Laboratory. More than twenty Americans worked there with him. He had a hand in the training of eight full professors at Harvard, and all but two of his students became professors or heads of departments. With the possible exceptions of Sir Joseph Barcroft and Sir Thomas Lewis, Cecil Drinker believed, August Krogh had more American students than any of his contemporaries. Among Krogh's Harvard students were Drinker, Edward Churchill, Eugene Landis, and Henry K. Beecher. Professor Krogh received an honorary degree from Harvard at the Tercentenary in 1936. He died in 1949.

In more recent years, John Pappenheimer, at first a career investigator of the American Heart Association, achieved fame for the application of the pore theory to capillary function. He now holds the George Higginson Professorship and in addition to his teaching, is engaged in the study of relations between brain circulation and respiratory function. Also to be noted is Professor Thomas H. Wilson's book, *Intestinal Absorption*, published in 1962, his major field of interest for some years. Professor A. Clifford Barger in this period was doing outstanding work on some aspects of kidney function. Professor Elwood Henneman is known for his research on neuronal function and his teaching of this subject.

A separate Department of Physiology was organized under Cecil Drinker at the Harvard School of Public Health in 1922.

BIOLOGICAL CHEMISTRY

This subject has had a history unlike that of the others in the medical curriculum. It seemed destined for a great future several centuries ago. For example, in the early 1600's, Jean Baptiste van Helmont found urea in urine and designated it as a result of digestion. A hundred years later, Hermann Boerhaave isolated it, and before the end of the eighteenth century Rouelle suggested that it was the end product of nitrogen metabolism. Later authors believed that the purpose of urine secretion was to separate the excess nitrogen from the blood. With beginnings like this, plus the fact that the seventeenth century also saw the recognition of sugar in the diabetic urine and the normal presence of phosphorus in the blood, it is difficult to understand why biological chemistry was so slow to develop as a scientific discipline. The lamentable state, in the mid-nineteenth century, of the uses of chemistry in medicine is described by Graves, but there have been extraordinary advances in the field of biological chemistry in the past half century. Two key figures played a great part in these advances, the first and the second Hamilton Kuhn Professors of Biological Chemistry, Otto Folin (1867–1934) and A. Baird Hastings (1895–).[30]

Otto Folin was born in Sweden but came to this country when young. After receiving a Ph.D. degree at the University of Chicago in 1898, Folin accepted an Assistant Professorship of Chemistry at West Virginia University but soon was offered, in 1900, a new position as Research Biochemist at the McLean Hospital near Boston. The Director of that institution, Dr. Edward Cowles, believed that chemical study of the insane might lead to an understanding of mental diseases, a hope that still exists. Folin was chosen for the post. Although he was not hopeful that Cowles' idea was feasible, he undertook to study in a quantitative way the protein metabolism of normal versus mentally disturbed individuals by measuring, as accurately as possible, all of the normal nitrogenous and other products excreted in the urine, in order first to learn the normal range of variation. Most of his life Folin concerned himself with blood and urine in an effort to understand protein metabolism. He believed that his best papers were the half dozen appearing in 1905, concerned with this subject. These today are often referred to as the "Classic Papers of Professor Folin."

In 1907 Folin was offered an appointment as Associate Professor of Biological Chemistry at Harvard. In 1909 he became the first Hamilton Kuhn Professor at Harvard. During his entire career Professor Folin was fascinated by problems of measurement, the quantitative approach to techniques for examining biological substances.

The second Hamilton Kuhn Professor, A. Baird Hastings, has this to say about his predecessor:

> My distinguished predecessor, Professor Otto Folin, became head
> of the Department of Biological Chemistry in 1907. He revolutionized
> chemistry in medicine, both by his ingenious development of accurate,
> usable methods for blood and urine analysis and by his conceptual
> contributions to our knowledge of intermediary metabolism. His
> methods permitted diseases and pathological states to be studied in
> quantitative, instead of qualitative, chemical terms. Indeed, it may be
> said that he and his two contemporaries, Benedict of Cornell and Van
> Slyke of the Rockefeller Institute contributed most of the chemical
> tools used in medicine up to the dawn of the Isotope Age we are now
> in.[31]

One of Folin's major contributions was to stimulate interest in biochemical research among medical students, graduates, or physicians from far and near. Among these, two (J. B. Sumner and Edward A. Doisy) are Nobel Laureates.[32]

Dr. Harry C. Trimble was associated with Folin for many years and wrote:

> To those who had the privilege of personal association with Folin
> he was always a modest, friendly and unassuming leader. Finding his
> chief delights in his family circle, his department at the Harvard
> Medical School, and in the game of golf at which he excelled, Folin's
> daily routine was simple and regular. Every morning of the school
> year he was early at his laboratory. There the young and struggling
> worker in biochemistry, whether from his own or other departments,
> or other universities, would always find the door unlatched. To all who
> entered, sympathetic listening, judicial discussion, and encouraging
> counsel were available. A quaint and always kindly humor made of
> every interview an occasion. Tall, erect, and spare of frame, possessed
> of a simple, innate dignity, he was always a striking figure, whether in
> his short white laboratory coat, in the lecture room, or at public meet-
> ings of scientific societies.[33]

Professor Folin will long be remembered as part of the great tradition of biological chemistry in the Harvard Medical School, not alone remembered by the Faculty, but also to twenty-six classes of medical students.

On the occasion of the twenty-fifth anniversary of Otto Folin's appointment as Professor of Biological Chemistry in Harvard University, several colleagues had planned a celebration to honor the man. What was to have been such a meeting became a memorial service, owing to his

Otto K. Folin, holder of the first chair of biological chemistry in America. Hamilton Kuhn Professor of Biological Chemistry at Harvard. His development of methods started clinical chemistry on its brilliant course. From a portrait in oil by Emil Pollak-Ottendorff (1934) in the Harvard Medical Portrait Collection.

death on October 24, 1934. Among those to comment was Henry A. Christian, who gave a warm tribute to Folin as a man, a "stimulating teacher and leader, above all as a wise, helpful and beloved colleague."

> You, my younger colleagues and students, scarce can vision medicine without the methods of blood analysis perfected by Folin and his pupils and those inspired by Folin's own accomplishments, so completely have these micro-methods of quantitative analysis become a factor integrated into the web and woof of the fabric of clinical medical and surgical lore . . .[34]

Stanley R. Benedict wrote in a letter to Professor Shaffer soon after Folin's death:

> One of the qualities which so impressed me in Folin, so rare among scientific workers, was the fact that he was able to drop out personalities when it came to a matter of difference of scientific opinion. I have known no one with whom it was possible to have such strenuous differences of opinion or viewpoint in scientific work and have this not interfere one iota in the close personal friendship which lasted over more than twenty-five years.[35]

Dr. Leo Loeb, in a letter to Professor Shaffer, commented that perhaps the most outstanding quality in Otto Folin was his imperturbable equanimity, but his relaxed dignity, and his refusal to take himself or anyone else too seriously, were also noteworthy characteristics. His shrewd judgment, which made him recognize that the orderly development of biological chemistry required more methods and standards than theories, kept American biological chemistry on the right track. Folin was not only a participant but a leader in the process whereby physiological and medical problems began to be referred more and more to chemistry. Owing in large measure to Folin's work at the beginning of the twentieth century, especially in the United States, the development of the biochemistries that pervade the biological and medical world today began to accelerate at an astounding pace. An important factor in the growth of biochemistry in this country was the development of Professor Folin's simple and accurate quantitative methods of analysis, enabling determinations to be made with small amounts of blood or other materials. Thus new and powerful tools were available to the student, a help in diagnosis as well as a guide to therapy.

There was no true biochemistry, in the current meaning of the term, until the chemists and the clinicians realized that each had something important to give to the other. This occurred at about the beginning of the twentieth century during the height of Folin's career.

Folin, working with Hsien Wu, introduced a system of blood analysis and established, in the process, the first truly quantitative laboratory course in biochemistry for medical students. The other who was particularly responsible for this early quantitative development was Dr. Donald D. Van Slyke of the Hospital of the Rockefeller Institute, who later, with John P. Peters, codified Quantitative Clinical Chemistry.

Folin and Van Slyke were not limited to devising techniques. There was Folin's work on intermediary metabolism and Van Slyke's on salts, water, and the acid-base balance in health and disease—both mere examples of a much larger body of work.

After Otto Folin's death in 1934, A. Baird Hastings became the second Hamilton Kuhn Professor of Biological Chemistry at Harvard. Coming out of a career that included a great deal of research, he chose at Harvard to expend most of his effort in organizing the available material in a solid course for medical students. A strong believer in individual responsibility, he chose to resign rather than to participate in the new "homogenized" first-year basic course, in which committees ruled but no man did. On December 12, 1958, just prior to his resignation, he addressed the Faculty in an emotion-laden and emotion-evoking speech. Believing that he had some heresies to present, he quoted President Conant's statement from his Tercentenary Address about the prevalence of heretics at Harvard. And in his initial remarks, Professor Hastings quoted another speech he had made to the Associated Harvard Clubs in Chicago, May 21, 1938, twenty years earlier, soon after coming to Harvard:

The present generation of first-year medical students is acquiring the habit of using Physiology in Anatomy, Chemistry in Physiology, and both Physiology and Histology in Chemistry. This break-down of the hard and fast divisions between the sciences of the first-year is, I am told, true also for the second-year subjects of Bacteriology, Pathology and Pharmacology.

It is to be hoped that the development of this habit of continuity of thought and the use of scientific information from course to course and year to year can be fostered through the clinical as well as the preclinical years. And then I told the following story: "I had an interview last week with the oldest member of our Department. I refer to our storeroom man, Mr. Henry Martin, whom many of you doubtless remember (20 years ago). In view of the fact that he has passed out unknowns to forty-three classes, I regard him as highly competent to brief me on 'Trends in teaching Biological Chemistry'." "You must have seen many changes in your period of service Mr. Martin," I suggested. "Well, I wouldn't say that things had changed very much," was his surprising reply. "When I came in '95, Professor Wood was interested in blood. Then Professor Folin came in 1908 and he introduced a lot of work on urine, and now you've come and we've gone back to work on blood again. No I wouldn't really say that there had been much change!"

Hastings believed that neither he nor Folin had been able to develop a course in biochemistry as good as might have been the case, owing to the fact that the entrance requirements in science were so low, and experience in quantitative analysis was not required.

In his frank discussion of problems viewed from the end of his career at Harvard, Hastings made a single recommendation: that the minimum preparation required in the natural sciences should be greatly increased from its then present 25 percent of college time. The requirements should include mathematics and quantitative analysis, he thought. His views on the matter were clearly in opposition to the trends of the times. He went on then to make clear his concept of biological chemistry, initiating the remarks with the sound question: "Is there a biochemistry?" One must bear in mind that there is not just one biochemistry; there are as many biochemistries as there are people who use chemical procedures and concepts in their study of living matter. Hastings goes on to say, "*Whatever* biochemistry is today—it owes as much to clinical medicine for its high place among the biological sciences—as medicine owes to *it*." He pointed out that "Its field of interest spreads from the structure and behavior of molecules to man, from the reaction of molecules with each other to the relation of man to his environment."[36]

In this address of 1958 Hastings commented that biophysics at that time was about where biochemistry was in 1900. Bold strides in this area had been made by Dr. Arthur Solomon, by Dr. Vallee in the Departments of Anatomy, Physiology, and Biophysics, and by Dr. Brownell at the Massachusetts General Hospital. "Diversity of approach was good for biochemistry—and diversity will be good for biophysics." Hastings hoped that there would be no urgency to define biophysics and thus, perhaps, limit its scope.

Baird Hastings gave a special tribute to Eric Ball. The upheaval in the world of science in wartime required Hastings' frequent appearance in Washington. For those four years, Eric Ball ran the Department with distinction, and again in 1952, when Hastings was on sabbatical leave. During World War II, Eric Ball served as Acting Head of the Department of Biological Chemistry, a post he held again in 1952 and in 1958–59. He was designated as official investigator for the Office of Scientific Research and Development in World War II, in which role he directed research programs on antidotes for the war gases and on the malarial parasite. The latter project led to the first cultivation of the malarial parasite *in vitro*.

Dr. Ball is a trustee of the Woods Hole Marine Biological Laboratory and is a member of the Corporation of the Woods Hole Oceanographic Institute, as well as the Bermuda Biological Station. He has held various editorial responsibilities; most important is that of the *Journal of Biological Chemistry*. Before his retirement, Dr. Ball was Edward S. Wood Professor of Biological Chemistry at Harvard Medical School. The group working under Dr. Ball had been especially interested in biological oxidations and intermediary metabolism. Dr. Ball became Chairman, in 1952, of the Division of Medical Sciences.[37]

Under his leadership, a revision of the program was made with a new course for first-year graduate students, entitled "Fundamentals of the Medical Sciences." This course has been taught jointly as a single enterprise by teachers from each of the basic science departments of the Medical School.

In addition to the two strong men, Folin and Hastings, there was Cyrus Fiske. He, along with Y. Subbarow, discovered phospho-creatine. They also discovered ATP at the same time as Lohmann. Thus our ideas of how muscles work were revolutionized.

The end of the Hastings era also marked the development of great changes in biochemistry. The advent of new techniques—chromatography, electrophoresis, electronic colorimeters and recording spectrophotometers, tracer methods, etc.—together with Government policies favoring basic research at the expense of clinical teaching, led to the accumulation of a vast number of bits of information, each part of a circumscribed area supervised by a specialist. The academic response to this crisis was the homogenized curriculum, where no one person had supervisory and planning responsibilities. Also, since specialists were favored over men of broad interest, the Department had to grow.

Accordingly, the third Hamilton Kuhn Professor had to be a different kind of person from the first two. Eugene P. Kennedy, the present incumbent, is an expert in the area of membrane biochemistry and was Chairman of the Department on a rotating system. He and his students have also been much interested in the biogenesis of membrane lipids. Their discovery of the cytidine coenzymes and their central role in the biogenesis of membrane phospholipids has led to investigations on the assembly of these complex molecules, investigations that some day will come to play a role in explaining clinical phenomena.

With the increased need of specialized teachers, the number of professors naturally grew. For example, Dr. Claude A. Villee, Andelot Professor of Biological Chemistry, has worked on and taught in the field of placental function. Professor Villee is also the author of a remarkable, highly popular biology textbook. Elkan R. Blout, Charles E. Harkness Professor of Biological Chemistry, is an expert in the structure of proteins and peptides.

An interesting phenomenon has been the development of a role for biochemists as leaders in certain types of hospital research. These men also taught at the School, although in some cases it was to give only one or two lectures a year. The practice began with the appointment to the staff of the Massachusetts General Hospital of Fritz Lipmann. He won a Nobel Prize, jointly with Sir Hans Krebs, and this event was considered a "recognition of the maturity of biochemistry in its ability to perform detailed chemical dissections of processes that for so many years had been known simply by the starting materials and the end products."[38]

Fritz Albert Lipmann was born June 12, 1899, at Koenigsberg, Germany. He received his education at the Universities of Koenigsberg, Berlin, and Munich, where he studied medicine, obtaining the M.D. degree in 1924 at Berlin. In his preclinical study, Lipmann was greatly impressed by Professor Klinger of Koenigsberg.

Lipmann, according to his biography, took a course in biochemistry in Berlin as early as 1923, but whether it was what is in this country now called biochemistry may be open to some doubt.[39] Following this, he held a fellowship in the Department of Pharmacology at the University of Amsterdam under Professor Ernst Laqueur. Lipmann, at this time feeling the need for further study of chemistry, returned to Koenigsberg to work under Professor Hans Meerwein, following which he returned to Berlin as an assistant in Professor Otto Meyerhof's laboratory in the Kaiser Wilhelm Institute. He decided then to stand for the Ph.D. degree, which he took in 1927. He then went with Meyerhof to Heidelberg, where he studied biochemical reactions in muscle. In 1930 he returned to the Kaiser Wilhelm Institute in Berlin as a Research Assistant in the laboratory of Albert Fischer. The plan was to apply biochemical methods to tissue cultures. Fischer, about to return to Copenhagen to occupy a new institute there, asked Lipmann to go with him, which he did in 1932. By this time anyone of the Jewish race was beginning to have difficulties or fear of difficulties in Germany. Lipmann spent 1931–32 as a Rockefeller Fellow in the laboratory of P. A. Levene at the Rockefeller Institute. On going to Copenhagen in 1932, he was given the title of Research Associate in the Biological Institute of the Carlsberg Foundation.

In 1939 Lipmann came to America to stay, but he was not interested in staking his entire future on a study of cancer research, as Dean Burke wanted him to do in his Cancer Unit at the National Institutes of Health. Following this, Lipmann had considerable difficulty in getting a suitable job. He was no longer young, although fairly well known, but, in his own words, he "unsuitably presented a certain self-reliance that often impressed others as arrogance."[40]

There was no place for him in the Department of Biochemistry in the Harvard Medical School. He landed in what he called a rather strange environment—the Department of Surgery at the Massachusetts General Hospital. This was arranged by Dr. Oliver Cope with the concurrence of the chief of the Department of Surgery, Professor Edward D. Churchill. It was there that he and his students discovered coenzyme A and identified pantothenic acid as one of its constituents.

Inevitably, such moving about and insecurity of position must have had a depressing effect on this gifted and sensitive man. His status was greatly enhanced, however, when, soon after his arrival in Boston, Dr. H. A. Barker, a well-known microbiologist of the University of California, indicated that he would like to spend a year with Lipmann. It was a great boon to this sorely tried man.

In 1949, uncomfortably close to the time he received the Nobel Prize (1953), Lipmann was named Professor of Biological Chemistry of the Harvard Medical School at the Massachusetts General Hospital. In 1957 he left to become a member and Professor at the Rockefeller Institute and now University.

In the late 40's and early 50's the discovery of coenzyme A opened up new areas of understanding of the mechanisms of biological phenomena. Lipmann also worked out the role of ATP in metabolic energy transfers.

Following his departure, Herman M. Kalckar filled the gap. During the 150th Anniversary of the Massachusetts General Hospital, Walter Bauer had, through his long friendship with Sir Henry Dale (who was, at that time, President of the Wellcome Trust) catalyzed a new development: a gift from the Wellcome Trust in London to the Massachusetts General Hospial for the salary of the Chief of the Biochemical Research Department. Dr. Kalckar was designated Professor of Biological Chemistry at the Massachusetts General Hospital, and Henry S. Wellcome, Biochemist. His work on the galactose transport system was a pioneering effort in a difficult field.

Another hospital-appointed Professor of Biochemistry was Jordi Folch-Pi, at the McLean Hospital. His work has been in the field of neural membranes and certain structural lipid-containing substances in the brain. The experiments were an outgrowth of his earlier experience with Donald D. Van Slyke at the Rockefeller Institute. Others included Bert L. Vallee, expert in metallo-enzymes at the Peter Bent Brigham Hospital; Dr. Roger W. Jeanloz, expert in glycoproteins at the Massachusetts General Hospital; Dr. Lewis Engel, steroid chemist at the Massachusetts

General Hospital; Paul M. Galop, connective-tissue investigator at the Children's Hospital and the Harvard Dental School; and Dr. W. Eugene Knox, enzyme chemist at the New England Deaconess Hospital.

All of these men, both those stationed at the Longwood Avenue Quadrangle and those at the various hospitals, trained Ph.D. candidates and postdoctoral fellows in their laboratories. Most of them spent far more time in these activities, in research, and in administration than in the teaching of medical students.

PHARMACOLOGY

The development of pharmacology was slow and complicated. As Dr. A. J. Clark pointed out in 1938, "Pharmacology is one of the youngest of the medical sciences; it is, indeed, a growth chiefly of the twentieth cenutry, and in consequence has very little history. Only three discoveries of major importance to pharmacology were made in the nineteenth century—namely, anaesthetics, antiseptics and endocrine therapy . . ."[41] Experience later supported the view that Harvard played a crucial role in the development of pharmacology. At the celebration of the One Hundredth Anniversary of the Harvard Medical School in 1883, Oliver Wendell Holmes, among other trenchant remarks, said that "it would be better if all drugs were sunk to the bottom of the sea, but worse for the fishes." Informed opinion of pharmacology in the early twentieth century was much the same:

> . . . the English apothecary, was able to accomplish the great ideal of the "surgery-boy" type,—the dispensing of immense quantities of "physic" in the most complicated prescriptions, to pass unquestioned down the willing throats of her Majesty's lieges.[42]

> . . . Of the four great remedies of Dr. Holyoke's and Dr. James Jackson's time, antimony has fallen from grace, and calomel, instead of being next the apothecary's right hand, as the letter *e* is to the printer's, has gone to an upper shelf, where it may be supposed to repent of its misdeeds, like Simeon Stylites. Cotton Mather had said a century and a half ago, "I am not sorry that antimonial emetics begin to be disused." He had said, too, more rhetorically, "Mercury, we know thee: but we are afraid thou wilt kill us, too, if we employ thee to kill them that kill us." This was a lively way of putting a thought long afterward made into a famous saying.[43]

> [If the] patient is [not] annoyed with over-medication,—painful and

Reid Hunt, Professor of Pharmacology. He helped develop modern pharmacology in America in the first third of the twentieth century. From an etching by Arthur W. Hentzelman, in the Harvard Medical Portrait Collection.

disgusting remedies,—the more tractable he is likely to be, and the less likely to throw his medicine out of the window, where it will kill the chickens instead of the fishes.[44]

Yet we must not be ungrateful to the pharmacist for the useful agents, old and new, which he puts in our hands. Opium and cinchona appear in our modern pharmacopoeia with all their virtues, but freed by chemical skills of the qualities which most interfered with their utility. Mercury is no longer considered a panacea, but it is still trusted for important special services. Most of the remedial plants have yielded their essential principles to chemical analysis, and have got rid of the useless portions which made them bulky and repulsive. Iodine, bromine, salicine, in their various compounds, have, within the present century, conferred inestimable aid in the treatment of some of the most formidable diseases. Many other new remedies, such as carbolic acid, glycerine, chloral, have been added to the list of those which are of daily use in combatting particular symptoms, or are adapted to certain exceptional conditions. The method of administering remedies by inhalation has been greatly extended, and the admirable invention of the process of subcutaneous injection—a method, I may remark, tried upon himself and made the subject of a thesis by the late Dr. Enoch Hale, a graduate of this School—has become, next to etherization, the most rapid and potent means of subduing pain and other forms of suffering. I need not speak of medical electricity, which has proved so serviceable in the treatment of nervous and muscular affections.[45]

A. J. Clark has defined pharmacology as "the study of the manner in which the functions of living organisms can be modified by chemical substances. The subject actually developed in a narrower field because its chief original aim was to provide a scientific basis for therapeutics. This study required [first] as its basis an adequate knowledge of the functions of the normal organism (physiology) and the derangements of these by disease (pathology), hence pharmacology developed later than the other medical sciences."[46] As pharmacology developed, an early task was to separate the folklore of therapeutic practice from demonstrable fact. The last half of the nineteenth century was largely given over to such tedious activities. In those days it must have been galling to have the physiologists patronize the pharmacologists as "mere collectors of uncorrelated data."

The modern era in pharmacology at Harvard began with the arrival of Reid Hunt in 1913. At that time all of his work on the thyroid and most of it on the choline derivatives had been completed, but remained the basis of much that he worked on and taught at Harvard. Hunt was born April 20, 1870, of Quaker parents and died March 10, 1948. After various academic experiences, he went to Johns Hopkins where he received his A.B. degree. In 1892 he enrolled as a medical student at the University of Bonn, and as a student of Professor C. Binz, his interest in pharmacology was aroused. There followed three years of graduate training in physiology under W. H. Howell at the Hopkins, where he took his Ph.D. in physiology in 1896 and received the M.D. the same year from the College of Physicians and Surgeons in Baltimore. Despite various other interests, he turned firmly to pharmacology in 1899 in the best possible American place: with J. J. Abel at the Johns Hopkins Medical School. He returned to Germany and worked with Paul Ehrlich in Frankfurt, after which he returned to the Hopkins. Shortly thereafter he was offered the Division of Pharmacology in the Hygiene Laboratory of the U.S. Public Health and Marine Hospital Service. For nine years he headed this division. After 1910 he was awarded a professorship. In September 1913 he was called to the Harvard Medical School as Professor of Pharmacology and Head of the Department. He became Professor Emeritus in 1936.

With his excellent background, and helped by the influence of Paul Ehrlich, it is not surprising that Hunt became a major figure in the Harvard Medical School, who achieved international fame with primary interest in the physiology and pharmacology of the autonomic nervous system and of the thyroid gland. While under Howell's influence, he had investigated the problem of the reflex blood pressure decrease and the relation of inhibitory to accelerator nerves of the heart. From this work, an important result emerged:

> ... the law of the antagonism of the cardiac nerves: when the accelerators and vagi are stimulated simultaneously the effect upon heart rate is determined by the relative strength of the two stimulating currents, and for submaximal stimuli the result is approximately the arithmetical mean of the effect of stimulating the nerves separately.[47]

While working in Abel's laboratory in 1900, Hunt observed that suprarenal extracts freed from epinephrine would lower the blood pressure, and that choline was one of the responsible substances. He also demonstrated that choline is a regular body constituent. This line of investigation had to be interrupted while he returned to Ehrlich in 1902, but on his return to America he soon found that acetylation increased the pharmacological activity of choline on blood pressure 100,000 times. It is doubtful that Hunt realized the importance of his discovery:

> The general conclusions he drew from this work in 1911 sound strangely modern, when he discusses the carrier function of the choline group for the esters and ethers of choline. "The role of this group

is probably to carry the compounds to definite cell structures—or, to use a comparison of Ehrlich's, to make them fit in a certain mosaic . . . The reasons for the efficiency of the group as a carrier and the low toxicity of its derivatives are perhaps to be found in the fact that choline is a constituent of probably all plant and animal cells; these have places into which the compounds can fit and the cells themselves containing such groups are not injured by them as they would be by new and unusual groups."
Ehrlich's concepts had entered the prepared mind of Hunt and he brought them to life in a new and independent manner that called forth the admiration of his teacher.[48]

It may surprise one today that the physiological implication of acetylcholine's powerful effect on the circulation should not have been recognized by him. The principal reason was probably that Hunt had assumed that the action of acetylcholine was purely a negative inotropic cardiac action. The situation became somewhat clearer when Sir Henry Dale in 1918 demonstrated the vasodilator action of acetylcholine, and Hunt then candidly admitted his error.

Hunt was a cautious man. His principal argument was that it had not been possible to show that acetylcholine was involved in the action of the depressor and other nerves. It required another five years before he could accept the important physiological role of acetylcholine after it was brought to light by Otto Loewi.

Hunt continued his interest in this field to the end of his academic career. In his systematic studies of the quaternary ammonium compounds and of related substances of particular theoretical interest, he broadened his contributions to the pharmacology of the autonomic nervous system. In his work with Ehrlich, he studied in mice the antagonistic action of various groups of substances to the poisonous action of the nitriles. He confirmed that mice could be protected against otherwise deadly doses by treatment with sodium thiosulfate and found that ethyl alcohol and dextrose had a similar protective effect.

On the hypothesis that an increase in basal metabolism should enhance the poisonous effect of acetonitrile by more rapid oxidation of the substance to hydrocyanic acid, he administered it to rats, guinea pigs, and mice, pre-treated for several days with thyroid. In agreement with his assumption, the lethal dose for rats and guinea pigs decreased. However, mice became very resistant to acetonitrile so that a multiple of the lethal dose for a normal animal was tolerated by a hyperthyroid mouse.[49]

This phenomenon in the mouse, which Hunt reported in 1905, has become widely known as the acetonitrile reaction of Hunt. He employed this reaction for the next twenty years as a tool for probing into various problems of thyroid physiology and pharmacology. He brought to light several important facts: Iodine compounds exert an action upon the organism through influencing the function of the thyroid gland. Some diets profoundly influence the incretory function of the thyroid. Preparations of thyroid gland have a physiological activity that is parallel to their iodine content. One can standardize, for therapeutic purposes, thyroid preparations by establishing a required percentage of iodine content.

Hunt worked in other fields as well. He was the pioneer in pointing out the dangers of methyl alcohol about the same time they had been recognized in Germany. His toxicity studies on arsphenamines, when these agents were first manufactured in this country, were highly important. He also showed that *Zygadenus venenosus* was responsible for the death of livestock because it contained substances similar to the veratrum alkaloids.

In the last half of Hunt's scientific life, he gave much thought to the problem of cancer and the hope of finding a specific remedy, but was able to make little or no progress. For many years he spent a great deal of time on the Pharmacopoeia, and his work on biological standardization was especially important. He did his best to promote the development of an internatonal Pharmacopoeia.

On all occasions, Reid Hunt showed a composure derived from the Quaker tradition of emotional control. He was a gentle and modest man, characteristics that belied the vigorous determination and persistence with which he fought against commercial exploitation of useless and dangerous drugs.

Pharmacology in America (and perhaps elsewhere as well) reached its peak during the Harvard career of Professor Otto Krayer, who served from 1939 to 1966. The remarkable achievements of Krayer and his staff placed his department at the very top.

It is interesting to compare the solitary, or almost solitary, scientist, Reid Hunt, working by himself in the nineteenth century, with Otto Krayer, who not only was a vigorous and imaginative "bench man" but one who guided and directed a formidable group of scholars, in the twentieth-century fashion. The concept of a group endeavor now occupies a much more prominent place than was true in the first years of this century. The men trained under Krayer, as will be noted later (page 264), have had a very great influence in this country and abroad.[50]

In 1939 the use of cholinesterase inhibitors *physostigmine* and *neostigmine* lacked a quantitative basis. Krayer used the inhibition of serum cholinesterase (in dogs and later in myasthenic patients) as a measure of the intensity and duration of the effect of the alkaloids in relation to dose. From this relationship, it became evident why the extremely high doses of the inhibitors were needed, *in vivo*, in order to achieve high degrees of inhibition of the cholinesterases with physostigmine and neostigmine (e.g., in cases of severe myasthenia gravis). This led to the study by Oliver H. Straus and Avram Goldstein, who made a fundamental contribution to the general problem of the enzyme-inhibitor-substrate relationship.[51] It can be added that the studies on physostigmine and neostigmine had their origin in the use of physostigmine in the earlier investigations, in which Loewi's demonstration of the Vagusstoff in the frog heart was successfully repeated in the mammalian heart. The prerequisite was an adequate inhibition of the cholinesterases of blood and tissue by physostigmine to prevent the breakdown of the acetycholine, released into the coronary circulation on electrical stimulation of the severed vagus nerves,[52] or on reflex vagal stimulation.[53]

Between 1940 and 1946 E. B. Astwood received particular encouragement from his chief as a member of the Department of Pharmacology. It was in this period that the group, in studying the effect of thiourea and *thiouracil* on thyroid function, constituted an enormous stimulus to the medical treatment of hyperthyroidism and to thyroid physiology and pharmacology.

A principal interest of Professor Krayer's after 1927 was the pharmacology of cardiac function. It was especially the versatility of the Starling Heart-Lung preparation which enabled Krayer to make many of his basic contributions to cardiac physiology and pharmacology. "The heart became the slave of the venous return," was a poetic way of describing how the amount of blood returning to the heart regulated the heart's action. Many of the studies in other areas resulted from Krayer's sustained interest in the function of the heart—for example, the work on Veratrum and Rauwolfia alkaloids. The investigation of Veratrum alkaloids over more than a quarter of a century (1940–1966) began with the rediscovery of the positive inotropic (force of contraction) action of the alkaloidal mixture "veratrine" on the heart. The work received additional impetus when pure substances became available (veratridine and protoveratrine) and from a critical evaluation of the earlier literature.[54] These studies resulted in the clarification of the mechanism of reflex action on the heart rate and blood pressure of the tertiary amine esters, veratridine and protoveratrine, originating from the heart itself (the so-called Bezold-Jarisch Effect) and from other sensory areas, the aorta and its branches, and the pulmonary artery. As a result of the long-lasting hypotensive action of protoveratrine, with its unique mechanism, Krayer suggested the use of this substance in the treatment of human hypertension.[55] This, in turn, stimulated the interest of several organic chemists in pure substances of this kind, and, as a result many new natural and partially synthetic substances became available for study. Much of the work in Krayer's laboratory became possible only when one of the leading organic chemists in the field, Morris Kupchan, received his initial impetus from, and continued to collaborate for many years with, the Department. The action of "veratrine" on skeletal muscle ("Veratrine Response") also was given renewed attention, on using pure compounds to study systematically their veratrine-like (*veratrinic*) action. The most important result was the recognition of substances which, *in vivo*, showed little or no hypotensive action while exhibiting the characteristic veratrine effect on muscle. This suggested the use of such compounds for the treatment of myasthenia gravis.[56]

Professor Krayer's first experiments with veratramine, which is a representative of the secondary amines among the natural Veratrum alkaloids and which previously had never been studied pharmacologically, led to the recognition of substances possessing a heart-rate decreasing action entirely different from that of the tertiary amine esters, through a direct action upon the pacemaker. Krayer named this phenomenon "autoaccelerator action" because it is most striking when the heart rate is elevated above normal. In the presence of veratramine, sympathomimetic amines exhibit full positive inotropic cardiac action, while the positive chronotropic action is reduced or abolished.

An offshoot of the work on the Veratrum alkaloids was the introduction of tetraethyl ammonium ion into the treatment of hypertension. Tetraethyl ammonia (T.E.A.) came to the attention of Drs. Krayer and Acheson as a veratrinic agent.[57] The subsequent study of circulatory action showed a hypotensive effect also reminiscent of that of the Veratrum esteralkaloids. The elegant analysis of the hypotensive action revealed a completely different mechanism: ganglionic blockade.[58] This gave the impetus for the clinical application in hypertension of T.E.A. and started the development of ganglionic blockers for this therapeutic indication in this country.

One of the first to suspect that *reserpine* had a peripheral effect, apart from its (initially at least) overemphasized action upon the central nervous system, Krayer demonstrated this in the isolated heart of the dog. In this preparation, reserpine had a rate-increasing effect that resulted from the release of norepinephrine. The mechanism of action and the dose response relationship of the norepinephrine-releasing and norepinephrine-depleting cardiac effects of reserpine and of other Rauwolfia alkaloids were thoroughly explored. This investigation was followed by, and run parallel to, systematic biochemical and physiological studies of the Department (guided especially by P. B. Hagen, N. Weiner, M. K. Paasonen, and U. Trendelenburg) on uptake, storage, and release of sympathomimetic amines in various tissues. Thus between 1958 and 1966 the Department made a large and important contribution to the explosive development of this field.

As Professor Krayer's career proceeded, he became increasingly aware of the necessity of having some departments of Pharmacology in which physiological, biochemical, and psychological methods would be in use side by side. An atmosphere could thereby be provided in which all aspects of drug action could be studied and the student of pharmacology made aware of the range and vast possibilities of exploration in this field. In the early 1950's, with the rare exception of Beecher's interest in this field,[59] psychological aspects of drug action (apart from drug addiction) were not widely studied in departments of Pharmacology. Partly this was due to the lack of appropriate methods for *quantitative* investigations, but mostly, it was owing to a general lack of interest in this field as an area of worthwhile scientific endeavor.

Krayer next turned his attention to the work of B. F. Skinner and realized the potential his techniques had for pharmacological studies. P. B. Dews, later Stanley Cobb Professor of Psychobiology, also explored this field.[60] His genuine interest in and application to the task enabled him and the Department to initiate a systematic study of *behavioral effects of drugs* as a recognized field of pharmacological investigation.

In the last decade of Krayer's career at Harvard, he became convinced of the importance of establishing a well-diversified Department of Pharmacology. The *psychological field* was developed by P. B. Dews and his colleagues, W. Morse and R. Kelleher, making the fundamental contributions to behavioral pharmacology. *Physiological* pharmacology was represented, in addition to Krayer himself, by U. Trendelenburg (autonomic pharmacology), John R. Blinks (cardiac physiology, pharmacology), Jean M. Marshall (electro-physiology, pacemaker activity in the heart and smooth muscle with automatic activity, i.e., uterus), D. R. Waud (receptor theory), W. Flacke (physiology and pharmacology of the circulation and of striated muscle), and Paul Munson (endocrinology). Biochemical pharmacology was represented by N. Weiner (storage, uptake, and release of the biogenetic amines, distribution of enzymes in the central nervous system); Martin Lubin (microbiological studies dealing with protein synthesis in bacterial mutants); H. Ryser (movements of large molecules, e.g., proteins—through cell membranes of certain cells in tissue culture); O. Jardetzky (introduction of new methods, nuclear magnetic resonance spectroscopy into the study of physical-chemical problems of pharmacology); and F. C. Uhle (synthetic organic chemistry in the fields of indoles and steroids). That the comprehensive and scientific atmosphere at last began to approach what Krayer had been aiming at may perhaps be seen from an outside appraisal of the department in regard to "quality of graduate faculty" and the "Rated Effectiveness of the Graduate Program." According to "An Assessment of the Quality in Graduate Education" by Allan M. Cartter, Vice President, American Council on Education, Washington, D.C., 1966, the Department of Pharmacology at Harvard ranked first among about forty departments of Pharmacology in this country which were evaluated.

Between 1939 and 1966 there were thirty-six professional members of the staff who remained in the Department for three years or longer. Of these, seventeen received headships of departments or equivalent administrative and academic positions, twelve in pharmacology and five in other branches of the medical sciences. Ten others reached the rank of full professor or associate professor, mostly in pharmacology at Harvard or in other academic institutions.

The graduate program in Pharmacology started slowly and developed only during the last ten years of Professor Krayer's tenure. As of this writing, of the eleven students receiving their Ph.D. in Pharmacology, four are full professors, three associate professors and one is an assistant professor—all in academic institutions. All together, during Krayer's tenure as head of the Department, there were thirty postdoctoral students in the Department from this country and forty from abroad.

It is curious indeed that notwithstanding Harvard's preeminence, the Department was allowed to disintegrate following Krayer's retirement in 1966. More than five years passed without a Chief. The staunch exemplars of physiological pharmacology, among whom Krayer stood at the top, were to some extent pushed aside by the molecular biologists. Without denigrating that field, one can still regret the lack of attention physiological pharmacology now receives. Whatever advances molecular (subcellular) biology may contribute to medicine, the fact remains that all of medicine, pharmacology included, needs the contributions derived from studies on organs and tissues at least as much as it needs studies on subcellular particles. When, if ever, Harvard will regain its place as a world leader in pharmacology remains an unanswered question.

THE PHARMACOTHERAPY COMMITTEE

On April 24, 1939, the President and Fellows of Harvard College voted, on recommendation of the Faculty of Medicine, to establish a University Committee on Pharmacotherapy. It was evident that recent activities in pharmacology and chemotherapy held promise of important developments in the treatment of disease, as pointed out by C. Sidney Burwell, then Dean of the Medical School. Adequate exploration of this field necessitated the close cooperation of various departments of the University. It was the hope that with the united action of investigators from various parts of the University, pharmacology and experimental therapeutics would be effectively cultivated and an opportunity made available for a new and improved training in the area. One of the purposes, perhaps the main purpose, of the organization of the Pharmacotherapy Committee was to bring together in a functioning organization representatives of Pharmacology, Chemistry, and Medicine. This was not to do work, however distinguished, which was simply chemical or pharmacological or medical, but to evolve a type of investigation which would be new and more effective than that which emanates from conventionally separated departments of Pharmacology, Chemistry, or Medicine.

The original members of this Committee were: Soma Weiss, Chairman, Walter Bradford Cannon, Frederick Lee Hisaw, Albert Baird Hastings, William Bosworth Castle, Louis Frederick Fieser, Otto Krayer, Fuller Albright, Reginald Patrick Linstead, Henry Knowles Beecher, Secretary, C. Sidney Burwell, *ex officio*, and James Bryant Conant, *ex officio*. The Pharmacotherapy Committee was indeed a unique instrument. While it functioned as a University Committee, it had many of the prerogatives of a separate faculty. For example, the Committee was empowered to grant Ph.D. degrees in its field.

A considerable controversy grew within the Committee as to whether, with the onset of World War II, the objectives of the Committee should, with profit, be turned away from truly basic scientific activities and redirected into areas relevant to the War effort. The "basic science" approach prevailed and may have contributed in no small part to the demise of the Committee after four years of successful life: The list of publications produced by members was creditable, however, and it seemed probable at that time and in retrospect that at least one important discovery had been made under the auspices of the Committee (E. B. Astwood, Thiouracil).

A depressing factor was the death of Soma Weiss at the outset of World War II. The return of Professor Linstead to England to participate in the British war effort was also a serious loss. Preoccupation with war problems at Harvard prevented several members of the Committee from devoting as much time to the endeavor as had been planned originally. President Conant regretted that his own absence from Cambridge prevented him from taking an active part in the enterprise, as he had originally hoped to do.[61]

It is clear that the Pharmacotherapy Committee was a casualty of World War II. Because the project was sound, one can hope that its purposes and plans can some day be effectively revived.

NEUROBIOLOGY

The Department of Physiology became one of the strongest departments in the Medical School when Cannon, Rosenblueth, Forbes, and Davis were all active there. With their departure, a great weakening of the effort in Neurophysiology occurred. Recognizing this, Professor Otto Krayer set out to find a young electrophysiologist to add to his staff. In this effort, he had the important support of Derek Denny-Brown and, later, Bernard D. Davis and others. The Department of Physiology, in the main, reacted coldly to Krayer's suggestion; he persisted, however, and having heard good things about Stephen Kuffler, looked into his background and believed that he would be an excellent choice for the position. Time has vindicated his judgment. In 1959 Kuffler and his co-workers arrived on the Harvard scene, and Kuffler received the title of Robert Winthrop Professor of Neurophysiology, and in 1964 Robert Winthrop Professor of Neuropharmacology. At the insistence of Kuffler, the laboratory space was at first called the "Laboratory of Neurophysiology in the Department of Pharmacology." The space and the group occupying it were to be under the administrative charge of the head of the Department of Pharmacology. The plan was that eventually the Neurophysiology Laboratory should, in matters of space and administration, be incorporated into a comprehensive Department of Physiology.[62]

The Laboratory of Neurophysiology continued under this official regulation until Professor Krayer's retirement. At that time, however, and with the active support of Dean Ebert, Dr. Kuffler succeeded in having a new department established in the Harvard Medical School—Neurobiology.

On July 1, 1966, the members of the Neurophysiology Laboratory of the Department of Pharmacology became the staff of the newly created Department of Neurobiology under the chiefship of Professor Kuffler.

Stephen W. Kuffler was born August 24, 1913, in Tap, Hungary. He received the M.D. degree at the University of Vienna, and subsequently various honorary degrees. He also received the Passano Prize ($7,500), awarded by The Passano Foundation, Inc. of Baltimore, Maryland, one of American Medicine's highest honors,[63] and in 1972 Columbia University awarded him the Louisa Gross Horwitz Prize ($25,000).

Born in Hungary, educated for medicine in Vienna, you embarked upon a career in Neurophysiology which has now spanned nearly three decades and has been productive over a remarkably wide range of scientific interests. In Sydney, Australia, in association with John Eccles and Bernard Katz, you developed the first isolated cell-to-cell junction and provided powerful evidence supporting the view that neuromuscular transmission is mediated by acetylcholine rather than by ionic currents. Later, you and your colleagues explored the inhibitory synapses of Crustacea and were leaders in establishing the role of gamma amino butyric acid as a neurohumoral transmitter. From your laboratory came the unexpected discovery that small diameter motor nerve fibers modulate the activity of sensory elements. Your elegant experiments on the receptive field structure of the cat retina have provided the foundation upon which many subsequent studies of vertebrate visual systems have been based. Finally, as the Robert Winthrop Professor of Neurobiology at Harvard, you have created a department and an environment renowned for scientific accomplishments and for exciting the interest and enthusiasm of countless young investigators who are already making major contributions to the future growth of the Neurosciences. Dr. Kuffler, Columbia University is privileged indeed to be able to present to you the 1972 Louisa Gross Horwitz Prize in Biology.[64]

His work constitutes a major contribution to the physiology of nerve cells.

It is characteristic of Professor Kuffler to say, "In our field there are innumerable ideas floating around, so that one really doesn't know whose they are . . . nor should it matter." Some attribution is in order, regardless:[65] David H. Hubel and Torsten N. Wiesel received the Rosenstiel Award in the Basic Medical Sciences, 1972, and in the same year the Jules Stein award for "distinguished ophthalmic research." These two investigators have collaborated in research on the neurophysiology of vision in an extraordinarily fruitful scientific partnership over more than thirteen years. Their work has had a profound effect on comprehension of how the brain functions, and on the general approach to perception, but particularly as it concerns the operation of the visual system. Their studies have also laid a sound foundation for the understanding, and possibly better treatment, of the effects of visual deprivation.

David Potter and Edwin Furshpan made a major contribution that was close to a great discovery. The first description of an electrically transmitting synapse in the nervous system was published by them in 1959. This was definitely the first authentic proof of a mode of transmission that had been theoretically supposed to exist over fifty years or much longer. Electrical synapses have later been found by Furshpan and Furukawa in vertebrates, and at the same time they discovered the first and only existing example of electrical inhibition. Out of these basic findings has come an entire related field that can be described as "coupling" of cells. Interestingly enough, such coupling is commonplace in most organs and is relatively rare in the nervous system, where it was first shown to exist. Edward Kravitz and his associates in the Department concentrated on identification of synaptic transmitter compounds and the mechanisms by which nerve cells regulate their accumulation, bringing together physiological and anatomical techniques with microbiochemical studies in a multidisciplinary study.

Chapter Twelve

The Preclinical Curriculum, II

P ATHOLOGY and bacteriology grew out of clinical medicine, and for years the two were closely related. The relationship of pathology has persisted, but that of bacteriology has fluctuated.

PATHOLOGY

The earliest pathologic writings were case reports. The two great compendia of pathologic material, Charles Bonet's *Sepulchretum* in the seventeenth century and Giovanni Morgagni's *De Sedibus et Causas Morburum* in the eighteenth century, were in large measure clinical-pathological correlations. In the mid-nineteenth century the clinical-pathological conference was a popular method of teaching in the clinic of Louis, where most of the leaders and teachers of Boston medicine studied. This approach to the understanding of clinical problems was therefore well-known at Harvard, but it needed an interest and a lively teacher to give it the prominence it deserved. Evidently, the case method of teaching clinical subjects at Harvard was pursued on an individual basis, although in the 1870's it had become official at the Harvard Law School under the influence of Professor Christopher C. Langdell. Walter Cannon, then a medical student, learned about this approach from his roommate, a law student.

The March 5, 1900, meeting of the Boston Society for Medical Improvement was historic. At that meeting Cannon proposed the adoption of the case system in medicine.[1] No less a person than Charles William Eliot of Harvard was greatly impressed by Cannon's proposal.[2] The method was first tried in a small class in neurology under Dr. G. L. Walton, but it was Richard C. Cabot who established the system, which led to the widespread recognition of its value. Not long before his death in 1939, Dr. Cabot described the history of the method's development in Boston.[3] He began using in private quiz exercises in his own office some of the printed case histories that had been contained in examinations in clinical medicine at the Harvard Medical School. When he later began his service on the wards of the Massachusetts General Hospital in 1908, he was troubled by the undesirable separation of the clinical man and the pathologist and his worry was increased by his discovery in an old volume of bound records a case diagnosed as neurasthenia, and his further discovery on checking the final record that the patient had died and had been autopsied, and that the correct diagnosis should have been cancer of the pleura.

At the beginning of 1910 Cabot, on his own initiative, began to hold exercises with the house officers and medical visitors to the Hospital. A weekly exercise was carried out in conjunction with Dr. James Homer Wright, modeled essentially on the later clinicopathological conferences. In 1915 Cabot adopted the practice of having these cases recorded stenographically. Copies were sent to interested physicians all over the United States and some to Europe, Asia, and Australia. It was not long before Cabot's informal and voluntary exercises with the house officers and graduate students had become a regular exercise for the third-year class in medicine at the Harvard Medical School. Later they were scheduled for the fourth-year class and continued up to Cabot's resignation as Professor of Clinical Medicine in 1933, at which time the exercises were taken over by Dr. Tracy B. Mallory and began to involve the entire staff of the Hospital. It was through Dr. Mallory's activities that the clinicopathological conference became firmly established in medical education.[4] The conferences, published in the *New England Journal of Medicine* as Case Records of the Massachusetts General Hospital, are widely regarded as an integral part of medical education today.

These formal—and often formidable—exercises have not obscured the fact that the work-a-day role of pathology is to support, enhance, and, on occasion, lead in the development of clinical knowledge. The formal instruction given Harvard medical students is in a second-year course of lectures that organize the vast field and explicate it; these are followed by periods in which gross and microscopical studies are made to exemplify what the lecturers have put forth. Although some of this instruction is given by Medical School teachers and research personnel engaged in the study of basic processes, most of it is in the hands of hospital-based pathologists. Moreover, third- and fourth-year students, in their clinical work in hospitals, receive less formal instruction from these same hospital-based pathologists. At times over the years the Pathology faculty at the Medical School has been made up largely of hospital pathologists.

This arrangement got off to a good start during the Eliot years, with William T. Councilman and Frank Burr Mallory at the Boston City Hospital and James Homer Wright at the Massachusetts General Hospital. When Dr. Councilman moved to the newly opened Peter Bent Brigham Hospital as Pathologist-in-Chief, Frank Mallory became Chief at the Boston City Hospital. Among Dr. Mallory's numerous contributions to the literature of pathology are studies on the classification of tumors, on technical methods, on cirrhosis of the liver, and on infectious diseases. Using his own staining methods, he contributed a great deal to the rational classification of tumors. He was always deeply interested in diseases of the liver, especially cirrhosis, and for the greater part of his life studied various aspects of this problem, using experimental as well as purely morphological approaches.

One of Dr. Mallory's outstanding contributions to medicine was his training of young men in pathology. Approximately 125 could be described as his trainees,[5] many of whom later became preeminent in various other branches of clinical medicine as well. He was close to his staff and took a great personal interest in them. His great desire was to instill in them his high ideals and his interest in pathology. Through them he exerted a profound influence on pathology throughout the country.

Dr. Mallory had continuous service at Harvard from 1901, at which time he was advanced to Associate Professor, to 1919, when he drops from sight, returning in 1928 as Professor of Pathology and retiring Emeritus in 1932. According to his son, Kenneth, this nine-year gap in his Harvard appointment occurred because Dr. Mallory considered that he should have been named Shattuck Professor instead of his former student, S. Burt Wolbach. Dr. Mallory's son, philosophical about the problem after the lapse of many years, says that it was probably a good thing that his father was not named Shattuck Professor, for he was able to get a great deal more accomplished than would otherwise have been the case.

In 1926 Frank B. Mallory's son, Dr. Tracy B. Mallory, replaced Dr. James Homer Wright as head of the Department of Pathology at the Massachusetts General Hospital and held the position for twenty-five years. During that time more than 100 physicians were trained in pathology. Dr. Mallory introduced the house officership and residency in his department and thus made it not only a service but also a teaching department. His major contributions to the field of pathology included the recognition of carcinoma-in-situ of the stomach, presentation of evidence that cancer of the stomach rarely develops from peptic ulcer, and, with Dr. Edward A. Gall, the tissue changes in patients exposed to benzene, which anticipate the entity of myeloid metaplasia. He also formulated a classification of the malignant lymphomas which is still the basis of present interpretations. In World War II he and Baldwin A. Lucké studied a large group of patients with hepatitis and described the anatomical changes, and this work remains the classic in the field. Tracy Mallory was the pathologist member of the Board for the Study of the Severely Wounded, which functioned in the Mediterranean Theatre.

In the meantime Dr. Councilman had retired and was succeeded as Pathologist-in-Chief at the Peter Bent Brigham Hospital by S. Bu t Wolbach. Following two years of instruction at the Lawrence Scientific School in Harvard, Professor Wolbach entered the Harvard Medical School, from which he was graduated in 1903. His apprenticeship in pathology was served under Drs. Councilman and Frank B. Mallory at the Boston City Hospital, 1904–05. His first association with the Harvard Medical School as a teacher began in 1905, when he acted as Assistant and then Instructor in Pathology. For a period of two years, 1908–10, he occupied positions as a pathologist in Albany but then returned to the Harvard Medical School in 1910 with the title of Assistant Professor in the Department of Bacteriology. He was promoted to Associate Professor in 1914.

In 1915 Dr. Wolbach accepted the appointment of Pathologist-in-Chief to the Children's Hospital, and in 1916 his association with Harvard's Department of Pathology was resumed. A year later he was appointed to the same position in the Peter Bent Brigham Hospital and the Boston Lying-in- Hospital. He was made Shattuck Professor of Pathological Anatomy in 1922 and held this post until his so-called retirement in 1947, following which he spent his last seven years in the Children's Hospital, where the position of Director of the Division of Nutritional Research was created for him.

Dr. Wolbach was a distinguished scientist. His contributions were especially numerous in the field of infectious disease, in which his most important original studies were concerned with two rickettsial diseases —Rocky Mountain spotted fever and typhus. His work on the former resulted in the first accurate description of the etiologic agent of this disease, its clinical symptoms, and its pathology. The studies demonstrated that the tick is the biological transmitter; they characterized the etiologic rickettsia and reported its unique ability to parasitize and distend nuclei in tick tissues, thus suggesting that ricksettsia might be the missing link between bacterium-like microorganisms and certain viruses that multiply within nuclei. Wolbach's pioneer studies on typhus were carried out in 1920 under the auspices of the League of Red Cross Societies. The work of the Commission sent to Poland to study this disease still stands as the definitive work on the etiology, pathology, and clinical aspects of typhus, and these studies gave Professor Wolbach world-wide fame as a medical scientist, an achievement which many believed to be more valuable than his works as a tissue pathologist.

Wolbach's investigations in tropical medicine, stimulated by a trip to Africa in 1911, resulted in his observations on the trypanosomes in the brain and the absence of cellular reaction to them in sleeping sickness. This important work was responsible for an insight of Hideyo Noguchi that led to an understanding of the pathology of general paresis.

Following his extensive work in infectious diseases, Wolbach's interest turned to vitamin research, where his basic contributions are everywhere regarded as classic. In his studies of the relationships of vitamins to tissue structure, he was not content until he understood and could summarize the basic processes involved in morphological change. His studies of the scorbutic state were an illustration. In them he showed that what appeared to many to be lesions of multiple character were essentially the failure of a single process: the inability of mesenchymal cells to lay down intercellular substance.

Wolbach's studies on Vitamin A deficiency were equally important. Here the fault was explained on a cellular level as being due to loss of specific chemical functions of the epitheliums concerned, while the power of growth became augmented. This resulted in a keratinizing metaplasia. The nervous lesions of this deficiency were shown to be of mechanical origin.

Wolbach's multiple activities led many to wonder how it was possible for him to accomplish so much. He often said that like Theobald Smith, he did his research "by stealth." In the Minute contained in the *Harvard University Gazette*, there is what sounds like an extravagant statement but is not:

> scientist, skilled manipulator of techniques, teacher, administrator, civic-minded citizen, loyal friend, advisor, sportsman, naturalist, conversationalist and raconteur . . . His uncompromising attitude toward untruths, his impatience with incompetence, his rigorous self-discipline—physical as well as intellectual—were characteristics that marked the man as well as the scientist.[6]

Professor Wolbach was succeeded by Gustave J. Dammin. While still a medical student, Dr. Dammin became interested in the pathogenesis of acute diarrheal disease in relationship to bacterial, protozoal, and viral pathogens. During five years in the Army as a Medical Laboratory officer, he had opportunities to further his interest in this field by studies in Puerto Rico, India, and Burma. His group has investigated many aspects of the pathogenesis of acute diarrheal diseases caused by the cholera vibrio, the Shigellas, and the Salmonellas—and, more recently, the toxic strains of *E. coli*. Detailed studies of fatal diarrhea in early life, carried out in Guatemala in 1958–60 by Dr. Dammin and his group, helped to foster the notion that there might be a variety of bacterial enteropathogens which could mimic the effects of cholera toxin on the intestinal mucosa.

Dr. Dammin has been closely identified as the pathologist of the group at the Peter Bent Brigham engaged in prolonging the survival of skin and kidney transplants. Their concern has been to modify the human and animal hosts so as to make them better recipients of transplants. The Dammin group have worked closely with their colleagues on transplantation also of liver, spleen, and bone marrow. Dr. Dammin has demonstrated that close support of the pathologist in clinical and laboratory research on tissue and organ transplantation is very important. His outstanding qualities as a teacher led in 1961 to his title of Elsie T. Friedman Professor of Pathology at the Medical School, which he holds at the present time.

The next Shattuck Professor of Pathological Anatomy was Arthur T. Hertig, appointed to that post in 1952. He had done highly important work at the Lying-in Hospital. Much of what is now known concerning the early human embryo is based on his definitive work. Before he joined Dr. John Rock in a study of the first two weeks of human embryological life, little was known of this period. Dr. Hertig overcame the obvious problem by searching diligently for early products of conception in removed uteri and Fallopian tubes of selected patients coming to operation. He found more than thirty early embryos for histochemical and developmental studies. The youngest ovum found was in the two-celled stage. Drs. Hertig and Rock have described the stages of human embryological development from the first division of the ovum until placental circulation becomes functional. Their studies have not been limited to the normal products of conception, but have also uncovered valuable information on several causes of spontaneous abortion. In 1968 Dr. Hertig was offered the opportunity to transfer his research interests to the New England Regional Primate Center—run by the Harvard Medical School in Southborough—where he continues study of the morphology of primate reproductive structures.

The next to hold the Shattuck chair was Benjamin Castleman, Pathologist-in-Chief of the Massachusetts General Hospital. Internationally known for his research and teaching in pathology and for his administrative and organizational abilities, Dr. Castleman's career included pioneering studies on the pathology of the parathyroid glands. In addition to his publications on a variety of pathological topics, he has served as editor of the Case Records of the Massachusetts General Hospital, published weekly in the *New England Journal of Medicine*, as noted above.

An outstanding example of the way in which a talented mind recognizes opportunities offered by clinical phenomena to develop new approaches is afforded by the career of Dr. Sidney Farber. He was a graduate of the Harvard Medical School who had become sufficiently interested in children's pathology as a student to create a pathological museum in a basement room at the Children's Hospital. He pursued his training, and after becoming Pathologist to the same institution, he became the first to describe cystic fibrosis as a generalized disorder. With colleagues he discovered eastern equine encephalitis in man. As far back as the early 1930's he recognized the importance of hyaline membrane disease in the newborn and began to study it. His attention was drawn, however, to the problem of childhood neoplasms, and in the early 1940's he defined what is meant by the total care of children with cancer. This statement of goals to be sought is one of the two great milestones which opened a new era in cancer research and care. His major contributions include the discovery that certain chemicals will limit the growth of many kinds of cancer cells and are thus able to prolong a good life and indeed to cure some previously incurable cancers.

In 1947 he made the important discovery that the drug aminopterin and the related chemical methotrexate have the power to cause complete (though temporary) remission of symptoms in acute leukemia. Aminopterin, a folic acid antagonist and antimetabolite that inhibits normal cell metabolism is the prototype of subsequent antileukemic chemicals that have greatly prolonged the lives of leukemia patients, sometimes for as much as fifteen years. The discovery made it clear that cancer control with the use of drugs is feasible, and thus initiated the era of cancer chemotherapy.

Following this important breakthrough, Farber discovered that Selman Waksman's first antibiotic, actinomycin D, was a specific in treating Wilms' tumor of the kidney. The agent reduced the size of the kidney tumor, killed the spreading cancer cells and destroyed metastases in the lungs. The combination of this drug with radiotherapy and surgery had a powerful effect in improving the prognosis in this disease.

In 1948 Dr. Farber established the Children's Cancer Research Foundation as an independent institution associated with the Children's Hospital Medical Center, the Harvard Medical School, the Peter Bent Brigham Hospital, and the Boston Hospital for Women in programs of chemotherapy of cancer. In this activity he established the first hospital and research institution devoted entirely to the care of children with cancer. He became the key figure in initiating far-reaching national and world research programs on the chemical treatment of cancer. In recognition of his outstanding past in teaching and research, he was appointed, S. Burt Wolbach Professor of Pathology.

Shields Warren,[7] Professor of Pathology at the New England Deaconess Hospital and the Harvard Medical School, is another example of the role of the dedicated scholar. In the middle of the 1920's Dr. Warren, then one of Dean David L. Edsall's bright young men, worked in the

Pathology Department. His principal effort at that time was to do what he could to stimulate teaching of all courses in the Medical School, and specifically to interest students in preventive medicine in the broad sense. An unexpected consequence of these activities was that Dr. Warren became convinced that schools of public health were detrimental to medical education because they separated from the medical curriculum a great deal that was relevant to the prevention of disease.

In the late 1920's Dr. Warren became impressed by the relative absence of information concerning the effects of ionizing radiation on human and animal tissues. This led to a series of studies based upon animal experiments and irradiated human tissues of surgical specimens and biopsies. Warren and his colleagues prepared a summary of the information then known concerning radiation effects, and were helpful in the Manhattan District project by establishing safety standards.

Warren's interest in this area continued after the War, when he was placed in charge of the Navy's investigating team concerned with the survivors of the bombings of Hiroshima and Nagasaki. These activities, with aid from other teams, laid the foundation for the Atomic Bomb Casualty Commission, which works with survivors up to the present time. He used his knowledge of irradiation to study problems of cancer control. In the last thirty-five years his research has been focused almost entirely on radiation carcinogenesis. He was the first Director of the Division of Biology in Medicine at the Atomic Energy Commission and later advised the National Aeronautics and Space Administration, as Chairman of its Committee on the Life Sciences, with regard to problems of space exploration, including the search for life on other planets. An important side-effort involved another area. Warren was stimulated by Dr. Elliott P. Joslin to study diabetes mellitus, and Warren's was the first monograph on the pathology of the disease published in America.

Still another hospital pathologist who made notable contributions to medical knowledge was Dr. Monroe J. Schlesinger, Clinical Professor of Pathology at the Beth Israel Hospital. He invented the injection-plus-dissection method of studying coronary and other arterial disease. Application of this method revolutionized the understanding of atherosclerosis. On his death he was succeeded by Dr. David T. Freiman, a notable teacher and an organizer of the teaching of pathology at the Harvard Medical School.

The high status enjoyed by Pathology at the School at the end of the Eliot era and in the first decades of the new century began to decline, as Professor Wolbach noted in a speech before the Alumni Association with the self-explanatory title "The Glorious Past, the Doleful Present and the Uncertain Future of Pathology."[8] The increasing daily demands of the clinical services at the hospitals took more and more of the time and facilities of the hospital pathology laboratories. The service function began to dominate. Moreover, the role of pathology as the way to gain understanding of clinical phenomena began to be rivaled by biochemistry and physiology. By 1954 the grand days of pathology were over.

BACTERIOLOGY

The beginnings of this part of the curriculum were during the Eliot era, when it appears that Drs. Harold C. Ernst, Professor of Bacteriology, and Theobald Smith, Professor of Comparative Pathology, both taught the subject. With the decline of Theobald Smith's activities, S. Burt Wolbach was recalled from his pathologist's position at Albany in 1910 to serve as Assistant and then Associate Professor of Bacteriology at the School. The Department was weakened when, in 1915, he resumed his position in Harvard's Department of Pathology. Moreover, changes in the concept of what bacteriology should do were becoming apparent. Whereas in earlier years physicians wanted to know mainly what bacteria *did* (and how this could be circumvented), with the passage of time they became aware of the importance of also knowing what bacteria *are*.

Professor Ernst's position became vacant, and a search was made for a bacteriologist who would develop and follow the necessary new directions. When the School was able to persuade Hans Zinsser to assume this responsibility, the Edsall period reached a high point. Born in 1878, Dr. Zinsser was educated at Columbia University with a bachelor's degree in 1899 and an M.D. degree in 1903. He received an honorary Doctor of Science degree from Columbia in 1929 and was the recipient of many other honorary degrees. From 1910 to 1911 he was Associate Professor of Bacteriology and Immunology at Stanford University but returned to Columbia University in 1913, where he remained for ten years as Professor of Bacteriology and Immunology. He was called to Harvard in 1923 as Professor of Bacteriology and Immunology. From 1935 to 1940 he held the newly created post of Charles Wilder Professor of Bacteriology and Immunology. He was Exchange Professor at Paris in 1935 and held a similar post at Peiping University Medical College in 1938.

Hans Zinsser was notable for a liberal attitude toward life and an open mind. These characteristics were eminently suitable for a man whose forebears were German Social Democrats. He was a man of broad culture with an excellent knowledge of the literature of America, England, France, and Germany. He had an understanding of and a keen appreciation for music. His textbooks on bacteriology and immunology set a high standard. They were frequently and scrupulously revised. His reputation as a scientist rests on a solid foundation of research which he guided into productive channels. His most notable contributions related to the bacteriology and immunology of typhus fever, which study he first undertook in Serbia in 1915. He extended these studies in the laboratory of Nicolle in Tunis, by expeditionary work in Mexico, and by intensive research carried out over a long period of years in his laboratory at the Medical School. The work of Zinsser and his associates laid a sound foundation for mass vaccination against both the European and the murine forms of typhus fever.

Zinsser's professional characteristics are best described as a militant scientific integrity, undeviating loyalty to his subject, and indefatigable application to the work at hand. Great scientist though he was, he became best known to many laymen as a man of lettters. Two books were written for them: *Rats, Lice and History*[9] and *As I Remember Him. The Biography of R. S.*[10] R. S. was, of course, Zinsser. These two books make clear his philosophy as a physician and scientist. Quite plainly, he was a clear scientific thinker and "learned essayist, a philosopher and a humorist. He ridiculed cant and pose, but he was not malicious."[12]

About a year before his death, Zinsser said of "R. S.":

He was not, at any time, tempted to seek strength in wishful surrender to a religious faith in which far greater men than he had taken refuge just before death. . . . Indeed, he became more firm in his determination to see things out consistently along his own lines of resignation to agnostic uncertainty—as his father had done before him. Moving further away, therefore, from faith in any comprehensible conception of God, he yet grew closer in conviction of the wisdom and guiding integrity of the compassionate philosophy of Christ.[12]

Another popular lecturer in the Department was William A. Hinton. After obtaining his early education in Kansas, he received his Bachelor of Science degree in 1905 and his Doctor of Medicine degree in 1912, both from Harvard University. After serving until 1915 as Voluntary Assistant in the Pathology Laboratory of the Massachusetts General Hospital, he became Director of the Laboratory Department of the Boston Dispensary and Chief of the Wasserman Laboratory, Massachusetts Department of Public Health; he held the latter post until 1923. At the Dispensary he helped to set up one of the first schools in the United States for training medical technicians. Under him the Wasserman Laboratory became a model of its kind, and he helped to establish over 100 new diagnostic laboratories when Massachusetts established prenatal and premarital laws.

In 1923–24, Dr. Hinton was Assistant in Preventive Medicine and

Hygiene in the Medical School, and for the next five years Instructor in Bacteriology and in Preventive Medicine and Hygiene. From 1929 to 1946 he was Instructor in Bacteriology and Immunology and in Preventive Medicine and Hygiene. In 1949 he was promoted to Clinical Professor of Bacteriology and Immunology. For many years Harvard has taken pride in the fact that this distinguished medical scientist was Harvard's first Black professor.

In 1927 Dr. Hinton reported a new blood test for the detection of syphilis, still widely used, and in further studies determined and improved its sensitivity and accuracy. Later, with Dr. John Davis, he developed a test on spinal fluids for the detection of syphilis. He also studied the clinical and pathologic aspects of this important disease and was often consulted by other doctors whose patients had venereal disease. In 1936 he published his authoritative textbook: *Syphilis and Its Treatment.*

In 1940 Dr. Hinton lost a leg following an automobile accident. He worked for another twelve years but failing strength and failing eyesight forced him to retire in 1953 to his home in Canton, Massachusetts, where he died in 1959. A Dwight D. Eisenhower Scholarship Fund for graduate students in Harvard University was established under his will. The fund is not yet complete, and in 1976 had an annual income of $4,835.18.[13] Hinton asked that the fund be named in recognition of the notable accomplishment during the administration of President Eisenhower toward the acceptance of the principle of equal opportunity for all. In a letter to President Nathan M. Pusey, General Eisenhower had said: "I cannot recall having been given a personal distinction that has touched me more deeply." The fund is a memorial to Dr. Hinton's Chicago father and mother, Augustus and Maria Hinton, "who, although born in slavery and without formal education, nevertheless recognized and practiced not only the highest ideals in their personal conduct, but also the true democratic principle of equal opportunity for all, without regard to racial or religious origins or to economic or political status."[14] The fund is "to be used in any department (of the University) by way of scholarship grants, prizes for scholarly treatises or other achievements, or otherwise."

Another in the galaxy of early leaders in bacteriology at the School was J. Howard Mueller. He had graduated in 1912 from Illinois Wesleyan University with honors in biology. At the University of Illinois he taught physiological chemistry for two years while he earned a master's degree. After a brief period in Louisville, where he became interested in pathology and bacteriology, he moved to Columbia University in order to gain further knowledge of pathology. He worked during the summer of 1914 at the College of Physicians and Surgeons of Columbia University, where his outstanding work led his instructors to urge him to continue his graduate studies. In 1916 he was awarded the Ph.D. degree in pathology with minors in biochemistry and bacteriology. His intention was to strengthen his understanding of the chemistry of disease.

Although Dr. Mueller continued to maintain an interest in the practical problems of diagnosis and control of disease as they appear at the autopsy table, in the clinical laboratory, and in the field, he was always searching for new relationships. In World War I he served with the Presbyterian Base Hospital Unit in France for two years. On his return from France in 1919 Hans Zinsser invited him to become an Assistant Professor and member of the Department of Bacteriology at Columbia. During his establishment there he initiated a long series of investigations on bacterial metabolism which continued throughout his life. He became an Associate Professor and, after Zinsser's death, the third occupant of the Chair of Bacteriology.

Although Mueller maintained that the sciences constituted a continuum, he believed in the primacy of chemistry, and he therefore returned to it and gave it his best thought. As Enders phrased it, Mueller, with the foresight of the pioneer, decided that bacteria, with their single-cell form and rapid growth and the ease with which conditions of their multiplication can be altered, were excellent material for biochemical investigation. As a practical man, he was led to select certain pathogenic organisms for study, for he believed that knowledge of their metabolism would very likely parallel, in fundamental ways, the metabolism of higher forms and might also reveal new or improved approaches to the prevention and therapy of infectious disease. In the beginning he explored the nutritional requirements of the hemolytic streptococcus. He found that a sulfur-containing component of a protein hydrolysate seemed to be essential for growth of this organism. This component, he discovered, did not contain cystine (cysteine)—the only sulfur-containing amino acid then known. It took him three years to acquire a mastery of the necessary but unfamiliar techniques and apply them to the isolation of this active material. Eventually he found that the unknown amino acid was in fact methionine, essential for the synthesis of choline and creatine. Many scientists consider that this discovery was Mueller's most important contribution to science and medicine.

In 1941 he took time to respond at once to a call for assistance from the Public Health authorities in Halifax, where a great epidemic of diphtheria had been raging for several months. This experience he put to good use after World War II in Germany, where diphtheria was a frequent occurrence among the occupation troops stationed there.

In the thirty-one years he served as Associate Professor and later Professor and Head of the Department of Bacteriology at the Harvard Medical School, many other important discoveries were made. For example, in collaboration with Zinsser he prepared from extracts of pneumococci and tubercle bacilli substances at first called "residue antigens." These agents were complex polysaccharides. Oswald T. Avery at the Rockefeller Institute, working simultaneously and independently, made similar observations. It had been the earlier belief that only proteins could act as antigens, but it was obvious that the earlier view had to be modified. Others picked up the polysaccharide problem, and study of it led to important advances in the immunological field. Later Professor Mueller undertook the analysis of the growth factors of the diphtheria bacillus. His work led to the production of toxin for immunizing purposes. With his techniques he could prepare toxoid free of large protein derivatives. Mueller also was able to prove that pimelic acid, nicotinic acid, and beta-alanine were essential growth factors for diphtheria. He made these observations before it had been demonstrated that nicotinic acid exerted a profound therapeutic effect in pellagra. Also, as the result of a productive study of the tetanus bacillus, he was able to define more clearly than heretofore the factors involved in the growth and toxin formation of the tetanus bacillus. His work in this area was not complete at the time of his death.

A successor of Harold Ernst and Hans Zinsser, Howard Mueller carried on their fine traditions in an admirable way. As Enders, his friend and colleague, put it, he was dedicated to the search for truth through the experimental method. He described Mueller as among those "who actively seek insight and meaning, whose minds are constantly on the alert to the possibility of new generalizations and new relationships . . ."[15]

Working without fanfare and with little in the way of academic reward during this period was John F. Enders himself. He first pursued an academic career in the field of English, but along the way he became aware of microbiology through his friendship with Hugh Ward, a graduate student in Bacteriology. He accompanied Ward to the laboratory and there met Zinsser, then Professor of Bacteriology and Immunology and one of Harvard's important teachers. As a result of Zinsser's contagious enthusiasm, Enders decided in 1927 to give up the teaching of English for a career of scientific research and investigation.

John Enders was graduated from Harvard University, where he received the Doctor of Philosophy degree in 1930. Since that time he has received a dozen or more honorary degrees and, above all, the Nobel Prize in Physiology and Medicine in 1954. Among the scores of other honors, he received the Presidential Medal of Freedom in 1963. He became Higgins University Professor, Harvard University, in 1962, a post he held until 1967. Since then he has been University Professor Emeritus. Dr. Enders was also former Professor of Bacterioolgy and Immunol-

John Enders, Higgins University Professor and Nobel Laureate. His contributions to virology developed new approaches that led to outstanding therapeutic and theoretical developments. Photograph from Harvard Medical Archives.

ogy at the Children's Hospital. However, his honors accumulated only after he won the Nobel; at that time he was only an Assistant Professor at the School.

After some work on hypersensitivity and on the factors that govern virulence in bacteria, Enders turned his attention in the late 1930's to viruses. His use of tissue cultures for study of the growth of viruses *in vitro* had begun earlier in work with Zinsser. Their early aim was to originate methods for preparing large quantities of typhus rickettsiae for use as vaccines. These efforts were not very successful in themselves but led to new techniques for the cultivation of viruses in tissue culture and to an examination of the effects of antibodies in viral infections of mammalian cells.

When World War II came, it was found that mumps was an important disease of recruits. Enders accordingly turned to a study of this disease. Beginning in 1942 he associated himself with various collaborators and established methods for the study of the ailment: the isolation of strains of the agent; the development of tests for detecting the presence of antibody in convalescent monkeys and human beings; the development of a skin test to identify immune individuals; the production of a formalinized vaccine, partly successful; and the adaptation of mumps and influenza viruses to tissue cultures. These fields and related ones covered six years of work—that is, until 1948.

With his background it seemed inevitable that as a next step Dr. Enders would try to cultivate poliomyelitis virus in cultures of other than nervous tissue. Success was reported in 1949 in the famous paper written in collaboration with Thomas H. Weller and Frederick C. Robbins. This is the work for which they were awarded the 1954 Nobel Prize in Physiology and Medicine. Following it, there was the successful cultivation of the three immunologic strains of poliomyelitis virus thus far identified; the demonstration of the killing effect of the virus on infected cells, by means of which the presence of the virus can be easily and quickly recognized; the neutralization of the virus by antibody; and the direct isolation of strains of virus from human beings. Thus the essential tools for the development of vaccines against poliomyelitis were developed.

Dr. Enders' laboratory work since the poliomyelitis activity continues with other viruses, principally measles. He and his colleagues have developed reliable methods for the propagation of these viruses, and have produced an attenuated live measles virus vaccine that is currently on trial in man. The strain of measles virus isolated in 1954 by Dr. Enders and Dr. Thomas C. Peebles, Instructor in Pediatrics at Harvard, formed the basis for the development of this vaccine, the development of which was directed by Dr. Enders, and Dr. Samuel L. Katz, Chief of the Newborn Division of the Children's Hospital Medical Center and Associate in Pediatrics at Harvard. Dr. Katz and his associates, in 1957, grew the virus in quantities and then made it less virulent by passage through chick embryos. The measles vaccine thus developed was first tested in monkeys and later in children.

Besides these history-making discoveries, the inspiration Dr. Enders has imparted to his students and collaborators has been a significant factor in assisting them to attain distinction for themselves. He claimed to be an intuitive thinker, but this simply means that his store of knowledge was so great and his ability to recognize connections between data so highly developed that he himself was not aware of how he conceived new ideas.

Another bacteriologist who got his start at Harvard during the Edsall years was Monroe D. Eaton. Dr. Eaton received his undergraduate training at Stanford with an A.B. and an A.M. in 1927. In 1930 he received his M.D. degree at the Harvard Medical School. From 1930 to 1933 he was an Assistant in Bacteriology in the Harvard Medical School, as well as Instructor and Tutor in Biochemical Sciences, Harvard College. In 1936–37 he was Assistant Professor of Bacteriology, Washington University in St. Louis, and then for ten years, 1937–47, he was a Staff Member of the International Health Division, Rockefeller Foundation, and also Director of the Virus Laboratory, California State Department of Public Health. He returned to Harvard in 1947 with the rank of Associate Professor of Bacteriology and Immunology and was promoted to a full professorship in 1969.

After a variety of early studies in diphtheria and tetanus toxins, and on the antigenicity of malarial parasites, Professor Eaton turned his attention to viruses, or what he thought were viruses. In 1942, with his co-workers, he isolated from patients with atypical pneumonia an agent whose presence in this disease was finally established. What seemed to be a virus—called by other investigators, *the Eaton agent*—turned out otherwise. The susceptibilty of the agent to tetracyclines made Eaton suspicious that this odd agent might not be a virus. This was finally proved when Robert Chanock and his associates were able to grow it in the absence of cells. The upshot was that Eaton established the etiology of atypical pneumonia, a disease that was found to be the cause of 10 percent of the disability of newly recruited Marines, frequently responsible for epidemics of pneumonia in schools, hospitals, and other institutions. Subsequently, he returned to his research on viruses and antiviral drugs.

A new direction was given the whole science of bacteriology by Albert H. Coons. He received his Bachelor's Degree at Williams College in 1933 and his M.D. degree at Harvard Medical School four years later. From 1939 to 1940 he was Research Fellow in Medicine in the School, after which he held various fellowships and residencies. Dr. Coons was stimulated as early as his second year in the Medical School by the work of Professors Zinsser and Enders. He carried out some laboratory work in the summer with Dr. Enders. During his training he continued to be interested in the cells that respond to an antigenic stimulus by synthesizing antibody specifically reactive with the antigen. With great help from Hugh Creech, an organic chemist, and Melvin Kaplan, at that time a Research Fellow, he developed a method, using a fluorescent dye, of labeling an antibody so that it can be detected under the microscope. This allowed the cytological localization of antigens or antibodies (by a reverse use) and enabled immunologists to study the specific histology and cytology of immune responses.

His studies were delayed somewhat by his miltary service from 1942 to 1945, but then he returned to Harvard and was an Instructor in Bacteriology and Immunology from 1947 to 1950. In 1950 he was named Silas Arnold Houghton Assistant Professor of Bacteriology and Immunology, and in 1953 was named Career Investigator of the American Heart Association, hence Visiting Professor of Bacteriology and Immunology in the Harvard Medical School. In 1970 he became Professor of Bacteriology and Immunology.

Since specific antibody molecules will react readily with a single microorganism, a labeled antibody can be used for diagnostic purposes. Moreover, an antibody against immunoglobulin can be used to detect an antibody specifically reactive with a chosen object (bacterium, virus-infected animal cell, etc.). By this means a few dead bacteria can be identified, or an antibody in a patient's serum can be sought for diagnostic purposes.

Of perhaps even more scientific interest, the fate of antigenic material can be traced after its injection into an experimental animal, and the resulting antibody, slowly accumultaing in a single cell, can be visualized. In this way Robin Fahraeus' observation that plasma cells are associated with antibody formation was confirmed and extended. Fahraeus described the rise and fall of plasma-cell populations in lymph nodes and spleen, and the differentiation of the plasmacyte family as its content of antibody increases. More recently it has been found that some lymphoid cells (B-cells) display immunoglobulin on the surface of their cell-membrane.

In the meantime, others have developed additional methods for labeling antigens and antibodies—for example, by means of ferritin molecules, which can be visualized under the electron microscope, or by the use of radioisotopes, which can be revealed by photographic emulsions examined under the light microscope. These methods and others, like the identification of antibody-secreting cells by suspending them in a gel with erythrocytes, have been put to hard use in an attempt to solve the riddle set by the very large number of antigenic determinants against which a mammal can produce specific antibodies. It has also become obvious that the immune system provides a very useful means for the study of differentiation, and it is already clear that specific reactions at the cell surface are fundamentally important. In short, the work of Dr. Coons and his co-workers has provided medical (and biological) research with one of its most useful tools. In addition to his research, Dr. Coons maintains an active role in the teaching of medical students.

Bacteriology took a sharply different direction under Dr. Bernard D. Davis, who became Professor of Bacteriology and Immunology at Harvard in 1957. He is an unusual man who has had an unusual career. Dr. Davis graduated from Harvard College in 1936 and from the Harvard Medical School in 1940. He received his M.D. degree *summa cum laude*, an accolade rarely conferred in the Harvard Medical School. As a student he carried out part-time research on protein chemistry for four years in association with E. J. Cohn and T. L. McMeekin in the Laboratory of Physical Chemistry. He received a medical internship and a research fellowship for 1940–41 at the Johns Hopkins Hospital. In 1942 he served at the National Institutes of Health in Aviation Medicine and in 1943–45 he worked in immunochemistry at the College of Physicians and Surgeons in New York with Elvin Kabat and in the immunology of malaria with Jules Freund at the Public Health Research Institute of the City of New York. In 1946–47 he worked at the Rockefeller Institute for Medical Research with René J. Dubos on the tubercle bacillus, which resulted in a period as a patient, with a spontaneous pneumothorax, in a sanatorium. From 1947 to 1954 he ran a Tuberculosis Research Laboratory for the United States Public Health Service at Cornell University Medical College.

During 1954–57 Dr. Davis began a new career as Professor of Pharmacology and Chairman of the Department at the New York University College of Medicine. In 1957 he became Professor of Bacteriology and Immunology and Head of the Department at the Harvard Medical School, and in December 1962 he was made the first Adele Lehman Professor in Harvard University. In announcing the establishment of the Professorship in 1962, Dean George Packer Berry emphasized that "knowledge of this chemical feed-back mechanism points to a new and extremely important type of genetic control of biological systems—the regulation of the synthesis of enzymes." [16] Dr. Davis is essentially a biochemist who uses the rapidly multiplying bacterial cell to study biochemical problems. He has devised ingenious methods for isolating mutants in his study of biochemical mutants. He has been an active student of the role of subcellular components—the cell membrane, ribosomes, etc.— in bacterial physiology and the manner in which they are affected by antibiotics. In November 1969 he moved from the Department of Bacteriology and Immunology to the Bacterial Physiology Unit.

Dr. Davis has commented that the possibilty of widespread and intentionally malevolent genetic tampering in man will become a reality is exceedingly remote.[17] He has emphasized that the potential benefits of genetic alterations greatly outweigh what he calls "overly dramatized" exaggerations of the dangers on the part of some scientists. In the article referred to, he writes:

> . . . however laudable the desire to improve our social structure, and
> however urgent the need to improve our protection against harmful
> uses of science and technology, exaggeration of the dangers from ge-
> netics will inevitably contribute to an already distorted public view,
> which increasingly blames science for our problems and ignores its
> contributions to our welfare.[18]

A major deterrent to the application of genetic control of such basic human traits as intelligence, temperament, and physical structure lies, in his view, in the fact that they are polygenic rather than monogenic in character. Monogenic traits, such as eye color and various hereditary diseases, result from genes which individually exert an all-or-none control over the trait. Such genes make up a small and special class. As Dr. Davis observes, "Most traits are polygenic: that is, they depend on multiple genes, and so they vary continuously rather than in an all-or-none manner. . . . if we eventually develop the ability to incorporate genes into human germ cells, and thus to repair monogenic defects, we would still be far from specifying highly polygenic behavioral traits."[19]

Another deterrent can be found in the fact that differences in behavior depend to a considerable extent on differences in the "wiring diagrams" of our individual brains. Added genes could not be expected to influence this diagram unless it is put into the germ cell before development. Dr. Davis has pointed out that in contrast, a gene for supplying a missing product—insulin, for example—could conceivably be effective whether introduced into a germ cell or into a fully developed individual.

There is a great need for education concerning the distinctions between monogenic and polygenic inheritance if the public is to distinguish between realistic and wild projections for future developments in genetic control in man. Dr. Davis continues: "If, in panic, our society should curtail fundamental genetic research we would pay a huge price. We would slow our current progress in recognizing defective genes and preventing their spread; and we would block the possibility of learning to repair genetic defects."[20] For example, the sacrifice would be great in the field of cancer. Dr. Davis believes that we are on the threshold of a revolutionary improvement in the control of malignant hereditary changes in somatic cells.

The benefits to be derived from studies of genetics extend beyond those in man to nonmedical benefits involving the production and improved quality of livestock and crops resistant to infections and greatly increased yields in antibiotic and other industrial fermentations.

In summing up some general implications for genetic research, Dr. Davis recognizes that there are dangers from genetics, small though they may be in comparison to the immense potential benefits, but such potential abuses cannot be prevented by curtailing genetic research. For one thing, there is the possibility that selective breeding could be used to influence the human gene pool even without further advances in the laboratory. He concludes:

> Moreover, since the greatest fear is that some tyrant might use genetic tools to regulate behavior, and especially to depress human potential, it is important to note that we already have on hand pharmacological, surgical, nutritional, and psychological methods that could generate parallel problems much sooner. Clearly, we shall have to struggle, in a crowded and unsettled world, to prevent such a horrifying misuse of science and to preserve and promote the ideal of universal human dignity.[21]

The emphasis in bacteriology that now pervades the Department at Harvard is on molecular biology, a change in direction that had serious adverse effects on the teaching of pharmacology at Harvard. Other bacteriology professors at Harvard who are devoting most of their time exclusively to research in subcellular particles—research that will, no doubt, some day become relevant to medicine—include Professor Luigi Gorini (Professor since 1964), Edmund Chi Chien Lin (Professor since 1969) and Jonathan R. Beckwith (Professor since 1969). Dr. Lin's title was established as Professor of Microbiology and Molecular Genetics, and in 1973 he became Chairman of the department that has that name. The activities of this department, praised as brilliant by informed scientists, cannot yet be evaluated with regard to their role in medical teaching. The most recent period has been one of confusing change in bacteriology, as the notion has developed that men who use bacterial cells solely to study subcellular chemical phenomena are bacteriologists (as if a physician who uses an automobile daily in his practice should come to be regarded primarily as an automotive engineer).

Professor Harold Amos, Chairman of the Department of Bacteriology since 1969, bears the main responsibility of teaching students the elements of that science. Dr. Amos received his undergraduate training at Springfield College in biochemistry in 1941 and his Ph.D. degree from

Harvard University in 1952. He entered the war and served from 1942 to 1946 in the European Theatre. After the war he was an Instructor in Bacteriology in Springfield College from 1947 to 1948. From 1950 to 1951 he was USPHS Predoctorate Research Fellow in Harvard University, and in 1951 he went to Paris to work at the Pasteur Institute. He returned to Harvard in 1952, where he went through the usual professional grades, and 1963 was named Associate Professor of Bacteriology and Immunology at the Harvard Medical School. In January 1968 he was Acting Chairman of the Department until June 30, 1968, and on July 1 became Chairman. He was promoted to a full professorship on July 1, 1969.

Dr. Amos began his research work with the study of inhibitors of herpes simplex virus, carried out under J. Howard Mueller. He made contributions to the mechanisms of several biochemical and genetic processes in bacteria. More recently he has been increasingly concerned with studies of virus synthesis in animal cell cultures, and in the course of working with this material he made a highly important discovery. It has long been known that when the nucleic acid of a virus enters a body cell or, for that matter, any kind of cell, it forces the cell to produce viral nucleic acids. Dr. Amos made the remarkable discovery that bacterial nucleic acids can also stimulate intact cells to manufacture bacterial genetic material. This finding has many as yet unexplored implications regarding the origin of the physiologic deviations that produce the manifestations of bacterial disease. It is also of obvious importance in biology in general and in molecular biology in particular.

Dr. Amos' research work has always been careful, critical, and, if anything, too modestly and briefly presented; his recent work demonstrates also a capacity for highly original and significant discovery. With the self-confidence that has come from his widespread recognition as an accomplished investigator, his self-disciplined and energetic approach to research, and his broad scientific background and interests, it seems likely that his scientific productivity is still in a phase of growth. At least equally important as this eminence in research are his qualities as a teacher. He combines his dedication to scientific work with an unusually gracious and warm relationship to people. These traits added to the gift of expressing himself clearly and with charm make him outstanding in the lecture hall. Not only do the medical students in his laboratory section frequently express appreciation for his contributions to their education, but students from other rooms soon beat a path to his door, knowing that he will unfailingly be interested in the problems they bring to him. To an unusual extent he is able to combine a sophisticated knowledge of the rapidly advancing frontiers of cell physiology and a real concern for meeting the educational objectives of the medical students. At a time when the emphasis in medical school teaching has veered away from the ills of man in his normal environment to the behavior of molecules in a test tube, this is a saving quality.

LEGAL MEDICINE

Dr. George Burgess Magrath became Medical Examiner for the Northern District of Suffolk County, Massachusetts, in 1907 and was appointed Lecturer in Legal Medicine at the Medical School. Dr. Magrath's connection with the School was not strong during most of his years, because of his heavy duties as Medical Examiner, and the course he taught was voluntary. From 1907 to 1932 he was not raised above the rank of Instructor. The great interest of Mrs. Frances Glessner Lee in the field of legal medicine, however, changed this entire picture in 1932. In that year Mrs. Lee made a gift to the University of $250,000 and also gave the School her large collection of books and other materials in the field. Dr. Magrath was raised to the rank of Professor and remained in that position until his retirement in 1937. He died in 1938.

With Magrath's retirement, the Medical School set out to develop a new program of scholarly quality in the medicolegal field. Some professors thought effort should be placed upon the broad aspects of the subject and upon crime prevention, but the interests of Mrs. Lee were at that time particularly concentrated upon the medicolegal investigation of death—the more traditional field—and her views prevailed. The University brought in, as the first Frances Glessner Lee Professor of Legal Medicine, Dr. Alan Moritz of Cleveland. Dr. Moritz was successful in building up the medical specialty field of forensic pathology. His primary emphasis was upon residency training. The Rockefeller Foundation took an interest in the field and supported the residency program for many years. Several of the leading figures in the field in the United States today are graduates of that program. Dr. Moritz was Professor and Head of the Department of Legal Medicine from 1932 to 1949, when he resigned from Harvard to return to Case Western Reserve University in Cleveland. During these years, he did not hold an official position as a medical examiner in the state. He and his residents were consultants to the medical examiners working through the Massachusetts Department of Public Safety. Dr. Moritz was succeeded as Department Head by Dr. Richard Ford, who was Medical Examiner for the Southern District of Suffolk County. Both were interested only in forensic pathology[22] and seemed unaware of the great changes taking place in medical-legal relationships—for example, in the importance of law in the field.

The next incumbent was William J. Curran, who has provided much material for this section. Dr. Curran was born March 16, 1925, and was an undergraduate in the pre-law course at Boston College in 1943 and 1946–48. He received a J.D. degree from Boston College Law School in 1950 and was awarded the LL.M. degree by the Harvard Law School in 1951 and the S.M. in Hygiene degree from the Harvard School of Public Health in 1958.

After practicing law in Boston from 1950 to 1952, Dr. Curran was in succession Assistant Director, Institute of Government, University of North Carolina (1952), Associate Professor of Law, Boston College Law School (1953–57), Director and Utley Professor of Legal Medicine, Law-Medicine Institute, Boston University (1957–66), and Dean and Director, Metrocenter and Metropolitan College, Boston University (1965–67). He was appointed Frances Glessner Lee Professor of Legal Medicine in the Department of Preventive and Social Medicine of the Faculty of Medicine and in the Faculty of Public Health at Harvard on July 1, 1968. His particular interests have been at the interface between law, medicine and public health. He now teaches courses in all of these three faculties. He has recently completed a historical survey of the medicolegal field in Europe and America.

Before Professor Curran took over, the emphasis in the Harvard Medical School as well as at most medical schools in the United States and Europe had been on forensic pathology. The Ad Hoc Committee[23] appointed to appraise the fitness of Dr. Curran for the Lee Professorship broadly explored the prerogatives and qualifications that candidates should have. Professor Otto Krayer had the following to say:

What we need is not a Professor of Legal Medicine but a Professor of Medical Law. It is antiquated to tie a Department of Legal Medicine at the Harvard Medical School to the Department of Pathology. But it would be equally wrong to tie it to any other department, Pharmacology, for example. Our Professor of Legal Medicine should be a lawyer, and his headquarters might just as well be in the Countway Library. However, his area of substantive involvement, because of the practical realities of his field, will require closer relations to some of the Medical School departments than to others. For example, because the corpse is an all-important element for one segment of his interests there must be ties to pathology; because poisons and use of drugs often play a very important role in his work, contact with Pharmacology and Toxicology is important. Of equal relevance is contact with the knowledge and concepts of preventive medicine and social medicine, for, after all, Law in a very large segment of its activities is nothing, more or less, than preventive medicine of social ills. Into this departmental framework of a medical school the problems of criminal law involving injuries and death from various causes can be fitted, so can human studies and the question of informed consent, iatrogenic diseases, the abuse of drugs and a host of entirely new problems arising from the new laws involving the activities of the Food and Drug Administration, industrial poisons and air and water pollution, narcotics control and even Medicare.[24]

Stimulated by Professor Krayer's comments, the Ad Hoc Committee examined many of the issues that bridge the gap between medicine and law:

— Population control, with such issues as abortion, birth control, and sterilization

— Tissues and organ transplantation

— Testing, utilization, and availability of artificial human organs

— Radiation control

— Environmental controls of air, water, and space

— Human and animal subjects in research

— Legal regulation of medical and paramedical professions

— Legal regulation of medical and scientific industries

— Legal and moral aspects of new discoveries and programs in in medicine

— Changing legal concepts of confidentiality in medicine

— Organized medical care programs

— Changing concepts pertaining to death

It should be apparent that no single medical specialty or single area of medicine can possibly encompass all of these issues. The common element remains legal. It was agreed by the Committee members that the Harvard Medical School needs a scholar in the law as part of its resident faculty to assure that the medical-legal matters just mentioned get a proper place in the curriculum.

The presence of a legal scholar in the Medical School could go far toward defining the medical point of view on important professional issues. Though in past times there have been government regulations or court decisions detrimental to good medical progress, at times seemingly conflicting laws, regulations, or decisions were right and proper, and the medical position had to be altered to meet these new requirements. At other times the legal restrictions imposed on medicine were not proper or justified, or they could possibly have been decided in a way that was less in conflict with medical standards. In such situations the medical position has either not been made clear by effective examination or has not been put forward in a balanced and reasoned manner, in such a way as to influence the legislature or the courts. If the Medical School were to have a medical-legal program worthy of the University, the Medical School could help to analyze such controversial facts, assess the areas of accommodation, and evaluate the specific restrictive interpretations and changes that might result from appropriate changes in the law.

In addition to the ordinary problems of legal medicine, we now have the medical-legal problems involved in human rights, in population control measures—birth control, for example—and very importantly, the problem concerned with the use of human beings in medical research. Professor Curran believes that "there is a need for the training of a new kind of medical-legal persons—specialists who can bridge the gap between the two disciplines. Law and medicine should mesh, not clash."[25]

Chapter Thirteen

Medicine

THE School's move to the Great White Quadrangle on Longwood Avenue had little direct effect on the primary clinical departments. The momentum produced by the optimism and enthusiasm of the Eliot era was maintained, however, and during the Edsall years was directed even more to teaching in the clinical setting. Men taken into the clinical faculty or, if already in it, given high posts during the Edsall years provided leadership for Harvard medicine and much of American medicine in general until past World War II.

MASSACHUSETTS GENERAL HOSPITAL

The first Jackson Professor of Clinical Medicine after David Edsall left in 1918 to become Dean was James Howard Means. Born in Boston, he was educated at Noble and Greenough, and spent a year at Massachusetts Institute of Technology under the biologist William T. Sedgwick. After graduating *cum laude* from Harvard College in 1907, he entered the Medical School, graduating with honors in 1911. His internship at the Massachusetts General Hospital was followed by periods with August Krogh in Copenhagen, Joseph Barcroft in Cambridge, and Francis Benedict and Eugene Dubois in this country. He returned to the Massachusetts General to work with Drs. Joseph Aub and L. H. Newburgh, and then established the first Basal Metabolism Laboratory for the study of clinical problems. After serving in France in World War I, he returned to the Hospital and a short time later established the Thyroid Clinic.

Space was needed for metabolic research, and during his tenure he established Ward 4 for this purpose, wrote extensively about his clinical observations and research on the thyroid gland, and in general fostered physiologic research in the clinical setting at the Hospital. A recipient of many high honors and a Boston aristocrat by birth and upbringing, he was notable for his outspoken fairness, attention to humane considerations, and decided liberalism in medical politics. In 1938, while President of the American College of Physicians, he used his presidential address to call attention to the deficiencies of the attitude of the American Medical Association to prepaid medical care. His objections were by no means purely theoretical—he called upon doctors to create an opposition group to foster the public welfare. In personality he was a man of relaxed, informal dignity who did the right thing as a matter of course. His actions in support of men he disliked personally were the wonder of all. Those he liked were shown no special favors; they were permitted to make their own way, and some of them did so brilliantly.

One of the latter was Paul Dudley White.[1] He took his M.D. degree at the Harvard Medical School and spent most of his professional life at or in connection with the Massachusetts General Hospital in the field of cardiology. As early as 1913 Dr. White was doing pioneer work with the electrocardiograph. In 1916 he was a member of the Harvard Unit of the British Expeditionary Force in France and later served with the American Red Cross. He finally returned to the United States and eventually became a Clinical Professor of Medicine at the Harvard Medical School and Chief of the Heart Service at the Massachusetts General. His clinical studies over the years made him one of the greatest cardiologists of all time. His text, *Diseases of the Heart* (1933), written with Dr. Edward Bland, has been a classic. It brought precision to a field that had long been largely a collection of clinical impressions.

In his early years White found difficulties in studying material in the United States relevant to heart disease, owing to the fact that there are few extremes for comparison in this country. His study of Harvard men who played football between 1900 and 1930, as to diet, exercise, occupation, and smoking and drinking habits, was not characterized by extremes. In 1940 he suggested that the habits of 100 New York bankers be compared with those of 100 Vermont farmers. Even this he found less illuminating than he had hoped. He continued to struggle for information that would make the onset of coronary thrombosis understandable, but a survey in Chicago showed that laborers there have as rich a diet as the well-to-do. A probably relevant observation concerning onset of coronary thrombosis is the fact that the American diet has jumped from 30 percent fat content to 42 percent, but the role of this factor has not been proved because in conjunction with the rise of fat, exercise has diminished all over the country.

White spent much of his life preaching the requirements for a healthy life, in which coronary thrombosis can be prevented or at least delayed. His life was devoted to practice, teaching, writing, and clinical research. He played key roles in the formation of several institutes for heart study. He probably traveled more widely than any other physician. After

World War II he became Chairman of the American Teaching Mission to Czechoslovakia (1946) and to Greece and Italy (1948). In 1948 Congress appropriated funds for the National Heart Institute, and White became Executive Director of the National Heart Advisory Council. He was already an internationally celebrated heart specialist when he became a household name on September 24, 1955, when President Eisenhower suffered a mild coronary thrombosis. During President Eisenhower's illnesses Dr. White's pronouncements were a daily occurrence in the news media, even to the description of the President's bowel activity. Paul White's homely manner, his calm demeanor, and the way he transmitted his confidence in his own experience was not only helpful to the nation during a trying period but showed it that a world-famous specialist from a famous institution could still be a good doctor without affectation or bluster.

Walter Bauer was another of Means's men, and although there was no great affection between the two, Dr. Means gave him every support. After receiving training at the Massachusetts General Hospital, for many decades Dr. Bauer studied the painful and disabling diseases that afflict the bones, joints, connective tissue, cartilage, and joint fluid. His early metabolic studies provided further evidence that bones are more than dead supporting structures. Their structure and chemical composition are influenced by such agents as diet, Vitamin D, and hormones. In his studies at the Hospital he elucidated the effect of the thyroid and parathyroid hormones on bones. He found that an excess of thyroid hormones pulls calcium and phosphorus out of the bones and that lack of those hormones results in excess retention of these salts in the bones. The parathyroid hormone, he discovered, has similar effects.

In 1926 Dr. Bauer participated in a study of the first case of hyperparathyroidism discovered in this country and the second case recorded in world literature. A tumor of one of the four parathyroid glands was responsible. In the early 1930's Dr. Bauer turned to the study of arthritis and other diseases that involve joints, and became notable for his work in joint metabolism and also for his persistent opposition to the use of steroids.

On the death of Dr. Means, Walter Bauer was chosen to succeed him as Jackson Professor. A man of cyclic mood, at times markedly so, Dr. Bauer nevertheless was also a man of inflexible opinion, which was likely to be stated repeatedly in a manner reminiscent of his ancestral god Thor dispatching thunderbolts. Among the opinions often reiterated was that steroids were of little use in arthritis, aspirin being preferable—a view not acceptable to most physicians. Another of his fixed notions was that progress in medicine depended on basic chemical research, and in his position of authority he reshaped the Medical Service at his hospital. In his later years he became severely ill. A heavy cigarette smoker, he ultimately developed emphysema, the disease that eventually killed him.

Another outstanding figure of the Means period was Joseph C. Aub, careful scientist, perceptive clinician, and man of culture. Dr. Aub was graduated from Harvard College in 1911 and from the Harvard Medical School in 1914. He then served as intern at the Massachusetts General Hospital. In his early days as a medical student he showed a keen interest in research, largely inspired by the great physiologist Walter B. Cannon, who became a lifetime friend. At the Medical School he soon caught the eye of the then full-time Chief of Medicine at the Massachusetts General, David Edsall. Dr. Edsall quickly recognized that Aub presented the kind of material for an academic career that he was always on the lookout for.

After finishing his internship, Dr. Aub went off to New York for a year to work under Graham Lusk and Eugene F. Dubois. Under this exceptionally fine guidance, Aub became adept at studying problems of calorimetry, after which he embarked on a residency, one of the very early ones at the Massachusetts General Hospital. At the same time, he studied the specific dynamic action of protein in liver disease. This took place in the rather primitive basal metabolism laboratory only very recently established by James Howard Means. With the declaration of World War I, Dr. Aub went off to France in Base Hospital No. 6, along with many other MGHers. This unit was stationed near Bordeaux, a very long way from the front, and Aub was delighted when he was ordered to an advanced region so that he could carry on research work on shock with Walter Cannon, whose department he entered after the War.

He continued for a time to work on shock, but at the instigation of Edsall decided on a long-range study of lead poisoning. Much of the basis for this work had already been done by Cecil Drinker. In 1924 Aub returned to medicine and the Massachusetts General Hospital. In 1925 the Research Ward 4 (now designated Mallinckrodt) was opened, and it was Aub who made the most of it in its early days. His high standards led to a pattern for excellence, since followed. The work on metabolism of lead was truly distinguished. It showed how lead enters the body, circulates in the blood, is stored in bones (where it is not especially dangerous), and is excreted. More important than this, it was discovered how the absorption of lead can be delayed and its excretion accelerated. This was a revolutionary advance in the treatment of plumbism.

From 1928 to 1942, Aub was in charge of the research at Harvard's Huntington Memorial Hospital, where the major concern was cancer. Undoubtedly, this move was basic in establishing his career in cancer research, which continued over many years. During those years he also held an appointment as Physician at the Peter Bent Brigham Hospital, which permitted him to keep in touch with general medicine. When Harvard closed the Huntington Hospital in 1942 and transferred its funds to the Huntington Laboratory at the Massachusetts General Hospital, Aub moved to the Massachusetts General, which was then and is still connected with the Huntington Laboratory. When the Massachusetts General opened its Research Building in 1951, Aub was assigned two floors in it. Under his leadership in cancer research, the Laboratory became one of the best recognized research centers in the country. In 1943 Aub was designated Professor of Research Medicine, and in 1956 he was obliged by the University rules to retire.

Closely associated with Dr. Aub in some of his earlier work on calcium metabolism was Fuller Albright. Dr. Albright, after joining the staffs of the Harvard Medical School and the Massachusetts General Hospital in 1928, became one of the University's outstanding investigators. He rose to the rank of Professor of Medicine in the former and of Physician in the latter. His most notable contributions were recognition of the disease produced by overactivity of the parathyroid glands; the effective treatment of rickets arising from resistance to vitamin D; the description of a disease since known as Albright's syndrome, in which patients have marked bone involvement and characteristic brown spots on their skin; the development of the proper treatment for uterine hemorrhage; the first description of a kidney disease known as renal tubular acidosis; the demonstration that the occurrence of thin bones in women after menopause can be effectively treated with female sex hormones; the description of the development of Cushing's syndrome, his conclusion forming one of the bases of the modern treatment of arthritis and asthma with cortisone and similar drugs; the description of pseudohypoparathyroidism, a new type of disease in which the endocrine glands are normal but the body fails to respond to the hormonal secretion; and a description of the physiological changes and the dangers of immobilization in Paget's disease, a relatively common disease of the bones. In 1949 and 1952 he published classical papers on the mode of action of ACTH.

In the quarter century between 1931 and 1956, Dr. Albright was associated with and trained some two dozen young investigators, many of whom now hold responsible positions throughout the United States. Since 1936 he himself waged a courageous battle against the inroads of Parkinson's Disease. This battle, a member of the Faculty of Medicine recently wrote, "has served as a source of inspiration to innumerable physicians and their families." He received many honors during his lifetime. Harvard University honored Dr. Albright in 1955 with the Doctorate of Science. His citation read: "Brilliant investigator in the complex field of nutrition and metabolism; your keen mind and enormous courage are a credit to this University and to medicine."

Dr. Chester Morse Jones was also a luminary of Dr. Means's tenure. Born in Portland, Maine, and a graduate of Williams College, he received his M.D. degree from Harvard in 1919. His professional association with it and with the Massachusetts General Hospital began two years later and continued until his retirement, at which time he held the rank of Clinical Professor of Medicine. A world-famous clinician in the field of gastroenterology, he also did notable research in the 1920's and 1930's on psychosomatic medicine, chiefly in reference to visceral pain and the influence of emotion on gastrointestinal function. For ten years, starting in 1948, he served on the American Board of Internal Medicine, first as Secretary and then as Chairman, and is generally acknowledged to be a prime mover in raising its standards. A brilliant bedside teacher, he used his urge to teach in his relations with patients, with remarkable results.

Dr. Means surrounded himself with other fine clinicians and bedside teachers, most of whom, led by their interest in clinical phenomena, carried out basic science research that was notable for its originality and quality, as well as clinical relevance. They will not be listed here, except for Arlie V. Bock, who deserves special notice. A pioneer in the measurement of cardiac output by the Fick principle in intact man (in the 1920's), he carried on his clinical work at the Hospital until he became Oliver Professor of Hygiene at Harvard College. Since retirement from that post he has become involved in the activities of a community hospital in the Nashoba Valley in central Massachusetts, and uses his clinical knowledge as expertly as ever as he continues to add decades to his life.

After Walter Bauer's death, Robert Higgins Ebert served briefly as Jackson Professor before becoming Dean of the Harvard Medical School. He was succeeded by Alexander Leaf. Dr. Leaf came to the Medical Services of the Massachusetts General Hospital in 1949 as a Clinical and Research Fellow with an interest in Nephrology, which was a new clinical and investigative area in medicine. Observations on the effects of vasopressin and other hormones in man led to an understanding of the pathophysiology of what was to become known as the Inappropriate ADH Syndrome. The opportunity to spend four months in Copenhagen with Professor Hans Ussing and the remainder of two years' leave with Professor Hans Krebs in Oxford gave Dr. Leaf a start in biophysical and biochemical aspects of ion transport and membrane function. During this leave he first discovered the usefulness of the histologically simple urinary bladder of the toad as a model upon which to study electrolyte and water transport and their hormonal regulation, and has become an expert on this matter.

Returning to the Massachusetts General Hospital and the Harvard Medical School in 1956, Leaf was appointed Chief of the Cardiovascular Research Laboratories by Dr. Bauer and continued his membrane studies and activities as clinical nephrologist for the Hospital. After Robert Ebert's appointment as Dean, Leaf served as Chairman of the Curriculum Committee at the Harvard Medical School for six years, during which time major changes were made to update the medical curriculum. More recently he has been involved in the joint Harvard Medical School – Massachusetts Institute of Technology Program in the Life Sciences.

Other men with distinguished careers in basic sciences have become Professors of Medicine at the Hospital. One is Kurt J. Isselbacher, Mallinckrodt Professor of Medicine at the Harvard Medical School and Physician, Chief of the Gastrointestinal Unit at the Massachusetts General Hospital. In the mid-1960's Dr. Isselbacher and his associates described a rare, hitherto unrecognized genetic disorder of amino acid metabolism which results in mental retardation and episodes of coma. He has also clarified the biochemical steps in intestinal fat absorption and has demonstrated the role of protein and protein synthesis in the transport of lipids by the inner lining of the intestines.

While at the National Institutes of Health (1953–56) Dr. Isselbacher, with Dr. Herman Kalckar, now Professor of Biological Chemistry at Harvard and Henry S. Wellcome Research Biochemist at the Massachusetts General Hospital, was the first to recognize and describe the defect in the uncommon hereditary disease galactosemia, and developed a specific enzymatic test for diagnosing the disease. With this test it is possible to diagnose the disorder at birth before any mental retardation occurs. The test is currently in use in most large pediatric and medical centers in the United States. Dr. Isselbacher and his associates have also been able to reproduce at the cellular level another rare human hereditary disorder known as congenital betalipoprotein deficiency (acanthocytosis). Recently they provided evidence that a special type of fat, a derivative of coconut oil, is successful in the treatment of this rare and previously fatal disease. Also, with his associates, Dr. Isselbacher first provided a new and important clue to the cause of Whipple's Disease, an uncommon disease of the intestinal lymphatic tissue in man. Their findings, since confirmed in other laboratories, suggest that Whipple's Disease is due to an infectious agent. Dr. Isselbacher has also worked in the controversial field of fat deposit in the liver of alcoholics. After returning from a sabbatical year (1970–71) at the Imperial Cancer Research Fund Laboratories in London, he directed his efforts to studies of oncology, especially the changes in cell surface membranes associated with cancer of the intestinal tract. He is an editor of Harrison's *Principles of Internal Medicine*.

Edgar Haber[2] is Professor of Medicine at the Harvard Medical School and Chief of the Cardiac Unit of the Medical Services at the Massachusetts General Hospital. He began his association with the Hospital as resident in medicine in the late 1950's, then spent three years in the laboratory of Christian Anfinsen (recent Nobel Laureate) at the National Institutes of Health in Bethesda, Maryland, where he carried on experiments in which he demonstrated that the secondary and tertiary structure of ribonuclease is entirely governed by the information contained in its amino acid sequence. This principle has been established as a fundamental tenet of molecular biology.

He returned to the Massachusetts General Hospital in 1961 as Senior resident in medicine and undertook the investigations in immunochemistry which continue today. Using immunologic techniques, he has studied a peptide substance held to be important in regulating the activity of blood vessels, and has investigated the usefulness of measuring blood digitalis levels in treated cardiac patients.

Quite a different type is John H. Knowles, who although no longer connected with the School is worthy of mention. He is former Professor of Medicine at the Harvard Medical School and former General Director of the Massachusetts General Hospital. Dr. Knowles was educated at Harvard College and Washington University Medical School (M.D. degree, 1951) and received clinical training at the Massachusetts General Hospital. Chiefly concerned with policy rather than administration, he directed Boston's enormous Massachusetts General Hospital from 1962 to 1971, during which time he became one of the severest defenders and, at the same time, sharpest critics of the American hospital. Some of his critical comments were considered poorly founded, and he was censured by the Massachusetts Medical Society. Not long before his resignation, Dr. Knowles directed a study group involved in analyzing, at its own request, the policies and procedures of the American Hospital Association. This resulted in the production of the "Knowles Report" and created a severe controversy within the Association. On July 1, 1972, Dr. Knowles became President of the Rockefeller Foundation.

BOSTON CITY HOSPITAL

The second decade of the twentieth century saw Dr. George G. Sears become Clinical Professor of Medicine at Harvard, with other well-known clinicians holding lesser ranks. These included E. P. Joslin, E. A. Locke, F. W. Palfrey, A. O. Hornor, W. R. Ohler, and B. B. Hamilton. All achieved fame in medical Boston, some in practice and others in hospital work. Locke and Palfrey continued to teach at the Boston City Hospital, the second oldest in the Harvard system. Joslin became a pioneer in the use of insulin at the Deaconess Hospital and the founder of a school of treatment of diabetes; Hamilton made outstanding contributions to the study of heart disease in pregnancy. The prevailing spirit was summarized by Abraham Shuman, the merchant prince who was President of the Trustees of the Boston City Hospital from 1892 to 1912. He said (in his 1899 report): "a large municipal hospital not only serves as a hospital for the care of the sick, but also as an institution for education in medicine, and the pursuit of medical science . . . and the trustees feel that it is their duty to assist this most laudable work"—a concept popularly supposed to have originated only in the mid-twentieth century.

In 1915 the Fourth Medical Service was created, with Dr. Sears in charge. He resigned in 1918. A research laboratory was started in 1918, where Dr. Ohler studied patients with nephritis, diabetes, thyroid, and other metabolic disorders. After the 1918 influenza epidemic, a research ward was set up to study patients with this disease and the secondary pneumonia; this was under the supervision of Drs. Edwin A. Locke and F. Dennette Adams. Next a special service was organized for patients with hematologic disorders. These laboratories were all run with private money. The situation failed to satisfy the staff, and in 1919 an earlier bequest made in memory of Dr. William H. Thorndike, Visiting Surgeon of the Boston City Hospital from 1866 to 1884, had accumulated to $200,000. To this the Trustees added $150,000 obtained as a loan and in 1921 voted to establish the world-famous Thorndike Memorial Laboratory, with Francis W. Peabody as its Director. Harvard appointed him Professor of Medicine. He was then forty-one.

Dr. Peabody had graduated from Harvard in 1907, interned in medicine at the Massachusetts General Hospital, gone on to an assistant residency under Llewellys Barker and in pathology under Welch at Johns Hopkins, studied in Berlin for a year, served as resident at the Rockefeller Hospital and then joined the staff of the Peter Bent Brigham Hospital, where he also served as Assistant Professor of Medicine at Harvard. While waiting for the Thorndike Memorial Laboratory to be built, he served as Visiting Professor of Medicine at the Peking Union Medical College in China. At the Thorndike Memorial Laboratory he appointed three physicians, Henry Jackson, Jr., Robert N. Nye, and a woman, Gulli Lindh Muller. One of the resident physicians was Herrman L. Blumgart. The opening ceremonies were marked by eloquent speeches by dignitaries, as well as the turning out of the lights when a sleepy guest leaned against a switch. The proceedings were also interrupted by an intrusion from the wings of a person with a mop and pail, thereby initiating one of the institution's most cherished traditions. Interruptions of this type became standard for all important meetings.

Dr. Peabody believed firmly that the research men should serve as clinicians on the wards. The list of early research projects by these clinician-researchers is most impressive. Many of the men went on to professorships elsewhere. Dr. Peabody put the spirit of the place into words: "The treatment of a disease must be completely impersonal; the treatment of a patient must be completely personal."

Among those who stayed was Herrman L. Blumgart, soon to be joined by Soma Weiss in studies of the circulation in patients. Weiss, after graduating from Cornell in 1923, had interned at Bellevue Hospital in New York. Both these men were to become Professors of Medicine at Harvard. In 1926 the Harvard community was stunned by the illness, and a year later the death, of Dr. Peabody. In 1963 a Faculty Professorship was established in his honor.

He was succeeded in 1928 by George Richards Minot, like Peabody a member of an old Boston family. After Minot's graduation from the Harvard Medical School in 1902 (with his cousin Francis Minot Rackemann), he interned at the Massachusetts General Hospital. Nevertheless, his interests were always of the most varied, ranging from the study of butterflies to the pursuit of Dr. Richard C. Cabot's social service approach to medicine. He took further training at Johns Hopkins in medicine with W. S. Thayer and in physiology with W. H. Howell. On his return to Boston he was appointed Assistant Professor of Medicine and soon became Physician-in-Chief of the Huntington Hospital, which in those days was across Shattuck Street from the Peter Bent Brigham Hospital. He developed severe diabetes in 1921, and his life was saved by the new availability of insulin in 1922. His interest in blood disease was awakened during his time with Howell, and he never gave it up. A case history written by Minot was well out of the ordinary: adhering strictly to fact, the report nonetheless sparkled with wit and bits of philosophy. He could be almost lyrical in discussing the beauties of a blood smear. Examination in his later years of notes from his early years makes it clear that even then he suspected a relationship of diet to pernicious anemia. As the *Harvard University Gazette* puts it, he was interested in blood and food—diseases of the former and deficiencies of the latter. His work on pernicious anemia aptly combined the two.

Outstanding characteristics of Dr. Minot were his inquisitiveness and his lively scientific imagination. He *had* to know the reasons for things, and if they were not superficially available, he went burrowing for them. His extraordinarily original work in hematology will doubtless be the longest remembered, but it must not be forgotten that he was also a

George R. Minot, Professor of Medicine, Director of the Thorndike Memorial Laboratory at the Boston City Hospital, Nobel Laureate. His concepts of conditioned nutritional deficiencies revolutionized clinical thinking. Photograph in the Harvard Medical Archives.

well-rounded physician, devoted to his patients. He was a superb clinical teacher who not only inspired his students by his remarkable scholarship and scientific acumen, but won them over by his kindliness and humor and a deep understanding of *their* problems.

William Howell's influence on Minot was undoubtedly very great, as was that of James Homer Wright and Francis Weld Peabody. Wright had made the observation that the bone marrow in pernicious anemia was "wildly hyperplastic." For some reason maturation of red cells did not take place. A block of some kind seemed to be obstructing their development. About this same time the work of George Whipple on experimental anemia came along, and Minot then showed that the ingestion of liver caused an almost immediate resumption of normal hematopoiesis in those suffering from pernicious anemia. This was accompanied by a wave of reticulocytes in the peripheral blood. It was Peabody who made bone marrow biopsies before and after liver treatment and showed that under the influence of whatever it was in the liver that was effective, the block to normal red cell formation was removed. These momentous studies reached a climax in 1926 and Minot, Murphy, and Whipple received the Nobel Prize in 1934. In general, Minot may be described as a Yankee of the Yankees, culturally an aristocrat, politically a conservative, but in behavior a democrat. He was cordial to all and kind to those who responded.[3] He served as Director of the Thorndike Memorial Laboratory and Professor of Medicine until 1948. Under him, at different times, were Joseph Wearn, Chester Keefer, and Harry Dowling, among others.

Dr. Minot shared a Beacon Street office with Edwin A. Locke, where they practiced medicine; Dr. Locke was Physician-in-Chief of the Fourth Medical Service from 1930. In 1932 Soma Weiss was made Director of the Fourth and the new Second Medical Service. During Dr. Minot's tenure, his own work took several new directions. William Castle demonstrated the intrinsic factor. With Drs. Mettier and Heath, George Minot studied the absorption of iron in certain nutritional anemias. Under him Maurice B. Strauss demonstrated the nutritional origin of anemias of pregnancy and of alcoholic polyneuritis. Dr. T. Hale Ham did his work on the mechanisms of hemolytic anemias. Drs. A. J. Patek, Jr., and R. P. Stetson showed that hemophilia could be controlled by a plasma globulin. The influence of George Minot seemed to pervade all of hematology.

Dr. Minot was succeeded by William B. Castle. Dr. Castle attended Harvard College and received his M.D. degree from the Harvard Medical School in 1921, followed by a medical internship at the Massachusetts General Hospital (1921–23). Following that, he became an Assistant in Physiology at the Harvard School of Public Health. He went through the ranks, in 1937 being named Professor of Medicine and later the Francis Weld Peabody Faculty Professor of Medicine at Harvard, effective July 1, 1963. This appointment was the first Faculty Professorship in the 181-year history of the Harvard Medical School.

Two especially important early influences on Dr. Castle were Dr. Peabody and a long affiliation with the Nobel Laureate Dr. George R. Minot, the second Director of the Thorndike Memorial Laboratory. At an early period in his career Dr. Castle directed his clinical and research interests to diseases of the blood. His most notable finding was that a substance normally secreted by the membrane that lines the stomach is lacking in patients who suffer from pernicious anemia. Dr. Castle named this the "intrinsic factor." It was found to be necessary for absorption of vitamin B_{12} in the diet, a vitamin required for the formation of blood and of other tissues. In the main, however, Dr. Castle will be remembered by 500 or more Thorndike and Harvard Medical Unit men as a wise administrator, critical questioner of research data, and humane physician. By the time he retired, the Harvard-Thorndike unit had contributed far more professors of medicine and of allied basic sciences to the medical world than any other institution in history.

Dr. Castle was succeeded by Maxwell Finland. The latter had been born in Russia in 1902, the young immigrant taking his bachelor's degree at Harvard College in 1922 and his M.D. from the Medical School in 1926. He worked up through the ranks in the Harvard Unit to become, in 1963, George Richards Minot Professor of Medicine and Director of the Second and Fourth (Harvard) Medical Services and Director of the Thorndike Memorial Laboratory at the Boston City Hospital. Only in America!

Respected internationally for his vast knowledge of the clinical and scientific problems concerned with infectious disease in man, Dr. Finland is one of the world's foremost authorities on the use of, and the dangers inherent in, antibacterial agents in the treatment of disease. Although he has studied many aspects of the incidence, communicability, immune responses, and pathologic physiology of a number of infectious diseases, his most persistent research interest has been in their treatment by specific antibacterial agents. His work in this area began in the late 1920's when, as Resident Physician for Pneumonia Patients at the Boston City Hospital, he undertook a pioneering study of the serum treatment of pneumococcal pneumonia.

Among Dr. Finland's research achievements are the clinical recognition of cold agglutinins (antibodies) in atypical pneumonia; the early clinical evaluation of many antimicrobial agents, including sulfadiazine, aureomycin, erythromycin, several tetracyclines, and novobiocin; the increasing resistance of bacteria to antibodies in relation to their usage; the recognition of the dangerous potentialities of secondary invasion of the lungs by staphylococci during influenza epidemics; the demonstration of the unsuspected chemical identity of streptonivicin and cathomycin purely on the basis of microbiological studies; the recognition of staphylococcal enteritis as a result of the alteration of the intestinal flora by broad-spectrum antibiotics; and a clear characterization of the role of ACTH and cortisone in infection.

Dr. Finland has made a major contribution to American and international medicine through the scores of Fellows working under his guidance and as his collaborators who have followed his example to become leaders in the fields of infectious diseases in such departments as medicine, preventive medicine, pediatrics, and microbiology. His widespread fame is based on his application of basic sciences to clinical research, but his other claim to fame, like that of Drs. Weiss and Castle before him, cannot be detected in his publications. As head of a clinical service where almost all the patients came in only when dreadfully sick— 20 percent of them *in extremis*—he and his senior staff had to provide leadership and instruction in how to make sound clinical decisions quickly and with a minimum of laboratory and roentgenographic study. That type of medicine can thrive only in a good municipal hospital, and there are few of them left.

Maxwell Finland was succeeded as Director of the Harvard Medical Services, Director of the Thorndike Memorial Laboratory at the Boston City Hospital, and Minot Professor, by Dr. James H. Jandl. A graduate of the Harvard Medical School, he became an internist who has spent the greater part of his professional life at the Boston City Hospital. Dr. Jandl has gained international renown by his research on disorders affecting the blood. His most recent research included the fundamental discovery, with Dr. H. Franklin Bunn, that heme, the nonprotein, insoluble iron-binding constituent of hemoglobin, undergoes continuous exchange between hemoglobin molecules under physiological conditions. Earlier, Dr. Jandl devoted considerable study to the metabolic abnormalities of the red cells in certain hemolytic anemias. Equal in importance to his research efforts has been the skillful guidance he has given to a growing number of young research fellows who have been attracted to his laboratory at the Hospital. He is held in high regard as a teacher at the Harvard Medical School.

To make things more difficult, all was not uniformly well at the Boston City Hospital. On several occasions, it came close to losing its accreditation because of poor housekeeping, deteriorating services, and inadequate records. There was clear evidence of ineptitude and rumors of corruption involving the city-appointed administrative officials. Harvard's sun was setting at the City Hospital, as Pathology, Gynecology, Pediatrics, and Radiology were given up in succession. A bankrupt city could no longer maintain it and decided to make it smaller. Only one medical school could be allowed to use the diminished facilities, and Boston University was chosen. After a hundred years, on July 1, 1973, Harvard's flag was hauled down.

Joining Dr. Jandl in this mournful retreat had been another Harvard Professor, Charles S. Davidson, Professor of Medicine at the Harvard Medical School, Visiting Physician at the Boston City Hospital, and Associate Director of the Thorndike Memorial Laboratory. Dr. Davidson is primarily concerned with understanding the pathogenesis, pathophysiology, and treatment of various liver diseases. His past experience and understanding in this field have been put together in a small book entitled *Liver Pathophysiology; Its Relevance to Human Disease.* In teaching and in patient care, before the debacle, Dr. Davidson had taken over the revitalization of the outpatient activities of the unit, a particularly important endeavor at that juncture because of the many aspects of the "revolution" in medical care which relate to ambulatory medicine. At the Boston City Hospital this was particularly important because construction of a new ambulatory activities department promised to be one of the most modern in the country.

We choose ten from among dozens of examples of the contributions to medicine of the Boston City:[4]

1. Dr. George R. Minot, Chief of the Fourth Medical Service and Director, Thorndike Memorial Laboratory, from 1928 to 1950, in 1934 received the Nobel Prize (shared with Dr. William P. Murphy of Boston and Dr. George H. Whipple of Rochester, New York) for the discovery of a cure for pernicious anemia.

2. The discovery of the specific plasma-protein, antihemophilic globulin (AHG), and the fact that its lack or deficiency is the cause of hemophilia, was made in the Thorndike Memorial Laboratory during the thirties by Dr. F. H. L. Taylor, Dr. Arthur Patek, and a number of associates, and can be ranked as one of the outstanding medical achievements of this century.

3. Dr. William B. Castle was the sole discoverer of the gastric "intrinsic factor," an essential product of gastric parietal cells that is required for the absorption of Vitamin B_{12}.

4. Drs. Clark W. Heath and M. B. Strauss provided the first conclusive evidence that iron was a quantitative requirement in the formation of hemoglobin and that the prevalent hypochromic anemia was curable by the use of iron salts in appropriate amounts.

5. Dr. William B. Castle, while working in Puerto Rico, demonstrated that crude liver extract had considerable therapeutic value in patients with tropical sprue, an effect mainly attributable to folic acid. In his

studies of liver extract, in pernicious anemia and in sprue, Dr. Castle prepared a deproteinized "crude liver extract" for parenteral use, and characterized the active agent for pernicious anemia patients as a B vitamin.

6. The development of electroencephalography as a clinical and diagnostic technique was made in the Neurological Unit of Boston City; it involved the collaborative efforts of Dr. and Mrs. Fred Gibbs and Dr. William G. Lennox, working at Boston City and at the Harvard Medical School, Department of Physiology.

7. The discovery of the anti-epileptic properties of diphenylhydantoin (Dilantin) was made in the Neurological Unit, Boston City Hospital, by Drs. Tracy Putnam and Houston Merritt. Jandl believes the discovery of diphenylhydantoin ranks among the top one or two dozen therapeutic discoveries in history.

8. Dr. John Harris first showed (in 1949) that stroma-free solutions of hemoglobin from sickle cell anemia blood formed elongated, watery crystals (or "tactoids") when deoxygenated. The molecular alignment on deoxygenation explained the rigid distortion of red cells underlying the pathophysiology of this disease process.

9. In 1950–52 Drs. George Gabuzda, Gerald Phillips, Charles Davidson, and their coworkers showed decisively that administering nitrogenous compounds, particularly ammonia, induced hepatic coma in patients with cirrhosis, and that blood levels of ammonia reflected the degree of coma. The neurological features of incipient hepatic coma (particularly the "liver flap" later given the arcane identification "asterixis") were described by members of the Neurology Unit at the same time.

10. Shortly thereafter, Dr. William V. McDermott and associates showed that the effects of ammonia and nitrogenous compounds on the sensorium arose from vascular circumvention of the liver, and that the effects of ammonia in cirrhosis was analogous to its effect in patients with surgically induced portacaval shunts.

This account of medicine at the Boston City Hospital would not be complete without reference to what promised to be an interesting development but which was never to come to full fruition. It should be remembered that in the first part of the twentieth century, Boston was a busy seaport with strong commercial connection with tropical countries. It seemed reasonable at that time to develop facilities for the study and treatment of diseases that might be brought back from tropical countries by mariners and travelers. Most readers will be amazed to learn that at the turn of the century, Boston was an area of endemic malaria. Moreover, during and after the Spanish-American War the United States Army became the world's leader in tropical medicine, and men trained in this work were coming back to this country. The story involves Dr. George Cheever Shattuck, the last of five generations of notable Boston physicians. George Shattuck, son of Frederick Cheever Shattuck and Elizabeth Perkins Lee, was graduated from Harvard College in 1901 and from the Harvard Medical School in 1905. Two years afterward, what was intended to be a brief visit to Dr. Richard Strong's laboratory in the Philippines developed instead into months of research and resulted in a paper by Dr. Shattuck on tropical ulcer. Following this, Dr. Shattuck went to Vienna for clinical training and returned in 1908 to receive his first appointment at Harvard as Alumni Assistant in Clinical Medicine. The association with Dr. Strong initiated in the Philippines continued until 1938, for Strong became, in 1913, Professor and head of the Department of Tropical Medicine.

George Shattuck often spoke of his father's role in the decision to initiate a School of Tropical Medicine at Harvard, the first of its kind in the United States. There can be little doubt that the warm relationship that had evolved between Richard Strong and George Shattuck played a considerable part in the decision.

In the winter of 1914–15, typhus fever broke out in the prison camps of Serbia and spread throughout the country. By March 1915 one third of the Serbian physicians had died. Within six months the Serbian epidemic had resulted in the death of 150,000 individuals, including five American physicians. Military activities had to be terminated.

The American Red Cross organized a Commission charged with the development of methods for controlling the epidemic. The membership of the appointed Committee was most distinguished: George Shattuck, Richard Strong, A. W. Sellards, S. Burt Wolbach, and Hans Zinsser.

There was some mystery about the etiologic agent in this disease. This was the situation when Shattuck became responsible for defining the clinical picture of the disease and for conducting autopsies. His report, which summarized observations of hundreds of cases, comprised a large part of the monograph material edited by Strong and published by the Commission. When the Commission was eventually broken up, Shattuck served with the Harvard Medical Unit attached to the British Expeditionary Forces in France. After the Armistice had been arranged, Strong brought Shattuck to Geneva as General Medical Secretary of the League of Red Cross Societies. This was the forerunner of the medical component of the League of Nations.

In 1921 Dr. Shattuck was appointed Assistant Professor of Tropical Medicine at Harvard and assigned the responsibility of organizing a Service for Tropical Diseases at the Boston City Hospital. Patients suffering from tropical diseases were scattered in significant numbers throughout the several Boston teaching hospitals, but because of reluctance to transfer patients to a specialized service, the beds assigned to Dr. Shattuck were rarely filled.[5] Many of these patients were at government hospitals, the Brighton Marine (USPHS) Hospital and the Chelsea Naval Hospital, and could not be easily transferred. Nevertheless, several major contributions emerged from the group at the City Hospital, in large part owing to Dr. Shattuck's persistent study. For example, pellagra and scurvy were recognized as common in the patient population,[6] and the first bacteriologically proved case of rat-bite fever which occurred in the United States and the cases of granuloma inguinale recognized in Massachusetts were reported from this Service. Shattuck, in what can only be called a prophetic paper, postulated that alcoholic neuritis and beri-beri were identical.

After 1928 the Service admitted patients to the wards of the Thorndike Memorial Laboratory and supported residents whose interests were similar to those of Drs. Minot and Castle. In the period beginning with World War I down to the mid-thirties, Shattuck played an important part in bringing Tropical Medicine at Harvard into preeminence in this country. His academic activities were reinforced by expeditions to the tropics. In 1924–25 he participated in the Hamilton Rice expedition to the upper Amazon, spending six months in previously unexplored territory. According to the report in the *Gazette*, travel through white water was by dugout canoe, and food supplies disappeared, either by accident or by thievery, so that the group became dependent upon what could be caught or shot. All acquired malaria, and one died. Hostile Indians harassed the explorers. Infected insect bites and machete wounds were common.

Dr. Shattuck's subsequent activities focused on Latin America. They began in 1929 and were carried out in collaboration with the Carnegie Institution of Washington. He was appointed Clinical Professor of Tropical Medicine at the Medical School and the School of Public Health in 1938. In 1951 his textbook, *Diseases of the Tropics,* was published. He received many honors throughout his long career, but for the man who more than any other can doubtless be credited with introducing the concept of deficiency diseases into America, he received far too little recognition. Discussions with this great man reveal adequate reason for his bitterness at not being given adequate hospital patients. Granted that shadows are longest at sundown, the world of Harvard and Boston medicine could have treated George Cheever Shattuck far more graciously than seems to have been the case. It must be borne in mind however, that malaria was wiped out. Boston ceased to be an important seaport, and the inflow of tropical disease ended.

Although Dr. Shattuck officially retired in 1947, he continued to enrich the lives of all who came in touch with him for twenty-five years more. When death came on June 12, 1972, in the 93rd year of his life, an end came to a remarkable career of service to society, to Harvard University, and to his chosen field of science, tropical medicine.

PETER BENT BRIGHAM HOSPITAL

The Peter Bent Brigham Hospital had a quite different history, involving fewer individuals but at times high drama. Things were quiet enough during Henry Christian's tenure. A superb clinician, trained previously as a pathologist, he ran a service in which the teaching and patient care were by himself, Reginald Fitz, Channing Frothingham, and Samuel A. Levine. The research consisted mainly in clinical studies that attempted to define syndromes and improve treatment by bedside observation correlated with clinical laboratory findings and postmortem findings.

Reginald Fitz, the son of Reginald H. Fitz mentioned previously, was born in Boston. He graduated from Harvard College and, in 1909, from the Medical School. After an internship at the Massachusetts General Hospital and a residency at the Brigham, he received further training at Johns Hopkins and the Rockefeller Hospital; he served in the Army in World War I, worked at the Mayo Clinic from 1920 to 1922, and was Associate Professor of Medicine from 1922 to 1936, after which he went to Boston University as Professor of Medicine. He held a great number of other posts, including that of University Marshall at Harvard.

Channing Frothingham graduated from Harvard in 1906; he rose to become Associate Professor of Clinical Medicine and Physician at the Peter Bent Brigham. Later he became Chief at Faulkner Hospital. In 1937 and 1938 he created a sensation, and some enmity, for his crusade in favor of prepaid medical care. A fine clinical teacher who delighted in upsetting pat diagnoses with innocent questions, he was an exponent of straightforward nontheoretical approaches.

Samuel A. Levine was born in Poland and brought to Boston at the age of three. He was a brilliant and indefatigable student at English High School and sold newspapers to help the family finances. His record won him a scholarship established at Harvard by the Newsboys' Union. Graduating from Harvard College in 1911, he entered the Medical School and became the first student to work (under Dr. Fitz) in the newly opened Peter Bent Brigham Hospital. He graduated in 1914 and served an internship at the same hospital. A period with Alfred Cohn at the Rockefeller Hospital followed, and during World War I he served with Sir Thomas Lewis and Frank Wilson (of Ann Arbor) at the British

Henry Asbury Christian. He was briefly Dean at the School, and then the first Hersey Professor of the Theory and Practice of Physic at the Peter Bent Brigham Hospital. A former pathologist, he made that discipline the basis of the development of clinical medicine at his hospital. He trained dozens of men who became leaders of American medicine. From a portrait in oil by Marie Danforth Page (1933) hanging in the Peter Bent Brigham Hospital.

Heart Hospital. Back in Boston after the War, he returned to the Peter Bent Brigham and served until his death. He became a world-famous cardiologist, and his pioneering writings on thyrotoxic heart disease and myocardial infarction were definitive. He wrote *Clinical Heart Disease* (1936) and, with Proctor Harvey of Georgetown, *Clinical Auscultation of the Heart* (1949). After his death his patients and friends established the Samuel A. Levine Professorship of Medicine. He was the only one of the group who stayed on for any length of time after Henry Christian's retirement.

In 1939 Soma Weiss was named Hersey Professor of Medicine at the Peter Bent Brigham Hospital. Born in Hungary, a graduate of Cornell University Medical School in 1923, and a former intern at Bellevue, he came to the Thorndike Memorial Laboratory after a period of training in pharmacology at Cornell. He had always dreamed of becoming a pharmacologist who would study the mechanisms of drug action in sick people who were responding to them. In 1930 he became Associate Director and instituted a series of researches on the clinical physiology of heart disorders which astounded and stimulated all who came near him. His familiarity with languages gave him access to a vast amount of European physiologic material, which he then applied to man. A brilliant clinical observer, he not only worked on hypertension and atherosclerosis but helped to define the Mallory-Weiss syndrome, carotid-sinus syncopes, neurogenic mechanisms in pulmonary edema, and a host of other newly recognized phenomena in studies that seemed to go on without end, He insisted at all times on service to the patients, and his magnetic personality and qualities of leadership stimulated the house staff and students to unanticipated efforts. When asked a question that (rarely) he could not answer, he was known to reply in English garbled by so atrocious a Hungarian accent as to be unintelligible. On arriving at the Peter Bent Brigham, he was the new broom. He died unexpectedly after a short period of service.

George W. Thorn was the next Hersey Professor of Medicine and later was also given the title of Samuel A. Levine Professor of Medicine and Physician-in-Chief at the Peter Bent Brigham Hospital. His pre-Boston period was spent in Baltimore working on adrenal steroids, and he continued this work here. His research has concentrated on endocrinology and metabolism. He pioneered in studies of salt and water metabolism, the effect of high altitude on adrenal function, and the myopathy of thyroid disease, and he has made significant advances in the medical knowledge of diabetes mellitus. Perhaps his greatest contribution is his research on cortisone and ACTH (adreno-corticotropic-hormone) and the development of its use in the treatment of numerous diseases. He was among the first to show that complete adrenalectomy could be performed in man, and he initiated the earliest work in human kidney transplantation at the Peter Bent Brigham Hospital.

In 1946 Dr. Thorn was attracted to the possibility of making an artificial kidney along the lines of that originally designed by Dr. Wilhelm Kolff, who, shortly after the war, told one or two American scientists about this new development. Dr. Thorn gathered around him an able team to construct this kidney and by 1948 and 1949 his Department was the first in the United States to have an active dialysis program for the treatment of renal failure. He used it not only to treat renal failure but as a basis for his later interest, adrenalectomy for hypertension, in the pathophysiology of advanced renal disease and for his collaborative work with the Department of Surgery in the initial trial of kidney transplantation. This was done in 1951 and could not have occurred without Dr. Thorn's interest in dialysis and his original and pioneering work in the use and construction of the kidney.

Above all Dr. Thorn was an outstanding administrator and organizer of teaching programs for postgraduates, and his service became a "medical U.N." After his retirement he continued to be active in clinical teaching by producing tapes and publications for practitioners. He surrounded himself with men of great competence, some in clinical medicine, others in basic research. One who combined both admirably, was Dr. John P. Merrill, Professor of Medicine at the Harvard Medical School and Director, Cardiorenal Section, Peter Bent Brigham Hospital.

John Merrill's interest in nephrology has had far-reaching consequences. It began with the artificial kidney, which he employed for the first time in the United States, not because of an original interest in kidney disease but because of an interest in electrolyte imbalance and what this might do to the electrocardiogram. It was in 1948 that Merrill and his group used an artificial kidney on a patient for the first time. A considerable stir was created in the lay press and among internists, but it was treated with great disdain by the physiologists. No less a man than Homer Smith once publicly stated that the artificial kidney did nothing but remove urea, and that everyone knew this was not important (he later apologized, and he and Merrill became good friends).

Merrill's point of view, which he defended for several years against considerable opposition, was that to embark on a crash program, doing nothing but treating patients at a fantastic cost, would so endanger developments in the field of renal disease that ten years hence he would have made considerably less progress than if he had proceeded at a much more leisurely pace, attempting not just treatment of all patients dying of renal failure, but coordinated programs of teaching and research. This view prevailed.

The ability to keep chronic uremic patients alive with an artificial kidney led to Merrill's and his group's ability to transplant kidneys in patients, and in 1950 Drs. David Hume and Merrill, along with Dr. Thorn and Dr. J. Hartwell Harrison did a number of cadaver transplants. This was followed in 1954 by the first successful kidney transplant in an identical twin, and in 1959 by the first successful true allograft. A large number of studies on various aspects of kidney disease continue to come out of Merrill's more spectacular pursuits.

BETH ISRAEL HOSPITAL

The fourth major Harvard-connected hospital for the teaching of medicine is the Beth Israel. It had an interesting beginning, which must be understood if one is to appreciate more recent developments. In the second half of the nineteenth century America began to lose its Protestant dominance with an influx of millions of Catholics and Jews, escaping poverty or persecution in Europe. The immigrants were, in general, poor. They worked hard and within one or two generations acquired enough security to engage in middle-class occupations. Jews especially had an intellectual tradition, with a special interest in medicine. To meet the needs of the immigrant community, the Mt. Sinai Dispensary was established August 1, 1902, in the West End of Boston. It had no inpatient facilities. Increasingly, the Dispensary became concerned with preventive medicine.

The poor and undernourished at that time were prime targets for tuberculosis, especially when they lived in overcrowded and unsanitary conditions. A tuberculosis clinic was established at Mt. Sinai in 1907. The building at the Dispensary was very soon outgrown, and in the early years of the present century the importance of the hospital became increasingly clear. The concept of a hospital became prominent in the thinking of the Jewish community in 1909. The *Jewish Advocate* acted as spokesman for the group. The Flexner Report, with its emphasis on medical education, was also a spur to the establishment of a Jewish hospital. With the passage of a few years the planning for the hospital had become increasingly sophisticated. It was clear that a dispensary, however improved, could never take the place of a hospital. In the years 1910–12 an attempt was made to consolidate the efforts of all Boston Jews interested in a hospital.

On May 21, 1916, the Commonwealth of Massachusetts closed the Mt. Sinai Dispensary, owing largely to the fact that the building had become structurally unsafe. After many fund-raising drives, sufficient money had been gathered to make it possible, on October 22, 1916, to dedicate the Beth Israel Hospital at the new site on Townsend Street in Roxbury. Forty-five patient beds were set up in the converted mansion. The bylaws of the Hospital were like those of the Massachusetts General in that the Hospital was to care for the sick and disabled of "any race, creed or color." It was to carry on "such educational, philanthropic and scientific activities and functions as are part of the efficient modern hospital . . ." The building soon became inadequate, and a new one was built in 1927 near the Medical School, on Brookline Avenue. This choice of location was to lead to a close relationship with the Medical School, although it was inconvenient for the Jews of Roxbury. In time, however, Roxbury became a slum area and the Jews moved to Brookline and other nearby suburbs.

In the 1927–37 period the Hospital developed its teaching affiliation with the Harvard Medical School. The first joint appointment was made in March 1927, when Dr. M. J. Schlesinger was named Pathologist-in-Chief. Next came, in 1938, the appointment of Herrman L. Blumgart as Associate Professor of Medicine at the Harvard Medical School.

Dr. Blumgart was born July 19, 1895, in Newark, New Jersey. He was graduated from Harvard in 1917 with the B.S. degree and received his M.D. degree from Harvard in 1921. His internship at Peter Bent Brigham Hospital from 1921 to 1922 was followed in 1923 by a year in London and Europe as Moseley Traveling Fellow of Harvard. He served under Francis Peabody and George R. Minot at the Thorndike Memorial Laboratory and from there was called to the Beth Israel Hospital in 1928 as Director of Medical Research and Visiting Physician. During World War II he served as Colonel in the Army Medical Corps. He was Medical Consultant to Headquarters of the Second Service, and Chief Consultant in Medicine to India-Burma and China Theaters. He became Physician-in-Chief to the Beth Israel on his return in 1946. At Harvard Dr. Blumgart started as Assistant in Medicine 1924–27, and was Associate Professor of Medicine 1929–46. He then became Professor of Medicine.

Many of Dr. Blumgart's published works, now numbering more than 130, have dealt with the normal and pathologic physiology of the circulation. Prior to 1920 it was possible to measure the output of blood from the heart but difficult to measure accurately its velocity in the body. Working as an assistant on the Harvard Service in the Thorndike Memorial Laboratory at the Boston City Hospital from 1924 to 1928, Dr. Blumgart devised a method of injecting a solution of radioactive salt into the left arm and measuring the time required to reach the right arm. Knowing the exact route to be followed provided an accurate means of measuring velocity.

His principal task, however, has been to change, often against resistance, a small, ethnically oriented, community hospital into an organization geared to medical teaching at the student, intern, and graduate levels. This he accomplished, and moreover made it world famous. His friends and patients established a professorship named after him.

During Dr. Blumgart's absence in military service, his functions were given to Dr. Mark D. Altschule, then Instructor in Medicine at the Harvard Medical School and Assistant Visiting Physician at the Hospital. All of Dr. Altschule's professional life has been spent in the service of Harvard and its affiliated hospitals. Following his graduation from the Harvard Medical School in 1933, he combined his residency training with laboratory research. In the half-dozen years following graduation, he had achieved a fine record as a productive clinical scientist. He became known especially for his contributions on the cardiovascular system. For some twenty years a constant stream of original publications on the cardiovascular system came from his laboratory.

In 1947, Dr. Altschule accepted the position of Director of Internal Medicine and of Research in Clinical Physiology at the McLean Hospital. He continued to teach at the Beth Israel Hospital and the Boston City Hospital, where he was acclaimed by the students as one of the finest teachers on the Harvard scene, but his main research activities were shifted to the McLean Hospital. Once again a steady stream of contributions dealing with metabolic and physiological changes in mental disease, especially schizophrenia, appeared. Simultaneously, observations were being made, for comparison, on other forms of stress. It was found that they all had biochemical features in common. As part of the study of biochemical responses to environmental change, he developed an interest in the pineal gland, and over the past two decades he, his students, former students, and coworkers have done much to clarify the role of that enigmatic gland in the body. He gradually rose to the rank of Clinical Professor of Medicine. In addition to teaching and research, Dr. Altschule has had a long-lasting interest in the history of medicine, where he has been a contributing scholar. The University has recognized his historical abilities by naming him Honorary Curator of Prints and Photographic Collections in the Countway Library.

A. Stone Freedberg, Professor of Medicine at the Harvard Medical School and Physician to the University Health Services assigned to the Medical Area Health Service, and Physician, Beth Israel Hospital, has long been a favorite teacher at that Hospital. He has also carried on work on the more subtle aspects of thyroid function in man. He served as Acting Physician-in-Chief for a time after Dr. Howard H. Hiatt's resignation.

Dr. Hiatt was successor to Dr. Blumgart and was given the title Herrman L. Blumgart Professor of Medicine at the Harvard Medical School and Physician-in-Chief, Beth Israel Hospital. Dr. Hiatt was graduated from Harvard College, and, in 1948, from the Medical School. He interned and served residencies at the Beth Israel Hospital. He has been associated with Harvard since 1955, when he became Instructor in Medicine, and with the Beth Israel Hospital during the same period. He became the Blumgart Professor and Physician-in-Chief in 1963. As chief physician of a major teaching hospital in a metropolitan center, Dr. Hiatt has focused his research on applying new knowledge to understanding and managing cancer in man. In his studies of cellular growth he has worked with two Nobel Laureates—James D. Watson of Harvard and Jacques Monod of the Pasteur Institute in Paris—and with the virologist Michael Stoker at the Imperial Cancer Research Unit in London. Dedicated to the view that basic science is primary in medical practice, he has built up his department with men trained in this area.

Dr. Hiatt resigned in 1972 to become Dean of the Harvard School of Public Health. This change in direction at first glance is startling, but consideration of the issues involved reveals that it should not be. There is a fundamental similarity between studying masses of anonymous molecules in their environment and masses of anonymous people in theirs.

Among the most interesting Clinical Professors of Medicine at the Beth Israel Hospital is Dr. Paul M. Zoll, who despite a full-time practice has found time to pioneer the development of the cardiac pacemaker.

OTHER TEACHING HOSPITALS

In addition to the major hospitals listed in this section there are others that played less dominant but still important roles in Harvard Medical teaching. One was the House of the Good Samaritan. Founded in 1861 for chronically ill children, it devoted itself almost exclusively in and after the 1920's to the problems of rheumatic fever. During this period it achieved international fame through the publications of Dr. T. Duckett Jones. He and his co-workers defined in terms that quickly became and remained authoritative the diagnostic features of rheumatic activity. His group also recognized the importance of the discovery by Dr. Alvin F. Coburn of the role of streptococcal infection in rheumatic fever recrudescence, and became pioneers in the prophylaxis of that disease. With the decline and severity of the disease (which antedated by several decades the development of the prophylactic approach), the hospital outlived its usefulness and was recently closed.

The Robert Breck Brigham Hospital was another one in the Harvard orbit. Founded in 1914 by the Brigham brothers, it devoted itself to the chronic care and treatment of the arthritic disorders. It was at all times an excellent clinical facility but decided to participate in the basic-science growth and development at Harvard and in 1966 became officially an affiliated hospital. Since the diseases in which arthritis occurs are usually those that show marked derangements in immune processes, it seemed reasonable to appoint Dr. K. Frank Austen Theodore Bevier Bayles Professor of Medicine at the Harvard Medical School and Physician-in-Chief, Robert Breck Brigham Hospital.[7] He has served most of his career at Harvard and has made a reputation as an outstanding student of the subtle intricacies and ambiguities of immune processes. He has been particularly active in changing immunology from a study of effects to a study of substances.

The New England Deaconess Hospital, for many decades a leader in diabetes studies and a pioneer in the use of the insulins has increased its stature in recent years through the appointment of George Cahill as Professor of Medicine at Harvard Medical School and Director of the Joslin Clinic. His work in intermediary metabolism in man has been perceptive in planning and expert in execution. The result has been a high level of clinically motivated biochemical research.

Chapter Fourteen

Surgery

THE Department of Surgery participated actively in the enormous development of medicine at Harvard partly through the leadership of David Edsall in encouraging scholars rather than technicians and partly because of what was beginning to happen in American surgery in general in the twentieth century. Surgery of the nineteenth century concentrated on technical and anatomical matters, but the twentieth century saw the increasing application of physiology and of biochemistry to clinical surgical problems. This revolution began slowly but soon reached explosive dimensions and is still going on.

MASSACHUSETTS GENERAL HOSPITAL

The tradition of outstanding surgical teachers was maintained at the Hospital in the person of Maurice Richardson and his colleagues. Dr. Richardson's leadership was exerted by enormous physical and intellectual energy. He was graduated from Harvard College in 1873 and from the Harvard Medical School, where he received his M.D. degree in 1877. From a very young age his great desire was to become a surgeon, and he rose through the ranks to attain the distinction of the Moseley Professorship of Surgery in 1907, a post he held until his death in 1912. He was also Visiting Surgeon at the Hospital.

Dr. Richardson was famed for his surgical skill, which he attributed to superior anatomical training and the later adaptation of sound surgical principles. At the beginning of his career, abdominal surgery amounted to little more than an occasional ovariotomy or herniorraphy. Surgery of the appendix, the gall bladder, and the stomach did not exist in his early days. Although not the discoverer of appendicitis or pancreatitis, both of which must be attributed to Reginald Fitz, Dr. Richardson was a pioneer in the development of the operation for appendicitis, and in later years he confined his work to abdominal surgery.

He was a great teacher and an excellent lecturer. He was both original and incisive. He was able to use his fundamental knowledge of anatomy by rapidly drawing accurate sketches on the blackboard, very often using both hands. His students were not only stimulated by his exuberance and great knowledge of technique, but inspired by Maurice Richardson the man.

His published papers cover nearly the whole range of abdominal surgery. He guarded jealously the good name of surgery as a specialty and the relationship between the surgeon and his patient. Most impressive, in addition to his surgical skill, were his integrity and honesty of purpose. His simplicity and straightforwardness had great influence on his contemporaries and his students. His physical strength and endurance were legendary. He walked one day from Fitchburg to the top of Mount Monadnock and back, a distance of some sixty miles. He enjoyed swimming in the open sea and swam across Vineyard Sound, and on another occasion swam nine miles from Salem to Magnolia. He was greatly interested in the woods and was especially interested in migrating birds. He played four instruments well: the piano, the flute, the cello, and the bassoon.

After a long day of operating, Dr. Richardson died in his sleep at 61 years of age. During the next generation clinical surgery continued to maintain its high status. A succession of outstanding clinicians like Edward Richardson, Homans Professor of Surgery, for all of whom the basic science of their specialty was anatomy, maintained the Massachusetts General Hospital tradition. Praised and respected by their contemporaries, their names and their work no longer arouse the recognition they deserve, nor did all the men who today deserve recognition achieve high position at the Hospital and in Harvard medicine. In fact, one who never rose above junior rank and whose idiosyncratic ways prevented enthusiastic acceptance of his ideas was perhaps the most influential of his contemporaries. This was Ernest Amory Codman, member of several old Boston families.

The man is often forgotten, but his contributions persist. "He stood 8 feet tall but was invisible," as one recent account put it.[1] His eccentricities were productive and, very often, far ahead of their time. His stubborn, uncompromising attitude was largely responsible for the difficulty his colleagues gave him when they did not simply ignore him. Nevertheless, he was largely responsible for insisting that the Massachusetts General Hospital pioneer in extending specialization in surgery.

Like several of his mature colleagues—for example, Walter Cannon and Robert Osgood—within a matter of weeks after the discovery of roentgen rays he was absorbed in their clinical use. From their experimental use of these, he and his colleagues received injuries that persisted throughout their lives.

Dr. Codman's principal obsession was what he called the End-Result System. He considered it "merely the commonsense notion that every hospital should follow *every* patient it treats, long enough to determine whether or not the treatment has been successful, and then to inquire, 'if not, why not?' with a view to preventing similar failures in [the] future."[2] Codman's system, complete with cards and charts, is clearly a forerunner of today's "new" Problem-Oriented Medical Record, the method being different from Codman's principally in that its concern is with problems instead of disease.

While Codman had undoubtedly been mulling over his system for some time, he was not fully engaged with it until the summer of 1910, when he was at a meeting of the Royal College of Surgeons in England. He and Dr. Edward Martin of Philadelphia had taken a hansom cab from the meeting site to the heart of London, and during the ride Codman described what he had in mind. Martin at once saw the possibility of the End-Result System as a venture around which one could build an American College of Surgeons. "[T]he tail is more important than the dog," Dr. Martin said, "but we shall have to have the dog to wag the tail."[3] Both Codman and Martin became founders of the American College of Surgeons, which was born in 1913. Its campaign to encourage use of the End-Result System was to be one of its major contributions.

In 1910 Dr. Codman had junior status in the Massachusetts General Hospital world.[4] He believed that this would hold back his efforts to spread the System there, and to overcome such difficulties he started the small Codman Hospital on Beacon Hill not far from the Massachusetts General. Clearly, he could not change the latter overnight, but he could guide the former. His hospital at once adopted and implemented the System.

In 1914 Dr. Codman, exasperated with the Massachusetts General and its failure to adopt his ideas, resigned as a protest against the seniority system of promotion, which had failed to recognize the value of the End-Result idea. His resignation was accepted, one supposes with alacrity, by the Trustees. The next day, however, he wrote to them seeking appointment as Surgeon-in-Chief "on the ground that the results of my treatment of patients at their hospital during the last ten years had been better than those of oher surgeons." The Trustees did not bother to reply.[5]

Codman at that time was Chairman of the county medical society, and he arranged a meeting at the Boston Medical Library. He failed to obtain the speakers he wanted, but ensured a crowd by inviting people like the notorious Mayor, James Michael Curley. At the end of this meeting he unveiled an 8-foot cartoon showing rich patients as a head-in-the-sand ostrich laying golden eggs.[6] The cartoon asked whether these people would continue to lay large medical fees if they knew the end results of hospital treatment. Dr. Codman's behavior was deemed a disgrace, and he was asked to resign as Chairman of the county medical society.[7]

When Codman returned from World War I, he found his hospital closed and in debt. He then set about organizing the important Registry of Bone Sarcoma. His hope was that this example might show the inadequacies of the then current methods. In addition, together with Harvey Cushing, he developed the first anesthesia records.[8]

Many people would say, in appraising Codman's productivity, that his book, *The Shoulder*, was his greatest contribution. Dr. Otto Aufranc said that "it remains a classic in concept and description . . . His basic understanding of the anatomy and the causes of pain and surgical indications have remained sound."[9] *The Shoulder* has been a reason for placing Dr. Codman with the orthopedists. Moreover, his original studies of fractures of the carpal scaphoid resulted in a monograph on the wrist. One difficulty with eccentrics is that it is difficult to know just where to place them.

Brilliant as Ernest Codman's clinical contributions were, his work on standards for evaluating the results of surgical care and anesthesia was more influential in the history of Boston medicine than his strictly technical works. The Massachusetts General Hospital, like all other leading hospitals, came to adopt the ideas of this man, one of its more aberrant sons.

The Massachusetts General was soon to experience even greater changes when Edward D. Churchill was appointed John Homans Professor of Surgery at the Medical School and Chief of the West Surgical Service at the Hospital. Dr. Churchill came to the Harvard Medical School with a Master's degree in biology, and was graduated from the School *cum laude* in 1920. Four years were passed as a member of the house staff at the Massachusetts General Hospital, following which he was a Dalton Scholar with Cecil Drinker and shortly thereafter received a Moseley Traveling Fellowship for work primarily with August Krogh in Copenhagen. During the European venture he trained himself in thoracic surgery, especially under Professors Ludolf Brauer and Ernst Sauerbruch. On returning to the United States he was appointed to a staff position under Edward P. Richardson, then Homans Professor of Surgery and Chief of the West Surgical Service in the Massachusetts General Hospital. Churchill was a biologist in surgeon's clothing, a leader in the "new biological surgery." His research activities at that time dealt with cardiopulmonary physiology and shock. More and more his clinical activities were concerned with surgery within the thorax. In collaboration with Paul D. White, he carried out the first successful pericardectomy in the United States for constrictive pericarditis. In the autumn of 1928 Dr.

Edward D. Churchill, Surgeon-in-Chief at the Massachusetts General Hospital and John Homans Professor of Surgery at the School. A pioneer in chest surgery and an outstanding medical educator. Photograph from the Harvard Medical Archives.

Churchill decided to accept the invitation to build up a full-time unit at the Boston City Hospital. He hoped that a surgical counterpart to the internists' famous Thorndike Memorial Laboratory could be developed. Alas, this was not achieved, and the recurrent problems of the Boston City Hospital resulted in failure of efforts to improve it.

At this time (1929), various offers of professorships came in from other institutions. Through the good offices of E. P. Richardson and Dean Edsall, but without Harvey Cushing's support, Dr. Churchill was invited to return to the Massachusetts General Hospital. He accepted.

Dr. Richardson fell ill, and Dr. Churchill succeeded him in the Homans Professorship and the Chiefship of the West Surgical Services. (It was only later that the General Surgical Services were merged under Dr. Churchill.) By the 1930s Churchill's international reputation was firmly established by his early operations on cancer of the lung, and particularly by his success with pulmonary resection for bronchiectasis.

Churchill's surgical feats were too consistent to be merely lucky breaks. For example, at a time when the surgical mortality of bronchiectasis was as high as 20 to 50 percent in various clinics, Churchill startled the thoracic world by carrying out either lobectomy or pneumonectomy in forty-nine patients with a case mortality of 6.1 percent.[10] His data were nearly everywhere disbelieved. Harsh things were said behind his back, and he was charged, in effect, with dishonesty, or at least with choosing less serious cases; yet he achieved an astonishing mortality rate of 2.6 percent in thirty-eight patients subjected to lobectomy by currently recommended methods. Indeed, by then he had carried out thirty successive cases without a death. It took some years before he was widely accepted as a new master. Although Churchill maintained a calm outward mien, he suffered grievously from the uncharitable acts of many of his colleagues.[11]

It was from his experience with bronchiectasis that Dr. Churchill evolved the concept of the bronchopulmonary segment as the basic surgical unit of the lung. His great interest was, at this time (the early 40's), his surgical approach to the cure of pulmonary tuberculosis. In those days, which preceded the introduction of antiotics, he realized that if he were to overcome the complex problems of surgery within the thorax, he would have to have better anesthesia than had been the case earlier. Fortunately, the application of physiologic and pharmacologic approaches to anesthesia provided him with what he needed. Much of this work originated at the Massachusetts General Hospital.

By the 1930's he had also begun to attack the problems of surgery of the esophagus. Churchill was a man of broad interests, and following E. P. Richardson as he was, it was not surprising that he had a keen interest also in thyroid disease. In association with Drs. Aub and Albright and Oliver Cope, original studies of the parathyroid glands were developed.

In a quiet way Churchill's development of the full-time Department of Surgery originated by Richardson took a leaf from Halsted's book. Halsted directed his pupils to enter special fields of surgery. Oliver Cope became interested in endocrine glands and later in burns. John Stewart was concerned with metabolic problems, Henry Beecher developed an Anesthesia Department, Champ Lyons was concerned with surgical infections. Edward Benedict took on endoscopy, and F. A. Simeone worked on vascular disease and shock.

At this period a lesser man might have ignored the clinical surgeons who were so needed to maintain balance in the Massachusetts General Hospital: Arthur Allen, Leland McKittrick, Joe Vincent Meigs, Marshall Bartlett, Grantley Taylor, Varaztad Kazanjian, Claude Welch, and Gordon Donaldson, to name a few. Churchill not only permitted but encouraged these men to develop their special interests and aptitudes in the various fields in which they later became famous.

Although, as noted above, there were similarities with the Halsted system, Dr. Churchill's approach to surgery differed sharply in other areas—for example, he never accepted the Johns Hopkins full-time system, sharing Dean Edsall's belief that it was not the best course to follow.

When the Coconut Grove disaster of 1940 struck, in which some five hundred people lost their lives, such a disaster had been prepared for, and many principles emerged during that terrible night which were useful in World War II, then rapidly approaching. Dr. Churchill went into the War as a Colonel and came out with the same rank. He was Surgical Consultant to the North African, later Mediterranean, Theater of Operations. His insistence on the use of whole blood marked a turning point in the handling of the severely wounded. His statement in Christopher's *Textbook* reads:

> Military surgery is not to be regarded as a crude departure from accepted surgical standards—"an awful business," as it has been called, but as a development of the science of surgery to carry out a specialized and highly significant mission. To keep this development sound in the midst of war, when emotional forces so commonly displace scientific motivation, is the prime challenge to the military surgeon. Military surgery is the surgery of trauma encountered in epidemic proportions.[12]

In terms of individuals who needed and got medical care during World War II, Dr. Churchill's contributions may have saved more lives than anything else he did. This was, in part, effected through the establishment (by him) of the Board for the Study of the Severely Wounded, North African – Mediterranean Theater of Operations. The Board was sometimes irreverently called "Churchill's traveling circus." The activities of the Board are described in *Physiologic Effects of Wounds*, edited by Henry K. Beecher.[13]

After he had returned to Harvard and the Massachusetts General Hospital following World War II, Dr. Churchill was in great demand in Washington, where the National Research Council, the Hoover Commission, and organization of the Department of Defense all had need of his wisdom. Speaking at the New England Medical Center one day, he said: "The master-apprentice training will always exist in a field so heavily weighted with handicraft, but the paradoxical situation may at times be recognized when the master surgeon by his operation saves the patient from succumbing to disease, but the apprentice saves the patient from succumbing to the operation."[14] Thus Churchill's postwar period was devoted to surgical education at the resident surgeon level. He was directly responsible for a revision of the cruel resident training program. Before Churchill the "pyramid" system was in vogue, where one surgeon of a group rose to the top. Churchill's rearrangement of the training program made it possible for all residents to pass through the chief residency.

His philosophy was set down in the course of editing J. Collins Warren's reminiscences, Dr. Chuchill using that framework for a series of comments on the surgical scene, as he saw it.[15]

In dedicating a book to him, Beecher said: "To Edward D. Churchill, M.D., who more than any other brought the standards of the University into the hospital. In no wise, in Churchill's view, could this be construed as a threat against the ancient humanitarian tradition of medicine. Dr. Churchill retired from the Hospital and the University in 1962. Shortly afterward, a fund was created for the establishment of a professorial chair in his name at the Harvard Medical School and the Massachusetts General Hospital. In his Presidential Address to the American Surgical Association, he said:

> In times of change there is need for wisdom both in the external social order and within the profession. Spokesmen who loudly proclaim measures based on self-interest will not be tolerated. A hold-fast in science is essential, but this represents only a part of the strength of surgery. By maintaining the ancient bond with humanity itself through Charity—the desire to relieve suffering for its own sake—Surgery need not fear change if civilization itself survives.[16]

His righthand man at the Hospital was then Oliver Cope, who received his education first at Harvard College and then at the Harvard

Medical School and the Massachusetts General Hospital. He was named Associate Professor of Surgery at Harvard in 1948, full Professor in 1963, and Emeritus in 1969. He is also Chief of Staff, Emeritus, Shriners' Burn Institute, Massachusetts General Hospital. His primary interest was in surgery of the endocrine glands. Of foremost interest was the anatomy, phyiology, and pathology of the thyroid gland, in which he made notable contributions.

More dramatic was his work with Dr. Churchill on the parathyroids. As Cope has said, the direction that surgical treatment of parathyroid disease should take was visualized by Dr. Churchill before he or Cope undertook an operation. Although Churchill and Cope very early went their separate ways, Cope adds generously that one of Churchill's remarkable capacities was to study a problem from the point of view of the difficulties of other surgeons.

The first step in preparing for parathyroid surgery was the acquisition of and the ability to identify parathyroid tissue, grossly and with certainty. At the time, 1931, when parathyroid dissections were undertaken, the outstanding pathologists Mallory, Bradley, and Castleman were no more sure of a parathyroid gland when grossly exposed than Cope was. In this 1931 period they had to depend on microscopic section for secure identification.

The next step was to determine the usual distribution of the parathyroids, with indications of where they were likely to be found. The precipitating factor can be attributed to a certain Captain Martel, who was brought to the Massachusetts General Hospital by Dr. Bauer. After preliminary studies on the normal anatomy of the parathyroid glands and their variations, Dr. Churchill planned an operation to search for an adenoma, and he found it in the right upper anterior mediastinum. Churchill acknowledged Cope's role in defining the wide distribution of the parathyroid glands. As the years passed, the surgeons at the Massachusetts General Hospital carried out some sixty-eight re-explorations, where the initial exploration had been done elsewhere.

As long ago as 1932 Fuller Albright realized that renal stones might be a complication of hyperparathyroidism. Late in the 1950's several cases indicated that pancreatitis was a possible clue to hyperparathyroidims. Hypertension with bizarre neurological signs was of interest, for one third of the first 250 patients who had hyperparathyroidism proved to have a clinical degree of hypertension, which was relieved by correcting the hyperparathyroidism.

Dr. Cope's next endocrine interest was in the adrenal cortex. He set about defining the adrenal cortical hyperplasia in Cushing's Disease. At that time (1938), cortisone was not available. One patient who entered the Hospital for the treatment of Cushing's syndrome was studied, and the circumstances led, for the first time, to the concept of subtotal adrenalectomy, comparable to subtotal thyroidectomy for Graves' Disease. After the first patient, a number of subtotal adrenalectomies were carried out in the years prior to the discovery of cortisone. In Cope's later years, he turned his attention to burns, being especially interested in the disaster management of pulmonary injury, as well as the surface burn and the protection of the damaged surface.

Without scanting any of the above studies, Oliver Cope focused a great deal of skilled attention on the education and graduate training of the surgeon. He observed that there seemed to be always plenty of surgeons interested in teaching surgical techniques. His own approach was far more philosophical, for as medicine and surgery have advanced, Cope believes, the teaching of surgical techniques has assumed less urgency and medicine and surgery, in his view, might now be dealt with as a single discipline. It is clear that Cope is simply another one of those men of distinction who, like Edward Churchill, are biologists in surgical clothing. The breadth of his view can be expressed by a quotation

> Thus, it happens that most clinical teachers of medicine and surgery emphasize the quantitative physiologic and clinical aspects of medicine. It is relatively easy to be sure about the metabolic aspects of thyroid disease or diabetes or the changes in the gastric content as a result of the vagus nerve activity. It is much more difficult to grapple with the emotional being of the patient or look into and identify those social aspects of the patient's life which may be leading to trouble. You can't do anything about them anyhow, so why pay attention in the face of so much that you can do about the chemical aspects! Encouraged and sometimes needled a bit by such wonderful people as Stanley Cobb, these deficiencies in the education of clinical medicine have led me to try to pick up the pieces, to fill in the gaps. It is not because I had any special aptitude or inclination, but simply the teaching wasn't there. The education of the student, portrayal of disease, has been lopsided, and for the last several years, therefore, I have been stressing the need for better awareness of the social aspects of the patient's life and the emotional problems which he has encountered. More and more do I see the need for fortifying our education in these regards.
>
> I have dwelt on the social aspects particularly in the Presidential Address before the American Surgical Association in 1963 entitled, "On Balance." More recently I co-sponsored and co-chaired the First Swampscott Conference on Behavioral Science in Medicine. This resulted in a monograph written by myself, *Man, Mind, and Medicine,*

and published by Lippincott in 1968. Perhaps when all is considered, this monograph is the most important contribution I have been able to make.[17]

Edward Churchill's retirement was a landmark in the history of the Massachusetts General Hospital. He was succeeded as Homans Professor of Surgery by Paul S. Russell, a graduate of the Medical School of the University of Chicago, who had received his surgical training at the Massachusetts General Hospital. He specializes in immune processes in relation to transplantation. The responsibilities of Chief of the Surgical Services at the Hospital were given in 1969 to W. Gerald Austen, Professor of Surgery. Dr. Austen is a pioneer in the study of the effects of cardiac necroses and how to prevent or ameliorate them, principally by surgical means.

The usefulness of the Massachusetts General Hospital to the community was greatly enhanced by the construction of the Shriner's Burns Institute across the street. The closeness of this Institute is more than geographic. John F. Burke is Chief of Staff of the Burns Institute and Visiting Surgeon at the Hospital, as well as Associate Professor of Surgery at the Medical School. In addition to his interest in antibiotic treatment developed at the Lister Institute in England while he held a Moseley Traveling Fellowship at Harvard, Dr. Burke has applied himself to biomedical engineering. He is Chairman of the Committee on Bioengineering. The Institute has studied burned tissue and how to handle it, and, in a more nearly unique enterprise, has developed a system of bacteria-free treatment units. This concept is utilized in clinical medicine. This approach, of course, goes far to reduce, or even prevent, cross infection.

BOSTON CITY HOSPITAL

The burdens of patient care, the policy ambiguities of a large municipal hospital, and the deplorable state of Boston finances kept some Harvard services from developing as remarkably as had the Harvard Medical Service. Nevertheless, the Medical Service insisted that it could not function optimally unless an equally strong surgical service was there as its partner. Finally, Harvard funds were made available to support a full-time Professor of Surgery at the City Hospital, and William V. McDermott was appointed David W. and David Cheever Professor as well as Director of the Sears Surgical Laboratories and of the Harvard Surgical

Service there. A graduate of the Harvard Medical School in 1942, Dr. McDermott received his surgical training at the Massachusetts General Hospital. He has been interested mainly in hepatic failure.

In 1953 Charles Davidson and his colleagues at the Boston City Hospital first really defined the deleterious effect of protein and other nitrogenous substances on certain patients with cirrhosis of the liver. McDermott also presented a report in 1953 at the Society of Clinical Investigation, later published in the *Journal of Clinical Investigation* with R. D. Adams, which defined the clinical syndrome of episodic stupor in a patient following portacaval shunting in which hyperammoniemia was related to the clinical symptoms and the syndrome shown to be induced by protein, urea, and ammonium salts; he showed that control could be gained by restriction of proteins or by the administration of oral antibiotics to suppress the urea-splitting organisms in the colon. The actual existence of the syndrome of ammonia intoxication remained controversial for several years, but eventually work by McDermott and other investigators clarified its pathogenesis. It is now well recognized that this type of intermittent encephalopathy occurs in at least 25 percent of all surgical shunts constructed, and it is particularly significant that if a shunt is constructed in the absence of portal hypertension or liver disease, the incidence is 100 percent. Hemodynamic studies have shown that existence of the clinical syndrome of post-shunt encephalopathy depends on (1) the shunting around the liver of portal blood that carries a high ammonia content after the ingestion of any nitrogenous material, and (2) the decrease in hepatic blood flow which occurs after diversion of portal blood unless compensatory increase in the arterial circulation has occurred in the course of progressive cirrhotic stricture of the portal bed within the liver. It is these hemodynamic changes which permit portal systemic shunting to be carried out without adverse effects in about three quarters of the cases of cirrhosis with bleeding varices. In the normal laboratory animal or in the normal human, the construction of a shunt is invariably followed by serious progressive and crippling encephalopathy due to the marked decrease in total hepatic blood flow. The attention directed toward this problem by McDermott's observations on patients with cancer of the head of the pancreas who had a resection of the portal vein and then a construction of a portal-systemic shunt was a significant conceptual advance.

In other work in the Department of Surgery at the Boston City Hospital, Paul Fredrick and Melvin Osborne showed for the first time that resection of the small bowel resulted in a tremendous gastric hypersecretion that was one of the major causes of the severe diarrhea and nutritional disorders that developed. This, in turn, led to the demonstration of a gastric inhibitory hormone secreted by the small bowel and was clinically productive in that a vagotomy and pyloroplasty could correct the gastric hypersecretion and also many of the nutritional disorders associated with this disabling operative procedure of massive small bowel resection.

With the collapse of Harvard's position at the Boston City Hospital (1973), Dr. McDermott and some of his staff have removed to the New England Deaconess Hospital.

PETER BENT BRIGHAM HOSPITAL

The opening of the Peter Bent Brigham was soon followed by the appointment of Harvey Cushing as Surgeon-in-Chief. There is no need to review here his remarkable career as one of the world's leading brain surgeons, in fact, as the man who did more than any other to create this specialty as a specialty. A thin, wiry man, he nevertheless found it possible to operate for as much as six or eight hours. His assistants were unable to keep up with him. His vast clinical experience with tumors of the brain, including the pituitary gland, greatly increased medical, neurological, and endocrinological knowledge. He trained most of the leaders in the field in the next generation but was a poor lecturer. His responsibilities as head of a general surgical service were not neglected, for his principal lieutenants included such outstanding general surgeons as David Cheever, known for his meticulous technique and his gentle handling of patients, and John Homans, famous for his textbook and for his studies of phlebitis.

Harvey Cushing was also an historian. He collected rare medical texts, wrote extensively about them, and gained fame with his biography of Sir William Osler. On his retirement in 1932 he took his valuable collections to Yale, which, unlike Harvard, was willing to make a place for him. He maintained his interest in medical history until his death.

Dr. Cushing was succeeded by Elliott Carr Cutler. A remarkable teacher of clinical surgery, accused at times of being more flamboyant than erudite, Dr. Cutler barely had time to get settled when World War II began to dominate his interests. After his military service, he returned to the Peter Bent Brigham, where he stimulated and guided others to develop approaches to cardiac surgery. But he soon developed signs of the illness that, after a protracted course, was to kill him. His clinical career included one of the first attempts to open a stenotic mitral valve.

Dr. Cutler was succeeded as Moseley Professor of Surgery in 1948 by a man in the tradition of Edward Churchill—that is, one who was equally physiologist and surgeon: Dr. Francis D. Moore.[18] A graduate of the

Harvey Cushing, first Moseley Professor of Surgery at the Peter Bent Brigham Hospital, and the founder of neurosurgery in America. He trained a generation of neurosurgeons both in this country and abroad. Famous medical historian. He fought unsuccessfully to have the Brigham made Harvard's university hospital, after the fashion of Johns Hopkins. Photograph in the collection of the Boston Medical Library.

Harvard Medical School, Dr. Moore early became interested in endocrine and metabolic research. In 1941–42 he was a Research Fellow of the National Research Council, working with Dr. Joseph C. Aub at the Huntington Hospital.

Dr. Moore returned to the Massachusetts General Hospital, where he completed the Senior Residency during the war. While there he participated in caring for the victims of the Cocoanut Grove fire. Prior to that time, however, he and Dr. Cope had already collaborated on work in capillary permeability in burns using radioactive dye. Drs. Moore and Cope at that time described for the first time the expanded extracellular fluid volume in burned patients. This was done by use of radioactive isotopes, a technique that later became the basis of many standard formulations for the treatment of burns. Dr. Moore has maintained a consistent interest in the pathophysiology and treatment of burns. When there was a shortage of young clinicians, he was called upon to assist Dr. Leland S. McKittrick in his private practice at the New England Deaconess Hospital. Dr. Moore was deemed unfit for military duty because of bronchial asthma, but working with Dr. McKittrick, he had extensive and valuable experience in several clinical problems.

During this time he began the application of stable and radioactive isotopes to a wide variety of other problems, and in 1946, in a small article in *Science*, he described the "Isotopic Dissection of the Human Body," employing multiple radioactive isotope dilution techniques. This application of isotopes led to the measurement of body composition in many pathological states and the further perfection of multiple tracer techniques.

At the same time, Dr. Moore became interested in the duodenal ulcer problem. He believed that subtotal gastrectomy was an unnecessarily mutilating operation for the disease. In the fall of 1943 he carried out his first vagotomy for duodenal ulcer, unaware of the simultaneous work of Dr. Lester Dragsted in Chicago, who had done the first operation a few months prior to Dr. Moore's. After completing an initial series of about 100 vagotomies, Dr. Moore became discouraged with the operation alone, but in 1960 he returned to it in combination with pyloroplasty and employed it widely in the treatment of duodenal ulcer, frequently referring to the lowered morbidity and mortality.

Dr. Moore did a great deal of student and resident teaching during this time and was content in his role as a Junior Attending Surgeon at the Massachusetts General Hospital, busy with his research in metabolism, isotope dilution, and duodenal ulcer treatment and at the same time with a growing private practice and a good deal of teaching. He was made Tutor in 1947.

In 1947 also Dr. Elliott Cutler died after a long illness, and Dr.

Moore was offered the position of Chief of Surgery at the Peter Bent Brigham Hospital and Moseley Professor of Surgery at the Harvard Medical School. He was only 34 years old. On coming to the Brigham in 1948, he asked the Trustees to establish a laboratory for surgical biochemistry and metabolism in the Hospital. In these laboratories a succession of young men have engaged in research and learned modern quantitative biology as applied to surgery. Many men who have been through these laboratory experiences are now Professors of Medicine, Surgery, and Pediatrics in other cities and other countries. In the course of twenty-five years, approximately 75 men have completed the Senior and Chief Residencies at the Peter Bent Brigham Hospital in General Surgery and an additional 50 in special fields. Approximately two thirds of these are in academic posts, and approximately one third are doing community practice.

The multiple isotope dilution techniques for body composition reached their peak development about 1958, and by 1963 *The Body Cell Mass and Its Supporting Environment* was published.[19] The book establishes norms and reports pathological findings by these techniques. They have since been used worldwide, most particularly the methods for total body water, total exchangeable sodium, and total exchangeable potassium—all of which were first developed extensively in Dr. Moore's laboratory. The endocrine and metabolic basis of surgical care, a continuing interest of Dr. Moore's, found its major expression in 1959 with the publication of *The Metabolic Care of the Surgical Patient*.[20]

Commencing in 1963, Dr. Moore's department devoted particular attention to the sort of pulmonary insufficiency that often was lethal in patients after severe injuries, wounds, and burns. In 1969 *Post-Traumatic Pulmonary Insufficiency* was published,[21] bringing together these studies and marking a major advance in the management of such cases. Studies carried out concomitantly in many other laboratories in this country and abroad have resulted in a remarkable reduction and incidence of this entity, largely because of recognition of its component physiologic mechanisms.

The treatment of renal failure by dialysis was developed during and immediately following World War II, and the medical department at the Peter Bent Brigham Hospital under Dr. George Thorn played a major role in bringing renal hemodialysis to a practical reality in this country. Shortly after his arrival in the Department of Surgery at the Brigham in 1948, Dr. Moore's department began to play an active collaborative role in the management of renal patients and soon took the lead in the development of kidney transplantation. Dr. David Hume and Dr. Joseph Murray, both members of the Department of Surgery, were key persons in this development, as well as Dr. Roy Calne, arriving for study from London in 1958.

The successful transplantation first done in the Department in 1954, between identical twins, was followed by transplants from unrelated persons. Following the introduction of chemotherapy by Dr. Calne in collaboration with Dr. Murray, it was possible in 1961 to do the first kidney transplant in immunosuppressed recipients, using asothiaprine. This component of the history of Dr. Moore's department was set forth in a book entitled *Give and Take*,[22] first published in 1964 and relating the history of kidney transplantation up to that time, which was largely a history of activities at the Harvard Medical School. By 1972 it was possible to update the book in another edition, entitled *Transplant: The Give and Take of Tissue Transplantation*.[23] It brought up to date the world experience of transplantation of all organs in a book for educated laymen. At present, in addition to his other clinical interests, Dr. Moore is engaged in a study to determine the optimal method of treating women with cancer of the breast.

The phenomenal output of Dr. Moore and his colleagues would seem to create the danger of all work and no play. The danger has been avoided by Dr. Moore's avocational efforts in the field of musical comedy. But not all his amusements were light or frivolous. His comment on the policies of some august granting agencies pointed out that today originality is not favored and that men like Louis Pasteur would have difficulty in getting support for their research. Dr. Moore stands out as a teacher whose lectures have been a model of orderly arrangement of the data needed to elucidate clinical problems.

CHILDREN'S HOSPITAL

The 1920's and 30's saw the growing fame of Dr. William E. Ladd at the Children's Hospital. Born in Milton, Massachusetts, and educated locally, he received his Bachelor's Degree from Harvard in 1902 and his M.D. from the Medical School four years later. He interned at the Boston City Hospital. He had been a varsity oarsman at the College and from 1908 to 1912 acted as the crew's physician and trainer. He became Assistant in Surgery at the School in 1917 and rose through the ranks there and at the City Hospital and Children's Hospital. He became Chief of the Surgical Service at the Children's Hospital in 1927, and Clinical Professor at the School in 1931. In 1941 his friends and the families of his former patients endowed a chair in his name. He achieved fame when he and forty other doctors with sixty nurses went from Boston to care for the victims of the Halifax disaster in December 1917. Hundreds of child victims came under the care of the group, and Dr. Ladd decided then to spend his life concentrating on surgery of infants and children. There was at that time no such specialty, and Dr. Ladd set about creating it.

He was a fine teacher, but he taught more by actions than by words. When, fully masked and gowned, he operated on the tiny draped abdomen of an undernourished newborn baby, his large hands, seemingly larger than the baby itself, told an eloquent story as they went about their skilled work with a gentleness that was also tenderness. Away from the patient, he was apt to be dour and uncommunicative, but if anything this heightened the dramatic effects of his result.

After his retirement his professorship passed to Robert E. Gross, who early in his career had begun to distinguish himself in the field of cardiac surgery. A graduate of the Harvard Medical School, he had for most of his professional life been associated with it and with the Children's Hospital. He rose through the ranks, and on January 1, 1947, he was appointed Ladd Professor of Children's Surgery and simultaneously Surgeon-in-Chief at the Children's Hospital. He held the latter post until 1966, when he was named Chief of the Cardiac Program at the Children's Hospital Medical Center. Although his interest in the general surgical problems of infancy and childhood has been great, he is especially known for pioneer work that deals with congenital cardiovascular abnormalities. Of his 200 publications, more than 70 relate to cardiovascular surgery.

It was on August 26, 1938, at the Children's Hospital Medical Center that Dr. Gross carried out the first successful closure of the patent ductus arteriosus. Before this time, the future for individuals with such congenital malformations of the heart was, to say the least, uncertain. Diagnosis was difficult, and there was no treatment. The surgical technique developed by Dr. Gross and his associates involved cutting the duct between the pulmonary artery and the aorta and firmly suturing it.

Dr. Gross has achieved international distinction for his corrective surgery of congenital stenosis of the aorta, and is also known for his contributions to the treatment of intra-auricular septal defects. He has developed techniques for the repair of congenital anomalies that involve the esophagus and trachea. His techniques for this type of surgery were developed through extensive animal experimental studies carried out in the Laboratory for Surgical Research at the Harvard Medical School. Like many other Harvard professors, he has been awarded many honors. However, he is the only physician who twice received the Lasker Award —a unique distinction.

BETH ISRAEL HOSPITAL

When this Hospital first became associated with the Harvard Medical School, there were no arrangements for a full-time Chief of Surgery, the administration of that department being first given briefly to Wyman Wittemore and then for a more protracted period to Charles G. Mixter. Dr. Mixter put the Surgical Service on a firm professional footing, but there was no research, and the teaching was not as well organized as at the other Harvard hospitals. This situation was remedied with the appointment of Dr. Jacob Fine as Professor of Surgery at the Beth Israel Hospital in 1948. A graduate of the Harvard Medical School, he had received training under Elliott Cutler in Cleveland before coming to Boston. His initial efforts involved attempts to relieve abdominal gassy distention by means of the inhalation of 100 percent oxygen, but within a short time, the study of hemorrhagic shock came to engross him and his associates, notably Drs. Howard Frank, Arnold Seligman, and Alexander Rutenburg, all of whom went on to professorships in their own right. Dr. Fine's own studies led him into the field of shock due to endotoxins and after his retirement from the Beth Israel Hospital, he became Director of the Shock Division of the Sears Surgical Laboratory at the Boston City Hospital.

He was succeeded as Professor of Surgery at the Beth Israel Hospital by Dr. William Silen, a 1949 graduate of the University of California Medical School. Administratively, Dr. Silen has believed that Harvard hospitals should pool their efforts and resources in regard to the surgical specialties: Orthopedics, collaborative residencies with the Massachusetts General Hospital in Neurosurgery and Cardiac Surgery, and a joint residency in Urology with the Brigham.

An enthusiastic and tireless bedside teacher, Dr. Silen has also made important contributions to the pathogenesis of gastrointestinal diseases. His group has worked on salt and water transport across the intestinal mucosa and on the nature of the factors that normally protect the gastric mucosa against the acid in the stomach.

THE CAMBRIDGE HOSPITAL

When, about a decade ago, the Trustees of the Cambridge City Hospital sought to give their institution the status of a university-connected hospital, the task of organizing the Surgical Service was given to Richard Warren. He is the most recent in a family of physicians that created Harvard medicine and has helped to mold it since. Richard Warren graduated from Harvard College in 1929 and from the Medical School in 1934. His surgical career involved chiefly work on vascular diseases, and he carried this out at the West Roxbury Veterans Administration and the Peter Bent Brigham before becoming Professor of Surgery at the Cambridge City Hospital.

He scored a notable first with his report in this country of a successful operation in 1958 for massive pulmonary embolism. Eight other surgeons, working in Europe from 1924, had reported their attempts, some successful and some not, to remedy the condition surgically. Dr. Warren's scholarly approach to this and other aspects of the surgical treatment of vascular disease has been evident in his many writings on the subject. In addition, Dr. Warren and his colleagues developed a surgical follow-up and home-visit program along new lines, though nonetheless reminiscent of E. A. Codman's earlier preoccupation with such matters:

> Two and one-half years of experience reveal an ability to follow up 90% of the patients leaving the hospital. A monthly newsletter has been circulated; a home visiting program has grown as an offspring. The program has promoted continuity of patient care, improved education of students and house staff, and has pointed to the needs of continued comprehensive patient care in the future. It further has made readily available data for specific follow-up information on certain surgical diseases. A 73% ambulation rate six months or later for patients treated for fractures of the hip by operation is cited as an example of the information derived.[24]

SCHOLAR-SURGEONS

There are, of course, many types of surgeons. Some can be distinguished by the limited fields in which they work, others by their breadth or by their research, teaching, or academic preferment. There is yet another category, the scholar-surgeon. Such individuals have scant or no interest in academic preferment. They do have a profound interest in all aspects of information concerning their special field of activity. Such individuals may have titles, generally that of Clinical Professor but often of lower rank. They are characterized by the breadth of their profound knowledge, as well as by their great skills. Although they may be considered to hold secondary status, below that of the full-time men, the contributions that some of them make to teaching, clinical research, and improvements in patient care may far outlast those of many academicians. They are important for another reason: they represent the persistence of a way of life that was the only one in the not-too-distant past of the Harvard Medical School and has been the traditional mode since the beginning of modern medicine. One should never forget that even Andreas Vesalius, today revered as the founder of modern anatomy, spent far more of his time practicing surgery that he did investigating and teaching anatomy. The same was true of all the pioneers whose advances created modern medicine—they were all practitioners of clinical medicine, whatever else they did within the confines of their specialty. The same was true of all the men who held the endowed chairs in medicine at Harvard during the nineteenth and, in a few cases, into the twentieth century.

The persistence of this mode in surgery is remarkable. It persists in medicine, as the large number of clinical professors of medicine attests, but for men who make no house calls and very few night visits, and whose practice in the main is either in an intern-served hospital or else in an office that has ready access to laboratory, roentgenologic, and consultant services, developing a scholarly status in one's medical specialty does not present overwhelming difficulties. This is not true of those who live on a surgical practice, for its demands in time in the operating room and in the handling of unexpected postoperative complications not only keep scheduled hours occupied but make the free ones unpredictable. That some of these men become medical scholars is worthy not merely of recognition but of the highest praise.

There is no small number of such men in the Harvard Medical Faculty and teaching staff. Mention will be made here of two. One individual who stands out is Dr. Claude E. Welch. Everyone who knows him will easily understand what is meant by the term "scholar-surgeon." His titles are Clinical Professor of Surgery, Emeritus at the Harvard Medical School and Senior Consulting Surgeon at the Massahcusetts General Hospital.

His earliest introduction to an intellectual life occurred in college, where he was completely immersed in the problems of chemistry. After graduation in 1927, he became an Instructor in Organic Chemistry at the University of Missouri and spent approximately a year and a half again submerged in chemistry. At this time radioactivity was assuming a great deal of interest, and Welch recalls how "we were boiling down the thorium at night, watching all of the pots glow in the dark and having white counts taken once a week to be sure that we were not contaminating ourselves as we were stirring these large vats." Dr. Herman Schlundt, who was in charge of the chemistry department at that time, was one of the outstanding authorities on radioactivity. Meanwhile, Welch was also carrying on a large number of experiments in organic chemistry in his large laboratory, and in the quest for an M.A. degree developed a number of new compounds which, to his knowledge, have had no use since. He found that he was spending from 6:00 A.M. to 12:00 P.M. in the laboratory or in the classrooms. "I felt it was drawing me completely away from the mainstream of human activities and I felt that if I continued in it very much longer that I might become a good scientist but not develop into a very good human being."

Accordingly, medical school followed, with a good deal of relief; patient contact proved most interesting and rewarding. Later, Welch became 50 percent of the so-called "pneumonia service" of the Thorndike and the City Hospital; his team developed a rapid blood-slide-typing test, and managed to treat all of the pneumonia in the hospital for a year. That was not easy in the pre-antibiotic days. It was followed by a few months in pathology under Dr. Mallory as an elective course. At that time, the pathology laboratory was a breeder of tubercle bacilli, and approximately half of the members of the Pathology Department dropped out at some time to be treated for tuberculosis. Fortunately, this did not happen to Welch, but it did make a clinical service of three months in the Raybrook Sanatorium in Saranac highly interesting.

One of the matters that stood out in Welch's mind in 1932 was the fact that he and his workers frequently plated staphylococci on agar and noted that there would be large blank spaces on the plate. They all knew what had caused it: some fungus had grown there and had inhibited the growth of the staphloccocus. "It is amazing how dumb we were and how smart Alexander Fleming was to realize the importance of that simple observation." With the increased clinical responsibility attending internship and residency, pure science was relegated to a secondary position. However, it had spawned a great interest in clinical research. Judged by the standards of today, most of such investigations done thirty years ago were poorly controlled. Nevertheless, they furnished collectively an important compendium of experience that pointed the way toward the proper therapy of many diseases.

Welch's interests have been chiefly in gastrointestinal disease and in cancer. If any of the numerous papers during this long period of time could be picked out as most important, he would include a group of statistical papers published with Ira Nathanson on the prognosis of all types of cancer in the late 1930's[25] and one on the treatment of combined intestinal obstruction and peritonitis by refunctionalization of the intestine in 1955.[26]

With the passage of time the necessity to evaluate critically the numerous papers that appear in abdominal surgery has led to the publication of a series of progress reports in the *New England Journal of Medicine* on abdominal surgery. This has been done biennially for the last thirty years. Meanwhile, one textbook on the surgery of the stomach and duodenum is now in its fifth edition and has been translated into several foreign languages.[27] Other textbooks on intestinal obstruction and on polypoid lesions of the colon also have had wide distribution.

The last decade has seen important developments in the social problems of medicine, and Welch has been intensely involved in many of these changes. It is very clear that if any changes are to be effected, they must be made through the agency of important organizations, since individual efforts these days are likely to be lost. Presidencies of the American College of Surgeons, the Massachusetts Medical Society, and numerous other scientific organizations, and many activities at the various councils and the House of Delegates of the American Medical Association have aided in this respect.

Other activities in which Welch had taken a great deal of pride include the chairmanship of the Committee on Publications at the *New England Journal of Medicine* for the past five years; this magazine undoubtedly is one of the outstanding medical publications in the world. Welch also served as editor of *Advances in Surgery* from its inception in 1965 until two years ago, when because of the press of other activities he relinquished it to a committee.

Medical School activities during this whole period have consisted of teaching the small groups of students that appear at the Massachusetts General Hospital. He has had a major role in postgraduate education not only in the courses given here in the Massachusetts General Hospital but in other areas. A number of faculty commitments have taken a great deal of time; the most onerous has been the Committee on Governance.

As President of the Harvard Medical Alumni, Welch tried to increase loyalties to the Medical School (they have not been prominent in the last few years), and also to promote the cause of continuing education in medicine as a life-long activity. In short, here was a man whose record as a student, a house officer, and subsequently must have afforded him a dozen opportunities to enter and pursue an academic career. He chose otherwise.

Another notable medical scholar is Dwight E. Harken. A graduate of Harvard College in 1931 and of the Medical School in 1936, he rose to the rank of Clinical Professor of Surgery at the School and Surgeon at the Peter Bent Brigham Hospital. He was completely engrossed in cardiac surgery and became an expert in the history of cardiology, including out-of-the-way early reports on cardiac operations. The background of his clinical work was obtained during World War II, and, of course, he had been stimulated by his chief, Dr. Elliott Cutler, late Moseley Professor of Surgery and Chief of the Surgical Services at the Peter Bent Brigham Hospital. Dr. Harken has, over the years, been a pioneer in many areas of cardiac surgery. He was one of those who developed surgery of the mitral valve at a time when the operative mortality of this operation was discouraging most other surgeons. At first he operated only on those hopelessly sick, and he made outstanding improvements in the quality of the lives of patients with very severe mitral valve disease in the late 1940's. This led to the development of open heart surgery and the use of mechanical valves. He was the first to use the caged-bell valve successfully (1960) in the natural anatomic site in man. This was an aortic valve and opened a wide field for use of prosthetic valves. Throughout the development of his operative techniques and of his principles of pre- and post-operative care, he worked closely with Dr. Laurence B. Ellis, Clinical Professor of Medicine.

For some years he gave attention to improving prostheses. With others, he was also interested in correcting fibrillation of the heart, returning the heart to a normal rhythm. He was long interested in the feat of totally implanting a "demand pacemaker" and he implanted the first such pacemaker on August 7, 1966. He emphasized that this was a greater engineering triumph than it was surgical, and he gave great criedit to Engineer Barouh V. Berkovits.

Dr. Harken, along with other leaders in cardiac surgery in Boston, elected not to carry out heart transplantation. He was not only a cardiac surgeon, however, but also a fine thoracic surgeon, with interest in the surgical treatment of tuberculosis and cancer of the lung. As regards patient care, he is the very model of the compassionate physician. He, too, chose a career of patient care and of the development of techniques tailored to individual patients in preference to the life of an academic professor. The contributions he has made in his pioneering work on the surgical treatment of valvular disease have justified his decision.

These men and dozens more like them in clinical departments are the backbone of the teaching staff, are responsible for vast amounts of patient care, and have contributed to the development of medicine, some to a degree scarcely perceptible, others to a degree that makes them outstanding in the world of research. They derive little or no income from what they do for Harvard, and what they do involves sacrifices of time, which means either money or else equally precious leisure.

UROLOGICAL SURGERY

Urological surgery became a specialty owing largely to the frequency of prostatic diseases and the necessity for their surgical treatment in most cases. Surgery of the kidneys and ureters, chiefly in relation to urinary stone formation or blockage from other causes, also involves special approaches and techniques. Harvard developed a number of outstanding technicians in these areas. The need for subtle diagnosis rarely arises in connection with these diseases because the diagnostic modalities are very exact and are widely available.

When, however, a need arose for developing approaches that would permit renal transplantation, the School and the Peter Bent Brigham Hospital assumed a position of leadership. This development occurred during the tenure of J. Hartwell Harrison. Dr. Harrison succeeded that able clinician William C. Quinby as Chief of Urology at the Hospital in 1941. A graduate of the University of Virginia, he received his M.D. degree in 1932 and served in the Harvard Unit, 105th General Hospital, for forty-six months. He was named Elliott Carr Cutler Professor of Surgery in June 1965. During these years a coordinated Residency Education Program in Urology has been developed and sustained among the following teaching hospitals, most of them associated with the Harvard Medical School: Peter Bent Brigham Hospital, The Children's Medical Center, the Beth Israel Hospital, Massachusetts General Hospital, and the Memorial Hospital, Worcester, Massachusetts.

Harrison's special interests have been in the area of surgery for renal failure, renal transplantation, the hormonal changes in the aging male, management of carcinoma of the prostate, renal hypertension, and disorders of the adrenal cortex and medulla. In 1952 he carried out with Dr. George Thorn the first bilateral total adrenalectomy in man sustained by cortisone acetate and desoxycorticosterone acetate substitution therapy. The first transplantation of the kidney between living donor and recipient in the human was performed by Murray, Harrison, and Merrill, in December 1954. A recent new position of Dr. Harrison's is member of the Kidney Advisory Committee to study the personnel facilities, and demands for the management of renal failure in the United States.

Chapter Fifteen

Pediatrics

HARVARD has extraordinarily strong and diverse facilities for teaching, research, and patient care in the field of pediatrics. There are two complementary administrative departments which offer different types of experience and environment to students. One department, at the Children's Hospital, has at its disposal the varied resources of a medical center almost entirely geared to the needs of children, where a group of independent clinical and laboratory services collaborate. This department also encompasses the academic activities on the Pediatric Service at the Beth Israel Hospital and teaching and research in pediatrics of the newborn at the Boston Hospital for Women (Lying-in Division). The other department uses the Children's Service at the Massachusetts General Hospital, where, in a more typical setting, the wide resources of a large general hospital can be focused by the pediatrician upon the health problems of children.

Pediatrics is not so much a specialty as a division of the whole field of medicine. It is concerned with the health of the individual from the time of conception throughout the period of growth and development. Its interests are closely linked with those of obstetrics in responsibility for the child during the later phases of intra-uterine life and of transition and adjustment to life in the external world, and merge into those of internal medicine and gynecology as the adolescent becomes an adult. In the medical curriculum, pediatrics provides a particularly good medium through which to illustrate the importance of genetics, the influence of the processes of growth and development upon physiologic functions and responses to disease and to therapy, the continuity and totality of optimal medical care, and the increasing opportunities for the prevention of disease and disability.[1]

Required work in pediatrics for third- and fourth-year students was instituted during the period after World War I. Creation of the full-time position of head of Pediatrics at the Children's Hospital led to the appointment in 1921 of Dr. Oscar Schloss to that chair. He held the position only briefly, but he made one notable decision, to bring James L. Gamble to Harvard in 1922.

Dr. Schloss was succeeded by Kenneth D. Blackfan in 1923. Dr. Blackfan had attended Albany Medical College, and during his third year came under the influence of Dr. Richard Pearce, Professor of Pathology there. He worked in Pearce's laboratory through the summer following his third year. Undoubtedly this friendly man later determined his future course in medicine. After graduation in 1905 Dr. Blackfan practiced country medicine, but he soon realized that he had certain deficiencies, and in 1909 the young country doctor set off for Philadelphia with the support of Richard Pearce. He was kindly received by Samuel Hamill and David Edsall, and a place was found for him as resident-in-charge of a foundling hospital. It was then that Kenneth Blackfan became a pediatrician. Two years later John Howland, who had just become Professor of Pediatrics in the new Medical School of Washington University, offered him a residency. When Howland succeeded Clemens Von Pirquet at the Johns Hopkins in 1912, he took with him a group of able young men, including Blackfan. There Blackfan had the advantages of a special hospital for infants and children, with laboratory equipment far in advance of any he had used up to that time. He soon found an opportunity to participate in the work going on. For example, with Walter Dandy he studied internal hydrocephalus, and published a work that in recent years has been designated a classic. He demonstrated that dehydration was a much more dangerous feature of diarrheal disease than is a state of acidosis, which Howland and W. McKim Marriott had just discovered. This shifted the emphasis from alkali therapy to fluid replacement.

Blackfan was still a resident at the age of 37, having held this modest designation for eleven years. Grim as that sounds, he had achieved his goal. He knew the existing body of knowledge and knew its boundaries. He knew, too, where to find the paths of progress. He was ready for larger duties. In 1920 he was invited to become the Professor of Pediatrics at the University of Cincinnati, and he accepted. In 1923 the results of his eighteen years of education toward leadership led Harvard to offer him a post. He was not a brilliant lecturer, but in the wards his teaching of students and interns has been described as close to perfection. He never used his great storehouse of experience and knowledge to dazzle but rather to point out sound appraisal of such evidence as could be obtained. His leadership was characterized by a gentle friendliness. His associates were made to feel that they were his comrades. He was not only a sympathetic chief but a good judge of people, and developed his department wisely by bringing in and encouraging good people.

One of the men he encouraged, indeed protected, was James Lawder Gamble. Dr. Gamble received his medical education at the Harvard Medical School. Following internships in medicine at the Massachusetts

General Hospital and in Pediatrics at the Children's Hospital, he went to Europe in 1913. There he was impressed by the extent to which quantitative chemical methods were being incorporated into the study of disease in the clinic. Under the influence of Drs. Otto Folin and Francis Benedict, James Gamble set out to carry on similar investigations under Dr. Fritz Talbot at the Massachusetts General Hospital. He fell under the spell of Professor Lawrence J. Henderson, and Henderson's physico-chemical approach to physiological processes had a tremendous influence on his development.

In 1914 he joined the Department of Pediatrics at the Johns Hopkins and from 1914 to 1922 established himself as an independent investigator. He then decided to give up clinical activities in order to devote his life to the study of disease through chemical methods. Following World War I he returned to Baltimore and resumed his enthusiastic attack on disease processes. His first investigations were concerned with nitrogen metabolism in infants. In 1920, with Kenneth Blackfan, he published a paper which proved that infants can synthesize cholesterol. He then carried out what has been called a classic study on "The Metabolism of Fixed Base during Fasting." When he came to Harvard in 1922 as Assistant Professor of Pediatrics, the Children's Hospital constructed a small building, the Laboratory Study, for him. As Allan Butler has phrased it: "the combination of Blackfan, the superb clinician and tactful administrator, and Gamble, the gifted investigator, each with full professorial rank, provided an unusual opportunity for both, as well as for all those who were fortunate enough to work under them."[2]

Gamble was made Associate Professor of Pediatrics in 1925 and Professor in 1932. In that period he was especially interested in the mechanism of acidosis and the effect of various lesions of the gastrointestinal tract upon body fluids. For example, in 1933, in association with Butler and Charles McKhann, he published a paper on "Intracellular Fluid Loss in Diarrhoeal Disease" which demonstrated that in addition to the loss of extracellular fluid and sodium, there was a loss of intracellular fluid and potassium which exceeded not only the extracellular loss but also the amounts that could be accounted for by the destruction of protoplasm. This was a most important paper; it indicated for the first time the therapeutic need for replacement of intracellular fluid and electrolytes, a practice that later was to reduce the morbidity and mortality of those who were subjected to starvation and dehydration. Dr. Gamble's fame became world wide. By 1939 he had put together his observations in a loose-leaf syllabus: *Chemical Anatomy, Physiology, and Pathology of Extracellular Fluid*. It is described as one of the great works of medicine.

The period of World War II was a most difficult one for Dr. Gamble.

Dr. Blackfan had died in 1941. This tragic situation was made even more difficult for Dr. Gamble by his having to assume administrative responsibility for the Department. The appointment of Richard M. Smith, an older clinician, to Blackfan's chair in 1942 relieved Dr. Gamble of his onerous administrative duties and rescued this brilliant laboratory scientist from the responsibility, which he could not meet satisfactorily, of running a clinical service.

Following World War II, Dr. Gamble studied some of the inconsistencies of metabolic balance data and the basic chemical phenomena of growth. In 1950 he retired but continued to visit the Hospital to guide the investigations of younger men. His work has had a tremendous impact on the development of medical thought and practice, which is sometimes described as momentous. His studies of supportive therapy, whether given by pediatricians, internists, obstetricians, or surgeons, influenced medical practice for all time. He strove for perfection not only in the "simple, decisive elegance" of his experimental work but also in its presentation to others. For example, his Lane Lectures at Stanford (1951) were felicitously entitled "The Companionship of Water and Electrolytes in the Organization of the Body Fluids." In accepting the Kober Medal, he modestly attributed his accomplishments to good luck: "I find in my Bartlett the statement that: 'Dame Fortune is a fickle Gipsey / And always blind and sometimes tipsey.' Perhaps you will say that is why we have been so companionable."[3]

Another of Kenneth Blackfan's righthand men was Louis K. Diamond. Dr. Diamond spent his whole professional life at Harvard and at the Children's Hospital except for a two-year period (1948–50) when he took a leave of absence to serve as Medical Director of the developing National Blood Program of the American Red Cross. He became Associate Professor of Pediatrics in 1949 and Professor in 1962.

During the three years after his residency training, Dr. Diamond, by working closely with Dr. Blackfan on blood problems in children, established the direction of his future career. Two papers, published in 1932 with Drs. Blackfan and James Baty, which contained one of the first descriptions of erythroblastosis fetalis and linked it with fetal hydrops, neonatal jaundice, and anemia of the newborn, set the stage for one of his subsequent major contributions to pediatrics. With the discovery of the Rh factor and its role in isoimmunization of the mother against the red cells of her fetus, he returned to this problem and with characteristic energy carried these fundamental discoveries of K. Landsteiner, A. S. Wiener, and P. Levine through to a clinical application that has saved thousands of lives and prevented large numbers of cases of cerebral damage. In order to apply the new knowledge of Rh typing to blood transfusion and to obstetrics and pediatric practice, a Blood Grouping

Laboratory was established at the Children's Hospital, with Dr. Diamond as Director, to serve several Boston hospitals and to promote research in this new field. Here advances in blood-grouping techniques were made, concentrated serum albumin was introduced as a diluent to make it possible to detect the "incomplete" Rh antibodies responsible for the disease in the fetus, and the technique of exchange transfusion was perfected as a means of removing indirect-reacting bilirubin from the infant in order to prevent kernicterus, with its resulting death or central nervous system damage. In 1946 Dr. Diamond received the Mead-Johnson Award of the American Academy of Pediatrics for this great therapeutic advance. Since then, the Blood Grouping Laboratory has made a number of contributions to knowledge of human blood groups, and its unparalleled collections of serum and access to donors of rare-type cells now makes it an extremely valuable facility for the rapidly expanding clinical studies in human genetics going on in the United States.

Another condition that Dr. Diamond recognized in his early studies with Dr. Blackfan—congenital hypoplastic anemia—later became the object of fruitful investigation by Dr. Diamond's group. This type of anemia, together with acquired aplastic anemia, which has become increasingly common in recent years, was shown to respond to intensive steroid therapy. The discovery that many cases of aplastic anemia would respond to the administration of testosterone was made because of Dr. Diamond's keen observation of spontaneous remission in a preadolescent boy upon reaching puberty. Dr. Diamond and his associates have also made important contributions to the use of blood fractions in the control of bleeding in hemophilia and afibrinogenemia, and to knowledge of the hemolytic anemias and of the hemoglobinopathies. With his associate, Dr. Park Gerald, Dr. Diamond has created one of the strongest foci in the Harvard area for the clinical study of human genetics.

In addition to his contributions to an understanding of the pathogenesis and treatment of blood diseases in children, Dr. Diamond created laboratories that have served as the principal training ground for younger pediatric investigators who are themselves now engaged in teaching and research in pediatric hematology. His work has given him an international reputation. In recent years his interest has shifted from hematology per se to human genetics on the one hand and to the interrelations of dietary deficiencies and anemia on the other. Dr. Gerald with Dr. Diamond's encouragement has developed a strong laboratory for clinical, biochemical, and chromosomal studies in human genetics, while Dr. Diamond has himself been exploring ways in which nutritional inadequacies in the developing countries affect the blood. Thus Dr. Diamond's interests in pediatric hematology are now taking him deeper and deeper into the biochemical activities of the macromolecules of the cell and more and more broadly into the socioeconomic and cultural problems of the newly developing countries. After 1950 Dr. Diamond shared the responsibility for supervising the operations of the medical service and the program of fourth-year pediatric teaching at the Children's Hospital.

Dr. Clement Smith was another of Kenneth Blackfan's protégés. Dr. Smith received his M.D. degree in 1928 at the University of Michigan and came to the Children's Hospital in 1931 as a Resident, remaining there in a teaching capacity until 1943. He then moved to Wayne State University in Detroit as Professor of Pediatrics and Medical Director of the Children's Hospital of Michigan, but in 1945 he returned to Harvard in order to devote a larger portion of his time to research upon newborn infants. In 1949 he was promoted to Associate Professor of Pediatrics at the Boston Lying-in Hospital and became Professor of Pediatrics at the Boston Hospital for Women (Lying-in Division) in 1963.

Dr. Smith has approached clinical investigation in his chosen field of pediatrics of the newborn primarily from the point of view of a physiologically trained physician with metabolic and biochemical interests. He recognized early that the major hazards to the newborn infant compromised the establishment of adequate respiratory function, and he has persistently investigated this critical aspect of neonatal physiology. His inquiries have led him into studies of fetal hemoglobin and iron metabolism, red blood cell carbonic anhydrase, the metabolism of water and electrolytes, maternal-infant nutritional relationships, and, more recently, an investigation of the disturbances in the circulation which may have an important bearing on the pathogenesis of the respiratory distress syndrome in newborn infants. His investigations have been thorough, stimulated by practical clinical problems and consistently focused on the critical basic mechanisms by which the infant successfully passes through what he has called in his Ratchford Lectures "The Valley of the Shadow of Birth."

Perhaps Dr. Smith's most important influence has been exerted as a teacher. Until Dr. Stewart Clifford went on a geographic full-time basis at the Boston Lying-in Hospital several years ago, Dr. Smith was the sole full-time representative of pediatrics in that institution. Starting in 1945, he was in the vanguard of the group of representatives of the various basic sciences and clinical disciplines whom Dr. Reid attracted to the Lying-in in recent years to broaden the scope of obstetrical teaching and research. In this capacity Dr. Smith has contributed richly to the teaching of neonatal pediatrics, particularly to Harvard Medical students and to pediatric residents from the Massachusetts General Hospital and the Children's Hospital. His clinical teaching is coupled with a deep concern for his small patients, which sets an example of the good physician, and he has always been much appreciated by the residents. An equally important contribution to teaching has been made through his scholarly book *The Physiology of the Newborn Infant*—now in its third edition—which is to be found in medical libraries throughout the world. This much-needed book, published in 1945, replaced the outdated standard work, William Feldman's *Antenatal and Postnatal Child Physiology.*

After World War II the return of many men from military service permitted the School to fill the gaps that had developed in the Faculty. In 1946 Charles A. Janeway was appointed Thomas Morgan Rotch Professor of Pediatrics at the Harvard Medical School and Physician-in-Chief at the Children's Hospital Medical Center in Boston. His major efforts since then have been devoted to focusing the development of the Department on the health needs of children throughout the world—by the creation of highly specialized clinical units based on advances in biomedical research, the training of men and women from this country and abroad for positions of pediatric leadership, and efforts to study and improve not only the diagnosis and treatment of disease in children, but also the practice and delivery of primary health and medical care.

Thus his group has emphasized two apparently opposite trends—increasing specialization within pediatrics, on the one hand, and attempts to make pediatrics more comprehensive, on the other. The first has led to the formation of a number of special divisions within the Department, three of which have finally become independent departments in the Hospital: Psychiatry, Neurology, and Cardiology. The second has extended pediatrics into close association with obstetrics, so that perinatal pediatrics, first developed by Clement Smith at the Boston Lying-in Hospital, is now a recognized field, for which a professorial post has been arranged. At the other end of the period of physical growth, the field of adolescent medicine, almost wholly created by Dr. J. Roswell Gallagher, who joined the Harvard Department in 1951, has brought increasing contact with internal medicine. In addition, increased emphasis has been placed on the social and psychological aspects of child health, a development which ultimately created the Hospital's second largest department—psychiatry—which works very closely with Janeway's. Finally, through the establishment of the Family Health Care Program in 1954, as an educational and research venture, Janeway has been exploring the special problems of delivering primary patient care to families in the community. This early program was a leader in the trend toward restoring the balance in medical education between research based on molecular biology and the delivery of patient care, and has now evolved into Harvard's focus of clinical experience for the training of family physicians, as opposed to teams of specialists.

Janeway's own research interests, kindled by training in the Department of Bacteriology under Hans Zinsser and under Edwin Cohn in physical chemistry, have led him into the fields of infectious disease, clinical immunology, nephrosis, plasma protein metabolism, and collagen diseases. During the war he collaborated with Edwin Cohn's group in their pioneering studies on the fractionation of the plasma proteins. It also led to Janeway's participation in the Commission on Plasma Fractionation and the Protein Foundation, which Dr. Cohn established to protect his patents for the public good. This interest has persisted, and Janeway has remained closely associated with the Blood Research Institute (the Protein Foundation's more recent name); Dr. Diamond and Dr. Janeway were instrumental in effecting its recent merger with the Blood Grouping Laboratory to create the Center for Blood Research, under the Scientific Directorship of Chester Alper, an Associate Professor in Janeway's Department. Dr. Janeway also worked with Dr. Louis Diamond to create a national blood program through the American Red Cross.

Allan Macy Butler succeeded Dr. Fritz Talbot, the part-time Chief of Pediatrics at the Massachusetts General Hospital in 1942, becoming its first full-time head. Dr. Butler was educated at Princeton (B.Litt., 1916) and received the M.D. degree from Harvard in 1926. During World War I he served with the First Division of the American Expeditionary Force and was discharged with the rank of Captain. He joined the staff of the Harvard Medical School in 1929 and also served as a member of the staff of the Children's Hospital from 1930 to 1942.

Under Dr. Butler's direction the Children's Medical Service at the Massachusetts General Hospital maintained a continuing interest in advancing knowledge of the effect of immaturity and disease on the internal milieu of the body and the application of this knowledge to the treatment of disease. He was regarded by his colleagues as an outstanding investigator who, like his mentor, Dr. Gamble, was prompt to apply new biochemical methods to the study of disease states. He was one of the first to call attention to the role of pyelonephritis in causing hypertension. His method for determining ascorbic acid led him to study the metabolism of this substance.

Dr. Butler, throughout his career, has shown to an unusual degree a philosophical approach to medicine and society. In his view,

As a major characteristic of our time is accelerating change, a major problem of society is trying to keep abreast of changing circumstances. Tolerant discussion and considered action may permit an evolutionary adaptation of traditional institutions that will avoid ill planned or abrupt revolutionary change. Thus, it is in the interest of conservatism, not radical change, that inquiry is here made concerning adaptation of our medical institutions to the increasing specialization demanded by the accelerating rate of scientific and technologic advances applicable to medicine.

While its increasing effectiveness has caused medical care to be considered a basic right of everyone and the concept of "separate but equal" to be recognized as unsound in medicine as it is in education, and while the increasing cost of care has relieved the individual patient and the philanthropist of the financial burden of illness by extending medical insurance and prepayment plans, how well are we adapting our professional services to realize more fully the potentialities for more effective and economical care? And how generally do the fiscal administrators and public recipients of prepaid or budgeted care appreciate that the return on the dollar spent is more important than the amount spent?[4]

Dr. Nathan B. Talbot succeeded Allan Butler as Charles Wilder Professor of Pediatrics at the Harvard Medical School and Chief, Children's Service, Burnham Division for Children, Massachusetts General Hospital. He was educated at Harvard University, receiving an A.B. degree in 1932 and the M.D. degree in 1936. His internship and residency were at the Children's Hospital. He was appointed Assistant Physician on the Children's Medical Service at the Massachusetts General Hospital in 1942, and was Chief later.

Dr. Talbot has been an outstanding investigator of the quantitative aspects of nutrition, metabolism, and endocrinology. Many of his observations have been included in his book *Functional Endocrinology from Birth through Adolescence*, which he and his associates at the Massachusetts General published in 1952. This text shows that disturbances of the endocrine system as an indicator of the stability of the normal body states occur with much greater frequency clinically than do the more dramatic but relatively rare diseases caused by a primary disorder of the endocrine system. In order to investigate these areas of pediatric endocrinology, Dr. Talbot established the Metabolic Unit at the Massachusetts General Hospital, and published a syllabus, *Metabolic Homeostasis*, in 1959.

More than half the patients having difficulties seemingly of a metabolic-endocrine nature were found to have in reality social or behavioral problems. He made unique studies on progeria, a condition that causes small stature and the appearance, mental attitude, and manner of old age. These studies suggested that the child was suffering from a functional disturbance of growth, secondary to such a high-energy requirement that it became physically impossible for him to maintain caloric balance. This clue suggested that short stature in basically normal people also might be caused by hypocaloricism. A collaboration with Dr. Erich Lindemann, Professor of Psychiatry at Harvard, led to a realization of the importance of social and behavioral factors in the diagnosis and management of nutritional, endocrine, and developmental disturbances.

Chapter Sixteen

Preventive and Social Medicine

O VER the years there has been an accumulation of knowledge concerning the early diagnosis and treatment of disease, as well as its control and prevention. A considerable milestone was passed when James Lind (1716–1794) carried out his epoch-making controlled study of the cause and cure of scurvy (1754). Of equal moment was Professor Benjamin Waterhouse's controlled clinical study (1802), in which he proved at Harvard the effectiveness of smallpox vaccination. A long time had to pass before the principles of Lind and Waterhouse were properly understood and put into effective action. In the past three quarters of a century, however, a tremendous amount of work has been done, especially in bacteriology, parasitology, and nutrition, which has led to a massive body of reliable information on these three subjects.[1]

Certain parts of this great accumulation of knowledge have been applied in important ways to specific methods of preventing disease, especially by increasing resistance to it. There is much still unknown or unsatisfactory, but the methods used are clear enough to enable the ordinary practitioner to put them into daily practice. Although it is everywhere agreed today that training in prevention should be an essential part of medical education, more needs to be said about how to teach it.

Until the beginning of the twentieth century, few teachers had had any instruction in the practical application of preventive measures, and there is still too little knowledge of the factors involved. Part of the difficulty lies in the fact that when preventive approaches are developed, they are quickly removed from general medicine or even from medicine as a whole. Thus today the problem of milk- and water-borne diseases no longer comes to the attention of ordinary physicians; it is now considered to be a concern of sanitation rather than medicine. Similarly, the development of substances that immunize against bacterial or viral diseases has placed this large segment of preventive medicine in the hands of pediatricians, particularly those involved in the care of infants and young children. The very serious problems of the diseases of industry and occupations are almost entirely left to industrial physicians employed by large corporations and to some government officials concerned with ecology. The medical practitioner is left with what is not known, or else so inadequately known as to constitute a mass of half-truths, superstitions and far-fetched statements based on admittedly inadequate statistics. Particularly distressing—and to the unwary, entrapping—is the forceful reiteration of undefined terms like "risk factor," which is meant to imply that it is an etiologic or preventive factor, when the very use of the term shows that it is not. The term is more likely the invention of a public relations mind than a medical mind. Any possibility of remedying this unfortunate situation is minimized by a grave defect of the medical school teaching of preventive medicine—it is taught entirely by one department, and it has not received the wide integration in all departments that should be the case. Beginning with the tenure of Dean David L. Edsall, however, the Harvard Medical School attempted to define the preventive aspects of pediatrics, obstetrics, mental disease, orthopedic surgery, and venereal disease, as well as industrial disease. An early attempt in 1929 to correct this situation can be found in *Synopsis of the Practice of Preventive Medicine*, by Shields Warren.[2]

Preventive medicine consists, of course, of two distinct phases: the protection of the individual's health and the protection of the health of the community. It is understandable that regular courses in preventive medicine in the past have emphasized the protection of the community rather than the protection of the individual. As Warren points out, because it has been necessary to devote so much time to broad questions, such as vital statistics, sewage, milk, and water, there has scarcely been time to give needed attention to the protection of the individual. This situation has had a bad influence on students, who have often held the point of view that a course in preventive medicine simply distracted their attention from the "major" issues—medicine, surgery, and obstetrics. In 1925 the Faculty of the Harvard Medical School adopted the policy of permeating the curriculum with preventive medicine, in the hope that this would be the major route through which the student would develop an integrated attitude toward all material in the curriculum. The noble enterprise atrophied soon after it was born. In retrospect, five decades later, it is easy to understand why.

The Department of Preventive Medicine was headed, beginning in 1909, by a man who was one of the world's greatest experts on the branch of preventive medicine that was soon to be removed from medicine. Milton J. Rosenau had a most distinguished career in this field before coming to Harvard. He received his principal education in the public schools of Philadelphia and the University of Pennsylvania, Department of Medicine, where he graduated in 1889. Following this, he undertook postgraduate work in Berlin, Paris, and Vienna. His early interest was in sanitation and public health. He became a member of the U.S. Public Health and Marine Hospital Service in 1890 and served until 1909. During the last ten years of this period he was Director of the Hygienic Laboratory and resigned in 1909 to become the Charles Wilder Professor of Preventive Medicine and Hygiene at the Harvard Medical School. President Eliot believed in 1909 that true preventive medicine should be included as an integral part of the training of medical students. To further this endeavor, Dr. Rosenau was invited to come to Harvard to inaugurate the first full-time chair of Preventive Medicine in an American medical school.

When Dr. Rosenau arrived in Boston, two men were living there who had been active in calling attention to the importance of environmental sanitation in the United States: Professor George C. Whipple at the Harvard Engineering School and Dr. William T. Sedgwick at the Massachusetts Institute of Technology. Dr. Rosenau, with these two scientists, founded in 1913 the first school of public health in the United States, the Harvard – Massachusetts Institute of Technology School. They gathered together a group of able young men who gave an impetus to the public health movement in America. The school continued until 1922, when Harvard founded its separate School of Public Health. Dr. Rosenau was one of the founders of that, and he was appointed Professor of Epidemiology in it while continuing to hold his post of Professor of Preventive Medicine in the Harvard Medical School. This combination was a good one, for Dr. Rosenau was able to introduce preventive aspects of medicine into the teaching of medical students and at the same time furnish ample clinical material. Dr. Wilson G. Smillie of the Harvard School of Public Health has commented that Dr. Rosenau did more to promote the field of preventive medicine and public health than any man of his generation. The stimulus for many more articles and books was initiated by his book, *Preventive Medicine and Hygiene*.[3] Following his retirement in 1935, he went to the University of North Carolina to direct the newly created Department of Public Health there. He served as Dean of the School of Public Health from 1940 to 1941 and then became Director of the School, a position he was holding at the time of his death, as well as a professorship in epidemiology. He also lectured on Preventive Medicine and Public Health at the Bowman Gray School of Medicine in Winston-Salem.

During his long and distinguished career, Dr. Rosenau served as a member of the Advisory Board of the National Health Council in the United States Public Health Service. Various other appointments were added to his activities; for example, in the Massachusetts State Department of Health he was Director of the Antitoxin Vaccine Laboratory and Chief of its Biological Laboratories. He was the author of *Disinfec-*

tion and Disinfectants, 1902; *Experimental Studies in Yellow Fever and Malaria*, 1904; the *Immunity Unit for Diphtheria Antitoxin*, 1905; a *Method of Inoculating Animals with Precise Amounts*, 1905; the *Cause of Sudden Death Following the Injection of Horse Serum*; the *Origin and Spread of Typhoid Fever*, 1907; *The Standardization of Tetanus Antitoxin*, 1908; the *Milk Question*, 1912; and *Preventive Medicine and Hygiene*, sixth edition, 1935. In association with others, he laid the foundations for the National Institutes of Health.

One of his best-known lieutenants was William Lloyd Aycock, who made major contributions, largely unrecognized, to our understanding of poliomyelitis. Dr. Aycock received the Doctor of Medicine degree from the University of Louisville in 1914. From 1914 to 1919 he was Instructor in Bacteriology at the New York Postgraduate Medical School and Hospital. From 1917 to 1919 he served as a first lieutenant in the United States Army and as Epidemiologist at the Central Laboratories of the American Expeditionary Forces. In the period 1919–31 he undertook investigations of poliomyelitis for the Vermont State Board of Health. In 1923 he returned to Harvard and was designated Director of Research of Harvard's Infantile Paralysis Commission. He went through the usual promotional grades to the rank of Assistant Professor of Preventive Medicine and Hygiene, Harvard Medical School and Harvard School of Public Health (1928–41). From 1941 to 1951 he held the post of Associate Professor.

Dr. Aycock's unshakable equanimity stood him in good stead when he failed to receive in his own lifetime adequate recognition for his superb work in the fields of epidemiology and poliomyelitis. He brought knowledge of many disciplines, as well as a wide acquaintance with the behavior of other infectious diseases, to apply to the epidemiology of infantile paralysis. His work was distinguished, and because of the breadth of his medical philosophy and "the force of his scientific imagination," as described in the Memorial Minute published in the *Harvard University Gazette*, he went far beyond the realm of immediate utility.

In 1924 his first epidemiologic study was published. In it he called attention to the fact that cases of poliomyelitis always occur during the months of winter and early spring. This and other similar investigations were derived from his basic thesis that poliomyelitis does not differ from other infectious diseases in any important way. He stressed this biologically sound hypothesis and supported it with evidence from many sources. A favorite method of procedure, which he applied as early as 1925, was comparing, under carefully selected situations, the epidemic behavior of poliomyelitis with that of other infections. These studies overcame much of the mystery that surrounded this disease, and it is largely to the insight and pioneering labor of Lloyd Aycock that one owes the knowledge that infection with the virus of poliomyelitis occurs as frequently as infection with the viruses of measles and mumps.

Dr. Aycock formulated a second generalization: the ubiquity of polio-myelitic infection as contrasted with the rarity of paralytic signs. He came to regard the development of paralysis as an unusual event, almost an accident, which depended upon factors intrinsic in certain individuals but which also might be influenced by extrinsic conditions—for example, season or climate.[4] A series of significant investigations and conclusions arose from this concept: (1) poliomyelitis virus is widespread in warm climates, and paralysis there is extremely uncommon; (2) many who recover from the disease exhibit signs of endocrine imbalance; (3) poliomyelitis may occur more frequently in pregnant individuals than in others; and (4) the bulbar form seems to follow the recent removal of tonsils. Dr. Aycock studied wisely and steadily to distinguish the host factors that render transformation of a common benign infection into a severe and crippling disease. Needless to say, these fundamental concepts stimulated further investigations by others.

> We have said little of his life or of his qualities as a man. It is sufficient to affirm that the Medical School is a better place because for thirty years he worked within its walls; that his friends while they live will gratefully preserve the memory of his modesty, his courage, and his intellectual enthusiasm. We believe he would have it so; that he would have chiefly remembered here that part of him which will surely endure. For, like Francis Bacon, "all other ambition whatsoever seemed poor in his eyes compared with the work he had in hand; seeing that the matter at issue is either nothing, or a thing so great that it may well be content with its own merit, without seeking other recompense."[5]

Perhaps, he was not appreciated for what he was, because he never was given the rank of full professor. At any rate he represents the great number of men who have contributed to the advancement of others in many parts of the world who received no recognition from their own institutions.

A turning point came in 1947. By that year, there was a certain amount of unrest in the Medical School in general and especially in the Department of Preventive Medicine, and an ad hoc committee was appointed to look into "what provisions should be made for the teaching of preventive medicine in Harvard Medical School" and the future of the Department of Preventive Medicine.[6] Many prominent persons in the field were consulted. It was the belief of the Committe that the size of the problem and its many implications for medical education and medical practice become more apparent when preventive medicine is defined. At the time of this report (1947), preventive medicine was the "prevention of disease, the prevention of the sequences of curable disease, the prevention, delay, or amelioration of the sequences of incurable disease." That is to say, preventive medicine was a philosophy, a discipline, or a point of view which can be applied to every phase of clinical practice. It can be applied as well, in direct relationship, to the basic sciences.

It was the unanimous belief of the Committee that the methods of teaching preventive medicine then being used in most medical schools were unsatisfactory, for these outstanding reasons:

1. There has been too much confusion of preventive medicine with public health and frequently unwarranted emphasis of the latter as it concerns the practicing physician.

2. There has been undue reliance on didactic methods, a situation comparable to the teaching of internal medicine a generation ago. This method of teaching, as well as the content of courses in preventive medicine is unpopular with students. They look upon these isolated lectures as being far removed from the thrilling experience of learning clinical medicine.

3. There has been too little participation in the teaching of preventive medicine by most of the clinical teachers—the striking exception being the pediatrician. Most clinicians center their interest on the cause and treatment of disease rather than its prevention. This lack of development of the clinical approach to the teaching of preventive medicine is in need of correction.

4. There has been insufficient integration of the teaching of preventive and curative medicine and the medical sciences. For example, if a system which permitted such integration were in effect, the teaching of rheumatic fever would be done jointly by representatives of at least the departments of medicine, pediatrics, psychiatry, bacteriology, and preventive medicine. The epidemiological aspects of the disease would be presented by representatives of the departments of preventive medicine and bacteriology; the clinical features of rheumatic fever by the pediatrician; the personal aspects by the psychiatrist; the natural history of rheumatic fever leading to rheumatic heart disease and the preventive aspects of the treatment of asymptomatic heart disease would be presented jointly by the internist and the representative from the field of preventive medicine; and the treatment of heart failure by the internist.

5. There has been too little demonstration that personal, social and environmental factors influence the incidence of disease and may adversely affect the course of disease. The patient is frequently considered another interesting case rather than a sick man urgently in need of help in conquering his fears as well as his physical disabilities.

6. There is need to focus attention on the natural history of disease, including its epidemiology, and the application of health knowledge for individuals and communities.

The committee believes this Medical School can make its greatest contribution by accepting an increasing responsibility in the application of health knowledge in the prevention of disease. Application of the advances in medical knowledge is dependent upon the product which the Medical School supplies to society. Hence, the medical faculty is in a position of primary importance in relation to deliverance of health knowledge. This imposes not only an increased responsibility, but also provides an increased opportunity to serve society more completely. This opportunity involves full acceptance of prevention as a natural correlate to diagnostic and curative medicine.

After due consideration of the above, the committee recommends:

1. The Medical School must accept this responsibility.

2. There should be a department of preventive medicine, as this seems the only effective way of accomplishing the following objectives:

(a) Correlation and integration of the knowledge of prevention simultaneously with the teaching of diagnostic and curative medicine.

(b) Demonstration to students and faculty of the benefits to be derived from the application of preventive knowledge.

(c) Research concerning the natural history of disease, its prevention, and the benefits to be derived from programs of care with service of a high quality.

The committee is of the opinion that any other organization based on existing departments could not give adequate emphasis to this major aspect of medicine.

3. The department should consist of a professor and a sufficient staff to provide at least one representative of the department in each of the teaching hospitals. The head of the department himself should hold an appointment in each of these hospitals. The staff should also include an epidemiologist and a medical statistician.

4. The headquarters of the department should be located in one of the teaching hospitals. The choice of hospitals should be left to the head of the department.

5. Recommendations 3 and 4 are made because it is essential that the clinical departments cooperate with the department of preventive medicine by mutual consent so as to make it possible to bring preventive medicine to the bedside.

6. The administrative organization necessary for the integration of the actual teaching should be formulated by the head of the department after consultation with the Dean and those responsible for the teaching of the clinical subjects and the basic sciences.

7. The head of the department must be well grounded in preventive medicine as a result of practical experience in the field. Moreover, it is of great importance that his knowledge of clinical medicine be sufficent to command the respect of his colleagues. His attitude must be in keeping with the policies contained in this report.

8. Adequate research facilities must be provided. The committee suggests that a considerable proportion of the research funds be devoted to supporting investigations in preventive medicine in collaboration with research units already in existence. Thus, reduplication will be avoided and great diversification of research made possible.[7]

The year 1947 also saw the appointment of Dr. David D. Rutstein as Professor of Preventive Medicine. Dr. Rutstein was born in 1909 at Wilkes-Barre, Pennsylvania. He received his M.D. degree *cum laude* from the Harvard Medical School in 1934. He started out in 1936–37 as a Research Fellow in Pediatrics at the School and at the Children's Hospital Medical Center, and Assistant in Bacteriology at the School. Thereafter he served in various other posts, including that of Deputy Commissioner of Health of the City of New York, where he was brought face to face with the social aspects of medical practice. He became Professor of Preventive Medicine and head of the Department at the Harvard Medical School in 1947. From 1966 to 1975 he held the position of Ridley Watts Professor of Preventive Medicine at the Harvard Medical School. He is now emeritus.

For a long time Dr. Rutstein has been recognized as a leader in the movement to reform America's system of medical care. In addition his original research activities dealt with respiratory tract infections, rheumatic fever, congenital heart disease, and, more recently, diseases associated with atherosclerosis. But his main effort has been directed toward establishing the criteria whereby the quality of medical practice and other aspects of medical care in a community may be evaluated. This was a necessary first step in the organization of efforts at prevention.

One can raise the question after examining the 1947 ad hoc committee's report as to what happened as a consequence of that study, and at least a partial answer can be found in a perceptive report by Dr. Rutstein to the Faculty of Medicine, May 2, 1952, in which he described plans for improving the teaching of preventive medicine.[8] A major objective at that time was to develop for the student an accurate realization of his future responsibilities as a practicing physician, his role in society, and his relationship to his patients and to his community. Since its reorganization in 1947, the Department of Preventive Medicine at the Harvard Medical School has been responsible for these aspects of the teaching of medical care.

Before that time the teaching of medical care and social medicine had been introduced in a fragmentary way by Dr. T. Duckett Jones in a series of lectures under the sponsorship of the Department of Preventive Medicine. These lectures were open to the University but were primarily intended for third-year medical students. At that time two concepts were formally introduced into the medical curriculum: (1) the role of preventive medicine in medical care of individual patients and (2) the definition and essentials of complete medical care.[9] In the third year a series of didactic exercises on the social aspects of medicine and the principles of medical care was presented by experts who represented a broad range of points of view in social medicine and medical care. It is evident that one answer to the question raised above is that "social medicine" was going to receive a far greater emphasis than had earlier been the case.

It was expected that the student would learn to apply the didactic teaching of the third year through a Health Resources Survey. He was given hypothetical cases and asked to report on the following: (1) optimal facilities desired for the complete medical care of the patients; (2) actual facilities present in the community; (3) differences between ideal and actual facilities; (4) practical suggestions for improving medical services, in an attempt to provide complete medical care.

The completed surveys presented at the beginning of the fourth year were discussed by a Departmental member in conference with a student. In the fourth year further teaching of social medicine was conducted by the Department at the bedside on ward rounds in the affiliated hospitals. During these rounds diagnosis and therapeutic recommendations were supplemented by discussions of the social and preventive factors related to the patient's illness and to his care following discharge from the hospital. Thus there was an integration of curative medicine and the medical sciences with a consideration of social and psychological aspects of the individual's disease.

In 1947–51 the initial response to this method of teaching was enthusiastic. A basic defect existed, however, as pointed out by Rutstein: the framework of teaching was didactic, and except for a few students in the fourth year it had usually not been possible to teach complete medical care at the time when the student was responsible for the care of the patient in the outpatient department or in the hospital ward. This defect resulted from lack of an adequate educational program tied to a total medical care program in the teaching hospitals. The student, although presented with a series of theoretical concepts, had not adequately absorbed the problems of complete medical care in the teaching hospitals. The serious student, no matter how hard he tried, found little opportunity to correlate available community services for the benefit of the patients under his care, nor could he, under the existing situation, maintain continuity in the medical supervision of his patients. An attempt to correct this defect was made by correlating activities of the Department of Preventive Medicine with ward experience in the Massachusetts General Hospital.

A representative sample of twenty-five students was assigned to the project. Each student was assigned to a family. He reviewed completely the Hospital record and any other available sources of information about his family and then conferred with all of those who had had any medical relationships with the family. The total family history was reviewed with the instructor, after which a visit was made to the family with the instructor for the purpose of getting acquainted. After this the student was expected to make regular visits whenever health emergencies arose. This was to be done alone or with an instructor or other consultant.

It was the plan that once a year the student would present to his entire class a family health problem he was familiar with. A physician at the level of Assistant Professor of Preventive Medicine would guide the students in their projects. Chiefs of services and their residents in the Massachusetts General Hospital were expected to participate. The Nursing and Medical Social Services were to be integrated into this program. Dr. Rutstein proposed that with a group of 400 to 600 families under close medical supervision by a well-coordinated group of physicians, basic scientists, and sociologists, an excellent opportunity for research studies of physical and mental growth and development would be created.

This ambitious plan does not seem to have had much influence on the teaching of social aspects of medicine, which continued to be unsatisfactory, nor did it spread to the other hospitals. In an attempt to strengthen the teaching, new appointments were made to the Faculty. They arose out of recognition of the need that something had to be done, although the social agitation that permeated the University in the late 1950's, uncritical as it was, was probably influential to some degree.

Dr. Osler Peterson joined the Faculty of Medicine in 1959, when, as a member of the Rockefeller Foundation, he set out to establish a teaching and research program in social medicine for undergraduate medical students. As one aspect of these activities, he undertook an investigation of the quality of surgery provided in New England hospitals. This study identified the major sources of error in diagnosis and error in decisions concerned with postoperative care. In 1962 Dr. Peterson was appointed Visiting Professor of Preventive Medicine at Harvard.

Dr. Peterson was educated primarily at the University of Minnesota, where he received the M.B. and M.D. degrees in 1938 and 1939, respectively, and the M.P.H. degree in 1947 from the Johns Hopkins University. He joined the Rockefeller Foundation Virus Laboratory staff at the Rockefeller Institute in 1943, and later served as a staff member of the Foundation. Following this, he spent several years in Europe as a representative of the Foundation. He returned to this country and became Director of Program Planning in the Division of Health Affairs at the University of North Carolina. In 1956 he became Assistant Director for Medical Education and Public Health in the Rockefeller Foundation. Until recently he served as Consulting Physician to the Second and Fourth (Harvard) Medical Services at the Boston City Hospital. In 1968 he became Professor of Preventive Medicine at Harvard.

Dr. Peterson's analytic surveys have been widely acclaimed. They focused attention on the weaknesses as well as the strengths of the general practice of medicine, of surgical diagnosis, and of the delivery of health care in the United States and abroad. More recently he has been involved in a survey of the variations in the provision, utilization, and economics of medical care in the State of Rhode Island. This study is being carried out through the cooperation of members of the Faculty of Medicine at Brown University and is of particular value because it involves a stable and relatively isolated population.

In 1970 Dr. Peterson generated consternation when he reported that there was a shortage of family physicians in Massachusetts, New Hampshire, and Rhode Island. In his view this situation had reached the critical stage. He noted great increases in specialists in certain fields, such as anesthesia, cardiology, child psychiatry, gastroenterology, general surgery, internal medicine, neurology, neurosurgery, obstetrics and gynecology, orthopedic surgery, pathology, pediatrics, psychiatry, radiology, and thoracic surgery; but there had been a decrease in the number of physicians capable of giving primary medical care.

Dr. Peterson also serves as Associate Director of Studies of the Medical Care and Education Foundation, Inc., a nonprofit organization concerned with research in regional planning in the states of New Hampshire, Massachusetts, and Rhode Island.

In 1961 he was made a member of the Faculty of Public Administration at Harvard. He has participated in the Harvard Inter-Faculty Medical Care, Teaching and Research Program.

The Department was further strengthened when Leona Baumgartner joined it. She had come to Boston as the bride of Dr. Alexander Langmuir, Visiting Professor of Epidemiology in the Faculty of Medicine, a world-famous expert in epidemic control and a regular consultant to the World Health Organization. Dr. Baumgartner, who is today one of the most distinguished members of the Harvard Faculty, was educated at the University of Kansas and Yale University. For nine years she was the City Commissioner of Health in New York City. From 1962 to 1965 she held the rank of Assistant Secretary of State in charge of technical assistance in the Agency for International Development (AID) Program. Today she is Visiting Professor of Social Medicine at the Harvard Medical School and Executive Director of the Tri-State (Massachusetts, Rhode Island, and New Hampshire) Regional Medical Program.

Dr. Baumgartner has commented that health does not have a very high priority in the United States "as far as either government or the private sector are concerned." In an effort to awaken more interest, she has lectured widely, repeatedly emphasizing that this nation faces a health crisis of major proportions. "The crisis," she says, "is in the system through which health care is delivered to the people." Unquestionably, some people receive as good care as can be secured anywhere in the world, but in some poverty-ridden areas care is negligible and the health of minority groups is no better than that in underdeveloped countries. "For these, and they number in the tens of millions, the crisis is more than real."

The inevitability of changes in the American health care system, Dr. Baumgartner believes, can be attributed to five key social and economic factors of contemporary American society:

(1) the rapid accumulation of scientific knowledge—biomedical as well as technological; (2) rapidly rising costs; (3) shortages of personnel—physicians, dentists, nurses and the many kinds of persons allied with them; (4) changes in people; and (5) changing professional attitudes.

Dr. Baumgartner has pointed out the changes that would be necessary if better health care is to be achieved:

1. Finding better ways to deliver health care. This must become as prestigious and well-supported a pursuit as research in molecular biology.

2. Making much greater use of allied health professionals and new types must be developed.

3. Increasing the collaboration of economist, engineer, behavioral scientist and health worker hopefully without loss of the tender loving care side of medical practice that means so much to patients.

4. Achieving regionalization of medical services. Isolated health facilities must be brought together to make the best possible use of scarce personnel and expensive facilities and equipment .The less sophisticated technologies must be made more accessible to those served—but decentralization and duplication of the more sophisticated must be avoided.

5. The incorporation of much more preventive care and screening into our health system.

6. Lowering the economic barriers to quality health care so that good care really will be available to all.

"We know what must be done," she declared, "and, difficult as the problems seem, they are not insoluble. If we invested no more energy, money and intellect in finding new ways and means than we now do in perpetuating the old ways and means—we might all surprise ourselves by achieving to a very great extent what we must achieve in the field of health care."[10]

In the late 1960's Dr. Rutstein expressed his wish to give up administrative responsibilities as head of the Department of Preventive Medicine and suggested to Dean Ebert that it would be wise to look into the future role of the Department within the framework of the Medical School and its associated hospitals. The Dean concurred and expressed the view that increasing interest of students and faculty in the social problems of medicine, the increasing number of programs directed toward the community, and the growing public and private concern with the delivery of medical care, made a review urgent. A committee was appointed and directed to "examine the scope, direction and organization of the Department" with particular attention to the opportunities for expansion and realignment of the Department's functions.

The Ad Hoc Committee made a thorough examination of the past role of the Department of Preventive Medicine. Its report summarized the erratic course of the teaching of preventive medicine; there is no better expression of the uncertainties that cloud the future of this subject. The report points out that there have been three eras in the history of such departments as Preventive Medicine. First, there was a bacteriologic era, wherein the several departments were concerned with microbiologic epidemiology. This shaded into the public health era, in the early part of the twentieth century, and the first and second eras continued together into the 1940's. In the public health era courses were generally taught by health officers and were, to a large degree, concerned with public health practices. Studies carried out in the 1940's by Dr. Hugh Leavell and Dr. Harry Mustard showed wide diversity of opinion over how and what should be taught and by whom. Student interest was lacking, and the programs were not very popular. By the 1950's, when the Association of American Medical Colleges held a conference at Colorado Springs on the teaching of preventive medicine, it was evident that although the prevention of illness was properly a major concern of departments of preventive medicine, there was a growing interest in community health problems especially those associated with the delivery of medical care.

By the 1960's the third and current era had developed. It was marked by expansion of concern for the diagnosis of community problems, the development of methods of determining illness in the population, and the delivery of health services. The application to these problems of scientific techniques was grounded in epidemiology and biostatistics, as well as economics and sociology. The term "preventive medicine" is no longer sufficient to describe the concerns, which deal with the relationship of medicine to society as a whole. It was therefore the belief of the Committee members that the name of the Department of Preventive Medicine should be broadened to the Department of Preventive and Social Medicine.

Society's expectations of health services have changed greatly in the last two decades. As a major interest of the establishment, medical schools, in addition to their classical tasks, are expected to be actively concerned with the rising costs of medical care, the poor distribution of health manpower, the lack of quality controls, and "above all the loss of human dignity suffered in the seeking of medical care by large numbers of the population."[11] If these concepts were to be put into operation, it was evident that radical changes in the institutional arrangements by which medical care is delivered to the population would be required.

In this third period the Medical School has a great challenge to preserve, deepen, and broaden the student's social conscience, so that his role as a physician will benefit not only the patients he sees but also the population from which these patients are derived. The basic aim of a Department of Preventive Medicine should be to help the student best fulfill his role as healer and as a preserver of health by emphasizing the means available to prevent disease and to treat it most effectively through early detection.

The teaching of clinical and social aspects of medicine requires integration by the faculty and the students, who must have access to both clinical and community settings. Clearly, the relationship of the Department to Harvard's associated hospitals, must, of necessity, be a key factor in achieving such integration. This is the case, not only because the hopital provides clinical material in its inpatient and outpatient areas, but also because the relationship of the hospital to the community is changing. To a large portion of the population in general, the hospital, especially the Emergency Room, is the only source of medical care. Such care is likely to be episodic and discontinuous. With knowledge of these problems, a number of the associated teaching hospitals have established community medical units within the hospital.

It is clear that the teaching program in Preventive and Social Medicine should be based upon sound epidemiological and biostatistical principles and not on temporarily popular slogans that put into words the demands of uncritical propagandists. Harvard's resources in terms of Departments of Health Services Administration, Behavioral Sciences, Poulation Sciences, Nutrition, Environmental Health, and the Center for the Prevention of Infectious Diseases should be widely utilized in the teaching of medical students. The problem still awaits solution.

As a result of the report of the Ad Hoc Committe, in 1971, Dr. Julius B. Richmond, a child physchiatrist, was appointed Professor of Preventive and Social Medicine. Former Dean of the Faculty of Medicine at the State University of New York at Syracuse, he is the author of a book entitled *Currents in American Medicine*, published in 1969. It is a critical analysis of the development of health delivery services in the United States from the beginning of the present century to the present time, and Dr. Richmond has emphasized that education for the health professions needs "to incorporate preparation for supervisory responsibilities while exploring the feasibility of new kinds of assistance," sentiments with which few will disagree. He also noted that "better understanding of the adequacy of community health services in terms of quality, quantity and distribution [is needed] . . . The problem is how to provide demonstrations in the delivery of health services without impairing the research and teaching functions of the medical center."

Chapter Seventeen

Radiology

THE development of radiology in the Harvard community occurred in the framework of hospital service rather than academic efforts. At the Massachusetts General Hospital the growth of the X-ray Department coincided with the career of Dr. George W. Holmes. He was appointed Assistant Roentgenologist in 1911, and he, with Dr. Walter J. Dodd, stressed, in 1913, the superiority of fluoroscopy over a series of films for evaluation of the gastrointestinal tract, a view widely held in Europe but generally rejected in the United States. Following Dodd's death, Holmes was appointed head of the Department. He always considered himself a physician appointed to the Department of Radiology, and emphasized the importance of a radiologist as a consultant to other physicians. In 1916 he established what was considered to be the first radiology residency in the country. In the early days, X rays were used to treat almost any condition appearing in the Hospital. Holmes always held to a conservative approach and went far to resist the abuse of radiation in treatment.

In 1925 the Tumor Clinic was established for the treatment of neoplastic disease. It was the first such clinic in a general hospital in this country. In 1940 the one-million-volt Van de Graaff generator was installed in the White Building. Dr. Laurence L. Robbins, in 1941, joined the staff as Assistant Radiologist on the completion of his residency and in the same year the Huntington Memorial Hospital (Harvard's only hospital devoted to the treatment of cancer) closed its doors and became a part of the Massachusetts General Hospital.

In 1941 Dr. Holmes retired, and Aubrey O. Hampton became head of the Department. In the wartime years there was a great loss of principal staff members to the military, and Dr. Holmes served again. He retired again in 1945, when Dr. Laurence L. Robbins was made Acting Chief. Dr. Holmes was noted for his quiet, scholarly discussions of clinical problems and his perceptive care in arriving at diagnoses. He held the rank of Professor of Radiology at the School and gave some lectures to the students.

He was greatly aided by Dr. Richard Schatzki, a brilliant scholar and teacher. Dr. Schatzki received his M.D. degree at the University of Berlin, subsequent clinical training at the University Hospital, Frankfurt, and training in roentgenology in Leipzig. Starting in 1933, he was Assistant Radiologist at the Massachusetts General Hospital. He was made an Instructor in Roentgenology in the Harvard Medical School in 1934 and rose through the ranks to become, in 1964, Associate Clinical Professor of Radiology at the Harvard Medical School.

Dr. Schatzki, who had come here as a refugee from Germany, was one of the truly important leaders in clinical radiology in America. His principal interest was the study of the gastrointestinal tract, where he made major contributions in the field of diagnostic radiology. He developed simple, reliable procedures for the detection of upper-stomach ulcers, ordinarily difficult to locate. He is well remembered for his elective course at the Harvard Medical School, where he taught radiology, and for his medical philosophy: "Radiology is only part of the equipment of diagnosis. The diagnostician uses his hands for palpation and he uses his sense of smell. He uses all of his senses. He listens to his patients and he uses all the information he accumulates this way before he even turns to the X-ray."[1]

Dr. Holmes was succeeded in 1946 by Dr. Laurence L. Robbins. He had gone through the usual clinical promotions and in 1960 was named Clinical Professor in Radiology. In 1969 he was elevated to Professor of Radiology at the Massachusetts General Hospital (Clinical Full-Time). Dr. Robbins strengthened the Department of Radiology there, having contributed greatly to undergraduate and postgraduate teaching and to scholarship, having assumed a major national role in his discipline.

In the meantime, the Peter Bent Brigham Hospital was going through a similar process. When Harvey Cushing insisted on the need for an expanded Department of Radiology, the Hospital appointed Merrill C. Sosman. Dr. Sosman received the M.D. degree from the Johns Hopkins in 1917. His first clinical experience was as a resident physician at the U.S. Soldiers' Home Hospital in Washington, D.C. He then joined the regular Army. By decision of the Surgeon-General he became involved in roentgenology and went overseas with the Army of Occupation. He returned to Walter Reed Hospital in 1921 and was sent to the Massachusetts General Hospital for training under Dr. George W. Holmes. Through Cushing's activities, Dr. Sosman was freed from military obligations and was appointed Roentgenologist at the Peter Bent Brigham in 1922. His entire career was virtually with two institutions, the Brigham and the Harvard Medical School.

At a period when the field of roentgenology was on trial to decide whether it deserved recognition apart from departments of medicine and surgery, Dr. Sosman never let anyone forget that the X-ray method provided more precise and accurate clinical diagnoses than was usually the case with other techniques. He described intracardiac calcification, work now characterized as classic. So also are his writings on the X-ray treatment of pituitary tumors. He worked with masters of the period: brain tumors with Harvey Cushing and Gilbert Horrax; genitourinary problems with William Quinby; surgery with David Cheever, John Homans, Elliott Cutler, Francis Newton (and, of course, Cushing); cardiology with Henry Christian, Samuel Levine, and Sidney Burwell; and pathology with S. Burt Wolbach. He retired in 1956.

A spectacular, at times flamboyant, teacher, Sosman remained at all times a sound and careful physician. He was a leader in the use of the X ray as an important diagnostic tool. His contributions to the science of radiology in the eyes of his colleagues and students not only widened the use of X rays but improved interpretation of X-ray films. Dr. Samuel A. Levine commented: "A great clinical teacher who has set the standard for radiology conferences. . . . His method of teaching has been unique —a mixture of keen erudition and a panoramic knowledge of general medicine, surgery, and pathology, combined with his own individual wit and humor."[2]

Aside from his expertise as a radiologist and an individual uniquely able to mobilize a broad comprehension of biological and physical principles as indispensable for efficiency in the field, Dr. Sosman exemplified the tradition of the great physician. He brought to bear unusual gifts as a teacher and clinician on the patient as a whole and on his effort to aid the patient as a human being. He was bound to influence favorably the careers of his students and colleagues. Among them was the late Philip H. Cook of Worcester, whose bequest to Harvard made possible, in 1955, the establishment at the Medical School of a fund for teaching and research in radiology. It was his hope that the President and Fellows might consider it desirable to establish the Philip H. Cook Professorship of Radiology. An ad hoc committee was later asked by Mr. Pusey to explore this situation.

Mention must also be made of the work of Dr. Felix Fleischner at the Beth Israel Hospital. A refugee from Europe, he brought to that hospital the advanced knowledge of German radiology, plus his own physiologically oriented interpretation of it. He made noteworthy contributions to our knowledge of pulmonary function as revealed by radiographic techniques. A memorial room in the Francis A. Countway Library of Medicine is planned for him.

The Department of Radiology was established as a separate department at the Harvard Medical School in 1944. This came about as a result of the growing stature of Dr. Sosman. Radiology had been functioning at first as a part of the Department of Surgery and subsequently as part of the Department of Medicine.

Notwithstanding the great clinical usefulness of the new technique at the Massachusetts General Hospital and other hospitals of the Medical School, there was considerable dissatisfaction with the work in radiology in the Harvard Medical School. Several attempts were made to overcome this. The first major committee effort was presided over by Dr. Shields Warren from 1958 to 1963. He initiated new and strong developments in radiobiology—for example, the appointment of Professor Henry I. Kohn as the Alvan T. and Viola D. Fuller – American Cancer Society Professor of Radiology (see below), and the construction under his guidance of an important new facility for radiobiological research: the Shields Warren Laboratories of the New England Deaconess Hospital.

The Ad Hoc Committee on Radiology and Radiation Biology was appointed by President Pusey in November, 1955 in anticipation of the retirement of Dr. Sosman.[3] Five years after the appointment of the Committee, it issued an interim report to the Committee of Professors. The impending retirement of Dr. Felix G. Fleischner had required a search for his replacement as Radiologist-in-Chief at the Beth Israel Hospital. The Trustees of that institution, acting in conjunction with the Medical School, provided the resources necessary to establish a professorship of radiology at the Beth Israel Hospital in the category of hospital full-time, and to build new facilities there. In 1962 Dr. Robert Shapiro was appointed Professor of Radiology at the Beth Israel and Radiologist-in-Chief in that institution.

In large part because of the discovery of atomic energy, as the interim report explained, there had been a growing demand for increased support of research in the field of radiation biology. Throughout the country investigators were being attracted to this field, and progress was evident at an accelerated pace. New interfaces among the established disciplines of radiology, medicine, and biology were becoming apparent and promised to become the basis for advances in therapeutic radiology, a field of great importance to progress in the treatment of cancer and some other conditions and to a greater understanding of the immunological mechanisms involved in the transplantation of tissues and organs. The discovery that the responses of certain cells to radiation could be influenced by drugs opened new opportunities for combining radiation and chemotherapy.

In an effort to increase the resources of the Department of Radiology and to provide for the relatively new field of radiation biology, the Ad Hoc Committee sought the aid of a number of distinguished consultants and studied many departments of radiology in this country and abroad. The conclusion was reached by the Committee that a single academic Department of Radiology at Harvard would be most conducive to good teaching, research, and patient care. It was expected that within the Department some separation of responsibility for diagnostic and therapeutic radiology would be present. In the view of the Committee, such a department would include a senior investigator in fundamental radiation biology, preferably one able to unite this field with physiology and pharmacology.

A second bold committee effort, under the chairmanship of Dr. A. Clifford Barger, 1963–65, concentrated particularly on the subject of therapeutic radiology. The first conclusion was that the time had come for Harvard University to make a formal separation between the two divergent disciplines of diagnostic radiology and radiotherapy. These two reports, excellent as they were, had not solved the problem of choosing a new chief for the Peter Bent Brigham Hospital. Accordingly, after President Pusey had studied the material presented to him by the two committees, he appointed a third (Harvard at work!) with the charge that it was to nominate the best possible candidate for the post of the new Philip H. Cook Professorship of Radiology, with the specification that the Cook Professor's primary interest be in Diagnostic Radiology. An agreement was reached between the University and the Trustees of the Peter Bent Brigham Hospital, stipulating that the Cook Professor would, at the time of his appointment, also assume the position of Radiologist-in-Chief at the Peter Bent Brigham Hospital.

The situation was complex. It was recognized that therapeutic needs involved at least two sequential phases: there was a mounting demand for radiotherapy because of the expanding work of the Tumor Clinic at the Peter Bent Brigham Hospital, and an immediate need for continuity in Radiotherapy as an interim measure, to be presided over by the Cook Professor. It was agreed that as the plans of the University for radiotherapeutic facilities and the appointment of a new tenure professor in this area matured, the responsibility of the Philip H. Cook Professor would pass into the hands of another individual and possibly another unit.

The foresight of President Pusey and the Brigham Trustees kept diagnostic radiology from becoming submerged. In fact, today diagnostic radiology is in a position stronger than ever because of the development of an investigative approach to the clinical methods themselves. A large factor in this change was the appointment in 1967 of Herbert L. Abrams as Philip H. Cook Professor of Radiology, Harvard Medical School, and Chairman, Department of Radiology, Harvard Medical School; also, Radiologist-in-Chief, Peter Bent Brigham Hospital and Director, Research Center in Diagnostic Radiology, Department of Radiology, Harvard Medical School.

Dr. Abrams received his M.D. degree at the State University of New

York, in 1946 and received radiological training at Stanford University Hospital. He went through the usual promotions until he became Director, Division of Diagnostic Roentgenology at Stanford and Professor of Radiology in 1961–62, retaining these posts until he came to Harvard. His particular interests had always been in cardiovascular radiology, particularly regional blood flow.

Dr. Abrams took immediate steps to strengthen and unify the School's program in radiology. New tenure professorships were established at the Beth Israel Hospital (Sven Paulin, M.D.), the Massachusetts General Hospital (Juan Taveras, M.D.), and the Peter Bent Brigham Hospital (Harry Z. Mellins, M.D. and S. James Adelstein, M.D.). A major effort was initiated to involve the entire department in undergraduate teaching at the Medical School. Radiology assumed an important role in the gross anatomy and human biology courses for the first- and second-year students. Beyond that, a considerable number of Harvard Medical students began to spend their clinical clerkships in the Department of Radiology at the affiliated hospitals.

At the Peter Bent Brigham Hospital, Dr. Abrams directed the expansion of the department from four to twenty-two radiologists and appointed distinguished specialists to head the divisions of diagnostic radiology, nuclear medicine, and physiologic research. A total equipment replacement program soon made it one of the most modern departments in the country, fully prepared to deal with all kinds of diagnostic radiology studies. A postgraduate training program was initiated for eighteen residents and seven fellows in diagnostic radiology, as well as three additional trainees in nuclear medicine, with major NIH support for three graduate training programs. "The appointment of Dr. Abrams," Dean Ebert said, "signals the first step in a formal separation of the disciplines of Diagnostic Radiology and Radiotherapy at the Harvard Medical School. The position of Diagnostic Radiology has been strengthened in recent years . . ."[4]

The Research Center in Diagnostic Radiology, of which Dr. Abrams is the head, has been funded by the National Institute of Health with a grant of one million dollars. It is the first such center in the country. New methods have been discoveerd for the study of the circulation of the blood, the blood supply of organs, lymphatic pathophysiology, radioisotope kinetics, and the use of both opacification and radioisotope techniques for dynamic clinical studies of the individual organs, or, indeed, the whole body. These new developments have thus provided what previously had been an empirical and diagnostic clinical field with a sound underpinning in basic science, biochemistry, and physiology.

As for the development of therapeutic radiology at Harvard, the Ad Hoc Committee carefully considered the qualifications and contributions of many able men already interested in therapeutic radiology. After a prolonged exploration, the Committee recommended for appointment as the first Alvan T. and Viola D. Fuller – American Cancer Society Professor of Radiology, Dr. Henry I. Kohn, then Clinical Professor of Experimental Radiology at the University of California.

Dr. Kohn was born in 1909. While still a student at Dartmouth, he had become interested in general physiology. He received his Ph.D. degree in biology at Harvard in 1935. For the subsequent two years he studied at Stockholm and Cambridge, following which he became an Instructor in, and later Assistant Professor of, Physiology and Pharmacology at Duke University School of Medicine. During this time he was involved in explorations of bacterial enzymes and the resistance of bacteria to the sulfa drugs that were being developed in that period. Because of an increasing awareness of medical relationships with physiology and pharmacology, Dr. Kohn decided to study medicine, first at Duke University, and then at Harvard. He received his M.D. degree in 1946. After an internship at Bellevue Hospital in New York City, he served for five years as a commissioned officer in the U.S. Public Health Service, first at the Oak Ridge National Laboratory and later in the Department of Radiology under Dr. Robert Stone at the University of California Hospital. Since 1953 he was not only Clinical Professor of Experimental Radiology at the University of California School of Medicine but, simultaneously, Research Radiologist at the Radiological Laboratory.

Dr. Kohn served as Secretary of the Advisory Committee on Biology and Medicine of the United States Atomic Energy Commission. He has been an adviser to the United States Delegation of the United Nations Scientific Committee on the Effects of Atomic Radiation. It was the opinion of the Ad Hoc Committee that he would bring to radiology at Harvard, at a favorable time, an unusual combination of talents, including a broad background in physiology and radiation biology and a keen comprehension of clinical radiation therapy. His radiological peers regard Dr. Kohn as an outstanding scientist.

Subsequent to his appointment to the Fuller – American Cancer Society Professorship, Dr. Kohn was named Davis Wesley Gaiser Professor of Radiation Biology. A Center for Human Genetics was established at the Harvard Medical School in January 1971, and Dr. Kohn was named its first Director. Dean Robert Ebert commented: "The Center for Human Genetics has been instituted in recognition of the fact that medical genetics has entered a period of rapid development and growth. The Center will form a unifying framework within which teaching and research in human genetics can be developed within the Medical School."[5] The thrust of the new Center is primarily medical and clinical. Genetics at the level of molecular biology has been fostered by the existing Medical School's Department of Microbiology and Molecular Genetics. The Center, according to the Dean, has been assigned the responsibility of teaching and research in the School, to enhance patient care and community service through the School's associated teaching hospitals and to facilitate programs held in common among faculty members.

The new center also is responsible for establishing effective liaison with such units as the Center for Population Studies of the Harvard School of Public Health, genetic programs of related interest in the Faculty of Arts and Sciences at Harvard and at the Massachusetts Institute of Technology, and the Laboratory of Human Reproduction and Reproductive Biology of the Medical School.

Taking the program for radiology at the Harvard Medical School as a whole, it can be seen that fifteen years of cogitation and planning resulted in the creation of a structure staffed with outstanding personnel. This new structure has probably come to equal the best currently in existence anywhere in the country. These developments grew out of an urge toward betterment, but the urge was activated not by a pioneering spirit but by awarness of the need to bring organized, up-to-date excellence to an area dominated by the extraordinary but solipsistic efforts of some unusual men who did not always understand how to use or implement the latest deevlopments. For Harvard this was an unusual course of events. Did it occur because this relatively late entry on the scene in clinical medicine could not, at the time, be conceptualized in terms of a basic science and so had to wait until it could? If so, this clearly shows how markedly the relations of basic science to clinical medicine had changed by the early twentieth century.

Chapter Eighteen

Neurology

SINCE neurology and neuropathology are clinical subjects, their history lies in the various hospitals that have been connected with Harvard. It will be recalled that James Jackson Putnam was the first Professor of Diseases of the Nervous System. His main interest was in psychoneurosis, and his hobby was the study of German philosophy. He was succeeded by his son-in-law, E. W. Taylor, who had the title of James Jackson Putnam Professor. Taylor functioned mainly as an outpatient physician at the Massachusetts General Hospital and gave clinics for the students.

The history of neurology at the Massachusetts General really begins, however, with James B. Ayer. The son, grandson, and great-grandson of New England physicians, he received his Bachelor's degree at Harvard in 1903, having distinguished himself as an oarsman there. (In 1914, when he went to the Henley Regatta as a substitute with a club crew, rather than remaining idle, he entered the Diamond Sculls on an impulse. He did not win, but his performance astounded the onlookers.) He received his M.D. degree from Harvard in 1907. While there, and subsequently, he became a close friend of Francis Weld Peabody, and the latter's death some years later at a young age filled Ayer with lasting grief.

Ayer began his clinical work at the Massachusetts General Hospital in 1911, working in neuropathology and developing a strong interest in the diagnostic value of spinal-fluid tests, some of which he had invented. During World War I he served under Dr. Lewis Weed of Johns Hopkins, a leader in spinal-fluid studies. Ayer's assignment was to study epidemic cerebrospinal meningitis. In 1921 he used combined lumbar and cisternal punctures to reveal spinal-fluid block. On Dr. Edward Taylor's retirement in 1926, Dr. Ayer was made James Jackson Putnam Professor. He started at once to obliterate the previous emphasis on psychiatry and philosophy and turn his department back to medicine. He organized a neuropathology laboratory under Dr. Charles Kubik in 1927 and an EEG laboratory under Dr. Robert Schwab in 1936. He was one of the greatest American clinical neurologists of his time, and his clinics, in which he modestly unraveled the most complicated clinical problems with seeming ease, were a model not only of diagnosis but of teaching. Those who were able to work with him were indeed fortunate, although some thought that he was too much the clinician and not enough the scientist. He retired in 1946, and the title went to Dr. Kubik, who exemplified the inseparability of neuropathology and clinical neurology. Raymond D. Adams became Bullard Professor of Neuropathology and soon the actual head of Neurology at the Hospital. (He had graduated with an M.D. degree at Duke University in 1936 and had made a reputation for himself as a microscopist.) He worked at Cornell and at the Boston City Hospital.

The Neurology Service of the Massachusetts General Hospital has adopted the philosophy that their activities should encompass the diagnosis and treatment of all identifiable diseases of the human nervous system proven to exist either by a visible lesion or by inferential evidence of one. No important distinction has been drawn between diseases that cause major alterations of behavior, thinking, mood, and personality and those which result in paralysis, sensory loss, aphasia, etc. Emphasis has been placed on the development of clinical criteria for accurate diagnosis and proper techniques for therapy and management.

When this Service was expanded in 1951, a large segment of neuro-psychiatric disease coming through the portals of the Massachusetts General was not, at that time, considered to be within the orbit of neurological disease. A considerable portion of patients with cerebrovascular diseases, for example, were being admitted to general medical services, where they were often not seen by physicians with special training in diseases of the nervous system. The disorders of the nervous system consequent upon alcoholism and malnutrition were not then considered to be of neurological origin. Children with mental retardation and developmental anomalies, some of which were affecting behavior, learning, and language, were left in psychiatry or pediatrics. Many of the major psychiatric illnesses, especially those resulting in a loss of intellectual function, were rarely being seen by the neurologists. Muscle disease was for the most part entirely neglected. One of the first tasks, therefore, was to single out clinical entities and diseases in these fields and to study them by the methods of neurological medicine.

Drs. Kubik and Adams had taken an interest in cerebrovascular disease, and Miller Fisher had been sent to work with them by Dr. Wilder Penfield. As this program of study was enlarged, Fisher returned to join Adams and Kubik full time; he has had a succession of very able young men collaborating with him. Their work has succeeded in defining for the first time atherosclerotic disease of the carotid arteries and the syndrome of amblyopia fugax, related to carotid stenosis. His original paper followed an earlier one by Kubik and Adams on atherosclerotic disease of the basilar artery, which at that time had not been clinically diagnosed or treated. (Now, accurate diagnosis is made regularly, and anticoagulant therapy has changed the outcome.)

Miller Fisher and Raymond Adams investigated embolization of the brain as a common vascular phenomenon which previously had been considered a rarity. They found it to rank foremost among the cerebrovascular diseases. Moreover, the syndrome of hemorrhagic infarction, a known type of ischemic necrosis in the human brain, was linked to migratory and disintegrating emboli, a concept vaguely entertained before but now widely accepted. This theory was also extended to the nebulous syndrome of vasospasm and "stroke without vascular occlusion." The clinicopathological entity known as cerebral Buerger's Disease was shown by Fisher to be a stagnation thrombosis of cerebral vessels due usually to atherosclerosis. The diagnosis of cerebellar hemorrhage had rarely been made during life until Fisher in a series of detailed clinical observations not only succeeded in doing it but, with the help of the neurosurgeons, salvaged a considerable percentage of the patients, restoring some of them to useful levels of function. The state known as *état lacunaire*, earlier delineated by French pathologists, was shown to have clinical equivalents and to be the basis of a series of neat cerebral syndromes. Pathogenetic factors were shown to be a combination of hypertension and atherosclerosis. The first classification of cerebrovascular disease composed by a national committee was largely written in the Neurology Service at the Massachusetts General Hospital, and the first large-scale national study of anticoagulation was directed by Dr. Fisher.

The work in alcoholic neurological diseases was carried on by Maurice Victor and Raymond Adams. Some thirty papers have been written and more than ten specific diseases of the human nervous system have been identified. A series of studies of the clinical picture, pathology, metabolic and nutritional basis, and therapy were undertaken of Wernicke-Korsakoff's Disease. It was shown finally that Korsakoff's syndrome is merely the mental part of Wernicke's Disease and that this seems to be entirely due to thiamine deficiency, preventable and correctable by the use of thiamine. Delirium tremens was clearly established as a withdrawal state correlating precisely with the fall of blood alcohol level in an addicted individual. It was proved that no nutritional factor was involved and that slower withdrawal would prevent the condition. Alcoholic auditory hallucinosis was more precisely defined as a form of psychosis related to withdrawal but sometimes persisting. (Residual Korsakoff's and auditory hallucinosis are responsible for one fifth of the long-term commitments to the Boston State Hospital.) An investigation of the clinical and pathological aspects of alcoholic cerebellar degeneration was carried out, and the comparison material for this study resulted in the publication of an atlas of the human cerebellum by Elliott Mancall, Jay Angevine, and Paul Yakovlev. These were the first pathologically studied cases of alcoholic cerebellar degeneration. Not only was the syndrome defined, but its precise correlation with Purkinje cell loss in the anterior lobe of the cerebellum was shown. Later it was ascertained that nutritional deficiency and not alcohol was the cause. Alcoholic epilepsy was the subject of another investigation by Dr. Victor and his associates. Finally, Marchiafava-Bignami's Disease was shown to be a nutritional problem not directly related to alcoholism even though it usually occurred in the alcoholic. The final paper in this series will be a definitive study of the clinical and pathological aspects of alcoholic polyneuropathy. All of this work is soon to be summarized in a monograph on the neurology of alcoholism.

Muscle disease became a primary interest in the Department about 1947–48, and it resulted in a monograph on the Pathology of Muscle by Carl Pearson, Derek Denny-Brown, and Raymond Adams. Several new muscle diseases were discovered, and a systematic investigation of chronic idiopathic polymyositis was summarized in a monograph by John Walton and Adams in 1955. It has since been determined to have an autoimmune basis involving a possible viral agent. Clinical myology was increasingly expanded as a subspecialty of medicine, and the major phenomenologies of all muscle diseases were brought together in the Thayer Lectures for 1972, given by Raymond Adams.

Dementia as a clinical state more recently became a subject of study, and the Neurology Service successfully defined a new condition known as "low pressure or normatensive hydrocephalus." Its universal recognition and the introduction of ventriculo-atrial shunting, has salvaged many hundreds of individuals from a disabling dementia. Many have been restored to an entirely normal mental function after having been incapacitated for a year or more. The concept of a hydrocephalic factor in a number of disorders of the human nervous system, even when the cerebrospinal fluid pressure is normal by accepted standards or only slightly elevated, had its origin in the Neurology Service of the Massachusetts General Hospital as a result of the work of Miller Fisher, Salomon Hakim, William Sweet, and Raymond Adams. Finding a method of treating one form of dementia has resulted in a more systematic study of all forms of intellectual failure in middle and late life, and the findings promise to change the treatment of hydrocephalus even in infancy and childhood. Of course, it not infrequently happens that a chronic subdural hematoma, a low-grade meningeal infection, or a metabolic disease will be found to have caused a form of dementia.

In the course of these studies Dr. Miller Fisher and Dr. Raymond Adams discovered a new clinical state known as episodic global amnesia, previously mislabeled as a form of stroke. The clinical state was made the subject of a monograph, and its benign character was proven by a series of observations on more than fifty patients.

A Pediatric Neurology Service was established. It was generously encouraged in the beginning by Alan Butler and later supported by funds obtained from the Kennedy Foundation and the Federal Government, which permitted the installation of several floors of laboratories and a clinical research center, the latter at the Fernald School. It is of interest that more than fifty of the better known pediatric neurologists in academic institutions in this country have had all or part of their training in this subdivision of the department during the past twenty years. The screening laboratory at the Massachusetts General Hospital for amino acid disorders of birth has resulted in the discovery of a whole series of new, inherited metabolic diseases, some of which are now preventable by dietary control during critical phases of myelination of the nervous system. The late Mary Efron was a recognized leader in this field, and her work is carried on by others. As a result, mental retardation, which was viewed as an end-stage of a large variety of human brain disease, was brought within the compass of the present activity.

Clinical neuropharmacology was vigorously promoted by the late Robert Schwab of the EEG laboratories. Many new therapies have been introduced, the most recent being amantadine for Parkinson's Disease. The EEG laboratory was the first such hospital laboratory in the United States and has now been expanded to include a wide variety of techniques applicable to humans. It was in this laboratory that the first observations of "brain death" were made by Schwab and Adams and later extended by Henry K. Beecher and others.

Because of ignorance of the cause of the majority of the cases of peripheral nerve diseases seen on the Massachusetts General Hospital wards, clinical and laboratory studies of the nerve fiber were begun in 1952–53. Byron Waksman and Adams found a means of inducing in animals an experimental allergic polyneuritis, and it is now the most widely used model of a polyneuritis. From observations of Fisher and Adams on diphtheritic polyneuropathy, the pathological basis of this condition was found and reproduced by Waksman and Adams in the laboratory animal. Myelomatous polyneuropathy was first described and uremic polyneuropathy was established as an entity. Autoimmune diseases of the central and peripheral nervous systems were studied intensively. The first cases of central pontine myelinolysis, an entity that had not previously been described, were found at about the same time as a new demyelinative disease of the human nervous system called multifocal leukoencephalitis. This latter proved to be a not infrequent cerebral disease for which the predicted viral etiology has now been found.

The Neurology Service has nevertheless maintained high level clinical study, considerate and courteous treatment of large numbers of patients with every type of neuropsychiatric disease, and integration of neuropathologic studies with clinical work, the latter being merely an extension of clinical studies of disease.

It is evident that modern Neurology developed in 1926 at the Massachusetts General Hospital, where a sound mixture of clinical observation and pathologic study led to immense changes in the field. The start of this process was, however, not sensational enough to please some medical educators, who maintained that up until that time the major advances in neurological disease in the United States had been made by neurosurgeons, particularly Harvey Cushing and his pupils. They not only had developed new surgical techniques but had described new syndromes, added to our knowledge of the functions of the nervous system and made great contributions to neuropathology and embryology through the microscopic study of brain tumors. Nonsurgical neurology appeared to have lagged behind, and lacked the grand figures who had graced the field in Germany, France, and England. It must be remembered that this was the period of the establishment of the Thorndike Memorial Laboratory, and many waited to see a similar enterprise in neurology at the Boston City Hospital.

The Harvard Neurological Unit at the Boston City was deliberately founded to fill this assumed gap. It was started with a grant from the Rockefeller Foundation which provided not only the salary of a director but funds for teaching and research. The Unit was built clearly as a research-oriented department with a staff primarily of full-time academicians. Dr. Stanley Cobb was chosen to be its first Director.

Stanley Cobb had been born near Boston and lived in the same house for much of his life. He received his Bachelor's degree at Harvard in 1910 and his M.D. degree in 1914. He served in World I and soon after his return started up the academic ladder, his first post being that of Instructor in 1919. He early distinguished himself with studies on the factors that control the cerebral blood flow in intact animals under anesthesia, surely a remarkable accomplishment. Dr. Cobb also received an appointment as Bullard Professor of Neuropathology.

At the time Dr. Cobb was appointed the first Director, the Medical Building, which was to house the Unit, was not completed. Dr. Cobb went off to Europe to visit notable European centers. In the meantime, Dr. Frank Fremont-Smith, who had been trained by James Ayer, was entrusted with the task of setting up the laboratories. The Unit offices on the ninth floor of the Medical Building were unusual for their day. Only one office, that of the Director, was strictly designed as an office. All of the other rooms were provided with benches and with gas, water, and air outlets, making them combined offices and laboratories.

Stanley Cobb in 1934 moved to the Massachusetts General Hospital as Chief of Psychiatry. This reflected his many interests. Although his title was Bullard Professor of Neuropathology, his own work had covered neuropathology, movement disorders, comparative neuroanatomy, and psychiatry. Later, after his retirement, he returned to an old interest as a naturalist by studying the brains of talking birds.

He was succeeded by a remarkable figure, Tracy Jackson Putnam, nephew of James Jackson Putnam, himself a major pioneer in American neurology and psychiatry. Tracy had received his M.D. degree from Harvard in 1920. As the new Director he was given the rank of Professor of Neurology in 1934 and held that post until 1939, when he resigned to go to Columbia University's New York Neurological Institute. Tracy Putnam is the only man ever to have been president of the American Neurological Association, the Harvey Cushing Society, and the American Association of Neuropathologists.

During the twelve years in which the Unit was under Cobb and Putnam, it established itself as the leading neurological research department in this country, and perhaps in the world. Houston Merritt and Frank Fremont-Smith carried out clinical studies on the cerebrospinal fluid as well as investigations on equilibria between the blood and the CSF, studies embodied in the standard monograph on the topic. William Lennox and the Gibbses, Frederic and Erna, made pioneering studies on the cerebral circulation, on cerebral metabolism, and on metabolic changes in epilepsy. That Dr. Abraham Myerson, who had pioneered in the study of cerebral metabolism by the use of carotid-jugular arterio-venous differences, was an Associate Director of the Unit in the early days was undoubtedly an added stimulus. Lennox and the Gibbses were also instrumental in developing the electroencephalogram as a standard tool in the study of epilepsy. Having found that the early electroencephalograph machines did not meet the requirements of clinical use, they commissioned a young engineer, Albert Grass, to build a better machine for the Unit. This started Grass on his career as the major manufacturer of electroencephalograph machines in the United States. The works of Lennox and the Gibbses are classic keystones of the newer knowledge of epilepsy.

Tracy Putnam's contribution to the experimental study of epilepsy is also classic. He developed a reproducible technique for the experimental production of convulsions, so that new anticonvulsants could be tested in animals. He surmised astutely that the anticonvulsant and sedative actions of phenobarbital were separable and set out on a deliberate search for modifications of the phenobarbital molecule that would diminish the lattter without effect on the former. The discovery of Dilantin came directly from this study, and it remains today, nearly forty years later, the most widely used anticonvulsant.

Putnam also pioneered studies of the pathology of multiptle sclerosis. He was an inventive neurosurgeon as well, developing new procedures for the treatment of hydrocephalus and pain. He was a pioneer in the surgical treatment of movement disorders and established the remarkable finding that excellent recovery of movement could occur in Parkinsonians who had undergone section of the pyramidal tract in the cord. Donald Munro, who joined the Unit early as Chief of Neurosurgery, was a pioneer in treatment of brain and spinal trauma. His unit for the care of traumatic paraplegias had a world-wide influence on the treatment of this previously neglected group of patients.

Alcoholism was naturally a major interest of the Unit. One of the remarkable figures involved in this area was Merrill Moore, a colorful and intensely energetic personality. (Moore's most striking accomplishment lay in his having written before his death over 100,000 sonnets—more, it has been stated, than have been written by all other poets in the history of English literature.)

Leo Alexander, later to become famous outside medicine for his role as the psychiatric adviser at the Nuremberg War Trials, made a major contribution by demonstrating that pigeons on thiamine-deficient diets developed the characteristic lesions of Wernicke's encephalopathy, a disorder to the understanding of which, Maurice Victor, another trainee of the Unit, made, in later, years, significant contributions. Alexander also made fundamental studies of the syndromes of the cerebral vessels. Merritt and John Romano described alcoholic cerebellar degeneration, an important contribution neglected for many years until Victor (by then working at the Massachusetts General Hospital) again called attention to it.

Following Putnam's resignation, Houston Merritt acted as Chief until the appointment of Derek Denny-Brown in 1942. This was a difficult time in which to assume the Directorship of the Unit. Because of the war, many staff and house officers had left, and Denny-Brown himself came only on the condition that he continued to be available to the British government, and he served in the Army, reaching the rank of Brigadier General. He went to India at the end of the War to study the neurological nutritional disorders of prisoners of war. He not only became Director of the Unit at the Boston City Hospital, but in 1946 was given the title of James Jackson Putnam Professor of Neurology, James Ayer having vacated the post by retirement. Despite the initial disruptions caused by the war, and the absence of the Director and many of the staff, the Unit flourished during his twenty-five years as Director, and his impact on American neurology was profound. Denny-Brown was a New Zealander who had worked with Sherrington at Oxford and was, in fact, a co-author of Sherrington's last book. His early contributions to neurophysiology, including his studies of red and white muscle, were major works. Denny-Brown, however, was a strong believer in the importance of the neurological clinician-researcher, and the leading theme of his research was the interplay between neurophysiology and the clinic. His contributions were many.

He was responsible for the introduction of electromyography as a clinical tool. He carried out basic research on the bladder and developed the technique of cystometrography. In a series of studies over many years, he clarified the physiology of the motor system and the disordered physiology of movement disorders. Even after his retirement, he spent five years in elucidating congenital double athetosis by a series of detailed studies on lesions of the putamen in the monkey. His work carried out during the war, on trauma to peripheral nerve and brain, remains a classic contribution in this area. He developed the first successful treatment of Wilson's Disease, with dimercaprol (BAL). He was the first to describe the nonmetastatic neurological complications of carcinoma, and the first to describe the syndrome of hereditary radicular sensory neuropathy. He was the author of the classic studies on parietal lobe diseases.

During this period many other contributions came out of the Unit. Adams and Joseph Foley described the syndrome of hepatic encephalopathy and its EEG changes. Lahut Uzman described the aminoaciduria of Wilson's Disease. Fundamental studies on the metabolic specializations of different types of muscle fiber, on complications of alcoholism, and on cerebrovascular disease were produced during this period.

As noted, the Unit had fulfilled its original aim to produce investigators and academicians. Nearly 800 papers have been published up to 1973. In forty-three years the Unit produced at least forty-four full professors. In fact, in 1964 Denny-Brown pointed out that nearly half of all the heads of university departments of neurology in the United States had spent significant periods there.

Dr. Denny-Brown retired in 1968. Norman Geschwind became James Jackson Putnam Professor of Neurology in 1969. Dr. Geschwind had studied under Denny-Brown as a medical student and had later been his chief resident in 1955–56. He had received his A.B. degree at Harvard in 1947 and his M.D. degree in 1951. He interned at the Beth Israel Hospital and then studied in England. For a time he was Chief of Neurology at the Boston Veterans Administration Hospital and later Professor of Neurology at Boston University. He brought a new interest to the Unit, involving the aphasias and related disorders and in a broader sense the study of behavior as related to the brain—an area that had received little interest among neurologists for many years. Dr. Geschwind is the only neurological department head for whom this long-neglected subject was a major area of interest and has been primarily responsible for the revival of research on it. He organized in the American Academy of Neurology the first course on the neurology of behavior, and has offered the first elective course in this area at the Harvard Medical School. The number of papers given in this field at the major neurological meetings has risen sharply in recent years, most of them by former trainees of Dr. Geschwind.

Dr. Geschwind's contributions include the description of the first modern patient with the syndrome of the corpus callosum, and detailed studies with pathological confirmation of other disorders of the higher functions, including pure alexia and isolation of the speech area. He described the first patient ever recorded to have epilepsy induced by his own speech, as well as presenting the first description of dementia in hereditary radicular sensory neuropathy. He described for the first time the common occurrence of pure writing disorders in confusional states.

His work has stressed the anatomical analysis of disorders of the higher functions, which has shown up in his analysis of the aphasias and callosal syndromes and of the apraxias, common and remarkable disorders that had previously been almost entirely neglected. He demonstrated that contrary to widely held views, cerebral dominance is the result of grossly evident anatomical asymmetries of the speech cortex, which opens new avenues of research on language, dominance, and recovery. He has been concerned with the evolution of language in relation to the evolution of the brain and has advanced a testable theory of the neurological alterations which may underlie language.

His work has been guided by the principle that in the field of the higher functions the clinician-researcher still remains an important and indispensable source of insights for basic research and that the understanding of behavior will lie most importantly in the understanding of cerebral circuitry. The stress in his training program has been on the production of clinicians who will be alert to the important stimuli from the clinic for basic research. Unlike many others, he believes that teaching hospital training centers should concentrate on the production of clinician-researchers. He believes that the great expansion of residency programs in academic centers has often led to the dilution of academic stimulation and has, therefore, reduced the size of his own programs. His emphasis an anatomy as basic to an understanding of behavior has led him to set up a neuroanatomy laboratory in the Unit, which became the leading contributor to the study of cortical connections in the primate. Dr. Geschwind maintained the last significant portion of the formerly glorious Harvard establishment at the Boston City Hospital. He hauled down the flag in June 1975.

The Children's Hospital also participated in the awakening of neurology which occurred in Boston in the mid-1920's. Dr. Bronson Crothers was appointed Neurologist there in 1920, and a separate department was organized around him in 1928. Dr. Crothers was born in upstate New York, the son of a clergyman. He received his M.D. degree at Harvard in 1909 and interned at the Children's and Massachusetts General Hospitals. At the start of World War I he volunteered for service in the Royal Army Medical Corps, later transferring to the United States Army. He worked with the famous English neurologists Henry Head and George Riddoch. On his return here he made the clinical study of cerebral palsy his specialty and was a pioneer in this field. He believed that in some cases cerebral palsy was due to unskillful obstetrical procedures, and he said so. He had few friends among obstetricians. He became Clinical Professor of Pediatrics in 1944 and held that post until his death.

In 1961 money was raised to endow a chair named in Dr. Crothers' honor. The first man to occupy it was Dr. L. Lahut Uzman, who was known to be fatally ill when appointed and who died soon thereafter. The second incumbent was Charles F. Barlow, who was appointed Bronson Crothers Professor of Neurology in 1963. He had received his M.D. degree from the University of Chicago and had been Associate Professor of Medicine (Neurology) there since 1952. The position also involved simultaneous responsibility as the Neurologist-in-Chief at the Children's Hospital Medical Center. The Neurology Service which had been established there by Dr. Crothers was continued by Dr. Randolph K. Byers, and a somewhat expanded service is now Dr. Barlow's principal base of clinical operation. In addition, he was encouraged by Dean George Berry and fully supported by Dean Ebert, as well as by Drs. George Thorn and Howard Hiatt, to incorporate and develop the Neurological Services at the Peter Bent Brigham and the Beth Israel Hospitals into a teaching unit for students and a postgraduate training program for residents. This was done, and for a time there was a fully integrated academic program utilizing the resources of the institutions, with a roster of twelve residents, three or four medical students for a one-month clerkship, and a faculty of twenty people appointed in the Harvard Departmental Unit.

The third major area of Barlow's activity centers on the Children's Hospital Medical Center Research Program for Mental Retardation and Related Aspects of Human Development, of which he is Program Director. In addition to the research in neuroscience, which is his principal interest, this involved the hospital research effort in human genetics, under the leadership of Dr. Park Gerald, and behavioral sciences, under Drs.

Julius Richmond and Peter Wolff. Recently, Dr. Richard Sidman, Bullard Professor of Neuropathology, joined this program and moved his departmental unit to the Children's Hospital Medical Center. He will have overall responsibility for the Neuroscience Research Program. The Mental Retardation Research Program occupies five floors and appropriate supporting facilities in the new Children's Hospital Medical Center Pediatric Sciences Buildings. He himself while at Chicago had studied permeability phenomena in the brain and the uptake of labeled drugs by the brain tissue of animals.

A formal neuropathology program was also instituted at the McLean Hospital, under the direction of Dr. Alfred Pope as Professor of Neuropathology. After he completed his postdoctoral training in general pathology and neuropathology, and in biological chemistry, Professor Pope was given the task, in 1946, of developing an independent unit in chemical neuropathology within the then newly established McLean Hospital Research Laboratory, with Dr. Jordi Folch-Pi as Director. The general goals of this unit have been investigations in quantitative neurochemical pathology having maximum capabilities for correlations between biochemical findings and normal or morbid microscopic anatomy. For this the principles and techniques of quantitative histochemistry as developed by K. Linderstrom-Lang and associates were adopted as the methods of choice. A program was undertaken utilizing this methodology for analysis of micro samples derived from the nervous systems of experimental animals and of man in health and disease. In recent years isolated cell lines of brain cellular constituents cultured *in vitro* by Dr. Harvey M. Shein were similarly studied.

Implementation of this program required the establishment of a full technological repertoire in micro-structural chemistry and enzymology, as well as neurohistology, and provided a facility with full possibilities for research and research training in microchemical neuropathology. From 1951 to 1971 Dr. Pope was fortunate to have as a close associate in both investigative and research training aspects, Dr. Helen Hess, now of the National Eye Institute.

Dr. Pope's special interest from the outset has been an approach to the molecular pathology of mental disease by means of a long-range core study on the microchemical anatomy and pathology of the human cerebral cortex. A systematic survey of the structural-chemical and enzymological fine structure of the frontal isocortex has been carried out in order to establish its elementary quantitative chemoarchitectonics. In addition, comparative observations have been made in relation to the major psychoses and presenile dementias. The general survey phase of this investigation has been completed and attention is now being focused on indices of protein turnover and its control by comprehensive studies on the enzymology of proteolysis within the architectonic layers and sublayers of the primate isocortex.

The final person to be discussed is Dr. Paul I. Yakovlev, one of the most brilliant minds ever to apply itself to the problem of synthesizing the complex phenomena that underlie brain function. He has brought to this enterprise not only a remarkable intellect and the ability to read many languages but also a massive knowledge of all the pertinent literature going back several centuries.

He came of a long line of military surgeons in the Czars' armies, and true to family tradition he entered the Military Medical Academy in St. Petersburg at the age of twenty in 1914. He graduated in 1919 and, the Russian revolution being in progress, made his hazardous way across the frozen sea to Finland. In 1920 he was able to get to London and then to Paris, where he studied with Pierre Marie and was given an M.D. degree in 1925. In Russia he had also studied under I. P. Pavlov, A. A. Maximov, W. M. Bekhterev, and L. I. Orbeli.[1] In France his chief became F. J. Babinski, under whom he prepared his doctoral thesis. In the United States he came under the protection of Stanley Cobb. He was buried in a succession of laboratory posts at a number of state hospitals in Massachusetts and Connecticut, and for a time was Associate Professor of Neurology at Yale. His research program took place on three planes: thalamocortical connections, development of the human forebrain, and neurological malformation.

Thalamocortical connections. The development of neurosurgery in the past thirty-five years fascinated Yakovlev as a natural means of investigating the anatomical cerebral mechanisms specifically of human motility and behavior. After the late thirties, he began systematically to collect the autopsy material and clinical biographical data of patients who have had surgical interventions for relief of grave societal maladaptions, crippling motor disorders, and unmanageable states of pain and chronic distress. The role of the thalamus and its connections with the cerebral cortex was the central problem in the rationalization of the neurosurgical interventions for therapeutic ends. His studies established a new concept of human brain function—namely, that in contrast to other primates the frontal lobes in man are *emancipated* from the thalamic afferents and therefore from the tutelage of the thalamic influences on human conscious activity (behavior). Thus there is an anatomical basis for the empirical fact that only man can interpose a symbolic representation of his conscious act between the instinctive drive to an act and the act that consummates the drive.

Development of the human brain. This also attracted Yakovlev's interest. In 1959 he welcomed the opportunity to collect and study in the following thirteen years a large and unique collection of autopsy material of fetuses and nonviable neonates through his participation in the peri-natal research project launched in 1958 on a national scale by the National Institutes of Health. The program of his studies of the autopsy material of the fetal nervous system followed his interest in the histo-anatomical criteria of the growth and development of the human brain in relation to the maturation of behavior. The contributions he regards with the most personal satisfaction are those which have contributed to comprehension of facts that were not new in themselves. He has cited the study (with A.-R. Lecours) of the "schedule" of myelination of different fiber systems and regions of the human forebrain. He and his colleagues have shown that myelination is not a finite process that terminates in the first year or two after birth but, in some fiber systems, continues well beyond the fourth decade of life. The chart of the "cycles of myelination" of the major fiber systems of the forebrain and brainstem in relation to age, in a large statistical sample of several hundreds of cerebra from the fourth fetal month to the ninth decade, has provided a normal standard for the studies of myelination in man.

On a sample of 181 fetal brains, from 14 fetal weeks to term, he has shown (with P. Rakic) that the pyramidal tracts from *both* hemispheres are distributed with a torque preferentially to the *right* side of the spinal cord in more than 80 percent of individuals.[2] The same ratio between the torques to the right and to the left side was found in the distribution of the pyramidal tracts below decussation in the brains of adults.

In a study of the development of nuclei of the thalamus and of the cerebral cortex, Yakovlev has shown the homology of structure and homeochrony of differentiation of the nuclei of the thalamus with the development and differentiation of the cortical areas to which they project. The data gathered in this study provided the basis for his conception of the development of the three longitudinal zones of the wall of the forebrain in relation to the development of the three spheres of motility (behavior): visceral, expressive emotional and effective transactional, and the *derived* modalities of the specifically human (societal) experience: symbolized thought, language, and manufacture (technology).

Malformations of the forebrain. A study of these was a means toward the end of unraveling the fundamental plan of morphological development of this area. In 1930, while working in the autopsy room of the Monson State Hospital (Palmer, Massachusetts), Yakovlev chanced to come across a grossly malformed yet symmetrical brain of a two-year-old child whom he had studied clinically. The malformation was baffling. Not having the necessary laboratory facilities nor sufficient experience, Yakovlev borrowed $1,000 and went to Switzerland, taking the specimen with him. The experience of about eight months under the late Professor M. Minkowski (1883–1972) at the Monakow's Institute in Zürich was the beginning of his planned anatomical studies and of a unique histoanatomical collection of the serial brain sections which he has built during the following forty years of peregrinations in different state institutions (1926–67), Yale Medical School (1947–51), and Harvard, to the present time.

He has published singly and in collaboration with his students some fourteen contributions to the study of different types of malformations. Of these contributions, he considers the most significant to be the studies of the congenital symmetrical clefts in the cerebral mantle ("schizoencephalies," 1946), and the studies of the failures of cleavage of the end brain into "paired" cerebral hemispheres ("arrhinencephalies" of Kundrat, 1886, or "holotelencephalies," as he has proposed calling them to designate this common type of malformation, 1959). In these investigations he started from the assumption that such malformations represent curtailments of the fundamental plan of brain development and can be regarded and simplified models of the "normal" human brain. The studies of schizoencephalies (with R. C. Wadsworth, 1946) dealt with symmetrical defects in the brain wall, generally referred to either as "porencephalies" (Kundrat, 1886) or "hydranencephalies" (Cruveilhier, 1835). In the studies he has clarified the confusion of two distinct issues involved in the origin of these symmetrical clefts: that of their formal origin (the "things caused") and that of their causal origin ("the causes" of things). He has shown the histopathological and anatomical features which permit distinguishing a telencephalic defect in the brain wall resulting from (caused by) a congenital or early acquired encephaloclastic lesions (vascular, infective-inflammatory, traumatic) from the symmetrical clefts arising as a result of the hemispheric evaginations, long before the embryonal brain walls are vascularized.

Studies of the failures of cleavage of the originally median telencephalic vesicle into paired olfactory buds and cerebral hemispheres, with a resulting "holospheric" (rather than hemispheric) brain, opened a new field for thought and investigation—the field of pro-morphology of the forebrain of vertebrates and man. Some of the baffling anomalies of brain development became understandable in the light of the results of these studies of "arrhinencephalies." His chief contribution is to have drawn to attention these malformations as evidence of the morphogenetic ablaterality of the forebrain.

The Collection of Normal and Pathological Anatomy and Development of the Human Brain is the product of Yakovlev's vision and enterprise over a period of forty-two years (1930–72). It represents approximately a quarter of a million preparations of whole brain serial sections of more than one thousand human cerebra prepared following a strictly uniform method. The variables due to technical artifacts are thus reduced to a minimum.

In the past twenty years of his work the Collection has become a national resource of histoanatomical research documentation and has been used by several hundred scholars and research workers in neurology in this country and abroad. The Collection is unique, not merely because of its size and volume (27 tons of glass) but because of the systematic method by which it has been built. The Collection holds a wide range of neuroanatomical information not available anywhere else:

(1) Normative cerebra from fourth week of gestation to tenth decade (over 300 cerebra)

(2) Stereotactically marked cerebra of adults without neurological or psychiatric disease (56 cerebra)

(3) Neurosurgical collection. Cerebra of individuals who have been operated on for relief of psychiatric or neurological symptoms and died from intercurrent disease with postoperative follow-up from a few months to several years (over 150 cerebra)

(4) Cerebrovascular collection. Cerebra of individuals who suffered a single stroke and survived from several months to several years (over 200 cerebra)

(5) Malformations (over 200 cerebra)

(6) Comparative Anatomical collection (primates and cetacea—over 100 cerebra)

(7) Neuropathological collection of cerebra of individuals with congenital or early acquired encephalopathies (cerebral palsies), extra-pyramidal disorders, and degenerative and metabolic disease (over 200 cerebra)

The Collection contains information to answer questions that require a large statistical sample of technically comparable exponent material for anatomical research in the following areas:

(1) Cranio-cerebral topography

(2) Rate of growth, development, and involution of the human brain

(3) Clinical localization of symptoms (lesions) in the brain and of function of the brain.

(4) Physical anthropology and encephalometry

The Collection is by far the greatest monument of classical neuropathology of all time and all places.

Dr. Yakovlev was Clinical Professor of Neuropathology during his later years of academic service. At the present writing he is 82 and is continuing his studies with undiminished vigor and undimmed brilliance.

Chapter Nineteen

Psychiatry

D URING the Eliot era, psychiatric disorders were the responsibility of neurologists, because all mental phenomena were considered—quite properly—to be manifestations of the function of parts of the brain, the main part of the central nervous system. However, with the move to the Great White Quadrangle in 1906, a different approach was initiated.

The decades of 1890–1910 saw ferment and enthusiasm in European psychiatry, owing largely to the remarkable clinical writings of Emil Kraepelin and the even more outstanding clinical discussions of Ernst von Krafft-Ebing, who unfortunately disgraced himself by writing a lurid book, *Psychopathia Sexualis*, and thereby lost his well-deserved former status. (The book, however, became a great success among American college undergraduates of the 1920's and 1930's.) The feeling of some at Harvard was that this new clinical material should be introduced into the curriculum, and the Commonwealth of Massachusetts cooperated by building the Boston Psychopathic Hospital as a branch of the Boston State Hospital and a part of the State Hospital System. It was opened in 1912 within easy walking distance of the School.[1] Its first Director was Elmer E. Southard, an extraordinarily perceptive and sympathetic clinician, who had received his Bachelor's degree at Harvard College in 1897 and his M.D. degree at the Medical School in 1901. While at the College and for years thereafter, he was much under the influence of William James and Josiah Royce. In 1904 he became Instructor in Neuropathology, and from 1909 until his death in 1920 he was Bullard Professor of Neuropathology. He was convinced that the microscope would ultimately reveal the secrets of his patients' illnesses. (It is worthy of note that the Medical School believed that clinical responsibilities were part of the duties of a neuropathologist.) In 1920 the Boston Psychopathic Hospital was made a separate entity, and a Professor of Psychiatry was sought to undertake the expanded teaching. Psychiatry became part of the required third-year curriculum.

The choice for the Professorship was Charles Macfie Campbell. Dr. Campbell had been born in Scotland in 1876 and received all of his higher education in Edinburgh, where he finally was granted his M.D. degree in 1911. After obtaining his Ch.B. degree in 1902, he studied in France with Pierre Marie and in Germany with Franz Nissl and Emil Kraepelin, following which he interned at the Royal Edinburgh Infirmary.

In 1904 he came to this country to work with Adolf Meyer at the Psychiatric Institute at Ward's Island, New York. He served there until 1911, went to the Bloomingdale Hospital (Cornell) as First Assistant Physician until 1913, and then went with Meyer to Johns Hopkins as Associate Professor of Psychiatry until 1918. After military service, he came to Harvard in 1920 as Professor of Psychiatry and also served as Director of the Boston Psychopathic Hospital. He held these positions until 1943. The most notable of his early publications was perhaps his 1914 paper on the psychogenic background of the manic-depressive psychosis. In this, and his many other writings, he emphasized the factors in life situations that might lead to mental disorders. He derogated both physiology and psychoanalysis in his interpretations of mental phenomena, choosing to stay close to the clinical manifestations that the patients presented. It should be remembered that, taking the country as a whole, the mental hospital beds were occupied almost entirely by persons either with pellagra or with cerebral syphilis, or both. Massachusetts had many patients with syphilis, but pellagra was rare. In the middle twenties, Dr. Julius von Wagner Jauregg discovered the fever treatment of cerebral syphilis, and Dr. Harry C. Solomon became an expert in this field. He was the logical successor to Dr. Campbell, although by the time the latter retired, cerebral syphilis had become much less of a problem.

Following the Harvard Medical School custom, Dr. Solomon held dual posts: at the Medical School and at the Boston Psychopathic Hospital. He very soon became distinguished in the field of psychiatry in the United States. At the Boston Psychopathic Hospital he was a leader in the inauguration of a series of children's clinics in mental health, all of which were important in training, research, and treatment. As a teacher Dr. Solomon provided an optimum setting for the teaching of medical students and young physicians and the conduct of research in the complex field of psychiatry. As a physician he minimized the bolted doors and prison-like atmosphere that had become common as a result of disappointment with the "milieu therapy"—called "moral treatment"—of the mid-nineteenth century. Of course, during his tenure, to the pellagra and cerebral syphilis that had already become curable were added the beneficial effects of electroshock therapy for depressions and of the phenothiazines and reserpine for schizophrenia.

For reasons never made clear Dr. Solomon suddenly came out strongly for the Freudian concept of brain function and its disorders, although he remained basically a neuropathologist and cannot be charged with the almost overwhelming presence of analysts in the United States.

At present the Massachusetts Mental Health Center is a psychiatric hospital operating under the supervision of the Commissioner of Mental Health of the Commonwealth of Massachusetts. The Center's budget is recommended by the Commissioner to the State Legislature. The Center is free to select its own University affiliations, but in general, since it is a state-supported institution, it encourages association with the three medical schools in Boston. The close relationship of the major portion of the teaching and research programs to Harvard was a matter of considerable interest to the directors, but there is no written agreement between the Center and the Medical School.

The development of centers for psychiatric study at the general hospitals in the Harvard orbit gave rise to an awareness of need for definitions of policy. An Ad Hoc Committee was formed. The concepts concerning the development of psychiatry at Harvard are very well stated in the "Report of the Ad Hoc Committee Appointed to Consider How Best to Strengthen Psychiatry at Harvard," October 23, 1958.[2] In its deliberations the Committee considered especially the need for maintaining a strong clinical unit for psychiatric teaching and research at the Massachusetts Mental Health Center, the need for a fundamental approach to psychiatry and the behavioral sciences at the Harvard Medical School, and the positions and relationships of the heads of the several psychiatric units in the Harvard Medical Center—that is, Dr. Erich Lindemann and the group at the Massachusetts General Hospital, Dr. Alfred Stanton and the group at the McLean Hospital, Dr. Elvin Semrad and the group at the Massachusetts Mental Health Center, Dr. George Gardner and the group at the Judge Baker Guidance Center and the Children's Hospital, Dr. Grete Bibring and the group at the Beth Israel Hospital, Dr. Henry Fox and the group at the Peter Bent Brigham Hospital, Dr. Philip Solomon and the group at the Boston City Hospital, and the relationship of the Boston Psychoanalytic Institute to the Departments of Neurology and Psychiary at Harvard.

As the Ad Hoc Committee pointed out, the Director of the Massachusetts Mental Health Center, in addition to his clinical responsibilities and interests in stimulating investigation in the field of mental disease, must, of necessity, perform a number of important functions with relationship to the Department of Mental Health and the Massachusetts Legislature. It has become clear that the quality of patient care, the level to which research studies were carried on, and the facilities of the Center made available for teaching are all directly related to a pleasant relationship between the Director of the Center and the Commissioner of Mental Health. The enthusiasm and interest of the Commissioner of Mental

Health for the Center can clearly influence in many ways the effectiveness of the Center.

A definite attempt had been made by Dr. Jack R. Ewalt when he was Commissioner of Mental Health (1952–58) to increase the fulltime senior personnel under the Center's Director in order to provide for the Director adequate support in directing the clinical and research activities of the Center as well as the Center's "hotel" functions. The building program at the Center, the rapid expansion in research facilities, the relationship with other psychiatric hospitals in the Commonwealth whereby the exchange of patients was remarkably facilitated by the Commissioner—all these have increased the effectiveness of the Center and have enhanced its national reputation for excellent clinical care, research, and teaching. They result, in part, from the activities of Ewalt when he was Commissioner of Mental Health and strongly supported Dr. Harry C. Solomon. These things together have helped to create an unusually stimulating and productive environment at the Massachusetts Mental Health Center.

It seemed unlikely to the Ad Hoc Committee that an individual primarily concerned with a large investigation program could meet other obligations basic to the successful administration of such a unit as the Massachusetts Mental Health Center. It appeared that the ideal candidate to head the Center would need to be an experienced clinician and teacher with broad interests in research and the capacity to deal easily with administrative matters. At the time the Committee's report was made, in 1952, Dr. Jack R. Ewalt was under consideration for the dual post as Dr. Harry Solomon's successor. He was accepted and designated Bullard Professor of Psychiatry. Dr. Ewalt has perhaps been best known in recent years for his work as Director of the Joint Commission on Mental Illness and Health.

The Commission's final report, *Action for Mental Health*, was released in March 1961. The American Psychiatric Association's Council had the following to say about it in January 1962:

The Council of the American Psychiatric Association agrees with and urges the implementation of the basic objectives of the national mental health program as outlined by ACTION FOR MENTAL HEALTH, the Final Report of the Joint Commission on Mental Illness and Health. This program, translated into action, will expand scientific knowledge of the mental illnesses; it will serve to overcome personnel shortages in psychiatric facilities of all kinds; it will harness all pertinent community resources to the task of treating and rehabilitating the mentally ill; and it will provide adequate financing to accomplish these purposes. The very publication of ACTION FOR MENTAL

HEALTH marks a turning point of momentous social and cultural significance in the history of the mentally ill in America. It signals a departure from an attitude of rejection of the mentally ill to one of acceptance and determination to solve this national problem.

The Center has a large staff, with diverse backgrounds and interests. One of its more noteworthy members is Dr. Daniel H. Funkenstein, who has made an intensive study over the past sixteen years of medical-student career choices. He has been preoccupied with the characteristics that mark students who eventually enter the field of primary medical care. His goal is to obtain data that will help in solving problems of delivery of such care. He has identified four eras (dating back to 1910) of social responsibility: the general practice era—1910–35; the specialized practice era—1935–59; and the scientific technological era—1959–68. He has also identified the appearance of a new era in 1969—the community era. In this last, medical students have demanded the delivery of adequate medical care to all segments of society without bothering to define "adequate." This means better community health services and the provision of medical care for minority groups, and, as a nonsequitur, the admission of more candidates from minority groups to medical schools.

Dr. Funkenstein has proposed (1970) guidelines to facilitate the learning and personal development of medical students. He has suggested that the guidelines might correct what he has seen as a "fundamental dichotomy between the current needs of medical education and the developmental needs of students." It is his belief that the principal impediments to bridging the dichotomy are

the failure to apply modern knowledge of learning and personal education to the education of students; the long dependency in which students are kept; difficulties in financing a medical education; the absence of role models; the marked differences in values between faculty and students; and the educational philosophy of the faculty.

It now remains to validate these ideas.

When Dr. James B. Ayer, Head of Neurology at the Massachusetts General Hospital, made it plain that his department was no longer interested in psychiatric problems, as it had been under James Jackson Putnam, it became clear that the Hospital would need to establish a Department of Psychiatry. As noted in the previous chapter, an interesting choice for its head was made: Stanley Cobb, Bullard Professor of Neuropathology and Director of the Neurological Unit at the Boston City Hospital. Who initiated this remarkable idea—Dr. Cobb was admittedly not a psychiatrist—is not clear today, but that it was enthusiastically supported is evidenced by a large grant from the Rockefeller Foundation and a smaller one from the Commonwealth Fund. Dr. Cobb took the post in 1934.

When the Massachusetts General Hospital sought a new Psychiatrist-in-Chief for their expanded and reorganized program after Dr. Cobb's retirement, the choice fell on Erich Lindemann. Before coming to Harvard as Research Fellow in Neuropathology in 1935, Dr. Lindemann had been actively working with psychotic patients. During this period he investigated the efficacy of a barbiturate, sodium amytal, in opening up the mental functions of depressed and schizophrenic patients. Barbiturates have been widely used in the techniques known as narcosynthesis— that is, treatment of neuroses in which the patient recalls his suppressed memories. The "sodium amytal interview" is widely used in amnesias and other hysterical reactions.

As an experimental psychiatrist and psychologist, Dr. Lindemann, a pioneer in the observation and study of reactions to loss and grief, concentrated his research on the application of social science approaches to psychiatric problems. He discovered that an essential component of an emotional crisis like, for example, that precipitated by death, is the change in the individual's social system. Adaptation to the loss of an important person in one's life demands a redefinition and reorganization of the whole scheme of roles.

Although Dr. Lindemann's first studies in emotional crises were based upon loss or grief, his interest in the sociological aspects of psychiatry developed throughout the thirty years he was associated with Harvard and the Massachusetts General Hospital. This interest in changes of social structures that affect an individual's mental well being actually began in 1942, when he was asked to aid victims of the Cocoanut Grove fire in Boston, where some 500 perished. In 1948 he was responsible for establishing the first community mental health center in the United States, the purpose of which was to study community conditions that might lead to mental disaster in certain individuals. As Director of the Wellesley Human Relations Service for many years, he focused on preventive psychiatry and preservation of mental and emotional health. The Center functions in clinical, consultative, and educational fields. The clinical staff provides help in planning the care of individuals with intense psychiatric disturbance, although it is geared first of all toward individuals and families seeking help with lesser emotional difficulties: support in unexpected life crises and guidance in ordinary daily situations. The Consultative service involves close working relationships with other professional individuals and groups. The Educational function embraces the hope that public understanding of an interest in mental health objectives might occur. It was Dr. Lindemann's finding that there is considerable variation in the adaptive processes among the several economic classes.

During this period the Department of Psychiatry received substantial additional funds by designating part of its space as the Hall-Mercer Hospital. With the support of the National Institutes of Mental Health, Dr. Lindemann was enabled to head the West End Research Project, the first project of its kind in the United States. In 1957 some 2,600 families in the West End of Boston were obliged to relocate. A systematic appraisal of the social and psychological stresses involved in relocation was made by Dr. Lindemann and his colleagues. The approach was effected through a series of interviews designed to study such problems as family life, community life, adaptation to stress, and the meaning of the physical environment. It is somewhat surprising that, as the investigator discovered, the financial aspect of relocation was a relatively minor consideration of the uprooted families. Much more significant was the fact that these families were being separated from a cluster of people upon whom they could depend. When the five-year project was completed in 1962, Professor Herbert Gans, a sociologist from the University of Pennsylvania and a member of the Advisory Committee of the West End Research Project, wrote a book, *The Urban Villagers*, which has come to be recognized as a blueprint of poignant and hitherto unrecognized human ties, needs, and behavior.[3]

In 1954 Dr. Lindemann was appointed to the position of Professor of Psychiatry at the Harvard Medical School and Chief of Psychiatry at the Massachusetts General Hospital. He retired in 1967, to be succeeded by Leon Eisenberg, formerly of Johns Hopkins. Dr. Eisenberg is known for having participated in activities relating to both public health and preventive psychiatry, and has devoted considerable time to studies of the public health implications of inadequate foster care provided by many welfare agencies. Other studies have been concerned with the basis of academic achievement as it relates to social class. In these he believes that he has demonstrated the importance of environmental factors on academic ability and achievement. His early studies in the field of child psychiatry were related to infantile autism and childhood schizophrenia. Somewhat later he investigated the effectiveness of pharmacologic and psychologic treatment of children. In this study he found that stimulant drugs were surprisingly effective in the treatment of hyperkinetic behavior disorders. Attention was improved by the treatment, and so were vigilance and learning.

About the same time that Dr. Eisenberg was appointed clinical head of psychiatry at the Massachusetts General Hospital, a great step forward was made in expansion of research on mental disease. Dr. Seymour Kety was appointed Professor of Psychiatry and given the mission of developing biochemical approaches to the problems of his field. Dr. Kety's early research on shock, in the Huntington Laboratories of the Harvard Medical School at the Massachusetts General Hospital in 1942–43, accompanied great interest in the field of cerebral circulation. While he was at the University of Pennsylvania, Dr. Kety developed a method by which inert gases like nitrous oxide in low concentrations could be used to determine quantitatively the rates of cerebral blood flow and metabolism in man and other animals. The resulting method has been utilized in a wide variety of physiological and pathological states.

By the time he came to Harvard, Dr. Kety had been recognized throughout the western world as a distinguished neuroscientist. In a speech delivered at the American Association for the Advancement of Science (1967), he commented on the difficulties that beset the investigator who seeks to examine the role of disturbed biochemical processes in mental illness—"the paucity of animal models and the inaccessibility of the brain."[4] The situation is different with many other disorders, such as infectious diseases, atherosclerosis, or cancer, for their occurrence in similar form in lower animals has greatly facilitated study of the disease process and made possible preclinical testing for therapeutic efficacy. Most psychiatric diseases have no counterpart in animals, requiring that crucial research on their etiology, pathogenesis, or treatment be carried out in patients suffering from the disorder. As Kety pointed out, cerebrospinal fluid is carefully protected against change in composition, and the brain's blood flow is so voluminous as to dilute to insignificance all but the metabolic outputs of its large energy requirements. A disturbed biochemical situation, however, such as that found in phenylketonuria or galactosemia, is "extracerebral in origin and affects the brain by virtue of its generalized effects . . ." These ailments can be discovered by analyzing the blood or urine. Continuing studies, particularly of mental illness, search for undescribed general defects must go on, but the fact must be faced that biochemical errors that are limited to the brain or its regions will not exhibit themselves under such examination. Johann Fichte wrote that the brain secretes thought and consciousness much as the liver secretes bile. Although this is a grand oversimplification, one studies mental states and behavior, and these evidences, one hopes, may provide sensitive indicators of biochemical processes which are subject to modification but which cannot be examined directly.

Dr. Kety has pointed out that formulation of a hypothesis that links mental state or disorder to a specific chemical component is one of the steps sought. Secondly, animal studies may have some use in indicating that the concentration of that component in the brain may be altered by administration of an appropriate precursor. Thirdly, clinical trial under proper precautions relative to safety and consent attempts to bring about the desired neurochemical change in association with controlled observation and objective evaluation of the psychological and behavioral changes that may presumably be associated with the chemical alterations. Such an approach has been employed in studies of schizophrenia, wherein a large variety of amino acids has served as substrates.

It must be agreed that, in many instances, one or more of the three ideal requirements of precursor-load studies were not fulfilled, and even where these can be carefully observed, the indirect nature of the approach restricts the extent of the conclusions to be safely drawn from such studies. It is impossible to transpose with surety animal doses to man, and very often chemical studies cannot employ the dosage levels that one may use in animals. Frequent sensitivity of peripheral tissues in humans limits the levels that can be safely induced. Consistent mental or behavioral effects associated with the administration of any precursor are not by themselves sufficient to validate hypotheses that attribute such action to one or another of their products. Kety comments, however: "Two interesting findings, relevant and perhaps significant to schizophrenia and depression, respectively, have recently come about by the use of the precursor-load concept." The strategy provides a useful and at this time unique approach to the neurochemistry of the mental state. The wide range of psychometric and performance evaluation that is possible in man, in addition to his ability to report some objective changes, makes such an approach especially useful for eliciting possible relationships between a considerable variety of metabolic intermediates in normal or pathological mental processes. It should be kept in mind that the "value of such techniques, as in the use of drugs for exploring etiology and pathogenesis, is in the development and exploration of hypotheses rather than their crucial testing."[5] Institutional support of the intensity and breadth given Dr. Kety for work in the field of the biochemistry of mental disease is in the tradition that was born at the McLean Hospital with Otto Folin and continued there.

The psychiatric accomplishments of the Massachusetts General Hospital should not omit the excellent studies in pain by Chester Jones and William Chapman, both internists. Similarly, there were in the 1920's and 1930's remarkable observations on neurocirculatory asthenia, a syndrome that occurs in anxious persons and some others. These studies of cardiorespiratory physiology made by Dr. Mandel Cohen, a psychiatrist, Dr. Paul D. White, and their colleagues showed that a defect in oxidative metabolism, of unknown mechanism, is at the root of the symptoms.

The development of psychiatry at the Beth Israel Hospital began with the Austrian refugee psychoanalysts, first Felix Deutsch and then, for a longer period, Grete Bibring. She is a remarkable woman, able to give understanding and comfort to other women and not overly concerned with precise Freudian explanations of the phenomena. She was succeeded on her retirement by Dr. John C. Nemiah who has studied especially the psychiatric problems often faced by medical and surgical patients, both in the hospital and at home. He has a paramount interest in the teaching of undergraduate medical students and postdoctoral fellows. Dr. Nemiah's textbook, *Foundations of Psychopathology* (1961), has become a standard text for many medical schools in the United States.

Psychiatry at the Boston City Hospital has undergone the expected vicissitudes and some that were not expected. At first it was more or less catch-as-catch-can, mainly diagnostic with respect to the huge number of confused, comatose, or aberrantly behaving patients who enter, with little or no opportunity for treatment. Considering the circumstances, this Service, organized in the 1950's by Dr. Philip Solomon, did very well. It was apparent, however, that alcoholism was a major problem among the Hospital's clients, and Dr. Jack H. Mendelson was appointed Director of the Alcohol Study Unit of the Department of Psychiatry there. While at the Hospital, he initiated and became a national figure in studies involving the physiological and psychological effects of alcohol administration in chronic alcoholics, and the drinking patterns of alcoholics. He left in 1964 to join the U.S. Public Health Service but in 1970 was invited to return to Harvard as Professor of Psychiatry, to succeed Dr. Solomon. Dr. Mendelson's group has studied drug and alcohol consumption and abuse in man. It has carried out a series of studies to assess the efficacy of beta-adrenergic blocking drugs in the treatment of alcohol-related disorders. It has also carried out a series of studies to determine the relationship between alcohol ingestion and aggressive behavior, and on the biological and behavioral concomitants of marihuana use in man.

Other studies have been concerned with the demonstration under metabolic ward conditions that the alcohol-withdrawal syndrome represents a specific abstinence phenomenon. This group has made the first demonstraton that behavioral tolerance is associated with induced metabolic tolerance, in studies of C^{14} (radioactive carbon tagged) ethanol metabolism by alcoholic subjects. These studies indicate that alcoholics do not possess a unique mode of metabolic degradation of ethanol. The group demonstrated that alcohol withdrawal is usually associated with respiratory alkalosis, which, in turn, affects intracellular-extracellular electrolyte balance. In short, many of the basic issues of the biochemistry of alcohol ingestion have been or are in the process of being elucidated.

The Children's Hospital has also had a psychiatric department. It was greatly strengthened in 1953 by the appointment of George E. Gardner as Clinical Professor of Psychiatry at the School and as Director of the Judge Baker Guidance Center. Dr. Gardner was born in West Bridgewater, a descendant of three Mayflower passengers. He received his Bachelor's degree at Dartmouth College in 1925 and thereafter had an unusual career. At Harvard he became Master of Education in 1926, then received a Ph.D. degree in 1930 and an M.D. degree in 1937. He was Research Fellow in Education at the College from 1928 to 1930, and then became first Research Fellow and then Assistant in Pediatrics from 1936 to 1946. He was Lecturer in Clinical Psychology at the College from 1946 to 1949 and at the Medical School from 1950 to 1953, then becoming Clinical Professor of Psychiatry. In 1965 he became Professor of Psychiatry, a post he held until his retirement in 1970. He was also Lecturer on Social Relations from 1969 on and, unofficially, a lecturer on Pilgrim history. His unusual professional accomplishment fitted him well to deal with the emotional problems of children and their mothers.

Dr. Gardner was succeeded by Julius B. Richmond, who was given the titles of Professor of Child Psychiatry and Human Development at Harvard, Director of the Judge Baker Guidance Center, and Psychiatrist-in-Chief at the Children's Hospital Medical Center. He had received his basic education at the University of Illinois and at the University of Chicago, and received the M.D. degree in 1939 from the University of Illinois. His clinical training was undertaken first at the Cook County Hospital in Chicago. He held a number of posts but finally was Professor of Pediatrics at the University of Illinois (1950–53). He was Dean of the Medical Faculty of the State University of New York at Syracuse (1965–70).

Dr. Richmond was nominated Head of the Department of Preventive and Social Medicine at the Harvard Medical School in connection with the preceding recommendations of the (1970) Ad Hoc Committee and began to occupy the post in July 1971. He was the first Director of Project Head Start in the Office of Economic Opportunity and later, as Director of Health Affairs for that Office, developed the concept of the organization's funded comprehensive health clinics. These have been held in high regard as new models for the delivery of health care.

This account of psychiatry at Harvard would be incomplete and to some extent misleading if the dominant role of psychoanalysis in it for several decades after World War II were ignored. At the turn of the century, a dozen or more distinguished physicians and psychologists of Boston became active participants in the discussion and, at times, in the clinical testing of Freud's early work. It must be noted that these men very often lost interest later or became hostile. By 1906, however, James Jackson Putnam, Professor of Diseases of the Nervous System at Harvard, had published the first reports in English of clinical cases treated by Freud's new method. In 1911 Dr. Putnam with Dr. Ernest Jones founded the American Psychonanalytic Association. In 1930 a new group of physicians interested in analysis founded the Boston Psychoanalytic Society.

The first great landmark in American analysis was the publication in April 1906 of the first paper in English on the clinical use of psychoanalysis, by the Bostonian Dr. James Jackson Putnam.[6] It is remarkable that at such an early stage of clinical development, Putnam was able to recognize the difference between psychoanalysis and other therapies. Putnam's analyzed cases were from a small ward for the treatment of psychoneuroses, which he had created at the Massachusetts General Hospital. Richard Cabot had mentioned in 1907 that Freud's psychoanalysis was one of the methods of treatment practiced in the Massachusetts General Hospital.[7] However, Putnam was the only Bostonian of his era to make psychoanalysis and its "stalwart defense" his principal work.

It is a curious fact that most of Putnam's medical colleagues who had shared his interest in the discussion of Freud before 1900 had now become "impassioned critics," or, even worse, indifferent. Morton Prince had given up his early interest in work with Freud. Stanley Hall, who had invited Freud to Worcester in 1909, had become an Adlerian, even though, as recently as 1920, Hall referred to Freud as "the most original and creative mind in psychology of our generation."[8]

The role of psychoanalysis underwent a sudden expansion after World War II. Although psychoanalysts had been given teaching posts at Harvard before this, the decision of Dr. Harry Solomon, then Professor of Psychiatry, to support the Freudian dogma, led during his tenure to the appointment of Freud's disciples to the main teaching posts at most of the Harvard hospitals.

Sharp criticism of the post-World War II Harvard (Boston) psychiatric scene was leveled by Dr. William Sargant of St. Thomas's Hospital, London. In Sargant's view, during the prewar years American psychiatry led the world, and the top positions in British psychiatry were most easily obtained by those who had gone to the United States to work and study, in many cases sitting at the feet of the great Adolf Meyer at the Phipps Clinic in Baltimore. According to Sargant, the trend has now been reversed.[9]

Major foundations, such as the Rockefeller and the Ford, have, in recent times, made large grants to psychoanalytically oriented departments of psychiatry, at Harvard (and elsewhere).

Chapter Twenty

Dermatology

Boston, like most large cities in this country, has had a number of men who specialized in diseases of the skin. There was a hint of something discreditable about the specialty, because dermatologists were also syphilologists, and in addition their remedies were largely irrational and their classification poorly founded. Many were nevertheless good physicians. From the academic viewpoint the situation was not satisfactory because these men depended upon their practices for their livelihood. Accordingly, in 1914 the Edward Wigglesworth Professorship of Dermatology was established, funds having been received in 1906.

The first man to occupy the post was Chester North Frazier, who had received his M.D. degree at Indiana in 1917 and was also a Doctor of Public Health. Most of his early career was spent at Peking Union Medical College investigating and teaching dermatology and syphilology in China. His earliest publication is in the *China Medical Journal* in 1926. He left China when the revolution began, by which time he had published a considerable amount of work on experimental syphilis. He came to Harvard in 1949 and at the same time was given the post of Chief of Dermatology at the Massachusetts General Hospital. A man of great personal charm and obvious erudition (he had been Honorary Librarian at Peking Union), he nevertheless did not strike the spark that Boston dermatology needed.

On his retirement, both his posts went to Thomas B. Fitzpatrick. After receiving his M.D. degree at Harvard in 1945, he had interned in medicine at the Boston City Hospital. Following a period in the Army, he had a three-year fellowship in dermatology at the Mayo Clinic, and obtained a Ph.D. degree from the University of Minnesota. After a brief period at Michigan, he became Professor and Chief of Dermatology at Oregon. Thirteen years after leaving Boston, he returned as Dr. Frazier's successor.

Dr. Fitzpatrick has been an innovative person since his days as a medical student. In 1945, with several of his classmates at Harvard Medical School, he was the main force in editing the *Handbook of*

Medical Emergencies, which was first privately printed and later published by the Harvard University Press. During his internship he envisioned the future of dermatology not as an isolated, externally oriented specialty but as an integral part of medicine. This ambition to bring about the rapprochement of dermatology and internal medicine has now been fulfilled, partially through his efforts. Dr. Fitzpatrick has edited a large and definitive textbook, *Dermatology in General Medicine*, published in 1971 by McGraw Hill. It is the first multi-authored, comprehensive book in the history of the field and has had a profound influence on attitudes and approaches to dermatology by the medical student, medical and pediatric intern, and internist.

In collaboration with Dr. A. B. Lerner of Yale, Dr. Fitzpatrick has made important contributions to the field of melanin biology. Working together from 1946 to 1955, the two established the mechanism of melanin formation in man and demonstrated that tyrosinase was the enzyme in mammals and man that was responsible for melanin formation. In addition, during this period, they were the first to demonstrate that melanocyte-stimulating hormone (MSH) can produce generalized hyperpigmentation of human skin. During the years 1952 to 1957 Dr. Fitzpatrick clearly demonstrated an important difference in the level of tyrosinase in normal cells vis-à-vis malignant melanoma cells. As a Commonwealth Fellow in the Department of Biochemistry, Radcliffe Infirmary, Oxford, he and his assistant, Dr. M. Seiji, first isolated and characterized the subcellular organelles that contain tyrosinase and the metabolic units of melanin formation in vertebrates. They called this particle a melanosome. In recent years he has concentrated on the application to man of some of this knowledge of melanin pigmentation. He has made three important contributions in this area:

(1) Delineation of the so-called "ash-leaf" white macules as the distinctive diagnostic sign of tuberous sclerosis, a serious dominant trait causing mental retardation. This finding has permitted the diagnosis of tuberous sclerosis at birth, inasmuch as the ash-leaf macules are present in over 90 percent of the patients and can be visualized with the aid of a Wood's light. Wood's lights are now routinely used throughout the world for screening the mentally retarded.

(2) Demonstration of a giant melanosome, or macromelanosome, in the cafe-au-lait macules in neurofibromatosis. This has permitted a distinction on a light-and-electron-microscopic basis between the cafe-au-lait type pigmentation seen in neurofibromatosis and polyostotic fibrous dysplasia.

(3) Delineation of the differences between various races of man based on the presence or absence of aggreation of melanosomes within keratinocytes; in the Negro skin the melanosomes remain undisturbed

when they are transferred to the keratinocytes, whereas in the other races the melanosomes become aggregated, are surrounded by a membrane, and undergo a degradation; this latter particle is, in fact, a lysosome. It has been shown by Fitzpatrick's group and others that this aggregation of melanosomes in keratinocytes is a size-dependent phenomenon; in other words, if the melanosome is longer than one micron, it will remain as an isolated particle when transferred to the keratinocyte, whereas melanosomes less than one micron become aggregated.

Perhaps Dr. Fitzpatrick's most important contribution to clinical medicine is the description of the gross pathology of early primary malignant melanoma of the skin, which has permitted the diagnosis of very early lesions, as small as 2–3 mm in diameter. The detection of melanomas in very early stages of their development has resulted in a significant increase in the five-year survival rate.

Chapter Twenty-one

Anesthesiology

ANESTHESIOLOGY is an ancient part of medicine which showed little or no change until the mid-nineteenth century. A glance through the early case records of the Massachusetts General Hospital or of any other nineteenth-century hospital before the advent of anesthesia can, through a few chilling phrases, suggest those ominous times ("having secured pulleys and straps and the patient was placed on a stout oak table [where he was] held by assistants . . . The patient had a disposition to faint. [At the end of the operation] he was untied and returned to his bed"). All of these phrases could have applied equally well to the events of a thousand years or more before the time they were written. In this period pitilessness was urged by Celsus as an essential trait of the surgeon.

Before the introduction of anesthesia, speed was also essential. Sir Clifford Allbutt noted that surgeons were pitted one against the other like runners. He was the best surgeon, both for patient and onlooker, who broke the three-minute record in an amputation. In record-breaking operations no one could take the time for antiseptic precautions. But with the introduction of anaesthetics came the end of slapdash surgery. The theories of Pasteur and Lister were put into practice.

Great as its effect on surgery was, the introduction of inhalation anesthesia into medicine as the discipline of anesthesiology remained almost stationary for three quarters of a century. Devices and procedures for administering ether or chloroform were changed and changed again, but they remained essentially the same. Anesthesiology in practice took form as an eclectic rather than a scientific branch of medicine, and it continued to be taught to students as such into the 1930's.

A little-known aspect of Edward D. Churchill's professional life as Chief of Surgery at the Massachusetts General Hospital in the 1930's and 1940's was his great concern with anesthesia and its development. This can be studied in two phases—first, to describe what his vision was, and second, to show, pragmatically ("things are what their results are"), the consequences of this vision. Dr. Churchill early was aware that surgery could not soundly advance until the anesthesia of the 1920's had improved. At the time this was not a clichè. As far as surgery in general is concerned, he and his contemporaries possessed the necessary anatomical knowledge for invasion: they had technical control of hemostasis and asepsis, and certainly no one would have the temerity to say that the pioneers in those far-off days lacked the requisite surgical judgment. They lacked experience in the unknown area of the chest, however, and this was principally so because the shortcomings of anesthesia at that time made intervention there a fearful thing. (It is probable that Eliott C. Cutler lost, owing in large part to inadequate anesthesia, the opportunity to initiate the era of intracardiac surgery with his early unsuccessful attempts at mitral valvulotomy.)

As Dr. Churchill has said,

> The quickening within the Art brought about by experts who held the conviction that Anesthesia was a vital area of activity highlighted the fact that surgeons had been so preoccupied with the development of their own technology that once again they had overlooked a potential source of safety and comfort for their patients.
> ... When I first became responsible for undertaking open-chest operations it was necessary to build a device with which positive pressure could be maintained, with my own hand, intubate the patient and after placing him in position on the operating table, scrub up and embark on the thoracotomy![1]

It would be very wrong to imply that Dr. Churchill was the only one of his time with a scholarly outlook. One can mention four leading American contemporaries. Many in other countries were also struggling with problems of anesthesia. So were others in America—but these four were outstanding: Evarts Graham, Frederick A. Coller, Alfred Blalock, and Churchill himself. (Coller was not especially interested in thoracic surgery, but he belongs in this quartet for reasons that will soon become evident.) None is now alive.

Whatever tribute one can pay these men is long past due. One should be as explicit as possible, for, paradoxically enough, these four have been the targets of severe and unjustified criticism from some anesthetists who did not understand what profound regard these men had for the importance of anesthesia. Their concern was to put anesthesia on such a basis that it could take an honorable place within the university curriculum. Theirs was not a lack of interest in or appreciation of the importance of anesthesia but, rather, a deeper and broader interest than their critics had. Their resolve was that anesthesia must be developed on a scholarly basis equivalent to that required of other medical disciplines. Technical excellence, essential as that is, was alone not enough.

It is essential that certain basic issues be appreciated. Anesthesia is the bridge between two great disciplines: pharmacology and surgery. More than any one else within the hospital, the anesthetist has the opportunity to be the pharmacologist in caring for the sick. In this role he has extraordinary possibilities for advancing the study of human pharmacology. The close link of pharmacology and anesthesia begins in their common history: Modern pharmacology is one of the youngest of the basic medical sciences.[2] The growth of both as formal disciplines has occurred chiefly in the twentieth century.

Any one of a number of points might be chosen as the true beginning of the present Anesthesia establishment in the Massachusetts General Hospital and the Medical School. Reasonable consideration could be given to the founding of the Henry Isaiah Dorr Chair of Research and Teaching in Anesthetics and Anesthesia in 1917—the first endowed chair in anesthesia (and still one of only a few in the world). Dean David L. Edsall, who started so many things of continuing significance in the Harvard Medical School, also had a hand in initiating the modern period: in a letter of February 7, 1931, he informed Dr. Edward D. Churchill that President Lowell had appointed a committee to consider the use of the Dorr bequest, and named Dr. Churchill Chairman. Dr. Churchill was able to lead the way, in part, because of his vision, but also because Harvard had the good fortune to have received the Dorr endowment. In 1936 Beecher established the first laboratory devoted to and limited to the study of anesthesia and related problems: the Anaesthesia Laboratory of the Harvard Medical School at the Massachusetts General Hospital. The laboratory was preceded by the appointment of Howard H. Bradshaw as head of anesthesia at the Hospital. His appointment was moved by the General Executive Committee and approved by the Trustees in March 1933. Dr. Bradshaw's tenure was, however, terminated by his resignation on September 1, 1936, to return to the practice of surgery.

Henry K. Beecher had received his M.D. degree at Harvard in 1932. He trained in surgery at the Massachusetts General Hospital and for a year in the physiological laboratory of Professor August Krogh in Copenhagen (1935), after which he returned to the Massachusetts General and was offered the possibility of contending for the Dorr Professorship, endowed but never occupied, with the expectation that he would be named the first occupant if, after a five-year trial period, he seemed to merit the post. Dr. Beecher's initial appointment was, as with all such positions there, a dual one: In April 1936 he was appointed

Instructor in Anesthesia in the Harvard Medical School, while at the Massachusetts General Hospital he was appointed Assistant Anesthetist on May 1, to be designated Anesthetist on September 1, upon Dr. Bradshaw's departure.

One other crucial date remains to be recorded. The unanimous recommendation by the Dorr Fund Committee to the Committee of Full Professors of the Medical School on January 27, 1941, five years later, was that Dr. Beecher be appointed Dorr Professor. This was submitted by the President and Fellows of Harvard College in February 1941, and consented to by the Board of Overseers at their next meeting. This latter meeting occurred at the College of William and Mary in Virginia, when for the first time in three hundred years the Overseers met outside of Massachusetts. It was agreed that the appointee would be designated Henry Isaiah Dorr Professor of Research in Anesthesia.

Throughout the following thirty years, Dr. Beecher took an active part in anesthesia, both clinical and investigative. It was his view that anyone with a clinical title should participate actively in that specialty, a situation unfortunately hardly ever the case in the field of anesthesia at this time (1975), as far as the professors are concerned.

Beecher construed his scientific responsibilities broadly, and in the course of doing so devised methods now in world-wide use for the quantification of the effects of drugs on subjective responses. Principally, he worked with pain, but many other responses were also involved, such as drowsiness, sleep, nausea, and anxiety. These activities led to his designation as a founding father of scientific psychopharmacology.

As time passed it became evident to Dr. Beecher that a good many activities in scientific work were of questionable ethics. A considerable bombshell was exploded in 1966 by his paper "Ethics and Clinical Research."[3] In the ten years since, the antipathy aroused in the scientific community by this 1966 paper has largely subsided. It is now widely agreed that some types of human experimentation were and are not proper.

Toward the end of Dr. Beecher's career, he, with others (R. D. Adams, A. C. Barger, W. J. Curran, D. Denny-Brown, D. L. Farnsworth, J. Folch-Pi, E. I. Mendelson, J. P Merrill, J. Murray, R. Potter, R. Schwab, and W. H. Sweet), devised "A Definition of Irreversible Coma,"[4] which amounted to a definition of death—brain death. Others had previously thought along these same lines, notably Dr. Raymond D. Adams, a participant in the study.

Dr. Churchill's vision encompassed the establishment of a laboratory. It was, as mentioned, the first to be founded by an anesthetist and devoted solely to the study of anesthesia and related problems. Of course, many illustrious men had worked in this field: In 1799 twelve years before the founding of the Massachusetts General Hospital, Sir Humphry Davy, in Beddoes' Pneumatic Institution, carried out what A. J. Clark has called "a model of pharmacological research complete in all its stages" on nitrous oxide. Others who come easily to mind are John Snow, Claude Bernard, Joseph Clover, H. H. and K. H. Meyer, Ernst Overton, Otto Warburg—the list is long and distinguished and has been followed by a younger and impressive group. But the Laboratory here was *de novo* an anesthesia creation, not only intellectually but also physically, with fine quarters (now crowded) occupied for a dozen years. April 27, 1936, marks the date of establishment of the Anesthesia Laboratory of the Harvard Medical School at the Massachusetts General Hospital. Although excellent work on anesthesia had already been done in conjunction with a number of physiology, pharmacology, and biochemistry laboratories elsewhere and prior to this time, this laboratory was the first to be established by an anesthetist for work solely on anesthesia and related problems.

The origins of anesthesia—and, one might add, every subsequent development in this field—have been immersed in controversy. The establishment of anesthesia at Harvard followed the same pattern. As mentioned, the initial grant establishing the Dorr Chair had been received a dozen years before any proposals for its use were made. No sooner had Dr. Churchill undertaken to employ this unused fund at the Massachusetts General Hospital than three other Harvard hospitals clamored for it. The controversy was in the usual vigorous Harvard tradition. It is referred to here only to point out that Dr. Churchill's characteristic far-seeing, long-range planning was in evidence. Without it, there would certainly have been no Department and Laboratory at the Massachusetts General Hospital, at least not in their present forms.

According to the late Mr. George E. Vincent of the Rockefeller Foundation, doctors don't reason, they just rearrange their prejudices. There is no deterrent as good as a laboratory in preventing the easy rearrangement of prejudices. Although the quality of teaching need not always be immediately influenced by nearby research activities, it is always improved in the long-run. It is clear that there is a better selection of residents to choose from because of these activities.

However brave the vision may have been, it could not have led to concrete events without money, in generous amounts, supplied over many years by the Medical Research and Development Board (now Command) of the United States Army, the Air Force, the Public Health Service's National Institutes of Health, and the National Research Council through its Committee on Drug Addiction and Narcotics. Mr. Edward Mallinckrodt for many years gave the Laboratory annual crucial financial support out of his own pocket; added to this was the warmth of his continuing interest in all things to do with anesthesia. It is possible that his generosity has made the difference between success and failure of the Laboratory.

It is evident that a great deal has been learned about the metabolic— and toxic—effects of anesthesia, about its "physiological trespass," in John Gillies' memorable phrase. But anybody who has followed the literature knows that we are scarcely a whit further advanced in understanding the nature of the anesthesia process than Morton was when he carried out the first public demonstration of clinical anesthesia. With investigators like Linus Pauling turning their attention to this basic problem, it is likely that the next twenty-five years will have more to show than at present. If the irritability of a cell—the response of a living cell to a stimulus—is the basic characteristic of life, then here is the central problem not only of anesthesia but of all biology, of life itself—a problem deserving of the attention of the ablest scientists.

There are three goals of the Anesthesia Laboratory: one is to study the problem of irritability (responsiveness) of the tissues to stimuli and the suppression of this irritability by drugs—as fundamental a problem as exists in all biology—and second, a practical problem, to lower the death rate from anesthesia. Third, the view is that a sound approach to problems in a laboratory must improve teaching and the conduct of the department.

Experimentation in animals has given rise in the past to very great discoveries; it will in the future. Without in the least minimizing the importance of animal experimentation now or in the future, it is fair to point out that there is rightly an increasing interest in human physiology and in human pharmacology. It is clear when one studies the effects of the depressants on the central nervous system that man has necessarily become the medium for much of such work.

Today, the anesthetist is no longer confined to the operating room. He is to be encountered in the pre- and post-operative wards, in the recovery room, in the respiratory unit, in the intensive-care unit. He is involved in bronchoscopy and oxygen therapy, and leads in the care of patients with problems of ventilation or acute circulatory disasters. He is present at general ward rounds and active in discussion there. Significantly, he has made a place for himself in pharmacology and in the care of pediatric, medical, and neurological patients; and in addition to his surgical responsibilities, he has found a place in scientific and medical societies not limited to his specialty. Anesthetists who have not done most of these things are behind the times. One can confidently predict further growth in all these directions. Once the anesthetist was confined to the operating room. His primary clinical responsibilities are still there, but his obligations are, justly, now far wider than that implies. In this broadening and deepening role, the physician-anesthetist achieves his long-sought but formerly denied status as physician-specialist. He has emerged from the operating room and has made a significant place for himself in the total care of the patient.[5]

The growth of the anesthesia establishment can be demonstrated not only by a comparison of 1936 with 1955 as far as staff numbers and budgets are concerned (personnel have quadrupled and expenses have mounted astronomically), but also by demonstrating the advancing age of the surgical patient material. For example, in the decade 1925–34 the average age of patients who died in the operating room was forty-two years; in 1935–44 it was fifty years; in 1945–54 is was sixty-one years. These data reflect the advancing age of patients and the increased complexity (older patients) of the problems presented to the anesthetist and the surgeon. The number of operations has increased in these two decades by about one third.

During the first thirty-five years of its existence, the Anaesthesia Department and Laboratory of the Harvard Medical School at the Massachusetts General Hospital have participated in many developments. Some of these have made anesthesia less unpleasant for the patient and more satisfactory for the surgeon; some have made it safer; and a few have made heretofore impossible surgical procedures possible.

For fifteen years a principal interest has been to study the pain process as a prototype for study of subjective responses in general. An understanding of the factors involved in the production and relief of pain is essential to an understanding of anesthesia, for just as one cannot understand sleep without understanding wakefulness, one might gain insight into the anesthesia process by study of the problems of pain and its relief. (It is necessary to add that this view has not been universally held by anesthesia colleagues over the country, but at least it has, after some stormy early years, been adopted by the pharmacologists.) Those who follow Lord Kelvin's view that science has not been approached until one can place meaningful numbers in front of his observations, have become interested in measuring subjective responses and in particular the quantitative effects of drugs on such responses. For years it has been puzzling that able pharmacologists would all agree that their proper field included study of the effects of drugs on the liver or the kidneys or the heart or the neuromuscular system, but *not* on the mind. The situation is now changing. It is evident that the Anaesthesia Laboratory had something to do with this change.[6]

The laboratory budget raised from sources outside the Hospital has increased nearly a hundredfold. It is reassuring to find that despite a total budget of nearly half a million dollars, the Anesthesia Service and Laboratory are essentially without cost to the Massachusetts General Hospital.

An unexpected but dramatic outgrowth of the advances in anesthesiology has been the development of new approaches to pulmonary hygiene and to resuscitation. Beecher's group played an active part in these developments, as have members of other Harvard hospitals and departments. Many of the procedures developed to treat postoperative pulmonary complications are now applied in cases of respiratory failure of any origin.

During 1959 Dr. Henrik Bendixen, one of the group, began to work with Dr. Jeremiah Mead of the Harvard School of Public Health. Dr. Mead had suggested that the standards of ventilation requirements proposed in 1954 by his colleague, Dr. Edward P. Radford, led to progressive alveolar collapse in animals. Mead encouraged Bendixen and his colleagues to test this hypothesis in anesthetized man. In order to do so it was necessary to have a clinically reliable oxygen tension electrode. Dr. Myron Laver, also one of the group, was sent to Buffalo, New York (1960), to work in Professor Herman Rahn's department. There, Laver perfected the use of the Clark oxygen electrode. After his return to the Massachusetts General, Bendixen, John Hedley-Whyte, and Laver showed that arterial oxygen tensions in patients undergoing abdominal surgery were unexpectedly low, and that this arterial hypoxemia persisted into the postoperative period. In 1963, after the opening of the Respiratory Unit under the direction of Dr. Henning Pontoppidan, repeated measurements of arterial blood gases showed that the inspired oxygen concentration of patients in acute respiratory failure had to be carefully titrated. Not only was there a large deficit in oxygenation, but the ventilation requirements of surgical patients in respiratory failure were increased by a factor of 2 or 3. This fact had been observed by L. J. Henderson in the same hospital sixty years earlier, but Henderson did not have a ventilator to provide the increased ventilation required by these patients. Gradually over the next four years, until 1967, respiratory therapists, blood gas technicians, physical therapists, and specialized nurses were trained. In 1962 the mortality of patients in acute respiratory failure at the Massachusetts General Hospital was over 90 percent; by 1967 the corresponding figure based on the 400 patients in acute respiratory failure in that year was 30 percent.

In 1967 the Harvard Medical School, at the request of Dr. William Silen, the new Professor of Surgery at the Beth Israel Hospital, transferred Hedley Whyte to that hospital. There, with Dr. Leonard Bushnell, the current management of respiratory failure was developed.

Previous to the advent of this new academic Anesthesia Department, no surgical patient in respiratory failure for more than twenty-four hours had survived at the Beth Israel. By 1970 the survival rate of the approximately 300 surgical patients a year who went into respiratory failure at the Hospital was 80 percent.

The Harvard Medical School has been fortunate in having superb clinicians and teachers in anesthesia (Leroy Vandam comes to mind) and superior investigators in the field, such as Myron Laver, Gene M. Smith, Henrik Bendixen, and John Hedley-Whyte. The record of their activities lies in the more than 300 publications in eleven languages from the Department and the Laboratory. It needs no further comment.

Chapter Twenty-two

Neurosurgery

CEREBRAL operations for the relief of pain, depression, and epilepsy are relatively new in neurosurgery. Although trephination had been practiced since ancient times, neurosurgery did not become a specialty until well into the twentieth century. Until that time the field remained a part of general surgery, and most craniotomies were related to trauma. A famous example, as previously noted, is provided by the "crowbar skull" in the Warren Anatomical Museum of the Harvard Medical School. An accidental dynamite blast in 1848 had hurled a 13-pound, 3½-foot tamping iron through the left frontal lobe of a railroad construction foreman in Vermont. He survived the accident, the operation performed by a country doctor, and the inevitable postoperative purulent infection, and lived until 1861, exhibiting only some personality changes.

Infection of the open cranial cavity was always greatly feared, and when Bradlee Ward E was opened for aseptic abdominal surgery in 1888 at the Massachusetts General Hospital, it was decided that "clean" craniotomies would also be performed in this facility.

At the beginning of the twentieth century, neurosurgery at the Massachusetts General Hospital was being performed mostly by Dr. Maurice Richardson and Dr. Samuel J. Mixter. In 1911, when a staff reorganization at the Hospital brought about the establishment of the General Executive Committee and the policy of Special Assignments, neurosurgery was turned over to Dr. Mixter and his son, Dr. W. Jason Mixter, as their special assignment. By 1917 from 80 to 100 neurosurgical operations were being performed by this team annually. Dr. Jason Mixter pioneered in the treatment of intractable pain and was one of the first to perform the retrogasserian neurectomy for the treatment of trigeminal neuralgia.

Jason Mixter had received his Bachelor's degree in 1875 at Massachusetts Institute of Technology and his M.D. degree at Harvard in 1879. He was an expert anatomist and taught the subject at the Medical School for some years. He was Assistant in Surgery from 1903 to 1916 and then rose to the rank of Lecturer. In 1933 he was appointed Chief of Neurosurgery at the Hospital; also, in the same year, a special neuro-surgical operating room was opened in the Baker Memorial Hospital (Massachusetts General Hospital). He is best known today for his definitive description, with Dr. Joseph Barr, of the ruptured-disc syndrome.

In the meantime, remarkable events were occurring at the Peter Bent Brigham. The first Surgeon-in-Chief, appointed even before the Hospital opened, was Harvey Williams Cushing,[1] a man destined to greatness and convinced of it while still young. He was born in Cleveland, Ohio in 1869, son, grandson, and great-grandson of physicians. The family had originally lived in Connecticut, but their first American ancestor had landed at Hingham, Massachusetts, in 1638. After graduating from Cleveland High School, where he learned, among other things, carpentry, he went to Yale and received his Bachelor's degree there in 1891. He was an excellent baseball player, reliable, unruffled, and certain in his movements, and was captain of the team.

Cushing came to Harvard and in 1895 received both a Master's degree and an M.D. degree. Something of a shocker is contained in his record of grades: the C− in clinical surgery contrasted sharply with eleven A's and three B's in other areas—a commentary on the grading system of those days and possibly of today as well. As a student he wrote a fine thesis on lung abscess but never again showed any interest in that subject. Following graduation from the Harvard Medical School, he went to the Massachusetts General Hospital as house pupil on the Surgical Service. Here his industry and his exquisite drawings to illustrate cases that he dealt with were early indications of an unusual man. For example, the earliest charts recording findings during anesthesia were presented by Cushing and Amory Codman.

As Cushing was nearing the end of his training at the Massachusetts General Hospital, he wrote to his friend W. S. Thayer and asked if there might be a position available to him under William Osler when his Boston service was completed. Thayer never replied. One wonders what the effect of a positive reply might have been on Cushing's career. It seems unlikely that a man with Cushing's endowment would be happy with medical practice, and it seems even more unlikely that neurology could have absorbed all of his energy. Instead of going to Osler when his work was completed, he went to the Johns Hopkins but as a member of the staff of William Stewart Halsted. Unquestionably, the impact of Halsted's teaching marked a turning point in Cushing's career and was perhaps one of the few instances when the influence of another played a major part in his development.

Boston surgery at the time Cushing had his training there was still based on speed, as though anesthesia had never been discovered. The speed may have been essential, since no blood replacement was available. The gentle, deliberate methods of Halsted were a life-long inspiration to his pupil, Cushing, who liked to tell the story that, coming from Boston, where a radical breast procedure was completed in twenty-eight minutes, he looked with considerable misgiving at Halsted's common four-and-a-half hour operation. He was amazed that stimulants were not necessary and was shocked when told not to dress a wound for ten days. He commented to himself, "I may not see the wound, but I shall smell it." When the ten days had passed, and the wound was exposed, well-healed and clean, it was clear that he had encountered a new world.

It is sometimes said that Dr. Halsted directed this one or that one into that or another field. Some say that Cushing was directed into neurological surgery by Halsted. This seems most unlikely, for Dr. Roy D. McClure, who had worked with Cushing during the first year the Hunterian Laboratory was open, made it certain that Cushing himself proposed to Halsted that he enter the field of neurological surgery. Halsted's reply was, "Why, Dr. Cushing, we had only two cases of brain tumor last year!" Cushing persisted, and finally Dr. Halsted remarked, "All right, the field is yours."

Shortly after completing his training as a general surgeon, Cushing went to Bern (1900–1901) and studied with Theodor Kocher and Hugo Kronecker. With these two men he carried out his first work in experimental neurology. Neurology was to become his life's work. While abroad, Cushing also worked in Sir Charles Sherrington's laboratory at Liverpool. There can be little question that the Sherrington influence furthered Cushing's interest in the nervous system. It is puzzling to observe that he found Victor Horsley too busy, and for that reason or another he did not work with the man who must receive the accolade of founder of neurological surgery. In many ways they were different men, Horsley and Cushing. Each one made his contributions.

Upon returning from Europe, Cushing became the Neurosurgeon of the Johns Hopkins Hospital group. They were discouraging days for him. Although his results were better than those of other surgeons, mortality was still very high. Rigorous attention to autopsies when possible often led to an explanation of the preceding catastrophe, and gradually technical performance improved. A happier experience came with surgery for trifacial neuralgia. Soon afterward he began to investigate the pituitary body. Tumors of that organ were discovered, and knowledge of its functions grew rapidly. At about the time Cushing returned to Boston, his first book appeared, *The Pituitary Body and Its Disorders* (1912).

During Cushing's formative years in Baltimore, he lived next door to William Osler and found him a never-ending source of stimulation and leadership. When discouraged and in need of advice, he often turned to Osler for help. It was from Osler that he acquired his love of books and his broad background of medical history. Osler left Hopkins for Oxford in 1905, but by that time Cushing was well started on his book-collecting adventures, and it may be that the independence engendered by the absence of Osler was a good thing for him. In any case, the two carried on a brisk correspondence.

As early as 1910, even before the Peter Bent Brigham Hospital was opened, Harvey Cushing was appointed Professor of Surgery at the Harvard Medical School and Surgeon-in-Chief at the Peter Bent Brigham Hospital, only four years after the new buildings of the Harvard Medical School had been occupied in 1906. The appointment of a specialist to a senior teaching position in the Department of General Surgery as Surgeon-in-Chief in a general hospital was most unusual. Cushing never taught under the title just mentioned, for by the time he had moved to Boston in 1912, Maurice Richardson of the Massachusetts General Hospital had died, and Cushing's title was changed to Moseley Professor of Surgery.

In 1913 the new Peter Bent Brigham Hospital opened its doors, and from that day onward, Harvey Cushing endeavored, so his peers have said, to establish the Peter Bent Brigham as *the* Harvard University Hospital. In this he failed. His successor, Elliott Carr Cutler, made the same attempt, with the same result. With the exception of the Huntington Hospital (for a brief period), Harvard never has had a single university hospital, a matter never comprehended by William Welch or Abraham Flexner, who, as noted, failed to see the true advantages in the Harvard system of numerous hospitals.

The first World War came, and in April 1915 Americans in Paris organized the American Ambulance Hospital. When the United States entered the War with Base Hospital No. 5 in France (May 1917 to May 1919), Cushing's great abilities soon led to his removal from the Base Hospital group to become the senior consultant in neurosurgery to the American Expeditionary Force. The work was grim and protracted, but there were happy occasions during the War. Cushing frequently was able to go to England, to see Osler and have long visits with him. This was before the death of Revere Osler, William's son. Following World War I, Cushing re-established himself in Boston. His slight interest in general surgery, evidently never very great, permitted his intense preoccupation with neurological surgery. About this time Sir William Osler died, and at the request of Lady Osler, Cushing took on the task of writing his biography. As with all of Cushing's activities, the achievement was brilliant, and the history received a Pulitzer Prize.

The Peter Bent Brigham Hospital became the training ground for neurosurgeons from all over the world. In the European tradition, Harvey Cushing's pupils dedicated a Festschrift to him as a special number in honor of his sixtieth birthday. The eighty-two papers contained in this volume were contributed by men holding some of the most important medical and surgical posts, not only in the United States but also in Europe. The contributions contained in it were not just in neurology and neurological surgery but ranged widely over the field of medicine. Historical essays as well as experimental and clinical observations were contained among the papers.

From a retrospective viewpoint, it is evident that Harvey Cushing's effect upon the Harvard Medical School Faculty was of considerable moment. At times the relationships were stormy indeed, for Cushing was not an easy man. He, along with Dean Edsall and Edward D. Churchill, led the opposition to a system that required "full-time clinical teaching" in the Hopkins or Rockefeller sense. Cushing also opposed the plan that the Medical School edit a textbook that purported to infiltrate all departments of the School with preventive medicine.

Hospital regulations established by Harvey Cushing and Henry Christian automatically retired the professional members of the Brigham Hospital staff at the age of 63. The awesome date arrived in 1932. At that time Cushing seemed to be at the top of his powers, although peripheral vascular disease, as well as the signs and symptoms of gastric ulcer, were plaguing him. The change from his intensely active life was accepted with more or less equanimity, and surgery was given up. The Brigham Hospital Trustees repeatedly asked him to remain in service as Surgeon-in-Chief. He refused. Attempts were soon made to lure him to many other places, although it was hoped that he would stay in Boston and work on his collection of brain tumors. He remained at the Hospital for a year, carrying on his work in uncomfortable circumstances, insisting that his successor occupy the quarters set aside for the Surgeon-in-Chief. After a year he returned to his Alma Mater, Yale, as the Sterling Professor of Neurology, a post he held from 1933 to 1937. This was an active post, not merely an honorary sinecure, and it turned his interest from Boston to New Haven.

At Yale, Cushing continued his diligent study of his great mass of material on brain tumors, a task that required unusual physical effort. It is true that some fragments had appeared in either book form or as a monograph—for example, acoustic neurinomata (1917) and with P. Bailey the classical study of the gliomata (1926). A final contribution in the field of pituitary disorders, "basophilism," was a syndrome that bore his name. Although Cushing described the disorder as one due to an increase in pituitary basophilic cells, causing adrenal cortical hyperactivity, Cushing's syndrome is now used to designate adrenal cortical hyperactivity of any origin. The Yale professorship was terminated in 1937, but the work continued, and he was as active from 1937 up to the time he died as at any time in the preceding five years. The monumental volume on the meningiomata appeared in 1938. The marvel is that the life of one man could contain so much achievement. If a single outstanding quality had to be chosen, it would probably be his curiosity. His accumulation of a great medical library is surely derived from that characteristic.

Cushing was indeed a superb teacher in the operating room and in his writings left a great legacy for generations to come. Young men were drawn to him because of his masterly handling of patients and their care, as exemplified in his accumulation of successful results. Within the hospital, the young assistants could not help being impressed by the beauty of his surgical technique. Nowhere else were tissues so exquisitely handled; nowhere else did wounds heal so kindly. Here again it was the apprentice system that allowed the man and his pupils to become the distinguished individuals they were. An unusual innovation for Boston was the type of resident hierarchy which Cushing and his medical colleagues instituted in the new Peter Bent Brigham Hospital. This plan permitted the master to retain at his side for years pupils who seemed to the Chief the most worthy of such an apprenticeship. This was the only kind of teaching that Harvey Cushing really concerned himself with. It is not surprising that his meticulous, thorough, hardworking approach to medicine evoked some antagonism. He tolerated fools not at all, and as his distinction grew, so also, according to some, did his authoritarian ways. There were many students who failed to appreciate Cushing's historical scholarship, who avoided his exercises except when they covered the nervous system or the ductless glands.

Cushing's statement about Osler applies to him also: "He advanced the science of medicine, he enriched literature and the humanities . . . He achieved many honors and many dignities, but the proudest of all was his unwritten title, 'the young man's friend.' " John Fulton at Yale wrote an excellent biography in 1946, which illuminates his work at Harvard from 1912 to 1933. It is also of interest to point out that the American Association of Neurological Surgeons, the largest society of this specialty in the world, was founded by his trainees and originally named the Harvey Cushing Society.

Whereas Cushing's continuing presence at the Peter Bent Brigham Hospital kept neurosurgical matters stable, things were much more fluid at the Massachusetts General Hospital. A special service was developed which included W. J. Mixter, whose major contribution was the recognition (with Dr. Joseph Barr) of rupture of the nucleus pulposus as the most common cause for low backache with sciatic radiation. In 1922 the Massachusetts General established a full-time teaching and investigative clinic called the Third Surgical Service and appointed Dr. Edward Richardson as Chief. Dr. Richardson selected a team of promising young investigators and sent them to European clinics for postgraduate studies. Among them was Dr. James C. White, who in 1927–28 studied under Professor René Leriche in the surgical clinic at Strasbourg. James White was the grandson of America's first Professor of Dermatology, James C. White, the elder. James White the younger was born in Vienna in 1895 and acquired a highly useful facility with languages in his youth. He received his Bachelor's degree at Harvard College in 1917 and his M.D. degree in 1923. After returning to Boston from Strasbourg, he joined the neurosurgical staff at the Massachusetts General Hospital under Dr. W. Jason Mixter and became Chief of Neurosurgery in 1941. He could not assume the duties of this post until 1946, when he returned from Naval duty. He became Professor of Surgery in 1955.

In his medical career, James White became absorbed in the possibilities of neurosurgical relief of otherwise intractable pain by himself and with Dr. William Sweet. This originated with the request of Dr. Paul D. White that they find pain-conducting pathways of angina pectoris. The work was carried out in dogs and established practical operations for the relief of pain in coronary disease by upper thoracic sympathetic ganglionectomy (instead of the ineffective cervical sympathectomies previously in use) or section of the corresponding upper four thoracic sensory spinal roots.

Donald Todd of the Department of Anesthesia made major contributions to the effectiveness of pain surgery by perfecting techniques for diagnostic blocking of the paravertebral sympathetic ganglia and spinal nerves under radiographic control, as well as in developing "wake-up" anesthesia (a special form of light anesthesia was involved), which made it possible to rouse the patient midway during the surgery and get his commentary on the site of action of the pain. From this, it was possible to test the distribution of pain by stimulating sensory nerve roots or axons in the spinal cord. The wake-up procedure was surprisingly nonpainful.

Much of Dr. White's investigation was carried out in the Surgical Research Laboratories of the Massachusetts General Hospital, largely financed in those days with Harvard funds. In 1933 these same funds were also used to establish a neurosurgical laboratory at the Hospital for the use of Dr. Tracy J. Putnam, but in the next year he resigned to become Chief of Neurosurgery at the Boston City Hospital.

It was early in the 1950's that James C. White and his associate, William H. Sweet, came to believe that the advancement of knowledge in clinical neurosurgery might be accelerated if such a neurosurgical service as theirs included basic scientists, especially those with an M.D. degree and clinical medical training. The first to join the service in this capacity was Dr. Adelbert Ames, III, who was subsequently appointed to a full professorship in physiology in the Harvard Medical School. He found that less than 20 percent of the retina was specialized for photoreception and that the remainder was a valid sample of normal brain tissue. He used this fact to study the effects of deprivation of oxygen on nervous tissue, using the more readily accessible retina instead of the brain.

Much of the work of Drs. White and Sweet has been devoted to the surgical control of pain. Two extensive monographs on pain in 1955 and 1969 were of great importance in keeping the medical world abreast of the neurological advances everywhere. White was the first to incise successfully the crossed-pain pathways in the medulla oblongata coming from the opposite torso and limbs. Pain relief was maintained in his patient for twelve years at the last follow-up. Other contributions of White and Sweet have included an analgesia of the spinal root entry zones for pain from the various viscera. These two investigators also developed an easy stereotactic method for control of pain and suffering by making radiofrequency heat lesions in the inferior medial white matter of the cerebral frontal lobes.

James White's professional career is an excellent example of how an expert clinician develops basic-science data to help him understand and treat clinical conditions. Both clinical medicine and neurophysiology benefited greatly from his studies.

Dr. White was succeeded by his long-time close associate, William H. Sweet, who became Professor of Surgery at the Harvard Medical School and Chief, Neurosurgical Service at the Massachusetts General Hospital. Dr. Sweet had graduated from the University of Washington in 1930 and won another Bachelor's degree at Oxford in 1934 after two years as a Rhodes Scholar. He received his M.D. degree at Harvard in 1936 and, later, a Doctor of Science degree, again at Oxford, in 1957. During World War II he served with British units. In 1958 he became Associate Professor at Harvard and in 1965 Professor of Neurosurgery and Chief of Neurosurgery at the Massachusetts General Hospital. With his broad experience in basic science, including a period at the Brookhaven National Laboratories, and his ingenuity in working out clinical problems, he has had a most productive career. In addition to his work with James White on pain and on the surgery of the autonomic nervous system, he has participated in a number of highly original enterprises. For example, he knew the possibilities of irradiation of tumors with heavy particles and with Dr. Raymond Kjellberg developed proton beam therapy, especially of the pituitary gland. He also used division of the pituitary stalk successfully to cause the remission of severe diabetic neuropathy.

Sweet did very important work with stereotactic surgery by means of a technique initiated in England by Sir Victor Horsley and R. H. Clarke in experimental animals at the turn of the century and subsequently developed by Ernest Spiegel and Henry Wycis of Philadelphia in the 1940's as a practical method of operating in deep structures of the human brain. The potential usefulness of this surgical tool was recognized by Sweet and supported by a Rockefeller Foundation grant; he studied the theoretical and technological aspects of stereotactic surgery in animals under the tutelage of Horace Magoun, Warren McCulloch, and Ray Snider in Chicago and aided in the development of the apparatus. One of the early problems was the development of a stereotactic brain atlas relating measurements in cadaver brain structures to landmarks, such as the third ventricle, which can be visualized on X-ray films by instillation of an appropriate contrast agent—for example, Pantopaque. Dr. Sweet was joined by Dr. Vernon Mark in 1949 to carry out this project.

The first clinical stereotactic operations on pain patients with terminal cancer were carried out in 1954 by Drs. Mark and Sweet at the Massachusetts General Hospital. Their stereotactic targets included the sensory and subsequently the parasensory areas of the thalamus, a procedure that was particularly effective in relieving the pain of patients with advanced cancer of the head and neck. Furthermore, it established a reticular pain pathway related to but separate from the chief sensory nucleus of the thalamus. These observations were confirmed by clinical anatomical investigations carried out by Dr. Paul Yakovlev[2] in patients who had been relieved of pain by thalamotomy and had subsequently succumbed to their cancer. Anatomical investigations by William Mehler and physiological findings of Denise Albe-Fessard confirmed these clinical observations of the Massachusetts General Hospital group.

Occasionally some pain patients had extreme depression and agitation because of obstructing cancer of the oropharynx, with impending strangulation. In these patients a radiofrequency lesion of the anterior nucleus of the thalamus was added to the lesion of the sensory or parasensory area in order to relieve the mental symptoms.

Stereotactic surgery was also used by Drs. Sweet and Mark to relieve some of the symptoms of temporal lobe epilepsy. Dr. Raymond Kjellberg at the Massachusetts General Hospital developed a stereotactic instrument and technique of his own for work on epileptic patients, although his chief interest was the relief of abnormal movement disorders, particularly in Parkinson's Disease. Dr. Frank Ervin, Director of the Psychiatric Research Laboratories at the Massachusetts General Hospital, called attention to the fact that the most disabling symptoms of temporal lobe epilepsy were often those of abnormal and unpredictable aggressivity of the patient. Radiofrequency lesions in the temporal lobe of some of these patients not only decreased their seizures but also decreased the interictal episodes of aggressivity in the successful cases.

With a number of colleagues, Dr. Sweet has worked on the use of a variety of beta- and positron-emitting isotopes. The technique has helped in the localization of brain tumors and abscesses. There seems to be no end in sight for the ingenious application of physical chemistry to the problem of the diagnosis and treatment of brain diseases in Dr. Sweet's group. Of particular recent note was the successful treatment of dementia caused by low-pressure hydrocephalus.

The work of Dr. Donald Munro at the Boston City Hospital took an entirely different direction. A graduate of Milton Academy and of Harvard College, he received his M.D. degree from Harvard in 1914. He interned at the Boston City Hospital from 1914 to 1916 and after further experience became one of the world's leading experts on the treatment of injuries to the brain and the spinal cord. His two books on the subject opened up new vistas in the treatment of these formerly hopeless conditions. In 1929, he took charge of the surgical part of the Neurological Unit at the Boston City Hospital in conjunction with Dr. Abraham Myerson and Dr. Stanley Cobb. He was Assistant Professor of Surgery at the School. He was Chief of Neurosurgery at the Boston City Hospital from 1941 until his retirement in 1956.

Dr. Vernon H. Mark, who had worked with William Sweet, later inherited the post at the City Hospital. He became Associate Professor of Surgery at Harvard Medical School and Director of the Neurosurgical Service at the City Hospital. Dr. Mark's principal surgical activities have been concerned with the definition of a pain center in the human thalamus not connected with other modalities of sensation, such as the discrimination of pin-prick. This work was done with Frank Ervin and William Sweet and accomplished at a time when the basic neurophysiologist and anatomist had not yet described this center. It has now been confirmed by anatomical and physiological work and by the results of stereotactic surgical therapy in Europe, South America, and other centers in the United States. The work is summarized in Chapter XVIII of White and Sweet's book *Pain and the Neurosurgeon—A 40-Year Experience* (1969). The initiation and suppression of attack behavior by electrical stimulation in various points within the limbic brain, in particular the amygdala, of patients with temporal lobe epilepsy, is described in Mark's new book, *Violence and the Brain*.[3]

The Peter Bent Brigham underwent a marked diminution in neuro-surgical activities after Harvey Cushing's retirement. The Brigham effort was combined with and, in a sense, was secondary to that which developed in the Children's Hospital. The story of Children's Hospital Neurosurgery begins with Dr. Franc D. Ingraham, a 1925 graduate of the Harvard Medical School. An internship with Harvey Cushing, a term at Johns Hopkins with Walter Dandy, and in 1928 a year with Sherring-ton in England gave him his training. He became Visiting Surgeon in Neurosurgery at the Massachusetts General Hospital in 1929. By that time he had already been characterized as technically the finest neurosur-geon ever seen. He also joined the staff of the Children's Hospital in the same year. In 1940 he founded the Laboratory of Surgical Research at that Hospital and developed the use of one of the Cohn fractions for the control of bleeding. From 1947 to 1964 he was Associate Professor of Surgery at the School and Neurosurgeon-in-Chief at the Children's and Peter Bent Brigham Hospitals. At first alone and then with Donald Matson, Dr. Ingraham worked out the treatment of congenital anomalies such as spina bifida and of the then largely intractable condition of hydrocephalus. In 1951 he and Dr. Matson published the standard work on the subject, *Neurosurgery in Infancy and Childhood*.

Dr. Ingraham was succeeded by Dr. Matson, a Harvard Medical School graduate of 1934 who joined the School's Faculty and the staff of the Children's and Peter Bent Brigham Hospitals in 1942 but then went for a period of training at the Lahey Clinic, to which Harvey Cushing's long-time associate Gilbert Horrax had gone on Cushing's retirement. When a professorship was named after Dr. Ingraham, Dr. Matson was made its first incumbent. He died in 1969 after a long and tragic illness.

He has been succeeded by Dr. W. Kearsley Welch as Franc D. Ingraham Professor of Neurosurgery at the Harvard Medical School and Neurosurgeon-in-Chief at the Children's Hospital Medical Center. Dr. Welch is also in charge of neurosurgery at the Peter Bent Brigham Hospital.

Chapter Twenty-three

Orthopedic Surgery

BOSTON's great School of Orthopedic Surgery (leaving aside Henry Jacob Bigelow, who was primarily a general surgeon) flourished as a world leader from the time Edward H. Bradford was named the first Professor of Orthopedic Surgery in 1903.[1] Leaders in this proud tradition cover continuously the last seventy years. The key figures will be discussed.

Dr. Bradford, who had graduated from Harvard College in 1869 and received A.M. and M.D. degrees four years later, became interested in orthopedic surgery about 1880, rose through the ranks, and became Professor in 1903. He held that post until 1912, resigning to become Dean at the School until 1918. During his tenure as Professor he trained or otherwise strongly influenced the next generation of leaders in the field.

One of these was Robert W. Lovett. Having received his A.B. degree at Harvard in 1881 and his M.D. degree in 1885, he turned to surgery for his career and entered the Department of Orthopedic Surgery in 1902. He rose to become Professor in 1914 and was named John Ball and Buckminster Brown Professor of Orthopedic Surgery in 1915; he carried on in this post until 1924. At the Children's Hospital he was greatly influenced by Dr. E. H. Bradford, and in the House of the Good Samaritan he encountered Dr. Buckminster Brown, who then was at an advanced age but was nonetheless young in spirit and eager as always to try to solve the problems of the cripple. Influenced by Bradford and Brown, Dr. Lovett, early in his career, resigned all hospital appointments except that of the Children's Hospital and from then on, devoted himself solely to Orthopedic Surgery. In medicine some gain prominence through research; others achieve eminence through clinical achievements, teaching, and ability to apply discoveries of medical science in the clinic. Dr. Lovett was of the latter type. As an able administrator, he reorganized the Department and established special clinics for the study and treatment of acute anterior poliomyelitis, scoliosis, and the paralyses that result from birth injuries. He was instrumental in establishing the Harvard Infantile Paralysis Commission for the study of poliomyelitis. He deserves great credit for his careful studies in the re-education of paralyzed muscles, although his greatest work was perhaps on lateral curvature of the spine.

Mention should be made of *A Treatise on Orthopedic Surgery* (1890) by Lovett and Bradford. It was the first notable American treatise on the subject and passed through five editions. *The Surgery of Joints* was written in 1910 with E. H. Nichols. In 1923 a new *Textbook in Orthopaedic Surgery* was published, written by Sir Robert Jones and Dr. Lovett. After Lovett's death in 1924, his colleague Sir Robert Jones wrote: "He represented the highest ideals of our art, and he brought to bear upon it the rich power of a cultured mind. An indefatigable worker, a keen and critical observer, he sought and paid unswerving fidelity to truth."[2]

He was succeeded by Robert B. Osgood. After receiving a Bachelor's degree at Amherst in 1895, he came to Harvard, receiving his M.D. degree there in 1899. From the beginning of his career, Dr. Osgood's interest was primarily in diseases of the bones and joints. This interest doubtless was stimulated by the training he had had at the House of the Good Samaritan. He became associated with Dr. Joel E. Goldthwait in the relatively new specialty of Orthopedic Surgery. With Dr. Walter J. Dodd, he took keen interest in applying the newly discovered roentgen ray to diseases of the bones and joints. He was the roentgenologist at the Children's Hospital from 1901 to 1902. Along with most of the other early workers on X rays, he received severe burns of his hands, which troubled him as long as he lived. He entered the Department of Orthopedic Surgery in 1909.

In World War I Dr. Osgood's record was notable. He collaborated closely with his friend Sir Robert Jones in establishing orthopedic hospitals in Great Britain. For a time he was Surgical Chief of Base Hospital No. 5 but was soon detached for duty with the Orthopedic Section of the American Expeditionary Force. He became Professor of Orthopedic Surgery in 1922 and was named to the Brown Professorship in 1924. He retired in 1931. In a foreword to a complimentary volume written by Osgood's associates, Sir Robert Jones, his friend and colleague says: "His logical mind—tempered and enhanced by a delightful imagination—has overcome all obstacles and he has never given cause for resentment. He has always been singularly unfettered by tradition and can throw light upon obscure problems from many unexpected angles."[3] His name is associated with the syndrome of separation of the tibial tubercle: Osgood-Schlatter disease. His technical brilliance made difficult procedures look easy.

On Dr. Osgood's retirement as Chief of Orthopedic Surgery at the Children's Hospital, Frank R. Ober succeeded him and held the post until 1946. A native of Maine and a graduate of Tufts College Medical School in 1905, he entered the Harvard Department of Orthopedic Surgery in 1914 and became Professor in 1931. He was designated John Ball and Buckminster Brown Professor in 1937 and held that title until 1946. He early saw the possibility of extending the range of orthopedic procedures to correct the effects of paralyses after poliomyelitis and of spasticity associated with cerebral palsy. To stimulate these developments, he brought in William T. Green, a 1925 graduate of the University of Indiana Medical School who interned in surgery at the Peter Bent Brigham Hospital.

Green's earliest publications, beginning in 1934, dealt with the serious problem of chronic arthritis in children. He was notably successful in impressing pediatricians and general practitioners, especially in New England, of the importance of recognition and treatment of various orthopedic conditions—for example, the importance of early drainage of a septic joint, especially the hip.[4] In the prevaccination era, poliomyelitis was often widespread in New England. Green was responsible for improving the care of the patient with this disease, not only through his personal activities, but through the training of other physicians who shared his principles. One of his outstanding contributions grew out of the early recognition of occasional discrepancy in the length of the lower extremities in the growing child. This is especially important, since recognition and management may well prevent a disabling deformity as growth continues.

In 1942 Dr. Green reported his results with the operative treatment of spastic cerebral palsy at the Children's Hospital and the Peter Bent Brigham. He called attention to various therapeutic errors that had been committed in this field. In 1943 he established the relation of neurofibromatosis to congenital pseudoarthrosis of the tibia. In 1946 he was appointed Orthopedic Surgeon-in-Chief of the Children's Hospital to succeed Dr. Ober and also Chief of the Orthopedic Division of the Peter Bent Brigham Hospital. In 1962 he was appointed the first Harriet M. Peabody Professor of Orthopedic Surgery at the Harvard Medical School, and he retired in 1968, leaving a legacy of hope for the possibilities of orthopedic repair of the effects of neurological diseases.

In the meantime, the Massachusetts General Hospital Department of Orthopedic Surgery was experiencing exciting developments under Dr. Smith-Petersen. As one traces the development of Orthopedic Surgery from the days of Henry Jacob Bigelow's occasional activities in the field (he was, of course, primarily a general surgeon) on through E. H. Bradford, R. W. Lovett, and R. B. Osgood, the developments are largely of a technical sort until Marius N. Smith-Petersen is encountered. He was able to take a new concept and develop it in the clinic. It is likely that no orthopedic surgeon exerted so great an influence upon his field than did Smith-Petersen when he was at the top of his activities.

He was a native of Norway and came to this country at the age of sixteen in 1903. Having received his Bachelor's degree at Wisconsin in 1910, he came to Harvard, where he won his M.D. degree in 1914. As early as 1917, while still an intern, he conceived the anterior supra-articular subperiosteal approach to the hip joint. Four years later he developed a new subperiosteal approach to the sacroiliac joint. In 1925 he first used the three-flanged nail to secure fractures of the femoral neck. Many of his colleagues believe this was his greatest contribution, but his 1930 acetabuloplasty of the hip may have been greater. Yet this was followed in 1938 by what others believe is the most important effort of all: vitallium mold arthroplasty of the hip. He focused a searching study on the hip, greater than that joint had previously received. In order to carry out these activities, he of necessity devised many instruments to facilitate the new type of surgery. He was a brilliant, intuitive improvisor whose wide-ranging imagination provided surgery with some of its most constructive innovations. From 1929 on, he was Chief of Orthopedic Surgery at the Hospital and Clinical Professor of Orthopedic Surgery at the Medical School.

His closest associate was Otto E. Aufranc. One of Dr. Smith-Petersen's greatest achievements was to prepare Dr. Aufranc, his devoted assistant and associate, to continue work on the hip. Aufranc's activities were mainly directed toward technical improvements, and there can be little argument that he was the world's outstanding authority on surgery of the hip. He had other interests centered around the Fracture Service. The origins of the Service go back to Dr. Charles Scudder, who gave the first postgraduate course in the management of fractures soon after the end of the first World War. Others who had a part in the development of fracture courses were Drs. Philip Wilson, Smith-Petersen, Van Gorder, and Cave. In 1947 Dr. Edwin Cave became the Chief of the Fracture Service and greatly enhanced its reputation. Aufranc approached the Service as Chief from a new point of view: it seemed to him that inasmuch as not many surgeons could afford to spend two weeks away from their practice, he pointed up the fact that there was need for a change of concept of management and teaching. Aufranc changed the postgraduate courses to three days on the weekend. Clearly, these brief courses fulfilled a need and became very popular. They were copied throughout the medical centers in the United States. Other short courses were developed, with Aufranc's example in mind. They dealt with the hip, shoulder, neck, spine, and hand. Several books were written by the group just mentioned on the treatment of fractures. A generation earlier the Fifth Surgical Service at the Boston City Hospital had made important contributions to the treatment of fractures, but their leadership had weakened, and the Massachusetts General Hospital became preeminent.

Aufranc's curiously low-level appointment, Lecturer in Orthopedic Surgery, emphasizes once more the failure to equate clinical distinction with academic rank at Harvard. The same can be said of Dr. Carter Rowe, who, until very recently, was Instructor in Orthopedic Surgery even though President of the American Orthopedic Association and famous all over the world.

In 1947 Joseph S. Barr became Chief of the Orthopedic Service at the Massachusetts General Hospital and was also designated John Ball and Buckminster Brown Professor of Orthopedic Surgery at the Medical School. Having received his M.D. degree at Harvard in 1926, he interned at the Peter Bent Brigham Hospital, went to the Children's Hospital and, in 1929, transferred to the Massachusetts General for training in orthopedics.

Of Dr. Barr's contributions to orthopedic surgery, undoubtedly his greatest achievement was the demonstration that rupture of a lumbar intervertebral disc is, in a large percentage of cases,[5] a cause of low back pain with sciatica. This classical paper, written with W. Jason Mixter in 1934, undoubtedly led to widespread understanding of the result of a ruptured intervertebral disc. Joel Goldthwait had, however, in 1911, called attention to the disc syndrome, and Walter Dandy, in 1929, had recorded, according to Edwin F. Cave, excellent descriptions of two cases.

Barr served with distinction in World War II. After his return this quiet, modest man revealed his greatest ambition—to establish an Orthopedic Research Laboratory at the Hospital. This, he did, in 1959. He retired in 1965 because of ill health.

The head of the new Laboratory was Melvin J. Glimcher. Born in Brookline, Massachusetts, and a graduate of the school system of Chelsea, he won two Bachelor's degrees at Purdue, one in mechanical engineering and another in physics. He took his M.D. degree at Harvard in 1950 *magna cum laude*, having presented a thesis on the engineering aspects of bone structure which amazed and enlightened the Faculty. He had his clinical training in orthopedic surgery at the Children's and Massachusetts General Hospitals. In the Laboratory, Dr. Glimcher was primarily interested in the various aspects of molecular biology and cellular biology concerning bone, cartilage, and other connective tissues. Under his aegis there was a rapid and extensive increase in knowledge of the structure, chemistry, organization, biosynthesis, degradation, and maturation of connective tissues, the nature of calcium phosphate solids, and their phase transformations. All have great potential significance in an understanding of bone diseases. In 1965, after Dr. Barr's retirement, Dr. Glimcher became Chief of Orthopedic Surgery at the Massachusetts General Hospital.

In addition to these men of high academic rank in Harvard's hierarchy, there are many other practicing orthopedic surgeons in Boston whose clinical and teaching performances are outstanding. One of the most interesting is Dr. Thomas B. Quigley, Clinical Professor of Surgery at the Harvard Medical School, Surgeon, Peter Bent Brigham Hospital, and Associate Director of Orthopedic Surgery at the Boston City Hospital. A graduate of the School in 1933, he has distinguished himself in sports medicine.

Harvard has made a number of contributions to sports medicine: "respectability [was achieved] through Thorndike's *Athletic Injuries*, 1938,"[6] but the *Bill of Rights of the Athlete* (1957) written by Thomas B. Quigley, was of first importance. It clarified the interrelationships between athlete, trainer, coach, and doctor and has had wide influence. When the theory was introduced that ligament rupture is at least as important as fracture and surgical repair is much to be preferred to immobilization, the theory was put into practice at Harvard, under the leadership of Dr. Quigley in 1949. Generally speaking, Harvard's experience with athletes has shown that study of them is valuable to the physician who must treat them and that to return an injured athlete to "normal" is to achieve much more than to enable him to regain a basic function. Dr. Quigley's writings on the recognition, treatment, and prevention of athletic injuries are world famous.

Chapter Twenty-four

Ophthalmology, Otolaryngology, and

Facial Surgery

OPHTHALMOLOGY

During the first quarter of the twentieth century, the successive Professors of Ophthalmology in the Harvard Medical School were Oliver F. Wadsworth, Myles Standish, Alexander Quackenboss, and George S. Derby. These men also functioned as Heads of the Department of Ophthalmology at the Medical School. In 1924 Dr. Derby became the first solo Chief of Ophthalmology at the Massachusetts Eye and Ear Infirmary, sharing his time between the Hospital and his private office in the Back Bay. After retirement he was succeeded by Dr. E. B. Dunphy, who served until 1962.

The evolution of ophthalmology from an empiric clinical specialty to an academic discipline resting on basic scientific foundations is one of the fascinating developments of the twentieth century. Two major threads of that development can be traced to the career of one man— Frederick Hermann Verhoeff—and the growth of one institution—the Howe Laboratory of Ophthalmology, both functioning within the orbit of the Harvard Medical School at the Massachusetts Eye and Ear Infirmary.

Dr. Verhoeff was born in Louisville, Kentucky, in 1874. He died in his 95th year, laden with honors. He had a paternal hand in developing two generations of ophthalmologists. He posed many questions and supplied many answers, and, was a powerful force in directing the course that ophthalmology was to take in the twentieth century. Emerson's words are relevant: "History is but the lengthened shadow of a great man."

The year Verhoeff was born marked a controversy in Europe. Rudolf Virchow had made leukocytes in the cornea the subject of an inaugural address. Whether these corneal leukocytes came from the circulation, as Julius Cohnheim believed, or from fixed tissue cells, as Friedrich von Recklinghausen thought, was a major issue in 1874. Four years later the origin of corneal leukocytes was still being hotly debated, and William

H. Welch, who was to influence Dr. Verhoeff's life many years later, was assigned the task of repeating Virchow's experiments in von Recklinghausen's laboratory. These results were not published: the cautious Welch was well aware of the inimical elements in the von Recklinghausen–Cohnheim conflict. It is possible that this earlier experience of Welch was one of the reasons why he guided Verhoeff into a career of opthalmic pathology a quarter century later.

From the age of twelve Verhoeff was interested in problems of optics. He studied at Yale, graduating in 1895, and enrolled in the third Johns Hopkins Medical School class, graduating in 1899. An accidental fact may have had further influence on his career: he lived in the same house as Dr. Welch. There is no evidence that Welch, a bachelor, took any particular interest in him at the time, or even directed his interests to pathology. However, when Dr. William Councilman, then the leading pathologist of the Harvard Medical School, asked Welch to suggest a full-time pathologist for the Massachusetts Eye and Ear Infirmary, Verhoeff was immediately nominated. The fact that Verhoeff had not, at that time, had much experience in pathology did not seem to weigh heavily. Welch rather blithely said Verhoeff could learn it—as, in fact, he did, and in so doing became America's most distinguished ophthalmic pathologist.

Verhoeff's reception in Boston was not cordial, nor was his salary of $650 a year more than adequate. Nevertheless, he not only learned eye and ear pathology but proved to himself and others that his interests in ophthalmology had many facets. He went abroad to study with Ernst Fuchs in Vienna, Otto Haab in Zurich, and Herbert Parsons in London. He became the American peer of these distinguished specialists.

Not long after he had returned to Boston in 1907, a pathology laboratory was constructed at the Infirmary according to his design. Studies on eye pathology began, and a center for training ophthalmic pathologists was developed. As Cogan has pointed out,[1] it would be hard to say whether the most significant product of this quarter of a century of the Infirmary's pathology laboratory was a stream of practical observations, the many trainees, or the example projected by Verhoeff's intellectual honesty and blunt address. In the same period he became a clinician and surgeon of distinction, as well as a pathologist. He proved that the practice of clinical ophthalmology and its correlation with ophthalmic pathology can be a fruitful symbiosis.

Dr. Verhoeff's interest in optics continued, and when he was relieved of his duties as pathologist, he returned energetically to the study of binocular vision and stereopsis. His *Theory of Binocular Vision*, published in 1935, is still the creed of many authorities in the field. Those who worked with him and knew him well developed a strong personal attachment amounting to affection as well as admiration:

> We knew he was not always right, but we knew his evidence was first-hand, and we respected his logic. We took no offense at his satire because we knew it to be warranted. We also knew that even when he was castigating us he had the same fondness for us that we did for him.[2]

On the laboratory side, Dr. Verhoeff became Professor of Ophthalmic Research in 1924, Scientific Director of the Howe Laboratory in 1931, and Director in 1932. On the clinical side, he began as an extern at the Johns Hopkins Hospital in 1899. In Boston, while a pathologist at the Massachusetts Eye and Ear Infirmary, he rose on the clinical ladder to the rank of Surgeon in Ophthalmology. He never became Chief of Ophthalmology at the Infirmary, nor Head of the Department at Harvard.

From 1900 to 1940, Dr. Verhoeff contributed articles of outstanding importance to almost every branch of ophthalmic interest. It has been estimated that his publication rate from 1899 to 1940 remained steady at some fifty articles per decade. The men he had trained were everywhere in positions of distinction.

Howe Laboratory of Ophthalmology[3]

In 1926 Dr. Lucien Howe, Professor Emeritus of Ophthalmology in the University of Buffalo, approached Dean Edsall with the proposal to found a center for eye research.[4] Shortly afterward the Howe Laboratory of Ophthalmology was established, in accordance with an agreement with Harvard University. It was Dr. Howe's intention to donate $250,-000 if Harvard would raise matching funds. This was accomplished with support from the General Education Board (Rockefeller Foundation) and the General Artemas Ward Memorial Fund. Signatories to the agreement were A. Lawrence Lowell (Harvard), Edward H. Bradford (Infirmary) and George Wigglesworth (Massachusetts General Hospital).

It was agreed that Dr. Howe was to be the first Director, and each succeeding Director was to be appointed jointly by the Corporation of Harvard University and the Managers of the Massachusetts Eye and Ear Infirmary by procedures that were customary for these institutions.

The Medical School provided temporary quarters initially, but the understanding was that the Laboratory would be moved to the Infirmary, which would supply space, light, and heat, and that the Laboratory would be attached to the Infirmary for as long as that arrangement appeared to be in the best interest of the Laboratory. It was the desire of the parties to this agreement that the Laboratory should "have a separate building whenever funds may be available for such a purpose."

The Director was to be responsible to University authorities, but mention of the Department of Ophthalmology or of any connection between this department and the Howe Laboratory was nowhere suggested in the agreement. Indeed, it was clearly implied in correspondence between Drs. Howe and Derby that these were separate departments. Dr. Howe was adamant that members of the Laboratory should not be committed to teaching or to other routine duties. (In the event, this was not always adhered to.)

The Laboratory began operation in 1927 at three locations: the Harvard Medical School, the Bussey Institution, Dr. Howe's home in Belmont. At that time the professional staff, in addition to Dr. Howe, consisted of Dr. Harry Messenger (physiological optics) and Dr. Clyde Keeler (genetics). In 1928 the Laboratory moved to the Infirmary, as indicated by a prominent plaque on the front entrance.

With Dr. Howe's death in 1928, a search was begun for a new Dirctor. Consideration was given to appointing Dr. George S. Derby, then Chief of Ophthalmology and simultaneously Director of the Howe Laboratory. It is clear from the correspondence of Dean Edsall and Dr. Derby that such a joint appointment was contrary to the intent of the gift. Dr. Edsall wrote in 1930:

> The authorities in Cambridge gave me the definite opinion that the director of the Laboratory should spend the major part, if not all, of his time in the laboratory itself—not in practice and not to any large degree in other University activities . . . the terms of the gift must be followed carefully.

It was further clearly pointed out that the individual in charge should not have other routine duties "of any moment" in connection with the Infirmary, so that he might devote himself exclusively to research.

The affairs of the Laboratory were put in the hands of a committee chaired by Dr. Blackfan, pending the search for a full-time Director. Limited operation continued with Drs. Messenger and Keeler, who comprised the staff. A new committee was formed in the 1930–31 season to operate the Laboratory and to find a Director. This committee, consisting of Drs. Derby, Verhoeff, and Zinsser, found it difficult to locate a director who would be content to function in a vacuum, removed from clinical medicine.

After Dr. Verhoeff was appointed Scientific Director in 1931 and later full Director, he reported directly to the Dean, but several staff appointments were held concurrently with the Infirmary. The Laboratory began to prosper, with emphasis on physiologic optics, pathology, and clinical studies. By the end of 1931 the staff consisted of Drs. Merrill King, Trygve Gundersen, Elek Ludvigh, and David Cogan, and Mr. Eugene McCarthy.

In 1940 Dr. Cogan was named Acting Director and later, on Dr. Verhoeff's retirement, full Director. The activities and staff are recorded in the Annual Reports, beginning in 1944. By this time, research was being carried out in the fields of biochemistry, physiology, neuro-ophthalmology, optics, toxicology, radiation, and applied research (especially glaucoma and cataracts). Reports concerning appointments, budgets, and research projects were made directly to the Dean.

At the end of World War II the new era of ophthalmic research began in earnest. Drs. Cogan and V. Everett Kinsey continued their studies on corneal permeability, which they had initiated during the war years. Drs. Cogan and S. Forrest Martin went to Japan to study the effects of radiation injuries to the eye among the survivors of the Hiroshima and Nagasaki atomic bomb explosions.

In 1949 Dr. Kinsey directed a nationwide investigation into variables associated with the development of retrolental fibroplasia of premature infants. The significant finding that emerged was the association of high concentrations of oxygen in the incubators of infants who developed this devastating retinopathy of prematurity. The reduction of oxygen concentrations subsequently led to a nearly total elimination of this disease.

In 1946 Dr. Cogan directed the first Harvard Basic Science Course in Ophthalmology, which was given twice in that year. Cogan's correlation of basic science principles with clinical manifestations has served as the model for all similar courses since that date.

Space continued to be a major concern of the expanding laboratory. In 1956 the Infirmary provided new quarters, which allowed expansion from 2100 square feet to 4500. In 1960 a penthouse was added, the construction being financed largely by the Lions Clubs of Massachusetts. During the 1950's Drs. Jin Kinoshita and Toichiro Kuwabara built the foundations of their brilliant careers respectively in ophthalmic biochemistry and experimental pathology. Dr. W. Morton Grant, who had discovered tonography in 1950, continued his studies on glaucoma and began collecting material for his textbook on toxicology of the eye, which was published in 1962. On the clinical side he collaborated with Dr. Paul A. Chandler in many important studies of glaucoma.

In 1962, on the retirement of Dr. Edwin Blakeslee Dunphy as Henry Willard Williams Professor of Ophalmology, Head of the Department at the Harvard Medical School, and Chief of Ophthalmology at the Infirmary, Dr. Cogan succeeded to these posts. Since he continued as Director of the Howe Laboratory, this represented a major departure from the philosophy expressed by Dean Edsall as reflecting the intent of the founding donor. Cogan's interests and aspirations were far too broad to be confined by the original terms of the gift. Not only did he proceed up the clinical ladder at the Infirmary to the rank of Surgeon in Ophthalmology, but his didactic talents led him to the teaching of medical students, fellows, and postgraduate students. He became active on the national and international scenes as visiting lecturer at other institutions and as consultant to the National Institute of Neurological Diseases and Blindness and the Atomic Energy Commission. He was appointed Chief Editor of the American Medical Association's *Archives of Ophthalmology* in 1961.

Dr. Cogan's acceptance of the positions of Chief of Ophthalmology at the Infirmary and Head of the Department at Harvard effectively integrated the Department and the Howe Laboratory under his administration. Thus he embodied the integration of research and teaching with patient care, his emphasis and special interests being in that order. Clinically, his interests centered on medical ophthalmology and neuro-ophthalmology, rather than ophthalmic surgery.

During the tenure of Dr. Dunphy as Head of the Department from 1941 to 1961, Cogan enjoyed a completely free hand in the administration of the Howe Laboratory. Dunphy always insisted, however, that there be room for other eye research at the Infirmary outside the Howe Laboratory. The wisdom of this philosophy was borne out by the fact that the Laboratory's interests were largely concerned with nonsurgical aspects of a specialty that in terms of inpatient activity is almost entirely surgical, at the same time that its outpatient activity is largely medical.

During the years 1962 through 1967, the Laboratory's influence and scope grew under the direction of Dr. Cogan. The distinction between the Laboratory and the Department of Ophthalmology became blurred by the overlapping activities of Laboratory members in training, research, and patient care. For example, Drs. Kupfer and Grant successively directed the Departmental training grant whereby certain four-year residents spent an extra year in the Laboratory. In addition to its research activities, the Laboratory established a fine record in the training of fellows, principally in the fields of neuro-ophthalmology, medical ophthalmology, and glaucoma. Many of these fellows accepted full-time academic positions at other institutions, and a number of them became department heads.

The philosophy of the Howe Laboratory stressed the application of basic science to the solution of clinical problems. Clinical research also depends heavily upon patient care. In this the members of the Infirmary's clinical staff excelled from the earliest days. Many of Dr. Verhoeff's contributions were clinical papers, some with a clinicopathological basis. Other members of the staff published significant results obtained from careful observation of large series of patients. Many, including Verhoeff himself during part of his career, were private practitioners with part-time academic affiliation with the Department of Ophthalmology at the Infirmary and, in recent years, at other teaching hospitals in the Harvard orbit. William Beetham, Virgil Casten, Paul Chandler, Trygve Gundersen, and many others reflect this trend in the 1930's and 1940's. In the 1950's and 1960's, Charles Schepens, Robert Brockhurst, Ichiro Okamura, H. Mackenzie Freeman, and J. Wallace McMeel appear in the forefront of clinical research in retinal detachment and related diseases. In cornea research and training, Claes-Henrik Dohlman and his co-workers became preeminent.

In the fall of 1946 Dr. Charles Louis Schepens arrived at the Infirmary. His ideas, abilities, and aspirations were directed toward revolutionizing fundus diagnosis, providing a new discipline for the diagnosis and surgery of retinal detachment, founding a distinguished independent research laboratory, and in the process largely reshaping the Department's clinical and surgical activities. Perhaps more than any other development, his efforts signalized the end of ophthalmology as a single specialty and its beginning as a collection of integrated subspecialties.

Although the existence of retinal detachment as a blinding disease had been known since the latter part of the nineteenth century, early attempts at repair were crude and without a scientific basis until the work of the great Swiss ophthalmologist Jules Gonin, in the 1920's. Gonin's contribution was his clarification of the role of retinal breaks (holes, tears) in the production of retinal detachment. He rightly insisted that locating and closing all breaks in the retina was essential to success in operative reattachment of the detached retina.

During the 1930's and early 1940's Dr. Gonin's principles were put into practice by the application of surface and penetrating diathermy to the scleral wall of the eye. Unfortunately, examination of the retinal periphery was inadequate or impossible with the hand-held (direct) ophthalmoscope. As a result, many small and peripherally located breaks went unrecognized, so that they were either not sealed by diathermy or were sealed accidentally by extensive barrages of diathermy applied over a wide area of the sclera. To this situation Schepens brought a new instrument, an organized approach, and a combination of surgical ability with the ability to obtain funds from governmental and private sources.

Born in Belgium in 1913, Dr. Schepens had served with distinction in the French and Belgian underground in World War II. During his prewar experience in ophthalmology he had recognized that retinal detachment and other diseases of the fundus periphery represented a major cause of blindness and a challenge both in diagnosis and in treatment. His interest in instrumentation had led him to the construction of a working prototype of his head-worn binocular indirect ophthalmoscope. This instrument combined an improved illumination and viewing system with the advantage of leaving one hand free for scleral depression while the other hand held the condensing lens, which also focuses a serial image viewed by the observer. With a well-dilated pupil this technique permits evaluation of fundus lesions, especially those of the extreme retinal periphery, which cannot be seen or can barely be seen with the hand-held direct ophthalmoscope.

Equipped with this tool and a broad conceptual program for (1) the diagnosis and treatment of retinal lesions, especially retinal detachment, (2) basic and clinical research on these subjects, and (3) training of fellows in this new discipline within the specialty of ophthalmology, Schepens began to examine patients with detached retinas and treat them surgically with diathermy after localization of retinal breaks. A superb observer and surgeon, he soon began to obtain results surpassing those previously achieved by others, and to cure patients who had been operated on unsuccessfully elsewhere.

In 1947 Dr. Schepens founded the Retina Service at the Infirmary, the first of its kind in the world specializing in retinal detachment and related conditions. Among the most significant developments of this new approach was the use of scleral buckling as a means of approximating the choroid to the retina in cases where vitreous traction prevented the retina from falling back into place. About 1953 he approached the Trustees of the Infirmary with the idea of founding a new laboratory for the basic and clinical study of the retina, vitreous, and cornea, all of which were at that time under vigorous study by the Howe Laboratory. Having met a cold reception, he founded an independent laboratory, the Retina Foundation, in a vacated tenement building on Chambers Street.

The Retina Foundation

Although not affiliated with the Medical School, the new Retina Foundation Laboratory was partially staffed with individuals holding part-time Harvard appointments in the Department of Ophthalmology. From the beginning it was looked at askance by those who believed that the Howe Laboratory was the only valid eye research enterprise within the University orbit. Very soon, however, the new seedling demonstrated its viability both scientifically and financially. The next ten years would see it move into a gleaming multimillion-dollar abode and would witness the growth of its several departments by the addition of several able scientists. One of these, a young Swedish ophthalmologist, Claes-Henrik Dohlman, was destined to found the Cornea Service at the Infirmary and to succeed to the leadership of the Department of Ophthalmology. In the meantime, the Retina Foundation underwent an internal schism, in which its departments of connective tissue research and muscle research split off to become the Boston Institute of Biomedical Sciences. These developments, although of related interest, are not properly part of the history of the Department of Ophthalmology, but they do indicate the processes that must be used to permit the development of new ideas and the functioning of independent minds which can find no place in the normally solidified academic structure.

By the 1960's it had become apparent that the Infirmary and its laboratories were bursting the seams of their antiquated building, which dated from the previous century. Paralyzed by apparent inertia and an ever-receding mirage that the Suffolk County Jail would be condemned, thus becoming available to the adjacent hospitals, the Infirmary's trustees temporized while pressures built up within the confines of the brick-walled compound. Never comfortable with the responsibilities of Chief of Ophthalmology at the Infirmary, Dr. Cogan requested relief from that position. The request was granted early in 1968, and he was replaced both as Chief and as Department Head by Henry Freeman Allen, who, in 1970, was appointed Henry Willard Williams Clinical Professor of Ophthalmology.

A clinician and teacher rather than an investigator, Allen saw the necessity for an integrated Department under a single head. During his six-year tenure he challenged the Howe Laboratory's claims to autonomy and agreed to step down on Dr. Cogan's retirement in favor of an individual who would wield the threefold authority of Departmental Head, Chief of Ophthalmology, and Director of the Howe Laboratory. He also supported the founding of a new Laboratory for the Study of Retinal Degenerations, under the direction of Dr. Eliot Berson. Unlike that of the Howe Laboratory, the enabling instrument clearly stated that the new laboratory would be under the authority of the Chief of Ophthalmology.

In 1972 Allen resigned as Chief of Ophthalmology, being replaced by Charles D. J. Regan, who functioned ably as Acting Chief of Ophthalmology during the interim period while a committee was searching for a new tripartite head. Their choice fell upon a member of the Department and a senior scientist of the Retina Foundation, Claes-Henrik Dohlman. Since he also succeeded in 1974 to the directorship of the

Howe Laboratory, a unified effort can be envisaged for the future of the Department in patient care, teaching, and research.

This account is more full of joinings and separations than are most departmental histories, but it is atypical only in the degree of academic disunity it reveals. There are two reasons, one accidental and the other inevitable. The accidental factor is the chance coming together of a number of men who had firm ideas about what they wanted linked with impatience with the frustrations induced by the seemingly arbitrary arrangements made by administrative officials who were not themselves engaged in clinical work. The inevitable result was the artificial separation of clinic from laboratory and the establishment of purely arbitrary boundaries between them.

Lucien Howe Library of Ophthalmology[5]

When Dr. Lucien Howe established the Laboratory of Ophthalmology, he expressed the wish that in conjunction with the Laboratory, a comprehensive library of books on ophthalmology and relevant periodicals be obtained. The wish was fulfilled, in part at least, in August of 1928, when such a library was opened in the Massachusetts Eye and Ear Infirmary. Its contents were made up of volumes from Dr. Howe's personal library and from the collection belonging to the Infirmary. An agreement between the Infirmary and Dr. Howe was made, which called for providing space and for a share of costs, responsibilities, and use of facilities. The agreement having weathered many vicissitudes, the Library is now a joint responsibility of the Harvard–Howe Laboratory and the Infirmary. When it first opened, it contained fewer than 3,000 volumes. Today the number has tripled. Another 3,000 volumes belong to the Infirmary's Library of Otorhinolaryngology.

The governing body of the Library is a committee composed of representatives of the Infirmary's staffs, Harvard's Department of Ophthalmology, the Howe Laboratory, and the University Library. In 1938 the committee asked Harvard to give the name Lucien Howe Library of Ophthalmology to the ophthalmic portion of the Library.

Members of the Howe family have had a deep interest in the history of ophthalmology. The intent of Dr. and Mrs. Howe in funding the Library was not clearly stated, but after a later review of the conditions the law firm of Ropes, Gray, Best, Coolidge and Rugg determined that the Library was intended to be an integral part of the Howe Laboratory. In accordance with this interest, the Howe Librarians have placed emphasis on the acquisition of classics of ophthalmic literature and the preparation of studies on the history of ophthalmology. It would be difficult to imagine the research and the clinical scene at 243 Charles

Street for the past half-century without the Lucien Howe Library of Ophthalmology.

OTOLARYNGOLOGY[6]

Stimulated by European investigation, chiefly German, otolaryngology had its beginnings at Harvard early in the Eliot era. For almost a century it remained a minor specialty, dedicated to serving patients competently but, at least in Boston, producing little in the way of pedagogic advances, although a great number of dissected temporal bones that showed the diseases of the middle and inner ear were accumulated.

The situation changed dramatically during World War II when Dr. Julius Lempert, a New York otolaryngologist, began to perform, in a primitive way, the operation that was to revolutionize otolaryngology. It came at a good time, for the chief mainstay of the specialty, the mastoidectomy, was to approach the vanishing point as antibiotics replaced the knife in the treatment of this dreaded disease. The new operations on the middle ear had the effect not only of curing—temporarily at least—a great many deaf people, but also of permitting one to think of otolaryngology in terms of basic science. By 1961, almost twenty years after the Lempert revolution, Harvard was ready to move. In that year it appointed Dr. Harold F. Schuknecht, Walter Augustus Lecompte Professor of Otology, as Professor of Laryngology at the Harvard Medical School. He also became Chief of Otolaryngology, Massachusetts Eye and Ear Infirmary. A research program in this subject was instituted.

Dr. Schuknecht was well qualified. He was graduated from the Rush Medical College, Chicago, in 1940 and had served as resident in otolaryngology at the University of Chicago Clinics from 1946 through 1948. During that time he came under the influence of Dr. William D. Neff, Chairman of the Department of Physiological Psychology, which was to play an important role in developing his interest in sensory physiology. Dr. Schuknecht was appointed to the full-time Faculty as Assistant Professor at the University of Chicago School of Medicine in 1949. For the next several years he was occupied with the study of Dr. John Lindsey's temporal bone collection, and his early attraction to head and neck surgery was supplanted by an interest in clinical otology. A six-week tutelage, under Dr. Julius Lempert, further determined his commitment to otology. He was the first clinical investigator to use consistently a conditioned-response method for the determination of auditory thresholds of experimental animals. From 1948 through 1951 he utilized behaviorly conditioned animals in a series of three classic experiments showing that (1) blows to the head create hearing losses having identical functional deficits and the same underlying pathology as that occurring from an explosion in air; (2) partial surgical section of the auditory nerve reveals that as many as 75 percent of the neurons can be lost without an elevation of puretone thresholds, a finding that provided the basis for a clearer understanding of the psycho-acoustic manifestations of neural lesions; and (3) low-tone hearing losses can be produced by creating lesions in the apex of the cochlea, showing that low frequencies as well as high frequencies have a special location along the cochlear duct.

In 1953 Dr. Schuknecht became Associate Surgeon at the Henry Ford Hospital, Detroit, Michigan, where he was provided with a research laboratory fully equipped to continue his investigations into the patho-physiology of deafness. During his first years in Detroit a one-stage fenestration operation devised by him remained the most spectacular otologic surgical procedure. Dr. Schuknecht observed stapes surgery by Samuel Rosen in New York and Dr. John Shea (Harvard Medical School 1943) of Memphis, as well as tympanoplasty surgery by Professors Horst Wullstein and Fritz Zollner of Germany, and was among the first to perform these procedures in America. In 1956 he developed and introduced the first metal prostheses for total replacement of the stapes. He subsequently developed the fat-wire, gel-wire, and tef-wire prostheses, all of which have been used extensively throughout the world in stapes replacement surgery for the management of deafness due to otosclerosis. He also became innovator, in America, of methods to reconstruct the middle ear sound-transmission system by the use of autogenous soft tissue and bone grafts, and designed numerous surgical instruments for this work which are widely used. From 1956 to 1959, in association with Dr. John Churchill, he showed that cholinergic nerve fibers were present in the organ of Corti and furthermore that these fibers are of efferent origin, coming from the olivocochlear bundle. Dr. Schuknecht also demonstrated that there is a system of channels in the osseous spiral lamina of the mammalian ear by which perilymph comes into direct continuity with the fluid surrounding the organ of Corti (the *canaliculii perforanti Schuknechtii*). Other experiments demonstrated the fluid dynamics of the inner ear, in particular the capability of the cochlear aqueduct to pass particular matter (erythrocytes), the independent origin of the endolymph in the auditory and vestibular systems, and the effects of fistuli of the cochlear duct. In 1956 he described a simplified transcanal labyrinthectomy for ablating vestibular function for the relief of vertigo due to Menière's disease, as well as a method by which vestibular function could be ablated by the intratympanic injection of streptomycin sulfate.

Having established himself as a pioneer and a world leader in the reborn science that underlay otolaryngology, Dr. Schuknecht was brought to Boston in 1961. In the area of research he expanded the ear pathology laboratory, added the Electronmicroscopy Laboratory under the direction of Mr. Robert Kimura, and lent his support to the already established Biochemistry Laboratory under the direction of Mr. Peter Marfey, the Microcirculatory Laboratory under the direction of Dr. John Irwin, and the Eaton-Peabody Laboratory of Auditory Physiology under the direction of Drs. Walter Rosenblith and Nelson Kiang. In 1962 he evolved the concept that positional vertigo of the paroxysmal type is due to a sediment of high specific gravity on the cupula of the posterior semicircular canal, making this structure sensitive to gravitational forces and causing vertigo with changes in the head position. In 1959 he presented histological evidence in the temporal bones of two patients which confirmed this concept and suggested that the disorder be termed cupulolithiasis.

In the first decade of his tenure at the Massachusetts Eye and Ear Infirmary, Dr. Schuknecht collected nearly 900 selected human temporal bones from the morgue of the Massachusetts General Hospital from individuals suffering from deafness or vertigo. These specimens were serially sections, stained, and mounted for histological study. From the studies of these specimens have come reports on the pathology of otosclerosis, acute and chronic otitis media, Menière's disease, Paget's disease, syphilis, leukemia, presbycusis (deafness of aging), congenital deafness, and noise deafness. In the collection are nineteen specimens from patients with Menière's disease, showing findings to support the theory first presented in 1962—that the acute vertiginous episodes are due to ruptures of the endolymphatic system and potassium paralysis of the vestibular nerve fibers, as had been previously proposed by others. Experimental work in the 1960's demonstrated, first in guinea pigs and then in cats, that ablation of the endolymphatic sac creates endolymphatic hydrops similar to that of Menière's disease. These findings support the view that the disease is caused by dysfunction of the endolymphatic sac and provide an animal model for further research on this common, disabling disorder.

Throughout his career at the Massachusetts Eye and Ear Infirmary, Dr. Schuknecht has remained clinically active, examining and treating about fifty outpatients per week and performing five major surgical procedures per week, in addition to consultations and surgical supervision on several service cases each week. He has published nearly 150 journal articles on both basic and clinical subjects, and four books: *Oto-*

sclerosis (1962), *Stereoscopic Atlas of Mastoidotympanoplastic Surgery* (1966), *Stapedectomy* (1971), and *Pathology of the Ear* (1974). The integration of knowledge acquired from clinical experience, pathological studies of the human temporal bone, and animal research has made him an authority on the pathophysiology and treatment of deafness and vertigo.

This perhaps overdetailed history of what is, or at least has been, a minor department in the School has several lessons. A brilliant *clinical* observation—Dr. Lempert's—revived a moribund subject and initiated a set of reverberations whereby basic sciences and clinical practice pushed each other forward. The new field is based on physiology rather than biochemistry, hence, in the eyes of some fanatics, is not merely old fashioned but intrinsically stodgy. It is evident, however, that physiology applied to clinical problems is dramatic enough to satisfy those who need this kind of stimulation and is, in fact, closer to clinical reality and therefore more directly applicable to it than is anything that goes on in the artificial environment of a test tube.

FACIAL SURGERY

Although there is no separate existence at Harvard of facial surgery as a department, the subject invites special comment. Facial surgery fortuitously was at first connected with dentistry, because the man who had a special interest in facial surgery at Harvard held the degree of Doctor of Dental Medicine for some years before he earned his M.D. degree at Harvard. Varaztad H. Kazanjian[7] who had been trained solely as a dentist, joined the first Harvard unit in France as Dental Chief. This unit was organized to treat the wounded of the British Expeditionary Forces. Dr. Kazanjian was destined to occupy himself with much more than the usual dental work. He early showed himself to be extraordinarily skillful in the treatment and reconstruction of shattered upper and lower jaws, and in short order he became a plastic surgeon. While he was with the British Expeditionary Forces in France, some 3,000 wounded men passed through his hands. Because of Dr. Kazanjian's great skill, more and more wounded were sent to his unit. He was described as "The Miracle Man of the Western Front." Recognizing his need for a Doctor of Medicine degree, he entered the Harvard Medical School in the autumn of 1919 and received the M.D. degree in 1921.

During a surgical clinic being conducted by Dr. Harvey Cushing while Dr. Kazanjian was a student, two high-ranking officers from the

Royal Army Medical Corps accompanied Cushing. On glancing up at the students, one of these officers grasped his companion's arm and pointed: they both climbed up the steps and literally dragged a very reluctant student to the floor of the amphitheatre. Dr. Kazanjian was introduced as the man who had taught these distinguished guests the technique they were about to demonstrate.

In the ensuing years, Dr. Kazanjian fought diligently for the recognition of plastic surgery in a professional atmosphere traditionally reluctant to accept any of the subspecialties of general surgery. He gathered about him a staff and students interested in dental collaboration in the care of deformities of the mouth and jaws. At these clinics methods of preparation of oral and facial prostheses were developed. Dr. Kazanjian's original approach to surgical problems has had a far-reaching effect. The psychological effects of the repair of a disfigured face are among the most gratifying in medicine.

Chapter Twenty-five

Obstetrics and Gynecology

THE development of obstetrics and gynecology has followed a wandering and circuitous course. At first joined, they were forcibly separated for a time in the years around World War II and then as forcibly brought together again. Moreover, the subject of diseases of women as taught in the nineteenth century included the nervous disorders that women then seemed to have commonly, postpartum psychoses (constituting 10 percent of all female admissions to mental hospitals, according to Philippe Pinel and his successors), and diseases of the breast—cancer and the terrible abscesses and tuberculosis that occurred during and after pregnancy.

It was twentieth-century endocrinology that in the main changed obstetrics and gynecology. Operative interventions still constitute a large part of their content, but a physiologic approach, involving chiefly the hormones, has come to dominate much of it.

The earliest clinical application of endocrinology to the medicine of women came with the development of a test for pregnancy developed by Selman Ascheim and Herman Zondek—a test that depended on the presence in the urine of large amounts of chorionic gonadotropin—the gonad-stimulating hormone that resembles that of pituitary origin but comes from the placenta. The hormonal aspects of diseases of women developed rapidly as endocrinologic studies and clinical observations stimulated each other. Not only did obstetrics and gynecology benefit but, in addition, hormonal factors are now used to treat disseminated cancers of the breast (and of the prostate gland).

Many of the older Harvard Medical School men will remember how obstetrics was taught as a matter of specialized mechanics. The men who taught and practiced it were competent and sympathetic teachers and physicians. Nonmechanical considerations were brought forward from time to time. For example, during the tenure of Franklin S. Newell there were interesting developments in cardiology. Dr. Newell, a graduate of Roxbury Latin School, Harvard College, and, in 1896, the Harvard Medical School, was head of Obstetrics and Gynecology at the

Boston City Hospital from 1912 to 1916, when it was still an important part of the Harvard teaching establishment. In 1916 he became Obstetrician-in-Chief at the Boston Lying-in Hospital and Clinical Professor of Obstetrics at the School, holding these posts until his retirement in 1931. His tenure saw the move of the Hospital to new quarters on Longwood Avenue and, perhaps more important, organization of the first cardiac clinic for pregnant women in this country. Under Drs. Burton E. Hamilton and Paul D. White, it not only helped scores of women with rheumatic or congenital cardiac lesions through their pregnancies but also made available, in the form of books and articles, information that doctors would need in handling such patients.

Dr. Frederick C. Irving succeeded Dr. Newell, becoming William Lambert Richardson Professor of Obstetrics at the School. He was a fine clinician in the traditional mode, with, in addition, a certain distinction as a versifier. His talents in the latter direction led him to create the famous *Ballad of Chambers Street*, which was recited for years at students' gatherings. This *Ballad* was not only outstanding for its exaggerated lyricism but also for its perceptive comments—usually uncomplimentary—about some of Boston's leading physicians. He also showed his skill in explaining obstetrics to the laity when he wrote his popular book called *Safe Deliverance* (1942).

Things changed with the appointment of Duncan E. Reid as Obstetrician-in-Chief of the Boston Lying-in Hospital and Richardson Professor of Obstetrics at the School in 1947. Dr. Reid was an unusual man. He was born in Burr Oaks, Iowa, in 1905, and his mother died six weeks later. His father died twelve years after that, and he was raised by relatives. An uncle, also named Duncan Reid, was a medical missionary in Africa and persuaded him to go into medicine, in opposition to the local minister, who thought that he should enter the clergy. Reid was an outstanding athlete at Ripon College—"The Ripon Flash" —and a notable scholar. He graduated from Northwestern University Medical School in 1931, having worked his way through first as a factory manager and then as a medical librarian. His early struggles left him not with bitterness and envy but with patience, understanding, and compassion. After early training in obstetrics and gynecology in Chicago, he came to Boston in 1933 to serve as resident under Frederick C. Irving. He was the first non-Harvard resident at the Hospital.

From 1947 to 1966 Dr. Reid served as Obstetrician-in-Chief at the Boston Lying-in Hospital and in 1959 was named Chief of Staff of the combined hospitals when the Lying-in and the Free Hospital for Women merged. He was responsible for the establishment of the Josiah Macy, Jr., Foundation Fellowships at Harvard for the training of men for academic careers in Reproductive Biology as related to obstetrics and gynecology. In 1964 he became the Kate Macy Ladd Professor of Obstetrics and Gynecology at the Harvard Medical School.

Dr. Reid has been concerned with fundamental studies of the lack of fibrinogen in the blood of pregnant women. He and his colleagues originally described the obstetrical states in which coagulation of the blood may become defective, owing to a deficiency of this protein. If the syndrome of hypofibrinogenemia goes undetected and untreated, it may mean the difference between survival and death from uncontrolled hemorrhage. Although the cause and mechanism by which hypofibrinogenemia develops remains uncertain, its diagnosis in the end depends upon a determination of the fibrinogen concentration of the patient's plasma. Dr. Reid found that the clot-observation test constituted a rapid and practical means for recognizing the hypofibrinogenemic state.

Twenty-five years of experience at the Harvard Medical School led to the publication, in 1962, of A Textbook of Obstetrics, a work widely hailed around the world for its sound scientific basis. Its dedication to "those who work together toward achievement of the initial right of man to be born without handicap and the privilege of woman to bear without injury" states Dr. Reid's professional concepts. He has been devoted to a study of the medical complications of pregnant women, such as hypertension and difficulties of coagulation. In his earlier years, Dr. Reid was concerned with defining more precisely the type of hypertension encountered as a complication of pregnancy. His paper on acute pulmonary edema in hypertensive toxemia has been important in making it clear how this ailment differs from acute pulmonary edema of heart failure in patients with valvular or hypertensive heart disease. He was intensely involved in a controversy of the day—namely, whether severe pregnancy toxemia initiates cardiovascular or renal disease. His views were subsequently upheld, and his conclusion was that if a patient was normal before an episode of hypertensive pregnancy, sequelae were rare and future pregnancies need not be regarded as hazardous. This was not then the view of the day.

Dr. Reid presided over the merger of two major hospitals—the Boston Lying-in and the Free Hospital for Women. The merger indicated that obstetrics and gynecology is a single discipline. To be sure, each of these institutions had singly attempted to broaden its medical base, but together the base was effectively and efficiently expanded. Divisions have now emerged—for example, Oncology, Radiotherapy, Endocrinology, Neonatology, Genetics, and Social Medicine—all in addition to the routine care of obstetrical and gynecological practice. The mission of the Boston Hospital for Women, as the amalgamated institutions are called, is to improve medicine as it applies to women.

Dr. Reid excelled as a teacher, clinician, and investigator. Throughout his career he has been interested in the care of women in pregnancy and childbirth with special attention to the medical complications of pregnancy, but he has also maintained an interest in the biology of reproduction. His approach has upgraded obstetrical care by taking it beyond the principles of midwifery. He used his professional eminence to improve the medical status of women, especially those who did not have access to good medical care. After his retirement at Harvard, he was Professor of Obstetrics and Gynecology at Arizona. He died of fulminating hepatitis, caught from a patient he was seeing. He left Obstetrics at Harvard, and in the country in general, better than he first encountered it.

At the present time, Gynecology at the Massachusetts General Hospital continues as a separate entity. Dr. Joe Vincent Meigs was one of its outstanding figures. Born in 1892, he received his M.D. degree from Harvard in 1919. The Vincent Memorial Hospital, a separate corporate organization, since 1939 situated within the Massachusetts General Hospital, was the scene of Dr. Meigs's distinguished services, starting in 1930. When he became Chief of Staff of that Institution, he was the first man to be chosen for the post. In 1941 he was also named Clinical Professor of Gynecology at Harvard. He held both posts until his retirement. He was a fine teacher, at both the undergraduate and the graduate levels, and very much interested in the diagnosis and treatment of cancer of the cervix. A disease associated with a specific benign tumor of the ovaries is now called Meigs' Syndrome. He published *Tumors of the Female Pelvic Organs* (1934); *Progress in Gynecology* (1946), Volumes I through IV, edited in collaboration with Dr. Somers H. Sturgis; and *Surgical Treatment of Carcinoma of the Cervix* (1954). Throughout much of his long career, he was associated with Dr. Langdon Parsons.

Dr. Meigs's life and career are well characterized in the citation given when he received an honorary Doctor of Science degree from Northwestern University in 1959:

A gifted teacher, a constant student, a skillful surgeon, he is one of the foremost gynecologists and pelvic surgeons in America. Efficient, industrious and respected by his contemporaries, he has contributed continuously during the past decade to progressive thinking and present knowledge about the treatment of cancer of the female genital organs; thereby making the life of many patients more secure and happier. Combining successfully the role of research investigator and clinical surgeon, he has been honored many times and in many ways by his colleagues at home and abroad.

In 1962 a group of friends and colleagues contributed funds to establish the Joe Vincent Meigs Professorship of Gynecology. The present incumbent is Dr. Howard Ulfelder. He was given his M.D. by Harvard in 1936 and received his surgical training at the Massachusetts General Hospital. In addition to the Meigs Professorship, he holds the title of Chief of Gynecology at the Vincent Memorial Hospital. Since 1955 Dr. Ulfelder has had the final responsibility for the supervision of the care of patients and the training of the staff on the gynecological service at the Massachusetts General Hospital. His responsibilities there have, over the years, shifted away from strictly surgical procedures to problems of contraception, family planning, venereal diseases, elective abortion, and medical-social problems. Since the Vincent Memorial Hospital has its own board and funds, the Chief of Staff functions to some degree as a Director of hospital activities in addition to other duties.

A considerable part of Dr. Ulfelder's responsibilities has fallen into the area of the research laboratories. In their early years emphasis was placed exclusively on malignant disease but with the passage of time a better balance has been achieved. Funds have been acquired to support studies in gonadotropins, steroids, sexual maturation, renal blood flow in nonpregnant and pregnant subjects, as well as a long-standing and thorough enterprise in the tabulation and follow-up of cancer cases, both ward and private. Recently, a registry was added for cases of clear cell adenocarcinoma of the genital tract in females below the age of 30. This was a direct outgrowth of the Ulfelder group's original observations, establishing a clear-cut relation between the occurrence of this tumor and the treatment of their mothers during pregnancy with stilbestrol to prevent miscarriage.

High on the list of Harvard's men of character and originality stands John Rock. Born in Marlboro, Massachusetts, in 1890, he graduated from Harvard College in 1915 and the Medical School in 1918. By 1922 he was Assistant in Obstetrics at the School, and he rose through various positions to become Clinical Professor of Gynecology in 1947, a post he held until his retirement in 1956. At first his career was that of a man who performed the usual procedures and recommended the usual treatments for his obstetrical and gynecologic patients. Early in his career, however, he showed his concern for the problems of some of his patients by establishing a Fertility Clinic, one of the first in the country. In the 1960's he astounded the medical community by his strong advocacy of oral contraceptives, for he was a devout Catholic. The development of "the pill" rose out of his collaboration with Dr. Gregory Pincus, a brilliant endocrinologist who had been let go by Harvard

University and had moved his laboratory to the Worcester Institute for Medical Research. The invention of the oral contraceptive had enormous sociologic consequences not the least of which was the demonstration that marked cultural changes were owing to technological changes. Thus, whereas the invention of the vacuum cleaner, the deep freeze food storage compartment, prepared foods, and clothes- and dishwashers liberated housewives and encouraged them to enter industry and politics, the invention of the pill liberated young women from constraints in which they had formerly lived. The only contribution that sociological theory made to the current social revolution was to institute child-rearing practices guaranteed to turn American children into horrors, a phenomenon that has markedly restrained any normal inclination to have babies.

In 1963 a John Rock Professorship was established in the Center for Population Studies at the Harvard School of Public Health. Roy Greep was the first incumbent. He was also the first Director of the Laboratory of Human Reproduction and Reproductive Biology at the Medical School.

Another outstanding innovator in the field of gynecologic practice was Dr. George Van Siclen Smith. Born in New York City in 1900, he graduated first from Phillips Andover Academy, and in 1921 from Harvard College. He was admitted to the Medical School in the fall of that year and in 1923 became a student house officer at the Free Hospital for Women. He remained connected with both the School and the Hospital thereafter, rising through the various ranks to become William H. Baker Professor of Gynecology in 1942 and Head of the Division of Gynecology at Harvard, and Chief Surgeon at the Hospital. With his wife, Olive, who had received a Ph.D. degree in biological chemistry in 1928 from the Harvard Medical School (and was known in the biochemical literature for some time thereafter as O. Watkins), he pursued a career of research combined with clinical practice in gynecology at the Hospital. A research laboratory, the Fearing Laboratory, was endowed by the sister of A. Lawrence Lowell, and this was the site of the work of the Doctors Smith thereafter. George Smith was the laboratory's Director. Their work was a systematic and meticulous study of the changes in the secretion of placental and ovarian hormones throughout normal and abnormal ovarian cycles and normal and abnormal pregnancies. The work led, in 1939, to the first identification of estradiol as a normal urinary constituent. The first description of ovarian cortical stromal hyperplasia, a change common in patients with cancer of the cervix, also came from this Laboratory. In addition, George Smith has written extensively about toxemia of pregnancy and cancers of the female genitalia. On becoming Chief Surgeon of the Hospital in 1947, he left the Directorship of the Fearing Laboratory, and his wife succeeded him as Director. He became emeritus in 1967 but has continued his private practice. The contributions of the Drs. Smith have enriched not only clinical gynecology but also the entire field of gonadal endocrinology.

Part IV
Noncurricular Factors in
Growth of The School

Chapter Twenty-six

Special Groups of Students

WOMEN

When Eliot assumed the Presidency in 1869, he inherited an angry controversy over the fitness of women to enter the Harvard Medical School. The origins of the debate go back at least to 1847, and by 1869 the conflict was full blown. An understanding of the scope and virulence of the arguments requires some pre-Eliot comment.

The problem was first posed at a meeting of the Medical Faculty on July 3, 1847,[1] at which time Professor Channing asked if a woman might be admitted to medical lectures, and to examination for a degree. This hot potato was hastily referred to the Corporation for reply. The President and Fellows, having considered the matter in a special meeting on August 14, 1847, concluded that the Corporation deemed it inadvisable to alter the regulations of the Medical School, which implied that the students were exclusively of the male sex.[2]

Notwithstanding Harvard's negative attitude, women in the mid-nineteenth century did invade the male medical scene. Samuel Gregory founded in Boston the first medical school for women in America (November 1848), and it became part of Boston University in 1874. Many of the problems given so much attention 125 years ago seem minor today. Their triviality suggests that they were no more than attempts to block the advent of women into the field: Would they be called doctor or "doctoress?"[3] Should they be allowed to dissect alongside men? Why not leave obstetrics to the midwives? Oliver Wendell Holmes said:

> I have always felt that this [nursing] was rather the vocation of women than general medical and especially surgical practice. Yet I myself followed a course of lectures given by the younger Madame Lachapelle in Paris, and if here and there an intrepid woman insists on taking by storm the fortress of medical education, I would have the gate flung open to her as if it were that of the citadel of Orleans and she were Joan of Arc returning from the field of victory.[4]

At a meeting of the President and Fellows of Harvard College, December 27, 1847,[5] the President submitted an application transmitted by

Holmes from Harriot Kezia Hunt with the request "to be permitted to attend the lectures at the Medical College." The reply was, "it is inexpedient to reconsider the vote of the Corporation of the 14 August relative to a similar request."

Miss Hunt was not so easily turned aside, however. After writing a long letter to the Medical Faculty, she had better luck, at least temporarily. At the meeting of November 23, 1850, it was "Voted that Miss Hunt be admitted to the lectures on the usual terms, provided that the admission be not deemd inconsistent with the Statutes." Five approved, with Dr. Bigelow, Sr., and Dr. Jackson dissenting.[6]

At a meeting of the Medical Faculty on December 12, 1850, consideration was given to two series of resolutions passed by "the Class" on December 10, 1850.[7] The first dealt with the admission of females, the second with the admission of "colored persons." Dr. Bigelow and Dr. Holmes were appointed a committee to look into the matter. They reported on December 13, 1850,[8] that they had received a "remonstrance" (1) against the attendance of a female (evidently unanimous) at lectures and (2) against the admission of colored persons (not unanimous) destined for Liberia. The upshot of this was that the "female" student (Miss Hunt) had, on the advice of the Faculty, withdrawn, and therefore no further action was required(!).[9] As for the "colored persons," they had paid for tickets to classes as arranged with the American Colonization Society and could not be "divested" of the rights involved. When the problem was again referred to the Corporation on December 26, 1850,[10] the "colored" problem was discussed at length and the Dean was instructed to inform the American Colonization Society that the Faculty deemed it "inexpedient" at the present course to admit colored students to the medical lectures.

On January 22, 1866, it was reported that Lucy E. Sewall and Anita E. Tyng, having already spent three years in medical study and having received M.D. degrees from the female medical colleges of Boston and Philadelphia, believed that they should have further medical education.[11] In 1862 Dr. Lucy E. Sewall, with others, had founded the New England Hospital. The matter was taken up by the Corporation. President Thomas Hill wrote to Dean G. C. Shattuck, April 4, 1866, instructing him to inform "Miss" Sewall and "Miss" Tyng that no provision had been made, or then existed, for the education of women in any department of the University.[12]

In 1867, stimulated by Susan Dimmock[13] and others, a further request for admission to the Medical Lectures was turned down by vote, seven in the affirmative and one in the negative: "that this faculty do not approve the admission of any female to the lectures of any professor." In 1872 officials of the New England Female Medical College approached Harvard in their search for a firm base and suggested in fact that the College be made a part of Harvard University. Harvard did not grant this wish, and in 1874 the ladies took their medical college into Boston University.

On April 8, 1878, the President and Fellows of Harvard College received a letter dated March 21, 1878, from Miss Marian Hovey, in which she offered the sum of $10,000 if the "advantage" of Harvard Medical School "can be offered to women on equal terms with men."[14] Her principal arguments were that a large number of graduates of the Medical School of Boston University were practicing in Boston, and the number was increasing. Many of these women were not well prepared. Few could afford to go to Europe for training. This offer was referred to the Overseers and produced extensive majority and minority reports. Miss Hovey's offer prompted a searching study of the matter.

The majority report (signed by Alexander Agassiz as Chairman, Morrill Wyman, Charles W. Eliot, and J. Eliot Cabot) showed signs of a great struggle of conscience. It described how the Committee had studied the medical education of women in England, Europe, and the United States. They found the evidence for action based upon these sources to be "inconclusive." They recognized the need for women in medicine but also observed that the University's resources were not yet adequate for men alone. This being the case, the University could hardly be expected to extend its resources to include women. The following questions were then sent to the members of the Massachusetts Medical Society:

1. Are you in favor of admitting women to the Medical School?

2. Are you in favor of admitting women on equal terms with men?

3. Are you in favor of a separate school for women?

4. If in favor of medical co-education, specify the subjects which, in your opinion, can be taught in common, and those in which men and women should receive separate instruction.

If we interpret the result by the answers to question 4: 138 wished to have nothing to do with the subject; 570 were in favor of the medical education of women physicians; 202 asked for an entirely separate school; and 320 were in favor of admitting women to the Medical School on the same terms as men, with separate studies wholly or in part. The majority of the committee therefore recommended "acceptance of the trust offered by Miss Hovey for the Medical School."[15]

An extensive minority report was signed by LeBaron Russell. Although he agreed with the majority that medical education should be provided for women, possibly in a separate school, which might or might not be created by Harvard, he opposed, in general, the report of the majority as being untimely and of dubious value, a threat to the well being of the School. That is to say, Harvard should not then accept the responsibility for educating women in medicine. It did not.

Miss Hovey's proposed grant of 1878 had a useful result: it flushed out President Eliot. It is now clear that he approved a trial period (he had signed the majority report, above) and was on the side of the liberals. This was emphasized a dozen years later when Miss Edith Varney raised the same questions. Her letter was answered on September 24, 1890, by Henry I. Bowditch:

Dear Madam

I am not surprised at the tenor of President Eliot's reply, which I enclose. I deem the position of Harvard in regards to the education of women, one of which *eventually* the University will be *thoroughly ashamed*. Even the word "Annex" which is connected with the Academic Department shows its low estimate of women. I never can think of it save with a certain contempt for the proud self-sufficiency evinced by the term—the Corporation virtually says "You women shall not join in the Academic Race because you are inferior to us; but as you want to learn something, we will have a small center created [illegible] our University; an "Annex" of the professors who choose are allowed to teach you in certain departments. But in this department of Medicine, certain courses of which woman is fitter than man to practice the art—we will never teach you."

Thank Heaven! other Universities in this country and in Europe have higher ideals in regard to women.

I regret that I cannot help you, but if you think any further counsel I can give you—I hope you will write again.

Respectfully yours,
Henry I. Bowditch[16]

President Eliot, ever careful in his use of words, did indeed regret the lack of a provision for giving a medical education to women at Harvard. He had written:

My dear Dr. Bowditch,—

I regret to say that there is as yet no provision for the medical education of women either in Harvard University or by the Society for Promoting the Collegiate Education of Women. . . .

Very truly yours,
Charles W. Eliot[17]

As the foregoing reports indicate, the matter of Miss Hovey's application was closed, as shown by the subsequent events that concerned Miss Varney. Other discussions of the role of women in medicine occurred, however. Various resolutions were presented. The final one, which was adopted, read:

> Whereas the Medical Faculty are now engaged in radically changing the plan of study in the School, an undertaking which will require several years for its completion, and will demand all the time and ability of the teachers which are available for the purpose, we deem it detrimental to the interests of the School to enter upon the experiment of admitting female students. Drs. Bigelow, Minot, Reynolds, Williams, Cheever, White, Porter, Warren, Richardson, Wood, Beach, Baker, and Hills voted Aye 13 in all—Drs. Ellis, Holmes, Edes, Bowditch, and Fitz voted No—5 in all. [Powerful men all. See votes and voters below.]

> 1. We the undersigned believe that the Medical School of Harvard University is intended to be a school for men: We believe that it is inexpedient to co-educate women in this medical school whether wholly or in part (i.e., in certain branches of study). (Signed)

H. J. Bigelow	James C. White
Edw. S. Wood	David W. Cheever
R. H. Fitz	M. L. Richardson
C. B. Porter	John P. Reynolds
J. Collins Warren	William B. Hills
F. Minot	H. H. A. Beach
H. W. Williams	Thomas Dwight

> 2. If the condition of admission of women to the Medical School of Harvard University is to be made in any way a pecuniary one, as it is, in the majority report of the Trustees, then we believe that $200,000 is the least sum for which such admission should be granted—(signed)

H. J. Bigelow	David W. Cheever
Edw. S. Wood	H. W. Williams
R. H. Fitz	John P. Reynolds
H. P. Bowditch	William B. Hills
C. B. Porter	James C. White
J. Collins Warren	H. H. A. Beach
F. Minot	Thomas Dwight

Dr. Reynolds presented in print four resolutions the first of which ... Resolved that it is not advisable to open the course of study at the Medical School to women—Drs. Bigelow, Minot, Reynolds, Williams, Cheever, White, Porter, Warren, Fitz, Richardson, Wood,

Beach, Baker and Hills voted in the affirmative—14 in all and Drs. Ellis, Holmes, Edes and Bowditch in the negative—4 in all. The remaining resolutions were withdrawn.

The following resolution was presented by Dr. Bowditch—"We see no objection to the organization for Harvard Medical School for women independent in government of the existing School for Men, but in which the instruction shall be united to that in the School for Men to such a degree as may be hereafter found to be practicable and expedient and we hereby express our willingness to become members of the Faculty of a School so organized"—Drs. Bigelow, Minot, Williams, Cheever, Warren & Beach 6 in all voted no. Drs. Ellis, Holmes, Reynolds, Edes & Bowditch 5 in all voted Aye—and Drs. White, Porter, Fitz, Richardson, Wood, Baker & Hills 7 in all were not prepared to vote.[18]

The deliberations of the Medical Faculty were passed on to the Overseers, who voted May 27, 1879, that:

In view of the state of opinion in the Medical Faculty, the Overseers find themselves unable to advise the President and Fellows to accept the generous proposal of Miss Marian Hovey . . . Thereupon the President of the University, in order to procure an expression of the views of the Board itself upon the general subject, proposed . . . "that, in the opinion of the Board of Overseers, it is expedient that, under suitable restrictions, women be instructed in medicine . . . in the Medical School" . . . It is obvious that both governing boards are in favor of giving medical education to women in the University under suitable restrictions; and it is also apparent that the reasons given by the Faculty for not admitting women to the School are temporary in their nature.

The President noted that since the above transactions, the Councilors of the Massachusetts Medical Society had

taken action which goes far to prove that the majority of the medical profession recognize the fact that there is a legitimate demand and an appropriate field of work for well-educated female physicians. [On October 1, 1879, 48 voted Yea and 32 Nay.] That the Councilors instruct the Censors of the Society to admit females to examination as candidates for admission to Fellowship.

This action cannot but suggest the inquiry whether it be expedient that Harvard University should make no provision for educating a class of persons who are admissible as members of so ancient and respectable a professional body as the Massachusetts Medical Society.[19]

The women were simply not going to accept defeat, however great the bitterness aroused by their importunate actions might be. The next blow against intolerance came in the form of a letter[20] from Marie E. Zakrzewska, M.D., and nine other women physicians asking if the President and Fellows of Harvard would accept $50,000 for the purpose of providing medical education of women leading to an M.D. degree. A ten-year plan was envisioned. The request was referred to the Overseers. On January 11, 1882, a committee of five was appointed to study the matter. It produced a majority report signed by three members, advising the Overseers against the acceptance of the fund mentioned—and a minority report signed by two members in favor of acceptance.[20] The Board adopted the minority report! When the matter was presented to the Overseers as a whole, eleven voted for the Board's decision and six against. The vote was returned to the Corporation where, in effect, it was tabled; evidently the adversaries hoped to delay until they could reverse the vote. A considerable state of confusion and some medical politicking ensued. The Medical Faculty surfaced with the recommendation (meetings of March 4 and 11, 1882) that money for the medical education of women and the granting of a medical degree to women not be allowed without the "advice and full concurrence of the Faculty of the Harvard Medical School."[21] Various committees produced various recommendations, but the gist of them is the Medical Faculty's wish to have a controlling role concerning women in Harvard Medicine.

There was considerable weakness in the application of Dr. Zakrzewska and her colleagues. In the first place, the $50,000 sum mentioned was grossly inadequate for the purpose stated, and second, even this sum was not in hand but was to be raised in the event that the President and Fellows consented to receive it. In fairness to a Faculty already preoccupied with many changes and confronted with expenses difficult to estimate in conjunction with the move into the new building, they can hardly be blamed for their reluctance at that time to take on the revolutionary changes pressed by the women.

On March 18, 1882, the Board of Overseers voted "That the President and Fellows be requested not to appropriate any money received for the purpose of giving a medical education to women without taking the advice of this Board."[22] The vote was transmitted to the Corporation at this meeting of March 27. Thus the Medical Faculty thwarted the ambitious women—for a time. There were many more votes by various groups, but they added nothing new. The repetitiveness of the proposals and counterproposals and the dwindling differences between the ayes and nays suggest that despite the positive statements made, some consciences were troubled, and increasingly so.

The new Boylston Street building was dedicated on October 17, 1883.

When the School moved from the North Grove Street building, November 24, 1883, Henry I. Bowditch wrote the Medical Faculty, asking on what terms the old building could be obtained for a Medical Department for women where degrees could be conferred under the same rules as for men.[23] The Faculty were not caught napping. They promptly replied that they had other uses in mind for the old building. They were supported by the Corporation, and, the women and their supporters having been defeated so many times, a considerable period of quiet ensued.

When World War I was near at hand, it was feared that in the event of war a grave shortage of physicians might develop. A remarkably different attitude from that of bygone years can be read in the *President's Report* for 1916–17. Although the change of attitude was not complete, as indicated by the condescending last line of the Report: "Many women are particularly well qualified for medical laboratory and research work." (The same can be said of male physicians.)

> For a time it was thought that a need existed for women physicians. This brought the subject of providing education for female students prominently before the Administrative Board of the School. Arrangements were made for the enrollment of female medical students under the direction of Radcliffe College, the teaching to be conducted by the regular teaching force of the Harvard Medical School.[24] A number of applications were received, but as the announcement of the proposed plan was made late in the summer, the applicants, with a few exceptions, who were qualified, were already enrolled at other medical schools. It was not, therefore, considered proper to consider these applications. Although the number of applications was not enough to make a recognized war exigency evident, there can be no doubt that if the war continues, there will be an urgent need of properly trained female physicians. Evidence of this is found in the experience of England, France, and Germany. The high standard of pre-medical scientific preparation and the arduous struggle demanded in modern medical practice at present seem to limit the number of suitable female applicants for medical study. There is no doubt, however, that a woman's claim for the best opportunity to study medicine is a just one and that no hindrance should be given to all properly qualified persons to enter upon such studies. Many women are particularly well qualified for medical laboratory and research work.[25]

In view of the ladies' many rebuffs, it is not surprising that a quiet period followed their efforts to obtain a medical education in the Harvard Medical School. Preoccupation with World War I doubtless had something to do with the slowdown. In any case, not much happened between 1918 and 1942.

The entry of the United States into World War II reopened the matter, albeit for other reasons. A committee was appointed by the Dean for the purpose of considering "Whether Women under Present Circumstances Should be Admitted to the Harvard Medical School," and on January 13, 1943, they submitted the report that follows:

Composition of the Committee
S. Burt Wolbach, Shattuck Professor of Pathological Anatomy,
  Chairman
Oliver Cope, Assistant Professor of Surgery
Chester M. Jones, Clinical Professor of Medicine
Charles C. Lund, Assistant Professor of Surgery
Robert S. Morison, Assistant Professor of Anatomy

As was to be anticipated, your committee was unable to find new premises of importance bearing upon the question, nor was it able to document the time-worn arguments, for and against, so familiar to this faculty. Although our deliberations, failing ponderable premises, do not merit characterization as scientific, there was much employment of logic and, without violation of its laws, conclusions were reached which seem as axiomatic and as incapable of proof as the "truths" held to be self-evident in the Declaration of Independence.

Three obvious aspects of the problem were considered.

(1) The question of adequacy of opportunities, regarded quantitatively and qualitatively, for medical education for women in this country.

(2) The possibility of advantages to the Medical School.

(3) The question imposed by our nationally important position of sharing responsibility for the medical education of women.

Concerning the present opportunities in this country for the medical education of women, the Committee can obtain no evidence of inadequacy from available statistics. The percentage of women applicants admitted is very slightly lower than that of male candidates. Harvard Medical School is the only one of outstanding merit refusing admission to women, so that the quality of instruction as a whole is on the same level as for men. (These statements are documented by tables in the appendix to this report.) President Ada L. Comstock of Radcliffe College has expressed the opinion (February, 1943) that "When and if the Harvard Medical School opens its doors, it will have to be, I believe, on grounds other than the inadequacy of opportunities for medical education for women in this country."

It may be argued, however, that the possibility of a medical career would attract a larger number of the ablest students in our eastern colleges for women if the Harvard Medical School admitted women.

There are a few advantages which the admission of women might bring to the Medical School. There would be a larger number of applicants to choose from and therefore a possibility of raising the intellectual level of the classes as a whole and of a reduction in the number of failures. There would be the possibility of securing students covering a wider range of aptitudes for the many branches of applied medicine and a larger number with research interests.

If the civilian admissions to each entering class during the war years ahead are to be limited to a small number, then the School and community will benefit by having a number of very superior women admitted to replace an equal number of mediocre men ineligible for military service.

On the question of duty to participate in the medical education of women, the committee has strong convictions, unhampered by any evidence that the quality of instruction has been lowered, or other untoward result experienced in the medical schools now accepting women. The presence of women in this medical school in those classes to which they have been admitted has not in any way detracted from classroom performance.

The members of the committee decided unanimously against seeking a solution in the interests of expediency or one not intended to be a permanent policy of the Medical School. All agreed that the opinion of this committee regarding the admission of women students to the Harvard Medical School should be expressed largely, if not entirely, on the merits of such a move as a proper educational policy in relation to the current world-wide trends. Education is a right of a democratic world and the right of women to higher education is intimately bound to the problem of human rights.

Recently, in Harvard University, the attitude toward women registered at Radcliffe College has become more liberal. They are now admitted to all university courses primarily offered to graduate students; the option of selection no longer resides with the heads of various university departments. Radcliffe students are eligible on an equal competitive basis with men to seminar courses with a limited enrollment.

Harvard Medical School has developed beyond the status of a New England institution. One of its chief functions is to train a body of representative able physicians for positions in all parts of the country, both in professional and educational life. As one of the few medical schools which set the standards for medical education in this country, it holds to a paradoxical policy in restricting its influence by the exclusion of women.

The Committee realizes that the admission of women would entail responsibility for providing post-graduate training for them, involving the difficult but not insuperable problem of interneships in first class hospitals.

Conclusions

The Committee unanimously recommends:

(1) The admission of women to the Harvard Medical School as an immediate and permanent policy.

(2) That the proportion of men to women admitted should be decided each year by the Admissions Committee solely on the basis of quality of the applicants.[26]

The Committee found itself in agreement, then, with the report of 1916–17 that women should be admitted on the grounds of general policy, and felt that it would be a serious misfortune from several points of view if, inadvertently, the impression were given that Harvard believed women as a class to be undeserving of the right to a medical education; whereas, as a matter of fact, it welcomed the opportunity to assume its share of the responsibility for the training of women in medicine, which could only lead to an improvement in medical practice and the advancement of medical science.

Realists familiar with the situation could not have overlooked the fact that almost all of the courses in the first two years in the Medical School were already open to women, and that every year several women took these courses, which led to the A.M. or Ph.D. in the Graduate School of Arts and Sciences. Not only this, but women were to be found in increasing numbers as interns and residents in all of Harvard's affiliated hospitals. When these facts are taken into account, the difficulties in the way of extension of these rights to the third and fourth years in qualification for the degree of Doctor of Medicine were not very great.

The arguments against the admission of women continued to be raised by individuals and groups from time to time; only one merits serious consideration: that women physicians frequently marry and do not utilize the fine medical training they have had. This statement, so often made, does not conform to available information. It is true that approximately 40 percent of women physicians marry, but half of this group continues to practice for a major portion of the time. Also, the Subcommittee called attention to the fact that women are particularly useful in positions of importance in social welfare, but that physicians of the same caliber are often not attracted to these positions, owing to the limited financial return. Women physicians are often found serving as consultants to juvenile courts or as part-time physicians to charitable institutions. Women in medicine enrich the cultural life of their communities by taking part in various lay activities, for example as members of hospital and school boards and directors of young groups, in which their medical training contributes to the general welfare.

The Committee of 1943 pointed out that at the time the report was written, it appeared that the number of first-rate students applying at Harvard had not been adequate to ensure a uniformly high quality in the student group. Each year the Admissions Committee had been forced to select some men who were less desirable than others. That this is no longer true, taking into account the massive number of applications, does not detract from the importance of the point at the time the Committee rendered its report. The Committee believed that the opening of opportunity to women would, to a significant degree, increase the quality of the Medical School classes.

One wonders how much importance should be attached to the last point made, for the last class accepted in the usual fashion in 1943 was from a pool of 1797 applicants. It seems unlikely that high diligence on the part of the Admissions Committee could not have found highly qualified candidates for admission in this large group. The Subcommittee persisted in its belief that, notwithstanding the number of applicants in normal times, qualification of students in each class would be improved if women were to be considered. In wartime, of course, it is to be expected that the numbers of applicants would fall, and this proved to be the case. At issue here was not only the immediate admission of women but the establishment of a long-range policy where women were to be admitted on the same basis as men. Owing to Harvard's policy of exclusion of women, grave shortages had appeared in the interns' and residents' staffs of the affiliated hospitals. In the wartime period of the Subcommittee report, it was necessary for the Harvard hospitals to call on women trained in more enlightened universities.

The Faculty of Medicine on April 2, 1943, by a vote of 66 to 12, accepted the report of the ad hoc committee and recommended to the governing bodies of the University that the admission of women to the Harvard Medical School be adopted, not only as an immediate but also as a permanent policy, and that the proportion of women to men admitted should be settled by the Committee on Admissions solely on the basis of the quality of the applicants.[27]

This represented a great change in the attitude of the Faculty of Medicine, which had, in earlier years, as the foregoing account shows, bitterly opposed the admission of women to the School, whereas in those earlier years women had more support in the governing bodies.

Surprisingly, the Corporation, at its meeting on June 21, 1943, voted "that this Board is unwilling at the present time to make the proposed change in regard to the admissibility of women to the Medical School." This rejection produced shock waves.

Nearly a year after the rejection by the Corporation, the manpower shortage was such that the matter, despite the negative ruling of the Corporation, was brought to the Administrative Board, which asked the Faculty and the Corporation to reconsider the question. In the spring of 1944 the Faculty of Medicine recommended to the Corporation "that beginning with the class entering in the autumn of 1945 women be eligible for admission to the Harvard Medical School."[28] The Minutes of the Meeting of April 18, 1944 (p. 206), record that it was "VOTED that the Administrative Board recommended that the question of admitting women to Harvard Medical School be reconsidered by the Corporation and that this recommendation should be supported by a statement drawn up by Dr. Morison on the figures of admission." This was approved by the Corporation in June 1944, and the Overseers consented in September. In September 1945 women entered the Harvard Medical School for the first time on an equal basis with men. The ladies had won their case. It took them ninety-eight years to do it, but Harvard's "shame" (Henry I. Bowditch) was at last expunged.

A series of interviews was conducted in 1972 by the MGH *News* concerning the attitude of various individuals to women in medicine, a situation of increasing prominence, owing, in part, to pressures from the Women's Liberation Movement. By way of comparison, 7 percent of the medical manpower in America is female, 15 percent in England, 20 percent in the Netherlands, 25 percent in Sweden, 30 percent in Germany, and 75 percent in the Soviet Union.[29]

In 1950, five years after women were accepted, 5.3 percent of students in all medical schools were females. In 1972 the figure was 13.6 percent. In the autumn of 1971 Harvard Medical School accepted 32 women, roughly one fifth of the class. There is a strong feeling among women that their qualifications have to be "exceptionally outstanding" for acceptance by the Harvard Medical School and postgraduate training programs.

At the Massachusetts General Hospital there is a conviction that the initial obstacles faced by women begin before medical school. It is also their belief that American society does not generally encourage women to enter medicine. Many of these same women report pressures from others not to attend medical school. Those who were admitted to the Harvard Medical School and the Massachusetts General Hospital were "strong, self-assured individuals who were certain of their goals."

There is the sometimes rather hotly debated question whether women medical graduates will devote enough of their lives to their profession to justify the time and money invested in them. Dr. Leon Eisenberg has said: "If we consider the obstacles that face women in entering medicine, in obtaining training in certain of its specialties, and returning to practice after bearing children, this record [of women in medicine] should be regarded as an extraordinary accomplishment rather than as any indication of limited potential. If we consider how much greater their professional output is likely to be once obstacles to training are removed, day care becomes more widely available for women with children, and problems of re-entry into professional life are simplified by the provision of rational job and retraining opportunities, it becomes abundantly clear that womanpower can contribute in a major way to meeting the national shortage of medical care."[30] Of the women in medicine at the Massachusetts General Hospital in 1972, all but one had been married, and all of those had at least one child; one had five children. Dr. Eisenberg spoke sadly of the "great loss of skill to the country" owing to current attitudes toward medical womanpower.

Those interviewed spoke of the difficulties of balancing the demands of family and career. The group at the Massachusetts General Hospital agrees that it is extremely difficult to have children and continue to work. They have found that the expenses of adequate care for their children consume nearly all of the salaries earned. Yet it is generally accepted that women have important contributions to make in such specialties as Pediatrics, Psychiatry, Neurology, Internal Medicine, and Anesthesia.

While surgery has occasionally been carried out by women on the staff of the Massachusetts General Hospital, the Department of Surgery, as such, had until July 1973 never accepted a female house officer, even though such may have existed in some of the surgical specialties. Surgery is still a male-dominated field.

It is probable, with changing health-care patterns, that women will become more active in the future than in the past in community health care and group practice, where their hours can be more easily regulated than at present (1975).

Unlike the situation 100 years earlier, however, none of the women interviewed at the Massachusetts General Hospital felt any personal prejudice in that institution because of her sex.

The Committee on Governance at the Harvard Medical School had this to say recently: "All appointments at all levels within the Harvard Medical School and its hospitals should be made on the basis of professional qualification and should specifically not take into account the race, religion, sex, marital status, or family relationship to other members of the same or different departments of the potential appointee."

BLACKS

In the preceding section reference was made to the admission of "colored persons." One documented case vividly tells the sad story of blacks in the Medical School until recently.[31]

At the Faculty meetings of November 2 and 4, 1850, Dean Oliver Wendell Holmes recorded that a letter from Charles Brooks and two letters from the Committee of the Colonization Society had been received in which inquiry was made in behalf of two "young men of color," Daniel Laing, Jr., and Isaac H. Snowden, concerning the possibilities of admission to the lectures in the Medical School. Their candidacy was supported by the managers of a Committee of the Massachusetts Colonization Society, Abraham R. Thompson and Joseph Tracy (letter of November 1, 1850).

The American Colonization Society was established in the United States in 1816 for the purpose of aiding emigration of freed Negro slaves from the United States to Africa. The Republic of Liberia owes its existence to the Society. Some 6,000 slaves were moved to Liberia between 1821 and 1867. About 1840, however, strong opposition to the Society developed in the United States, and after 1865 it functioned chiefly as a trustee for the Liberian settlements.

At the November 4th meeting noted above, the Faculty accepted the two blacks as students to attend the regular courses of lectures. In a letter of November 6, 1850, Professor Tracy and Dr. Thompson were united in their expression of appreciation to Dr. Holmes, but they were short on money and asked for a little delay in paying the tuition for their two candidates, Laing and Snowden.

Shortly afterward, this letter was received:

> To the faculty of Harvard Medical College—,
> As a movement has of late arisen in this institution for the purpose of admitting a negro as a student of Harvard Med. College—& as a paper to that effect has been signed by some of its members, & presented to the faculty, some effort is necessary on the part of those opposed, to prevent this inexpedient action.
> We therefore students of Harvard Med. Col. placing all confidence in the judgment of our preceptors; would respectfully request of them that they would decide the matter unbiased by the opinions of others—
> [Signed by F. M. Lincoln and seven others]
> [Not dated, but from the context about November–December, 1850]

> To the Medical Faculty of Harvard University;
> Gentlemen,

The undersigned, members of the medical class, would respectfully submit to the Medical Faculty their desire to be informed whether colored persons are to be admitted as students at another course of lectures. This request is offered not with the view of influencing any action of the Faculty [certainly not!] but simply that the undersigned may have opportunity to make such arrangements for the future as shall be most agreeable to their feelings in the event of negroes being allowed again to become members of the school.
  (Signed)
  C. A. Robertson   E. P. Abbe [and fourteen others]. [Not dated, ca. November 1850]

Notwithstanding the disclaimer, it is clear that a threat is contained in the comments. Those writing stated subsequently in a resolution of December 10 that the admission of blacks to the medical lectures would be "highly detrimental to the interests, and welfare, of the Institution of which we are members, calculated alike to lower its reputation in this and other parts of the country, to lessen the value of a diploma from it, and to diminish the number of its students." [32] They go on to say that "we cannot consent to be identified as fellow-students, with blacks; whose company we would not keep in the streets, and whose society as associates we would not tolerate in our houses." Moreover, the dissenting group felt its grievances were merely the "beginning of an evil, which, if not checked will increase, and that the number of re-spectable *white* students will, in future, be in an inverse ratio to that of *blacks*." They requested that the Faculty spare them "the necessity of being in such company, or of compelling us to complete our medical studies elsewhere."

To add to the complexity of the situation, other medical students dissented from the preceding recommendation concerning the admission of colored students (December 11, 1850). They requested that the Dean place their statement before the Medical Faculty, and their request was transmitted to the Faculty on December 12, 1850. There were two aspects worthy of note to this protest. One was that reasons for the cause adopted were stated by these dissidents, whereas the earlier group restricted themselves to a simple expression of disapproval of the resolutions referred to. Although this second group did not wish to appear as trouble-makers, they did wish to make it clear that the number of those who signed their protest was much greater than the majority who voted for the resolutions (December 12, 1850, Richard J. Gimory, Chairman, Adams Wiley, Secretary).

While the Faculty are desirous of doing full justice to the claims of all who apply to them for medical education, they feel bound to remember that all causes of irritation introduced among their students interfere at once with the success of their teaching and their means of being useful to those who require their assistance. The presence of colored persons at the Medical Lectures had proved a source of irritation and distraction during the present session more general and serious than might have been apprehended. It becomes the duty of the Faculty therefore, to request the gentlemen who represent the Colonisation Society not to renew an application which it is evidently incompatible with the welfare of the School under their charge to grant.

[not dated or signed]

The material was placed before the Faculty, and it was concluded that

The result of this experiment has satisfied them that the intermixing of [the white and black races] different races on a footing of equality & personal proximity [in their active rooms] during this course of lectures, is distasteful to a large fraction of the class, & injurious to the interests of the school . . .

In the Minutes of the Faculty Meeting of December 17, 1850, it was

VOTED—That whereas arrangements were made at the beginning of the course, with gentlemen representing the American Coloniza-tion Society, for the attendance this year of certain colored persons, destined for Liberia, and whereas all persons who have purchased tickets, have thereby acquired rights of which they cannot properly be divested—therefore the Faculty do not feel themselves authorized to revoke this arrangement, or to recede from this former vote on the subject.

The Dean, Oliver Wendell Holmes, was instructed to communicate these proceedings to the medical class, some of whose members had challenged the propriety of allowing blacks to attend the Harvard Medi-cal School. Professor Walter Channing, recognizing the controversial possibilities, wished to pass the problem on to the President and Fel-lows, but the Faculty would not agree to that.

At a meeting of December 26 further discussion of the "colored per-sons" was resumed, at length. A remarkable flip-flop was arranged, the thrust of which was to inform the agents of the Colonization Society that "this Faculty deem it inexpedient, after the present course, to admit colored students to attendance on the medical lectures. Affirmative: Drs. Bigelow, Jackson, Holmes, and Bigelow, Jr. Negative: Drs. Channing, and Ware. (Dr. Horsford not voting.)" Perhaps a little softening of the harsh attitude of December 1850 can be seen in a letter of Novem-ber 5, 1853, where it was stated that the medical students, believing the intention of Mr. Isaac H. Snowden to be sound, had no objection to his attendance upon a course of lectures and asked that the Faculty would grant him the right of attendance. This petition was signed by Samuel A. Green and 73 others.

The unpleasant situation was summarized in the *Boston Journal* in an editorial December 10–13, 1850. When it was discovered at the beginning of lectures that two "colored students" were to be present, and a few weeks later another black made his appearance, the report was circulated that a woman had taken tickets for the lectures! This was the last straw. The pent-up indignation now broke out. Two series of resolutions were passed, remonstrating against this conjunction of sexes and races. One series concerned the "female Aesculapius" and protested her presence. This complaint was unanimously supported. The other series did not achieve such unanimity, not because the presence of blacks was agreeble to anyone, but because some were opposed to supporting a measure that was likely to bring out the hostile feelings of a part of the community. The resolutions were passed by a large majority and sent to the Faculty. A protest was made by the minority and also sent to the Faculty. The Faculty examined both of these resolutions and made a report to the class. Some eloquent individual had induced the *lady* to change her mind. The blacks had their tickets and could not be deprived of them.

The class had assumed that because the catalogue said nothing about it, they would not be forced to deal with persons whose presence would be unwelcome, but they found themselves deceived or mistaken and were annoyed by having the blacks present among them. They felt that their feelings should have been consulted in a matter concerning them so personally. Clearly, they were affected by prejudice, but an honest prejudice. Indeed, the policy was to avoid the mingling of blacks and whites in the public schools. It was common to hear disparagement of the blacks, who were considered inferior. The editorialist goes on to suppose that the case were altered and instead of black students attending lectures, a black professor were to be appointed to deliver some of them. One cannot doubt for a moment that the entire Faculty would indignantly resign their posts. Their aversion to the society of blacks was very firmly established.

The medical students said, "It is not for the physician to crush any. It is his mission to heal the sick and relieve the suffering . . ." The writer of the editorial concludes that blacks should be educated for any and all professions, but his plea was that no one would compel white men to become martyrs and fraternize with them. If any chose this course, so be it. If some protested against it, their feelings and prejudices as white men should be respected. The writer signs his name "COMMON SENSE."

We can, since our arrival at the Harvard Medical School in 1928, attest to the desire of the School to include blacks in its student body. One or two were generally on hand. The explanation for this poor showing was that only rarely did a black candidate appear with background preparation sufficient to enable him to compete with white applicants for admission to the School. The situation in which ignoring color was a matter of policy was still ambiguous because other disadvantages connected with being born and raised a black in this country were evaded.

In May 1968, in response to a petition signed by 278 medical students, the Faculty of the Harvard Medical School voted to establish a commission on relations with the black community in Boston.[33] The students' initiative, stimulated by the assassination of the Rev. Martin Luther King, Jr., urged that the School undertake an examination of its contributions to the "training of black physicians, to health services in the black community, to employment opportunities for black citizens, to research in teaching in Social Medicine and to the establishment of liaison with organizations in the black community." (In September 1968, of some 570 students working for the M.D. degree at Harvard, five were American blacks). A report of a committee headed by Dr. Leon Eisenberg said that "To the tens of millions of medically disadvantaged people in this country, Harvard's claim that it trains the leaders of American medicine is a source of condemnation; we have been training the leaders of a grossly inequitable system." This long and carefully constructed report stimulated the Medical School to adopt a new policy in May 1968. By 1969 the policy was in operation, which meant that for the first time the Harvard Medical School was really coming to grips with the problem of the education of black physicians, as well as other disadvantaged students. It was decided to increase by twenty places opportunities for blacks. In the beginning Harvard did not wish to take in students from all-black schools, since they were often not well prepared. That policy has since been modified.

It was agreed that black students, although they might not compete at once in intellectual terms with the white candidates, must show potentiality for making safe and sound physicians. Special handling, itself a kind of racism, is evidently necessary for a time. It is anticipated that the specialized treatment will not be necessary after 1985.

There is a conviction on the part of some members of the Faculty that blacks are handled too gingerly. As one man put it, instructors toss "snowballs" to the black students—that is, easy questions, it is hoped they can answer. If this is true, it will last only a very few years. Clearly, some blacks have difficulty in adjusting to the School in the first and second years. Many have a good deal of self-doubt and insecurity. By the third year, however, they have usually developed enough self-esteem and security to carry on better work. Some believe that the blacks have more emotional disturbances in general than whites, but data are not yet available to establish or reject that view.

At the time this is being written, it is not what has been done for them that needs attention, but what has not yet been done. Quite commonly, they wanted and expected special treatment; they wanted their needs to be recognized by the Harvard Medical School, especially their poor preparation, but their problems remain and are various. Blacks seem to have more financial difficulties than do whites. Whites often create environments that lead to cliquishness on the part of blacks. Nevertheless, the statistics show improvement:

> Although efforts are made to increase the number of students from groups which historically have had few members in medical schools, the Harvard Medical School does not have a separate program for students from minority groups. The School does, however, actively recruit qualified students from minority groups, and a significant number have been admitted. Presently, in the Class of 1973, there were 16 Black students, one American Indian, and three Oriental students. The Class of 1974 includes 26 minority students: one Mexican-American and one Cuban, three Orientals, and 21 Black students. The Class of 1975 includes 30 minority students: three American Indians, five Orientals, seven Spanish-American (Mexican-American, Puerto Rican, and Cuban), and 15 Black students. In the Class of 1976, thirty minority students have been offered places. Of these, 5 are Oriental, 9 are Spanish-speaking, one is American Indian, and 15 are Black. The Committee on Admission admits 140 students each year.[34]

In a postlude to the black students' problems, one can do no better than to quote the distinguished Professor Walsh McDermott. He has had this to say (1971):

> ... forty years ago [i.e., early 1930's], when I was a first-year medical student, there were two black students in our class of around one hundred. In those days half the U.S. schools were in the Eastern Time Zone and most schools in the whole country were in the northern states. As a practical matter, therefore, most of the schools were in a position where they had a free hand as to whom they would admit. If you talked to the admissions office in any one of these schools you would hear that the policy was to apply honestly and

courteously the same criteria for all applicants irrespective of race
and so far as I could see this was done. No special efforts were made
to recruit black students; neither were there any efforts to recruit
whites. The people at each school would sometimes express regret
that educational deprivation lower down in the school system made
the numbers of qualified black applicants rather small. But the feeling generally was: "Well, that is a part of our national tragedy; at
least at *our* school we do what we can, we play it fair." With this
policy the admission rate for black students remained at essentially
the same low level for thirty-five years or so, until positive efforts
to increase it significantly were made in the schools in quite recent
times.

The point is that during the period in question, the faculties of
the individual separate schools would have been absolutely and quite
genuinely horrified if any one had accused them of holding to a policy of racial exclusion in medical educaion. And viewed from the
standpoint of any one school they were right. Yet in actual fact, considered as members of a medical education establishment they were
countenancing a policy of almost complete apartheid; because the
great majority of black students received their medical education at
either one of only two schools.

It was one of life's tragic instances where the sum of individual
innocence turns out, in reality, to be collective guilt.[35]

Perhaps for today's shock value, nothing can quite equal a statement
by Abbott Lawrence Lowell which appeared in the *New York Times* of
January 12, 1923:

> Like the proposed religious quotas, the color ban became a *cause
> célèbre*. Negro civil rights groups agitated against it, and 149 Har-
> vard alumni signed a protest petition, but to no avail. As Lowell said
> in a letter to the father of one of Harvard's black freshmen: ". . . I
> am sorry to have to tell you that in the Freshman Halls, where resi-
> dence is compulsory, we have felt from the beginning the necessity
> of not including colored men. . . . we have not thought it possible to
> compel men of different races to reside together.

In the past twenty years there have, indeed, been enormous advances.

JEWS

Until the second half of the nineteenth century, America was unmistakably a Protestant country. Its colleges had been founded, for the most

part, by Protestant religious organizations with a dual purpose: the production of an educated ministry and the training of missionaries. Calvinism dominated the scene. In the beginning of the second half of the nineteenth century, the situation began to change with the influx of millions of Catholics and Jews.[36]

Although the great wave of Catholic immigration occurred before that of the Jews, it was not until much later that the Catholics made significant inroads into American higher education. By 1880, however, it was common for Jews to be engaged in middle class occupations, and the more ambitious ones were intent on getting a medical education.[37] Jews had an intellectual tradition that facilitated adjustment. Jewish immigrants sent their children off to college, whereas Catholic leaders took an ominous views of the evils that might be encountered in secular education. Jews, somewhat stubbornly, refused to build their own colleges even when threatening restrictive quotas were present. Catholics preferred to develop a complex system of parish shools and Catholic colleges. Jews produced many scholars. This was not true of the early Catholics.

Samuel Morison held the view that the arrival of Russian and Polish Jews at Harvard marked the beginning of the "Jewish problem." This applied pretty well to the country as a whole. In 1881 Jews numbered approximately a quarter of a million in a population of 63,000,000. It is Nathan Glazer's view, also, that before 1880 or 1890 there were too few American Jews to be much of a "problem."[38] Their number continued to be regarded as too small to constitute a target for denunciation.[39] Oscar Handlin has found that "the prevailing temper of the nineteenth century [to Jews] was overwhelmingly tolerant."[40] All historians do not agree with this. For example, John Higham believes that Jews of the early nineteenth century in America got along very well with their non-Jewish neighbors, "although American conceptions of Jews in the abstract at no time lacked the unfavorable elements embedded in European tradition."[41]

Discrimination gradually became common in clubs, however, including some university alumni clubs and in some private schools in the East.[42] It would perhaps be more accurate to say that there was, at this time, an absence of overt hostility except in social arenas. As Oscar and Mary Handlin point out, the economic expansion after the middle nineteenth century was responsible for creating a class of wealthy capitalists. Some members of this group were Jews who were ready to challenge the upper-class establishment. After 1880, longings for higher status increasingly found satisfaction in associations with a hereditary basis.[43] It was in 1922 that Harvard University introduced regional quotas as a device for limiting its Jewish enrollment.[44] The "Jewish problem" at Harvard was a manifestation of a larger problem for early twentieth-century America. Morison observed that after the Civil War, Southerners avoided Harvard because it admitted Negroes on the same terms as whites.[45] They were allowed to eat at Memorial Hall and room in College dormitories.

In 1880 the Jewish population of the United States was 250,000, less than one percent of the population; by 1924 the Jewish population had grown to approximately 4,000,000.[46] In 1920, according to Steinberg, a pattern of anti-Jewish discrimination had become established.[47] This was particularly evident in the northeast part of the country. Discrimination was now common in clubs, resorts, and schools. According to Steinberg, most writings in the period 1920–30 referred to the establishment in many schools of some kind of restrictive device.[48]

An article in the *New York Times* described how both Columbia and New York Universities had taken steps to restrict their Jewish enrollment.[49] This was done covertly. They relied on character tests and regional quotas to hide their intentions. Harvard differed only in that it was the only university to advocate openly the quota system. In June 1922 the University issued a statement that described the recent increase in students and the shortage of facilities to care for them. It is not surprising that these attitudes apply equally to the Medical School.

By 1920 Harvard College's Jewish enrollment had reached 20 percent. No obvious restrictions were then in effect. Other colleges had much smaller proportions of Jewish students. At Dartmouth, for example, in 1930 it was 7 percent.

> Why did Harvard not proceed more discreetly and simply adopt the subterfuge employed elsewhere? The reason is to be found in the personality of President Lowell, perhaps in his New England candor, more likely in his naïveté and underlying prejudice. Lowell believed that he was acting courageously. As he wrote on one occasion: "This question is with us. We cannot solve it by forgetting or ignoring it." [50] In his commencement address a week later he added a touch of eloquence: "To shut the eyes to an actual problem of this kind and ignore its existence, or to refuse to grapple with it courageously, would be unworthy of a university." [51] The "problem" was that Jewish enrollment at Harvard had increased from 6 percent in 1908 to 20 percent in 1922. Lowell, however, was determined to avoid the "indirect methods" [52] employed elsewhere. The storm of protest that ensued must have given him occasion to question the practicality of such moral rectitude.[53]

In the *New York Times* of June 17, 1922, Lowell told Alfred A. Benesch that if the number of Jews were limited at colleges, they [Jews] would be better off, although it is the function of the University to discourage discrimination.

The Harvard Medical School has many facets. Most of them reflect credit, but occasionally some attitude, some deed, some failure of probity reminds us that it is a human institution created by men and fallible, as witness Judge Sewall's seventeenth-century double-dealing in the Corporation with the first endowed professorship. Then there was, of a different nature, the intolerance of women and blacks as candidates for medical education at Harvard (see above). So with Jews.

It is far easier to document the injury done to blacks than to Jews. There was, in 1928, when the writers entered the Harvard Medical School, a commonly heard assertion that Jews were admitted in numbers up to 10 percent of the class, but not more. Every effort to document this has proved futile, although there is support for the 10 percent quota that many people believed existed. But one can approach the Jewish matter in a much more positive way: there is, for example, the considerable number of Jews admitted to the Faculty about Dean Edsall's time (1918–35)—men who proved their worth in illustrious careers: Herrman Blumgart, Edwin Cohn, Soma Weiss, Joseph Aub, Samuel A. Levine, Milton Rosenau, Harry Solomon, and many others. Although antisemitism may have existed, it clearly was not a dominating factor in Dean Edsall's time at the faculty level. The student level is another matter. In a field so highly charged with emotion and individual value judgments, one strives in vain to find objective data. Many if not most scientists hold[54] that there is no such thing as truly objective scientific observation, for there is always a subjective element. Data of the following kind, even if subjective, can be found.

If one examines the record of each fourth-year class over a fifty-year period, counts the patently Jewish names, and from the total number of students in each fourth-year class calculates the percentage, a surprisingly smooth curve emerges:

YEAR	PERCENTAGE
1910	5.5
1920	6.6
1932	8.0
1939	9.5
1953	22.3
1960	15.6
1968	16.0
1972	20.0

The percentage of Jewish students shown is, of course, minimal: some names may have been anglicized, but others not typically Jewish could have been overlooked. The 1910 data were obtained in the same way as the subsequent material. What is of special interest is the 3.6-fold increase over the 52 years. Changed attitudes arising from World War II may have influenced the greatly increased percentage between 1939 and 1953. Similar data for the Faculty members with tenure (137) show the percentage as of January 1, 1972 to have been 34.3.

Although a variety of factors can account for the low incidence of Jews in the student body from 1910 to 1939 inclusive, it is difficult to escape the view that anti-Semitism was an important element but now it is happily greatly minimized—if, indeed, it is operative at all.

At least there is no question that Jewish physicians have an easier time now and as a group are more respected than was earlier the case. Inquiry of leading Jewish physicians as to whether they have suffered indignities because of antisemitism brought out staunch denials. This would not have been the case thirty or forty years earlier.

Chapter Twenty-seven

Special Enterprises

Dr. John Collins Warren, throughout a busy surgical life, collected many interesting and unusual anatomical specimens. As early as 1799, when he was a medical student at Guy's Hospital, London, the value of such collections had been long recognized in Europe, and he had realized their importance.[1] In 1809 Warren and a colleague formed the Anatomical Theatre and Dissecting Room at 49 Marlborough Street. It was a source of teaching material. As various collections of human specimens came on the market in Europe or America, they were purchased. By 1834 the need for space was so great that Warren appealed through the Harvard Treasurer to the Corporation. They agreed that if Warren would contribute $1,000, the Corporation would create new space for the collection.

Warren's interests broadened to include wax representations of smallpox and other skin diseases made in Paris. An interesting item in the Museum is the so-called crowbar skull, as noted above (page 38). Skeletons of fish fascinated Warren, and he collected them, too. President Quincy expressed the wish that the Museum be made available to medical students "and others"; even the public was later allowed to visit it; but the Corporation remained, for a time, loath to spend further money on better accommodations. Warren used his fees from lectures to support it.

When he resigned his professorship in 1847, most of his collection was presented to Harvard College, and with it the sum of $6,000 (or $5,000—the accounts vary) for its preservation and development. His intention was that all diseases should be represented at various stages. In recognition, the Corporation of the University gratefully accepted the collection and voted that the Museum be named after him. In 1870 Dr. J. B. S. Jackson, Curator of the Warren Anatomical Museum and Shattuck Professor of Morbid Anatomy in Harvard University, published a *Descriptive Catalogue* of the Museum with a brief history of it, followed by comment on the thousands of human specimens there (in 1870, 3,689; in 1906, 10,000).[2]

Following Dr. Warren's initial gift, the collection continued to grow. Dr. Oliver Wendell Holmes contributed many valuable preparations, especially chosen to illustrate healthy anatomy, including many microscopic specimens. Professor Henry Jacob Bigelow was an ardent collector. So also, in the early days, were Professors George Hayward, John Ware, and R. M. Hodges.

When the Medical School moved in 1847 into the North Grove Street Building, adjoining the Massachusetts General Hospital, a large room was made available for the Museum material. When, in 1883, the School moved once again, this time to the Boylston Street Building, the Museum moved too. The specimens were especially valuable in the midnineteenth century, when bodies for dissection could be obtained only with difficulty.

Dr. Warren, wishing to present himself as an example to medical students and to the public, bequeathed his body to the School. The skeleton is in the Museum but can be seen only by members of the Warren family.

Professor J. B. S. Jackson, the first Curator, held this post for thirty-two years, resigning in 1879. As a splendid custodian, he had doubled the original endowment by the time of his retirement. When the School and the Museum moved to Longwood Avenue, the Henry Jackson Fund was given to provide a curator's salary. It was named the John Barnard Swett Jackson Curatorship.

The present Curatorial Associate in the Warren Museum, David L. Gunner, is making a valiant effort to restore the Museum to a useful state.

THE HARVARD CANCER COMMISSION AND THE
COLLIS P. HUNTINGTON MEMORIAL HOSPITAL

Collis P. Huntington (1821–1900), a railroad magnate and capitalist, was born in Connecticut[3] of English stock that had emigrated to America in the seventeenth century. He claimed that he started out in life with several advantages: no money and a limited education. He went to California in 1849 and by shrewd buying and selling made a name for himself as an entrepreneur. In 1860 he was asked to build a railroad across the Sierra Nevada Mountains. Teaming up with Leland Stanford, Mark Hopkins, and Charles Crocker, he obtained government grants and commenced construction. By 1869, when the Central Pacific Railroad was joined to the Union Pacific, Huntington was a very rich man and continued to expand his fortune by similar ventures. Opinions differ as to his character. According to the *Dictionary of American Biography*, "he was [probably] vindictive, sometimes untrulthful, interested in few things outside of business." He denied social responsibility. His wife, however, took a different view.

To appreciate the consequences of her different view, it is necessary to understand the Cancer Commission of Harvard University. It was based on a gift in 1899 from Caroline Brewer Croft, and at that time it incorporated her name in the title. In 1909 the name was changed, and it became the Cancer Commission. It was designed to guide a multidisciplinary approach to cancer. Prior to the establishment of this group, cancer investigations were principally etiological. A direct method of attack was generally employed. In subsequent research, the experimental method was more often used.

After the death of her husband, Mrs. Collis P. Huntington made a generous gift to the Commission for the building of a hospital to bear the name of her husband, and this new hospital was under the control of the Cancer Commission of Harvard University. The first annual report of the Collis P. Huntington Memorial Hospital covers the period from its opening, March 1912, to June 30, 1913.[4]

At its establishment Professor E. E. Tyzzer was named Director, with Thomas Ordway as Physician-in-Charge. Even in the early years notable discoveries have been made possible by the Cancer Commission. Dr. Tyzzer is said to have discovered the first evidence of heredity of cancer in 1907. Dr. William Duane, Harvard Professor of Physics, defined the international X-ray unit. He also developed high-voltage X ray and was the pioneer of the 200,000-volt machine in America. The electrosurgical knife was invented by William T. Bovie, and in 1937 a million-volt X-ray machine was installed in the Hospital. It was said to be the first successful constant current machine of its kind in the world.

The primary purpose of the Hospital was to provide an optimal opportunity for the study of malignant tumors in human beings. Although principally designed for investigation, the Hospital, it was hoped, would finally offer diagnosis and a means of gaining familiarity with various types of tumors—in effect acting as a clearinghouse for tumor cases.[5]

The Huntington Hospital moved, in 1942, to the Massachusetts General Hospital, and in one sense is the only Harvard Hospital. Its laboratory was named for John Collins Warren. Dr. Joseph C. Aub and many other notable physicians have been on its staff. Currently, the Director is Dr. Paul Zamecnik, a graduate of Dartmouth College who received his M.D. degree from Harvard in 1936. As a portent of the future, he spent the following year next door to the Medical School at the Huntington Memorial Hospital, where Dr. Joseph C. Aub and a group of gifted younger men were caring for cancer patients and studying the biology of cancer.[6]

In 1939, just before World War II, Dr. Zamecnik went to the Carlsberg Laboratory in Copenhagen, where he worked with the celebrated K. Linderstrøm-Lang, who, more than any other man of his day, stimulated protein chemists throughout the world. In the following year, at the Rockefeller Institute, he carried on further related activities.

During World War II Zamecnik, Aub, and others carried out a long series of studies of possible toxic factors in experimental traumatic shock, and shortly afterward, he joined with Fritz Lipmann and others to study the toxin of *Clostridium Welchii*. By this time a considerable interest had been aroused in protein biosynthesis. Protein molecules were so complex, so delicate, and so easily damaged that study of them was difficult. As Dean Edsall said:

> A few distinguished investigators were trying to bring light into this darkness, but most of them, I think, had their lanterns pointing in the wrong direction. They were looking to see whether the enzymes that broke proteins down to amino acids would also catalyze the reverse reactions under suitable conditions, in spite of the formidable free energy barriers that would have to be overcome by this route. Paul Zamecnik looked in a very different direction. Guided by the insights already expressed by Linderstrøm-Lang, by Herman Kalckar, and by Fritz Lipmann, he believed from the beginning that phosphate bond energy must somehow be coupled with the biosynthesis of peptide bonds to make a protein, and that the great specificity of protein structure could hardly be attained by the mediation of the relatively non-specific proteolytic enzymes.[7]

The role of genetic coding in protein synthesis was greatly clarified by the work of Dr. Zamecnik and his group.

PHYSICAL CHEMISTRY AND BIOPHYSICAL CHEMISTRY AT THE SCHOOL

In 1919 the Medical School received a gift of $2,000,000 (later increased to more than $5,000,000) from the Joseph R. DeLamar Bequest. The Department of Physical Chemistry of the Harvard Medical School was then created, and existed from 1920 to 1954.[8] Its successor was the University Laboratory of Physical Chemistry Related to Medicine and Public Health. This Department was instructed to engage in research fundamental to medicine but without the usual requirement of teaching medical students. That, of course, was a very uncommon provision. From John T. Edsall's account of the Department of Physical Chemistry at the Harvard Medical School, written in 1950,[9] it appears that Lawrence J. Henderson, Professor of Biological Chemistry in Harvard University, recommended Dr. Edwin J. Cohn to initiate the work of this independent research department. That apparently is an error, for John T. Edsall has since stated that he knew that his father, Dean Edsall, was eager to keep Henderson at Harvard.[10] The Dean believed that most people in the University had underestimated Henderson's importance, and since Henderson had received a most attractive offer from Johns Hopkins, Dean Edsall made Henderson the titular head of the Department in its formative years, although Cohn conducted its affairs. The record shows, in fact, that Dean Edsall created the Department as a place for Henderson, who later (1927) became head of the Fatigue Laboratory at the Harvard Business School.

Dr. Dickinson W. Richards, who had a long and close relationship with Henderson, described "Professor L. J." as a rather stout man of middle stature, usually adorned with a red necktie and brown tweed suit. At the time when Richards knew him, he had thinning red hair and a red beard flecked with gray. His eyes were wide and very blue, his cheeks pink. Habitually, he had a somewhat surprised expression, and he looked cherubic. His voice was high, his diction precise. Among the guiding principles of his life, according to Richards, was the intent to protect his own time and keep those who bored him at a distance. He claimed that he was constitutionally lazy, and liked to avoid doing things. This was, of course, a pose, for his penetrating and restless mind was never still. He loved a good epigram and a sharp and true generalization. He dismissed an earnest German physiologist as "a good third-rate man." He was devoted to James Gamble and described him as pathologically modest. A distinguished but somewhat stuffy geologist was described as "the perfect example of the man who became famous because he thought he was."

Henderson had a great admiration for the distinguished school of British physiologists—Henry Dale, Ernest Starling, Joseph Barcroft, and others, but this did not prevent his taking an occasional shot at them. "A. V. Hill," said Henderson, "is a remarkable mathematician: He can construct a formula that will fit any set of data, however erroneous."[11] Sidney Burwell has commented that any time he was bold enough to express an idea to Henderson, the latter would reply, "Why, yes, obviously," and that was the end of that. One day the celebrated physiologist Joseph Barcroft was doodling with a pencil on a piece of log paper. He happened to plot out some points on a carbon dioxide dissociation curve, and they fell on a straight line. Somewhat amused, he

Lawrence J. Henderson, Professor of Biological Chemistry at Harvard University. One of the first to apply methods and concepts of physics to human physiology, to the betterment of physiology. Also notable for his contributions to the sociology of medicine. Photograph in the Harvard Medical Archives.

sent off a letter to Henderson. Henderson's reply read, "Dear Barcroft: By intellectual processes of a low order, you have arrived at a conclusion of some importance."[12]

L. J. Henderson was born in Lynn, Massachusetts, June 3, 1878. At the age of sixteen he entered Harvard College, and subsequently the Medical School. Following four years at the School, he went to Europe for two years and passed his time chiefly in Franz Hofmeister's laboratory in Strassburg. Four years later he wrote two long essays, *The Fitness of the Environment*[13] and *The Order of Nature*.[14] These two essays constitute a careful description of Henderson's scientific philosophy and provide a useful background for his later physiological writings. *The Fitness of the Environment*, better known than *The Order of Nature*, consists mainly of an examination of the properties of hydrogen, oxygen, and carbon; their combinations, water and carbonic acid; and the demonstration that it is owing to the unique properties of these substances that living beings can be formed and can exist. As Richards says, it is a "logical proof of the adaptability of matter to life, and life to matter."[15]

The second volume is more philosophical; Henderson attacked the problem of teleology and concluded that the functional relationships found in nature in living organisms cannot be owing to mere contingency. They are ordered, evolutionary, and therefore, of necessity, teleological. This, of course, is teleology as a general philosophic principle and not simply a convenient explanation for small individual events. In the course of these studies, Henderson became intensely interested in the papers of J. Willard Gibbs,[16] whose ideas on systems and phases were important in Henderson's later analysis of the complex system of the physical chemistry of the blood.

The principal event in Henderson's life after World War I was his dawning appreciation of the full significance of the interaction of oxygen and carbon dioxide in the blood. It was a matter of surprise to him that physiologists who were studying the respiratory function of the blood should not have drawn from the discovery of the variation of oxygen saturation with carbon dioxide pressure the (to him) obvious conclusion that since carbon dioxide influences the oxygen equilibrium in blood, oxygen must influence the carbon dioxide equilibrium. When he studied the interaction between oxygen and carbon dioxide, he recognized that it was of major importance not to regard the change in one substance as cause and the change in the other as effect, for when one thinks of these terms mathematically as variables and functions, no problem arises. This is a general statement. In a period of a dozen years, Henderson's concept of acid-base balance and neutrality regulation took shape. In the end, he was able to formulate this equilibrium into a single diagram. After that, the basic integration moved rapidly forward. As early as 1921 the general outline of the blood nomogram had been devised.

Donald D. Van Slyke was at this time busily engaged in investigating the distribution and movement of electrolytes between red blood cells and plasma, and a profitable collaboration between Henderson and Van Slyke arose. During the same period a group of physiologists in Boston under Bruce Dill and Arlie V. Bock were busily engaged in studying the respiratory functions of the blood. Most of Henderson's normal nomogram was derived literally from the blood of Bock (and some from one of the present authors).

Richards recounts that although cardiac output was measured by an indirect method, Bock learned that the Germans were determining cardiac output by direct right-heart punctures. Bock had planned to try this on himself in order to obtain mixed venous blood. Henderson heard about it, marched into the laboratory, and said, "Arlie, are you thinking of directly puncturing your own heart?" Bock admitted that he was. "Arlie," said Henderson, "I forbid it," and stalked out. Later, German physiology developed cardiac catheterization, and the objection ceased to be valid.

In 1927 Henderson was invited to give the Silliman Lectures at Yale, and from his preparation for these lectures a classic study emerged: *Blood: A Study in General Physiology* (New Haven, 1928).

Henderson used to claim that he had just one procedure with his students: "I neglect them." This, of course, was not entirely true. He disliked certain things in the German character, especially the Germans' tendency to be subservient and obsequious to authority.

On returning to Harvard, he was appointed Lecturer in Biological Chemistry. Thus his association with Harvard began and continued throughout his lifetime. He was Lecturer only one year, 1904–05, Instructor 1905–10, Assistant Professor of Biological Chemistry 1910–19, Professor 1919–34, and Abbott and James Lawrence Professor of Chemistry from 1934 until he died of a pulmonary embolism.

In Henderson's later years, he was concerned with the complex relationships of human beings on the social level. His thinking in this area was initiated by Vilfredo Pareto's *Treatise on General Sociology* (Paris, 1917).[17] In Cannon's view it is likely that Pareto's analysis of human motives appealed to Henderson because it resulted in a constructive system in which variable constituents influenced one or another.[18] In 1932 Henderson was invited to conduct a seminar on Pareto in the Harvard Department of Sociology. He accepted this invitation and repeated the seminar each year thereafter. One of its values was that Henderson was able to maintain a consistent approach to social problems and thus to render the study of sociology concrete and specific.

The famous Fatigue Laboratory of the Harvard School of Business Administration was one of Henderson's creations (see below, page 514). His last important contribution to the advancement of scholarship at Harvard was his role in founding the Society of Fellows. In doing this, he was greatly stimulated by his knowledge of Trinity College, Cambridge.

Throughout Henderson's association with Harvard, he continued to be a highly effective instigator and supporter of new concepts in Harvard's educational and institutional developments. He was elected Foreign Secretary of the National Academy of Sciences, and thereby attracted and informed many European scientists of what was going on in American science.

Several other points concerning Henderson's philosophy of science should be mentioned. In particular, attention should be given his thoughtful essay, "The Study of Man." [19] The scientific study of man is ancient and respectable, going back at least to Aristotle and Hippocrates. In this more than thirty-year-old essay, the study of man takes a principal place in the studies of the learned. It may be divided into two parts: the successful part and the unsuccessful. Speaking generally, Henderson pointed out that "the successful part of the scientific study of men is related to medicine, the unsuccessful part to philosophy and to the social sciences. These relations are not only historical, they are also to be seen in methods, attitudes and traditions." [20] The craftsman does not need theoretical science nor does the descriptive scientist. They deal with "common sense." But theory, in terms of an abstract conceptual scheme, seems to be necessary if one is to exploit effectively even descriptive science. On the basis of experience, it is evident that there are two kinds of human behavior, and it is important to distinguish them in all thinking, talking, and writing associated with two kinds of subjects: (1) concrete observations and experiences which can be represented by accurately defined unambiguous words, together with the more general considerations that are clearly and logically related to such concrete observations and experiences. (2) Thinking, talking and writing about general ideas or concepts which do not clearly related to concrete observations and experiences and which cannot be precisely defined. The Hippocratic writings belong to the first class, and the works of Plato to the second.

In Henderson's view, the Hippocratic conceptual scheme, although it works, suffers from a particular difficulty:

It presents a view of the physiological system in a state of equilibrium, without giving a satisfactory picture of the constituent parts of the system or of the forces that operate between these parts. We now know that it is convenient and reasonably satisfactory to think of the constituent parts as chemical substances, fluids, cells, tissues and organs; and of the forces as the forces with which theoretical physics and theoretical chemistry are concerned. Such a conception was not available to Hippocrates. Nevertheless, his conceptual scheme worked and for a long time worked well. This is, in fact, the test of a conceptual scheme and the only test: it must work well enough for the purpose of the moment.[21]

The medical sciences have suffered from Whitehead's "fallacy of misplaced concreteness." [22] The rise of bacteriology and its influence upon medical thought and practice may be considered in this connection. The discovery of specific pathological microorganisms seems to have been responsible for an oversimplification of thought about the origin and nature of disease. It led to a great tendency to think of diseases as entities, perhaps as definite as atoms of oxygen. It was pleasant to think of the specific organism as the sole cause of a specific disease, originating from a single cause and curable by the use of a single remedy. Henderson pointed these things out in his 1941 essay, "The Study of Man." It is interesting to observe that Dubos fourteen years after Henderson's statements used almost the same words in a long series of impressive data to demonstrate that the nineteenth-century doctrine of Pasteur and Koch, as to the specific etiology of disease, is no longer tenable in any inclusive sense.[23] One of the present writers pointed out to Dr. Dubos that the newer doctrine of no specificity of etiology of disease could be extended to a symptom of disease—pain—where the pain experienced bears great relationship to the significance of the wound but little or none to the extent of the wound. Dubos replied that it was his "conviction that 'specificity,' while an essential concept in the formulation of scientific medicine during the nineteenth century, often tends to prevent us from gaining a comprehensive view of the problem of disease." [24] An obvious sign is that the practice of medicine by the tedious process of trial and error in time eliminates fallacies of misplaced concreteness. Henderson concludes his essay by saying

When we reflect upon these differences between the two kinds of studies of men, shall we not do well to think also of the fruitfulness of the medical sciences and of the unfruitfulness of the social sciences? But let us not try to say what is here cause, what effect. Human interactions are intricate and obscure, and the art of studying them is difficult . . . The social sciences will become more fruitful when in certain ways the thought and procedures of social scientists conform more closely to those of medical scientists.[25]

This great mind not only defined and clarified abstract concepts dealing with science and medicine but also developed concrete mechanisms that applied them to practical problems. The Department of Physical Chemistry was one of these concrete mechanisms. In 1927 Edwin J. Cohn became titular as well as de facto head of this department. Dr. Cohn had become interested in biological science as an undergraduate at Amherst College. He then transferred to the University of Chicago, with a major interest in physics and chemistry, and later on he went to Harvard, where he specialized in physical chemistry. He had become convinced by 1916 that one could not understand the specificity and organization of biological systems merely by investigating the variables of the environment common to all cells. It became clear to him that his life work would be centered on proteins. He thereupon went to Yale to study with T. B. Osborne, who was at that time the foremost American authority in the field.

The first World War came, and Henderson and Cohn were directed to study breadmaking in a scientific way, which they did in the laboratory of Dr. Theodore J. Richards, at Harvard Univeristy in Cambridge. They also carried out a study of the isoelectric point of vegetable juices related to their drying. As soon as World War I was over, Cohn went to Europe as one of the earliest National Research Council Fellows. He studied with Sir William Hardy and Joseph Barcroft in England, with S. P. L. Sørensen in Denmark and with Svante Arrhenius in Sweden, and in 1920 he returned to the Harvard Medical School.

In the first decade of its existence, 1920–30, the Laboratory concentrated on studies of well-known plant and animal proteins, casein in milk, the serum albumin and various globulins of blood plasma, the hemoglobin in red blood cells, the zein of corn, and the myosin of muscle. The aim of this work was to define the size of the molecules, their properties as acids and bases, and the nature of the forces that determine their solubility in different solvents. In these studies a great deal was learned about the preparation of proteins for study. Dr. Cohn, with his teachers Osborne and Sørensen, believed that, contrary to the general view, proteins were enormous molecules with molecular weights in the thousands.

From 1927 to 1931 Dr. Cohn studied a practical problem. He extracted from liver a concentrated substance that was effective in the treatment of pernicious anemia. After George Minot and William Murphy had shown that such a substance existed, Cohn undertook its chemical separation. A liver extract was finally made clinically available; it had life-saving potential in treating pernicious anemia.

Despite the excursions mentioned, the primary objectives of the laboratory remained the study of proteins and their interactions. The first study of a tissue protein was carried out in 1925 by W. T. Salter, while a medical student, on the muscle globulin later shown to be myosin. In 1929 A. von Muralt and John T. Edsall continued the study of myosin, demonstrating that it was an elongated molecule of fibrous shape. This was responsible for the double refraction of the muscle fiber itself. Subsequent studies have confirmed their deductions and have indicated that this protein is the fundamental contractile substance of muscle. When purified preparations of fibrinogen were obtained, as they were at about this time, M. Florkin (later of Liège) was the first to make a laboratory study of a protein component found in the blood-clotting system. A. A. Green amplified the earlier studies of Cohn and Adela Prentiss and carried out extensive studies of the solubility of the oxygen-transporting agent of blood, hemoglobin. They studied various conditions of pH, ionic strength, and temperature, and produced, according to John Edsall, a classic.[26]

In the decade 1930–40 it became evident that the unknown structure of the proteins and the complexity of their chemical reactions made any interpretation of their solubility relations difficult. This led to a series of investigations on the simpler compounds which make up proteins, the amino acids and peptides. These experimental studies led to the development of a more precise elaboration of Peter Debye's theory to the so-called dipolar ions. Professors George Scatchard and John G. Kirkwood of the Massachusetts Institute of Technology were principally responsible for this development. It is interesting to observe, in passing, that it was characterisic of the Laboratory that various investigators who collaborated with the personnel of the Laboratory had actually no formal relationship to it. This policy has existed from its earliest days. Dr. Scatchard, for example, as Dr. Edsall has said, has been a member of the Laboratory in an intellectual sense since 1923. Clinicians as well as scientists have participated in such unofficial ramifications of the Laboratory's work.

Jeffries Wyman, Jr., returned from Europe in 1927, where he studied dielectric properties of amino acids and peptide solutions. At about this time studies of Raman spectra by Edsall revealed the dipolar ionic structure of amino acids and peptides by direct measurement of characteristic molecular vibration frequencies. In the decade 1929–1939 a systematic picture emerged which allowed correlation of the structure of these simple models with their physical and chemical properties, and a basis was thus established for a systematic and rational approach to the study of protein molecules themselves.

> The methods would appear to be at hand . . . for the study of all proteins. There is no theoretical obstacle to the isolation of all the protein constitutents of any given tissue, or to their characterization as chemical substances, and to the study of their interactions as biological components. Proceeding thus, often with new techniques, but employing the classical methods of physical chemistry, we may hope in time to achieve an understanding of the morphology and physiology of biological systems in terms of the properties of their components.[27]

Although studies of amino acids and peptides continued until about 1939, a return to the study of proteins themselves had been undertaken in 1935. J. L. Oncley came into the Laboratory and developed an excellent method of studying dielectric constants. His method was applicable not only to amino acids but also to large protein molecules.

Stimulation in these areas followed the development of new tools. Theodor Svedberg had created the ultracentrifuge in Sweden, and Oncley had built one driven by air. The Ultracentrifuge Laboratory, opened in 1939 under the direction of Oncley, was involved with the war effort long before the United States entered the war. It was clear that the problem of blood transfusion was very great indeed, and the resources of the Laboratory were quickly mobilized for the separation and production from blood of the serum albumins. The separation of other proteins of plasma was also begun.

The observation that the denaturing effects of organic liquids on protein disappear at very low temperatures was the beginning of the development undertaken in reply to a request of the National Research Council early in 1940. At that time the problem of blood supply was urgent. Protein separation was accomplished by new methods, which utilized the precipitating action of cold alcohol. These methods made possible the fractionation of blood plasma on a very large scale. The National Research Council, in April 1941, made a grant for the development of a pilot plant for processing human plasma and its component fractions. The Harvard Pilot Plant was inaugurated within a few months and made possible the study of intermediate stages between research and full-scale production. The advances made in the research laboratory were immediately incorporated into the Pilot Plant procedures.

A nationwide blood collection program was inaugurated by the American Red Cross on an enormous scale. Other specialties joined the Laboratory, and the products of fractionation could be studied by chemists, immunologists, and clinicians. As the Laboratory became more expert in developing practical procedures, the Pilot Plant activities were steadily expanded by seven pharmaceutical firms, under naval contracts. A Committee on Medical Research of the Office of Scientific Research and Development was formed and offered a contract to Dr. Cohn as responsible investigator of chemical, *clinical*[28] (emphasis added), and immunological studies on blood and blood derivatives. This work was supported by the OSRD from August 22, 1941, to June 30, 1946.[29]

On the advice of Dr. Cohn, the Committee on Medical Research awarded contracts to the Universities of Wisconsin, Stanford, Columbia, and the Massachusetts Institute of Technology. The laboratories were very busy places. Crisis followed crisis. Their tentative specifications had to be submitted to the Harvard Pilot Plant. The material had to pass tests for sterility as well as animal safety. The sterility part was easy enough to manage, but for some puzzling reason, guinea pigs injected with albumin for the safety test died with worrisome frequency. The problem was solved when it was learned that an "expert" who was visiting the Laboratory had recommended that a mercury compound be used as a preservative. Study of the guinea pig deaths showed that nearly all of the mercury introduced into the animal had separated into the albumin part.

When World War II was over, the question arose whether the dried plasma that had been prepared with mercury could be salvaged. Dr. Walter L. Hughes, Jr., undertook to answer the question, and his work led to a discovery of fundamental importance: Hughes was able to show that in the chemical grouping in the albumin molecule, a sulfhydryl group gave the albumin an affinity for mercury. One mercury atom binds two albumin molecules through their sulfhydryl groups. Hughes's discovery led to further important studies.

During the war a physicist, chemist, and organic chemist worked as a team in conjunction with a physiologist, biochemist, bacteriologist, pharmacologist, pathologist, anatomist, clinician, and surgeon. In times of peace such collaboration is hard to achieve. As John Edsall has pointed out, it is important that this experience be incorporated into our educational pattern.

> The need for training a new generation to attack the problems of
> our society with the new knowledge born of mathematics, physics
> and chemistry, became increasingly acute during and at the end of the
> last war. There was a dearth of scientists whose training in both
> organic chemistry and pharmacology rendered them especially fitted
> for the synthesis and appraisal of new drugs and other chemical compounds; of those trained both in physical chemistry and bacteriology

and thus especially fitted for the preparation of natural products destined either for prophylaxis or therapy; of those trained both in physics and physiology and thus especially fitted to analyze and protect against the influence of high altitude; to analyze and to learn to make the best possible use, under new conditions, of the sense organs of hearing or of vision. Even training in biophysics and biochemistry, as it was interpreted a quarter of a century ago, was often inadequate, both at the theoretical and experimental level, for research involving the physics of sound or of radiation; the physical chemistry of the separation of radioactive isotopes or of proteins; or the organic chemistry employed in the synthesis of the smaller natural products, or of the molecules with which they interact.[30]

When the war was finally over, in 1945, the Laboratory concentrated its principal study on problems of fundamental importance not determined by immediate practical medicine. The urgent need then was for scientists to return to basic problems. One could be certain that practical applications later on would flow from some of their activities, but this possibility could not dominate. The Laboratory once again became international, with investigators from Argentina, Australia, Belgium, Chile, China, England, Finland, France, Holland, Israel, Sweden, and Switzerland. Twenty-four of these investigators in the period 1946–49 came from foreign lands.

In one aspect of postwar work it was decided to study protein crystals by X-ray diffraction, which, it was hoped, would lead to a deeper understanding of the detailed construction of the protein molecule. Two experts in this area, Drs. Barbara W. Low and Dorothy Crowfoot (Hodgkin) joined the Laboratory in 1948. There was no thought that this work would lead to immediate practical knowledge, but it was believed that a long-term investigation in the X-ray field would lay a foundation for true understanding of many of the phenomena common to pharmacology and to medicine.

The years 1947-48 were marked by developments of importance to blood collection and fractionation. The methods employed during the war were far from perfect, and the new methods were calculated to lessen the damage to some important unstable compounds in blood. The system of plasma fractionation was sharply revised, and the new methods were found applicable, with some modification, to the study of many kinds of tissue, of which the liver was the first. Soon after the War, in 1946, a group undertook the separation of liver proteins in an almost undenatured state. This work led to separation of fractions containing several enzymes, including xanthine oxidase and phosphatases, and to the separation of two nucleoproteins. Shortly afterward, on July

1, 1949, Dr. Cohn was appointed to the Higgins University Professorship. He was the first scientist to hold a University Professorship. He bent all his efforts to the study of proteins, "for the structure of the proteins remains the greatest unsolved problem in biochemistry."[31]

John T. Edsall's history of the Department carried it up to 1950, when it became a University Laboratory, only a little more than three years before Dr. Cohn's death. Edsall reports that the University Laboratory continued essentially as it had before its change in title. But there was one unfortunate aspect of the situation which must be mentioned.[32] Beginning in the spring of 1952, Cohn, insofar as can be judged now, was the victim of a series of minor strokes, which seem to have produced in him grandiose ideas. Life at the University Laboratory of Physical Chemistry was difficult for most people during the last year and a half of Dr. Cohn's life. At that time he was, in many respects, still able to function very ably. For example, it was during the last year of his life that he established the Protein Foundation, which has now become the Blood Research Institute, and he acquired a distinguished group of individuals to work there.

He died of a massive brain hemorrhage on October 1, 1953. Some time before that, Edsall had reached the conclusion that he could no longer work with Cohn and had made his plans to move to the Biological Laboratories in Cambridge. This move did not take place, however, until after Cohn's death.

Lawrence Oncley then became the head of the Department at the Medical School. At that time the Laboratory had been renamed the Department of Biophysical Chemistry. Not long afterward, having lost its excuse for a separate existence, it merged with the Department of Biological Chemistry under the headship of Baird Hastings.

Although the University Laboratory of Physical Chemistry is ordinarily associated with the name of Edwin J. Cohn, it would be a great mistake to underestimate the importance of Professor John T. Edsall as a productive and stabilizing influence in the rather hectic milieu of that Laboratory.

John T. Edsall was born in Philadelphia in 1902, the eldest of three sons of the man who was Dean of the Harvard Medical School from 1918 to 1935. After being educated at Harvard College and the Harvard Medical School, Edsall, in the company of Jeffries Wyman, sailed in June 1924 for two years of study in Europe. A summer in Graz polished their German to the point where they could converse in that language with ease. In Graz, Edsall became acquainted with Otto Loewi; Fritz Pregl, the founder of microanalysis; and Fritz Reuter, Professor of Legal Medicine and a man of great charm and cultivated tastes. By that time, Loewi had carried out the famous experiment for which he later received the Nobel Prize, in which it was shown that stimulation of the vagus nerve of a frog produced a chemical substance later shown to be acetylcholine. Wyman and Edsall then went to Cambridge University, living at St. John's College. Edsall took the Part II Course in Biochemistry, which was then, in 1924, being given for the first time. Biochemistry had been presented before as a part of Physiology. A new building to house Sir Frederick Hopkins helped attract a group around him, but it was his inspiration that made Biochemistry in Cambridge taught and practiced from a breadth of outlook at the time unparalleled.

Hopkins' second in command was J. B. S. Haldane, a formidable character with an impressive physique and tremendous voice, as well as vast learning, which he was not averse to passing on to others. With considerable insouciance he carried out various experiments on himself. While Edsall was there, Haldane was ingesting large amounts of strontium salts and observing the metabolic effects. His lectures on enzymes formed the basis of his famous book on the subject, which appeared a few years later. There were many other young and stimulating individuals in the Laboratory.

Important influences came from outside of Biochemistry: Sir William Hardy, who had started as a histologist, had become one of the great pioneers in the physical chemistry of proteins. This foreshadowed John Edsall's later career. A. E. Mirsky and M. L. Anson had been at Harvard but were now carrying out important work on hemoglobin in Barcroft's laboratory. G. S. Adair showed his beautiful work on osmotic pressure in the Low Temperature Research Station and demonstrated that the molecule of hemoglobin was four times as big as people had supposed it to be. He set forth his famous equation for the binding of oxygen to hemoglobin. These and others influenced Edsall.

While at Cambridge, and with the help of Hopkins, Edsall started on a study of phosphates in muscle. According to Edsall, the study became completely irrelevant within a year or two with the discovery of phosphocreatine by Cyrus Fiske and Yellapragada Subbarow, and of ATP not long after. Jeffries Wyman had started working in Biochemistry at Cambridge but decided after one term that A. V. Hill's laboratory in London was the best place for him. There he studied the physics of muscular contraction. During the Christmas vacation of 1925, Wyman and Edsall met in Austria to visit friends, and in the spring vacation of April 1926 they added Robert Oppenheimer, whom they had known as a freshman at Harvard when they were seniors, and went off to Corsica. Oppenheimer, studying at the Cavendish Laboratory in Cambridge, was solving problems in physics in a way that gave Edsall a feeling of awe. Heisenberg's first great paper on quantum mechanics had just appeared, and Schrödinger's work was to appear only a few months later. Dirac was a fellow graduate student of Edsall's at St. John's College. Something of the excitement of the laboratory was conveyed to Edsall by Oppenheimer in his discussion of quantum mechanics, but Edsall felt that his mind was too slow to grasp quickly Oppenheimer's discussions. These things are mentioned only to give some idea of the forces that played on Edsall at this time. "Those two years in Cambridge," he has said, "were of profound importance in my life. In science, they immensely widened and deepened my vision of the scope of biochemistry."[33]

In the summer of 1926 Edsall returned to Boston to start his first clinical year at Harvard Medical School. He was dissatisfied with the instruction he received and the contents of the courses available to him then. To make use of free afternoons at Harvard—Tuesday, Thursday, and Saturday—he undertook a study suggested by Alfred Redfield, who believed that the most neglected part of the muscle problem lay in muscle proteins. Since Edwin Cohn had already started some work in this area, Redfield suggested that Edsall go to work with Cohn in the unique Department of Physical Chemistry at the Harvard Medical School.

Cohn welcomed Edsall. (It should be remembered that Edsall was, at that time, still a medical student.) Cohn set him to extracting what was then called simply muscle globulin from beef muscle from a nearby slaughterhouse.

A turning point in Edsall's scientific life came with the arrival of Alexander von Muralt from Switzerland, whose purpose was to work on the double refraction of muscle. With the polarizing microscope and samples of muscle, which he immersed in fluids having different refractive indexes, the orderly structure of the submicroscopic fibrillar elements was shown.

Muralt received a considerable shock one day while looking through the *Chinese Journal of Physiology* to find that the same research had already been carried out by a German physiologist, Hans Stübel, while working in China.

The Department of Physical Chemistry at the Harvard Medical School was first and always a research department; Edwin Cohn gave an occasional lecture only when he felt like doing so. Following receipt of his M.D. degree in 1928, Edsall was engaged both in Harvard's tutorial system and in formal lecturing. The tutorial work took place at Harvard College in Cambridge, four miles distant from the Medical School laboratory. It was difficult fulfilling one's responsibility as a member of two faculties and in association with two very different groups of people, but Edsall found this a rewarding experience, for it permitted him to be in close touch with both places. Ronald Ferry invited both Wyman and Edsall to join the staff of John Winthrop House as two of its charter members. Friendships therefore developed with historians, economists, philosophers, political scientists, and others who would otherwise never have been known.

Edsall found the tutorial work to be a great intellectual stimulus. It involved constant discussions and interchange of ideas with a small group of able undergraduates each year, and no less stimulating guidance of research for seniors who were striving for honors degrees. This work with gifted students became a fascinating part of Edsall's life. He also gave a few lectures each year in L. J. Henderson's course. About 1940 Henderson decided to give up the course, and Wyman and Edsall established a new course on the biophysical aspects of biochemistry within the Biology Department. Except for a break during the war years, they continued to teach it together until Wyman resigned from Harvard in 1952 to become science attaché at the United States Embassy in Paris. Activities in this course led to their later book, *Biophysical Chemistry*, which appeared in 1958.

Edsall continued to lecture at Harvard, principally on proteins, enzymes, and biological chemistry in general. In addition, he took on the editorship of the *Journal of Biological Chemistry*.

Professor Cohn wrote much of the book *Proteins, Amino Acids and Peptides, as Ions and Dipolar Ions* (New York, 1965), with co-author George Scatchard, a constant adviser and helpful critic. Essential chapters were contributed by John G. Kirkwood and J. L. Oncley. In the end it was Edsall who did most of the final writing, supported by a Guggenheim Fellowship in 1940–41. During this time the Edsall family passed a year at the California Institute of Technology, where he could work almost without interruption on the book.

By 1941, when Edsall had returned from his sabbatical at the California Institute of Technology, Edwin Cohn had placed the Laboratory on a war footing, even though the United States was not to be officially at war for some months. The Laboratory was already fractionating blood plasma in order to obtain human serum albumin and other plasma proteins for use by the Armed Forces. In Edsall's view albumin had great advantage over whole plasma as a plasma expander, especially after they learned to pasteurize it, killing the virus of serum hepatitis. Gamma globulin was useful for temporary immunization against measles and, later, infectious hepatitis.

Cohn's driving energy was just what was needed to obtain the necessary government support so that large groups of scientists and clinicians working in a common cause could be drawn together with seven major pharmaceutical firms engaged in the large-scale production of plasma fractionation. This story can be found in various publications.[34]

Edsall's activities involved chiefly fibrinogen and fibrin. Two products were obtained and found to be useful, especially by neurosurgeons: fibrin foam with thrombin, and fibrin film. The first proved to be of great value in checking hemorrhage during operations, especially in brain surgery. The second provided the first safe and effective materials for replacement of the dural membrane. In the war years these products were made on a large scale. Without a doubt, they saved many lives.

For some years following the death of Edwin Cohn in 1953, Edsall served on the National Research Council Committee on Blood Plasma and Plasma Expanders. Part of that time he was Chairman.

When the war was over, the laboratory returned to its basic work on proteins. Edsall moved back to Cambridge, as mentioned above. Soon afterward the University established a Committee on Higher Degrees in Biochemistry. Edsall was the first chairman. This Committee has since grown into the Department of Biochemistry and Molecular Biology at Harvard University.

The breadth of Edsall's thinking can best be indicated by the last paragraph of his "Reflections of a Biochemist":

We have been living through a period, unique in the world's history, of rapid growth of population, of material goods, and of energy supply. Soon, within a few moments of geological time, this growth must come to an end. Population will be stabilized at some reasonable level, or else population growth, after proceeding unchecked for another generation or two, will lead to catastrophe as mankind becomes more and more crowded and the earth's resources become increasingly exhausted. The liberation and utilization of energy by man must also be stabilized at a level that will avoid intolerable thermal pollution and other hazards. Waste products and valuable minerals must be recycled rather than discarded. We must aim to preserve the richness and variety of the world in its splendid diversity of landscape and of plant and animal life, if our descendants are to have at least as rich and full a life as the best lives that men can lead today. We should seek to maintain a world that will be a better place to live in than today, a thousand or a million years from now; for mankind will never find another home to compare with this ravaged but still magnificent planet.[35]

Blood Fractions and the University Laboratory of Physical Chemistry

Some of the work done in the Cohn laboratory has had such important clinical connotations as to require separate discussion. The fractionation of whole blood during World War II represents both scientific success and an industrial triumph. (Clinically, a mixed blessing was at hand.) The success of the fractionation program made possible the preparation, and distribution to the battlefield, of vast quantities of plasma.[36] In certain situations plasma was life-saving—in burns, for example; in other cases its administration was an unmitigated disaster because of a tragic error. A wounded man would bleed, his blood pressure would fall, bleeding would cease, and intravenous plasma would be administered *before definitive surgical treatment was available*. The blood pressure would then rise and bleeding would resume. His remaining precious hemoglobin would be washed out, and he would die. When definitive surgical treatment is soon to be available, the administration of enough plasma to raise the blood pressure to 85 mm. is indicated, while *whole blood* is obtained and injected.[37]

The Committee on Transfusions of the National Research Council took the position that "most instances of shock are associated with hemoconcentration, and a given quantity of plasma is more effective than an equal quantity of whole blood, in treatment." The basis for this dangerous conclusion apparently stems from World War I work by Cannon, Fraser, and Hooper.[38] They reported that in shock there is a concentration of red blood cells in the periphery—earlobe, finger, toe— as compared with that found in venous blood in the arm. This finding led to the belief that there is a generalized increase in capillary permeability. It was believed by some (in controlling positions) that in shock the blood becomes concentrated, and therefore the proper treatment of shock involves dilution of the blood with plasma. The erroneous concept of increased capillary permeability and hemoconcentration was perpetuated in the Manual prepared under the direction of the National Research Council by the Committee on Surgery of the Division of Medical Sciences. Others also endorsed it.[39]

The American Army entered North Africa in 1942 without suitable facilities for blood transfusion. Reliance was placed on plasma for treatment of those suffering from blood loss. The tragic error of this approach was soon demonstrated on the African battlefield: Whole blood was essential in the treatment of those severely wounded who were suffering from blood loss, and this was ultimately acknowledged. After the war, Norman Kirk, Surgeon General of the American Army, took full responsibility for the lack of whole blood facilities in North Africa.[40] This honorable man should not have been allowed to do so. No one man was responsible.

The British had whole blood available in the battle area. The *New York Times* of August 27, 1943, quoted Professor E. D. Churchill (who had leaked the information to the press) as saying that whole blood was urgently needed and that plasma alone was not adequate:

Col. Edward D. Churchill of Boston, Professor of Surgery at Harvard, and now consulting surgeon for the troops here, has pioneered in setting up blood banks similar to the Red Cross blood deposits in the United States. In a report to the surgeon's office Colonel Churchill declared: "There is need for whole blood transfusions in the treatment of a significant proportion of wounded. Plasma is not an adequate substitute in these cases."

The outgrowth of Colonel Churchill's report was the setting up of a far-flung system of blood banks in the rear echelons of medical support. The blood bank method—result of an extensive survey among units that were in combat in North Africa—will be another rung in the ladder of curative medical science.

Prisoners of War Contribute

Approval of the blood-storage program was announced by the Surgeon's Office of the North African Theatre of Operations after four months of research and questioning of medical officers in the combat area. As "live blood" transfusions are difficult to safeguard in front-line medical service, adequate blood banks are being set up in evacuation and general hospital areas, some of which are as close as three or four miles to the combat zone.

Functioning much the same as the Red Cross collection agencies' blood bank teams in the United States, the Army's evacuation and general hospitals will collect in bottles live blood from volunteer donors. Donors, the Surgeon's Office reported, will come from noncombatant troops, convalescent and mildly wounded patients and soldiers from medical detachments . . .

The article so disturbed the plasma advocates that Edwin J. Cohn said: "What in God's name does Pete [Churchill] mean by saying this? He's wrecking our entire program!"[41] This program was not sufficiently proven to have been tried out in a combat area. The National Research Council had plenty of opportunity to give the plasma matter comprehensive checking before plasma was introduced *de novo*, but this was not done.

World War II was started with the concept that plasma for the intravascular space and sodium chloride solution for the interstitial space were therapeutic measures adequate to re-establish equilibrium in a wounded man. Experience in North Africa immediately demonstrated the inadequacy of this therapy and showed the necessity for whole blood. As soon as equipment could be obtained a blood bank, organized by the Theater with service troops as donors, supplied the full needs of the Mediterranean forces to the end of the war.

The loss of whole blood following wounding far surpassed that estimated at the beginning of the war, and the degree of shock closely paralleled the amount of blood lost. The obvious explanation of why whole blood is needed rather than plasma is that replenishment of red cells maintains the required oxygen-carrying capacity.[42]

Churchill was too able, too strong, to be ignored by the military. As he made clear in his diary, the authorities finally recognized the validity of his views and at the onset of the Anzio campaign ordered that adequate supplies of whole blood be made available (the British also were vociferous in their demands for whole blood).

J. D. Stewart's preliminary report to the Surgeon of March 17, 1944, on thirty-five seriously wounded men described no hemoconcentration or shock.[43] The same was true of the much more extensive report of the Board for the Study of the Severely Wounded.[44]

HISTORIC APPLICATIONS OF BIOPHYSICS IN MEDICINE

November 12, 1936, was an important date little appreciated at the time by those who sat at a luncheon table at a colloquium in Vanderbilt Hall when Dr. Karl Compton, then President of Massachusetts Institute of Technology, addressed them on the subject "What Physics Can Do for Biology and Medicine."[45] He described how Fermi had tagged iodine and other elements with radioactivity, which could be measured at a distance from the body, and referred them to the report in *Nature* describing this exciting discovery.[46] Immediately, those at the table (J. H. Means, Saul Hertz, Jacob Lerman, and Earle Chapman), knowing the avidity with which the thyroid takes up iodine, recognized the potential of this new tool, and a mutual, kinetic force thrust their leader, Means, toward Compton. Immediately Means started negotiations for a cooperative venture in physics and thyroid physiology and disease between the Massachusetts Institute of Technology and the Massachusetts General Hospital. Soon thereafter this cooperative enterprise was established and led to continued, productive investigations. Dr. Saul Hertz pursued studies, under Professor Robley D. Evans' direction, which yielded the preliminary physiological data before the first attempts at therapy in January 1941. Through 1941–42, Hertz treated about twenty-six patients with a combination of radioactive and the time-honored stable iodide. But those in the clinic who saw these patients did not share Hertz's enthusiasm, and, indeed, when he joined the Navy late in 1942 he was hard pressed to find someone to follow up his cases or to continue the program started in conjunction with the Massachusetts Institute of Technology. In December 1942 he approached Dr. Earle M. Chapman because of his experience in radiation therapy and his contact with the thyroid clinic. Meanwhile, Rulon Rawson had replaced Hertz as the Director of the Thyroid Clinic, and he agreed to continue Hertz's efforts, although, based on his own observation of Hertz-treated cases who had been presented before the Clinic, he was skeptical of the clinical potential of radio-iodine.

In February 1943 Dr. Chapman assumed active direction of the program with Robley Evans. The radio-iodine was I^{130} with only twelve hours half-life, a product of the cyclotron at the Massachusetts Institute of Technology. It was apparent that the definitive use of radio-iodine should be established by bracketing the single effective dose in hyperthyroidism and producing myxedema or near total destruction of the gland by this method. This had to be done without the addition of ordinary iodine, which Dr. Means had insisted upon for amelioration of the toxic thyroid symptoms. Their immediate review of the twenty-six patients of Hertz revealed that six were in chronic hyperthyroidism while on iodide and that early subtotal thyroidectomy was indicated. Meanwhile, the upward trend of their dosages through 1943–44 revealed that indeed myxedema could be produced with single dosages that were significantly greater than those employed by Hertz. No ordinary iodide was used. By June 1946 the results of their new series in contrast to Hertz's series were presented at the American Medical Association meeting in San Francisco.[47] The definitive use of this single agent in therapy was established.

In August 1946 the Atomic Energy Commission released I^{131} (eight-day halflife) for use in qualified centers across the country, and their source of nuclear energy shifted from Cambridge to Oak Ridge. Through the next two decades Chapman continued to observe the biologic effects of radiation from I^{131} and wrote several reports with various younger men who came to the Thyroid Clinic, which was then directed by John Stanbury.

In 1961 the National Center for Radiological Health started the Cooperative Thyrotoxicosis Therapy Follow-up Study, to test for an increase in the incidence of leukemia and cancer in hyperthyroid patients treated with radio-iodine. Despite Chapman's pleas in the formative meetings, no effort was made to look for genetic defects in the offspring of treated patients. The scientists vowed that no adequate control data for this could be obtained, so why look! After many years of dire threats of I^{131} causing leukemia, cancer, and genetic defects, the publications to disprove the first of these came in the *Journal of the American Medical Association*,[48] and more recently in the *Journal of Clinical Endo-*

crinology and Metabolism.[49] Chapman was able to publish data that suggest that the incidence of genetic defects in children of parents treated with radio-iodine is no greater than in the general public.

The problem of contamination from radioactive fallout created mild hysteria in 1960–61, and government health agencies began searching for countermeasures. Surprisingly, a search of the literature as well as consultation with the subcommittee on countermeasures of the National Advisory Committee on Radiation revealed the stark fact that the minimal effective oral dose of iodide for suppression of radioactive iodine uptake by the normal thyroid was unknown. George Thorn was named Chairman of a subcommittee of the National Advisory Committee on Radiation to explore this in mid-1961, and Chapman was asked to head a research team to define the minimal allowable dosage to protect children especially. The result was published in *Science.*[50] Fortunately, the fallout scare subsided as above-the-earth explosions were stopped.

In the meantime, in the middle 1940's, Drs. Howard A. Frank and Arnold Seligman at the Beth Israel Hospital made plasma albumin tagged with radioactive iodine and used it to measure plasma volume in shock. Modifications of this method are widely used today.

THE BIOPHYSICAL LABORATORY

Very soon after the end of World War II, and under the leadership of A. Baird Hastings and Shields Warren, the Biophysical Laboratory was established, July 1, 1946. The original staff consisted of Dr. Arthur K. Solomon and one graduate student, who were soon joined by an electronics technician and a secretary. Educated at Princeton, Harvard University, and Cambridge University in England from 1934 to 1964, Dr. Solomon received the Ph.D. degree in physical chemistry under Professor George Kistiakowsky in 1937, and then the Doctor of Science degree from Cambridge University. He held various research fellowships and chairmanships in the field of physics and biological chemistry. From 1957 to 1968 he was Associate Professor of Biophysics at the Harvard Medical School, and in 1968 he was promoted to a full professorship.

To the task of organizing the Laboratory of Biophysics, Dr. Solomon brought an impressive background of experience and training. At the Cavendish Laboratory he had participated in the construction of the cyclotron, and in 1939 he returned to Harvard and assisted with the same task.

The production of C^{11} from boron in the cyclotron led to his participation in metabolic studies with this isotope, in association with Professors Hastings, Conant, Kistiakowsky, and others. These studies were interrupted by the war, and Dr. Solomon returned to England at the request of the Director of the Cavendish Laboratory to take part in their wartime projects. At this time he played a major role in the development of close-range, anti-aircraft radar.

At first, the aspect of biophysics of most interest to the medical community was the application of radioactive isotopes to problems of biology and medicine. Radioactive isotopes were just becoming available on a modest scale from the Oak Ridge National Laboratory, and there were no commercially available means of detecting them, neither counters nor scalers nor any of the ancillary equipment used to handle isotopes. In the early years the Biophysical Laboratory was the major source of expertise in this field, not only for preclinical departments but also for departments of medicine in the hospitals. For roughly the first two years of its existence, the Biophysical Laboratory made in its shop all the radioactive counters for the preclinical departments. During this period new kinds of counting equipment were designed and built, including low background counters, special systems for measuring radioactive hydrogen, and a variety of very small probe counters for use in studies of the human brain. Before mass spectrometers became commercially available, the Laboratory, in collaboration with Dr. Francis D. Moore of the Peter Bent Brigham Hospital, built its own instrument, which played a prominent role in numerous experiments on the total body water in man.

After the first year Dr. Solomon was joined by two other professional colleagues, Dr. Dewitt Stetten to represent the Department of Biochemistry and Dr. Seymour Gray to represent the Department of Medicine. This tripartite division of the Laboratory continued for some years. Dr. Stetten remained but a single year and was followed by Dr. Christian Anfinsen for Biochemistry, who stayed for about two years. After this Professor Manfred Karnovsky represented the biochemical interest in the Laboratory until about 1962. When Dr. Gray left the Laboratory after five years, there was no further formal representation of the Department of Medicine.

In these early years the Laboratory was instrumental in developing rules regulating the amounts of radioactive isotopes that could be safely handled, and making recommendations for the doses that might appropriately be given to patients in hospitals for investigational purposes. The Laboratory staff was also responsible for lectures to the medical students on the use of radioactivity and for many years ran the first-year laboratory on radioactive measurements. Even in those early days it was directly planned that the activities of the Laboratory would be broader than the use of isotopes.

As radioactivity and its measurements became commercially available and widely disseminated, the Laboratory intensified its interest in biological membranes. The teaching shifted from biochemistry to physiology, and the Laboratory staff became responsible for teaching first-year medical students about ion transport and biological membranes. Many medical students were attracted to carry out research in the Laboratory during their Medical School years, and several returned as postdoctoral fellows before going on to positions in other universities. Graduates of the Laboratory now hold tenure positions in medical schools not only in the United States but all over the world. Dr. Stetten has, of course, played a prominent role in the development of the National Institutes of Health, and Dr. Anfinsen won a Nobel Prize.

The Department of Biophysics is also a Division of the Faculty of Arts and Sciences, where Arthur K. Solomon and Elkan R. Blout serve as part of the Faculty of the Committee on Higher Degrees in Biophysics. The Biophysics Program by 1968 offered nine courses to students in the University. One of these, given by Dr. Solomon, attracted, in the preceding year, seventy-six undergraduates and eleven graduate students. Thus the Laboratory has provided teaching at all academic levels.

Later, the Massachusetts General and the Peter Bent Brigham Hospitals established biophysics laboratories under, respectively, Drs. Gordon L. Brownell and Bert L. Vallee, to support research based on biophysical techniques. Professor Vallee and others have also participated in teaching biophysics.

Chapter Twenty-eight

Associated Institutions

THE GRADUATE SCHOOL OF ARTS AND SCIENCES: DIVISION OF MEDICAL SCIENCES[1]

Each of the basic science departments of the Harvard Medical School comprises one component of the Division of Medical Sciences. The Division is the formal linkage between those departments and the Graduate School of Arts and Sciences of Harvard University. As can be imagined, the Division also provides mechanisms for interdepartmental activities, as mentioned below.

The Division of Medical Sciences was established in the Harvard University Faculty of Arts and Sciences as early as 1908. It provides facilities for advanced study and investigation leading to the degrees of Master of Arts and Doctor of Philosophy in the basic medical sciences—anatomy, biochemistry, immunology, microbiology and molecular genetics, neurobiology, experimental pathology, pharmacology, and physiology. The Division enjoys the facilities of the departments and research laboratories of the Harvard Medical School, its affiliated hospitals, and other related parts of the University. As part of the Faculty of Arts and Sciences of Harvard University, the Division also has close relations with the Departments of Biology, Chemistry, and Physics in Harvard College.

The aim of the Division is to ensure a broad education in the biological fields mentioned above, and specialization in one of them, for those who wish to pursue careers of research and teaching. The Division is uniquely equipped for this aim because it brings together the facilities of a group of departments in the Medical School. It can provide opportunities for correlating research activities that often require a wider range of experience and techniques than can be found in any single discipline or department. Furthermore, because it has active contact with many of the clinical problems under investigation in the several hospitals of the complex affiliated with the Harvard Medical School, it maintains its position as a meeting place for the biological, medical, physical, and chemical sciences.

THE HARVARD FATIGUE LABORATORY

The Harvard Fatigue Laboratory had its origin in the mind of one man: Lawrence J. Henderson. It could claim some degree of parentage from J. B. S. Haldane of Oxford and J. Barcroft of Cambridge. The University of Strassburg played a role (1902–04), for it was there that Henderson and Carl L. Alsberg (1877–1940) became acquainted and had many stimulating conversations relevant to the later establishment of the Laboratory.

Alsberg came to the Harvard Medical School in 1902 as an Assistant in Biological Chemistry. A year later, Henderson came as an Instructor. It was widely recognized that they were many years ahead of their time in trying to teach medical students some physical chemistry, including the law of mass action (Henderson's students called him "little k"). It was Alsberg who suggested to D. Bruce Dill (who later became Director of the Fatigue Laboratory) that he should work with Henderson. Dill did so, shortly after receiving his Ph.D. at Stanford in 1925. Henderson explained that his principal interest was then in the physico-chemical properties of blood.

Much of the relevant research was going on in Arlie V. Bock's laboratory at the Massachusetts General Hospital. Bock's interest in respiratory matters had been greatly stimulated by his membership in Barcroft's expedition for high altitude studies in Peru in 1921–22. His skill as a clinical investigator and his interest in human physiology in health and in disease made the 1925–27 period a stimulating one. Dill commented that he soon learned how indebted they all were to Barcroft, Haldane, Donald Van Slyke, and A. V. Hill.

Dill dates the concept of the Fatigue Laboratory as 1926. The physical establishment of the Laboratory was the product of several individuals' industry. Wallace Donham (1877–1954) had been Dean of the Harvard Graduate School of Business Administration since 1919 and had raised money to build a new school across the Charles River and adjoining the Harvard Stadium. Support became a certainty on receipt of a short letter and check for $5,000,000 from George Fisher Baker for the construction of the School. Dean Donham, with Henderson and the backing of President Lowell, organized a small committee to obtain support for the incorporation of a laboratory of human physiology in the Business School. Other committee members were William Morton Wheeler, representing Harvard College, David L. Edsall, Dean of the Medical School, Elton Mayo, Professor of Industrial Research in the Business School, and Arlie V. Bock of the Medical School and the Massachusetts General Hospital. Dean Donham sequestered a part of Morgan Hall for the site of the Fatigue Laboratory. Laura Spelman

Rockefeller gave $25,000 for equipping the Laboratory, and the Rockefeller Foundation made $500,000 available over a ten-year period for operations. Equipment was obtained and installed early in 1927. Soon after this, work was progressing well. The committee continued to function by providing administrative guidance for the Laboratory.

An unsigned article on the Laboratory, published in the *Harvard Alumni Bulletin*[2] was written, in large part if not entirely, by Henderson. From it we learn that the Laboratory was a physiological institute devoted to experimental research. A principal aim of its investigators was to set up "quantitative descriptions of the physiological experiences of every-day life."[3] A further aim was to illuminate the psychological and sociological work of Professor Mayo's department in the Harvard Business School, with a certain part of the work carried out in the laboratories and clinics of the Massachusetts General Hospital. The hope was that progress could be made toward a generalized scientific description of the experiences of individuals in their environments. This amounted to a study of human biology.

The Fatigue Laboratory was founded to support physiological, applied physiological, and sociological investigations. It was established by Drs. L. J. Henderson, A. V. Bock, and D. B. Dill,[4] whose laboratories had already made progress in the synthetic study of the respiratory function of the blood and the related functions of circulation, breathing, and metabolism. They had succeeded in applying quantitative methods not only to analytical but also to synthetic studies. They had, therefore, a promising beginning in the field of quantitative description of physiological findings. Their purpose was to carry on research, within the range of their experimental competence, which might lead on an even larger scale than formerly to quantitative synthetic results. Such studies, when applied to individuals, yielded quantitative description of differences among individuals, and until this work was undertaken had been pursued for the most part by physical anthropologists. These scientists had to rely largely on measurement of bones, whereas the physicians relied on the study of their cases. Anthropological studies have not been very satisfactory, in part because individual traits tend not to be highly correlated with the form of the skeleton. Illness is usually more or less accidental. It was obvious that a broad understanding of individual differences among persons was likely to rest upon a foundation that is chiefly physiological and psychological. From other points of view, this subject clearly involved the study of human genetics, but the geneticist must know what physiological characters to look for, and this he must learn, if at all, from the physiologist.

It is evident that the physiological status of the individual is an important factor in determining fitness for work, but it is just as important to understand the kind of changes which work produces in a worker. Undoubtedly, work determines to some extent the diseases that a man may have, and the work he does is bound to modify the course and result of all his diseases. The psychological pattern is related to his physiological status. Problems of applied physiology must include, on the one hand ,studies of what is vaguely called "fatigue," arising in the actual condition. On the other hand, studies leading toward diagnosis of normal differences of physiological pattern are also important. These facts are especially relevant to some of the chronic diseases. One must take into account the problem of the physiological experiences of men as data related to sociology.

Elton Mayo's studies in the field of industrial psychology and sociology had led him to look for association with the physiological work and familiarity with the methods and reasoning involved in synthetic studies. Dr. Henderson's curiosity had been aroused by this field, following his interest in the teachings of Vilfredo Pareto's *Treatise on General Sociology*. Henderson found it to be a remarkable application of logical methods, with which he was acquainted as a physiologist, to the problems of sociology. However difficult work in this field might be, it is evident that many conditions of interest to the physiologist are closely connected with physiological and psychological findings, as well as those specifically sociological. Thus association between the work of Professor Mayo's department and that of the Fatigue Laboratory seemed desirable. It was evident that collaboration could be expected. The Fatigue Laboratory was constructed with these ideas in mind. The founders knew that work in the field would be tedious and laborious, and that progress would be slow.

L. J. Henderson's monumental *Blood: A Study in General Physiology*, published in New Haven in 1928, provided a starting point for all of the other work of the Laboratory. An extensive series of researches on muscular activity was carried out, and the work was incorporated in the second edition of Bainbridge's *Physiology of Muscular Exercise* (London, 1931). This second edition was almost completely rewritten by A. V. Bock and D. B. Dill at the request of the English physiologist. Next, the group of phenomena vaguely indicated by the word "fatigue" have been widely studied.

In earlier years it had been suggested that the supposedly definite state indicated by the word "fatigue" was dependent upon, or caused by, a fatigue toxin. The work of the Fatigue Laboratory has shown, however, that the various unpleasant sensations referred to by the word "fatigue" are associated with a variety of physiological states which have in common only the fact that the physiological equilibrium of the body is somewhere breaking down. It is well known that fatigue in such forms of muscular activity as speed in running is associated with a lack of oxygen and the accumulation of lactic acid in the body. Other factors emerge after long, hard, muscular work—for example, lack of fuel for the muscles may become of primary importance, but not as serious as lack of oxygen. Other situations—such as standing at attention for long periods with a resulting accumulation of lymph in the legs and sometimes an inadequate return of blood to the heart—are also important. It has been discovered also that when work is performed at high temperatures or humidities, a great deal of blood is to be found in the skin. Heat has another effect, namely, causing the loss of salt from the body in sweat, leading to fatigue and muscle cramps.

The researchers hoped to find a single cause or a simple effect, but there is not much in common among the above states except the result understood by "fatigue," which turns out to have little objective meaning. There is at hand a changing condition of the organism tending toward breakdown. It is possible to describe the facts only as simultaneous changes of many things tending toward a condition in which it is no longer possible to persist in the activity causing the condition.

The Fatigue Laboratory has sent out four expeditions under Dr. Dill, one to Colorado, to study physiology at high altitudes, and three for the study of the effects of heat, conducted on the Isthmus of Panama, at Boulder Dam, and in the steel works of Youngstown, Ohio. There were ordinarily more than 100 cases of heat cramps each summer at Youngstown. Dr. J. H. Talbott was principally responsible for the Youngstown studies. An understanding of the situation led to treatment and prompt relief of heat cramps by the ingestion of sodium chloride. The Fatigue Laboratory soon became a center for international research, and an expedition with collaborators from the universities of Cambridge and Copenhagen went to the Andes.

Dr. Dill had not only planned and carried out researches of the kind mentioned, but also trained technicians for the War and Navy departments of the federal government. This work involved defense against poison gases, the physiology of diving, and life in submarines. The Fatigue Laboratory cooperated with the laboratories of Massachusetts General Hospital in clinical reserches related to these problems, under the leadership of Drs. Bock and Talbott.

In summing up the work of the Fatigue Laboratory, one may describe it as an attempt through experimental research and collaboration with others to make contributions toward the establishment of what can be called Human Biology. It was believed that the time will come when study of men's many activities and their interrelations will be recognized as associated with human welfare in the normal activities of life as well as in the treatment of the sick. In such studies, physiological work is bound to be important—more important, it seems, than morphological work.

> Something like this is the inevitable tendency of science when things as they are are studied. Simplicity is attainable through abstraction, separation, isolation, and by making other things equal. But in everyday life other things are never equal, isolation is impossible, separation difficult, and abstraction dangerous. If we are to know the event or process that we call the life of a man, we must strain every effort to synthesize the results of abstract analysis.[5]

Dr. J. H. Talbott played a major role in the Laboratory from its beginning. He had begun work in the School with Arlie Bock in 1926 as a medical student. When the Fatigue Laboratory was opened, he moved to the Business School, where he had quarters. Talbott was a member of the Laboratory's first high-altitude study group in 1929 and the first desert study group in 1932. As noted, he was responsible for the study of heat illness in the steel industry in Youngstown. He also was a clinical investigator in the high-altitude study of 1935. Bock carried out some of his activities in the Fatigue Laboratory and took part in the desert study in 1932.

The international reputation of Henderson was a magnet that attracted foreign fellows, some of them distinguished, like F. J. W. Roughton, Peter Scholander, and Sir Hubert Wilkins. Many United States physiologists who worked in the Laboratory, some postdoctoral and others candidates for degrees, now hold professorships. Another group participated in collaborative efforts, notably with Walter Cannon.

The oncoming war had a major effect on the Laboratory. Studies relevant to the miltary began to take shape with the approval of Henderson, Donham, and Dill. By this time, funds from the Rockefeller Foundation were running out, but Henderson was able to raise money needed for wartime research from the National Academy of Sciences–National Research Council or directly from the Quartermaster Corps. At this time W. H. Forbes was responsible for the concept of a climatic research laboratory at Lawrence, Massachusetts. Paul Siple guided its early development, and it soon became a first-rate facility for testing and appraising cold weather clothing and equipment. The program of that venture was coordinated with the activities of the Fatigue Laboratory.

When Dill returned from military service in 1945, the momentum of the war years continued to carry the Laboratory ahead. Several severe changes occurred: L. J. Henderson died from a pulmonary embolus in 1942, and Dean Donham retired. President Conant returned from his wartime activities. He had been doubtful about the value of the

Fatigue Laboratory from its inception, and it was generally believed that he thought Henderson had gone too far afield in this venture. He was also dubious about the value of Henderson's interest in Pareto and human behavior and about the Business School as a proper place for the Fatigue Laboratory. Donald K. David, who was appointed Dean of the Business School in 1942, was told that he must finance the Fatigue Laboratory or close it. Government funds for research of the type carried out in the Laboratory were available, but University policy after the war opposed the use of government funds for such a purpose.

In this period of uncertainty the interests of the Laboratory were shifted from research in military physiology to industrial physiology and psychology. It was also during this period that senior members of the staff received offers which, considering the uncertain future of the Fatigue Laboratory, they could not refuse. Dill was appointed Scientific Director of the Medical Laboratories of the Army Chemical Corps. After his departure, the University closed the Laboratory and turned its assets over to the School of Public Health. The dissolution of the Laboratory and distribution of its assets was carried out by W. H. Forbes, who completed it in 1946.

The part the Fatigue Laboratory played in the careers of many physiologists can never be measured; in some cases it was doubtless minor, but in others it was a major influence. Unquestionably, the success of those who were trained in the Laboratory has been, as Dill has said, a lasting reward to those who participated in that training. Although L. J. Henderson has long since died (1942), Dill likes "to think that both his spirit and the spirit of the Fatigue Laboratory will be perpetuated by those who came under their influence." [6]

> The studies initiated at the Fatigue Laboratory are far from being completed. It is gratifying to observe that many of the ideas initially occupying the Laboratory's attention are still being actively pursued by what appears to be a large and continually expanding number of investigators. The extent to which they base their investigations upon the foundation laid by the results of the Fatigue Laboratory's rerearch program offers concrete evidence of the high quality and innovative activities of the group. [7]

AFFILIATED HOSPITALS OF THE HARVARD MEDICAL SCHOOL 1970

The major teaching hospitals of the Harvard Medical School are:

Beth Israel Hospital, 1916
Boston City Hospital, 1864

Includes the Thorndike Memorial Laboratory, 1923
   the Neurological Unit, 1926
   the Mallory Institute of Pathology, 1933
Boston Hospital for Women, formed by the merger in 1966 of the Lying-in Hospital, 1832, and the Free Hospital for Women, 1875
Children's Hospital Medical Center, 1959
  Includes: Parents and Children's Services of the Children's Mission, 1849
    The House of the Good Samaritan, 1861
    The Children's Hospital, 1869
    The Hospital and Convalescent Home for Children, 1873
    The Infants' Hospital, 1881
    The Sharon Sanitarium, 1891
    The Judge Baker Guidance Center, 1917
    The Children's Cancer Research Foundation (Jimmy Fund), 1947
Massachusetts Eye and Ear Infirmary, 1827
 Associated with the Harvard Medical School since 1866
Massachusetts General Hospital, established 1811, opened 1821
  Includes: McLean Hospital, 1811
    Collis P. Huntington Memorial Hospital, 1912
    (In 1941, Harvard University and the Massachusetts General Hospital agreed with the Collis P. Huntington Memorial Hospital that the work on treatment and research in the field of cancer would be transferred to the Massachusetts General Hospital. This was done in 1943. The concept was that the care and treatment of medical specialties could be better dealt with in a large general hospital rather than in smaller units.)
    Hall Mercer Hospital, 1941
    Vincent Memorial Hospital, 1942
    Burnham Memorial Hospital for Children, 1946
Massachusetts Mental Health Center, 1912
Peter Bent Brigham Hospital, 1913
Robert Breck Brigham Hospital, 1914 (affiliated 1966)
In addition to these, the following carry out some teaching and/or research identified with the School:
    New England Deaconess Hospital, 1896
    Veterans Administration Hospital, West Roxbury, 1944
    (the Veterans Administration was established in 1930)

Unlike most medical schools, no single hospital was ever designated as the University hospital for Harvard. As demonstrated in the preceding observations, the hospitals are spread widely. This multiplicity, on occasion, has worked to Harvard's disadvantage: At the time the Harvard Medical School and the Johns Hopkins Medical School were competing for large sums from the Rockefeller Foundation to found a school of public health (1914), the point of view was put forward, principally by W. H. Welch of the Hopkins, that Harvard, having no university hospital, was less well equipped than Hopkins, where everything was under the control of a single hospital institution. Harvard's point of view was that a number of hospitals provided a far greater diversity of material and richness of opportunity for study.

From time to time various individuals—for example, Harvey Cushing and his successor, Elliott C. Cutler—were reported by Edward D. Churchill to have tried to establish the Peter Bent Brigham Hospital as the official University hospital. The efforts were unsuccessful.

Insofar as one can judge by hindsight, the forces leading to the multiple-hospital system were (a) the geographic need for widespread medical care as the population increased, and (b) the development of special techniques and the recognition that certain diseases could be best handled by these techniques as provided by a specialized hospital— for example, the Boston Lying-in Hospital, the McLean Hospital, and the Pediatric Services at several hospitals.

THE FRANCIS A. COUNTWAY LIBRARY OF MEDICINE
AND THE BOSTON MEDICAL LIBRARY

According to an agreement dated January 14, 1960, this Library is operated by two corporations, that of the Boston Medical Library and that of Harvard University. The Countway Library opened its doors on June 16, 1965. It combines the collections, services, and staff of two formerly separate libraries, the Boston Medical Library and the Harvard Medical Library. It is administered by a joint Library committee.

The Boston Medical Library was founded in 1805 and reestablished in 1875 by distinguished Boston physicians, including Oliver Wendell Holmes. Its constitution was granted in 1877 by the General Court of Massachusetts. It was enlarged in 1928, and its purpose is "to establish and maintain a Library of Medicine and the Allied Sciences and the promotion and advancement of medical science and education."[8] The Boston Medical Library has been officially affiliated with the Massachusetts Medical Society since 1947.

The history of the Harvard Medical Library begins in 1782, on which date the Harvard Medical School was founded. The Corporation of Harvard University adopted a plan that specified "enriching the library of the University with medical and chemical books."[9] The creation of a strong library at the Medical School dates from 1914, when a number of departments there combined their collections for the use of the entire School. The Library collections of the Harvard School of Public Health and the Harvard School of Dental Medicine were merged with the Harvard Medical Library in 1928 and 1969 respectively.

In 1958 Miss Sanda Countway made a large gift to Harvard to build the Francis A. Countway Library of Medicine as a memorial to her brother.

The Oliver Wendell Holmes Endowment

Notwithstanding the achievement of housing the collections in an efficient new building and the realization of operating economies resulting from the unification of services and the creation of a Rare Books Department, it was soon obvious that a larger financial outlay would be necessary to ensure the "preservation, enhancement and ready availability of the manuscripts, books and pamphlets which contain the significant ideas of the medical past."[10] Because the greatest portion of the Countway retrospective collections is owned by the Boston Medical Library, the Trustees of that institution have assumed the responsibility of providing the urgently needed financial base by creating the Oliver Wendell Holmes Endowment.

The Collections

The number of bound volumes in the Library is greater than 450,000. This total includes sets of periodicals representing more than 20,000 different titles, of which approximately 6,000 are being received at this time. The time span between the oldest and the most recent covers more than seven centuries. The books come from the major centers of education and culture which have existed throughout the world.

Some 100,000 books and 100,000 pamphlets, as well as a large number of manuscripts, are separately housed in special quarters for the protection and care of rare and valuable items. These collections are so rich and varied that it is difficult to single out highlights and individual treasures. In general, it can be said that the Library contains nearly all the landmark works in the literature of medicine. Examples are Avicenna's *Canon* (Strassburg, 1473), Vesalius' *Fabrica* (Basel, 1543), Harvey's *De Motu Cordis* (Frankfurt A.M., 1628), Morgagni's *De Sedibus* (Venice, 1761), Auenbrugger's *Inventum Novum* (Vienna,

1761), Withering's *Account of the Fox-Glove* (Birmingham, 1785), Jenner's *An Inquiry into the Causes and Effects of the Variolae Vaccinae* (London, 1798), Parkinson's *Essay on the Shaking Palsy* (London, 1817), and Laennec's *De l'auscultation mediate* (Paris, 1819). The original articles describing landmark medical discoveries published in periodicals or their rarer reprints are well represented in the collections. Examples are Morton's initial use of ether anesthesia, reported in *the Boston Medical and Surgical Journal* by Bigelow in 1846, and Roentgen's article announcing his discovery of X Rays to the Physico-Medical Society of Wurzburg in 1895.

Medical and renaissance manuscripts. The collections include more than fifty manuscripts of medical interest written between 1200 and 1600. Many of these manuscripts, including four important thirteenth-century items, were purchased with funds given by the Godfrey M. Hyams Trust in June 1930 to establish the Solomon M. Hyams Collection of Jewish Medicine and Science, which has been described by William C. Quinby in the March/April 1938 issue of the *Journal of the Mount Sinai Hospital, New York.*

Incunabula. Of exceptional quality and renown is the Boston Medical Library's collection of incunabula (books published before A.D. 1501), which numbers over 800—more than exist in any other medical library anywhere—and which places the Countway Library eleventh among all libraries of any kind in the United States in the possession of fifteenth-century books. Two great collections have provided the majority of these important and beautiful volumes, the William Morton Bullard Collection (541 items) and the Solomon M. Hyams Collection (31 titles).

Subjects. Most of the medical specialties and the disciplines related to medicine are well represented in the historical collections. The Countway Library contains one of the largest and most comprehensive collections of medical and medically related manuscripts in this country. Materials dating from the medieval period and from the Renaissance (previously described) are represented, as are manuscripts of local origin and more recent times. A large and significant part of the Library's manuscript collections derive from the records and archives of the Harvard Medical School, and from the accumulated manuscripts, papers, and correspondence of its faculty. The nearly two-hundred-year existence of this school and the eminence of its faculty make these papers a major resource for studying and documenting the development of American medicine and American medical education.

Another major resource is the collection of early manuscript records of the Massachusetts Medical Society from 1781 to 1900, which were presented to the Boston Medical Library in 1971 for safekeeping and scholarly use. The manuscripts, letters, and official records of this Society, many of whose leaders played major roles in the development of American medicine, give a fine picture of medicine, and particularly its regulation by a parent body, in the period before germs were considered a causative factor in disease.

Paintings. The Library has an important collection of paintings by such first-rate artists as Gilbert Stuart and John Singleton Copley, and also by men who did more primitive work. For example, the portrait of Cotton Tufts has had wide circulation in exhibits throughout this country. The Countway Library also possesses the portrait of John Clark, who practiced in Newburyport in the 1660's, the portrait being the second oil painting made in North America. Included among some as yet unidentified paintings may be the long-missing portrait of Dr. Crawford Long, believed by some to have discovered ether anesthesia.

Epilogue

THIS account of three hundred years of Harvard medicine falls into several divisions. The precursor period covered approximately one hundred and twenty years. The next main period, also approximately one hundred and twenty years in duration, covered its formation, its early developmental stages, and the Eliot era. It ended with the visible move of the School to the Great White Quadrangle on Longwood Avenue, and the not yet visible beginnings of a revolutionary change in Harvard medicine. The second main period of the School's history has several distinguishing characteristics. Most of the leaders of Harvard medicine during that period had chosen to go to France for training and had come back convinced of the soundness of the French view of medicine. This view was that although the basic sciences were extremely important, they were so only insofar as they were usable in explicating clinical problems. The same view prevailed at the famous nineteenth-century clinical schools of Dublin, London, and Vienna.

Another feature of this second period of medicine at Harvard was that the faculty was comprised of members of a small number of related Boston families, and the third characteristic, not unrelated to the second, was that the School was run as if it were a private club. The club was abolished by President Eliot when he instituted regulations governing student admission, attendance, and tuition fees, as well as faculty salaries. Some of the faculty were appointed full time during his era, and the University came to have a controlling voice in their appointment.

The history of medicine at Harvard became complicated by changing views of the nature of medicine that began to develop in the late nineteenth century. Indications of the impending revolution that was to change American medicine in the twentieth century had appeared long before that in Europe, but its manifestations at Harvard were so fragmentary and tentative as to go unrecognized there. This revolutionary view was that medicine had to be subservient to the basic sciences rather than the reverse. The notion actually had had its earliest modern expression in the sixteenth century. It is true that the remarkable advances in chemistry in the fifteenth century had affected medical thinking in the sixteenth. It led some physicians—like Silvius, Peyer, and Brunner—to pursue researches that afforded important data on the secretory activity of glands and on digestion; it led Willis to suggest the nature of diabetes mellitus; and so forth. Other physicians, however, preferred instead to apply various broad, vague—hence mystical—interpretations of chemical findings to medical thinking. Paracelsus had been a leader in this kind of thinking, and on the Continent one of his disciples, the Belgian physician (and former Capuchin mystic) Van Helmont, founded the iatrochemical school of medical practice. In England, on the other hand, Paracelsus received only passing and generally unfavorable notice until 1585, when one R. Bostocke, Esq., published his book entitled *The Difference between the Ancient Phisicke and the Latter Phisicke.* Bostocke believed that medicine and indeed all of observable Nature exemplified the chemical theories of Paracelsus. In effect, Bostocke believed that medicine was nothing but applied chemistry. If his notion sounds familiar, that is because today it is the official dogma of some powerful medical educators.

The seventy-five years after Bostocke's publication witnessed a violent controversy between the Paracelso-Helmontian physicians and the traditional physicians. Careful experiments performed during this period gradually discredited the extreme views of the former group but led, on the other hand, to the inclusion of demonstrably sound chemical data and methods in the thinking of the latter group of physicians. Nevertheless, the notion that medicine is best considered a branch of chemistry did not die (although it had no important adherents until later): it resurfaced once more around the middle of the nineteenth century in the form of a movement in Germany whose followers held that they were the only ones able to practice "rational medicine," defined as medicine derived solely from the basic sciences. It is easy to understand why that notion arose at that time in that place. German medicine in the years after the Napoleonic upheavals was probably the most backward in Western Europe. It refused to recognize the advances of French medicine—then the greatest in Europe—and even refused to acknowledge the need for a physical examination! At that time clinicians maintained that taking the patient's history was more than enough. It was not until after the student riots of the revolution of 1848 that the physical examination was made a part of medical teaching and the value of ausculation and percussion grudgingly acknowledged. The peculiar state of German medicine at the time is indicated by the career of Carl Schelling, who gave up teaching medicine to become a full-time philosopher and one of the founders of the absurd *Natur-*

philosophie that made German medicine of the period even more ridiculous. It is easy to understand why the young revolutionary physicians and medical students of Germany should want to change things. Like most revolutionaries, however, they were ignorant of history, hence, when they needed a positive program, they adopted a regressive and restrictive dogma that had been discredited long before.

It would be well to point out at this time that medicine is actually the mother of all the sciences, as Canon Charles Raven so clearly showed in his lecture before the Faculty of the History of Medicine and Pharmacy of the London Worshipful Society of Apothecaries on December 2, 1959. Good clinical observation always stimulates the most fruitful medical research: It is hard to imagine much in today's biochemistry that was not initiated and to some degree developed by bedside observations. The results of these sciences that grow out of medicine hark back to the field that first created them, thereby enriching their source also. Nevertheless, in medicine clinical phenomena are the primary data, and data from the basic sciences are merely supportive, explicatory, and at times questioning. The young German revolutionaries of 1848 knew nothing about all this, and their crusade for "rational medicine" seemed new and wonderful to them. (Observe also the choice of the adjective "rational." It had no primary relation to what they were preaching, but it did serve the important function of making all who opposed them guilty of irrationality.) The new superstition made little headway in Germany until the rise of the Ph.D. system that was to make German universities famous in the late nineteenth century provided them with a procedure for pursuing their aims. The German "rational medicine" later aroused the admiration of a number of powerful American medical educators, none of whom was a clinician and some of whom were not even physicians. The result in the twentieth century was the Flexner Report.

Harvard, with its predominantly French attitude toward medicine, did not take to the Flexner Report. Nevertheless, after World War II it was greatly influenced by it, despite the strong warnings against its tenets given in 1936 by L. J. Henderson, one of the most distinguished basic medical scientists produced by Harvard, and indeed by the world as a whole. After World War II, the prevailing atmosphere, the huge amounts of money provided for research (and not one cent primarily for bedside teaching), and perhaps the fact that the dean at the Harvard Medical School from 1949 to 1965 was not a clinician all led at Harvard to the growth of the role of basic sciences at all levels of medical teaching.

This growth has had a number of consequences other than the increase in emphasis on the basic sciences. For one thing, clinical bedside teaching has inevitably suffered, and attempts to bring the basic sciences closer to clinical experience have not been as successful as hoped. Another consequence has been an enormous accumulation of bits of data derived from the force-fed research effort. In this way, a crisis was produced that led two decades ago to the attempt to organize the clouds of data by means of the homogenized curriculum—an ordered collection of what purported to be facts. This collection had a serious fault: it attempted to fuse all data, regardless of the methods used to obtain them and in disregard of the fact that the method, to a large extent, determines the outcome. Moreover, it still did not satisfy the students' unsatisfied need for bedside teaching. The response to the latter complaint has been the introduction into the curriculum of social material, consisting mainly of depressing statistics and sentimental anecdotes. It is scarcely possible for this situation to be regarded as satisfactory, but when it will change, or what direction the change will take, cannot at this writing be stated.

As for the overwhelming amount of information the physician and the aspiring physician must learn, this is an old source of complaint. For example, the monk Theodoric, later Bishop of Bitanto and then of Cervia, almost eight hundreds years ago in his famous treatise on the extraction of arrows complained: "Every day a new instrument and a new method is invented by the cleverness and ingenuity of a physician." A hundred years ago the English version of Virchow's *Cellular Pathologie* stated "Day by day do those who are obligated to consume their best energies in the frequently so toilsome and so exhausting routine of practice find it becoming less and less possible for them not only to closely examine, but even to understand the more recent medical works." For today's full-time academic physicians, the word "practice" has had to be replaced by "conferences" and "committee meetings," but in all other respects they are in the same position. Moreover, as Francis Bacon commented in 1620, great accumulations of data are stultifying because they "rather incline us to admire our wealth than perceive our poverty." The problem is that approximately half of what is taught at medical school is wrong. This erroneous old material is supplanted by the new, some of which is also erroneous. And how much that is correct and useful is pushed out by the new, which may or may not be correct and useful? The total amount of material that is taught has not increased measurably in the present century—it has only changed. This problem has no solution except to have men of experience, broad learning, knowledge of the past, and an instinct for the future plan the content of the courses.

What has kept Harvard from going as far down the Flexner road as some other schools is not entirely clear, but clearly it *has* kept clinical medicine from becoming monotonous in content and in approach (basic science vs. bedside practice, patient care vs. intern care, etc.). The avoidance of the large, monolithic university hospital is another factor. One of Francis Bacon's most interesting comments (1620) bears on the disadvantages of the megahospital. The situation arose when Thomas Sutton, an extremely wealthy coal-dealer and money-lender, died and left a huge sum to support an institution for the care of the poor in London. The will came before Sir Francis, as Solicitor General, and he recommended that the King, James I, disallow it.[1] Bacon wrote: "Some number of hospitals with complete endowments will do far more good than one hospital of an exorbitant greatness." By placing hospitals in areas where there is most need "the remedy may be distributed as the disease is dispersed. . . . Chiefly I rely upon the reason that in these great hospitals the revenues will draw the use, and not the use the revenues; and so through the mass of their wealth they will swiftly tumble down to a mis-employment." One badly conceived or badly run hospital can seriously retard medical teaching.

Another phenomenon that should be noted is the discrepancy in increases in the sizes of the student body and the faculty. In the past thirty years, the former increased only slightly (until the establishment of selective admission of a fixed number of candidates recruited from specially chosen population groups led to a somewhat larger increase). The faculty, on the other hand, increased more than tenfold. Also increased were the budget for their salaries and the space for their offices and laboratories. Today, despite a great deal of building, there is a serious shortage of classroom space. There is also a continual rise in tuition fees. There is absolutely no evidence to suggest, much less prove, that the Harvard Medical School is today turning out better physicians than it did thirty years ago. In fact, the Harvard Medical School today is being run for the benefit of the faculty and not the students. It is ironic that what Mr. Eliot drove out has come back in through another door.

The current overcommitment to basic science that has characterized the last two or three decades of medical teaching (and patient care) has produced a discontent in two important groups—patients and students. These dissatisfactions were entirely predictable and can be expected to persist as long as the notion of "rational medicine" prevails. However, an additional and unexpected type of destructive change in medicine has also occurred. Once the idea that basic science was the sole road to advances in clinical medicine became dominant, clinical research was given a secondary role, and, in fact, has now come to be regarded as unlikely to be very productive. What was unexpected was the rise to a position of dominant influence of the notion that clinical research is intrinsically immoral. The ethics of clinical research were extensively discussed two decades ago.[2]

Recently there has been a change. Ideas that have become highly important in the civil rights movement, although clearly valid as such, do not always apply to the relation between a doctor and a patient. The noise about this matter has come almost entirely from laymen and from basic scientists, and has had confusing and disrupting effects. Recent efforts in the direction of clarification and codification of ethical concepts by medical practitioners are not only sound but helpful, whereas the recommendations, or rather the demands, of these others are not, and in fact they violate the civil rights of some patients who want to participate in research for the benefit of mankind. Accordingly, not only are students dissatisfied with their training while still at school, but they find themselves unable to deal satisfactorily with patients afterward. The latter situation has aroused a public outcry, and the schools, without admitting that they were wrong, declare that everything will be all right once they start training men for "primary care" and "family practice." That the schools should have shown so much persistence in recent decades in not training physicians for clinical practice is scarcely mentioned and certainly not criticized. Many men now in practice, finding themselves unable to deal with patients, claim they are too busy to do so, and enlist nurses and nonprofessional paramedical persons to do much of it for them. The crowning irony is that the few remaining clinicians still engaged in teaching are prevented by nonsensical restrictions from making efforts to improve patient care.

Medical education is in a state of crisis. How it can be forced to prepare students for the best patient care is far from clear today, but one thing *is* clear—that the lessons of the past have been ignored too long. The future of the Harvard Medical School is today unpredictable. It seems likely to participate in the changing medical education in this country in general, but the School always has gone—and, it is to be hoped, always will go—its own way more often than not. The future changes at Harvard will necessarily be influenced by the decreasing supply of money, the dissatisfaction with current ideas about the theory and practice of medicine, and the appearance of men with persuasive personalities who will gain support for their proposed reforms, whatever they may prove to be. In the past, Harvard has been the leader in medical education in this country, and it maintained this position for over a century without the help of money from the federal government or from foundations. When it accepted huge sums—sometimes conditionally—from both, it may have impaired its ability to make decisions. Will this prevent it from ever becoming an outstanding leader again? Was it ever an *outstanding* leader? It was certainly an innovator, most strikingly in President Eliot's day, but to what extent were its innovations accepted by other schools? This highly important question must remain unanswered, for the data that might provide the answer are not to be found in our sources. On the other hand, there is no question that Harvard's leadership was evidenced by the large numbers of its graduates who, in the past, became clinical and academic leaders in other places after leaving Harvard. However, since Harvard had the pick of the students, its leadership may have depended as much on the intrinsic qualities of its graduates as on the training they received.

One of the functions of a history is to predict the future, not in terms of specific happenings but in respect to trends. Had Harvard's history gone only to 1950, this would have been possible. The marked changes in its policies under its last two deans have, however, removed it from the track it had followed so successfully since 1782 and has made its direction unpredictable. Will it ever return to its traditional directions? Will it pursue its present courses, which have made it almost unrecognizable in all but name? Does the future of society demand these changes, or are they ill-advised? These questions may be answered in future volumes, to be published perhaps one hundred years from now. In the meantime, this volume, we hope, provides a valid account of how Harvard became great as it pursued its own particular course of development as a training ground for both medical practitioners and their teachers.

Notes

Preface

1. The men who taught at the School in the nineteenth century had almost all been trained in France. This seems to have been the result of deliberately seeking for the best, as Boston elitism required. The faculty members in that era were, for the most part, members of elite Boston families and were, in fact, related to each other by blood or marriage or both. The dominating influence of these Brahmins began to decline before World War I and was almost entirely dissipated after World War II. With them the old French view of medicine also became submerged. Were the old Boston medical families replaced because their traditional views of the primacy of bedside medicine ceased to be as attractive as the German "rational medicine" concept, which made medicine a laboratory science? Or did the German view become dominant because the old Boston medical families withdrew, as in the case of Richard Cabot? In short, were the two happenings causally related? If so, which is cause and which effect? These items of sociological history clearly pertain to the genesis of change at Harvard, and they need separate study.

2. Boston Athenaeum, Rare Books Department of the Boston Public Library, Francis A. Countway Library of the Harvard Medical School, Rare Books Department of the Harvard Law Library, Harvard University Archives, Houghton Library, Library of the Massachusetts Historical Society, Massachusetts State Archives, Archives of the Rockefeller Foundation, and Society for the Propagation of the Gospel (London). We owe a great debt to the librarians and archivists involved.

PART I. THE EARLIEST STAGES

1. Awareness of Need

1. The Medical "Department" of the College of Philadelphia (1765) and the Medical School of King's College (1767) were the first and second. Legalists could argue that the Harvard school did not exist until the Board of Overseers had approved it, which they did on November 4, 1782. The consent of

the Overseers was and is required for all college statutes and appointments, hence was necessary for the creation of the Medical School as an entity in the University.

2. John Duffy, *Epidemics in Colonial America* (Baton Rouge, 1953). We are greatly indebted to this scholarly study.

3. For a fuller description of the colonists' problems of disease, see material stored in the Countway Library under the title "Medicine at Harvard," pp. I–4 thru I–20.

4. "The CLEARE SVNSHINE OF THE GOSPELL, Breaking forth upon the INDIANS in New England," Massachusetts Historical Society, *Collections*, Ser. 3, Vol. 4 (1833), 56–57; originally published in London, 1648.

5. Cotton Mather, *The Angel of Bethesda*, in Otho T. Beall, Jr., and Richard H. Shryock, *Cotton Mather: First Significant Figure in American Medicine*, (Baltimore, 1954).

6. Ralph and Louise Boas, *Cotton Mather, Keeper of the Puritan Conscience* (New York, 1928), pp. 46, 47. Library of Congress, "Jones Papers," *Virginia's Magazine of History and Biography*, 26 (1918), 70–80.

7. Thomas Prince, *A Chronological History of New England*, 2 vols. (Boston, 1736, 1755), 1:171, 2:19. Vol. 2 was published under the subtitle *Annals of New England*.

8. Francis R. Packard, *History of Medicine in the United States*, Vol. 1 (New York, 1931), 273.

9. William Byrd to the Royal Society, Virginia, April 20, 1706, in Sloane MSS (40–40 fol. 151), B. Miscel., copy; Library of Congress. John Oldmixon, *The British Empire in America*, Vol. 1 (London, 1741), 429. William Smith, *The History of the Province of New York* (London, 1776), pp. 272–273. Will Bradford to Secretary, New York, September 12, 1709, in S.P.G. MSS, A 5, Item 53. (The volumes and item numbers or pages are as now recorded in the present files of the United Society for the Propagation of the Gospel, London. The system is not consistent.)

10. Lucas to the Secretary, Newbury, New England, July 24, 1716, in S.P.G. MSS, A 11, p. 403.

11. A letter from the Church Wardens of Perth Amboy, New Jersey, June 16, 1769, to the Rev. Dr. Barton, in S.P.G. MSS, B 24, Item 278.

12. R. P. Stearns, "Remarks upon the Introduction of Inoculation for Small Pox in England," *Bulletin of the History of Medicine*, 24 (1950), 103–122. Letter from Emanuel Timonius, Constantinople, December 1713, in *Philosophical Transactions*, 29 (1714–16), 72–76.

13. Duffy, p. 28.

14. William Douglass, *A Summary, Historical and Political*, Vol. 2 (London, 1755), 406. Some thirty-four years after the great epidemic of 1721 (where Zabdiel Boylston boldly risked his reputation and his neck), Douglass came around: "The novel practice of procuring the small-pox by inoculation, is a very considerable and most beneficial improvement in that article of medical practice." And now the alibi: "It is true, the first promoters were too extravagant, and therefore suspected in their recommendations of it." After a good look at Boylston's overwhelming data of 1721–22, Douglass had only to

rearrange his prejudices, but evidently, he was too stiff-necked at that time to do so.

15. Worthington Chauncey Ford, ed., *Diary of Cotton Mather*, 2 vols. (Boston, 1911–12), in Massachusetts Historical Society, *Collections*, Ser. 7, Vol. 8, 1709–24, pp. 634, 657–659.

16. Packard, 1:81.

17. The issue of legality is reminiscent of the questions raised 250 years later when kidneys were taken for transplantation.

18. Donald Fleming in P. A. Freund, ed., *Experimentation with Human Subjects* (New York, 1970), pp. 379–382.

19. Zabdiel Boylston, *An Historical Account of the Small-Pox Inoculated in New England. Upon All Sorts of Persons, Whites, Blacks, and of all Ages and Constitutions, Etc.* (London, 1726), p. 40. There can be little doubt that considering the hysterical temper of the people, Boylston's very life was at stake in this demonstration.

20. *New England Weekly Journal*, No. 153, February 23, 1730; No. 156, March 16, 1730. *Boston Gazette*, No. 538, March 23–30, 1730. "Description of Boston" in Massachusetts Historical Society, *Collections*, Ser. 1, Vol. 3 (1794), 292.

21. William Pepper, *The Medical Side of Franklin* (Philadelphia, 1911), pp. 15, 34–39.

22. Henry Newman, "The Way of Proceeding in the Small Pox Inoculation in New England," in *Philosophical Transactions*, 32 (1722–23), 33, 34.

23. William Currie, *An Historical Account of the Climates and Diseases of the United States of America . . .* (Philadelphia, 1792), pp. 3, 39, 40. *William Cheever's Diary*, 1775–76, in Massachusetts Historical Society, *Proceedings*, 60 (1927), 95.

24. Packard, 1:577–578. Morris C. Leiking, "Variolation in Europe and America," *Ciba Symposium* III (1942), p. 1124.

25. Adams Papers, July 17, 1776, Massachusetts Historical Society.

26. Ibid., July 24, 1776.

27. James Thatcher, *American Medical Biography, or Memoirs of Eminent Physicians who have Flourished in America*, 2 vols. in one (Boston, 1828), 18.

28. *Diary of Cotton Mather*, p. 229.

29. Duffy, p. 111.

30. Albert Deutsch, "The Sick Poor in Colonial Times," *American Historical Review*, 46 (1941), 560–579.

31. Boston Registry Department, *Records Relating to the Early History of Boston*, 11 (1876–1909), 33, 222.

32. Deutsch, pp. 565, 566.

33. Samuel A. Green, *History of Medicine in Massachusetts* (Boston, 1881), p. 48; see also Deutsch, p. 571.

34. Alexander Brown, *The First Republic in America* (Boston, 1898), pp. 156, 377–378. Boston Registry Department, *Early Boston Records*, 2:148.

35. *Early Boston Records*, 7:64, 76.

36. Deutsch, pp. 578–579.

37. General Court Records, Sessions of March 1647–48, Archives of the Commonwealth of Massachusetts, State House, Boston.

38. General Court Records, Session of May 16, 1649.

39. James Lloyd's Ledger, p. 40, February 24, 1764; Countway Library of Medicine, Harvard Medical School.

40. *Address of the Board of Trustees of the Massachusetts General Hospital to the Public* (Boston, 1814), p. 7. The copy in the Archives of the Massachusetts Historical Society contains the handwritten notation that the *Address* was written "By Josiah Quincy, Esq."

2. Education of Physicians

1. Whitfield J. Bell, Jr., "Medical Students and Their Examiners in Eighteenth Century America," *Transactions and Studies of the College of Physicians of Philadelphia*, 21 (1953–54), 14–24.

2. Such a limited background led those who could afford two or three years' study in England, Scotland, Holland, or Italy to take a superior, even angry, view of these inadequately trained men. The Virginians at Edinburgh in 1761–62 and 1765, for example, petitioned the Virginia Council and House of Burgesses to "prevent anyone for the future from professedly practising medicine who has not received a public testimony of his abilities, by being properly licensed and honored with a doctor's degree." Nothing came of this. See W. B. Blanton, *Medicine in Virginia in the Eighteenth Century* (Richmond, 1931), p. 401. Also, "Early Letters of Arthur Lee," letter to his father, R. H. Lee, Edinburgh, March 20, 1765, published in the *Southern Literary Messenger*, 29 (1859), 71–72. For a scholarly discussion of medical education and training, see R. H. Shryock, *Medicine and Society in America* (New York, 1960), pp. 3, 8, 9, 16–19, 21–29, 33, 127, 129, 135, 137–151, 154, **159**.

3. Letter of Dr. James Lloyd to his father, May 22, 1752. Houghton Library.

4. Letter of May 25, 1761.

5. Thomas Neville Bonner, *American Doctors and German Universities* (Lincoln, Nebraska, 1963), p. 3.

6. Letter from George Ticknor to Alexander von Humboldt in Paris, April 24, 1832, in Vincent Y. Bowditch, *Life and Correspondence of Henry Ingersoll Bowditch*, Vol. 1 (Boston, 1902).

7. Bowditch, p. 49.

8. Letter from Henry I. Bowditch to his sister, Mary, Paris, November 1833, in Bowditch.

9. Bonner, p. 7.

10. Betsy Copping Corner, *William Shippen, Jr.* (Philadelphia, 1951), p. 98.

11. We acknowledge our debt to George W. Corner's scholarly history of the School of Medicine of the University of Pennsylvania, *Two Centuries of Medicine* (Philadelphia, 1965).

12. Not only the Shippens against Morgan and vice versa, but Thomas Bond against Morgan; Shippen, Jr. vs. Benjamin Rush and Morgan; the Congress against Morgan; Morgan vs. the Army; Rush vs. the Army; Rush and the Army against Shippen. Rush hated both Shippens. He was against John Ewing for Provost, and Adam Kuhn and Benjamin Barton were against Rush; Granville Pattison was against Nathaniel Chapman and Philip Physick. The charges involved not only envy and jealousies but questions of competence, popularity, lying, and even charges of adultery. It is doubtful if the stormy times that surrounded the establishment of the first medical school have ever been equaled.

13. Minutes of the Meeting of the Trustees of the College of Philadelphia, May 3, 1765.

14. The Countway Library of the Harvard Medical School has the presentation copy to Dr. John Warren, from his "respectful and affectionate friend, John Morgan," Philadelphia, February 27, 1783. It was first published in Philadelphia in 1765.

15. G. W. Corner, pp. 29–30.

16. Ibid., p. 21.

17. Rev. John M'Vickar, A.M., *A Domestic Narrative of the Life of Samuel Bard, M.D., LL.D.* (New York, 1822), pp. 37–40.

18. G. W. Corner, p. 57.

19. Letter in the Colden Papers, February 17, 1735–36. New-York Historical Society.

20. *Transactions of the American Philosophical Society*, Vol. 1 (2nd ed., corrected, Philadelphia, 1789), p. 5.

21. The charters of the American Academy of Arts and Sciences and the Massachusetts Medical Society are remarkably similar. At the time of incorporation eight men belonged to both organizations.

22. Graph. Iatroon Letter, "Utopia 2d. of 2d. Moon, 1765." Massachusetts Medical Society.

23. Walter L. Burrage, *A History of the Massachusetts Medical Society*, Privately Printed (Norwood, Mass., 1923), p. 19.

24. Warren Papers, New England Historical Society and the Countway Library.

25. It is not surprising that the young (28) John Warren, vigorous, apt, well trained and of prominent family, was the target of some unfriendly muttering. See Burrage, p. 20.

> One night Dr. Rand returned home from one of his professional meetings and, addressing himself to me, he said, "Eliot, that Warren is an artful man, and will get to windward of us all. He has made a proposition to the club that, as there are nearly a dozen pupils studying in town, there should be an incipient medical school instituted here for their benefit, and has nominated Danforth to read on materia medica and chemistry; proposed that I should read on the theory and practice of physic, and some suitable person on anatomy and surgery. He was at once put up for the latter branches; and after a little maiden coyness, agreed to commence a course . . .

This may have been the earliest plain statement of Warren's plans for a medical school. It is reminiscent of John Morgan sixteen years earlier (1765) during the foundation of the Medical School of the University of Pennsylvania. The older man sent Warren a warmly inscribed copy of his *Discourse*.

26. Burrage, p. 15.

27. Letter to the Public upon the Institution of the Medical Society, in the handwriting of John Warren, as attested by his great grandson, J. Collins Warren. Archives of the Massachusetts Medical Society, undated but presumably 1782. See H. I. Bowditch, Vol. 1, Paper 5, Original Letter, 1852.

3. Beginnings of the Harvard Medical School

1. John Warren, Letter to the Public upon the Institution of the Medical Society, Massachusetts Medical Society Papers, Bowditch, Vol. 1, p. 5. Countway Library.

2. Report submitted on September 19, 1782, to the President and Fellows of Harvard College by Joseph Willard and Edward Wigglesworth.

3. The Harvard Medical School has occupied seven different locations from 1782 to the present: 1782: Harvard Hall, Cambridge. The first lectures were given in the basement of this building. 1783: Holden Chapel, Cambridge. Occupied as soon after the opening of the School as it could be fitted. 1810: 49 Marlborough Street, Boston (now 400 Washington Street). No illustration of this building can be found. 1816: The new building on Mason Street, Boston. This was the first building constructed especially for the School. 1847: The North Grove Street building adjoined the Massachusetts General Hospital. 1883: 688 Boylston Street, "expected to be the home of medicine for generations," was the home for 23 years. 1906: Longwood Avenue, Boston. These superb buildings were dedicated September 25 and 26, 1906, and occupied by the School at the opening of the term, September 27, 1906.

4. Chapter 71 of the General Laws of Massachusetts, Section 30A [St. 1935, chapter 370, section 1, amended by St. 1948, chapter 160, section 2].

5. Samuel E. Morison, *Three Centuries at Harvard* (Cambridge, 1936), p. 170.

6. Memorial of the President and Fellows to the General Court, February 5, 1784. State House Archives, House File No. 1405.

7. James Thacher, *American Medical Biography*, Vol. 2 (1828), p. 261.

8. Thomas Dwight, "The Department of Anatomy," in *The Harvard Medical School*, 1782–1906, (Boston, 1906), p. 1.

9. Fielding H. Garrison, *An Introduction to the History of Medicine* (4th ed., Philadelphia and London, 1929), p. 331.

10. Thacher, pp. 263, 264.

11. *Laws of the Commonwealth of Massachusetts*, chap. 175 (1815), 684, 685.

12. Chap. 57 (1831), 574–576.

13. "An Act Concerning the Study of Medicine," *Acts and Resolves Passed by the General Court of Massachusetts*, chap. 242 (1845), 571, 572.

14. "Of the Promotion of Anatomical Science," *General Statutes of the Commonwealth of Massachusetts*, chap. 27 (1859), 195.

15. "An Act Relative to the Promotion of Anatomical Science," *Acts and Resolves of the Commonwealth of Massachusetts*, chap. 479 (1898), 436, 437.

16. A. K. Stone, "The Department of the Theory and Practice of Physic," in *The Harvard Medical School*, 1782–1906 (Boston, 1906), pp. 15–30.

17. Ibid., p. 15.

18. Benjamin Waterhouse, *The History of the Variolae Vaccinae or Kine-Pox commonly called the Cow-Pox* (Boston, 1800), p. 8.

19. James Lind, *A Treatise of the Scurvy* (Edinburgh, 1753).

20. Thomas F. Harrington, *The Harvard Medical School*, 1 (New York, 1905), p. 90.

21. A. de Wilder, *History of Medicine* (New Sharon, Maine, 1901), p. 455.

22. See Minutes of the Corporation, May 18, 1812. For a further discussion of the charges, see William Coolidge Lane, Librarian of Harvard University, "Dr. Benjamin Waterhouse and Harvard University," reprinted from *Proceedings of the Cambridge Historical Society*, 4 (January 1909), 17–22.

23. J. C. White, "The Department of Chemistry," in *The Harvard Medical School*, 1782–1906, p. 31.

24. Records of the Council of the Massachusetts Medical Society now deposited in the Countway Library of the Harvard Medical School. Included with these records are the work sheets and full recommendations of the various committees involved.

25. Walter L. Burrage, *A History of the Massachusetts Medical Society* (Norwood, Mass., privately printed, 1923), pp. 75, 76.

26. Warren, Report of the Committee on the Pharmacopoeia, May 31, 1818. Manuscript in the Countway Library. Proposal approved, June 2, 1818. Those especially interested in the National Convention from Massachusetts were J. C. Warren, M.D., John Gorham, M.D., Jacob Bigelow, M.D., James Thacher, M.D., and George C. Shattuck, M.D. The intimate relationships of the Massachusetts Medical Society and the Harvard Medical School are evident in these names.

27. *The Pharmacopoeia of the United States of America*, 1820 (Boston, 1820), p. 17.

28. Not the first publication, but, as mentioned, the longest sustained in terms of continuity. New York had its *Medical Repository* which first appeared in 1797, only to die twenty years later. Philadelphia's *Medical Museum* was born in 1804; it lasted nine years. It was revived in 1820, and in 1827 it became the well-known *American Journal of Medical Sciences*. As such, it continues to the present time. Baltimore's *Physical Recorder* had a brief existence in 1809.

29. Garland, "*The Boston Medical and Surgical Journal*, 1828–1928," *New England Journal of Medicine*, 198 (1928), 1–13. Garland, "*The New England Journal of Medicine* and the Massachusetts Medical Society," ibid., 246 (1952), 801–806. Garland, "*The New England Journal of Medicine*, 1812–

1968," *Journal of the History of Medicine*, 24 (1969), 125–139. See also Garland, "Medical Journalism in New England, 1788–1924," *Boston Medical and Surgical Journal*, 190 (1924), 865–879.

30. Garland, "A Voice in the Wilderness, *The New England Journal of Medicine* since 1812," *British Medical Journal*, 1 (1962), 105–108. H. R. Viets, "A Score of Significant Papers Published in the *Journal* during the Last One Hundred and Fifty Years," *New England Journal of Medicine*, 266 (1962), 23.

31. Walter B. Cannon, "The Case Method of Teaching Systematic Medicine," *Boston Medical and Surgical Journal*, 142 (1900), 31–36. Cannon, "The Case System in Medicine," *Boston Medical and Surgical Journal*, 142 (1900), 563, 564.

32. C. W. Eliot (President of Harvard), "The Inductive Method Applied to Harvard," *Boston Medical and Surgical Journal*, 142 (1900), 537–558. Read at a meeting of the Boston Society for Medical Improvement, March 5, 1900.

33. The writers have leaned heavily on notes and other material provided by Professor Curran, Frances Glessner Lee Professor of Legal Medicine, July 1, 1968, and an outstanding authority widely recognized. Professor Curran's interests have been at the interface of law, medicine, and public health. The Department of Legal Medicine has suffered from lack of a good historian in the department. The field has, in the recent past, been dominated by practitioners, who frequently copied each other's inaccurate historical notes.

34. Malcolm Storer, "The Department of Obstetrics," in *The Harvard Medical School*, 1782–1906, p. 37.

35. Ibid., p. 37.

36. Ibid.

37. Ibid., p. 38.

38. Unless otherwise noted, we are indebted to Thomas F. Harrington for this information in *The Harvard Medical School*, Vol. 1 (New York, 1905), pp. 335 ff.

39. Welch, "The Relation of Yale to Medicine," Address at the Two Hundredth Anniversary of the Founding of Yale, October 21, 1901. In *Papers and Addresses*, Vol. 3 (Baltimore, 1920), pp. 1256, 1257.

40. Nathaniel W. Faxon, *The Massachusetts General Hospital*, 1935–1955 (Cambridge, 1959), p. 4.

4. The Second Phase

1. Oliver Wendell Holmes, "The Contagiousness of Puerperal Fever," *New England Quarterly Journal of Medicine and Surgery*, 1 (1842–43), 503–530.

2. Thomas Dwight, "The Department of Anatomy," *The Harvard Medical School*, 1782–1906, p. 8.

3. W. T. Porter, "The Department of Physiology," ibid., p. 87.

4. Ibid., p. 89.

5. One day many years ago, the Bigelow Amphitheatre of the Massachusetts General Hospital was crowded, as usual, and a young surgeon, Dr. Charles Scudder, was preparing a patient for surgery. He said portentously, "And NOW, I shall place the patient in TrenDEL/enburg position" (head down). A voice from the crowded stands: "Tren/del/en/burg." Scudder: "WE say TrenDEL/enburg." Gruff voice from the stands: "I am Tren/del/en/burg."

6. Richard C. Cabot, "The Department of Clinical Medicine" in *The Harvard Medical School, 1782–1906*, p. 73.

7. Ibid., p. 75.

8. Ibid.

9. F. B. Mallory, "The Department of Pathological Anatomy," in *The Harvard Medical School, 1782–1906*, p. 63.

10. Walter Channing, "Two Cases of Inhalation of Ether in Instrumental Labor," *Boston Medical and Surgical Journal*, 36 (1847), 313.

11. Walter Channing, *A Treatise on Etherization in Childbirth* (Boston, 1848).

12. Fleetwood Churchill, *The Diseases of Females: Including Those of Pregnancy and Childbed* (Philadelphia, 1850). Francis Ramsbotham, *The Principles and Practice of Obstetric Medicine and Surgery, in Reference to the Process of Parturition* (London, 1857).

PART II. THE ELIOT YEARS, 1869–1909

5. A New Broom

1. See the *Harvard Catalogue of* 1838. See also the *Circular of the Medical School for* 1838. The situation was much improved a few years later: *Boston Medical and Surgical Journal Extra* (August 10, 1842), Medical Lectures in Boston, 1841–42. Instruction was given in the use of the stethoscope, ophthalmoscope, and laryngoscope, first noted in the *Catalogue of the Harvard Medical School, 1867–68*, p. 90. The microscope was first mentioned the following year, 1869–70. Pathological Anatomy was recognized in the Harvard Medical School in 1870 when Dr. R. H. Fitz was appointed to an instructorship in that field.

2. Henry J. Bigelow, *Medical Education in America* (Cambridge, 1871), p. 79. The Annual Address read before the Massachusetts Medical Society, June 7, 1871. Also, in Henry J. Bigelow, *Surgical Anaesthesia, Addresses and Other Papers* (Boston, 1894), pp. 279–341.

3. It may be of some comfort to able young men whose Harvard appointments are terminated at the Assistant Professor level, to know that this is what happened to Eliot in 1863—*Dictionary of American Biography*, 6 (New York, 1931), 71. Discouraged, he considered giving up teaching, went to Europe for two years to pursue his studies in chemistry; but could not stay away from a

firsthand study of European education while on this journey. In this way he learned how far behind the great European universities Harvard and other American universities were. A second European trip in 1867 served the same purpose. These European experiences culminated in two articles published in 1869 in the *Atlantic Monthly* on "The New Education: Its Organization." These attracted great attention and undoubtedly influenced the Harvard Corporation, just then searching for a successor to President Thomas Hill. Eliot was not the wholehearted choice of the Corporation; in fact, it at one time rejected him, but later reversed itself in a divided vote. In retrospect, it seems as if each step in his career, even what seemed like a backward step, namely the termination of his Harvard appointment, only served to prepare Eliot for his great role in life, the Presidency of Harvard University and especially his monumental revision of medical education, not only at Harvard but in the whole country.

4. Abraham Flexner, *Medical Education in the United States and Canada* (New York, 1910), p. 12.

5. Ibid., p. 8.

6. Minutes of the Meeting of the Medical Faculty, Countway Archives.

7. Something of the 20-year-old Eliot's quality and thoughtful approach to life is revealed in a letter to his mother:

March, 16, 1854

DEAR MOTHER,—I have chosen the profession of a student and teacher of science, and it is you who should first know my choice, and understand the grounds of my decision. I shall try to write out here the pith of all the thought which I have given to the subject for the last year and a half, and to show you the steps which led me to this conclusion.

"To do all to the glory of God" should be the ruling motive of a Christian's life.

Man glorifies God, 1st by being *useful*, 2nd by being *happy* . . . (Harvard University Archives)

8. Rosamond Warren Gibson, daughter of J. Mason Warren, personal statement to Henry K. Beecher, 1931.

9. A notable area of disagreement between Eliot and Bigelow was in the field of technical training—see Samuel C. Prescott, *When M.I.T. was "Boston Tech,"* 1861–1916 (Cambridge, 1954), p. 70. Though it is true that Bigelow enjoyed and appreciated classical studies (or so he said), he had a strong belief that the aims and educational standards represented in Boston Tech were most likely to lead to progress. Harvard was officially sympathetic with the ideals of technical education but took the strong view that such studies belonged with a University. As evidence of Harvard's good faith in this direction, it is to be remembered that as early as 1847, the Lawrence Scientific School had been established within Harvard. There was considerable vacillation on the part of Harvard in this matter, according to Prescott; for details see his pp. 72–76, 77, 82. Eliot pressed his plan of uniting the Institute of Technology with Harvard College. According to Prescott, "the administration always showed a bias toward the pure rather than the applied sciences, and the pre-

vailing opinion within the University was that professional training should be added to rather than combined with the traditional liberal arts curriculum" (p. 70).

10. James Clarke White, *Sketches from My Life* (Cambridge, 1914), p. 53. (As a dermatologist, he was inevitably called "Skinny" White.)

11. Eliot's first contact with the Harvard Medical School was as an Instructor in Chemistry in 1856.

12. Editorial, unsigned, by James Clarke White, "Election in Harvard University," *Boston Medical and Surgical Journal* 74 (1866), 508–509. All three editorials are unsigned and are to be found also in James Clarke White, *Sketches from My Life* (Boston, 1914). First editorial, pp. 123–125; second editorial, "Medical Education," pp. 125–128; third editorial, "Censorial Duties—Medical Education," pp. 128–131. (These editorials are presented in the order they appear in White's *Sketches*, not as originally published.)

13. James Clarke White, "Medical Education," *Boston Medical and Surgical Journal*, 74 (1866), 63–65.

14. When Louis Agassiz heard the best of them read at Commencement, a "look of mingled wonder, pain, and disgust at their flimsy badness [was] amusing to observers." *Dictionary of American Biography*, 6 (New York, 1931), 75.

15. James Clarke White, "Censorial Duties—Medical Education," *Boston Medical and Surgical Journal*, 75 (1866), 105–107.

16. President's *Report* (1871–72), pp. 25, 26.

17. Nearly everybody has been attempting to reduce the length of the physician's training except Stanford, where, in some apparent confusion, the four-year course has been extended to five years.

18. President's *Report* (1879–80), p. 33.

19. Frederick C. Shattuck and J. Lewis Bremer, "The Medical School, 1869–1929," in S. E. Morison, *The Development of Harvard University, 1869–1929* (Cambridge, 1930), p. 561.

20. See *Memorials of Calvin Ellis* (14 pp., Cambridge, 1884), and Thomas F. Harrington, in *The Harvard Medical School, 1782–1905*, Vol. 2, pp. 902–910.

21. Ibid.

22. Calvin Ellis, Dean, in the *Annual Report of the President of Harvard College*, 1876–77 (Cambridge, 1878), pp. 100–101.

23. Shattuck and Bremer, p. 562.

24. Thomas Dwight, "The Department of Anatomy," in *The Harvard Medical School, 1782–1906*, p. 12.

25. W. T. Porter, "The Department of Physiology," ibid., p. 87.

26. Professor W. T. Porter has provided much helpful information concerning the early days of the Department of Physiology. At the time of the great physiological conference at the Harvard Medical School in 1929, Dr. Frederick W. Ellis—"Henry Pickering Bowditch and the Development of the Harvard Laboratory of Physiology," *New England Journal of Medicine*, 219 (1938), 819–828—reflected sadly that probably not more than one other member of the International Physiological Conference could, with his own

recollection, recall the modest beginnings of physiological research in the Harvard Medical School. What is true of Harvard University, of course, is often true of other institutions in this country. Physiology came into its own in the last quarter of the nineteenth century. With advances in the field has come realization by the medical profession that physiology *is* the basis of scientific medicine.

Physiology began its spectacular rise in Massachusetts in 1871 with Henry Pickering Bowditch's arrival. Ellis recalled that Reginald H. Fitz, then Professor of Pathology, encountered him on a train, sat down beside him, and asked him what he was doing. When told that his principal interest was physiology, Fitz expressed the view that physiology had done about all it could for medicine. Fitz, as the discoverer of appendicitis and pancreatitis, was renowned, and his judgments had to be listened to. He believed that physiology had little promise for medicine. Fitz's science was then an anatomical one; now, it is largely physiological. According to Ellis, clinical research is simply applied physiology. Beecher arranged a score of Lowell lectures by distinguished scientists (four were Nobel Laureates) who presented their work in terms of its origin at the bedside. These lectures were collected in a book, *Disease and the Advancement of Basic Science*, edited by Henry K. Beecher (Cambridge, 1960). Pure physiologists have too long held the view that they were the only scientists, and all others were downstream and applied scientists. Beecher's thesis was that basic science is concerned with the discovery and establishment of new truths, and all else is applied science.

27. Sir Henry Dale, *Obituary Notices of Fellows of The Royal Society*, 5 (1945–48), 407.

28. Walter B. Cannon, "Biographical Memoir, Henry Pickering Bowditch, 1840–1911," Vol. 17 of the *Eighth Memoir* (Washington, D.C., National Academy of Sciences, 1922), 184.

29. Alfred C. Redfield, "The Laboratories of Physiology of the Harvard Medical School" in *Methods and Problems of Medical Education*, Third Series N (New York, Rockefeller Foundation, 1925), pp. 21, 22.

30. Thomas E. Cone, Jr., "Dr. Henry Pickering Bowditch on the Growth of Children: an Unappreciated Classic," *Transactions and Studies of the College of Physicians of Philadelphia*, 42 (1974), 67–76.

31. Richard C. Cabot, "The Department of Clinical Medicine," in *The Harvard Medical School, 1782–1906*, p. 73.

32. W. B. Cannon, H. A. Christian, and R. P. Strong, "Minute on the Life and Services of Frederick Cheever Shattuck, 1847–1929," *Harvard University Gazette*, 24 (1929), 116.

33. Cabot, p. 85.

34. S. B. Wolbach, H. A. Christian, and W. B. Cannon, "William Thomas Councilman," *Harvard University Medical Faculty Minutes of the Meetings*, Vol. 9, 1920–1938, pp. 204–206.

35. Harvey Cushing, "Biographical Memoir of William Thomas Councilman, 1854–1933," *National Academy of Sciences, Biographical Memoirs*, Vol. 18, *Seventh Memoir* (Washington, 1937), p. 164.

36. F. B. Mallory, "The Department of Pathological Anatomy," in *The Harvard Medical School*, 1782–1906, p. 71.

37. Mallory, p. 72.

38. F. W. Draper, "The Department of Legal Medicine," in *The Harvard Medical School*, 1782–1906, p. 45.

39. Ibid., pp. 46, 47.

40. Malcolm Storer, "The Department of Obstetrics," ibid., p. 38.

41. Karl Schroeder, *Handbuch der Krankheiten der Weiblichen Geschlechtsorgane* (Leipzig, 1874).

42. William Playfair, *A Treatise on the Science and Practice of Midwifery* (Philadelphia, 1876). Franz Winckel, *A Handbook of Diseases of Women* (Philadelphia, 1889), or *Lehrbuch der Fraven-krankheiten* (Leipzig, 1886). Edward Parker, *The Handbook for Mothers: A Guide in the Care of Young Children* (New York, 1866). Robert Barnes, *A Clinical History of the Medical and Surgical Diseases of Women* (Philadelphia, 1878).

43. William Lusk, *The Science and Art of Midwifery* (New York, 1882).

6. Appearance and Growth of New Specialties

1. James C. White, *Sketches from My Life*, 1833–1913 (Cambridge, 1914).

2. J. T. Bowen, "The Department of Dermatology," in *The Harvard Medical School*, 1782–1906, p. 100.

3. O. F. Wadsworth, "The Department of Ophthalmology," ibid., p. 105. For what follows we are indebted to Dr. Wadsworth.

4. C. F. Harrington, "The Department of Hygiene," ibid., p. 109.

5. C. S. Minot, "The Department of Histology and Embryology," ibid., p. 113.

6. Algernon Coolidge, Jr., "The Department of Laryngology," ibid., p. 117.

7. C. M. Green, "The Department of Gynecology," ibid., p. 121.

8. C. J. Blake, "The Department of Otology, ibid., p. 129.

9. "The Cover," *Massachusetts Physician* 34 (October 1975), 7.

10. T. M. Rotch, "The Department of Pediatrics," in *The Harvard Medical School*, 1782–1906, p. 145.

11. Ibid., p. 146.

12. T. M. Rotch, *Pediatrics, the Hygiene and Medical Treatment of Children* (Philadelphia, c. 1895).

13. Harold C. Ernst, "The Department of Bacteriology," in *The Harvard Medical School*, 1782–1906, p. 133. We are indebted to Dr. Ernst for special notes about those early days.

14. Ernst was well known in his student days for his baseball prowess. He introduced curve-ball pitching. The remarkable speed of his delivery led to the

invention of the catcher's mask. Ernst was supreme in college baseball in his undergraduate days.

15. S. Burt Wolbach, "Harold Clarence Ernst (1856–1922)," *Proceedings of the American Academy of Arts and Sciences,* 60 (1924–25), 623.

16. At one of the early confrontations between the Harvard Medical School and the antivivisectionists, the following took place: The lawyer for the antivivisectionist group looked over the contingent from the Harvard Medical School and said scornfully to the audience at the State House, "As you can see, nobody of any consequence comes from Harvard to support vivisection." Perhaps the Harvard contingent did not look like much, but all the same, those present included Dr. Harvey Cushing, Dr. Walter Cannon, Dr. Milton Rosenau, and others.

17. Wolbach, p. 624.

18. E. W. Taylor, "The Department of Neurology," in *The Harvard Medical School,* 1782–1906, p. 137.

19. E. H. Bradford, "The Department of Orthopedics," ibid., p. 143.

20. Theobald Smith, "The Department of Comparative Pathology," ibid., p. 157.

21. Ibid., p. 160, 161.

22. R. J. Dubos, "The Gold-Headed Cane in the Laboratory," *Public Health Reports,* 69 (1954), 365–71. Dubos, Personal communication, letter of January 20, 1956, to Henry K. Beecher; see Beecher, *Measurement of Subjective Responses* (New York, 1959), pp. 182, 183.

23. Smith, p. 161.

24. M. V. Tyrode, "The Department of Pharmacology," in *The Harvard Medical School,* 1782–1906, pp. 165, 166.

25. A. J. Clark, "Aspects of the history of Anesthetics," *British Medical Journal,* 2 (1938), 1029–34.

26. Frederic A. Washburn, *The Massachusetts General Hospital, Its Development,* 1900–1935 (Boston, 1939), pp. 459–467. See also Ida M. Cannon, *On the Social Frontier of Medicine* (Cambridge, 1952).

27. Washburn, p. 460.

28. James J. Putnam, "Not the Disease Only, but also the Man," the Shattuck Lecture delivered at the Annual Meeting of the Massachusetts Medical Society, June 13, 1899.

29. *Dictionary of American Biography, Vol. XV,* p. 283.

30. Henry A. Murray, "Morton Prince: Sketch of His Life and Work," *Journal of Abnormal and Social Psychology,* 52–53 (1956), 291–295.

31. Ibid., p. 292.

32. Otto M. Marx, "Morton Prince and the Dissociation of a Personality," *Journal of the History of the Behavioral Sciences,* 6 (1970), 123.

33. Ibid., p. 123.

34. Murray, p. 292.

35. Ibid., p. 293.

36. Morton Prince, "A Critique of Psychoanalysis," *Archives of Neurology and Psychiatry,* 6 (1921), 610–621. Marx, p. 129.

37. Murray, p. 295.

38. Walter B. Cannon, "The Movements of the Stomach Studied by Means of the Röntgen Rays," *American Journal of Physiology*, 1 (1898), 359–382.

7. The Era Ends—Brilliantly

1. *Addresses and Exercises at the One Hundredth Anniversary of the Foundation of the Medical School of Harvard University* (Cambridge, 1884), p. 38.

2. See Henry K. Beecher's preface to *Disease and the Advancement of Basic Science* (Cambridge, 1960).

3. Frederick C. Shattuck and J. Lewis Bremer, "The Medical School, 1869–1929," in S. E. Morison, *The Development of Harvard University*, 1869–1929 (Cambridge, 1930), p. 569.

4. Walter B. Cannon, "Biographical Memoir, Henry Pickering Bowditch, 1840–1911," Vol. 17 of the *Eighth Memoir* (1922), p. 193.

5. Shattuck and Bremer, p. 571.

6. Ibid., pp. 572, 573.

7. William Allan Neilson, *Charles W. Eliot, the Man and His Beliefs* (New York and London, 1926), pp. ix–xxvii.

PART III. THE GREAT WHITE QUADRANGLE: FROM 1906

8. Changing Harvard

1. Knud Faber, "Nosography in Modern Internal Medicine," *Annals of Medical History*, 4 (1922), 1–63.

2. Abraham Flexner, *Medical Education in the United States and Canada* (New York, 1910), p. 12.

3. Morris Fishbein, *A History of The American Medical Association, 1847 to 1947* (Philadelphia, 1947), pp. 891, 1198.

4. Flexner was born in 1866 into a German Jewish family in Louisville, Kentucky. He was taught reverence for authority very early in his life. Flexner studied at Hopkins in its first decade. That institution was dominated by others who had a great reverence for Germany; Osler, Halsted, Mall, Kelly, Abel, Welch. Flexner spent two years in Germany (around 1908). It is not surprising that with all of this German influence in his genes and at his elbow, he had a high regard for authoritarianism of the German type (one can only wish it were possible to present Dr. Flexner with a copy of Santayana's *Egotism in German Philosophy*). For all the adulation of Flexner and his Report, however, it is possible to find here and there a balanced view: "The truth is that the Report added force and direction to a movement that had existed for four

decades"—Saul Jarcho, "Medical Education in the United States—1910–1956," *Journal of the Mount Sinai Hospital*, 26 (1959), 339. Harvard Medical School's reforms had begun more than forty years before the Flexner Report was published.

5. Abraham Flexner, *Henry S. Pritchett, A Biography* (New York, 1943), p. 108.

6. *The Rockefeller Foundation, International Health Commission, First Annual Report, June* 27, 1913 – *December* 31, 1914, p. 10.

7. Flexner (1943), p. 112.

It is amusing to observe Flexner's doubtless unconscious biases: In his book *Medical Education, A Comparative Study* (New York, 1925), Harvard is not mentioned in the index although the text contains several important references to Harvard. On the other hand, Hopkins is well represented in the index.

8. Flexner (1943), p. 113.

9. Ibid., p. 114.

10. Report of the Overseers' Committee to Visit the Medical and Dental Schools, February 26, 1913, *Bulletin* 44, p. 167.

11. It is informative to examine the Hopkins Faculty and to compare it with Harvard Medical School's in 1893. Of the twenty-seven listed at Harvard as Professors, the following are names to conjure with: Charles William Eliot, President, whose devotion to the welfare of the Medical School was legendary. The Dean was William L. Richardson, who was also Professor of Obstetrics. James C. White, Professor of Dermatology, was the strong right arm assisting President Eliot in his reforms. Henry P. Bowditch, Professor of Physiology, founded the first physiological laboratory in America. Charles B. Porter was Professor of Clinical Surgery. J. Collins Warren was a distinguished Professor of Surgery. Reginald H. Fitz, Hersey Professor of the Theory and Practice of Physic, was the discoverer of appendicitis and pancreatitis. Thomas Dwight was the celebrated Parkman Professor of Anatomy. James J. Putnam, Professor of Diseases of the Nervous System, was one of the great figures of his time. Edward S. Wood was Professor of Chemistry. Frederick C. Shattuck was Jackson Professor of Clinical Medicine. Edward H. Bradford was Assistant Professor of Orthopedics and later Dean. T. M. Rotch was Professor of the Diseases of Children. William T. Councilman was Shattuck Professor of Pathological Anatomy. Charles S. Minot was Professor of Histology and Human Embryology. Maurice H. Richardson was Professor of Anatomy and later of Surgery. Harold C. Ernst was Assistant Professor of Bacteriology. William T. Porter was Assistant Professor of Physiology. Franklin Dexter was Demonstrator of Anatomy. *One Hundredth and Eleventh Annual Catalogue of the Medical School (Boston) of Harvard University*, 1893–94 (reprinted from the *Catalogue of the University* (Cambridge, 1893), p. 8. In addition to these eighteen names, there were nine others in the category of Faculty and forty-five in the category of "other instructors." Many of these attained great distinction. In 1893 they were, in general, the vigorous younger group.

The entire Faculty of the Johns Hopkins Medical School in 1893: William H. Welch, M.D., Professor of Pathology and Dean; Ira Remsen, M.D., Ph.D., Professor of Chemistry; William Osler, M.D., F.R.C.P., Professor of the

Principles and Practice of Medicine; Henry M. Hurd, M.D., Professor of Psychiatry; William S. Halsted, M.D., Professor of Surgery; Howard A. Kelly, M.D., Professor of Gynecology and Obstetrics; Franklin P. Mall, M.D., Professor of Anatomy; John J. Abel, M.D., Professor of Pharmacology; William H. Howell, Ph.D., M.D., Professor of Physiology; George H. F. Nuttall, M.D., Ph.D., Associate in Bacteriology and Hygiene; Simon Flexner, M.D., Associate in Pathology; John M. T. Finney, M.D., Associate in Surgery; Hunter Robb, M.D., Associate in Gynecology; J. Whitridge Williams, M.D., Associate in Obstetrics; and B. Meade Bolton, M.D., Acting Associate in Bacteriology and Hygiene. *The Johns Hopkins University School of Medicine, 1893–1943* (Baltimore, 1943), pp. 12, 13.

Each institution had a distinguished faculty, but the Harvard Teaching Staff was larger than Hopkins by 35 percent. The laboratories were "unexcelled" in both institutions, according to Flexner. The endowment was of about the same size in each, but the annual budget of the Harvard Medical School was more than twice that of the Johns Hopkins. The Harvard Medical School was 111 years old when the Hopkins School was founded. At that time, 1893, Charles William Eliot had been in control of the situation for twenty-four years, with its reforms well established.

12. Flexner (1910), p. 109.

13. Ibid., pp. 109, 110.

14. Walter Edward Dandy, formidable neurosurgeon, received the M.D. degree from the Hopkins in 1910, coincident with the publication of the Flexner Report. He was roundly exposed to the beauties of the spartan life there but in some way avoided its strictures. Perhaps these strictures were not so universal even at the Hopkins as one might suppose from reading Flexner: The same issue of the *Baltimore Sun* which contained Dandy's obituary mentioned that he had accumulated a fortune while in practice at Hopkins. (What better evidence could one find of an escape from the requirements of the local "laws?") Ironically, in a column of the *Sun* adjacent to the obituary is a moving article describing the precarious financial state of the Johns Hopkins. Dandy flourished; Hopkins did not.

15. Lawrence S. Kubie, "The Half-Failure of the Full-Time System as an Instrument of Medical Education," *The Pharos* of Alpha Omega Alpha, Honor Medical Society (1971), p. 64.

16. Kubie, p. 65.

17. Ibid.

9. David Linn Edsall

1. Chief sources of information concerning Edsall are the Archives of the University of Pennsylvania, Washington University in St. Louis, the Harvard Medical School, the Archives of the Rockefeller Foundation, and personal papers in the custody of his son, Dr. John T. Edsall.

2. Edsall was denied what he considered adequate laboratory space for his

own work. More important, his view of the breadth of preventive medicine was shared by few. He believed that this new discipline should include not only serum and vaccine treatment and the prevention of disease, but also eugenics, occupational diseases and their prevention, infant mortality, the prevention of infectious diseases, the study of various obscure conditions, and new methods of treatment—as, for example, the use of meningococcal serum and Ehrlich's "606." He moved on to St. Louis as Professor of Preventive Medicine and was "a second time ambushed." Local jealousies were once again too much for him. For an interesting review of the Philadelphia and St. Louis periods, see Joseph C. Aub and Ruth K. Hapgood, *Pioneer in Modern Medicine, David Linn Edsall of Harvard* (1970), pp. 84–102, 103–123.

3. David L. Edsall, "The Clinical Study of Respiration," *Boston Medical and Surgical Journal*, 167 (1912), 639–651 (Shattuck Lecture).

4. George W. Corner, *A History of the Rockefeller Institute, 1901–1953: Origins and Growth* (New York, 1964).

5. "State Board Statistics for 1907," *Journal of the American Medical Association*, 50 (1908), 1845.

6. Reginald H. Fitz, "The School During the Twentieth Century," *Harvard Medical Alumni Bulletin*, 10 (1935), 2.

7. Edsall (1912), p. 639.

8. Fitz, p. 2.

9. President Eliot's Farewell Speech to the Medical School (May 1, 1909), p. 1. Widener Archives, Harvard University.

10. Ibid., p. 3.

11. Ibid.

12. Hans Zinsser, "Dr. Edsall and the Harvard Medical School," *Harvard Medical Alumni Bulletin*, 10 (1935), 1.

13. Ibid.

14. David Linn Edsall, "Statement of the Dean to the Faculty of Medicine," (April 7, 1919), p. 1.

15. Ibid., p. 3.

16. Ibid.

17. Ibid., p. 5.

18. D. L. Edsall to President Lowell, May 26, 1921. Also, Edsall, Dean's Report, Harvard Medical School, 1927–28.

19. David L. Edsall, F. P. Wilbur, and Cecil K. Drinker, "The Occurrence, Course and Prevention of Chronic Manganese Poisoning," *Journal of Industrial Hygiene*, 1 (1919), 183–193.

20. Alice Hamilton, *Exploring the Dangerous Trades* (Boston, 1943).

21. Jean Alonzo Curran, *Founders of the Harvard School of Public Health, with Biographical Notes, 1909–1946* (New York, 1970), p. 18.

22. Cecil K. Drinker, "Development of the School of Public Health," *Harvard Medical Alumni Bulletin*, 10 (1935), 10.

23. Edsall (1919), p. 7.

24. Ibid., p. 10.

25. Ibid., pp. 12, 13.

26. Harvard University Medical Faculty, Minutes of Meetings, Volume 6, 1899–1907, pp. 230 ff.

27. These letters are in the Rockefeller Foundation Archives, Division 1107.

28. Abraham Flexner, *I Remember* (New York, 1940), pp. 176–178.

29. Ibid., p. 178.

30. Harvard Faculty of Medicine to General Education Board, March 28, 1913, General Education Board files.

31. Eliot to Buttrick, April 23, 24, 1917, General Education Board files.

32. Fitz, p. 7.

33. Ibid.

34. Ibid., p. 8.

35. Interview with Mason Ham, *Boston Herald*, November 28, 1929.

36. Ibid.

37. James H. Means, "David Linn Edsall," *New England Journal of Medicine*, 233 (1945), 543.

38. Walter A. Jessup, "Harvard in Medical Education," *Science*, 82 (1935), 471.

39. Jessup, p. 472.

40. Ibid.

41. Ibid.

42. Means, pp. 542–544.

43. Lawrence J. Henderson, "The Relation of Medicine to the Fundamental Sciences," *Science*, 82 (1935), 477.

44. Ibid., p. 479.

10. Curriculum Changes

1. "Education in Medicine," *Harvard Bulletin*, 12 (1909), 1–6.

2. Ibid., p. 1.

3. Ibid.

4. Ibid., p. 6.

5. In the postscript to a letter written June 29, 1946.

6. Frederic A. Washburn, *The Massachusetts General Hospital, Its Development*, 1900–1935 (Boston, 1939), p. 460. See also, Ida M. Cannon, *On the Social Frontier of Medicine* (Cambridge, 1952).

7. Washburn, p. 461.

8. Ibid., p. 462.

9. Ibid.

10. Ibid., p. 463.

11. Lawrence J. Henderson, "Physician and Patient as a Social System," *New England Journal of Medicine*, 212 (1935), 819–823. Lawrence J. Henderson, "The Practice of Medicine as Applied Sociology," *Transactions of the Association of American Physicians*, 51 (1936), 8.

12. David Linn Edsall to Samuel Eliot Morison, November 22, 1928 (HMS).

13. David Linn Edsall, Autobiographical Notes, p. 2 (Countway Archives), "The Story." The story recounted has not been found. It is not in the letter to Professor Morison. Dr. Aub has seen the letter, which has subsequently disappeared.

14. David L. Edsall, "The Handling of the Superior Student," *Proceedings of the Association of American Medical Colleges*, 35 (1925), 119, 120.

15. Ibid., p. 114.

16. Edsall to Locke, May 25, 1934, in the Countway Library.

17. Arlie V. Bock to Edsall, October 29, 1924 (HMS).

18. Edsall to A. Flexner, January 23, 1925 (HMS).

19. Walter Bauer, "The Tutorial System in the Harvard Medical School," *Journal of the Association of American Medical Colleges*, 15 (1940), 118.

20. Ibid., p. 120.

21. Ibid., pp. 120, 121.

22. Edsall to Locke.

23. Harvard University Medical Faculty, Administrative Board Records, 3 (1917–1923), 473.

24. Harvard University Medical Faculty Minutes of Meetings, 9 (1920–1938), 26.

11. The Preclinical Curriculum, I

1. Frederic T. Lewis and J. L. Bremer, *A Textbook of Histology Arranged Upon an Embryological Basis* (Philadelphia, 1927). A revision of the 2nd edition of Lewis and Stöhr's textbook of histology based on the 15th German edition of Stöhr's *Histology*.

2. George B. Wislocki, "A Report on Research Work in the Department of Anatomy of the Harvard Medical School from 1931 to 1943, with Thoughts regarding possible future Developments," September 28, 1943. Countway Library Archives.

3. Don W. Fawcett, *The Cell and Its Organelles and Inclusions, An Atlas of Fine Structure* (Philadelphia, 1966). We are indebted to Professor Don W. Fawcett for much of the material presented in this section.

4. William Bloom and Don W. Fawcett, *A Textbook of Histology* (Philadelphia, 1962).

5. We are indebted to Professor Elizabeth D. Hay for assistance with the material presented in this section.

6. Letter of December 15, 1942, by William T. Porter to his colleagues. Countway Library Archives.

7. Joseph Garland, "Walter Bradford Cannon, George Higginson Professor of Physiology," *Harvard Medical Alumni Bulletin*, 46 (Sept./Oct. 1971), 4–8.

8. Garland, p. 5.

9. Robert S. Morison, "Walter Bradford Cannon," in *International Encyclopedia of the Social Sciences*, ed. David J. Sills, 2 (1968), 260–262.

10. Garland, p. 6.

11. Morison, p. 262.

12. Walter B. Cannon, *The Way of an Investigator* (New York, 1945), p. 165.

13. Henry K. Beecher passed many frustrating hours, especially in the damp summertime, with this galvanometer, when resistance would go to pot.

14. Wallace O. Fenn, "Alexander Forbes—May 14, 1882–March 27, 1965" in *Biographical Memoirs*, of the National Academy of Sciences of the United States of America 11 (New York and London, 1969), 118, 119.

15. Fenn, pp. 117, 118.

16. Hallowell Davis, Alexander Forbes, David Brunswick, and Anne Mc-Henry Hopkins, "Conduction without Progressive Decrement in Nerve under Alcohol Narcosis" in Proceedings of the American Physiological Society, Thirty-Seventh Annual Meeting, *American Journal of Physiology*, 72 (1925), 177–178.

17. G. Kato, *The Theory of Decrementless Conduction in a Narcotized Region of Nerve* (Tokyo, Nankodo, Japan), 1924.

18. "Alexander Forbes—Memorial Minute Adopted by the Faculty of Medicine of Harvard University, September 24, 1965," *Harvard University Gazette*, 61 (October 16, 1965), 32, 33 (Written by John R. Brooks, Stanley Cobb, Hallowell Davis, William H. Forbes, Eugene M. Landis, John F. Perkins, Jr., George Wald, and John R. Pappenheimer, Chairman).

19. A. Forbes, W. B. Cannon, J. O'Connor, A. McH. Hopkins, and R. H. Miller, "Muscular Rigidity with and without Sympathetic Innervation," *Archives of Surgery*, 13 (1926), 303–328.

20. J. Reboul, H. B. Friedgood, and H. Davis, "Electrical detection of ovulation," *American Journal of Physiology*, 119 (1937), 387. J. Rock, J. Reboul, and J. M. Snodgrass, "Electrical Changes Associated with Human Ovulation," *American Journal of Obstetrics and Gynecology*, 36 (1938), 733–746. J. M. Snodgrass, "Factors Influencing Bioelectric Skin Potentials," *American Journal of Physiology*, 129 (1940), 467.

21. F. A. Gibbs, H. Davis, and W. G. Lennox, "The Electroencephalogram in Epilepsy and in Conditions of Impaired Consciousness," *Archives of Neurology and Psychiatry*, 34 (1935), 1133–1148.

22. P. A. Davis, "Effects of Acoustic Stimuli on the Waking Human Brain," *Journal of Neurophysiology*, 2 (1939), 494–499.

23. H. Davis, C. T. Morgan, J. E. Hawkins, Jr., R. Galambos, F. W. Smith, "Temporary Deafness Following Exposure to Loud Tones and Noise," *Acta Otolaryngologica, Supplementum LXXXVIII* (1950), 1–57.

24. H. K. Beecher and F. K. McDonough, "Cortical Action Potentials during Anesthesia," *Journal of Neurophysiology*, 2 (1939), 289–307.

25. Eugene M. Landis, "Physiology for Medical Students at Harvard, A Description of the New Course," *Harvard Medical Alumni Bulletin*, 19 (1944), 9–13.

26. Ibid., p. 9.

27. Ibid., p. 11.

28. Ibid.

29. Ibid., p. 13.

30. In 1791 William Erving left £ 1,000 to endow a professorship in his name. It remained in the Medical School until 1850, when Josiah Cooke succeeded Webster. It was then transferred to the Department of Chemistry in Cambridge, where it has remained ever since. Efforts to return it to the Medical School were not successful.

31. A. Baird Hastings, "Atoms in the Medical School: An Address Given at the Alumni Day Symposium, 1956," *Harvard Medical Alumni Bulletin*, 31 (1957), 16.

32. A Memoir prepared by Philip A. Shaffer for the National Academy of Sciences and presented at the Annual Meeting, 1950, *Vol.* 27, *Third Memoir* (published 1952), p. 62.

33. Harry C. Trimble, "Otto Folin, A Life Work in Biochemistry," in Otto Folin in Memoriam, 1867–1934 (a collection), p. 11. In the Countway Library Archives.

34. H. A. Christian, "Tribute to Professor Folin," *Science*, 81 (1935), 37.

35. Philip Anderson Shaffer, "Otto (Knut Olof) Folin, 1867–1934," in *Biographical Memoirs* of the National Academy of Sciences of the United States of America, 27 (Washington, 1952), 48, 49.

36. A. Baird Hastings, "Biochemistry's First Century," *Quarterly Bulletin of the Indiana University Medical Center*, 21 (1959), 40.

37. "Ph.D. Program in the Department of Biological Chemistry," Harvard University, Graduate School of Arts and Sciences, Division of Medical Sciences.

38. Theodore L. Sourkes, *Nobel Prize Winners in Medicine and Physiology*, 1901–1965 (London, New York, Toronto, 1966), pp. 311, 312.

39. *Nobel Lectures, Physiology or Medicine*, 1942–1962 (Amsterdam, London, and New York, 1964), p. 439.

40. Fritz Lipmann, *Wanderings of a Biochemist* (New York, London, Sydney, and Toronto, 1971), p. 39.

41. A. J. Clark, "Aspects of the history of Anaesthetics," *British Medical Journal*, 2 (1938), 1029–1034.

42. Oliver Wendell Holmes in *Addresses and Exercises at the One Hundredth Anniversary of the Foundation of the Medical School of Harvard University, October* 17, 1883 (Cambridge, 1894), p. 16.

43. Ibid., p. 17.

44. Ibid., p. 18.

45. Ibid., pp. 20, 21.

46. A. J. Clark, "General Pharmacology," in *Handbuch der Experimentellen Pharmakologie*, Begründet von A. Heffter (Berlin, 1937), Ergänzungswerk, Vol. 4, p. 1.

47. Based upon extracts from the Memorial Minute of the following committee: J. Howard Mueller, George B. Wislocki, S. Burt Wolbach, and Otto Krayer, Chairman, in Harvard University Medical Faculty, Minutes of the Meetings, 10 (1938–48), 208–214.

48. Ibid., p. 210.

49. Ibid., p. 211.

50. We have been greatly assisted by Professor Krayer's meticulous comments concerning his Department of Pharmacology.

51. O. H. Straus and A. Goldstein, "Zone Behavior of Enzymes," *Journal of General Physiology*, 28 (1943), 559. A. Goldstein, "The mechanism of enzyme-inhibitor-substrate reactions," *Journal of General Physiology*, 27 (1944), 529.

52. W. Feldberg and O. Krayer, "Das Auftreten eines acetylcholinähnlichen Stoffes in Herzvenenblut von Warmblütern bei Reizung der Nervi Vagi," Nauyn-Schmiedberg's *Archiv für experimentelle Pathologie und Pharmakologie*, 172 (1933), 170.

53. O. Krayer and E. B. Verney, "Reflektorische Beeinflussung des Gehaltes an Acetylcholin in Blute der Coronarvenen," Nauyn-Schmiedeberg's *Archiv für experimentelle Pathologie und Pharmakologie*, 180 (1935), 75.

54. O. Krayer and G. Acheson, "The Pharmacology of the Veratrum Alkaloids," *Physiological Reviews*, 26 (1946), 383–446.

55. E. Meilman and O. Krayer, "Clinical studies on the pure Veratrum alkaloids," *41st Annual Meeting of the American Society for Clinical Investigation*, May 2, 1949.

56. W. Flacke and R. P. Blume, "The Effects of Germine Monoacetate in Patients with Myasthenia Gravis," *Federation Proceedings*, 29 (1970), 280.

57. G. H. Acheson and G. K. Moe, "Some Effects of Tetraethyl Ammonium on the Mammalian Heart," *Journal of Pharmacology*, 84 (1945), 189–195.

58. G. H. Acheson and S. A. Pereira, "The Blocking Effect of Tetraethyl Ammonium on the Superior Cervical Ganglion of the Cat," *Journal of Pharmacology*, 87 (1946), 273–280. See also G. H. Acheson and G. K. Moe, "The Action of the Tetraethyl Ammonium Ion on the Mammalian Circulation," *Journal of Pharmacology*, 87 (1946), 220–236.

59. Henry K. Beecher, *Measurement of Subjective Responses, Quantitative Effects of Drugs* (New York, 1959).

60. P. B. Dews and W. H. Morse, "Behavioral Pharmacology," *Annual Review of Pharmacology*, 1 (1961), 145–174.

61. Letter of James Bryant Conant to Henry Knowles Beecher, dated November 24, 1943.

62. Letter from Professor Otto Krayer of September 9, 1972, to Henry K. Beecher.

63. The Passano Award is sustained by annual contributions from Williams & Wilkins, publishers, and the Waverly Press, printers of books and periodicals in medicine and its allied sciences. The Passano Foundation was formed by the late Edward Boteler Passano, founder of the two companies.

64. Citation from William J. McGill, President of Columbia University, to Dr. Stephen W. Kuffler upon Dr. Kuffler's being awarded the Louisa Gross Horwitz Prize in Biology, October 4, 1972.

65. Letter of June 6, 1972, from Professor Stephen W. Kuffler to Henry K. Beecher.

12. The Preclinical Curriculum, II

1. Walter B. Cannon, "The case method of teaching systematic medicine," *Boston Medical and Surgical Journal*, 142 (1900), 31–36. Walter B. Cannon, "The case system in medicine," *Boston Medical and Surgical Journal*, 142 (1900), 563–564.

2. Charles W. Eliot, "The Inductive Method Applied to Medicine," *Boston Medical and Surgical Journal*, 142 (1900), 557–558.

3. F. A. Washburn, *The Massachusetts General Hospital, Its Development* 1900–1935 (Boston, 1939), pp. 115–116.

4. B. Castleman, *The Clinicopathological Conference, Proceedings of the First World Conference on Medical Education, London, 1953* (London, 1954), pp. 435–443.

5. Frederic Parker, Jr., Chairman, S. Burt Wolbach, and Robert N. Nye, "Frank Burr Mallory," Harvard University Medical Faculty, Minutes of Meetings, Vol. 10, 1938–1948, pp. 57–59.

6. D. Cheever, S. Farber, R. Gross, J. Homans, F. Newton, M. Sosman, S. Warren, and A. Hertig, Chairman, "Simeon Burt Wolbach," *Harvard University Gazette*, 11 (1954), 401–405.

7. Letter to Henry K. Beecher from Shields Warren, dated April 18, 1973.

8. S. Burt Wolbach, "The Glorious Past, the Doleful Present and the Uncertain Future of Pathology," *Harvard Medical Alumni Bulletin*, 28 (1954), 45–48.

9. Hans Zinsser, *Rats, Lice and History* (Boston, 1925).

10. Hans Zinsser, *As I Remember Him. The Biography of R. S.* (Boston, 1940).

11. George Cheever Shattuck, "Hans Zinsser, 1878–1940," *Harvard Medical Alumni Bulletin*, 15 (1940), 3.

12. Shattuck, p. 4.

13. Latest available figure, *Treasurer's Report, Fiscal Year* 1971–72.

14. We are indebted to the Harvard Medical School Archives for assistance with this material.

15. John F. Enders, "John Howard Mueller, 1891–1954," *Harvard Medical Alumni Bulletin*, 28 (1954), 36.

16. We are indebted to the Harvard Medical School Archives for assistance with this material.

17. Bernard D. Davis, "Prospects for Genetic Intervention in Man," *Science*, 170 (1970), 1279–83.

18. Ibid., p. 1279.

19. Ibid., pp. 1279–80, 1281.

20. Ibid., p. 1282.

21. Ibid.

22. Personal communication to Henry K. Beecher from Professor Curran.

23. The Ad Hoc Committee to consider the promotion of Dr. Curran to the Frances Glessner Lee Professorship consisted of Robert H. Ebert, M.D. (ex officio), Jack R. Ewalt, M.D., Livingston Hall, LL.D. (Harvard Law School), Arthur T. Hertig, M.D., Otto Krayer, M.D., David D. Rutstein,

M.D., Shields Warren, M.D., and Benjamin Castleman, M.D., Chairman.

24. Report of the Ad Hoc Committee for the Frances Glessner Lee Professorship of Legal Medicine, May 1968.

25. An announcement by the Harvard Director of Medical Information, July 9, 1967.

13. Medicine

1. Mary Ellen Thomsen, "You've Heard of Dr. White," *Harvard Alumni Bulletin*, 58 (1955), 146–150. I am also grateful to the Countway Library Archives for assistance. See also Paul Dudley White, *My Life and Medicine* (Boston, 1971).

2. We are indebted to the Countway Library Archives for assistance with the material in this section.

3. Herrman L. Blumgart, C. S. Burwell, R. Fitz, J. H. Means, G. W. Thorn, and W. B. Castle, Chairman, "George Richards Minot," *Harvard University Gazette*, 45 (1950), 176–178. See also Francis M. Rackemann, *The Inquisitive Physician: The Life and Times of George Richards Minot, A.B., M.D., D.Sc.* (Cambridge, 1956).

4. We are greatly indebted to James H. Jandl for assistance with the material in this section.

5. Dr. Shattuck met obstacles in every direction. Finally, we asked him why. He said, rather cryptically, "Because I am my father's son." Evidently, rather unattractive factors entered into the difficulty Dr. Shattuck had in getting material for study. His reasons for bitterness at this situation are not altogether clear. It does seem that those (George Minot, for example) who could have helped him obtain material for study did not do so. At that time Dr. George Gray Sears was Chairman of the Board of Trustees of the Boston City Hospital.

6. It was claimed by young residents that the young men in training at the Massachusetts General Hospital got pellagra, whereas the disease was found in patients at the City Hospital.

7. We are greatly indebted to K. Frank Austen for assistance with the material in this section.

14. Surgery

1. The MGH *News*, 31 (1972), 2–3.

2. Ernest A. Codman, *The Shoulder* (Boston, 1934), p. xii.

3. Ibid., p. xiii.

4. Ibid., p. xv, xvi.

5. Ibid., p. xxi.

6. Ibid., p. xxiv.

7. The Massachusetts General Hospital continued to function in its deliberate way. The End-Result cards and follow-up system and the extension of practice through surgical specialties continued.

8. Henry K. Beecher, "The First Anesthesia Records (Codman, Cushing)," *Surgery, Gynecology and Obstetrics*, 71 (1940), 689–693.

9. Letter of Otto Aufranc to Henry K. Beecher, December 23, 1970.

10. Edward D. Churchill, "Lobectomy and Pneumonectomy in Bronchiectasis and Cystic Disease," *Journal of Thoracic Surgery*, 6 (1937), 286–311.

11. Comment to Henry K. Beecher, 1936.

12. Edward D. Churchill, "Military Surgery," in *A Textbook of Surgery*, ed. Frederick Christopher (Philadelphia and London, 1945), pp. 144–145.

13. The Board for the Study of the Severely Wounded (North African – Mediterranean Theater of Operations), *The Physiologic Effects of Wounds*, ed. Henry K. Beecher (Washington, D.C., 1952).

14. Edward D. Churchill, "The Quality of Surgery," *Bulletin of the New England Medical Center*, 11 (1949), 22.

15. J. Collins Warren, *To Work in the Vineyard of Surgery*, ed. Edward D. Churchill (Cambridge, 1958).

16. Edward D. Churchill, "Science and Humanism in Surgery," Address of the President to the American Surgical Association, *Annals of Surgery*, 126 (1947), 396.

17. Letter of Oliver Cope to Henry K. Beecher, March 20, 1973.

18. We wish to thank Dr. Moore for his assistance in preparing this section.

19. Francis D. Moore, Knud H. Olesen, James D. McMurrey, H. Victor Parker, Margaret R. Ball, and Caryl Magnus Boyden, *The Body Cell Mass and Its Supporting Environment* (Philadelphia, 1963).

20. Francis D. Moore, *The Metabolic Care of the Surgical Patient* (Philadelphia, 1959).

21. Francis D. Moore, John H. Lyons, Jr., Ellison C. Pierce, Jr., Alfred P. Morgan, Jr., Philip A. Drinker, John D. MacArthur, and Gustave J. Dammin, *Post-Traumatic Pulmonary Insufficiency* (Philadelphia, 1969).

22. Francis D. Moore, *Give and Take, The Development of Tissue Transplantation* (Philadelphia, 1964).

23. Francis D. Moore, *Transplant: The Give and Take of Tissue Transplantation* (New York, 1972).

24. A. R. Spievack, K. J. Masters, B. L. Rubin, M. R. Godley, and R. Warren, "A Surgical Follow-Up and Home Visit Program," *Archives of Surgery*, 102 (1971), 119.

25. E. M. Daland, C. E. Welch, and I. T. Nathanson, "One Hundred Untreated Cancers of the Rectum," *New England Journal of Medicine*, 214 (1936), 451–458. I. T. Nathanson and C. E. Welch, "Life Expectancy and Incidence of Malignant Disease—I. Carcinoma of the Breast," *American Journal of Cancer*, 28 (1936), 40–53. C. E. Welch and I. T. Nathanson, "Life Expectancy and Incidence of Malignant Disease—II. Carcinoma of the Lip, Oral Cavity, Larynx, and Antrum," *American Journal of Cancer*, 31

(1937), 238–252. I. T. Nathanson and C. E. Welch, "Life Expectancy and Incidence of Malignant Disease—III. Carcinoma of the Gastrointestinal Tract," *American Journal of Cancer*, 31 (1937), 457–466. C. E. Welch and I. T. Nathanson, "Life Expectancy and Incidence of Malignant Disease—IV. Carcinoma of the Genito-urinary Tract," *American Journal of Cancer*, 31 (1937), 586–597. I. T. Nathanson and C. E. Welch, "Life Expectancy and Incidence of Malignant Disease—V. Malignant Lymphoma, Fibrosarcoma, Malignant Melanoma and Osteogenic Sarcoma," *American Journal of Cancer*, 31 (1937), 598–608.

26. C. E. Welch, "The Treatment of Combined Intestinal Obstruction and Peritonitis by Refunctionalization of the Intestine," *Annals of Surgery*, 142 (1955), 739–751.

27. C. E. Welch, *Surgery of the Stomach and Duodenum: A Handbook of Operative Surgery* (Chicago, 1951).

15. Pediatrics

1. We are indebted to the Harvard Medical School Archives for the source of this material, which was a Committee Report under the Chairmanship of Duncan E. Reid, dated November 19, 1962.

2. We have been greatly assisted in preparing this material by the Minute in the *Harvard University Gazette*, 55 (1960), 181–183.

3. Ibid., p. 182.

4. Allan M. Butler, "Medicine and Changing Times," *New England Journal of Medicine*, 274 (1966), 119–120.

16. Preventive and Social Medicine

1. Introduction by David L. Edsall in the book *Synopsis of the Practice of Preventive Medicine*, by Shields Warren (Cambridge, 1929), pp. xi–xv.

2. Warren, preface to *Synopsis of the Practice of Preventive Medicine*, pp. v–vi.

3. Dr. Rosenau was never one to overlook the humor in a given situation. Some time after the publication of his book *Preventive Medicine and Hygiene* (New York, 1913) a lady from Montana wrote to him: "I understand you have published a book on preventive medicine. Well, I have ten children, and that is enough. Please send me one copy of your book."

4. John F. Enders, John E. Gordan, and David Rutstein, "William Lloyd Aycock," *Harvard University Gazette*, 47 (1952), 193.

5. Enders, p. 194.

6. Report of the Ad Hoc Committee on Preventive Medicine, February 19, 1947. The Committee consisted of Walter Bauer, M.D., Chairman; Charles S.

Davidson, M.D.; John F. Enders, Ph.D.; Henry M. Fox, M.D.; Charles A. Janeway, M.D.; and George R. Minot, M.D.

7. Ibid.

8. Report of Dr. David D. Rutstein, "Plans for Improvement of Teaching of Preventive Medicine," April 28, 1952, for Meeting of the Faculty, May 2, 1952.

9. Ibid.

10. Address by Dr. Leona Baumgartner at a meeting of the American Philosophical Society on the topic "Medicine and Society—New Issues," November 12, 1970.

11. Report of the Ad Hoc Committee on the Future of the Department of Preventive Medicine, July 1970. The Committee consisted of K. Frank Austen, Albert H. Coons, Paul M. Densen, James M. Dunning, Leon Eisenberg, John F. Enders, Daniel D. Federman, Park S. Gerald, Alexander Leaf, Sidney S. Lee, William McDermott, Jr., Mitchell T. Rabkin, Robert B. Reed, George W. Thorn, and Alonso S. Yerby.

17. Radiology

1. We are indebted to the Harvard Medical School Archives for help with this section.

2. Ibid.

3. The Ad Hoc Committee consisted of Dr. George P. Berry, Dr. Gustave J. Dammin, Dr. Bernard D. Davis, Dr. Otto Krayer, Dr. Eugene M. Landis, Dr. Francis D. Moore, Dr. George W. Thorn, and Dr. Shields Warren, Chairman.

4. Press Release, Harvard University News Office, Tuesday, January 17, 1967.

5. Press Release, Harvard University News Office, Tuesday, April 27, 1971.

18. Neurology

1. Orbeli, the late distinguished Russian neurophysiologist, has, for years, been well known in this country. Some years ago, he and Alexander Forbes were having a brisk conversation in fluent English. Another Russian approached, and suddenly, Obeli could not speak English at all. When Henry K. Beecher met him in 1956, he was wearing the uniform of a Major-General. Beecher said, "Professor, I have been told that Russian scientists do not accept the probability theory." "That is not entirely true," said the distinguished Professor. "We do not believe that an average of 1 plus 49 is 25 has any meaning." Beecher said, "Neither do we." He said, "Of course, when Forster

was analyzing the causes of the first World War, he had to deal with vast numbers and, in that case, made some use of probability theory."

2. P. I. Yakovlev and P. Rakic, "Patterns of Decussation of Bulbar Pyramids and Distribution of Pyramidal Tracts on Two Sides of the Spinal Cord," *Transactions of the American Neurological Association*, 91 (1966), 366–367.

19. Psychiatry

1. The name Boston Psychopathic Hospital was later changed to the Massachusetts Mental Health Center, a curious name typical of the later period.

2. The members of the Ad Hoc Committee were Eric G. Ball, George P. Berry, Herrman L. Blumgart, Derek Denny-Brown, Charles A. Janeway, Talcott Parsons, and George W. Thorn, Chairman.

3. Herbert Gans, *The Urban Villagers* (New York, 1962).

4. A speech delivered by Seymour Kety in 1967 on "The Precursor-Load Strategy in Psychochemical Research," manuscript in the Harvard Medical School Archives.

5. Ibid.

6. James Jackson Putnam, "Recent Experiences in the Study and Treatment of Hysteria at the Massachusetts General Hospital, with Remarks on Freud's Method of Treatment by 'Psychoanalysis'," *Journal of Abnormal Psychology*, 1 (1906), 26.

7. Richard C. Cabot, "Suggestions for the Reorganization of Hospital Outpatient Departments," *Maryland Medical Journal*, 50 (1907), 81.

8. Ernest Jones, *The Life and Work of Sigmund Freud*, abridged by Lionel Trilling and Steven Marcus (New York, 1961), p. 297.

9. William Sargant, M. B., "Psychiatric Treatment—Here and in England," *Atlantic Monthly*, 214 (1964), 88–95. See also Nathan G. Hale, Jr., *Freud and the Americans: The Beginning of Psychoanalysis in the United States, 1876–1917* (New York, 1971).

21. Anesthesiology

1. Edward D. Churchill, foreword, in H. K. Beecher and C. Ford, *A Bibliography of the Publications of the Anesthesia Laboratory of the Harvard Medical School at the Massachusetts General Hospital, 1936–1962* (Baltimore, 1962), pp. ix–xi.

2. A. J. Clark, "Aspects of the History of Anaesthetics," *British Medical Journal*, 2 (1938), 1029.

3. Henry K. Beecher, "Ethics and Clinical Research," *New England Journal of Medicine*, 274 (1966), 1354–60.

4. Report of the Ad Hoc Committee of the Harvard Medical School to

Examine the Definition of Brain Death, "A Definition of Irreversible Coma," *Journal of the American Medical Association*, 205 (1968), 337–340.

5. Henry K. Beecher, "Trends in Anesthesia," *Journal of the American Medical Association*, 180 (1962), 43.

6. Henry K. Beecher, *Measurement of Subjective Responses. Quantitative Effects of Drugs* (New York, 1959).

22. Neurosurgery

1. Early in his career Cushing dropped the Williams, which came to him through a maternal ancestor. After he had taken the surgical examinations for house pupil at the Massachusetts General Hospital, he was not informed of the result until long after other candidates. The reason was that the notification of his success had been mistakenly forwarded to one Hayward Warren Cushing.

2. In order to avoid distortions of the brain caused by fixation with formalin, Dr. Yakovlev decided to try the technique of freezing the brains and sectioning them on a freezing stage supported by an inflow of carbon dioxide. These whole brain sections were carried out on a giant microtome on the main floor of the Warren Anatomical Museum. One evening when Dr. Yakovlev was carrying out his anatomical work on a cadaver brain with the assistance of Mr. Forest Eastman and Dr. William Chapman of the Massachusetts General Hospital, the outflow valve apparently became obstructed, and the entire apparatus, together with the brain, exploded, the debris narrowly missing Dr. Chapman's head, ascending like a rocket, and emerging through the skylight of the roof.

3. Vernon H. Mark, *Violence and the Brain* (New York, 1970).

23. Orthopedic Surgery

1. Bradford's professorship extended from 1903 until 1912, when he resigned to become Dean of the Medical School.

2. John G. Kuhns and Robert B. Osgood, "Robert Williamson Lovett," in *American Explorers in Orthopaedic Surgery* (Battle Creek, Michigan, 1931), section IX.

3. Sir Robert Jones, "Foreword," in "A Tribute to Dr. Robert B. Osgood," *New England Journal of Medicine*, 209 (1933), 51.

4. Henry H. Banks, "Our Orthopedic Personality," *Bulletin of the American Academy of Orthopedic Surgeons*, 19 (1971), 17–19.

5. Edwin F. Cave, "Joseph S. Barr, M.D.," *The News of MGH*, 24 (1965), 7.

6. Letter to Henry K. Beecher from Thomas B. Quigley, October 4, 1971.

24. Ophthalmology, Otolaryngology, and Facial Surgery

1. We are indebted to David G. Cogan for much of the information contained in this section. See David G. Cogan, "Dr. Frederick H. Verhoeff, Ophthalmology's Senior Citizen," *Harvard Medical Alumni Bulletin*, 37 (1962), 10, 11.

2. Ibid., p. 11.

3. We are indebted to Dr. Henry Freeman Allen for assistance with this material.

4. We are indebted to Dr. David G. Cogan and Mr. Charles Snyder for assistance with this section.

5. We have been particularly indebted to Mr. Charles Snyder for help with this section.

6. We are indebted to Harold F. Schuknecht for assistance with the material in this section.

7. Bradford Cannon, "Special Awards of the American Society of Plastic and Reconstructive Surgery, and of the Foundation of the American Society of Plastic and Reconstructive Surgery," *Plastic and Reconstructive Surgery*, 9 (1952), 294–298.

PART IV. NONCURRICULAR FACTORS IN THE GROWTH OF THE SCHOOL

26. Special Groups of Students

1. Minutes of the Meetings of the Medical Faculty, 2 (1847), 5. Countway Library Archives.

2. President and Fellows in special meeting, August 14, 1847, Harvard University Archives (Widener Library).

3. Samuel Gregory, *Doctor or Doctoress?* (Boston, 1868).

4. *Addresses and Exercises at the One Hundredth Anniversary of the Foundation of the Medical School of Harvard University, October* 17, 1883 (Cambridge, 1884), p. 19. Countway Library Archives.

5. Harvard Archives, December 27, 1847. The original letter from Harriot Kezia Hunt is in the Countway Archives.

6. Minutes of the Meetings of the Medical Faculty, 2 (1850), 73.

7. Ibid., p. 74.

8. Ibid., p. 75.

9. For Miss Hunt's rather emotional response to her problems with the Harvard Medical School, see Harriot K. Hunt, *Glances and Glimpses* (Boston, 1856), especially pp. 23–72.

10. Minutes of the Meetings of the Medical Faculty, 2 (1850), 77.

11. Letters in Countway Archives.

12. Letter, April 4, 1866, in Countway Archives.

13. Minutes of the Meetings of the Medical Faculty, 3 (1867), 16.

14. Harvard Archives. Countway Archives have a photostat.

15. In the Board of Overseers of Harvard University, the Majority Report, signed at Cambridge, May 3, 1879. Photostat in Countway Archives.

16. Letter to Miss Varney, September 24, 1890, from Henry I. Bowditch. Countway Library Archives.

17. Letter to Dr. Henry I. Bowditch from Charles W. Eliot. Countway Library Archives.

18. Minutes of the Meetings of the Faculty of Medicine, 3 (1879), 322 ff. Countway Library Archives.

19. Both extracts are from the *President's Report*, 1878–79, (1880), pp. 29–32.

20. Letter received by the President and Fellows on September 26, 1881, and recorded in the *President's Report for* 1881–82 (1882), pp. 32–38.

21. Curiously, neither of the meetings of March 4 and 11 is recorded in the Minutes of the Faculty Meetings. The information recorded is found in the *President's Report*, 1878–79.

22. *President's Report for* 1881–82 (1882), p. 33. See also appendix I and appendix II, pp. 133, 134.

23. T. F. Harrington, *The Harvard Medical School*, Vol. 3 (1905), 1244.

24. Unfortunately, the women were not prepared to take advantage of the long-sought opportunity: Only twenty candidates applied. Of these, sixteen clearly did not have the requisite preliminary training. Three elected to go to other schools. It is not known what happened to the lone survivor. The plan was abandoned, but President Lowell remarked that nevertheless the question of admitting women to the Harvard Medical School was still open. R. H. Fitz, "Votes for Women," *Harvard Medical Alumni Bulletin*, 17 (1943), 30–32.

25. *President's Report*, 1916–17 (1918), pp. 144, 145.

26. January 13, 1943. Countway Library Archives.

27. Report of a Subcommittee of the Administrative Board on the advisability of admitting women to the Harvard Medical School. Committee members: A. Baird Hastings, William E. Ladd, and Robert S. Morison, Chairman (Countway Library Archives). See more recent articles relevant to the general problem: Helen S. Pittman, "Admission of Women to Harvard Medical School," *Harvard Medical Alumni Bulletin*, 43 (1969), 3; "Dr. Alice, First Lady of Harvard," Ibid., pp. 4, 5; "Opportunities for Women in Medical Research," Ibid., pp. 6, 7; Phoebe A. Williams, "Women in Medicine: Some Themes and Variations," *Journal of Medical Education*, 46 (1971), 584–591.

28. *President's Report*, 1943–44 (1947), pp. 169, 170.

29. From MGH *News*, 31, No. 3 (March 1972), 1–7.

30. Ibid.

31. All of these documents are in the Countway Library Archives.

32. Minutes of the Meetings of the Faculty of Medicine, 2 (December 13, 1850), 75, 76. A photostat of the original is in the Countway Library Archives.

33. A letter from Leon Eisenberg, Chairman, Commission on Relations

with the Black Community, to the Dean, Robert H. Ebert, dated April 1, 1969: "Leon Eisenberg, Chairman, Preliminary Report to the Dean of the College on Relations with the Black Community submitted to the Faculty of Medicine, April 1969."

34. "Information for Students from Minority Groups," a memorandum from the Office of the Committee on Admission, Harvard Medical School (1973).

35. Walsh McDermott, "Do Medical Schools Have to be Restructured to Produce the Doctor of the Future?" in *Proceedings of Anglo-American Conferences on Medical Care*, Royal Society of Medicine, London (April 5–7, 1971), pp. 65–73.

36. Stephen Steinberg, *The Religious Factor in American Higher Education*, Ph.D. dissertation, University of California at Berkeley (1972), p. 1.

37. Nathan Glazer, *American Judaism* (Chicago, 1957), p. 42.

38. Nathan Glazer, "Social Characteristics of American Jews, 1654–1954," *American Jewish Yearbook*, 56 (1955), 9.

39. Gustavus Myers, *History of Bigotry in the United States* (New York, 1960), p. 71.

40. Oscar Handlin, "How U.S. Anti-Semitism Really Began," Commentary, 11 (1951), 541.

41. John Higham, "Social Discrimination Against Jews in America, 1830–1930," *Publication of the American Jewish Historical Society*, 47 (1957), 3.

42. Higham, p. 13.

43. Oscar and Mary F. Handlin, "The Acquisition of Political and Social Rights by the Jews in the United States," *American Jewish Yearbook*, 56 (1955), 43–98.

44. Steinberg, p. 3.

45. Samuel E. Morison, *Three Centuries of Harvard* (Cambridge, 1965), p. 416.

46. Glazer, *American Jewish Yearbook*, 56, 10–11.

47. Steinberg, p. 10.

48. Ibid., p. 11.

49. *New York Times*, June 2, 1922, p. 1.

50. Ibid., June 17, 1922, 1:6.

51. Ibid., June 23, 1922, 1:2.

52. Lowell thus alluded to quotas in a letter reprinted in the *New York Times*, June 17, 1922, p. 3.

53. Steinberg, p. 30.

54. Glass contends that science itself is "an evolutionary product and a human organ produced by natural selection . . ." He does not hold the view that either the processes or concepts of science are strictly objective. "They are as objective as man knows how to make them, that is true; but man is a creature of evolution, and science is only his way of looking at nature. As long as science is a *human* activity, carried on by individual men and by groups of men, it must at bottom remain inescapably subjective." B. Glass, *Science and Ethical Values* (Chapel Hill, N.C., 1965).

27. Special Enterprises

1. John Collins Warren, scribe's manuscript in the Countway Library of Medicine.

2. J. B. S. Jackson, *Descriptive Catalogue of the Warren Anatomical Museum*, (Boston, 1870).

3. C. P. Huntington was born in a community known informally as "Poverty Hollow," Connecticut.

4. J. Collins Warren, Report of the Chairman of the Commission to the Cancer Commission of Harvard University. C. P. Huntington Memorial Hospital for Cancer Research, *Annual Reports*, 1–6 (1912–18), 7.

5. E. E. Tyzzer and Thomas Ordway, "The Huntington Hospital and the Scope of Its Work," *Boston Medical and Surgical Journal*, 166 (June 13, 1912), 887–889.

6. We have been greatly assisted in preparing this brief report by the statement of John Edsall, "*The Achievements of Paul C. Zamecnik*, Remarks on the Occasion of his Receiving the *Passano Award*, Atlantic City, New Jersey, April 13, 1970," pp. 1, 2.

7. Ibid., pp. 4, 5.

8. We are greatly indebted to Professor John T. Edsall for much of the historical material presented here.

9. John T. Edsall, "A Historical Sketch of the Department of Physical Chemistry, Harvard Medical School: 1920–1950," *American Scientist*, 38 (1950), 580–593.

10. Letter from John T. Edsall to Henry K. Beecher, September 28, 1972.

11. Dickinson W. Richards, "Lawrence Joseph Henderson," *The Physiologist*, 1 (1958), 36, 37.

12. Ibid., p. 36.

13. Lawrence J. Henderson, *The Fitness of the Environment* (New York, 1913).

14. Lawrence J. Henderson, *The Order of Nature: An Essay* (Cambridge, 1917).

15. Richards, p. 34.

16. It is the belief of many that J. Willard Gibbs was one of the greatest scientists America has produced. His sister-in-law would not have agreed. Her husband was also a professor at Yale, and his work was so demanding that his wife was obliged to take J. Willard on shopping tours with her, for, according to her, *he* was not really important.

17. Lawrence J. Henderson, "Physician and Patient as a Social System," *New England Journal of Medicine*, 212 (1935), 819–823.

18. Walter B. Cannon, "Biographical Memoir of Lawrence Joseph Henderson, 1878–1942," National Academy of Sciences, *Second Memoir* (Washington, D.C., 1943), 43.

19. Lawrence J. Henderson, "The Study of Man," *Science*, 94 (1941), 1–10.

20. Ibid., p. 1.

21. Ibid., pp. 3, 4.
22. Ibid., p. 5.
23. R. J. Dubos, "The Gold-headed Cane in the Laboratory," *Public Health Reports, Washington,* 69 (1954), 365–371.
24. Dubos, letter to Henry K. Beecher of January 20, 1956.
25. Henderson (1941), p. 10.
26. Edsall (1950), p. 583.
27. Ibid., p. 584.
28. The clinical mandate by Doctor of Philosophy Cohn, that brilliant, strong-willed, and arrogant man, may have been at least a partial source of the disastrous overemphasis on plasma.
29. Edsall (1950), p. 587.
30. Ibid., p. 590.
31. Ibid., pp. 592, 593.
32. Edsall, letter to Beecher.
33. John T. Edsall, "Some Personal History and Reflections from the Life of a Biochemist," *Annual Review of Biochemistry,* 40 (1971), 8.
34. Edwin J. Cohn, "The History of Plasma Fractionation," in *Advances in Military Medicine,* Vol. 1 (Boston, 1948), 365–443. John T. Edsall, "Edwin Joseph Cohn," in *Biographical Memoirs, National Academy of Sciences,* 35 (New York, 1961), 47–84. John T. Edsall, "Edwin J. Cohn," *Ergebnisse der Physiologie Biologischen Chemie und experimentellen Pharmakologie,* 48 (1955), 23–48. John T. Edsall, "The Plasma Proteins and Their Fractionation," *Advances in Protein Chemistry,* Vol. 3 (New York, 1947), 383–479.
35. Edsall, *Annual Review,* p. 27.
36. By December 1943, 5,652,387 bleedings had been recorded, of which 5,472,797 had been processed into dried plasma and serum albumin. The remainder was dispensed as liquid plasma. Unpublished data of E. D. Churchill.
37. Henry K. Beecher and Charles H. Burnett, "Field Experience in the Use of Blood and Blood Substitutes (Plasma, Albumin) in Seriously Wounded Men," *Medical Bulletin of the North African Theater of Operations,* 2, No. 1 (July 1944), 2–7. Henry K. Beecher, "Preparation of Battle Casualties for Surgery," *Annals of Surgery,* 121 (1945), 769–792.
38. Walter B. Cannon, John Fraser, and A. N. Hooper, "II. Some Alterations in the Distribution and Character of the Blood," *Reports of the Special Investigation Committee on Surgical Shock and Allied Conditions* (December 25, 1917), pp. 27–40.
39. Norman E. Freeman, "The Mechanism of Shock," in *Burns, Shock, Wound Healing and Vascular Injuries* (Philadelphia, 1943), pp. 107–130 (p. 117).
40. Unpublished notes of E. D. Churchill and provided to the writer.
41. Ibid.
42. Ibid.
43. Fifth Army, near Mignano, Italy.
44. The Board for the Study of the Severely Wounded, Mediterranean Theater. The five Harvard members (out of seven) are italicized.

45. Personal letter from Earle M. Chapman, M.D., to Henry K. Beecher, M.D., dated January 4, 1971.

46. E. Fermi, "Radioactivity Induced by Neutron Bombardment," *Nature* 133 (1934), 757.

47. E. M. Chapman and R. D. Evans, "The Treatment of Hyperthyroidism with Radioactive Iodine," *Journal of the American Medical Association*, 131 (1946), 86.

48. Eugene L. Saenger, George Thoma, and Edythalena Tompkins, "Incidence of Leukemia Following Treatment of Hyperthyroidism," *Journal of the American Medical Association*, 205 (1968), 855–862.

49. Brown Dobyns, Glenn Sheline, Joseph Workman, Edythalena Tompkins, William McConahey and David Becker, "Malignant and Benign Neoplasms of the Thyroid in Patients Treated for Hyperthyroidism: A Report of the Cooperative Thyrotoxicosis Therapy, Follow-up Study," *Journal of Clinical Endocrinology and Metabolism*, 38 (1974), 976–998.

50. Krishna M. Saxena, Earle M. Chapman, and Charles V. Pryles, "Minimal Dosage of Iodide Required to Suppress Uptake of Iodine-131 by Normal Thyroid," *Science*, 138 (1962), 430.

28. Associated Institutions

1. We are indebted to Dr. Eric G. Ball for the material used in this section.

2. "The Harvard Fatigue Laboratory," *Harvard Alumni Bulletin*, 37 (1935), 548–551.

3. Ibid., p. 548.

4. D. Bruce Dill, "The Harvard Fatigue Laboratory," *Supplement* 1 *to Circulation Research*, 20 (March 1967), 1-161–1-170.

5. *Harvard Alumni Bulletin*, p. 551.

6. Dill, p. 1-170.

7. Steven M. Horvath and Elizabeth C. Horvath, *The Harvard Fatigue Laboratory: Its History and Contributions* (Englewood Cliffs, N.J., 1973), p. 181.

8. From information prepared in the Countway Library.

9. Ibid.

10. Ibid.

Epilogue

1. N. R. Shipley, Ph.D. dissertation, Harvard University, 1967.

2. Henry K. Beecher, "Ethics and Clinical Research," *New England Journal of Medicine*, 274 (1966), 1354–60. Henry K. Beecher, *Research and the Individual* (Boston, 1970). Mark D. Altschule, *What Medicine Is About: Using Its Past to Improve Its Future* (Boston, 1975).

Index